iPhone
The Missing Manual

Thirteenth Edition

iPhone: The Missing Manual, 13th Edition BY DAVID POGUE

Published by O'Reilly Media, Inc., 1005 Gravenstein Highway North, Sebastopol, CA 95472.

O'Reilly books may be purchased for educational, business, or sales promotional use. Online editions are also available for most titles *(http://oreilly.com)*. For more information, contact our corporate/institutional sales department: 800.998.9938 or *corporate@oreilly.com*.

Copy Editor: Julie Van Keuren

Indexers: David Pogue, Julie Van Keuren

Cover Designers: Monica Kamsvaag and Phil Simpson

Interior Designer: Julie Van Keuren (based on a design by Phil Simpson and Ron Bilodeau)

Print History:

November 2019.	First Printing.
December 2019	Second Printing
January 2020	Third Printing

ISBN: 978-1-492-07514-1

[TI]

Contents

Part Three: The iPhone Online

Part Four: Connections

Part Five: Appendixes

The Missing Credits

David Pogue (author, illustrator) has been a *New York Times* columnist since 2000 (although somewhere in there, he took a five-year detour at Yahoo Finance).

He's also a five-time Emmy-winning correspondent for *CBS News Sunday Morning,* the host of 17 *NOVA* specials on PBS, and the creator of the Missing Manual series. He's written or co-written more than 100 books, including dozens in this series, six in the *For Dummies* line (including *Macs, Magic, Opera,* and *Classical Music*), two novels (one for middle-schoolers), *The World According to Twitter,* and three books of essential tips and shortcuts: *Pogue's Basics: Tech, Pogue's Basics: Life,* and *Pogue's Basics: Money.* In his other life, David is a former Broadway show conductor, a magician, and a funny public speaker. He lives in Connecticut with his wife, Nicki, and three awesome children.

You can find a complete list of David's columns and videos, and sign up to get them by email, at *authory.com/davidpogue*. His website is *davidpogue.com.* He welcomes feedback about his books by email at *david@pogueman.com.*

Julie Van Keuren (editor, indexer, designer) spent 14 years in print journalism before deciding to upend her life, move to Montana, and live the freelancing dream. She now works for a variety of clients who understand that skilled editing, writing, and book layout don't have to come from inside a cubicle. She and her husband have two adult sons. Email: *JulieVanK@gmail.com.*

Rich Koster (technical reviewer) bought an iPhone on the first evening it was available. He began corresponding with David Pogue, sharing tips and observations; eventually, David asked him to be the beta reader for the first edition of *iPhone: The Missing Manual*—and hired him as the tech editor of subsequent editions. For this book, he accomplished all the work on the iPhone 11 Pro. Rich is a husband, father, retired graphic artist, writer, and Disney fan (@DisneyEcho on Twitter).

Kellee Katagi (proofreader) has devoted most of her 20-plus-year writing and editing career to covering fitness, nutrition, travel, and outdoor sports. A former managing editor of *SKI* magazine, she now smiths words from her Colorado home, where she lives with her husband and three kids. Email: *KelKatagi@gmail.com*.

Diana D'Abruzzo (proofreader) is a Virginia-based freelance editor with more than 20 years of experience in the journalism and book publishing industries. More information on her life and work can be found at *dianadabruzzo.com*.

Acknowledgments

The Missing Manual series is a joint venture between the dream team introduced on these pages and O'Reilly Media. I'm grateful to all of them, especially to the core of the iPhone Missing Manual team.

The work done on previous editions lives on in this one; for that, I'm grateful to Phil Simpson, Jude Biersdorfer, Matt Gibstein, Brian Jepson, Apple's Trudy Muller and Teresa Brewer, Philip Michaels, and O'Reilly's Nan Barber.

Thanks also to David Rogelberg and Tim O'Reilly for believing in the idea; to Apple's Jacqueline Roy for chasing down dozens of technical answers; to Aaron Woodwell for the cool nighttime beach shot on page 295; to Judy Le for assistance with creating the many symbol characters; and above all, to Nicki, Kell, Tia, and Jeffrey. They make these books—and everything else—possible.

—*David Pogue*

Also by David Pogue

- *macOS Catalina: The Missing Manual*
- *Windows 10: The Missing Manual, 2nd Edition*
- *David Pogue's Digital Photography: The Missing Manual*
- *The World According to Twitter*
- *Pogue's Basics: Tech*
- *Pogue's Basics: Life*
- *Pogue's Basics: Money*

Introduction

How do you make the point that the iPhone has changed the world? The easy answer is "use statistics"—2.5 billion sold, 2.2 million apps on the App Store, 200 billion downloads.... Trouble is, those statistics get stale almost before you've finished typing them.

Maybe it's better to talk about the aftermath. How the invention of the iPhone changed society, business, and culture forever. With the iPhone (and Google's imitator, Android), we became, for the first time, a society of people who are online continuously. Our communications blossomed from text messages to video calls, WhatsApp, FaceTime, and Skype. Billion-dollar businesses like Uber, Snapchat, and Instagram sprang into existence. Distracted driving, distracted walking, distracted eating, distracted dating, and even distracted sex all became "things."

Apple introduces new iPhone models every fall. In September 2019, it introduced the 22nd, 23rd, and 24th models, the iPhone 11, 11 Pro, and 11 Pro Max.

There's also a new, free version of the iPhone's software, called iOS 13.

You can run iOS 13 on *older* iPhone models without having to buy a new phone. This book covers all the phones that can run iOS 13, from the iPhone SE through the iPhone 11 family.

About the iPhone

What is the iPhone? The better question is what *isn't* the iPhone?

It's a cellphone, obviously. But it's also a full-blown multimedia player, complete with a dazzling screen for watching videos. And it's a sensational pocket internet viewer. It shows fully formatted email (with attachments, thank you) and displays entire web pages with fonts and design intact. It's tricked out with a tilt sensor, a proximity sensor, a light sensor,

Wi-Fi, Bluetooth, GPS, a gyroscope, a barometer, and that amazing multi-touch screen.

The iPhone is also the most used *camera* in the world. Furthermore, it's a calendar, address book, calculator, alarm clock, ebook reader, stopwatch, podcast player, stock tracker, video viewer, traffic reporter, and weather forecaster. It even stands in for a flashlight, a tape measure, and—with the screen off—a pocket mirror.

And don't forget the App Store. Thanks to the 2.2 million add-on programs that await there, the iPhone can also be...everything *else*. A medical reference, a musical keyboard, a time tracker, a remote control, a sleep monitor, a tip calculator. Plus, the App Store is a portal to thousands of games, with smooth 3D graphics and tilt control.

Calling this thing a phone is practically an insult. (Apple probably should have called it an "iPod," but that name was taken.)

About This Book

You don't get a printed manual when you buy an iPhone. Online, you can find an electronic manual, but it's free of details, hacks, workarounds, tutorials, humor, and any acknowledgment of the iPhone's flaws. You can't easily mark your place, underline, or read it in the bathroom.

The purpose of this book, then, is to serve as the manual that should have accompanied the iPhone. (If you have an iPhone 5s or an earlier model, then you really need one of this book's previous editions. And if you do have an iPhone SE or later model, this book assumes that you've installed iOS 13.2 or later; see Appendix A.)

Writing a book about the iPhone is a study in exasperation, because the darned thing is a moving target. Apple updates the iPhone's software fairly often, piping in new features, bug fixes, speed-ups, and so on.

About the Outline

iPhone: The Missing Manual is divided into five parts:

- Part One, **The iPhone as Phone**, covers everything related to phone communications: dialing, answering, voice control, voicemail, conference calling, text messaging, iMessages, MMS, and the Contacts (address book) program. It's also where you can read about FaceTime, the iPhone's video-calling feature; Siri, the voice-operated "virtual assistant"; and the surprisingly rich array of features for people with disabilities—some of which are also useful for people without them.

- Part Two, **Pix, Flix & Apps**, is dedicated to the iPhone's built-in software, with a special emphasis on its multimedia abilities: playing music, podcasts, movies, and TV shows; taking and displaying photos; capturing photos and videos; using the Maps app; reading ebooks; and so on. These chapters also cover some of the standard techniques that most apps share: installing, organizing, and quitting them; switching among them; and sharing material from within them.

- Part Three, **The iPhone Online**, is a detailed exploration of the iPhone's ability to get you onto the internet, either over a Wi-Fi hotspot connection or via the cellular network. It's all here: email, web browsing, and Personal Hotspot (letting your phone serve as a sort of internet antenna for your laptop).

- Part Four, **Connections**, describes the world beyond the iPhone itself—like using your Mac or PC to sync or back up the phone. These chapters also cover Apple's iCloud service, Continuity (the wireless integration of iPhones and Macs), and the Settings app.

- Part Five, **Appendixes**, contains two reference chapters. Appendix A walks you through the setup process; Appendix B is a master compendium of troubleshooting, maintenance, and battery information.

About→These→Arrows

Throughout this book, you'll find sentences like this: Tap **Settings→ General→Keyboard**. That's shorthand for a much longer instruction that directs you to open three nested screens in sequence, like this: "Tap the **Settings** icon. On the next screen, tap **General**. On the screen after that, tap **Keyboard**." (In this book, tappable things on the screen are printed in **orange** to make them stand out.)

About MissingManuals.com

Missing Manuals are witty, well-written guides to computer products that don't come with printed manuals (which is just about all of them). Each book features a handcrafted index; handy cross-references to specific page numbers; and an ironclad promise never to put an apostrophe in the possessive pronoun *its*.

To get the most out of this book, visit *missingmanuals.com*. Click the **Missing CDs** link, and then click this book's title to reveal a neat, organized list of the shareware, freeware, and bonus articles mentioned in this book.

The website also offers corrections and updates to the book; to see them, click the book's title, and then click **View/Submit Errata**. In fact, please submit corrections yourself! Each time we print more copies of this book, we'll make any confirmed corrections you've suggested. We'll also note such changes on the website, so you can mark important corrections into your own copy of the book, if you like. And we'll keep the book current as Apple releases more iPhone updates.

iPhone 11, 11 Pro: What's New

The three 2019 iPhones aren't radical upgrades from the previous year's models; most reviewers advised iPhone owners that this time, there was no pressing need to upgrade. Here's a rundown:

- **iPhone 11.** This model is last year's iPhone XR—same size, price ($700 and up), and screen—with one juicy enhancement: a second lens.

    Yet this isn't a 2x zoom like the one on last year's iPhone XS. It doesn't zoom in—it zooms *out*. It's an ultra-wide angle lens. And because there are two lenses now, this phone can take Portrait-mode photos of people, pets, and things (page 308).

    You can get the 11 in six colors: White, black, yellow, red, purple, and green. Apple says it's slightly more waterproof and slightly more shatterproof than before—and gets one more hour of battery life per charge.

- **iPhone 11 Pro,** the high-end phone, adds a *third* lens. Now it's got ultra-wide, standard, and telephoto. This phone ($1,000 and up) has a nicer screen (OLED instead of LCD technology), contains a bigger battery (four hours longer per charge than last year's iPhone XS), and comes with an 18-watt charger that "fast charges" the phone to 50 percent in 30 minutes.

- **iPhone 11 Pro Max** is the exact same thing as the 11 Pro, but bigger. It's basically the size of last year's XS Max model—but because Apple eliminated the margins above and below the screen, the screen is much bigger. For something that's 6.5 inches diagonal, the Max (as some are calling it) feels surprisingly small in the hand. Maybe that's because it gains its area mostly in height, not width. It costs from $1,100 to a staggering $1,450.

All three new phones introduce substantial photography enhancements. They include these:

- **Night mode** (captures incredible color and detail even in pitch-dark conditions), **Smart HDR** (better highlights and detail), and **Deep Fusion** (a computational feature for even better detail).

- **Video in Photos mode.** All these phones let you start recording video even when you're in still-photos mode, just by holding down the shutter button, without having to switch modes. They also offer audio zoom, which attempts to zoom into the audio source as you zoom in with the video.

- **First-class front camera.** The front-facing camera is now almost identical in quality to the back cameras: 12 megapixels and capable of recording 4K video at 60 frames a second. For the first time, the front-facing camera can shoot slow-motion video, too. It also makes Face ID recognize you faster—and from more angles.

What's New in iOS 13

You'd have to write an entire book to document everything that's new or changed in iOS 13; it's a *huge* upgrade. But here's a quick rundown.

Dark Mode

This one gets most of the press, mainly because it's so visible. It's one of the most arresting and radical design changes in iPhone history.

Dark mode is a dark-gray color scheme. Once you turn it on, most of Apple's built-in apps—Home screens, Settings, Mail, Calendar, Photos, Messages, Reminders, Notes, and so on—take on a stunning, white-on-black design. Even your wallpaper images shift when Dark mode is on.

Here's what *doesn't* change in Dark mode: photos, web pages in Safari, and preexisting non-Apple apps. Software companies will have to update their programs if they want them to take on Dark mode's dusky hues.

You'd really have to stretch to say Dark mode is a useful change. Mainly it's just cool-looking.

You can try Dark mode for yourself in any of three ways. First, there's a Control Center button for it (page 614), which is the quickest way to turn it on and off. Second, you can open **Settings→Display & Brightness** and tap **Dark**. Third, you can set Dark mode to kick in automatically at sunset, or on any time schedule you prefer.

In this book, you'll mostly see illustrations of Light mode, the traditional white-background screens. That's so you won't lose your bearings as the pictures flip back and forth.

Light mode

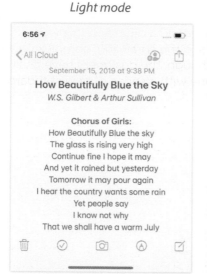

Dark mode

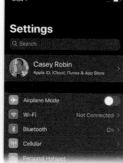

Photos

Apple's elves gave Photos a massive renovation. The browsing mode (Years, Months, Days, All Photos) is gorgeous, employing artificial intelligence to pluck your best shots from out of the haystack.

The editing mode in particular is infinitely better. There are more color correction tools, more flipping and perspective adjustments, more Portrait-mode effects. You can now control (and measure) the intensity of any edit, effect, or lighting style. And, for the first time, you can zoom in or out as you're editing.

Above all, you can apply all these edits to videos, too. Color-correct them, brighten them up. And flip them! No more being stuck with a video rotated 90 degrees because the camera was confused when you shot it.

Interface Overhauls

For many years, Apple has tried to maintain a difference between the small, sweet simplicity of the phone and the sprawling, complex universe of the desktop computer. In iOS 13, though, the designers have finally given up. They've equipped the iPhone with a series of new standard navigation and selection techniques:

- **Long-Pressing.** For a few years there, Apple heavily promoted its Force Touch screens, which can summon different effects depending on how hard you press the glass. But with the iPhone 11 family, Apple has abandoned the idea.

  In iOS 13, *long*-pressing—leaving your finger down on some icon or button for about a second—achieves the same thing, and works on every single phone. You can now pop up a preview of an email message, Messages chat, or Safari web link just by long-pressing it. App icons on your Home screen produce shortcut menus when you long-press them, too. (The **Edit Home Screen** command is one of them. In other words, it now takes an extra step—or an extra half-second—to put your app icons into wiggling mode, for moving or deleting them.)

  Awkwardly enough, *hard*-pressing (pressing extra-hard) still works in many places in iOS 13—on the phone models equipped with Force Touch. Hard-pressing takes less time than long-pressing—and lots of people are used to it. When this book mentions hard-pressing, you'll know it means "on models with Force Touch screens."

  In related news: Many apps let you choose multiple items simultaneously (emails in a list in Mail, conversations in Messages, files and folders in Files). In the past, you'd tap **Edit** and then tap selection circles one by one. And you can still do that.

  But now you can select batches of them with one smooth move: a *two-finger tap and drag*.

- **Editing text.** Apple has put a lot of effort into making text easier to edit. To precisely position the insertion point, you just drag it (it grows a bit so you can see it). The loupe magnifier, which helped you move the insertion point for the first 12 years of the iPhone's existence, is gone.

  There are new, three-finger gestures for Cut, Copy, Paste, and Undo, plus another formatting bar. It's gotten easier to select addresses, phone numbers, and email addresses, because iOS recognizes them; just double-tap.

Scroll bars are on the phone now, too. They appear in Safari, Messages, long Notes, documents, and many other scrollable apps. Grab that tiny bar at the right edge of the screen and drag; now you can leap all the way to the beginning or end, or anywhere in the middle, without having to swipe-swipe-swipe-swipe.

You can read more about all these features starting on page 99.

- **Command panels.** The iPhone has never had a menu bar, as a Mac or PC does. Over the years, Apple has had to cram more and more options into weirder and more awkward places. So in iOS 13, Apple introduced a menu-like concept called (at least in this book) command panels. You'll spot them in many of Apple's standard apps.

  Usually, command panels open when you long-press something: an email message in a list, a person or device in the Find My app, a place in Maps, a song in Music, a message in the list in Messages, a file in Files, a link in Safari, the 􀈂 button in any app. You can see the effect on pages 511 and 536.

  Often, a preview of your work appears in an upper bubble, and the panel appears below. You can drag up to enlarge the command panel. Or tap the gray background to make the whole thing disappear.

Sign In with Apple

You know those "Sign In with Facebook" and "Sign In with Google" buttons that appear on thousands of websites, to save you time when signing up for a new account? Apple has introduced its own version. The difference is that Apple promises it won't track or profile you.

To use this feature, you'll need an Apple ID, a device signed into iCloud, and a website that actually offers it.

Maps

Apple's long-suffering Maps app is—dare we say it?—finally getting somewhere. In several U.S. cities, the maps show far more detail, right down to individual buildings. A new **Look Around** feature rivals Google's Street View, in that it lets you see a photograph of an address, taken from the street—and look around you, or move forward down the road. (This feature, too, is available in only a few cities.)

There's real-time bus and subway info in many cities, a handy **Share ETA** feature that texts your progress updates to someone you specify, one-tap Favorite places, and more.

Reminders

This app has been gutted and rebuilt. You can attach photos, scanned documents, and web link reminders for reference, and if your to-do title includes dates, times, and places, Reminders correctly parses them.

There are sub-tasks (indented to-dos underneath the primary ones), too, and message groups. And not only can a reminder pop up at a certain time or place—now it can pop up the next time you're chatting with a certain person in Messages!

Voice Control

It's now possible to do *everything* on the phone by voice alone—an enormous engineering accomplishment. You can press buttons, tap things, swipe or pinch, scroll, dictate, make text edits—all with very natural voice commands, all hands-free. This feature is primarily intended for people who can't hold the phone, but it turns out to be useful in all kinds of situations, especially when you're trying to fix dictation mistakes. (You can say, for example, *Replace "Mr. Trannidy" with "missed her train today."* No fussy finger dance on glass!)

Messages

Used to be, everyone you chatted with could paste in whatever image they wanted to represent you. But now Messages automatically offers to share your chosen avatar image with the other guy.

iOS 13 includes more Animoji and more ways to use Memoji (the cutesy animated character you've designed to resemble you).

Search in Messages is better, too, because it gives you quick access to photos, web links, and attachments as well as messages.

Files

The Files app, the iPhone's "desktop" for organizing files and folders, has come a long way. Now it can "see" the files on a memory card or flash drive—and even create folders on them. It's got a Downloads folder to hold your downloads from Safari and Mail. You can compress and decompress zip files.

Notes

What a beefy upgrade! There's a new thumbnail view of your notes, so you can see them like little Post-it pages instead of just a list. Checklists are easier to process: You can swipe to indent a line, or drag and drop them into a new order, or have them fall to the bottom of the list automatically when you check them off.

You can now create folders to organize your notes. And you can now *share* notes folders—and mark them "view only," if you like.

Safari

The iPhone's browser grows more like a desktop computer every day. Now there's even a Downloads menu that lets you start, stop, track, and find file downloads. You can set up standard settings for each individual website: type size, Reader view, Desktop Site view, ad-blocker status, privacy settings, and so on.

You can also save an entire batch of open tabs as a single bookmark so they'll all open at a tap later. Oh, and there's a new Start page—the one that appears before you type in a web address—filled with shortcuts to recent sites, favorite sites, and suggested sites.

Mail

When you hit ↩, you now get a command panel filled with options for processing a message—**Reply**, **Reply All**, **Forward**, **Print**, **Notify Me** of replies, **Mark as Unread**, **Move to Junk** (or a different folder), **Flag**, and the new **Mute Thread**—all in one place.

Your outgoing messages now have full, desktop-class formatting options, complete with fonts, styles, paragraph alignment, bulleted or numbered lists, photos, scanned files, and finger drawings.

Now, when you flag messages to get your attention later, you can also choose *colors* for those flags.

And, if some idiot is harassing you, there's a **Block Sender** command that can dump those inbound messages straight to the Trash before you even see them.

The Speed Round

Frankly, the category where Apple put the most effort into improving iOS 13 is Miscellaneous. Here's a sampling:

- **Quicker sharing.** When you tap the 🔼 button to share something, the Share sheet now offers a list of the people you most often share with—and how you share with them. There'll be an icon for **Mom/ Messages**, for **Casey/Email**, and **Your Mac/AirDrop**, for example. This single change saves so many taps!

- **Hotspot fixes.** You can choose a Wi-Fi hotspot right from the Control Center now, without having to burrow into Settings!

Meanwhile, when the iPhone discovers a new Wi-Fi hotspot, it doesn't interrupt you with a full-screen alert. If you wish, it can offer a subtle notification at the top of the screen.

- **Personal Hotspot** is now available to your Family Sharing members—either automatically or when you grant them permission. And it doesn't shut down the connection when you put your laptop to sleep; you'll still get messages and notifications when the lid is closed.

- **The Health app** has been blessed with sophisticated menstrual-cycle tracking and audiogram (hearing test) tracking, and new graphs show your various fitness stats over time.

- **Swipe typing.** Aficionados swear they can type faster and more accurately by sloppily dragging their finger across the keys instead of tapping them individually. As you go, you can type some and swipe some, without ever having to change keyboards or modes.

- **Free radio.** You can ask Siri to play any radio station. Also, Siri's voice has been improved for more natural inflections.

- **The Shortcuts app** is now included with iOS 13 (rather than being a separate download), and includes an option to trigger Shortcuts (automated actions) automatically at certain times or places.

- **Apps open faster**—and also download faster—because they're as little as half the size on the App Store.

- **Calendar attachments.** You can add photos or files to individual calendar appointments.

- **Do Not Disturb While Driving** is now smart enough *not* to turn on when you're on the bus or the subway.

- **Find My** is a new app—the bizarrely named melding of two older apps, Find My iPhone and Find My Friends. Furthermore, you can now find your phone even when it's not online—it can share its whereabouts with passing iPhones and iPads over Bluetooth, which gets relayed back to you, securely and privately.

- **Controllers.** You can connect an Xbox or PlayStation controller to your phone for game use.

- **Separate Emoji and Language keys.** Much better.

- **Scrolling lyrics** in the Music app.

- **38 new keyboard languages,** two new translation dictionaries (Thai–English and Vietnamese–English), and seven new next-word prediction languages.

- **Auto-dump robocalls.** When you turn on **Silence Unknown Callers**, your phone rings and buzzes only if the caller is in your Contacts, Mail, or Messages collections—or you've called that number before. All other calls are automatically sent to voicemail.

- **Screen Time** now lets you limit your kids' time on individual apps (not just in broad categories). And when their time is up, they can tap "One more minute" so they have a chance to save their work or say goodbye.

- **Low Data Mode** is like Low Power Mode, but for data. It makes your phone consume a lot less data when it's on cellular networks (or even specified Wi-Fi networks). For example, it pauses app updates, pauses syncing photos to iCloud, turns off auto-video playback, chooses lower-quality settings for streaming music and FaceTime, and stops background apps from using data.

- **Volume indicator.** When you use the volume keys, the volume indicator no longer blocks your entire screen. It's now a subtle vertical bar near the volume buttons themselves.

- **The screenshot mechanism** has had another overhaul. For example, you can capture a screenshot of an entire Safari web page, email, or long Note, even if, in real life, it would require scrolling.

- **Eight new wallpapers!**

What It All Means

Let's be honest: iOS has become a very dense operating system, with more features than you could master in years.

But never mind. iOS 13 is better, smarter, faster, clearer, and more refined than everything that came before. It takes hundreds of steps forward, and only a couple of tiny steps back.

That's a lot of tweaks, polishing, and finesse—and a lot to learn. Fortunately, 700-plus pages of instructions now await you.

PART ONE

The iPhone as Phone

The Guided Tour

You won't believe how much is hidden inside this sleek, thin slab. Microphone, speaker, cameras, battery. Processor, memory, power processing. Sensors for brightness, tilt, and proximity. Twenty wireless radio antennas. A gyroscope, accelerometer, and barometer. And on the Face ID phones—that is, the recent phones that don't have a home button—the face-recognition system includes an infrared lamp, an infrared camera, and a tiny projector.

For the rest of this book, and for the rest of your life with the iPhone, you'll be expected to know what's meant by, for example, "the side button" and "the Lock screen." A guided tour, therefore, is in order.

Sleep and Wake

For most of its existence, your iPhone will be neither on nor off. It will be asleep. It sleeps whenever you don't touch the screen for a while (you choose the interval), or when you press the side button.

In sleep mode, the screen is dark, yet the phone stays on alert to take an incoming call or message. If you're *on* a call, it continues. If music is playing, it keeps going. If you're recording audio, the recording proceeds.

But with your phone asleep, you preserve battery power. And you don't have to worry about accidental button presses. (You wouldn't want to discover that your iPhone has been sending texts or taking photos from the depths of your bag. Nor would you want it to dial a random number from your back pocket, a phenomenon that's earned the unfortunate name *butt-dialing*.)

Waking the Phone

You could argue, though, that knowing how to *wake* the phone might be a useful skill. The technique depends on whether you have a Face ID phone (iPhone 11, 11 Pro, 11 Pro Max, X, XR, XS, XS Max) or one with a home button:

- **Face ID phones:** Press the side button, or just lift the phone to a vertical position.

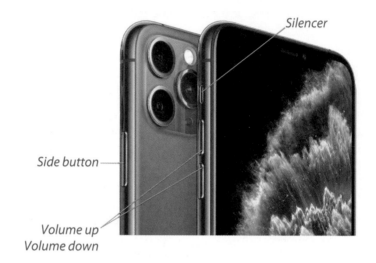

Silencer

Side button

Volume up
Volume down

- **Home-button phones:** Press the home button or the side button, or just lift the phone upright. On the iPhone 6s and later, the side button is on the right edge; on the iPhone SE, it's on the top. (That's right—on the iPhone SE, the *side* button is on the *top*. Keep up.)

Home button

No matter which model you have, the screen lights up, and you're looking at the *Lock screen*.

The Lock Screen

When you wake the phone, you don't bring it *fully* to life. You land instead at a halfway point called the Lock screen (below, left).

That's a state of being somewhere between asleep and on. You can get a lot done here even before you reach the Home screen: check the time, read your new messages, consult your calendar, take a photo, and more.

Chapter 2 goes into exhausting detail about how to manage and customize your notifications, the little Lock screen banners that inform you about missed calls, texts, emails, Facebook posts, or whatever you specify.

Unlock the Phone

Often, you'll wake your phone only to check the time or your notifications; then you'll just put it back to sleep again (hit the side button, or just toss it in your pocket and wait for it to auto-sleep).

But other times you'll want to finish turning it on, proceeding to the Home screen. Here's how that works:

- **Face ID phones:** Swipe up from the bottom of the screen. It can be a very short, light, quick swipe. If the phone's front camera system recognizes your face (page 57), or if you enter the passcode correctly, you arrive at the Home screen.

- **Home-button phones:** Click the home button. If the phone recognizes your fingerprint (page 54), or if you enter the passcode correctly, you arrive at the Home screen.

Now, remember: You can do a lot on an iPhone even *before* you've fully awakened it. Bad guys don't need a password to view the notifications on your Lock screen; to talk to Siri (Chapter 5); to control your Apple-compatible door locks and lights; to take a picture; and so on. For privacy, you can turn those features off individually. See page 67.

iOS offers a buried but powerful option for home-button phones: **Rest Finger to Open**. (It's in **Settings→ Accessibility→ Home Button**.) When you turn this on, the second click—the one to get past the Lock screen—is no longer necessary.

If your phone is asleep, then just lifting it (with your finger resting on the home button) wakes *and* unlocks it; you barely even see the Lock screen. Or you can click the home button and just leave your finger on it. In each case, you save at least one home-button press.

So what if you *do* want to visit the Lock screen? Just raise the phone, or click the side button, *without* touching the home button.

<table>
<tr><td>Lock screen</td><td></td><td>Home screen</td></tr>
</table>

Apps

Badge

Dock

The Home Screen

The Home screen is the launching pad for every iPhone activity. It's what appears when you press the home button or swipe up on the screen (Face ID phones). It's the immortal grid of colorful icons.

It's such a software landmark, in fact, that a quick tour might be helpful:

- **Icons.** Each icon represents one of your iPhone apps (programs)—Mail, Maps, Camera, and so on—or a folder you've made to *contain* some apps. Tap one to open that app or folder.

Your iPhone comes with a couple of dozen apps preinstalled by Apple; you can't remove them. The real fun, of course, comes when you download *more* apps from the App Store (Chapter 10).

- **Badges.** Every now and then, you'll see a tiny, red number "badge" (like ❷) on one of your app icons. It's telling you something new awaits: new email, new text messages, new updates for the apps on your iPhone. It's saying, "Hey, you! Tap me!"

- **Home screen dots.** The standard Home screen can't hold more than 20 or 24 icons. As you install more and more apps on your iPhone, you'll need more and more room for their icons. Fortunately, the iPhone makes room for them by creating *additional* Home screens automatically. You can spread your new programs' icons across 11 such launch screens.

  The little white dots are your map. Each represents one Home screen. If the third one is "lit up," you're on the third Home screen.

  To move among the screens, swipe horizontally—or tap to the right or left of the little dots.

  And if you ever scroll too far from the *first* Home screen, here's a handy shortcut: Press the home button, if you have one, or do the "go home" swipe up from the bottom (yes, even though you're technically already home). That takes you back to the first Home screen.

- **The Dock.** At the bottom of the Home screens, four exalted icons sit in a row on a light-colored panel. This is the Dock—a place to park the most important icons on your iPhone. These, presumably, are the ones you use most often. Apple starts you off with the Phone, Mail, Safari, and Music icons there.

  What's so special about this row? As you flip among Home screens, the Dock never changes. You can never lose one of your four most cherished icons by straying from the first page; they're always handy.

- **The wallpaper.** You can replace the background image (behind your app icons) with a photo. A complicated, busy picture won't do you any favors—it will just make the icon names harder to read—so Apple provides a selection of handsome, relatively subdued wallpaper photos. But you can also choose one of your own photos.

  For instructions on changing the wallpaper, see page 617.

It's easy (and fun!) to rearrange the icons on your Home screens. Put the most frequently used icons on the first page, put similar apps into folders, and reorganize your Dock. Full details are on page 365.

Turning the Phone On and Off

Most of the time, you'll just put the phone to sleep when you're not using it. You'll very rarely turn the phone fully *off*. But just in case:

- **Turning the phone on.** The phone does come from the factory turned fully off, so it's good to know: To turn on a fully off phone, hold in the side button for a few seconds—until the logo appears. Then wait for about a minute.

- **Turn the phone fully off.** You might turn the iPhone off whenever you're not going to use it for a few days. In this condition, the phone uses no power at all, and all calls go straight to voicemail.

  If you have a Face ID phone, hold in the side button *and* either of the volume buttons across from it for a few seconds.

  If you have a home-button phone, just hold in the side button (which may be on the top, remember).

  The screen changes to say, among other things, **slide to power off**. Confirm your decision by placing a fingertip on the and sliding to the right. The device shuts off completely.

  If you change your mind about turning the iPhone off, tap the Cancel button.

- **Answer call/Dump to voicemail.** The side button has another function, too: When a call comes in, you can tap it *once* to silence the ringing or vibrating. After four rings, the call goes to voicemail.

You can also tap it *twice* to dump the call to voicemail immediately. (Of course, because they didn't hear four rings, some people will realize you've blown them off. Bruised egos may result.)

In combination with other buttons, the side button is also involved in turning off fingerprint or face recognition (page 57), capturing a screenshot (page 357), speaking to Siri (page 158), and restarting a locked-up phone (page 666).

Silencer Switch, Volume Keys

Praise be—this phone has a silencer switch! This tiny flipper, on the left edge near the top (shown on page 16), means no ringer or alert sound will humiliate you in a meeting, at a movie, or in church. To turn off the ringer, push the flipper toward the back of the phone.

NOTE: Even when silenced, the iPhone still makes noise in certain circumstances: when an alarm goes off; when you're playing music, video, or a podcast; when you're using Find My (page 424); when you're using VoiceOver; or, sometimes, when a game is playing. Also, the phone still vibrates when the silencer switch is engaged, although you can turn that off in **Settings→Sounds & Haptics**.

On the left edge are the volume controls. They work in five ways:

- **On a call,** these buttons adjust the speaker or earbud volume.

- **When you're listening to music,** they adjust the playback volume—even when the phone is locked and dark.

- **When you're taking a photo or video,** either one serves as a shutter button or a camcorder start/stop button.

- **When a call comes in,** they silence the ringing or vibrating.

- **At all other times,** they adjust the volume of sound effects like the ringer, alarms, and Siri.

In each case, a volume graphic appears to show you where you are on the volume scale. In iOS 13, it's no longer a huge block that covers up whatever you're doing; it's a subtle, quickly collapsing slider at the left side of the screen, right next to the volume keys.

Screen

The touchscreen is your mouse, keyboard, dialing pad, and notepad. You might expect it to get fingerprinty and streaky.

But the iPhone has an *oleophobic* screen. That may sound like an irrational fear of yodeling, but it's actually a coating that repels grease. A single, light wipe on your clothes restores the screen to its right-out-of-the-box crystal sheen.

The iPhone's screen has crazy-high resolution (the number of tiny pixels per inch). It's really, really sharp, as you'll discover when you try to read text or make out the details of a map or a photo. The actual number of pixels depends on your phone: It's 1136×640 in the iPhone SE, 1334×750 in the iPhone 6/6s/7/8, and 2436×1125 in the XS and 11 Pro. The massive XS Max and 11 Pro Max models supposedly pack an awe-inspiring 2688×1242 tiny dots, but nobody's ever counted.

> **TIP:** If your puny thumb is too small to reach the top of your mammoth iPhone screen, consider turning on Reachability (page 247).

The front of the iPhone is a special formulation made by Corning, to Apple's specifications—even better than the Gorilla Glass used on previous models, Apple says. It's unbelievably resistant to scratching. You can still crack it if you drop it just the wrong way, though.

If you're nervous about protecting your iPhone, you can always get a case for it, or a "bumper"—a silicone band that wraps around the edges.

Face ID Phones: The Notch

If anyone grumbles about the Face ID iPhones at all, it's about the notch. That's the dark area at the top center that contains the front-facing camera, the earpiece, and the phone's Face ID sensors (page 57). Apple decided that, to keep the phone as small as possible, this notch would interrupt the standard status bar, splitting it into two "ears."

The notch

You can't see the notch when the status bar is black—on a black Home screen, for example. You don't see it when you're looking at photos or videos, either, unless you zoom into them. You do see the notch when the status bar is white or another color, and it's also noticeable when you're using an app that hasn't been updated for Face ID phones. Sometimes those apps try to display information right where the notch sits!

In any case, on the ears, there's very little room for status icons. The left ear shows the time and, sometimes, the location services logo (➶); and the right ear shows icons for your cellular bars, Wi-Fi strength, and battery level. (The left ear turns red, green, or blue to provide privacy warnings from background apps, as described in a moment.)

To see the full range of status icons, *swipe down from the right ear* to open the Control Center (page 42). Everything, including the cell network name, appears on this screen—although, if you're having a bad day, you'll see the words "No Service" instead.

Home-Button Phones: The Status Bar

The icons you may see in the status bar at the top of a home-button iPhone screen can convey a huge range of information—if you know how to interpret them. Here they are, from left to right.

- **Cell signal (.ıll).** The number of bars indicates the strength of your cell signal, and thus the likelihood of losing the connection. If there are no bars, then the dreaded words "No Service" appear here.

- **Network name and type.** These days, different parts of the country—and even your street—are blanketed by cellular internet signals of different speeds, types, and ages. Your status bar shows you the kind of network signal it has.

  From slowest to fastest:

  E or **○** means your iPhone is connected to your carrier's slowest, oldest internet system. You might be able to check email, but you'll lose your mind waiting for a web page to load.

  If you see **3G**, you're in a 3G network—still slow compared with **4G**, which offers speed in between 3G and LTE.

  And if you see **LTE** up there—well, get psyched. You're in a city with a 4G LTE cellular network. And that means *very* fast internet.

NOTE: If you're an AT&T customer, you might also see a **5GE** logo. Don't be fooled—that's not 5G, the superfast network coming to iPhones in 2020. That's just sneaky AT&T's version of LTE.

You may also see a notation like "T-Mobile Wi-Fi" or "VZW Wi-Fi." The iPhone can make free phone calls over a Wi-Fi network—if your cellphone carrier has permitted it, and if you've turned the feature on (page 592). It's a great way to make calls indoors where the cell signal is terrible.

- **Airplane mode (✈).** If you see this instead of cell-signal and Wi-Fi bars, then the iPhone is in airplane mode (page 494).

- **Do Not Disturb (☾).** Nothing can make the phone ring, buzz, or light up except calls from the most important people. See page 70.

- **Wi-Fi signal (📶).** You're connected to a wireless hotspot. The more "sound waves" you see, the stronger the signal.

- **10:19 PM.** When the iPhone is unlocked, a digital clock appears on the status bar.

- **Alarm (⏰).** A valuable reminder that you have an alarm set.

- **Wireless earbuds (🎧).** The iPhone is connected wirelessly to a Bluetooth earpiece, earbuds, or headphones. (You may even see the device's battery gauge: ▯.)

- **TTY (☎).** You've turned on Teletype mode, meaning the iPhone can communicate with a Teletype machine. (That's a machine that lets deaf people make phone calls by typing and reading text. It hooks up to the iPhone with a special cable Apple sells from its website.)

- **Call forwarding (↪).** You've told your iPhone to auto-forward any incoming calls to a different number. This icon explains at a glance why your iPhone never seems to get calls anymore.

- **VPN (▬).** You corporate stud! You've managed to connect to your corporate network over a secure internet connection, probably with the assistance of a system administrator—or by consulting page 612.

- **Syncing (✷).** The iPhone is currently syncing with some internet service—iCloud, for example (Chapter 16).

- **Battery meter (▬⚡).** When the iPhone is charging, the lightning bolt appears. Otherwise, the battery logo "empties out" from right to left to indicate how much charge remains. (You can even add a "% full" indicator to this gauge; see page 621.)

- **Navigation active (➀).** You're running a GPS navigation app, or some other app that's tracking your location, in the background (yay, multi-tasking!). Why is a special icon necessary? Because those GPS apps slurp down battery power like a thirsty golden retriever. Apple wants to make sure you don't forget you're running it.

- **Rotation lock (➁).** This icon reminds you that you've deliberately turned off the screen-rotation feature, where the screen image turns 90 degrees when you rotate the phone. See page 45.

From time to time, you'll see the left ear or the entire status bar change color. That's its way of saying, "Hey, watch what you're saying or doing, because an app in the background is observing you!" Here's your key:

- **Red** for when you're recording in the background—either using the Voice Memos app to record audio or the screen-recording feature described on page 359.

- **Green** for when you're on a phone call or FaceTime call in the background. They can still hear you!

- **Blue** for when an app is actively tracking your *location*. If you're using GPS or something, well, that's fine. But if it's some evil app that's tracking you, now you'll know.

> **TIP:** In each case, you can tap that colored status bar (or, on Face ID phones, that colored ear) to jump into the app responsible.

Cameras and Flash

On a Face ID phone, the front-facing camera is hiding inside the notch (page 22). On a home-button phone, above the screen, there's a horizontal slot. That's the earpiece. Just above it or beside it, the tiny pinhole is the front-facing camera.

This camera's primary purpose is to let you take selfies and conduct video chats using the FaceTime feature, but it's also handy for checking for spinach in your teeth.

Until the iPhone 11 family came along, the front camera was never as good as the back cameras, though; it's always been worse in low light and taken much lower-resolution shots.

A tiny LED lamp appears next to this back lens—actually, it's two lamps on the 6 and 6s iPhones, and *four* on the 7, 8, and Face ID phones. That's the flash for the camera, the video light when you're shooting movies, and a darned good flashlight for reading restaurant menus and theater programs in low light. Open the Control Center (page 42) and tap the 🔦 icon to turn the light on and off.

The pinhole nestled near the lenses is a microphone. It's used for recording clearer sound with video, for better noise cancellation on phone calls, and for better directional sound pickup.

The iPhone Plus models and Face ID models actually have two or even *three* lenses on the back, for different degrees of zoom. Details on this feature and everything else on the iPhone's cameras are in Chapter 9.

Sensors

Behind the glass above the screen are two sensors. (On the black iPhones, you can't see them except with a flashlight.) First, there's an ambient-light sensor that brightens the display when you're in sunlight and dims it in darker places.

Second, there's a proximity sensor. When something (like your head) is close to the sensor, it shuts off the screen and touch sensitivity. It works only in the Phone app. With the screen off, you save power and avoid dialing with your cheekbone when you're on a call.

SIM Card Slot

On the right edge of the iPhone, there's a pinhole on what looks like a very thin slot cover. If you push an unfolded paper clip straight into the hole, the *SIM card* tray pops out.

A SIM card is a tiny memory card that stores your account info— things like your phone number and calling-plan details. (SIM stands for "subscriber identity module.")

By removing the card from one phone and putting it into *another* phone, you can transplant a phone's brain. The other phone now knows your number and account details, which can be handy when your iPhone goes in for repair. For example, you can turn a Verizon iPhone 11 into a T-Mobile iPhone 11 just by swapping in a T-Mobile SIM card.

Knowing about SIM cards is also smart when you travel overseas, because you can rent a cheap local SIM card to use while you're there. You'll avoid racking up hundreds of dollars in international roaming fees on your own plan, but of course you'll have a different phone number temporarily.

TIP: If you'd rather keep your own plan and number overseas, contact your carrier before you go. Tell them where you plan to travel, and ask for a temporary international plan. If you fail to make this call, you may (a) not be able to use the phone at all, or (b) pay through the nose, ears, and eyeballs for the roaming surcharges. (One exception: On T-Mobile, international texting and internet are free.)

There are some situations when swapping SIM cards from one iPhone to another isn't straightforward. Here are some of the gotchas:

- **If your objective is to switch carriers** (for example, Verizon to T-Mobile), you'll need an *unlocked* iPhone. A locked phone is married, by software, to your original carrier; that's how they make sure you're not going to ditch them while you still owe them money.

  If you bought your iPhone from your original carrier, it's probably locked. Contact customer service; they'll unlock it for you by remote control (assuming you don't owe them money). If you bought it new from any other source, and paid for it up-front, it's already unlocked.

- **If you have a GSM iPhone from T-Mobile or AT&T,** it won't work on the Sprint or Verizon networks, alas.

- **The iPhone XS, XS Max, 11, and 11 Pro models** can, incredibly, have two phone numbers. You might have one for work and the other for personal use.

  There's a physical SIM card, plus an *electronic* SIM (eSIM). There's some fine print here: The feature works only if your carrier offers it, and it requires an unlocked iPhone. But it's been done right; for example, you can specify which line gets dialed for each person in your Contacts. (And if you don't specify, the iPhone just uses the number you used last time.)

If you were curious enough to open the SIM card tray, you can close it simply by pushing it back into the phone until it clicks.

Headphone Jack

Until the iPhone 7 came along, iPhones contained a standard jack for plugging in earbuds or headphones.

No Headphone Jack

Why did Apple remove the headphone jack from the iPhone 7 and later models? Well, that jack may not seem very big—but on the *inside* of the phone, the corresponding receptacle occupied an unnerving amount of nonnegotiable space. Apple wanted that space back: for a bigger battery, for a better camera, for new features.

So how are you supposed to listen to music without a headphone jack? Apple offers three ways:

- **Use the adapter.** Apple makes a 2-inch adapter cord that connects any headphones to the phone's Lightning (charging) jack. It came in the box with iPhone 7, 8, and X models; it's a separate purchase for later models (how rude!).

- **Use the earbuds.** The phone also comes with white earbuds that connect to the Lightning jack.

> **TIP:** Of course, if your headphones are plugged into the Lightning jack, you can't charge your phone while listening over them. Fortunately, Amazon is full of cheap adapters that let you charge and plug in headphones simultaneously.

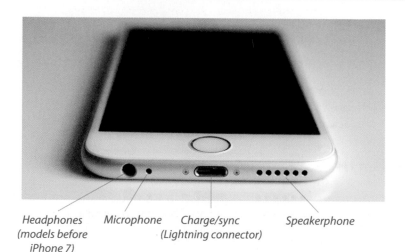

Headphones   Microphone   Charge/sync   Speakerphone
(models before   (Lightning connector)
iPhone 7)

- **Use wireless headphones.** You can also use any Bluetooth wireless earbuds—from $17 plastic disposable ones to Apple's own, impressive AirPods. Page 154 has more on Bluetooth headsets.

In theory, those three approaches should pretty much cover you whenever you want to listen.

In practice, though, you'll still get zapped by the occasional inconvenience. You'll be on a flight, for example, listening to your laptop with headphones—and when you want to switch to the phone, you'll realize your adapter cord is buried in the overhead bin (based on a true story).

But this kind of hassle is the new reality. Samsung, Motorola, Google, HTC, and other companies have already ditched the headphone jack on their phones, and other phone makers will follow suit.

Microphone, Speakerphone

On the bottom of the iPhone, Apple has parked some important audio components: the speaker and a microphone or two.

On the iPhone 7 and later models, actually, there are two speakers, on the top and bottom of the phone. Stereo sound has come to the iPhone. (Face ID phones even *record* video in stereo.)

NOTE: On the bottom edge, inside a perforated grille, a tiny second microphone lurks. It's the key to the iPhone's noise-cancellation feature. It listens to the sound of the world around you and pumps in the opposite sound waves to cancel out all that ambient noise. It doesn't do anything for *you*—the noise cancellation affects what the *other* person on the phone hears.

That's why there's yet *another* microphone at the top back (between the camera and flash); it's designed to supply noise cancellation for you, so the other person sounds better when you're in a noisy place.

Lightning Connector

On the bottom edge of the phone, right in the center, you'll find the connector that charges and syncs the iPhone with your computer.

For nearly 10 years, the charge/sync connector was the famous 30-pin connector. But starting on the iPhone 5, Apple replaced that inch-wide connector with a far-smaller one it calls Lightning. The Lightning connector is a great design: It clicks nicely into place (you can even dangle the iPhone from it), yet you can yank it right out. You can insert the Lightning into the phone either way—there's no "right-side up." It's much sturdier than the old connector. And it's tiny, which was Apple's primary goal—only 0.3 inches wide.

30-pin connector (iPhone 4S)

Lightning connector (iPhone 5 and later)

You may still occasionally encounter a car adapter or hotel-room alarm clock with the old kind of connector. (For $30, you can buy an adapter.)

Over the years, a new ecosystem of accessories based on the Lightning connector has arisen. We'll enjoy a new era of standardization—until Apple changes jacks again.

Antenna Band

Radio signals can't pass through metal. That's why there are strips or panels of plastic or glass on every iPhone.

And there are a *lot* of radio signals going into this phone. All told, there are *20* different radio transceivers inside the modern iPhone. They tune in to the LTE, 3G, and 4G signals used in various countries around the world, plus the three CDMA signals used in the U.S.; and one each for Wi-Fi, Bluetooth, American GPS, and Russian GPS.

In the Box

Inside the minimalist box, you get the iPhone and these items:

- **A Lightning cable.** When you connect your iPhone to your computer using this cable, it simultaneously syncs and charges. See Chapter 15.

- **The AC adapter.** When you're traveling without a computer, you can plug the dock's USB cable into the included two-prong outlet adapter, so you can charge the iPhone directly from a wall socket.

TIP: Apple's 18-watt adapter offers fast charging for the iPhone 8 and later, meaning 30 minutes to a 50 percent charge. It's $30—or included right in the box with the iPhone 11 Pro.

- **The earbuds.** Every iPhone comes with a pair of the iconic white earbuds that announce to the world, "I have an iPhone!" These days, they're what Apple calls EarPods. They sound great, although their bulbous shape may get uncomfortable in smaller ears. A volume control/clicker is right there on the cord, so you can answer phone calls and pause the music without even taking the phone out of your pocket. (The EarPods that come with the iPhone 7 and later plug into the Lightning jack, since there's no headphone jack. The 7, 8, and original X phones also come with that 2-inch adapter cable for existing earbuds.)

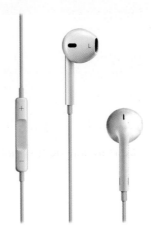

- **Decals and info card.** iPhone essentials.

Finger Techniques

On the iPhone, you operate all your software using the touchscreen instead of physical buttons.

Tap

The iPhone's onscreen buttons are big, giving your fingertip a fat target.

You can't use a fingernail or a pen tip; only skin contact works. (You can also buy an iPhone stylus. But a fingertip is cheaper and harder to misplace.)

Double-Tap

Double-tapping is generally reserved for two functions:

- **In the Safari, Photos, and Maps apps,** double-tapping zooms in on whatever you tap, magnifying it. (At that point, double-tapping means "Restore to original size.") Double-tapping also zooms in to formatted email messages, PDF files, Microsoft Office files, and other things.

- **When you're watching a video,** double-tapping switches the aspect ratio (video screen shape).

Swipe

In some situations, you're asked to confirm an action by *swiping* your finger across the screen. That's how you confirm that you want to shut off the phone, for example. Swiping is also a great shortcut for deleting an email or a text message.

Drag

When you're zoomed into a map, web page, email, or photo, you scroll around by sliding your finger across the glass in any direction—like a flick (read on), but slower and more controlled. It's a huge improvement over scroll bars, especially when you want to scroll diagonally.

Pinch and Spread

In apps like Photos, Mail, Safari, and Maps, you can zoom in on a photo, message, web page, or map by *spreading*.

That's when you place two fingers (usually thumb and forefinger) on the glass and spread them. The image magically grows, as though it were printed on a sheet of rubber.

NOTE: English has failed Apple here. Moving your thumb and forefinger closer together has an appropriate verb: *pinching*. But there's no good word to describe moving them the opposite direction. Apple uses the expression *pinch out* to describe that move (along with the redundant-sounding *pinch in*). But in this book, the opposite of "pinching" is "spreading."

Once you've zoomed in like this, you can zoom out again by putting two fingers on the glass and pinching them together.

Flick

A *flick* is a faster, less-controlled *drag*. You flick vertically to scroll lists on the iPhone. The faster you flick, the faster the list spins downward or upward. Lists have a real-world sort of momentum; they slow down after a second or two, so you can see where you wound up.

At any point during the scrolling of a list, you can flick again (if you didn't go far enough) or tap to stop the scrolling (if you see the item you want).

Edge Swipes

Swiping your finger inward from *outside* the screen has a few variations:

- **From the top edge.** Opens the Notification Center, which lists all your missed calls and texts, shows your appointments, and so on.

- **From the bottom edge.** On home-button iPhones, opens the Control Center, a unified miniature control panel for brightness, volume, Wi-Fi, and so on. (On Face ID phones, swipe down from the right ear instead.)

- **From the left edge.** In many apps, this means "Go back to the previous screen." That works in Mail, Settings, Notes, Messages, Safari, Facebook, and some others. At the Home screen, it opens the Today screen (page 76).

It sometimes makes a difference whether you begin your swipe *within* the screen or *outside* it. At the Home screen, for example, starting your downward swipe within the screen area doesn't open the Notification Center—it opens the iPhone's search function.

Quick Actions (Long-Press)

If you long-press an app's icon (touch until you feel a little vibration on most phones), you get a shortcut menu of useful commands. Apple calls them *quick actions*, and each is designed to save you a couple of steps. Sometimes, above the commands, you get a bubble of information, too. (That bubble may offer an Add Widget button; see page 76.)

Some examples:

- **The Camera app** icon offers Take Selfie, Record Video, Take Photo, and Take Portrait Selfie commands.

- **Photos** offers a bubble of icons for the four most recent Memories it's come up with (page 320), as well as Most Recent, Favorites, One Year Ago, and Search commands.

- **Notes** gives you **New Note**, **New Checklist**, **New Photo**, and **Scan Document** commands. In the bubble, you see the last note you edited.

- **Maps** offers **Mark My Location**, **Send My Location**, and **Search Nearby** (for restaurants, bars, shops, and so on). When you're at home, you may see your travel time to work and the current traffic situation.

- **The Phone app** sprouts icons for people you've called recently, as well as **Create New Contact**, **Search for Contact**, **View Most Recent Call**, and **View Most Recent Voicemail** (handy!).

- **Calendar** opens a bubble that displays your next appointment, plus an **Add Event** command.

- **Reminders** displays whatever deadline is coming up next. It also lists some of your reminder categories, so you can create a new to-do directly inside one of them (for example, **New in Family**).

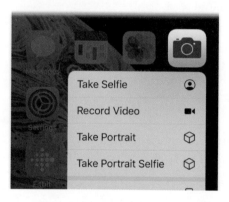 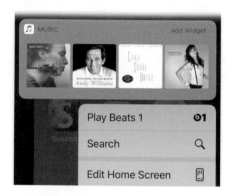

- **Mail and Messages** offer **New Message** commands. Mail also offers **Search**, **New Message**, and an inbox or two. Both apps display an icon (or several) representing recent correspondents.

- **Music** displays a bubble of four recent album-art icons, along with commands for **Play Beats 1** and **Search**.

- **Home-screen folders** sprout a **Rename** command at your fingertip. Sometimes you're offered the names of a couple of apps inside, too.

Similar quick actions also sprout from these Apple apps' icons: Clock, Measure, Wallet, iTunes Store, App Store, TV, Health, Weather, Calculator, Books, News, Safari, FaceTime, Podcasts, Contacts, and Find My.

Non-Apple apps often offer shortcut menus, too. For example, the Fitbit app offers one-tap ways to log your weight, water or food intake, or exercises. The Delta app offers quick links for **Check In**, **Flight Status**, and

My Trips. The Uber app offers one-tap buttons for booking a ride to your **Home** or place of **Work**.

> **TIP:** The **Edit Home Screen** command appears in the shortcut menu for *every* app. Tap it to commence dragging your icons around as described on page 365. (Alternatively, just keep pressing past the point of the shortcut menu's appearance.)

And, of course, you can use long-presses to respond to notifications: Reply to a text message, accept a Calendar invitation, or see where your Uber is on a map.

You can long-press a message in a list in Mail; you get both a preview bubble and a shortcut menu of handy commands like **Reply**, **Reply All**, **Forward**, and so on. Drag upward on the preview to see the hidden shortcut commands.

You can also long-press in Maps (preview information about a pushpin), Calendar (see details of an event), Photos (preview a photo in a screenful of thumbnails), Safari (preview the page hiding behind a link), Weather (add a new city or see weather details for a name in the list of cities), Music (shows you albums you can play with a tap on the cover art), TV (read details about a movie in a list), Notes (see the contents of a note's name in a list), the Messages list (see quick replies like "Yes" and Thanks"), and News (preview the body of an article in a list).

> **NOTE:** 3D Touch is on its way out.
>
> The screens on iPhone models from the 6s to the XS can detect *how hard* your finger is pressing, thanks to a technology Apple called 3D Touch. For example, you can hard-press a message in your email inbox to see a preview of its contents. (You can no longer press even *harder* to open the message full-screen, though, the feature called Peek and Pop.)
>
> Unfortunately, people found 3D Touch *plus* long-pressing to be one interface technique too many; they were confused and frustrated. So in iOS 13, hard-pressing still works in most contexts on 3D Touch phones. But *long*-pressing works in all those same places—and on *all* iOS 13 phone models.

Charging the iPhone

The iPhone has a built-in, rechargeable battery that fills up most of its interior. How long a charge lasts depends on what you're doing—music playback saps the battery the least; games and GPS navigation sap it the most. But one thing is for sure: You'll have to recharge the iPhone regularly. For most people, it's every night.

> **NOTE:** The iPhone's battery isn't replaceable. It's *rechargeable*, but after 400 or 500 charges, it starts to hold less juice. Eventually, you'll have to pay Apple to install a new battery. (Apple says the added bulk of a protective plastic battery compartment, a removable door and latch, and battery-retaining springs would have meant a much smaller battery—or a much thicker iPhone.)

Charging with the Cable

You recharge the iPhone by connecting the white Lightning cable that came with it. In general, people plug the far end into either of two places:

- **A computer's USB jack.** In general, the iPhone charges even if your computer is asleep. (If it's a laptop that itself is not plugged in, though, the phone charges only if the laptop is awake. Otherwise, you could come home to a depleted laptop.)

- **The AC adapter.** The little white two-prong cube that came with the iPhone connects to the end of the cradle's USB cable.

Unless the charge is *really* low, you can use the iPhone while it charges. The battery icon in the upper-right corner displays a lightning bolt to let you know it's charging.

> **TIP:** If you have an iPhone 6 or later, it'll charge much faster if you charge it with the 2.1-amp wall adapter that comes with an iPad, instead of the 1-amp adapter that comes with the phone. How does a 90 percent charge in two hours sound?
>
> Better yet: If you have an iPhone 8 or later, you can get *really* fast charging—along the lines of 50 percent charge in 30 minutes—but only if you connect it to a USB-C power brick plugged into the wall. Apple sells one, the 18W USB-C Power Adapter, for $29—but the cable you need (USB-C to Lightning) isn't included. Fast charging is cool, but it ain't cheap. (The 18-watt charger is included only with the iPhone 11 Pro.)

Charging on a Pad (iPhone 8 and later)

iPhone fans can stop looking at Samsung owners with envy: Now you, too, can charge your phone by setting it down on a Qi charging pad.

> **NOTE:** Qi, pronounced "chee," is the Chinese word for the life force in everyone and everything. It's also a great word for Scrabble.

You can buy one of these tabletop charging pads from any company; they cost about $12 on Amazon. You have to plug the pad into a power outlet, of course—wireless charging isn't really wireless at all. But at least you're spared the hassle of plugging and unplugging a cable every night. You just place the iPhone face-up onto the pad, and boom: The little lightning-bolt icon appears, and the "now charging" chime sounds.

Some fun facts about speed:

- **Charging a dead iPhone** for two hours brings it to about 40 percent charge on a standard 5-watt Qi pad, or to about 50 percent if you use a "fast-charging" 7.5-watt pad. (For comparison, two hours brings it to 80 percent charge using the standard Lightning cable.)

- **If you plug in the Lightning cable** *and* put the phone on the charging pad, you don't cut the time in half. In that situation, the cable wins. The pad does nothing.

Battery Life Tips

For most people, the battery life of the iPhone is about a day. But if you can't even make it to bedtime, knowing how to scale back your iPhone's power appetite should come in extremely handy.

These are the biggest wolfers of electricity: the screen and background activity (especially internet activity). Therefore, when you're nervous about your battery on an important day, here are your options:

- **Low Power Mode** can squeeze another three hours of life out of a charge.

  In Low Power Mode, your iPhone quits doing a lot of stuff in the background, like fetching new mail and updating apps. It also stops playing most of iOS's cute animations and stops listening for you to say

"Hey Siri" (page 160). The processor slows down, too; it takes longer to switch between apps, for example. And the battery indicator turns yellow, to remind you why things have suddenly slowed down.

Unless you've fiddled with the settings, you get an invitation to turn on Low Power Mode when your battery sinks to 20 percent remaining, and then again at 10 percent. You can also turn on this mode manually, using the Control Center (page 42) or the switch in **Settings→Battery** (below, top right).

If your phone is plugged in, it exits Low Power Mode automatically once it has enough juice (lower right).

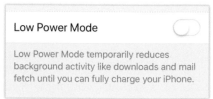

At any time, you can also shut down juice-guzzling features manually. Here they are, roughly in order of power appetite:

- **Dim the screen.** Turning down your screen saves a lot of battery power. The quickest way is to open the Control Center (page 42), and then drag the brightness slider.

  On a new iPhone, Auto-Brightness is turned on, too. In bright light, the screen brightens automatically; in dim light, it darkens. That's because when you unlock the phone after waking it, it samples the ambient light and adjusts the brightness.

NOTE: This works because of the ambient-light sensor near the earpiece. Apple says it experimented with having the light sensor active all the time, but it was weird to have the screen constantly dimming and brightening as you used it.

(You can turn this auto-brightness feature off in **Settings→ Accessibility→Display & Text Size**.)

TIP: You can set things up so a triple-click on the home button or side button instantly dims your screen. It doesn't save any power, but it's great for use in the bedroom, movie theater, or planetarium— without having to fuss with settings or sliders. See page 257 for this awesome trick.

- **Turn off "push" data.** If your email, calendar, and address book are kept constantly synced with the internet, then you've probably gotten yourself involved with Yahoo Mail, iCloud (Chapter 16), or Microsoft Exchange. Unfortunately, all that continual sniffing of the airwaves, looking for updates, costs you battery life. If you can do without the immediacy, visit **Settings→Passwords & Accounts→Fetch New Data**. If you turn off the Push feature for each email account and set it to **Manually** instead, your iPhone checks for email and new appointments only when you actually *open* the Mail or Calendar apps. Your battery goes a lot further.

- **Beware GPS.** GPS navigation, in Maps or Google Maps, drains your battery power like a hole in a water bucket. So as you drive, once your guidance app has led you to a place you recognize, by all means shut it off.

  But there's more. In **Settings→Privacy→Location Services**, there's a list of all the apps on your phone that are using its location feature to know where you are. It's a combination of GPS, cell-tower triangulation, and Wi-Fi hotspot triangulation. And it uses battery power.

  Some apps, like Maps, Find My, and Yelp, don't do you much good unless they know your location. But plenty of others don't really need to know where you are. Facebook and Twitter, for example, want that information only so they can location-stamp your posts. In any case, the point is to turn off Location Services for each app that doesn't really need to know where you are.

TIP: In the list of apps under Location Services, tiny ➍ icons show you which apps are using GPS right now and which have used it in the past 24 hours. These icons can guide you in shutting off the GPS use of various apps.

- **Beware processor gluttons.** 3D games and other graphically intensive apps are serious power hogs, too.

- **Turn off background updating.** Non-Apple apps check frequently for updates, too: Facebook, Twitter, stock-reporting apps, and so on. Not all of them need to be busily toiling in the background. Your best bet for battery life, then, involves visiting **Settings→General→Background App Refresh** and turning the switch off for each app whose background activity isn't strictly necessary.

- **Turn off Wi-Fi.** If you're not in a wireless hotspot, you may as well stop the phone from using its radio. Open the Control Center and tap the 📶 icon to turn it off. Or at the very least tell the iPhone to stop *searching* for Wi-Fi networks it can connect to. Page 492 has the details.

- **Turn off Bluetooth.** If you're not using a Bluetooth gadget (headset, fitness band, or whatever), then for heaven's sake shut down the Bluetooth radio. Open the Control Center and tap the ✳ to turn it off.

- **Turn off cellular data.** This option (in **Settings→Cellular**, but there's also a Control Center button for it: 📡) turns off the cellular internet features of your phone. You can still make calls, and you can still get online in a Wi-Fi hotspot.

  This feature is designed for people who have a capped data plan—a limited amount of internet use per month. If you discover you've used up almost all your data allotment for the month, and you don't want to go over your limit (and trigger an overage charge), you can use this option to shut off all data. Now your phone is just a phone—and it uses less power.

- **Consider airplane mode.** In airplane mode, you shut off *all* the iPhone's power-hungry radios. Even a nearly dead iPhone can hobble on for a few hours in airplane mode—something to remember when you're desperate. To enter airplane mode, tap the ✈ icon in the Control Center (page 42).

TIP: For sure turn on airplane mode if you'll be someplace where you *know* an internet signal won't be present—like on a plane, a ship at sea, or Wyoming. Your iPhone never burns through a battery charge faster than when it's hunting for a signal it can't find; your battery will be dead within a couple of hours.

- **Turn off the screen.** With a press of the side button, you can turn off the screen, rendering it black and saving power. That won't interrupt audio playback—like music or podcasts—or Maps navigation.

If your battery still seems to be draining too fast, check out the table on the facing page at right, which shows you exactly which apps are using the most power.

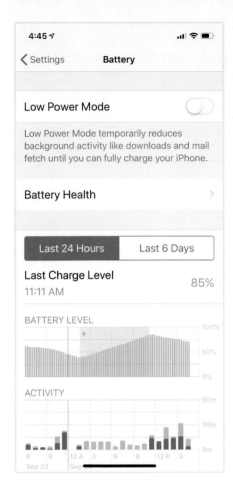

To see it, open **Settings→Battery**. You can switch between battery read-outs for the past 24 hours, or for the past six to ten days.

Keep special watch for apps bearing these labels:

- **Low Signal.** A phone uses the most power of all when it's hunting for a cellular signal, because it has to amplify its radios in hopes of finding one. If your battery seems to be running down faster than usual, the "Low Signal" notation is a great clue—and a suggestion that maybe you should use airplane mode when you're on the fringes of cellular coverage.

- **Background activity.** Background internet connections are especially insidious. These are apps that do online work invisibly, without your awareness—and drain the battery in the process. Here you can clearly see which apps are doing it.

Once you know the culprit app, it's easy to shut its background work down. Open **Settings→General→Background App Refresh** and switch off each app whose background activity isn't strictly necessary.

TIP: If you tap **Settings→Battery →Show Activity** (previous page, right), the screen shows you how much *time* each app has spent running—both in the foreground and in the background. It's an incredibly informative display if you've been wondering where all your battery power has been going.

There is, by the way, another kind of battery life: the battery's lifespan. In iOS 13, for the first time, Apple has given you a feature to prolong it: **Optimized Battery Charging**. If you turn this feature on in **Settings→Battery→Battery Health**, the phone can limit its charging to 80 percent full most times—a classic trick for making lithium-ion batteries last longer. It studies your charging habits, though, so it's supposed to give you a full charge when you need it.

Control Center

For such a tiny device, there are an awful lot of settings you can change—*hundreds* of them. Trouble is, some of them (volume, brightness) need changing a lot more often than others (language preference, voicemail greeting).

That's why Apple invented the Control Center: a panel that offers quick access to the controls you need the most.

To open the Control Center, no matter what app you're using, do like this:

- **Face ID phones:** Swipe down from the upper-right ear.

TIP: On the Lock screen, a faint underline appears beneath the right ear to remind you the Control Center is there.

- **Home-button phones:** Swipe upward from beneath the screen.

You can even open the Control Center, using these techniques, from the Lock screen (unless you've turned off that feature in **Settings→Face ID & Passcode→Allow Access When Locked: Control Center**).

Now, it's worth pointing out that many of the Control Center's settings are even faster to change using Siri, as described in Chapter 5. When it's not socially awkward to speak to your phone (like at the symphony or during a golf game), you can use spoken commands to adjust settings without even touching the screen.

The Starter Set

You can customize what appears on the Control Center, but the following controls are nonnegotiable. They're your starter set, and you can't remove most of them.

> **TIP:** In many cases, you can *long-press* one of these buttons to open a subpanel that offers even more controls, as shown below at right. The following write-up dives into those long-press options in detail.

Airplane mode, Cellular data, Wi-Fi, Bluetooth

What you get when you long-press that top-left tile

- **Airplane mode (✈).** Tap to turn the icon orange. Now you're in airplane mode; the phone's wireless features are all turned off. You're saving the battery and obeying FAA regulations. Tap again to turn off airplane mode.

  Sample Siri command: "Turn airplane mode on." (Siri warns you that if you turn airplane mode on, Siri herself will stop working. Say, "OK.")

- **Cellular data (ᵗ).** This icon is the on/off switch for your iPhone's connection to the internet over the cellular airwaves (rather than

Wi-Fi). Cellular data, after all, costs you money—especially when you're roaming (page 602)—and you may have a monthly limit. So it's good to be able to control when you're using it up.

Sample Siri command: "Turn off cellular data."

- **Wi-Fi (◌).** Tap to turn your phone's Wi-Fi off (white) or on (blue).

Sample Siri commands: "Turn off Wi-Fi." "Turn Wi-Fi on."

> **NOTE:** The **Wi-Fi** and **Bluetooth** buttons here in the Control Center turn off those wireless features only *partly* and only *temporarily*.
>
> The first time you use these buttons, a message appears, letting you know that Wi-Fi or Bluetooth will be off only until tomorrow (namely, until 5 a.m.). Apparently, a lot of people forgot to turn these features on again—when, for example, getting into their Bluetooth-equipped cars the next day.
>
> Meanwhile, some aspects of these technologies remain on— enough Wi-Fi to let AirDrop (page 380), Personal Hotspot (page 495), and Location Services (page 623) work, and enough Bluetooth to let the Apple Watch, Apple Pencil, Personal Hotspot, and Handoff connect.
>
> Bottom line: Turning off Wi-Fi or Bluetooth in the Control Center doesn't save you as much battery, or block as many radio signals, as *really* turning them off. If that's your goal, go into Settings→Wi-Fi or Settings→Bluetooth and do it the hard way.

- **Bluetooth (✳).** Tap to turn your Bluetooth transmitter off (white) or on (blue).

Sample Siri commands: "Turn Bluetooth on." "Turn off Bluetooth."

Long-press options: If you long-press anywhere in this cluster of four wireless buttons, you pop open a new panel. It offers the same buttons—**Airplane Mode, Cellular Data, Wi-Fi, Bluetooth**—with labels, this time, along with two more.

First, there's **AirDrop** (◉). This feature gives you a quick, effortless way to shoot photos, maps, web pages, and other stuff to nearby iPhones, iPads, iPod Touches, and even Macs. (See page 380 for details.) Tap this button to see the AirDrop controls.

Second, there's **Personal Hotspot** (◉), which lets your phone act as a Wi-Fi hotspot for your laptop or other gadgets (page 495).

> **TIP:** Once you've opened this mini-panel, long-press again on the ◌ button to specify *which* hotspot you want to join—or long-press ✳ to specify which Bluetooth gadget to connect to. These are nifty iOS 13 shortcuts. See page 33.

- **Music.** On this little tile, you see information about the current song, plus playback controls (◀◀, ▶, ▶▶).

  These controls govern playback in whatever app is playing music or podcasts in the background: the Music app, Pandora, Spotify, whatever it is. You can skip a horrible song quickly and efficiently without having to interrupt what you're doing, or pause your podcast to chat with a colleague.

  Sample Siri commands: "Pause the music." "Skip to the next song." "Play some Billy Joel."

  Long-press options: The subpanel offers a scrubber bar that shows where you are in the song, the album art, and a button (◉) that lets you choose what speaker you want to use. It always lists **iPhone** (the built-in speakers), but it may also list things like a Bluetooth speaker, earbuds, or AirPlay, which sends music or video to a wireless speaker system or TV (see page 285).

  There's also a volume slider. It lets you make big volume jumps faster than you can by pressing the volume buttons on the side of the phone.

- **Rotation lock (⟲).** When rotation lock is turned on (red), the screen no longer rotates when you turn the phone 90 degrees. The idea is that sometimes, like when you're reading an ebook on your side in bed, you don't want the screen picture to turn; you want it to stay upright relative to your eyes. (A little ⟲ icon appears at the top of the screen to remind you why the usual rotating isn't happening. On iPhones with Face ID, you'll have to open the Control Center to see that icon.)

  The whole thing isn't quite as earth-shattering as it sounds—first, because it locks the image in only one way: upright, in portrait orientation. You can't make it lock into widescreen mode. Furthermore, many apps don't rotate with the phone to begin with. But when that day comes when you want to read in bed on your side, your iPhone will be ready. (Tap the button again to turn rotating back on.)

  There are no Siri or long-press options for this control.

- **Do Not Disturb (☾).** Do Not Disturb mode, described on page 70, means the phone won't ring or buzz when people call—except a few handpicked people whose communiqués are allowed to ring through. Perfect for sleeping hours; in fact, you can set up an automated schedule for Do Not Disturb (midnight to 7 a.m., say).

  But what if you wake up early or want to stay up late? You can tap to turn Do Not Disturb on (blue moon) or off (white).

Long-press options: Here's a brilliant feature: Do Not Disturb can turn itself *off* automatically. Long-pressing the Control Center icon offers you choices like **For 1 hour** (great for meetings), **Until tomorrow morning** (great for dates), and **Until I leave this location** (great for movies and plays). If the iPhone knows you're in a meeting, based on your calendar, you get a fourth option, which names the current appointment so that DND will turn off as soon as whatever-it-is ends.

An option to jump to your daily automatic **Schedule** for Do Not Disturb is here, too; it takes you to the screen described on page 70.

Sample Siri commands: "Turn on Do Not Disturb." "Turn Do Not Disturb off."

- **Brightness (☀).** Here's a screen-brightness slider—in the form of a big, fat vertical bar that's easy to operate. Drag anywhere within it, up or down, to change the brightness.

  Sample Siri commands: "Make the screen brighter." "Dim the screen."

  Long-press options: The subpanel presents an on/off button for three features: **Night Shift**, which makes the screen yellower before bedtime to prevent sleep disturbance (page 615); **True Tone**, a feature of the iPhone 8 and later phones that tweaks the screen colors to make them look consistent in whatever ambient light you're in (page 615); and **Dark Mode**, a new iOS 13 look described on page 5.

- **Volume (◀))).** Here it is, next to brightness: an equally big, fat volume slider. Slide your finger up or down to adjust the audio volume.

  Long-press options: Long-pressing doesn't gain you any *new* controls. It does, however, open up a much bigger version of the volume slider. It's now easier to make finer adjustments.

The bottom row of the starter icons, described next, are removable. If they're not floating your boat, see the next section for instructions on how to get rid of them.

- **Flashlight (🔦).** Tap to turn on the iPhone's "flashlight"—actually the LED lamp on the back that usually serves as the camera flash. Knowing that a source of good, clean light is a few touches away makes a huge difference if you're trying to read in the dark, find your way along a path at night, or fiddle with wires behind your desk.

NOTE: On the Face ID phones, there's also a flashlight button right on the Lock screen. Long-press it to turn it on.

Long-press options: You get a four-segment "slider" that controls the flashlight's brightness. The top segment means full brightness; the bottom one means Off. That's supercool, especially on the iPhone 7 and later, where the LED flashlight is enough to light up a high-school football game at night.

Sample Siri commands: "Turn on the flashlight." "Turn it off"

- **Timer (◉).** Tap to open the Clock app—specifically, the Timer mode, which counts down to zero. Apple figures you might appreciate having direct access to it when you're cooking, for example, or waiting for your hair color to set.

  Long-press options: Long-pressing gets you a cool "Set timer for" slider, so you can start a timer for anywhere from one minute to two hours with a single finger swipe. Hit **Start** to start, or tap outside the slider to cancel the whole procedure.

  Sample Siri commands: "Open the Timer." Or, better yet, bypass the Clock and Timer apps altogether: "Start the timer for three minutes." "Count down from six minutes." (Siri counts down right there on the Siri screen.)

- **Calculator (▦).** Tap to open the Calculator app—a handy shortcut if it's your turn to figure out how to divide up the restaurant bill.

  Long-press options: A Copy Last Result button appears, so you can snag whatever.

  Sample Siri commands: "Open the calculator." Or, better yet, without opening any app: "What's 106 divided by 5?"

- **Camera (▣).** Tap to jump directly into the Camera app. Because photo ops don't wait around.

  Long-press options: Handy! Here are the Take Selfie, Record Video, and (on Plus and Face ID models) Take Portrait commands. Each saves you a little fiddling in the Camera app.

  Sample Siri commands: "Take a picture." "Open the camera." "Scan QR Code." "Record video."

- **Home (⌂).** Here's instant access to your HomeKit smart-home gadgets, if any. Door locks, lights, thermostats, what have you. Tap to open a page of icons for the ones you've identified as your favorites (page 430); from here, tap to turn them on and off, or long-press to open their settings pages. (There aren't any long-press options on the Control Center icon itself.)

Sample Siri commands: "Turn on the kitchen lights." "Set the down-stairs to 70 degrees." You know.

Customizing the Control Center

Make Control Center your own! You can add all kinds of buttons to it.

The Center for Control Center Customization, as it turns out, is **Settings→ Control Center→ Customize Controls** (below, left). Here's a giant list (right) of the buttons you're allowed to add or remove. It's very simple: Tap ⊖ and then **Remove** to remove a button that's already installed. Tap ⊕ to install a button that's not yet on the Control Center.

And drag the little ☰ handles up or down to choose an *order* for your icons on the Control Center.

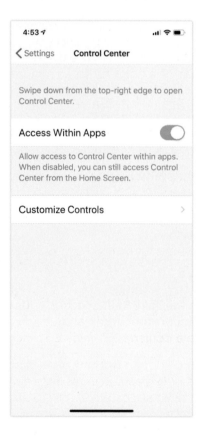 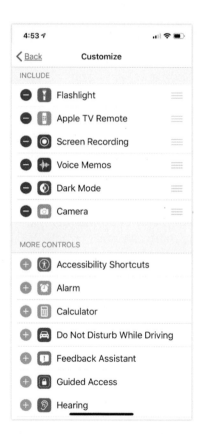

Here are your options (except as noted, none of them offer further options when you long-press):

- **Flashlight, Timer, Calculator, Camera, Home.** As described previously.

- **Accessibility Shortcuts.** Opens the same list of accessibility shortcuts (Zoom, VoiceOver, AssistiveTouch, and so on) you've chosen to list for quick access when you triple-click the home button. These options, and the triple-clicking business, are described on page 255.

- **Alarm.** Tap to open the Clock app, this time set to Alarm mode (page 414), where you can set (or turn off) an upcoming alarm.

- **Apple TV Remote.** This pops open an onscreen version of your Apple TV remote control, complete with Menu, Play, and Siri buttons—plus a large trackpad area for scrolling around. This item is fantastic when you can't seem to dig your actual Apple TV remote from under the couch cushions.

- **Dark Mode.** Turns on iOS 13's new Dark mode (page 5).

- **Do Not Disturb While Driving.** Apple is very proud of this feature, which prevents notifications, calls, or texts from lighting up your phone or making it ring whenever you're behind the wheel and in motion.

  You can read all about this feature on page 74. There you'll learn that you can (and probably should) set it to turn on *automatically* when you're driving. In other words, this button is primarily useful for turning DNDWD *off*—when you're in the passenger seat.

- **Guided Access.** Opens the on/off switch for Guided Access, otherwise known as "kiosk mode." It locks the phone into one particular app, so that (for example) your toddler can play with it without wreaking any havoc. See page 253.

- **Hearing.** Turns on Live Listen, the feature that turns your iPhone into a remote microphone for your AirPods wireless earbuds (page 256).

- **Low Power Mode.** Here's a one-touch way to manually switch on the battery-saving feature known as Low Power Mode (page 37).

- **Magnifier.** Turns the entire phone into a powerful, illuminated magnifying glass, as described on page 237.

- **Notes.** This is a big, big deal. The idea is to give you immediate access to Notes, so you can jump in, no matter what you were doing, to write down something quickly: a phone number someone's giving you, dosage instructions your doctor's rattling off, or a brainstorm you've just had for a million-dollar product.

TIP: One tap opens directly into the Notes app. But if you long-press instead, you get a list of commands like New Note, New Checklist, New Photo, and Scan Document.

Now then. If you make Notes part of the Control Center, it will be available even when the phone is locked. Clearly, that could be a privacy disaster if your phone falls into the hands of some passing evildoer.

Apple has given that scenario a lot of thought, though. First of all, if you open Notes from the Lock screen, there's no way to see any *existing* notes. You're stuck on a single page.

But that's not the end of the privacy control—oh, heavens, no. Open **Settings→Notes→Access Notes from Lock Screen**.

At the top, you have three choices. **Off** means forget it—you can't open Notes from the Lock screen at all. (So why bother putting the Notes button on the Control Center? Because you can still use it when the phone *isn't* locked.)

Always Create New Note means every time you open Notes from the Lock screen, you wind up at another fresh, empty Notes page.

And **Resume Last Note**…well, if you choose this option, Settings has a whole bunch more questions for you.

For example, if you open Notes from the Lock screen, do you want it to reopen the last note you viewed in the app? Or just the last note you opened *from the Lock screen*? That second option is another security precaution, keeping your Lock screen doodlings separate from your other stuff.

You also get a bunch of time settings, like **After 5 Minutes**, **After 15 Minutes**, and so on. What Apple is saying here: "Even though you've selected **Resume Last Note**, you're still going to get a new, *empty* note if it's been at least five minutes since the last time you looked at it. Just in case you wander off during a meeting and some idiot picks up your phone six minutes later to see what you were writing."

Never ignores all these options. It means that *every* time you open Notes from the Lock screen, you'll return to whatever Note page you've been working on.

If all these options make perfect sense to you, there are many fine career opportunities awaiting you at the Internal Revenue Service.

- **QR Code Reader.** Opens the Camera app in QR Code mode (page 647).

- **Screen Recording.** Here's a freak of iOS nature: a Control Center button for a feature you can't trigger in any other way. The idea, of course, is to let you record videos of what's happening on the iPhone screen—with narration, if you like. See page 359 for details.

- **Stopwatch.** Tap to open the Clock app, already tuned to the Stopwatch mode (page 418). You're all ready to time that 50-yard dash or teenage room-cleaning.

- **Text Size.** There are all kinds of ways to make text bigger and more readable on the iPhone's screen (see page 239). But this Control Center option gives you a more immediate way of making adjustments—say, when you find yourself on some web page in 3-point type. Tap to see a vertical slider, whose segments indicate increasingly larger type sizes. Slide your finger accordingly.

- **Voice Memos.** The Voice Memos app has always been handy for recording speeches, interviews, song ideas, and so on. What *hasn't* been handy is the long slog to get into the app and start recording.

  No more! Tap this button to open the Voice Memos app, where another tap begins the recording. Better yet, a long-press on this Control Center button produces a menu that lists your three most recent recordings (for instant playback)—and a **New Recording** button. In other words, you can get the audio capture going with only one tap-and-slide in the Control Center.

- **Wallet.** Here's another way to jump into your Apple Wallet—usually because you want to use Apple Pay (page 579). Tap this button to open the Apple Pay screen with your preferred card selected; at this point, you'll use your fingerprint—or on Face ID phones, your face—to complete the transaction.

Closing the Control Center

The Control Center closes when any of these things happen:

- **You tap one of the buttons** that opens an app (Timer, Calculator, Camera, Notes, and so on).

- **You tap anywhere** *except* on a button.

- **You swipe upward** (Face ID phones) or downward (home-button phones) anywhere on the Control Center.

- **You press the home button,** if you have one.

In some apps, on home-button phones, swiping up doesn't open the Control Center on the first try, much to your probable bafflement. Instead, swiping just makes a tiny appear at the edge of the screen. (You'll see this behavior whenever the status bar—where the time and battery gauge appear—is hidden, as in the full-screen modes of Books, Maps, TV, and so on. It also happens in the Camera app.)

In those situations, Apple is trying to protect you from opening the Control Center accidentally—for example, when what you really wanted to do was scroll up. No big deal; once the appears, swipe up *again* to open the Control Center.

If you find yourself opening the Control Center accidentally too often—when playing games, for example—you can turn it off. Open **Settings→Control Center**. Turn off **Access Within Apps**. Now swiping opens the Control Center only at the Home screen.

Passcode Protection

Like any smartphone, the iPhone offers a first line of defense if it ever winds up in the wrong hands. It's designed to keep your stuff private from other people in the house or the office, or to protect your information in case you lose the iPhone.

Some iPhone owners don't bother setting up a passcode. Maybe they never set the thing down, so they don't worry about privacy. Or maybe there's just not that much personal information on the phone—and meanwhile, having to enter a passcode every time you wake the phone can get to be a hassle.

TIP: If you ever do lose your phone, you can put a passcode on it by remote control; see page 573.

Everyone else figures that the inconvenience of entering a passcode many times a day is a small price to pay for the knowledge that nobody can get into your stuff if you lose your phone.

Of course, you can also protect your home-button phone with a fingerprint or your Face ID phone with face recognition. But both of those require that you *first* create a passcode, which will always be the fallback.

Even if you *usually* unlock the phone with your finger or face, you'll still be required to use that passcode, for added security, after any of these things occur:

- **You've restarted or shut down** the phone.

- **You've made several failed attempts** to log in with a finger or face.

- **It's been two days** since you unlocked the phone.

- **It's been six days** since you last entered your passcode, and you haven't used your finger or face in eight hours.

- **You started to turn off** the phone as described on page 20 but tapped Cancel instead.

None of that will be on the test. The point is that sometimes, even with finger or face recognition, you'll need your passcode.

Setting Up a Passcode

Now, you probably created a phone passcode the first time you turned your iPhone on; the iPhone practically insists on it.

But if you skipped that step, here's how to do it now.

Open Settings→Touch ID & Passcode. On iPhone Face ID models, it's called Face ID & Passcode.

Tap Turn Passcode On. iOS proposes that you make up a six-digit passcode. But if you tap Passcode Options, you can choose instead a Custom Alphanumeric Code (any password, any length), Custom Numeric Code (an all-number code, any length), or 4-Digit Numeric Code (you know—ATM style).

You're asked to type the passcode you want twice, to make sure you didn't make a typo.

NOTE: Don't kid around with this passcode. If you forget the code, you'll have to *restore* your iPhone (page 667), which wipes out everything on it. You've probably still got most of the data on your computer or backed up on iCloud, of course (music, video, contacts, calendar), but you may lose text messages, mail, and so on.

Once you confirm your passcode, you return to the Passcode Lock screen. Here you have a few more options.

The Require Passcode option lets you specify how quickly the passcode is requested before locking somebody out: anywhere from immediately after the iPhone wakes to as long as four hours later. (These options are a convenience to you, so you can quickly check your calendar or missed messages without having to enter the passcode—while still protecting your data from, for example, criminals who pick up your iPhone while you're out getting coffee.)

If you use Touch ID or Face ID, **Immediately** is your only option. Just keep your fingers or face handy.

Certain features are accessible on the Lock screen even before you've entered your passcode: the **Today** and **Notifications** tabs of the Notification Center, the **Control Center**, **Siri**, **Home Control**, **Reply with Message** (the ability to reply to text messages right from their notification bubble on the Lock screen), and **Return Missed Calls** (the option to return a missed call from *its* bubble, without unlocking the phone).

The **USB Accessories** option is meant to add security. **Off** means that, starting an hour after the phone has gone to sleep, anything you've plugged into the Lightning jack is electronically disconnected (aside from charging).

What Apple is worried about is that your family will wait till you've gone to bed, grab your iPhone, and then connect it to a computer, open iTunes, and sneakily get access to your data. Now they can't. (They can't sneakily connect your phone to earbuds or speakers, either.) If that seems a little far-fetched to you, then turn this on so you won't wonder why your plug-in gadgets don't seem to be working.

These are huge conveniences, but also, technically, a security risk. Somebody who finds your phone on your desk could, for example, blindly voice-dial your colleagues or use Siri to send a text. If you turn these switches off, nobody can use these features until after unlocking the phone with your passcode, fingerprint, or face.

Finally, here is **Erase Data**—an option that's both scary and reassuring. When this option is on, if someone makes 10 incorrect guesses at your passcode, the iPhone erases itself. It's assuming that some lowlife burglar is trying to crack into it to have a look at all your personal data.

This option, a pertinent one for professional people, provides potent protection from patient password prospectors.

And that is all. From now on, each time you wake your iPhone (if it's not within the window of repeat visits you established), you're asked for your passcode.

Fingerprint Security (Touch ID)

All home-button iPhones offer the option of using a more secure and convenient kind of "passcode": your fingertip.

The lens built right into the home button (clever!) reads your finger at any angle. It can't be faked out by a plastic finger or even a chopped-off finger. You can teach it to recognize up to five fingerprints; they can all be yours, or some can belong to other people you trust.

Before you can use your fingertip as a passcode, though, you have to teach the phone to recognize it. iOS asks you to set up a fingerprint the first time you wake your new phone (or newly upgraded one). But if, at that juncture, you hit **Skip**, here's how you can add one now:

1. **Create a passcode.** You can't use a fingerprint *instead* of a passcode, only in *addition*. You'll still need a passcode from time to time to keep the phone's security tight. For example, you need to enter your passcode if you can't make your fingerprint work—maybe it got encased in acrylic in a hideous crafting accident), if you restart the phone, and so on.

   So open **Settings**→**Touch ID & Passcode** and create a password, as described earlier.

2. **Teach a fingerprint.** At the top of the Touch ID & Passcode screen, you see the on/off switches for the four things your fingerprint can do: unlock the phone (**iPhone Unlock**); pay for things (**Apple Pay**);

serve as your password when you buy books, music, apps, and videos from Apple's online stores (**iTunes & App Store**); and automatically enter your password into websites and apps (**Password Autofill**; see page 513).

But what you really want to tap here, of course, is **Add a Fingerprint**.

Now comes the cool part. Place the finger you want to train onto the home button—your thumb or index finger are the most logical candidates. You're asked to touch it to the home button over and over, maybe six times. Each time, the gray lines of the onscreen fingerprint darken a little more, as shown on the previous page.

Once you've filled in the fingerprint, you see the Adjust Your Grip screen. Tap **Continue**. Now the iPhone wants you to touch the home button another few times, this time tipping the finger a little each time so the sensor gets a better view of your finger's *edges*.

Once that's done, the screen says "Success!"

You're ready to start using the fingerprint. Try it: Put the phone to sleep. Then wake it by pressing the home button, and leave your finger on the button for about a second. The phone reads your fingerprint and instantly unlocks itself.

And now, a few notes about using your fingerprint as a password:

- **Yes, you can touch your finger** to the home button at the Lock screen. But you can also touch it at any Enter Passcode screen.

  Suppose, for example, that your Lock screen shows that you missed a text message. And you want to reply. Well, you can swipe across that notification to open it in its native habitat—the Messages app—but first you're shown the Enter Passcode screen. Ignore that. Just touch the home button with the finger whose print you recorded.

- **Apple says the image** of your fingerprint is encrypted and stored in the iPhone's processor chip. It's never transmitted anywhere, it never goes online, and it's never collected by Apple.

- **If you return to the Touch ID & Passcode screens,** you can tap **Add a Fingerprint** again to teach your phone to recognize a second finger. And a third, fourth, and fifth.

- **On the other hand,** it makes a lot of sense to register the *same* finger *several* times. You'll be amazed at how much faster and more reliably your thumb (for example) is recognized if you've trained it as several different "fingerprints."

- **To rename a fingerprint,** tap its current name ("Finger 1" or whatever). To delete one, tap its name and then tap **Delete Fingerprint**. (You can figure out which finger label is which by touching the home button; the corresponding label blinks. Sweet!)

- **You can register your toes** instead of fingers, if that's helpful. Or even patches of your wrist or arm, if you're patient (and weird).

- **The Touch ID scanner may** have trouble recognizing your touch if your finger is wet, greasy, or scarred.

- **The iPhone's finger reader** isn't just a camera; it doesn't just look for the image of your fingerprint. It's actually measuring the tiny differences in electrical conductivity between the raised parts of your fingerprint (which aren't conductive) and the skin just beneath the surface (which is). That's why a plastic finger won't work—and even your own finger won't work if it's been chopped off (or if you've died).

Fingerprints for Apps, Websites, and Apple Pay

So if your fingerprint is such a great solution to password overload, how come it works only to unlock the phone and to buy stuff from Apple's online stores? Wouldn't it be great if your fingerprint could also log you into secure websites? Or serve as your ID when you buy stuff online?

That dream is finally becoming a reality. Software companies can now use your Touch ID fingerprint to log into their apps. Mint (for checking your personal finances), Evernote (for storing notes, pictures, and to-do lists), Amazon (for buying stuff), and other apps now permit you to substitute a fingerprint touch for typing a password.

What's really wild is that password-storing apps like 1Password and LastPass have been updated, too. Those apps are designed to memorize your passwords for all sites on the web, of every type—and now you can use your fingerprint to unlock them.

Moreover, your fingerprint is now the key to the magical door of Apple Pay, the wireless pay-with-your-iPhone technology described on page 579.

This is all great news. Most of us would be happy if we never, ever had to type in another password.

Face ID

When Apple decided to cover the entire face of the iPhone X and its successors with screen, there was an obvious problem: the home button.

Were they really going to interrupt that gorgeous ocean of screen with a cutout for the home button?

Nope. The home button went away. In place of its functions, Apple came up with the various swipes and side-button presses described in this book. And in place of the fingerprint reader, the Face ID models have a *facial recognition* system. You unlock the phone by looking at it.

You can't fool Face ID with a photo, a mask, or even a 3D model of your head. It works in the dark. It works if you change hairstyles, glasses, makeup, or facial hair. It works through most sunglasses. It works if you're wearing a hat and scarf (it just has to see your eyes, nose, and mouth).

If you grow fat, or skinny, or old, it will still work, because it gradually updates its model of your face as you use it. (And if you have radical plastic surgery, well, you'll have to retrain it. Takes about a minute.)

It can't be forced on you when you're sleeping, because you have to be *looking* at the phone. It can't be forced on you by a police officer, because you can disable it with a quick, secret button press (page 82).

Whereas one in 50,000 people might be able to get into your phone with a fingerprint, Face ID's miss rate is one in *a million*. (The exception: Your identical twin might be able to fool it. You've been warned.)

You'll use Face ID wherever you used to use your fingerprint: triggering Apple Pay, for example, or logging into apps like Mint, 1Password, and E-Trade.

TrueDepth

So how does the phone recognize your face? Using a mass of sensors Apple calls TrueDepth. They hide in the notch at the top of the iPhone.

When you wake the phone, an infrared lamp (called the *flood illuminator*—but you knew that) blasts invisible light forward to see if a face is in range. If so, a tiny *dot projector* blasts 30,000 pinpoints of infrared light onto your face, and an infrared camera reads the distortion of their spacing and shape to find its contours. (That's why Face ID works in the dark—it relies on infrared light.)

If the infrared camera confirms that you're you—if the mathematical model of your facial contours matches what it captured when you trained it—then the phone unlocks. Only the tiny opening of a padlock on the Lock screen signifies that facial recognition has done its thing.

Training Face ID

In most ways, Face ID works exactly like Touch ID, described earlier. For example, you must create a passcode as a backup before you can turn on Face ID.

You'll need that passcode from time to time, for added security—after you've restarted the phone, after five failed attempts to log in with facial recognition, and so on (see page 52).

After creating your passcode in **Settings**→**Face ID & Passcode**, tap **Set Up Face ID**. Center your face in the circle, and then trace a circle in the air with your nose, so the frame of the circle fills in. You're asked to do this a second time; it has now created its model of your face.

(Apple stresses that the scan of your face is never transmitted, not even to Apple, and is not part of any backup. It's stored in a protected piece of memory called the Secure Enclave.)

You can even train the cameras to recognize a second face (tap **Set Up an Alternative Appearance**). That might be a second person (your spouse, your kid), or it might be you with a dramatically different look. Either way, it means more flexibility.

Using Face ID

From now on, you can unlock your iPhone like this:

- **Wake the phone** by tapping the screen, pressing the side button, or tipping the phone upright.

- **Look at the phone.** A white padlock at the top of the screen opens to show you that Face ID has recognized you and unlocked the phone.

  If all you wanted to do was check your notifications or something, that's all there is to it. In fact, what's especially cool is that when you wake the phone, message and mail notifications don't reveal their contents—but once the phone recognizes you, they expand in place!

  If you actually want to *proceed*—to go to the Home screen, for example—then there's one more step:

- **Swipe up from beneath the screen.** It can be a short, quick swipe. The Home screen (or whatever app you were using) appears. You're in.

Every now and then, Face ID doesn't unlock when you look at it, and asks that you enter your passcode.

If you do, that's a good thing; Face ID learns from its mistake and is more likely to recognize you the next time.

But if you're in a hurry, you can just tell Face ID to try scanning you again: A quick swipe up from the bottom of the screen makes the phone perform a new scan. (Of course, putting the phone to sleep and waking it again will do the same thing.)

TIP: There are some useful options to change in Face ID: See page 620.

2

The Lock Screen & Notifications

The Lock screen—the first thing you see when you wake the iPhone—is more than just a big Do Not Disturb sign. It's a lively bulletin board for information about your life. It's possible to have complete work sessions right at the Lock screen, without even fully unlocking the iPhone.

For starters, you can use the iPhone as a watch—millions of people do. Just lift the sleeping phone, or press the side button, to consult the Lock screen's time and date display, and then shove the phone right back into your pocket. It goes back to sleep after a few seconds.

Better yet, the Lock screen gives you a handy status report. Here you see a record of everything that happened while you weren't paying attention. It's a list of missed calls, text messages received, notifications from your apps, and other essential information.

Lock Screen Swipes

The Lock screen is the centerpiece of two other important screens. You can swipe left or right to bring them into view.

- **Swipe left** to open the Camera app (page 287).

- **Swipe right** to reveal the Today (Widgets) screen (page 76).

Actually, there two *more* screens you can reach from the Lock screen:

- **The Control Center.** You reach it by swiping up from the bottom of the screen (home-button phones), or down from the right ear (Face ID phones); see page 42.

- **The Notification Center.** Get here by swiping up—but this time from the middle of the screen; see page 67.

Keep this map in your head every time you wake your phone:

Notifications

A notification is an update from an app trying to get your attention. You get one every time a text message comes in, an alarm goes off, a calendar appointment is imminent, your battery is running low, and so on. Almost every app can display a notification, if you let it.

Notifications show up in two places, or maybe 2½:

- **On your screen, while you're working.** They pop up individually to get your attention.

- **On the Lock screen,** in a scrolling list of alerts that came in while you were away (facing page, left). Unlocking the phone wipes them away. The *next* time you unlock the phone, that batch will be gone.

- **On the Notification Center.** If you swipe down from the top of the screen, you open another list of notifications. It's almost identical to the Lock screen, complete with wallpaper, day, and date. You can even swipe left for the Camera or swipe right for the Today screen.

  But there are two key differences. First, this screen (facing page, right) shows *all* the notifications that have come in recently—both the new ones from the Lock screen and ones you've already seen, even if they're several days old.

> **TIP:** On the actual Lock screen, you can swipe up to see these older ones.

Second, you can specify, for each app, where its notifications appear. You can make them appear on the Lock screen, in the swipe-down notifications screen, on both, or on neither; see page 67.

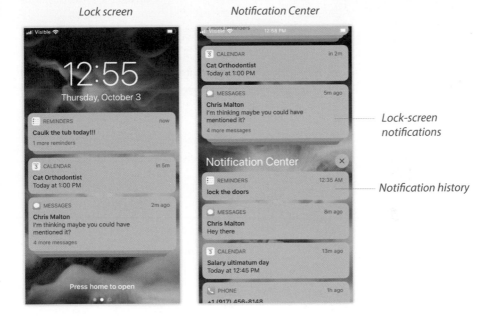

Lock screen   *Notification Center*

Lock-screen notifications

Notification history

Apple doesn't really have a name for the swipe-down-from-top screen, and "kind of like the Lock screen except that you get it by swiping down, and it also shows your notifications history" is too clumsy to use repeatedly in this chapter. So let's just call it the Notification Center, even though the Notification Center is *technically* only the bottom part of it, as shown above.

To close this screen, swipe any empty area up and away, or press the home button (if you have a home button), or do a quick up-swipe (if you have a Face ID phone).

Your options for dealing with incoming notifications are dizzying these days. They depend on which kind of phone you have, what your settings are, whether the phone is locked, and so on.

The following pages tackle the 2½ notification situations one by one.

While You're Working

Here are your options if the phone is unlocked and you're using it.

- **Flick it away.** If a notification banner appears, flick it upward to make it vanish. (If it's a "Temporary" banner, as described on page 69, just wait; it'll go away momentarily.)

- **Process it in place.** You can take direct action on many kinds of notifications—incoming text messages, emails, or calendar invitations, for
example. Without leaving the notification banner, you can reply to
the text message, delete the email, accept the calendar invitation, see
where your Uber car is, mark the Reminder as done, and so on.

Just *long-press* the banner to expand it and see your action options.
If it's a text message, you get a miniature version of Messages
in the window, so you can reply (below, right). If it's a reminder,
you can choose **Mark as Completed**, **Remind me in 1 Hour**, or
Remind me Tomorrow. And so on.

You can also swipe to the left on the banner to reveal some option
buttons instead. For a text message, they include **Clear**, **View** (which
produces the insta-reply screen shown above at right), and **Manage**
(read on). If it's an email, they say **Trash** and **Mark as Read**; and so on.

- **Open it.** Finally, you can tap a notification to open the app it came
from. Tap an email notification to open the message in Mail; tap a
text-message notification to open the text in Messages; and so on.
That's handy when you want to dig in and see the full context of the
notification.

On the Lock Screen

When notifications appear while you're *not* using your phone, they accumulate on the Lock screen.

Here's what you can do with them:

- **Ungroup them.** Notifications stack up in groups, by app. If you have eight text messages and three reminders waiting, you see only *two* stacked-looking bubbles, one per app. It's a triumph of software engineering over chaos. (You can see some of these stacked notifications in the illustration on page 63.)

  With a tap, you can expand a stack to view the individual notifications within it. (Depending on how you've fiddled with your privacy settings, you may first have to unlock the Lock screen—with your face, fingerprint, or passcode, as described on page 17. This doesn't mean getting *past* the Lock screen to the Home screen; it just means the padlock icon on the Lock screen must be open.)

  At that point, you can process each one individually, or you can nuke them all at once.

> **TIP:** If the iPhone thinks there's enough room to fit all the expanded notifications—for example, if all you got were two missed calls— you don't even have to tap to expand it. The stack expands automatically, as soon as your face or fingerprint has unlocked the phone.

- **Clear them.** Apple has made sure you can delete notifications in convenient units.

  Delete an *individual* notification by swiping it to the left; tap the **Clear** button that appears.

  Delete a *whole stack* (a whole app's worth) by swiping it all the way to the left. (The long way: Drag partway to the left, and then tap the **Clear All** button that appears.)

- **Tune this app's notifications.** iOS lets you shut up a certain app right here in the list of notifications, without having to burrow into Settings. Just long-press on a bubble stack, or an individual notification, from that app. (The long way: Swipe left, and then tap **Manage**, as shown on the next page at left.)

> **NOTE:** This operation, too, requires that you've unlocked the Lock screen with your face, fingerprint, or passcode.

A screen appears, offering two massive blue buttons. **Deliver Quietly** means that, from now on, this app's notifications will no longer make sounds, vibrate, display a badge like this ❷ on its icon, or appear on the Lock screen. The only place you'll see the notifications is in the Notification Center, the swipe-down list. That's a much quieter, more out-of-the-way place.

If you silence enough apps, the notifications from the apps you really *do* consider important will stand out that much more.

NOTE: If iOS notices that you always ignore a certain app's notifications, it might even *suggest* that you turn on Deliver Quietly for it. Now that's proactivity!

The other big button here, **Turn Off**, means this app's notifications won't show up anywhere. It's dead to you.

The **Settings** button opens the app's corresponding page in Settings, where you can make much finer adjustments to its notifications' behaviors (read on).

- **Process notifications in place.** You can long-press an expanded notification bubble to view the action buttons, exactly as described on page 64. (Alternatively, swipe left and then tap **View**.)

TIP: If you swipe left on a stacked bubble and then hit **View**, you're processing only the *topmost* notification.

- **Open the app.** Swiping all the way to the right opens the app itself. (The long way: Swipe a bit to the right and then tap **Open**.)

The Notification Center

When the phone is awake, and you swipe down from the top edge of your screen, you get another variation of the notification list.

When those notification bubbles are staring you in the face, you can process them using all the techniques you'd use on the Lock screen: Ungroup them, clear them, tune them, open them.

There are a few differences:

- **This is a more complete list** than what you see on the Lock screen, because it also shows you *older* notifications (under the heading "Notification Center"). These are bubbles that you've already seen on the Lock screen but haven't yet cleared or opened. (You can see the Notification Center at right on page 63.)

- **This screen may show** the alerts from many more apps, because you may have told certain apps to "Deliver Quietly," as described.

- **You don't have to worry** about unlocking anything before you process the notifications on this screen. After all, the phone is already on. You've already unlocked it.

- **In addition to clearing notifications** individually or by app, you can also clear everything under the words "Notification Center" at once—your whole history. To do that, tap the ✖ button and then hit **Clear** to confirm. (Or long-press the ✖ button and then tap **Clear All Notifications** to confirm.)

Customizing Notifications

You can (and should) specify *which* apps are allowed to junk up your notification screens. Open **Settings→Notifications** to see the master list, with one entry for every app that might ever want your attention. (Or just tell Siri, "Open notification settings.")

At the top of this screen, you get the master **Show Previews** switch (next page, left). This is a privacy thing. When someone sends you a text, do you want the notification banner to include *the message itself*, right there on your locked phone? (That's the preview.) Or do you want the banner to indicate only that a person has sent *some* message, which you can read only after unlocking the phone?

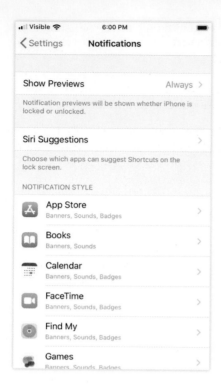

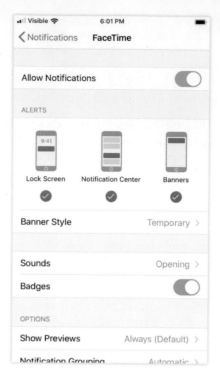

And it's not just texts. Do you want Uber information to appear in the banner? How about the Facebook alerts? The name of your alarm or reminder?

You have three choices here: **Always** (always show the message in the notification banner), **When Unlocked** (show only if I'm using the phone—not when it's locked), and **Never**.

NOTE: This **Show Previews** switch is a global switch—but individual apps can override it. You'll also find a separate **Show Previews** switch for each app that's capable of displaying information.

You'll quickly discover that *every* app thinks it's important; *every* app wants its notifications to blast into your face when you're working. You, however, may not agree. You may not consider it essential to know when your kid's Plants vs. Zombies score has changed, for example.

So: Tap an app's name to open its individual Notifications screen. Here you'll find settings that vary by app, but they generally run along these lines (above, right):

- **Allow Notifications.** If you don't want this app to make any notifications pop up at all, turn this off.

- **Lock Screen, Notification Center, Banners.** As you now know, there are three places where alerts may appear: the **Lock Screen** (when you're first waking your phone), the **Notification Center** (swipe down from the top of the screen), or the **Banners** that appear when you're using the phone. Using these three buttons, you can specify, just for this app, where you'll permit the notifications to appear.

  Maybe you want the Lock screen to show only missed calls, new text messages, and new email—but you'd like the pull-down Notification Center to be fully stocked with Twitter and Facebook updates. Or maybe you'd rather not permit passing evildoers to pick up your phone and see your notifications without even having to unlock it.

- **Banner Style** appears as an option only if you've turned on **Banners**.

  A **Temporary** banner appears at the top of the screen, holds still long enough for you to read it, and then goes away after a few seconds. Facebook and Twitter updates and incoming email messages do well as temporary banners.

  A **Persistent** banner stays on your screen until you tap or swipe it. You might use this option for apps whose messages are too important to miss, like alarms, flight updates, or texts.

- **Sounds.** Some apps try to get your attention with a sound effect when a notification appears. Turn this off if you think your phone makes too many beeps and burbles as it is. (Some apps also let you choose *which* sound effect plays to get your attention. You can change the sound or choose **None**.)

- **Badges.** A badge is a little red circled number (❷, for example). It appears right on an app's icon to indicate how many updates are waiting for you. Turn it off if you really don't need that reminder.

- **Show Preview.** This setting allows this app to override your global Show Previews setting (described earlier). If you *generally* don't want your apps displaying private information while the phone is locked, but it's OK for the Uber app to do so (for example), here's your ticket.

- **Notification Grouping.** You've already seen iOS's alert-bubble stacking feature at work. What you may not realize is that you can turn that on or off independently for each app.

  Off means every notification appears in its own bubble; no grouping for you! **By App** means all banners from a single app appear in a stack. And **Automatically** groups banners logically: separate stacks for individual conversations in Messages, correspondents in Mail, news sources in News, and so on.

As you poke around in the Notifications settings, you'll discover that certain apps offer oddball options that don't match up with the settings you see for most apps. Don't freak out. It's all part of Apple's master plan to put controls where it hopes you'll find them.

Do Not Disturb

When you turn on Do Not Disturb (in **Settings→Do Not Disturb**, shown on the next page at left, or on your Control Center), the phone is quiet and dark. It doesn't ring, chirp, vibrate, light up, or display messages. A ☾ appears on the status bar to remind you why it seems so uncharacteristically calm.

Airplane mode does the same thing, but there's a big difference: In Do Not Disturb, *the phone is still online*. Calls, texts, emails, and other communications continue to arrive; they just don't draw attention to themselves.

Do Not Disturb is what you want when you're in bed, in a meeting, in a movie, or on a date. You don't really want to be bothered with chirps for Facebook status updates and Twitter posts, but it's fine for the phone to collect them for the morning or your next free moment.

Over the years, Apple has made DND smarter and more flexible. Today, for example, it offers these options:

- **Do Not Disturb on a schedule.** You can set things up so that DND turns on and off automatically on a schedule, so the phone goes dark each night at the same time you do.

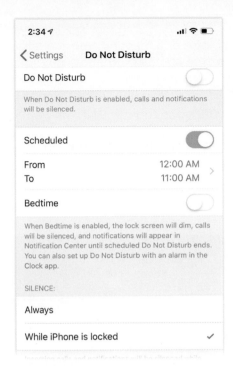

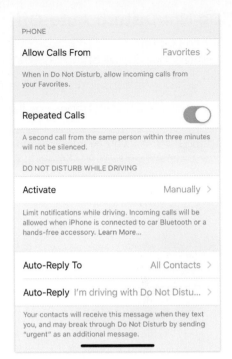

- **Do Not Disturb auto-off.** Do Not Disturb can shut itself off, returning your phone to full noisiness, according to a time interval or place—like when the movie is over, or when you leave a meeting.

- **Do Not Disturb at Bedtime.** This feature prevents even any *visual* indication that notifications have arrived.

- **Do Not Disturb exceptions.** You can designate important people whose calls and texts are allowed to get through Do Not Disturb. You know—for emergencies.

- **Do Not Disturb While Driving.** The phone can auto-detect when you're in a car—and prevent incoming rings and dings from distracting you.

Turning on Do Not Disturb

To turn on Do Not Disturb manually, you have three options:

- **Tell Siri,** "Turn on Do Not Disturb."

- **Open the Control Center** (page 42), and tap 🌙 so that it turns blue.

- **Open Settings,** tap Do Not Disturb, and turn on Do Not Disturb (above, left).

Do Not Disturb Auto-Off

When you turn on DND as you enter a movie or a meeting, you can tell it to turn itself off automatically when the time comes.

To see your options, long-press the ☾ on the Control Center.

A pop-up menu appears (below, left), offering to turn off DND after an hour; until later in the day or night; as you leave your current location; or—if iOS knows from your calendar that you're at a meeting or appointment—when that appointment time slot ends.

This is really excellent. You'll never again miss calls and texts because you forgot to turn off DND.

Scheduled Do Not Disturb

In **Settings**→**Do Not Disturb**, turn on **Scheduled**, and then tap the **From/To** block to specify starting and ending hours. (There's no separate setting for weekends; Do Not Disturb will turn on and off for the same hours every day of the week.)

Bedtime

Once you set up a schedule, the **Bedtime** switch appears. It's intended to solve a real-world problem: You wake up to pee in the middle of the night, you can't help checking your phone, you see a bunch of notifications on the screen, and you wind up getting so sucked in that you can't get back to sleep.

With Bedtime turned on, these exciting changes take place during your scheduled sleeping hours:

- **The Lock screen is solid black.** No more colorful wallpaper to jangle you awake.

- **No notification bubbles show up at all.** Instead, if you wake the screen, you see nothing but the time, date, and the little message shown on the facing page at right.

You can exit DND During Bedtime by long-pressing that bubble (or swiping to the left) and tapping **Turn Off**. Or just unlock your phone as usual and swipe down from the top to see your missed notifications. But you might sleep better if you resist that temptation.

Locked or Unlocked

The Silence option on the **Settings→Do Not Disturb** screen works like this: If you choose **Always**, then Do Not Disturb works exactly as described.

But if you choose **Only while iPhone is locked**, then the phone *does* ring and vibrate *when you're using it*. Because, obviously, if the phone is awake, so are you. It's a great way to ensure that you don't miss important calls if you happened to have awakened early today and started working.

Allowing Special Callers Through

What if your child, your boss, or your elderly parent needs you urgently in the middle of the night? Turning the phone off completely, or putting it into airplane mode, would leave you unreachable in an emergency.

Fortunately, you can create wormholes through your Do Not Disturb blockade for specified callers and texters:

- **Allow Calls From.** When you open **Settings→Do Not Disturb** and then tap **Allow Calls From**, you're offered options like **Everyone** (all calls and texts come through), **No One** (the phone is still online, but totally silent), or **Favorites**, which may be the most useful option of all.

  That setting permits calls and texts from anybody you've designated as a favorite in the Phone app (page 116). Since those are the people you call most often, it's fairly likely they're the most important people in your life.

  You can also create an arbitrary group of people—just your mom and sister, just your boss and kids, whatever. You have to create these address-book groups on your computer (page 122)—for example, in Contacts on the Mac. Once you've done that, their names appear on the Allow Calls From screen under Groups. You can designate any one of them as the exception to Do Not Disturb.

- **Emergency Bypass.** This feature lets you designate any person in your Contacts list as an "It's OK to Disturb" person. That person's calls and texts will always go through. See the Tip on page 127.

One More Safety Measure

The Do Not Disturb settings screen also offers something called **Repeated Calls**. If you turn this on, then if *anybody* tries to call you more than once within three minutes, she'll ring through.

The idea here is that nobody *would* call you multiple times unless she needed to reach you urgently. You certainly wouldn't want Do Not Disturb to block somebody who's trying to tell you that there's been an accident, that you've overslept, or that you've just won the lottery.

Do Not Disturb While Driving

According to the latest statistics, 100 percent of all car accidents are caused by *people*. Human beings are the *worst* drivers.

One of our chief idiocies is attempting to handle text messages and calls while we're driving; fortunately, Apple has tried to do something about it.

If you turn on the Do Not Disturb While Driving feature, then whenever you're driving, notifications from your apps don't show up to distract you. Your phone remains dark and silent. (Alarms and timers still ring, and you still see and hear Maps navigation instructions. Incoming phone calls follow whatever Do Not Disturb exceptions you've set up as described on the previous pages.)

You can set it up so that if someone texts you, they get an auto-response like, "I'm driving. I'll see your message when I get where I'm going." A second text from you then says, "(I'm not receiving notifications. If this is urgent, reply 'urgent' to send a notification through with your original message.)"

Isn't that smart? Now senders know that if this really is an emergency, they can send an "urgent" text. Now you'll see that and the original text, and you can pull over to see what the issue is.

How to Turn on DND While Driving

The first time you drive with your phone, an introductory screen appears. "Your iPhone can detect when you may be driving and automatically silence your incoming alerts and notifications." Tap the big, fat **Turn On While Driving** button to make sure this feature is always on when you're behind the wheel.

If you missed that opportunity (by tapping **Not Now**), then here's how you set up DND While Driving: Open **Settings→Do Not Disturb→ Activate**. Here you have four options:

- **Automatically.** This is by far the best option. Let Do Not Disturb turn itself on every time you're driving. The phone will use its motion and network sensors to figure out when it's in motion.

TIP: This setting engages DND even when you're or in the passenger seat of a car. In that situation, wake the phone. Long-press the **Do Not Disturb** bubble on the Lock screen (or swipe left on it and then tap **View**) to view the **I'm Not Driving** button. Tap it to let messages through. This feature was intended to prevent you from being distracted behind the wheel, not to ruin your life.

- **When Connected to Car Bluetooth.** If your car has Bluetooth—if, for example, you make calls and play music wirelessly through its sound system—this is a better option. It means the phone will know it's in your car by recognizing its Bluetooth. As a bonus, you'll still be able to make and receive phone calls through the car's audio, using the car's buttons.

- **Manually.** This option means that you intend to turn DND While Driving on and off manually, using the Control Center. See page 48 for instructions on adding the DND While Driving button to the Control Center.

  But you know what? Don't use this option. It's much easier and safer to let DND While Driving switch on automatically. If you have to do it manually, you'll forget. You'll fall out of the habit. You won't enjoy its life-saving safeguards.

- **Activate With CarPlay** means you won't be disturbed while driving in your CarPlay-equipped car.

Auto-Reply Settings

Who should receive those "I'm driving; I'll get back to you later" text messages? That's up to you.

Open **Settings→Do Not Disturb→Auto-Reply To**. Here you can choose **No One** (nobody gets an auto-reply), **Recents**, **Favorites** (page 116), or **All Contacts**. In other words, total strangers (people not in your Contacts, whom you've never communicated with before) never get the auto-reply, no matter what you choose here.

You can also tap **Auto-Reply** on this screen to edit the actual message. You can make it say, for example, "I'm sorry, my car can't talk right now." Or "Your text is very important to us..."

> **NOTE:** You can't, however, edit the second text reply, the one that says "I'm not receiving notifications. If this is urgent, reply 'urgent' to send a notification through with your original message." That one always goes out as you see it here.

Making DNDWD Mandatory

If you're the parent of a teenager, you might wish DND While Driving weren't quite so optional. You might wish you could require that it be turned on when your newbie driver is behind the wheel.

You can. Do Not Disturb While Driving is now one of the options in **Settings→Screen Time→Content & Privacy Restrictions**, which means your offspring won't be able to turn off DNDWD without your special password (see page 387).

The Today Screen (Widgets)

To the left of the Lock screen or the Notification Center screen, you'll find what Apple calls the Today screen. It's a motley assortment of panels that Apple calls widgets.

Some are quick-access buttons that launch related apps, like quick-dial (or quick-text) buttons for your favorite contacts; others are info-bits that you might want to check throughout the day, like your calendar, news, sports, stocks, and weather.

This entire wonderland is available before you've even unlocked the phone. Just swipe right from the Lock screen. Great when you want to check your calendar for your next thing.

It's also available when you've opened the pull-down Lock screen (swipe right, above or below the notification banners), and even when you're at the Home screen (swipe right).

Truth is, many people don't even know the Today screen is there; even if they do, most people don't use it. That's partly because this feature doesn't really become useful until you customize it: Rearrange the widgets, remove the ones you'd never touch, and install more useful ones.

The very first time you open the Today screen, you see things like the search bar (page 111), Up Next, Siri App Suggestions, and News.

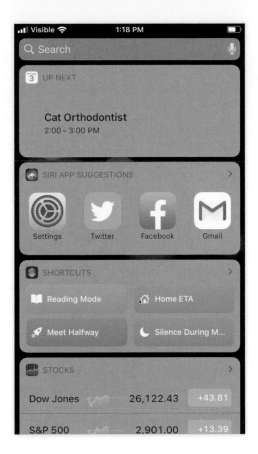

(They're described on these pages.) But the key to the real magic is the **Edit** button, which is hiding below all the widgets, several scrolls down.

The list you find here has two parts: the widgets that are currently installed and the ones that aren't. Delete a widget by tapping its ⊖; add one by tapping its ⊕. Rearrange the installed ones by dragging their ☰ handles. When you're finished, tap **Done**.

So what widgets are available? Here's a rundown:

- **Up Next.** The next couple of things on your calendar. Tap to log in and open the Calendar app, which shows you details of the event.

- **Siri App Suggestions.** This little row of app icons actually has nothing to do with Siri, the voice-controlled assistant. Instead, these are the iPhone's suggestions of apps you may want to use right now, based on your location, the time of day, and your typical routine. For example, if you open the Music app every evening during your 6:30 p.m. gym workout, then the Music app appears at that time, ready to open. If you check your Fitbit app every morning when you wake, then this screen offers its icon at that time of day. The idea is to save you from having to hunt for these apps when you need them again.

If you find these icons unhelpful, you can turn off this widget. You can also prevent *certain* apps' icons from appearing here. Open **Settings→ Siri & Search**. Here, if you scroll down, you'll find the names of all apps that might be inclined to appear as a Siri App Suggestion; you can tap them to turn them off, one at a time.

- **News.** Headlines from the News app (page 449).

- **Weather.** You guessed it.

- **Maps Destinations.** If you use Apple's Maps app, and routinely enter the addresses of your appointments on the Calendar, here's the pay-off: a list of upcoming and predicted destinations, including your next calendar appointment and where you parked your car (page 443).

- **Stocks.** The latest on whatever stocks you follow (page 475).

- **Tips.** This is the closest Apple comes to offering a manual for iOS 13.

- **Screen Time.** This one's a color-coded time-o-meter, showing how many minutes and hours you've sucked away using your phone— and what you've been doing. It's a reflection of the Screen Time app described on page 383.

- **Calendar.** Today's agenda. Tap an appointment to unlock your phone and see its details screen.

- **Favorites.** This is your speed-dial list. The first four people you've designated as favorites appear here, for quick speed-dialing.

  But it's not just about phone calls—who does *that* anymore? You can also designate a texting or email address, Skype handle, or other communication address as a favorite (page 116). Which means that, using this widget, you can insta-text your spouse or your kid without having to open the app, access the address book, choose the person's name, and so on. Shortcuts, baby!

- **Files.** Here are the most recent files you've moved to or from your iCloud Drive (page 421).

- **Find Friends.** This widget shows a map that pinpoints the location of any loved ones you're tracking (page 424).

- **Mail.** A speed-dial list of the people you've designated as VIPs (page 531), for quick emailing.

- **Maps Nearby.** These icons are shortcuts for time-appropriate searches, like coffee in the morning or nightlife after dark.

- **Maps Transit.** If you use Maps' public-transportation feature, this widget lets you know about delays and service interruptions.

- **Music.** Playback controls for whatever you were playing last.

- **Notes.** You see the first couple of lines of the Notes page you most recently edited.

- **Photos.** Thumbnails that, after you unlock the phone, open Memories (automated slideshows of recent time periods).

- **Podcasts.** Here are the icons for podcasts you've been listening to. It's a quick way to jump back in without fumbling through the app.

- **Reminders.** Your unfinished to-dos. You can mark one as done here, without having to unlock the phone and open the app. That's a big deal.

- **TV.** Shows any shows you've been watching in the TV app (page 280).

You probably have many other widgets, too, installed by your apps. Waze, Yelp, *The New York Times*, NPR, Google Maps, Kindle, Evernote, Dropbox, Chrome, Amazon, and many other apps put widgets here for your quick-glancing pleasure.

TIP: Many widgets are expandable. If you see a **Show More** button on a widget, it means a larger area, showing more information, is available to you. For example, expanding the Favorites widget shows icons for *eight* speed-dial people instead of four; expanding the Notes widget shows the *three* notes you've most recently viewed instead of one; and so on.

Widgets on the Home Screen

You don't have to swipe onto the Today screen to view a widget you need right now. You can long-press (page 33) an app's *Home screen icon* to view not just its shortcut menu but also its widget, for quick consultation. (This pop-up panel also includes a tiny **Add Widget** button, should you decide to install it on the Widgets *screen*.)

In Case of Emergency

Apple has turned the iPhone into an ingenious, smart emergency beacon. When you're in trouble—you're being followed, you're being attacked, you've fallen and you can't get up—the phone can automatically dial both 911 *and* send text messages to specified loved ones, letting them know you have an emergency and including your location. (If you move, they get additional texts letting them know where.)

When you need help, trigger the automatic emergency call like this:

- **iPhone 7 and earlier.** Click the side button five times fast. Drag the **Emergency SOS** slider on the resulting Shut Down screen.

- **iPhone 8 and later.** Hold in the side button *and* either volume button for two seconds. Drag the **Emergency SOS** slider on the Shut Down screen.

> **TIP:** In **Settings→Emergency SOS**, you'll find a fascinating option for your newer phone called **Call with Side Button**. If you turn it on, then pressing the side button five times rapidly *also* works to trigger the emergency dialing, just as it does on older iPhones. In times of danger, this method may be faster than pressing and waiting.

In all cases, a big red five-second countdown starts. At 3, a whooping audio alarm begins. At zero, the phone dials 911. (This countdown is designed to give you a chance to change your mind.)

Then, after a 10-second countdown, the phone texts your designated contacts, accompanied by a little map. "Emergency SOS," it says. "[Your name] has made an emergency call from this approximate location. You

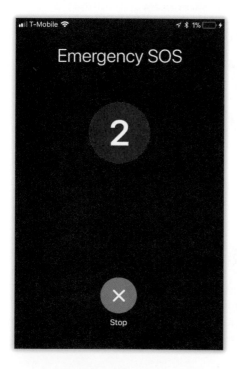

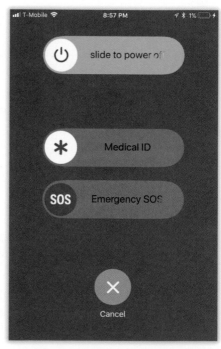

are receiving this message because [your name] has listed you as an emergency contact."

> **TIP:** If you have a newer iPhone, you have a sneakier method of triggering this feature: Just keep pressing the side and volume keys. If you press those buttons long enough, the whole thing is automatic, even if you can't see the big red countdown on the screen. After five seconds, the whooping alarm starts; two seconds later, the phone dials 911.
>
> The advantage of this method, of course, is that you can do it entirely in your pocket. You don't have to be looking at your phone, which might be useful when an unpleasant human is staring you in the face.

To set this up, open Settings→Emergency SOS. Here you can:

- **Turn off "Call with Side Button."** That's the five-click side-button trick.

- **Turn off Auto Call.** That's the part that dials 911 automatically when the countdown ends. If you're worried about that, turn it off. In this case, there's no countdown, alarm, or auto-dialing. You must swipe your finger across an Emergency SOS slider to place the call, and the call goes to the nearest police office line (not 911).

- **Set Up Emergency Contacts in Health.** Tap this, then Create Medical ID, and then add emergency contact to specify who gets called when you trigger the Emergency SOS feature.

- **Countdown Sound.** Lets you turn off the whooping alarm (available only if Auto Call is turned on). On one hand, you no longer have an audible alert that your phone is about to call 911—if, for example, you triggered Emergency SOS accidentally. On the other hand, there's no alarm sound to warn a bad guy that you're calling.

Medical ID on the Shutdown Screen

It's worth noticing that on the Emergency SOS screen (previous page, right), you get more than the Emergency SOS slider; you also get a Medical ID slider.

Swipe to open a screenful of essential medical information about you. And where does the Medical ID screen get this information? You've filled it out in the Health app (page 427).

Note that both of these features are available even if the phone is locked. Anyone can bring up this screen on any iPhone in the world—click the side button five times fast (iPhone 7 and earlier), or press the side button and volume button together for three seconds (iPhone 8 and later). You can get help on the way, even if it's not your phone.

The "Forcible Unlock" Situation

When the public first heard about Face ID, there was panic. "Oh, *great*," people said. "So now a mugger can force me to unlock the phone by holding it up to my face!" (There were also variants: "So now a *cop* can force me to unlock the phone by holding it up to my face!")

Apple has you covered. If anyone demands your phone under threat, bring up the shutdown screen described above (five clicks, or side button + volume key). What your antagonist probably doesn't realize is that when that screen appears, *Touch ID and Face ID are turned off*. Neither your face nor your fingerprint will unlock the phone at this point—only the passcode will work.

Of course, the mugger or rogue officer could still try to force you to enter your passcode—but now you've got bigger problems.

3

Typing, Editing & Searching

The modern iPhone's onscreen keyboard is smart in all kinds of ways—automatically predicting words and correcting typos, for example. And if you don't like the keyboard, you can just choose one designed by a different company.

This chapter covers every aspect of working with text on the iPhone: entering it, dictating it, fixing it, and searching for it.

The Keyboard

The iPhone keyboard appears whenever you tap in a place where typing is possible: in an outgoing email or text message, in the Notes app, in the address bar of a web browser, and so on.

As your finger taps the glass, a "speech balloon" appears above your finger, showing an enlarged version of the key you actually hit (since your finger is now blocking your view of the keyboard).

TIP: If you worry about spies nearby figuring out what you're typing by watching those bubbles pop up over your fingertips, you can turn them off. Open **Settings→General→Keyboard**, and turn off **Character Preview**.

In gray, surrounding the letters, you'll find these special keys:

- **Shift (⇧).** When you tap this key, the arrow turns black to indicate that it's in effect. The next letter you type appears as a capital. Then the ⇧ key returns to normal—the next letter will be lowercase.

Caps Lock (⇪). The iPhone has a hidden Caps Lock "key." To engage it, double-tap the ⇧ key; it changes to ⇪. You're now in Caps Lock mode, and you'll type in ALL CAPITALS until you tap the ⇪ key again (or 123 or 😀 or 🌐). If you can't seem to make Caps Lock work, try double-tapping the ⇧ key *faster.* Or see if maybe Caps Lock got turned off in **Settings→General→Keyboard**.

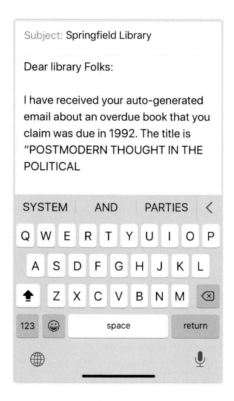

- **Backspace (⌫).** This key actually has three speeds:

  Tap it once to delete the letter just before the blinking insertion point.

  Hold it down to "walk" backward, deleting as you go.

  If you hold down the key long enough, it starts deleting *words* rather than letters, one whole chunk at a time.

- **123.** Tap this button when you want to type numbers or punctuation. The keyboard changes to offer a palette of numbers and symbols. Tap the same key—which now says ABC—to return to the letters keyboard.

  Once you're on the numbers/symbols pad, a dark-gray button appears, labeled #+=. Tapping it summons a *third* keyboard layout, containing the less frequently used symbols, like brackets, the # and % symbols, bullets, and math symbols.

- ☺. Hey, cool! In iOS 13, the Emoji key (☺) no longer shares a spot with the ⊕ key (for switching languages)! They're both visible all the time. Anytime you want to pop in a little smiley or symbol, tap this one to open the Emoji palette described on page 93.

NOTE: This key appears at the lower-left corner of the screen, next to the 🎤 button, *unless* you've installed the ⊕ button described on page 96. In that case, the ☺ key jumps up and wedges itself beside the space bar as shown on the facing page. It's all more logical than it sounds.

- ⊕ is the layout-switcher key. It appears only if you've installed additional keyboard (language) layouts as described on page 96.

- 🎤. Tap this button to dictate spoken text to your iPhone in lieu of typing. See page 104

- **return.** Tapping this key moves to the next line, just as on a real keyboard. (There's no Tab key or Enter key in iPhone Land.)

Tips for Better Typing

Some people have no problem tapping those tiny virtual keys; others struggle for weeks. Either way, here are some tips:

- **Use the whole pad of your finger or thumb.** Don't try to tap with only a skinny part of your finger to match the skinny keys. You'll be surprised at how fast and accurate this method is. (Tap, don't mash.)

- **This may sound like New Age hooey,** but *trust* the keyboard. Don't pause to check the result after each letter. Just plow on.

NOTE: Although you don't see it, the sizes of the keys on the iPhone keyboard change all the time. The software enlarges the "landing area" of certain keys, based on probability.

For example, suppose you type *tim*. The iPhone knows no word in the language begins with *timw* or *timr*—and so, invisibly, it enlarges the "landing area" of the E key, which greatly diminishes your chances of making a typo on that last letter.

- **Don't bother using the Shift key** to capitalize a new sentence. The iPhone does that capitalizing automatically. (To turn this feature on or off, use **Settings→General→Keyboard→Auto-Capitalization**.)

- **Don't type a period** at the end of each sentence, either. Because the period is such a frequently used symbol, there's an awesome short-cut that doesn't require switching to the punctuation keyboard: At the end of a sentence, *tap the space bar twice*. You get a period, a space, *and* a capitalized letter at the beginning of the next word. (This, too, can be turned off—in **Settings→General→Keyboard→"." Shortcut**—although it's hard to imagine why you'd want to.)

- **You can save time** by leaving out the apostrophes in contractions. Type *im*, *dont*, or *cant*. The iPhone proposes *I'm*, *don't*, or *can't*, so you can just tap the space bar to fix the word and continue.

- **Many beginners hold the phone** with one hand and tap keys with the index finger of the other. As you become more proficient, though, you may prefer two-thumb typing—or, faster yet, type with your left thumb (so that your left hand can grip the phone) and right index fin-ger (which is more agile).

Autocorrect: Your Typing Assistant from Hell

The iPhone, like all smartphones, offers autocorrect. Whenever it thinks you've made a spelling error, it *automatically* substitutes the "correct" word or spelling. For example, if you type *imsame*, the iPhone realizes you meant *insane* and replaces it automatically.

Most of the time, that's helpful; autocorrect even finishes long words for you sometimes. But be vigilant; many times, autocorrect substitutes the *wrong* word! And sometimes you don't notice it, and you wind up texting gibberish to your correspondent. The internet is filled with hilarious examples of autocorrect gone wrong.

So here's the important thing: The iPhone always shows you the replace-ment it intends to make before making it—as the highlighted (middle)

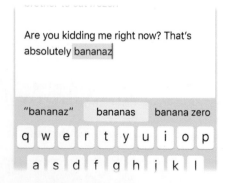

QuickType suggestion (facing page, left). To accept its suggestion, tap the space bar or any punctuation. To prevent the replacement, tap the *first* QuickType word (the one in quotes).

> **TIP:** If you turn on Speak Auto-text (in **Settings→Accessibility→Spoken Content→Typing Feedback**), the iPhone even speaks the suggested word out loud. That way, you can keep your focus on the keyboard.

And by the way: If you *accidentally* accept a QuickType suggestion, tap the Backspace key. A word bubble appears, which you can tap to reinstate what you'd originally typed.

> **TIP:** If you think autocorrect is doing you more harm than good, you can turn it off in **Settings→General→Keyboard**. Turn off **Auto-Correction**.

The QuickType Bar

What Apple calls its QuickType bar can save you a *lot* of time, tapping, and errors.

The idea is simple: As you type a sentence, the software *predicts* which word you might type next—the three most likely words, actually—and displays them as three buttons above the keyboard.

If you begin the sentence by typing *I really*, then the three suggestions might be *want*, *don't*, and *like*.

But what if you intended to type *I really hope...?* In that case, type the first letter of "hope." Instantly, the three suggestions change to *"h"*, *hope*, and *have*. (The first button always shows, in quotes, whatever non-word you've typed so far, just in case that's what you intend. To place it into your text, you can tap that button *or* tap the space bar or some punctuation.)

In other words, QuickType is autocorrect on steroids. Frankly, it's a rush when it correctly proposes finishing a long word for you.

With QuickType, you can produce a sentence like "I'll gladly pay you Tuesday for a hamburger today" with 26 taps. (If you had to type out the whole thing, you'd have tapped 50 times.) QuickType also adds spaces for you.

QuickType is smart in several ways:

- **QuickType's suggestions** are *different* in Messages (where language tends to be casual) than in Mail (where people write more formally).

- **Similarly, QuickType modifies** its suggestions based on whom you're writing to. It *learns*.

- **Sometimes, QuickType offers** you several words on a single button, to save you even more time (for example, *up to* or *in the*).

- **When you're in the Messages app,** QuickType suggests an emoji (a tiny cartoon symbol) when you've typed a corresponding word. Page 207 has the details.

- **QuickType automatically adds** a space after each word you select, so you don't have to mess with the space bar.

- **QuickType's suggestions** may offer movie names, song names, or place names you've recently viewed in other apps.

- **You can hide the QuickType bar** if it's getting on your nerves. Hold down the ☺ button; from the shortcut menu, tap **Keyboard Settings**. You wind up in **Settings→General→Keyboard**, where you'll find the **Predictive** on/off switch.

QuickType does mean you have to split your focus. You have to pay attention to both the keys you're tapping and the ever-changing word choices above the keyboard. With practice, though, you'll find that QuickType offers impressive speed and accuracy. You won't miss the little autocorrect bubbles of old.

QuickPath: Swipe to Type

For people who'd rather eat sand than type on glass buttons, iOS 13 brings some excellent news: Now you can *swipe to type*.

For years, fans of smartphone keyboards called Swype, SwiftKey, and Gboard have raved about the joy they get from swipe-typing—and now, at last, it's a built-in iPhone feature.

Apple calls it QuickPath. To use it, you don't tap each key to spell out a word. Instead, you can rapidly and sloppily *drag your finger across* the keys, hitting the letters you want along the way and lifting your finger only at the end of each word. Somehow, the software figures out what you were going for.

In this example (left), you're typing *winter*. You're hitting all kinds of non-essential letters along the way, like Y, U, and K, but iOS ignores them. It realizes *winter* is the only word that makes sense.

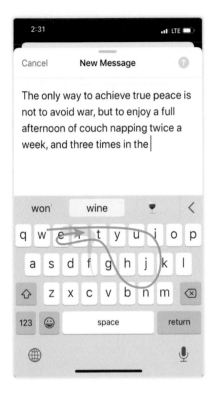 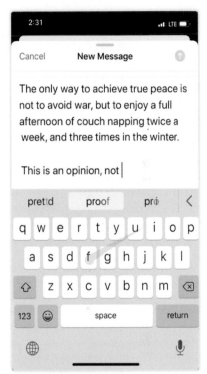

Sounds bizarre, but fans say this system is satisfying and freakishly fast, especially with practice. And it's pretty—your finger leaves a sort of fire trail as it slides across the glass (right).

The best part of Apple's version is that you don't have to switch modes when you want to swipe; you can alternate between swiping across the keys and tapping them without changing a single setting. You might decide to swipe for common words and use tapping for weird names or acronyms.

And now, some QuickPath tips:

- **Don't put in spaces.** You get a space every time you finish a word.

- **Don't worry about double letters.** If you slide out *Fed my toth a litle blod*, iOS types *Feed my tooth a little blood*. It's smart that way. (In the illustration at right on the previous page, you got *proof* by swiping through the letters *PROF*.)

- **You can swipe to type words** in English, Simplified Chinese, Spanish, German, French, Italian, and Portuguese—without ever changing keyboards or settings! iOS recognizes all of those languages' swiped words.

NOTE: To make this work, you need to have added the language to your phone. Go to **Settings→General→Language & Region** and add a language, as described on page 96.

- **You can turn off the QuickPath swipe-typing feature** in Settings→ General→Keyboard→Slide to Type. You might do that if, for example, you never use QuickPath and find that it just gets in your way when you're trying to use the keyboard-as-trackpad trick described on page 99.

- **As you begin going down the QuickPath path,** you may sometimes enter the wrong word by mistake. In those situations, tap-tap-tapping the Backspace key (⌫) letter by letter would feel frustratingly inefficient. So when you're swipe-typing, the *first tap* of the ⌫ key deletes the *entire* word you've just typed. (Subsequent taps delete one letter at a time as usual.)

  You can turn this feature off with Settings→General→Keyboard→ Delete Slide-to-Type by Word.

Not everyone is a fan of swipe-typing. And it's not flawless; there's no way to specify "setup" versus "seep," "met" versus "meet," or "god" versus "good," for example, because QuickPath decides for itself whether a letter should be doubled. (Online rumors swirl that you can hesitate or wiggle on a letter to double it. In the real world, that's iffy.) And sometimes, there's just no way to get the word you want. If you try to swipe out the word *sine*, for example, it's almost impossible to avoid the G key, so you get *singe*—or something else entirely, like *some*.

If you decide that tapping is faster and more accurate, that's your call.

Teaching the Dictionary

If you start typing a word the iPhone doesn't recognize, the first of the three suggestion buttons displays your word in quotation marks. If you really do intend to type that nonstandard word, tap its button. You've just allowed the "mistake" to stand—and you've added it to the iPhone's dictionary. The phone assumes you've just typed some name, bit of slang, or terminology that wasn't in its dictionary originally.

From now on, it will accept that bizarre new word as legitimate—and, in fact, will even *suggest* it the next time you start typing it.

The Spelling Checker

Here's the world's friendliest typo-fixer. Apple calls it a spelling checker, but maybe that's stretching it.

Anytime the iPhone doesn't recognize something you've typed, it draws a dotted red underline beneath it. Tap the word to see a pop-up balloon with one, two, or three alternate spellings. Often, one of them is what you wanted, and you can tap it to fix the mistake. (Equally often, none of them is, and it's time to break out the keyboard.)

TO DO TODAY

Buy a tube of caulk at
hadware store

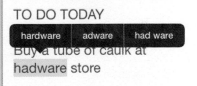

Punctuation with One Touch

On the iPhone, the punctuation and alphabet keys appear on two differ-ent keyboard layouts. That's a hassle, because each time you want, say, a comma, it's an awkward three-step dance: (1) Tap the 123 key to get the punctuation layout. (2) Tap the comma. (3) Tap the ABC key or the space bar to return to the alphabet layout.

Imagine how excruciating it is to type, for example, *a P.O. box in the U.S.A.* That's 37 finger taps and nine mode changes!

Fortunately, there's a secret way to get a punctuation mark with only a *single* gesture. The iPhone doesn't register most key presses until you *lift* your finger. But the Shift and punctuation keys register their taps on the press *down* instead. So here's what you can do, all in one motion:

1. **Touch the** 123 **key, but don't lift your finger.** The punctuation layout appears.

2. **Slide your finger onto the period or comma key, and release.** The ABC layout returns. You've typed a period or a comma with one touch instead of three.

> **TIP:** If you're a two-thumbed typist, you can also hit the 123 key with your left thumb and then tap the punctuation key with your right. It even works on the #+= sub-punctuation layout.

In fact, you can type any of the punctuation symbols the same way. This technique makes a *huge* difference in the usability of the keyboard.

> **TIP:** This same trick saves you a finger-press when capitalizing words. Put your finger down on the ⇧ key and slide directly onto the letter you want to type. Or hold the Shift key down with your left thumb, type a letter with your right, and then release both.

Accented Characters

To produce an accented character (like é, ë, è, ê, and so on), keep your finger lightly pressed on that key for one second. A palette of diacritical marks appears; slide onto the one you want.

Not all keys sprout this pop-up palette. Here's a list of the ones that do:

Key	Alternates
a	à á â ä æ ã å ā
c	ç ć č
e	è é ê ë ē ė ę
i	ì į ī í ï î
l	ł
n	ń ñ
o	õ ō ø œ ó ò ö ô
s	ß ś š
u	ū ú ù ü û
y	ÿ
z	ž ź ż
?	¿
'	` ' '
"	« » „ " "
-	– — •
$	₱ ¥ € ¢ £ ₩
&	§
0 (zero)	°
.	…
%	‰
/	\
!	¡
=	≠ ≈

The Emoji Keyboard

Don't miss the emoji keyboard. It gives you a palette of smileys and fun symbols to use in your correspondence. (If you know someone under 25, you may know all about them.)

When you tap the ☺ key, you're offered thousands of emoji. They're spread across eight categories (plus a Frequently Used category), each represented by a tiny icon at the bottom.

Most of these emoji categories scroll sideways—they're several screens wide. To return to a category's first page, you don't have to swipe; just tap the category's icon.

NOTE: These symbols show up identically on Apple machinery (phones, tablets, Macs) but may look slightly different on other kinds of phones. An international organization determines which symbols are included in the standard emoji set, but each tech company draws its own interpretation of each symbol.

At the left edge of the emoji keyboard, by the way, a new panel awaits. These are any *stickers* or *Memoji* you've created, as described on page 219.

Text Replacement (Abbreviation Expanders)

Here's a feature hardly anyone ever talks about—probably because nobody knows it exists. But it can be a huge time- and sanity-saver.

You can program the phone to expand abbreviations that you type. Set up *addr* to type your entire mailing address or *eml* to type out your email address. Create two-letter abbreviations for big legal or technical words you have to type a lot. Set up *goaway* to type out a polite rejection paragraph for use in email. And so on.

This feature has been in Microsoft Office forever (called AutoCorrect). And it's always been available in add-on apps. But since it's now built right into the operating system, it works anywhere you can type.

You can start building your list of abbreviations in **Settings→General→Keyboard→Text Replacement**. Tap the + button. On the resulting screen, type the expanded text into the **Phrase** box. (It can be long, but it has to be one continuous blob of text; it can't contain returns.) In the **Shortcut** box, type the abbreviation you want to trigger the phrase.

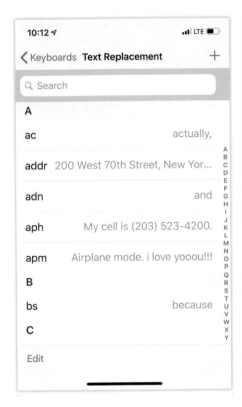

That's it! Now, whenever you type one of the abbreviations you've set up, the iPhone proposes replacing it with your substituted text.

The One-Handed Keyboard

It's a rare operating system with the foresight and vision to acknowledge morning coffee.

For the first time, you can carry a cup in one hand while typing on your iPhone with the other. That's because there's an optional keyboard lay-out (except on the smaller iPhone SE): an extra-skinny one that huddles against one side, within reach of a single thumb.

To make it so, hold down the lower-left key (🌐 or 😊). From the shortcut menu, choose one of the outer two keyboard icons, as shown here. (They represent the left- and right-huddling keyboards, respectively.)

International Typing

Because the iPhone is sold around the world, it has to be equipped for non-English languages—and non-Roman alphabets. Fortunately, it's ready. You can, in fact, set up two lists: one for the languages you'll be writing in and another for the keyboard layouts you'll be using to type those languages. (For example, the traditional QWERTY keys don't do you much good when you're trying to type in Mandarin.)

- **Writing languages.** To prepare the iPhone for language switching, go to Settings→General→ Language & Region. Tap iPhone Language to set the iPhone's primary language (for menus, button labels, and so on).

  If you plan to incorporate other languages into what you type, tap Other Languages and choose from the newly massive list (iOS 13 adds 38 new typeable languages). For each new language you add, you get a prompt asking if you would like to change the iPhone default to that language or Keep English. After you've made your choice, your phone will return to the Language & Region screen, where you can tap a new prompt, Add Language, to add any additional languages. If you tap Edit here, you can drag the language names into the order you prefer to see them in the 🌐 menu or remove them from the list entirely.

- **Keyboard languages.** To make other *keyboards* available, go to Settings→General→Keyboard→Keyboards, tap Add New Keyboard, and then turn on the keyboard layouts you'll want available: Russian, Italian, whatever. (In iOS 13, there are 15 new Indian-language keyboards.)

If you choose Japanese or Chinese, you're offered the chance to specify which *kind* of character input you want. For Japanese, you can choose a QWERTY layout (Romaji) or a Kana keypad. For Simplified or Traditional Chinese, your choices include the Pinyin input method (which uses a QWERTY layout) and handwriting recognition, where you draw your symbols onto the screen with your fingertip; a palette of potential interpretations appears above what you've written. (That's handy, since there are thousands of characters in Chinese, and you'd need a 65-inch iPhone to fit the keyboard on it.)

Once you've installed some keyboard languages, you can exploit the ⊕ key. Each time you tap it, you rotate to the next keyboard you requested earlier. Or long-press it to produce a *menu* of languages.

Thanks to that ⊕ key, you can freely mix languages and alphabets within the same document without having to duck back to some control panel to make the change. And thanks to the iPhone's virtual keyboard, the actual letters on the "keys" change in real time.

SwiftKey, Gboard, and Other Keyboards

You're not stuck with Apple's onscreen keyboard. You can, if you like, install virtual keyboards from other companies.

There's much less reason to do so now that QuickPath is available in iOS; people who liked to swipe-type often would switch to the SwiftKey or Gboard keyboards. Still, rival keyboards may have some advantages: For example, SwiftKey can sync what it's learned to your other gadgets (iOS learns, but its education is locked on your iPhone). The Minuum keyboard is weird-looking but compact, leaving a lot more room for your writing. Then there are Fleksy, TouchPal, Kuaiboard 2, and a raft of others.

To install an alternate keyboard, get it from the App Store (page 361). Then go to **Settings→General→Keyboard→Keyboards**. When you tap **Add New Keyboard**, you'll see your newly downloaded keyboard's name. Turn it on by tapping it and then turning on **Full Access**.

Now, when you arrive at any writing area in any app, each tap on the ⊕ button summons the next keyboard you've installed—or you can hold your finger down on it for a pop-up list (previous page, left).

Connecting a Real Keyboard

This iPhone feature barely merits an asterisk in Apple's marketing materials. But if you're any kind of wandering journalist, blogger, or writer, you might flip your lid over this: You can type on a real, full-size, physical keyboard and watch the text magically appear on your iPhone's screen—wirelessly.

That's because you can use a Bluetooth keyboard (the Apple Wireless Keyboard, for example) to type into your iPhone.

To set this up, tap **Settings→Bluetooth**. Turn Bluetooth on, if it's not already.

Now turn on the wireless keyboard. After a moment, its name shows up on the iPhone screen in the Devices list; tap it. You'll know the pairing was successful, because when you tap in a spot where the onscreen keyboard would usually appear—well, it doesn't.

Typing is a lot easier and faster with a real keyboard. As a bonus, the Apple keyboard's brightness, volume, and playback controls actually work to control the iPhone's brightness, volume, and playback.

> **TIP:** The Apple keyboard's ⏏ key even works: It makes the iPhone's onscreen keyboard appear or disappear. And to switch languages, press ⌘-space bar on the wireless keyboard. You'll see the list of languages. Tap the space bar again to choose a different language.

When you're finished using the keyboard, turn it off. The iPhone goes back to normal.

Editing Your Writing

On a regular computer, you probably know how to edit what you've typed: Use the mouse or trackpad to move the insertion point; drag to highlight words; use the menu commands for Cut, Copy, Paste, Undo, and Redo.

Well, that's great. But the iPhone doesn't *have* a mouse, trackpad, or menus. So now what? You can't ever edit what you've typed? It's first drafts forever?

Not at all. Apple has come up with sneaky touchscreen methods for selecting and manipulating text—and in iOS 13, it has given them more juice than ever.

Moving the Insertion Point

How are you supposed to edit something you typed a few sentences ago? By dragging the little blinking insertion point with your fingertip. (You don't have to pause before moving your finger.) Release when that insertion point lands exactly where you want to delete or add text, just as though you'd clicked there with a mouse.

The loupe—the magnifying glass that made this process easier for the first 12 years of the iPhone, is no longer with us in iOS 13. Still, the insertion point does get gigantic while you're moving it, for ease in positioning.

The Secret Trackpad

Dragging the insertion point is one way to move it. Using your iPhone's invisible trackpad is another.

You can make it appear in either of two ways:

- **The 3D-Touch trackpad.** On phones with 3D Touch—the 6s, 6s Plus, 7, 7 Plus, 8, 8 Plus, X, XS, and XS Max—you can use this trick.

  Whenever text is on the screen and the keyboard is open, press firmly anywhere on the keyboard. All the keys go blank, as shown below.

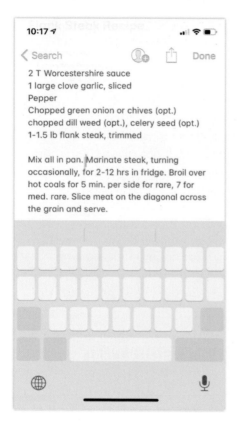 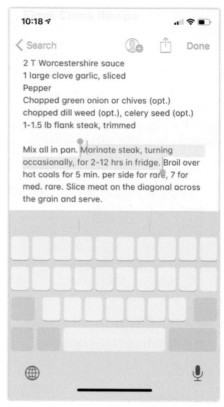

You can ease up on the pressure, but *don't lift your finger* from the glass. You can now move the insertion-point cursor through the text just by dragging your finger across the keys. If it hits the edge of the window, it scrolls automatically.

Still keep your finger down. At this point, a harder press—a little jolt of additional pressure—lets you select (highlight) text:

Hard-press once to select the adjacent word.

Hard-press twice to select an entire sentence.

Hard-press three times to select an entire paragraph.

After performing any of these techniques, you can expand the selection by dragging up or down. (Again, you don't have to keep pressing hard, but you do have to keep your finger on the glass.)

- **The space bar trackpad.** Here's another way to trigger the trackpad, which works on all iPhone models: Long-press the space bar. You may feel a little click, and then the keys go blank.

  Now, without lifting your finger, slide it to move the insertion point. When it's where you want it, lift your finger. The key labels return.

  If you're clever, you can even *select* text this way. Long-press the space bar with your index finger; without lifting it, slide to the beginning of the desired selection. *Still* without lifting your index finger, tap and release with a second finger anywhere on the keyboard to enter text-selection mode. Now you can drag your index finger (which has never left the glass) to select text.

Using either trackpad method, once you've selected text, the command bar (**Cut**, **Copy**, **Paste**, and so on) appears for your text-manipulation pleasure.

Little by little, the iPhone is revealing its secret ambition to be a laptop.

Selecting Text

Before you can cut, copy, or mass-delete something you've typed, you first have to highlight it (select it).

In the absence of a mouse, you can use the secret trackpad methods described above—or you can use the older tapping methods:

- **To select some.** Double-tap the first word (or last word) you want in the selection. That word is now highlighted, with colored dots at diagonal corners. Drag these handles to expand the selection.

Double-tap...

...drag the handle.

On a web page, you can't double-tap to select a word, because double-tapping means "zoom in." Instead, *hold your finger down* on a word to produce the selection handles. (Slide your finger to expand the selection.)

However, if you're zoomed out to see the whole page, holding down your finger highlights the *entire block* of text (a paragraph or even a whole article) instead of one word. Now you can expand the selection to include a photo, if you like; that way, you can copy and paste the whole enchilada into an outgoing email message.

- **To select all.** Suppose you intend to cut or copy *everything* in the text box or message. Tap anywhere in the text to place the insertion point. Then tap the insertion point itself to summon the selection buttons— one of which is **Select All**.

Selecting text is even easier when you use the secret trackpad; see page 99.

Cut, Copy, Paste (Editing Toolbar)

Copy and Paste do just what you'd expect. They let you grab some text from one place and dump it somewhere else. For example, you might want to copy something from a web page and paste it into an email message, copy directions from email into Notes, paste a phone number from your address book into a text message, and so on.

You start by highlighting the material you want, as described. At this point, a special editing bar appears—and the Cut and Copy buttons are staring you in the face (below, left).

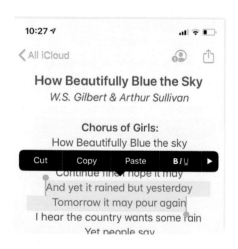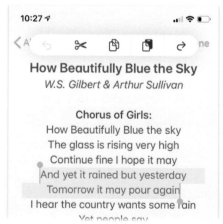

Tap **Cut** (to copy and remove the selected text) or **Copy** (to leave it but place a duplicate on your invisible Clipboard). If you want to get rid of the text *without* copying it to the Clipboard—because you want to preserve something else you copied there, for example—just tap the ⌫ key.

> **TIP:** And what if you want to copy text without the formatting (bold, italics, underlining) that it might have? After selecting the text, tap **Share** and then tap **Copy** in the Share sheet.

Finally, switch to a different spot in the text, even if it's in a different window (for example, a new email message) or a different app (for example, Calendar or Notes). Tap in any spot where you're allowed to type. Tap the **Paste** button that appears to paste what you cut or copied. Ta-da!

Cut, Copy, Paste (Three-Finger Gestures)

New in iOS 13: three-finger gestures for performing the Cut, Copy, and Paste. It's a little nuts—is there even room for a three-finger gesture on a screen that's 2½ inches across?—but if you're a power user, well, go for it.

Begin by selecting some text, as already described. Then:

- **Cut** by pinching three fingers inward *twice*. On the second pinch, the word "Cut" appears briefly—and the text vanishes. It's now on your invisible Clipboard, ready to paste.

- **Copy** by pinching three fingers inward on the glass. (Use the entire screen as your canvas—the keyboard as well as the text above it.) The word "Copy" appears briefly at the top of the screen.

- **Paste** (once you've tapped within the text to indicate *where*) by *unpinching* with three fingers—that is, spreading them outward simultaneously.

> **TIP:** If you *tap and hold* with three fingers simultaneously, you summon the new editing toolbar. This is, believe it or not, a *different* editing toolbar from the *traditional* editing toolbar. The old editing toolbar uses words like **Cut**, **Copy**, and **Paste**. *This* editing toolbar has icons for those functions (facing page, right).
>
> Why did we need a second editing toolbar? Because some people prefer icons. Obviously.

Undo, Redo

Everyone makes mistakes. Fortunately, the iPhone harbors an Undo command, which can come in handy when you type, cut, copy, or paste something by mistake. In fact, you can even undo the Undo—with the Redo command.

iOS 13 gives you three ways to trigger these commands:

- **Shake the phone.** Yes, you *shake* the iPhone. It offers you an **Undo** button, which you can tap to confirm the backtracking. (This feature has to be turned on in **Settings**→**Accessibility**→**Touch**.)

  Shake the phone again, and the screen offers you a **Redo** button. Fun! (Except when you shake the phone by accident and get the Nothing to Undo message. But still.)

- **Open the new toolbar.** Rest three fingers on the screen simultaneously. On the new editing toolbar at the top of the screen, tap ↶ (for Undo) or ↷ (for Redo).

- **Swipe with three fingers.** Swipe left with three fingers to undo, or swipe right with three fingers to redo.

You can perform any of the new three-finger gestures anywhere on the screen, even on (or partly on) the keyboard. Many of them are fairly fussy to get working well, though—they're clearly most at home on an iPad.

Dictation

The iPhone's speech-recognition feature, sometimes called Siri (even though Siri is also the voice *command* feature), lets you enter text anywhere, into any program, just by *speaking*. (Behind the scenes, it's using the same Nuance recognition technology that powers the Dragon line of dictation programs.)

It's extremely fast and, usually, remarkably accurate. Suddenly you don't have to fuss with the tiny keyboard. The experience of "typing" is no longer claustrophobic. You can blather away into an email, fire off a text message, or draft a memo without ever looking at the screen.

Now, before you get all excited, here are the necessary footnotes:

- **Voice typing works** even if there's background noise, but you get the best results if it's fairly quiet.

- **Voice typing isn't always practical,** since everybody around you can hear what you're saying.

- **Voice typing isn't always accurate.** Often you'll have to correct an error or two.

All right—expectations set? Then here's how to type by speaking.

First, fire up someplace where you can call up the keyboard: Messages, Notes, Mail, Safari, whatever. Tap, if necessary, so that the onscreen keyboard appears. Tap the 🎤 below the keyboard.

When you hear the xylophone note, say what you have to say (below, left). If there's background noise, hold the phone up to your head; if it's relatively quiet, a couple of feet away is fine. You don't have to speak slowly, loudly, or weirdly; speak normally.

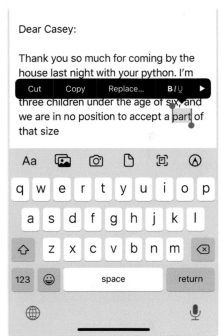

As you speak, the words fly onto the screen. You have to speak your own punctuation, like this: "Dear Dad (colon): Send money (dash)—as much as you can (comma), please (period)." The table at the end of this section describes all the punctuation you can dictate.

After you finish speaking, tap anywhere in the big gray sound waves area. Another xylophone note plays—higher, this time—and you may see some of the words *change* right before your eyes, as though Siri is changing her mind. In fact, she is; she's using the context of *all* the words you said to revise what she *originally* thought you said, as you said it. See?

After you stop transcribing, the keyboard returns. Now you can tap in the text to edit any mistakes (above, right), exactly as you would fix an error in something you typed. (If you're using Voice Control, as described on page 228, you can just speak to correct the mistakes.)

Or, if the whole thing is a mess, you can Undo your transcription (page 248).

> **TIP:** Often, the iPhone knows perfectly well when it might have gotten a word wrong—it draws a dashed underline beneath words or phrases it's insecure about. You can tap that word or phrase to see the alternative interpretation, which is often correct.

Usually you'll find the accuracy pretty darned good, considering that you didn't have to train the software to recognize your voice, and considering that your computer is a *cellphone*, for crying out loud. You'll also find the accuracy is better when you dictate complete sentences, and that long words fare better than short ones.

Punctuation

Here's a handy table that shows what punctuation you can say and how to say it.

> **NOTE:** If you've ever used Dragon NaturallySpeaking (for Windows) or Dragon Dictation (for the Mac), you already know these commands; they're the standard Nuance dictation-software shortcuts, because that's what the iPhone uses behind the scenes.

Say this:	To get this:	For example, saying this:	Types this:
"period" or "full stop"	. [space and capital letter follow]	"Best (period) date (period) ever (period)"	Best. Date. Ever.
"dot" or "point"	. [no space follows]	"Email frank (dot) smith (at sign) gmail (dot) com"	Email frank.smith@gmail.com
"comma," "semicolon," "colon"	, ; :	"Mom (comma) hear me (colon) I'm dizzy (semi-colon) tired"	Mom, hear me: I'm dizzy; tired
"question mark," "excla-mation point"	? ! [space and capital letter follow]	"Ellen (question mark) Hi (excla-mation point)"	Ellen? Hi!

Say this:	To get this:	For example, saying this:	Types this:
"inverted question mark," "inverted exclamation point"	¿ ¡	"(inverted question mark) Que paso (question mark)"	¿Que paso?
"ellipsis" or "dot dot dot"	…	"Just one (ellipsis) more (ellipsis) step (ellipsis)"	Just one… more…step…
"space bar"	[a space, especially when a hyphen would normally appear]	"He rode the merry (space bar) go (space bar) round"	He rode the merry go round
"open paren," then "close paren" (or "open bracket/ close bracket," or "open brace/ close brace")	( ) or [ ] or { }	"Then she (open paren) the doctor (close paren) gasped"	Then she (the doctor) gasped
"new line"	[a press of the Return key]	"milk (new line) bread (new line) quinoa"	Milk Bread Quinoa
"new paragraph"	[two presses of the Return key]	"autumn leaves (new paragraph) softly falling"	autumn leaves softly falling
"quote," then "unquote"	" "	"Talk about (quote) alternative facts (unquote)"	Talk about "alternative facts"
"numeral"	[writes the following number as a digit instead of spelling it out]	"Next week she turns (numeral) eight"	Next week she turns 8

Say this:	To get this:	For example, saying this:	Types this:
"asterisk," "plus sign," "minus sign," "equals sign"	*, +, −, =	"eight (asterisk) two (plus sign) one (minus sign) three (equals sign) fourteen"	8*2+1−3=14
"ampersand," "dash"	&, —	"Logan (amper-sand) Dexter (dash) the best (exclamation point)"	Logan & Dexter—the best!
"hyphen"	- [without spaces]	"Don't give me that holier (hyphen) than (hyphen) thou attitude"	Don't give me that holier-than-thou attitude
"backquote"	'	"Back in (backquote) (numeral) fifty-two"	back in '52
"smiley," "frowny," "winky" (or "smiley face," "frowny face," "winky face")	:-) :-(;-)	"I think you know where I'm going with this (winky face)"	I think you know where I'm going with this ;-)

You can also say "percent sign" (%), "at sign" (@), "dollar sign" ($), "cent sign" (¢), "euros sign" (€), "yen sign" (¥), "pounds sterling sign" (£), "section sign" (§), "copyright sign" (©), "registered sign" (®), "trademark sign" (™), "greater-than sign" or "less-than sign" (> or <), "degrees sign" (°), "tilde" (~), "vertical bar" (|), and "pound sign" (#).

The software automatically capitalizes the first new word after a period, question mark, or exclamation point. But you can also force it to capitalize words you're dictating by saying "cap" right before the word, like this: "Dear (cap) Mom (comma), I've run away to join (cap) The (cap) Circus (comma), a nonprofit cooperative for runaway jugglers."

Here's another table—this one shows the other commands for capitalization, plus spacing and spelling commands.

TIP: Speak each of the on/off commands as a separate utterance, with a small pause before and after.

Say this:	To get this:	For example, saying this:	Types this:
"cap" or "capital"	Capitalizes the next word	"Give me the (cap) works"	Give me the Works
"caps on," then "caps off"	Capitalizes the first letter of every word	"Next week (caps on) the new england chicken cooper- ative (caps off) will hire me"	Next week The New England Chicken Cooperative will hire me
"all caps on," then "all caps off"	Capitalizes everything	"So (all caps on) please please (all caps off) don't tell anyone"	So PLEASE PLEASE don't tell anyone
"all caps"	Types just the next word in all caps	"We (all caps) really don't belong here"	We REALLY don't belong here
"no caps"	Types the next word in lowercase	"See you in (no caps) Texas"	See you in texas
"no caps on," then "no caps off"	Prevents any capital letters	"I'll ask (no caps on) Santa Claus (no caps off)"	I'll ask santa claus
"no space"	Runs the two words together	"Try our new mega (no space) berry flavor"	Try our new megaberry flavor
"no space on," then "no space off"	Eliminates all spaces	"(No space on) I can't believe you ate all that (no space off) (comma) she said excitedly"	Ican'tbelieveyou ateallthat, she said excitedly
[alphabet letters]	Types the letters out (usually not very accurately)	"The stock symbol is A P P L"	The stock sym- bol is APPL

You don't always have to dictate these formatting commands, by the way. The iPhone automatically inserts hyphens into phone numbers (you say, "2125561000," and get "212-556-1000"); formats two-line street addresses without your having to say, "New line" before the city; handles prices automatically ("6 dollars and 32 cents" becomes "$6.32").

It formats dates and web addresses well; you can even use the nerdy shortcut "dub-dub-dub" for the "www" part of a web address.

The phone recognizes email addresses, too, as long as you remember to say "at" or "at sign" in the right spot. You'd say, "harold (underscore) beanfield (at) gmail (dot) com" to get "harold_beanfield@gmail.com."

> **TIP:** You can combine these formatting commands. Many iPhone owners have wondered, "How do I voice-type the *word* "comma," since saying "comma" types out only the symbol?"
>
> The solution: Say, "No space on, no caps on, C, O, M, M, A, no space off, no caps off." That gives you the *word* "comma."
>
> Then again, it might just be easier to type that one with your finger.

The "Look Up" Dictionary

On page 90, you can read about the spelling dictionary that's built into iOS—but that's just a dumb list of words. Your iPhone also has a *real* dictionary, one that shows you definitions.

In many apps, you can look up any word that appears on the screen. Double-tap it to get the editing bar (facing page, left); then tap Look Up. (You may have to tap ▶ to bring that button into view.)

(If no definitions are found, then tap Manage Dictionaries at the bottom of this screen for a list of dictionaries you can download: English, French, Simplified Chinese, and so on. Tap the ones you think you'll use to download them.)

But there's more to Look Up than definitions. Depending on what you're looking up, you may also see listings for Wikipedia entries, movie titles, sports scores, App Store apps, Twitter tweets, songs from Apple Music, web videos, and the web at large. It's all meant to put the power of iOS search—including the entire internet—behind any word you see.

> **TIP:** If you'd prefer just to look up definitions, open Settings→Siri & Search, and turn off Suggestions in Look Up. Now tapping Look Up means only "Check the dictionary." (Then again, it still offers a Search Web button in case you change your mind.)

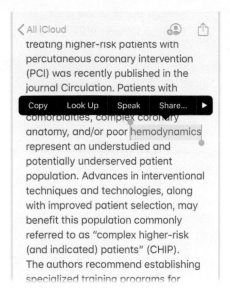

Speak!

The iPhone can read to you, too. Visit **Settings→Accessibility→Spoken Content** and turn on **Speak Selection** and/or **Speak Screen**. Choose a language (or accent), a voice, and a speaking rate. (The more realistic voices, like Ava and her brother Alex, require you to download audio files from Apple. Just tap the ☁ to begin the download.)

It's fun to turn on **Highlight Content**, too. (Each word will light up in color as the phone speaks it. Great for kids learning to read!)

From now on, among the other buttons that pop up when you select text, a **Speak** button appears. Or, if you swipe down the screen with two fingers (and you've turned on **Speak Screen**), your iPhone reads the entire screen.

You can use these features whenever you want to double-check the pronunciation of a word, whenever you want to have a web article or email read to you while you're getting dressed for the day, or whenever you lose your voice and just want to communicate with the rest of the world.

Searching Your iPhone

The iPhone's global search feature can find information on your phone within any app—but it's also something like a typed version of Siri, in that it can call up information about movies, restaurants, news, and so on.

How to Use Search

Start at the Home screen. From here, you have two options:

- **Swipe down.** Don't swipe from the top of the screen, which brings up the pull-down Lock screen (page 62). Instead, drag down on the *middle* of a Home screen.

- **Swipe to the right** from the first Home screen. Lurking to its left is the Today screen (page 76)—with, once again, a search box at the top.

When you tap into the search box, the keyboard opens automatically. Type or dictate to identify what you want to find and open. For example, if you were trying to find a file called *Pokémon Fantasy League*, typing just *pok* or *leag* would probably suffice. (Search doesn't find text in the *middles* of words; it searches from the beginnings of words.)

There are two stages of results: what you see *before* you tap the **Search** button on the keyboard and what you see *after*.

- **Before you tap** Search (while you're typing), you get, just below the typing box, a list of autocomplete suggestions (facing page, left). It's composed of data bits actually on your phone: app names, people's names, calendar appointment names, and so on. For example, if you've typed *app*, the suggestions may include *apple*, *appearance schedule*, and so on.

> **TIP:** If you tap an app's name in this list, you get to see which *folder* contains that app. (We're talking about the text list just under the search box—not the rows of app names that display their icons.)

Below that, iOS makes additional guesses at what you're seeking, grouped by category: Applications, Voice Memos, Mail, Contacts, Notes, News, Safari, Dictionary, and so on. In fact, these suggestions may even come from within non-Apple apps. All this is part of what Apple calls Siri Suggestions. You can turn them off, either globally or one app at a time; see page 114.

At the very bottom, you get buttons for **Search Web**, **Search App Store**, **Search Maps**, and **Ask Siri**, for the sake of completeness.

> **TIP:** If you drag your finger to scroll the list, the keyboard helpfully vanishes so you can see more results.

- **After you tap Search,** you get a list of results that contain *exactly* what you typed (facing page, right). If you've typed *app*, the suggestions may include **App Store**, **Train App**, and so on. (If the search can't

find many matches, it may show you some autocompleted suggestions, of the *apple* and *appearance schedule* sort.)

Either way, you wind up with a list of tappable search results, organized
by category or app. This list may reveal matching terms from these
categories:

- **Apple's apps.** Music, Podcasts, TV, and Audiobooks (song, performer, and album names, plus the names of podcasts, videos, and
  audiobooks); Notes, Messages, Reminders, and Voice Memos (text of
  your notes, texts, and to-do items; names and descriptions of voice
  memos); calendar events (including meeting invitees and locations);
  and Mail (To, From, and Subject fields of all accounts; body text in
  some accounts).

- **Other companies' apps.** Search can also find recent destinations
  you've used in Google Maps, Uber, or Lyft; photo album names in

Flickr; and so on. (Not all apps are searchable—only those updated since iOS 11 came along.)

- **To find your apps.** If you have lots of apps, this is a superefficient way to find them. The results even identify which *folder* an app is in.

- **Siri suggestions.** The Search feature can find movies, music, apps, and results from Wikipedia (when you search for, say, "rhubarb" or "Thomas Edison"); news; restaurants, shops, and businesses; the App Store; the iTunes Store; and the Book Store.

  The results list identifies which category each hit comes from. Tapping a result does what you'd expect: for a web article, opens it; for a business, opens its Maps page so you can call it or get directions; for something from an Apple store, opens the appropriate store.

  Really, don't miss this. When you hear about a cool app, don't open the App Store to look for it. When you want to know a sports score, don't start with Safari. When you need the phone number of a restaurant, don't call 411. Instead, use Search for all those things.

- **Web results.** You can tap **Search Web** at the bottom of the results list to hand off to Safari for a search.

> **NOTE:** Many apps have their *own* search boxes (usually hidden until you scroll to the top of their lists). Those search functions are great when you're already *in* the program where you want to search.

If you see the name and icon of whatever you were hoping to dig up, tap to open it. The corresponding app opens automatically.

Controlling What Shows Up

Apple lets you limit which apps' data shows up in search results. If you don't think you'll search your email from this screen (and maybe, for privacy reasons, you'd rather not see email snippets show up in the results), you can turn it off.

In **Settings→Siri & Search**, you'll find a master list of apps that Search can "see into." Tap one and turn off its switch to exclude it from search results. (You can still find that app's icon by typing its name—you just won't see any information from *inside* that app.)

4

Phone Calls & FaceTime

With each successive iPhone model, Apple improves the iPhone's antennas, circuitry, speakers, microphones, and software. Meanwhile, features like Siri, autoreply, and Do Not Disturb have turned Apple's phone from an also-ran into one of the most useful gadgets ever to hop onto a cellular network.

Dialing from the Phone App

Suppose you're in luck. Suppose the bars at the top of the screen tell you that you've got cellular reception. You're ready to start a conversation. To make a phone call, open the Phone app. It's usually at the bottom of the Home screen. (The tiny circled number, like ❷, tells you how many missed calls and voicemail messages you have.)

> **TIP:** Using Siri is often faster. You get good results saying things like, "Call Casey Robin's cell" or "Dial 866-2331." Truth is, you don't even need the verb. If you utter *only* a phone number to Siri, she'll figure out what to do.

Now you've arrived in the Phone app. The icons at the bottom represent your voicemail (page 131) and the four ways of dialing from here:

- **Favorites.** Here's the iPhone's version of speed dial: It lists up to 50 people you think you call most frequently. Tap a name to make the call. (Details on building and editing this list begin on the next page.)

- **Recents.** Every call you've recently made, answered, missed, or even just dialed appears in this list. Missed callers' names appear in red lettering, which makes it easy to spot them—and to call them back.

  Tap a name or a number to dial. Or tap the ⓘ to view the details of a call—when, where, how long—and, if you like, to add this number to your Contacts list.

- **Contacts.** This program also has an icon of its own on the Home screen; you don't have to drill down to it through the Phone button. It's your phone book; tap somebody's name or number to dial it.

- **Keypad.** This dialing pad's big, fat buttons are easy to hit even with big, fat fingers. Punch in a number and then tap 🔵 to place the call.

Once you've dialed, no matter which method you used, either hold the iPhone up to your head, put in the earbuds or AirPods, turn on the speakerphone, or put on your Bluetooth earpiece—and start talking!

This, however, is only the Quick Start Guide. Here's a more detailed look at each of the Phone app modules.

The Favorites List

You may not wind up dialing much from Contacts. That's the master list, all right, but it's too unwieldy when you just want to call your spouse, your boss, or your lawyer. Dialing by voice (Chapter 5) is almost always faster. But when silence is golden, at the very least use the Favorites list—a short, easy-to-scan list of the people you call most often (facing page, left).

Actually, *calling* is only the beginning. A favorite can be any kind of "address": for an email, text message, video call, even an internet voice call in an app like WhatsApp, Skype, or Cisco Spark. In other words, you can set things up so one tap on a favorite opens an outgoing text to your beloved, and a different tap triggers a Skype call to your boss.

 Once you've set up these favorites, you can add them to the Today screen (page 76), so that placing one of these calls or text communications is only a swipe and a tap away.

You can add names to this list in any of three ways:

- **From the Favorites list itself.** Tap + to view your Contacts list. Tap the person you want. If there's more than one phone number or email address on the info screen, then tap the one you want to add to Favorites.

 Each favorite doesn't represent a *person*; it represents a *number or address*. So if your best friend Chris has both a home number and a cell number, then add two items to the Favorites list. Gray lettering in the list lets you know whether each number or address is mobile, home, Skype, Messages, FaceTime, or whatever.

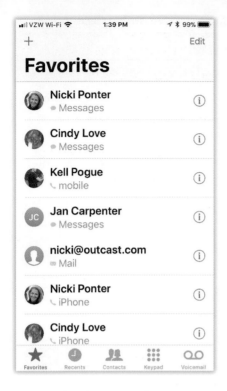
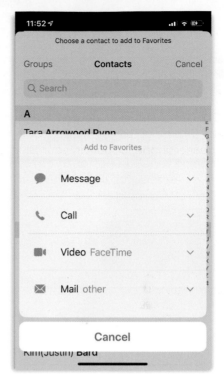

- **From the Contacts list.** Tap a name to open the info screen, where you'll find a button called **Add to Favorites**. It opens the Add to Favorites panel shown above at right. For each of its four communication methods—Message, Call, Video, Mail—you get a pop-up menu that lists your available apps for performing that sort of human contact.

  Tap the one you want to add to Favorites.

- **From the Recents list.** Tap ⓘ next to any name or number in the Recents list. If it's somebody who's already in your Contacts list, you arrive at the Call Details screen, where one tap on **Add to Favorites** does what it says.

  If it's somebody who's not in Contacts yet, you'll have to *put* her there first. Tap **Create New Contact**, and then proceed as described on page 123. After you hit **Save**, you return to the Call Details screen so you can tap **Add to Favorites**.

TIP: To help you remember that a certain phone number or email address is already in your Favorites list, a gray star appears next to it in certain spots, like the Call Details screen and the Contact Info screen.

The Favorites list holds 50 numbers. Once you've added 50, the **Add to Favorites** and + buttons disappear.

> **NOTE:** The face of each favorite peeks out of a round frame next to the name. If your Contacts card for that person doesn't have a photo—or Animoji!—the circle shows the person's initials instead.

Reordering Favorites

Tapping that **Edit** button at the top of the Favorites list offers another handy feature, too: It lets you drag names up and down, so the most important people appear at the top of the list. Just use the grip strip (≡) as a handle to move entire names up or down the list.

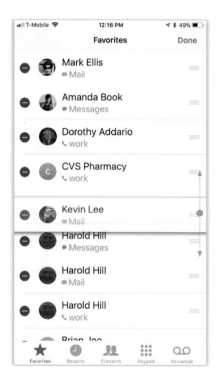

Deleting from Favorites

To delete somebody from your Favorites—the morning after a nasty political argument, for example—use the iPhone's standard shortcut: Swipe leftward across the undesired name. Tap **Delete**.

(If you're paid by the hour, you can use the slow method, too. Tap **Edit**. Now tap the ⊖ button next to the unwanted entry and tap **Delete** to confirm.)

The Recents List

Like any self-respecting cellphone, the iPhone maintains a list of everybody you've called or who's called you recently. The idea, of course, is to provide you with a quick way to call someone you've been talking to lately.

To see the list, tap **Recents** at the bottom of the Phone app. You see a list of the last 75 calls you've received or placed, along with each person's name or number (depending on whether that name is in Contacts or not), city of the caller's home area code (for callers not in your Contacts), time or date of the call, and what kind of call it was—mobile, home, work, FaceTime, FaceTime Audio, Skype, or whatever.

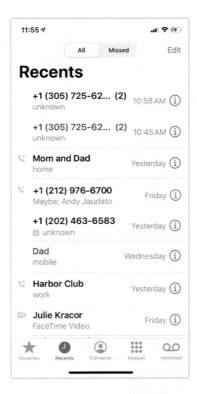

Here's what you need to know about the Recents list:

- **Calls you missed** (or sent to voicemail) appear in red type. If you tap Missed at the top of the screen, you see *only* your missed calls. The color-coding and separate listings are designed to make it easy for you to return calls you missed, or to try again to reach someone who didn't answer when you called.

- **A tiny** 📞 **or** ↗️ **icon** lets you know which calls you *made* (to differentiate them from calls you *received*).

- **To call someone back**—regardless of whether you answered or dialed the call—tap that name or number in the list.

- **"Maybe: Casey Robin"** appears when the iPhone guesses at the caller's name—by looking for a matching phone number in the signature portion of your received email! For example, if Casey Robin has called you from 213-292-3344, and there's also an email from Casey that includes a phone number as part of the signature, the Recents list says: *Maybe: Casey Robin.* Clever!

- **Tap** ⓘ **next to any call** to open the info screen. At the top of the screen, you can see a list of recent calls, and whether each was incoming, outgoing, missed, or canceled (in which you chickened out and hung up before your callee answered).

  What else you see here depends on whether the other person is in your Contacts list.

  If so, the info screen displays the person's whole information card (below, left). A little table displays all the incoming and outgoing calls to or from this person that day. A small gray star denotes a phone number that's also in your Favorites list, and a Recent label indicates which number that recent call came from (or went to).

  If the call *isn't* from someone in your Contacts, you get to see a handy notation at the top of the info screen: the city and state where the calling phone is registered (below, right).

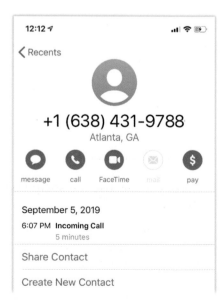

- **To save you scrolling,** the Recents list thoughtfully combines consec-utive calls to or from the same person. If some obsessed ex-lover has been calling you every ten minutes for four hours, you'll see "Chris Meyerson (24)" in the Recents list. (Tap ⓘ to see the exact times of the calls.)

- **You can erase one call** from this list exactly the same way you'd delete a favorite: Swipe leftward across the undesired name. Tap the Delete button that appears. (Once again, there's also a long way: Tap Edit, tap ● next to the unwanted entry, and then tap Delete.)

  You can also erase the *entire* list, thus preventing a co-worker or significant other from discovering your illicit activities: Tap Edit, and then tap Clear at the top of the screen. You're asked to confirm your decision.

Contacts

The Phone app may offer four ways to dial—Favorites, Recents, Contacts, and Keypad—but the Contacts list is the source from which all other lists spring. That's probably why it's listed several times: once with its own icon on the Home screen, again at the bottom of the Phone app, and also in the FaceTime and Messages apps (when you tap the ⊕).

Contacts is your address book—your master phone book.

> **NOTE:** Your iPhone's own phone number appears at the top of the Contacts list. That's a much better place for it than deep at the end of a menu labyrinth, where it is on most phones.

If your social circle is longer than one screenful, you can navigate this list in any of three ways:

- **First,** you can savor the distinct pleasure of flicking through it.

- **Second,** if you're in a hurry to get to the V's, use the A-to-Z index down the right edge of the screen. Just tap the first letter of the last name you're looking for. Or slide your finger up or down the index. The list scrolls with it.

- **Third,** you can use the search box at the very top of the list, above the A's.

  Tap to make the keyboard appear. As you type, Contacts pares down the list, hiding everyone whose first, last, or company name doesn't match what you've typed so far. It's a really fast way to pluck one name out of a haystack.

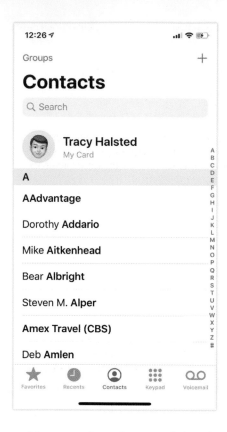
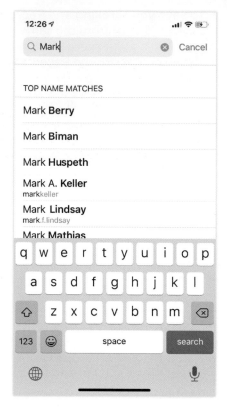

(You can clear the search box by tapping the ✖ at its right end or restore the full list by tapping **Cancel**.)

In any case, when you see the name you want, tap it to open its information card. Tap the number you want to dial.

Groups

Many computer address book programs, including the Mac's Contacts app, let you place your contacts into *groups*—subsets like Book Club or Fantasy League Guys. You can't create or delete groups on the iPhone without a special app, but at least the groups from your Mac, PC, Exchange server, or iCloud account can get synced over to it. To see them, and to switch them all on or off at once, tap **Groups** at the top of the Contacts list.

Here's where groups come into play:

- **If you can't seem to find someone in the list,** you may be looking in the wrong list. Tap **Groups** at the top-left corner to return to the list of accounts. Tap **Show All Contacts** to view a single, unified list of everyone your phone knows about.

- **If you use the Groups feature,** remember to tap the group name you want *before* you create a new contact. That's how you put someone into an existing group.

NOTE: Contacts imported from Facebook and Twitter are no longer groups that you can hide or show at will. If you've given those apps access to Contacts, you may find the list hideously bloated with hundreds of people you never actually call. If you don't want to see them, you have to remove them individually. Too bad!

Adding to the Contacts List

Every cellphone has a Contacts list, of course, but the beauty of the iPhone is that you don't have to type in the phone numbers one at a time. Instead, the iPhone sucks in the entire phone book from your Mac or PC, iCloud, and/or an Exchange server at work.

It's infinitely easier to edit your address book on the computer, where you have an actual keyboard and mouse. The iPhone also makes it easy to add someone's contact information when she calls, emails, or text messages you, thanks to a prominent **Add to Contacts** button.

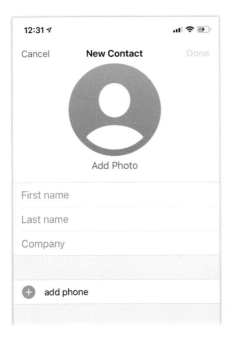
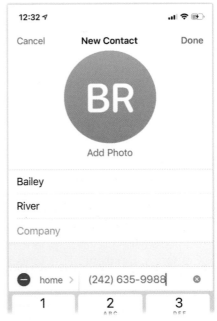

But if, in a pinch, on the road, at gunpoint, you have to add, edit, or remove a contact manually, here's how to do it:

Make sure you've selected the right group or account, as described already. Now, on the Contacts screen, tap +. You arrive at the New Contact screen, which teems with empty boxes.

It shouldn't take you long to figure out how to fill in this form: You tap in a box and type. But here are a few tips for data entry:

- **The keyboard opens automatically** when you tap in a box. And the iPhone capitalizes the first letter of each word for you.

- **Phone numbers are special.** When you enter a phone number, the iPhone adds parentheses and hyphens for you. (You can even enter text phone numbers, like 1-800-GO-BROWNS; the iPhone converts the letters to digits when it dials.)

  If you need to insert a pause—for dialing access numbers, extension numbers, or voicemail passwords—type #, which introduces a two-second pause in the dialing. You can type several of them to create longer pauses.

  To change the label for a number ("mobile," "home," "work," and so on), tap the label that's there now. The Label screen shows you your choices. There's even a label called "iPhone," so you and your buddy can gloat together.

TIP: If you scroll down the Label screen, you'll see you can also create *custom* labels. You might prefer someone's cellphone number to be identified as "cell" instead of "mobile," for example. Or you might want to create a label that says "Skype," "Google Voice," "Line 2," "Yacht Phone," or "Bat Phone." The secret: Tap **Add Custom Label**. (Once you've created a custom label, it's there in the list of options for your use later.)

- **Expand-O-Fields mean you'll never run out of room.** Almost every field (empty box) on a Contacts card is infinitely expanding. That is, the instant you start filling in a field, another empty box (labeled ⊕ add phone or whatever) appears right below it, so you can immediately add *another* phone number, email address, URL, or street address. (The only nonexpanding fields are First name, Last name, Company, Ringtone, Text Tone, Notes, and whatever oddball fields you add yourself.)

  For example, when you first tap **add phone**, the phone-number box you get is labeled "home." (If that's not the right label, you can tap it to choose from one of almost a dozen others—or add a custom label.)

A new **add phone** button appears so you'll have a place to enter a second phone number for this person. When you do that, a *third* **add phone** button appears. And so on.

In other words, you can never run out of places to add more phone numbers, addresses, URLs, and social media profiles.

- **You can keep track of social.** In iCloud accounts, there's also the **social profile** field, where you can list somebody's address for social media (Twitter, LinkedIn, Flickr, Facebook, and so on) and any communication apps you have installed (Messenger, Zoom, WhatsApp, Skype, Amazon Alexa). There's an **instant message** field, too, where you can record addresses for chat networks Skype, MSN, and so on.

- **Relationships are here.** Then there's **add related name**. Here's where you can list this person's mother, father, spouse, partner, child, manager, sibling, and so on—or even specify a different type of relationship (tap the existing label and then **Add Custom Label**).

- **You can add a photo of the person, if you like.** Tap **add photo**. If you have a photo of the person on your phone already, tap **All Photos**. You're taken to your photo collection, where you can find a good headshot.

  Alternatively, tap 📷 to activate the iPhone's built-in camera. Frame the person, and then tap the white camera button to snap the shot.

  In either of those cases, you wind up at the **Move and Scale** screen (next page, right). Here you can frame up the photo so the person's face is nicely sized and centered. Spread two fingers to enlarge the photo; drag your finger to move the image within the frame. Tap **Use Photo**; now you're offered a bunch of color filters to enhance the shot. Tap one (or tap **Original**). Back on the info screen where you started, the photo now appears. Tap **Edit** if you want to duplicate the photo (so you can make further edits), edit the Move and Scale screen, or get rid of it altogether.

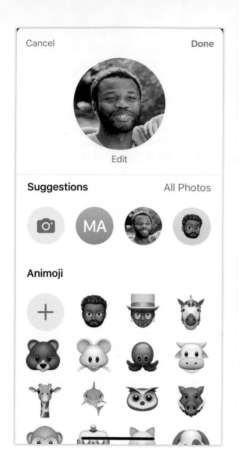

Instead of a photo, you're also offered a wealth of Animoji (above, left)—Apple's set of cute, cartoon, interactive animal faces, along with any you've created yourself (page 219). If you tap one of these, you're asked to "Strike your favorite pose," meaning make a face into the camera. The cartoon mimics your expression; tap the white, round shutter button to freeze the icon that way. If it looks good, make your adjustments on the Move and Scale screen, hit **Choose**, and then choose a background color. Tap **Done**.

From now on, this photo or Animoji will pop up whenever the person calls. It also appears next to the person's name in your Favorites list.

- **You can choose a ringtone.** You can choose a different ringtone for each person in your address book. The idea is that you'll know by the sound of the ring who's calling you.

NOTE: It's one tone per person, not per phone number. Of course, if you really want one ringtone for your buddy's cellphone and another for his home phone, you can always create a different Contacts card for each one.

To choose a ringtone, tap **Default**. On the next screen, tap any sound in the Ringtones or Alert Tones lists to sample them. (Despite the separate lists, in this context, these sounds are all being offered as ringtones.) When you've settled on a good one, tap **Done** to return to the info screen where you started.

TIP: Here, on the ringtone selection screen, you're offered an **Emergency Bypass** switch. Turn it on to say, "Whenever this person calls or texts, I want my phone to ring or vibrate *even* if I've turned on Do Not Disturb" (page 70).

- **You can specify a vibration pattern for incoming calls.** This unsung feature lets you assign a custom vibration pattern to each person in your Contacts, so you know by *feel* who's calling—without even removing the phone from your pocket, even if your ringer is off. It's a surprisingly useful option.

  To set it up, start on the Ringtone screen described already; tap **Default** next to the word **Vibration**. You're offered a choice of canned patterns (Alert, Heartbeat, Quick, Rapid, and so on). But if you tap **Create New Vibration**, you can then tap the screen in whatever rhythm you like. It can be diddle diddle dee…or the opening notes to the Hallelujah Chorus…or the actual syllables of the person's name. ("Maryanna Beckleheimer." Can you feel it?)

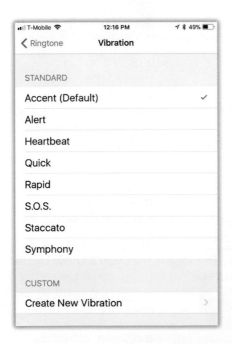

The phone records your pattern, which you can prove to yourself by tapping Play. If you tap Save and name that pattern, then it becomes one of the choices when you choose a vibration pattern for someone in your Contacts. It's what you'll feel whenever this person calls you. Yes, it's tactile caller ID. Wild.

- **You can also pick a text-message sound (and vibration).** Just as you can choose sounds and vibrations for incoming phone calls, you can tap Text Tone to choose sounds and vibrations for incoming text messages and FaceTime invitations.

- **You can add new fields of your own.** Very cool: If you tap add field at the bottom of the screen, then you go down the rabbit hole into Field Land, where you can add any of 13 additional info bits about the person whose card you're editing: a prefix (like Mr. or Mrs.), a suffix (like M.D. or Esq.), a nickname, a job title, a phonetic pronunciation for people with uncommon names, and so on.

  When you tap one of these labels, you return to the info screen, where you'll see that the iPhone has inserted the new, empty field in the most intelligent spot. For example, if you add a phonetic first name, that box appears just below the "First name" box. The keyboard opens so you can fill in the blank.

- **You can link and unlink Unified Contacts.** As noted earlier, your phone can sync up with different accounts. Your Contacts app might list four sets of names and numbers: one stored on your phone, one from an iCloud account, one from Facebook, and a fourth from your corporate Exchange server at work. In the old days, therefore, certain names might have shown up in the Contacts list two or three times— not an optimal situation.

  Now, as a favor to you, the iPhone displays each person's name only once in that master list. If you tap that name, you open a unified information screen for that person. It includes *all* the details from *all* the underlying contact cards.

NOTE: The iPhone combines cards only if the first and last names are exactly the same. If there's a difference in name, suffix, prefix, or middle name, then no unifying takes place. Remember, too, that you see the unification only if you view the All Contacts list.

To see which cards the iPhone is combining for you, scroll to the bottom of the card. There the Linked Contacts section shows you which cards have been unified.

You can tap a listing to open the card in the corresponding account. For that matter, you can manually link a card, too; tap Edit, tap link contacts, and then choose a contact to link to this unified card—even if the name isn't a perfect match.

NOTE: It's OK to link Joe Carnelia's card with Joseph Carnelia's card—they're probably the same person. But don't link up *different* people's cards. Remember, the whole point is to make the iPhone combine all the phone numbers, email addresses, and so on onto a single card—and seeing two sets on one card could get confusing fast.

This stuff gets complex. But, in general, the iPhone tries to do the right thing. For example, if you edit the information on the unified card, you're changing that information only on the card in the corresponding account. (Unless you *add* information to the unified card. In that case, the new data tidbit is added to *all* the underlying source-account cards.)

NOTE: To delete any info bit from a Contacts card, tap the ● next to it, and then tap the Delete button to confirm.

Adding a Contact on the Fly

There's actually another way to add someone to your Contacts list—a faster, on-the-fly method that's more typical of cellphones. Start by bringing the phone number up on the screen:

- **In the Phone app,** open the Keypad. Dial the number, and then tap Add Number.

- **You can also add a number** that's in your Recents (recent calls) list, storing it in Contacts for future use. Tap the ⓘ button next to the name.

In both cases, finish up by tapping Create New Contact (to enter this person's name for the first time) or Add to Existing Contact (to add a new phone number to the card of someone who's already in your list). Off you go to the Contacts editing screen shown on page 123.

Editing Someone

To make corrections or changes, tap the person's name in the Contacts list. In the upper-right corner of the info card, tap Edit.

You return to the screens already described, where you can make whatever changes you like. After you tap **Done** (or **Cancel**), you can return to the Contacts list by swiping to the right.

Deleting Someone

Truth is, you'll probably *add* people to your address book far more often than you'll *delete* them. After all, you meet new people all the time—but you delete them primarily when they die, move away, or dump you.

To zap someone, tap the name in the Contacts list and then tap **Edit**. Scroll down, tap **Delete Contact**, and confirm by tapping **Delete Contact** again. (Weirdly, the **Delete Contact** option doesn't appear if you open someone's info card from the Recents or Favorites lists—only from the main Contacts list.)

Sharing a Contact

There's a lot of work involved in entering someone's contact information. It's a nice touch, therefore, that you can spare the next guy all that effort—by sending a fully formed electronic business card to him.

To do that, open the contact's card—it can be yours or anyone's—and tap **Share Contact**. Here's the usual array of ways that you can electronically send things to other phones—the Share sheet, described on page 378. You can send this contact "card" by **AirDrop**, **Messages**, **Mail**, and so on.

Tap your choice, address the message (to an email address or, for a message, a cellphone number), and send it. The recipient, assuming he has a half-decent smartphone or address-book program on the receiving end, can install that person's information with a single tap on the attachment.

The Keypad

The fourth way to place a call is to tap **Keypad** at the bottom of the screen. The standard iPhone dialing pad appears.

To make a call, tap out (or paste) the phone number—use the ⊗ key or a left swipe to backspace if you make a mistake—and then tap the 📞 button.

You can also use the keypad to enter a phone number into your Contacts list, thanks to the **Add Number** button, described earlier.

> **TIP:** If you tap the 📞 button before touching any digits, you call up the last number you dialed on the keypad, ready to call again.

Visual Voicemail

On the iPhone, you don't *dial in* to check for answering-machine messages people have left for you. You don't enter a password. You don't sit through some Ambien-addled recorded voice saying, "You have...17...messages. To hear your messages, press 1. When you have finished, you may hang up..."

Instead, whenever somebody leaves you a message, the phone wakes up, and a notification lets you know who it's from. You also hear a sound (unless you've turned on the silencer switch).

That's your cue to open **Phone→Voicemail**. There you see all your messages in a tidy chronological list. (The list shows the callers' names if they're in your Contacts list; otherwise it shows their numbers.) You can listen to them in any order—you're not forced to listen to three long-winded friends before discovering that there's an urgent message from your boss. It's a game changer.

iOS even makes an attempt to *transcribe* your voicemails—to understand them and type out what they say. It's pretty crude, with lots of wrong and missing words. But it's usually enough to get the gist.

Setup

To access your voicemail, open the Phone app; tap Voicemail.

The very first time you visit this screen, the iPhone prompts you to make up a numeric password for your voicemail account—don't worry, you'll never have to enter it again, unless you plan to actually dial in for messages (page 135). Record a "Leave me a message" greeting.

You have two options for the outgoing greeting:

- **Default.** If you're microphone-shy, or if you're famous and don't want stalkers calling just to hear your famous voice, then use this option. It's a prerecorded female voice that says, "Your call has been forwarded to an automatic voice message system. 212-661-7837 is not available." *Beep!*

- **Custom.** This option lets you record your own voice saying, for example, "You've reached my iPhone 11 Pro. You may begin drooling at the tone." Tap Record, hold the iPhone to your head, say your line, and then tap Stop.

   Check how it sounds by tapping Play.

Then just wait for your fans to start leaving you messages!

Using Visual Voicemail

In the voicemail list, a blue dot (●) indicates a message you haven't yet played.

> **TIP:** You can work through your messages even when you're out of cellular range—on a plane, for example—because the recordings are stored on the iPhone itself.

When you tap the name of a message, you instantly see the date and time it came in, the person's name (if it's in your Contacts) or the cell-phone's registered city and state (if not), and a rough transcription. The Play slider tells you how many seconds long the message is.

And all the controls you need are right there, surrounding the message you tapped:

- **Share ( ).** Yes, you can send a voicemail recording to someone else (or to your laptop)—by email, text message, or whatever (page 378). Preserving important voicemails like this can be supremely useful—in, for example, a lawsuit.

- **Open this person's Contact card** by tapping ⓘ.

- **The transcript.** This is a crude transcript (Apple labels it *beta*, after all). There's no punctuation. There may be missing _____ and phrases. Some words might be completely wrong. But it's usually good enough that you can tell if a message is some robocall asking for money, or a message from the school nurse saying your kid has a broken rib.

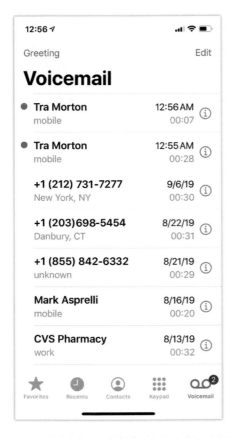
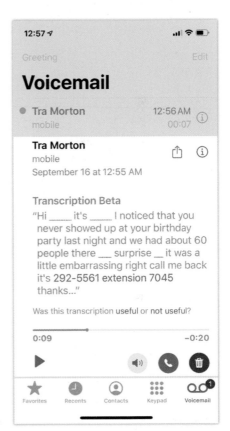

- ▶. Tap to listen to the message.

- ◀)). As the name "Visual Voicemail" suggests, you're *looking* at your voicemail list—which means you're *not* holding the phone up to your head. The first time people try using Visual Voicemail, therefore, they generally hear nothing!

  But if you hit Speaker (◀))) before you tap ▶, you can hear the playback *and* continue looking over the list.

- ☎. Tap to return the call. Very cool—you never even encounter the person's phone number.

- 🗑. You might want to keep the list manageable by deleting old messages. That's what this button does.

  If you have a lot of messages to delete, here's a faster way: Swipe across the first one's name right to left, and then tap **Delete**. The message disappears instantly. You can work down the list quickly this way.

- **Rewind, Fast Forward.** Drag in the scrubber bar (beneath the message) to skip backward or forward in the message. It's a great way to replay something you didn't catch the first time.

To collapse the expanded message, tap another message in the list, if it's visible, or just tap the caller's name.

Even before you've expanded a message's row to view the ▶, ◀), ☎, and 🗑 buttons, a few other Visual Voicemail buttons are awaiting your inspection:

- **Greeting.** Tap **Greeting** (upper-left corner) to record your voicemail greeting.

- **Call Details.** Tap ⓘ to open the info screen—the Contacts card—for the message that was left for you.

  If it was left by somebody who's in your Contacts list, you can see *which* of that person's phone numbers the call came from (indicated in blue type), plus a ★ if that number is in your Favorites list. Oh, and you can add this person to your Favorites list at this point by tapping **Add to Favorites** (at the bottom of the screen).

You can return the call right from the info screen, fire off a text message, send an email, place a FaceTime audio or video call, or even send that person some money via Apple Pay (page 579).

If the caller's number *isn't* in Contacts, you're offered a **Create New Contact** button and an **Add to Existing Contact** button, so you can store it for future reference.

Dialing In for Messages

Gross and pre-iPhonish though it may sound, you can also dial in for your messages from another phone.

To do that, dial your iPhone's number. Wait for the voicemail system to answer. As your own voicemail greeting plays, dial * (or # if you have Verizon), your voicemail password, and then #.

You hear the Uptight Carrier Lady announce how many messages you have, and then she'll start playing them for you. After you hear each message, she'll offer you the following options (but you don't have to wait for her to announce them):

- **To delete the message,** press 7.

- **To save it,** press 9.

- **To replay it,** press 4. (On T-Mobile, it's 1.)

Conveniently enough, these keystrokes are the same on Verizon, Sprint, and AT&T.

> **TIP:** If this whole Visual Voicemail thing freaks you out, you can also dial in for messages right from your own iPhone. Open the keypad and hold down the 1 key, just as though it were a speed-dial key on any normal phone.
>
> After a moment, the phone connects; you're asked for your password, and then the messages begin to play back, just as described already.

Answering Calls

When someone calls your iPhone, you'll know it; three out of your five senses are alerted. Depending on how you've set up your phone, you'll *hear* a ring, *feel* a vibration, and *see* the caller's name and photo on the screen. (Smell and taste will have to wait until iOS 14.)

NOTE: For details on Vibrate mode and on choosing a ringtone, see page 606.

How you answer depends on what's happening at the time:

- **If the iPhone is asleep or locked,** the screen lights up and says slide to answer. If you slide your finger as indicated by the arrow, you simultaneously unlock the phone and answer the call.

- **If you're using the iPhone,** tap the green Accept button. Tap the red hang-up button when you've both said enough.

- **If you're wearing earbuds,** the music fades out and then pauses; you hear the ring both through the phone's speaker and through your earbuds. (If you have a vibration pattern set up, then the phone vibrates, too). Answer by squeezing the clicker on the earbud cord or by using either of the methods already described.

When the call is over, you can click again to hang up—or just wait until the other guy hangs up. Either way, the music fades in again and resumes from the spot where you were so rudely interrupted.

Same thing if you were watching a video or listening to a podcast; it pauses for the duration of the call and resumes when you hang up.

Online and on the Phone, Together

Don't forget that the iPhone is a multitasking master. Once you're on the phone, you can dive into any other program—to check your calendar, for example—without interrupting your call.

You may even be able to use the phone's internet functions (web, email, apps, and so on) without interrupting the call. To be precise, you can be online and on the phone simultaneously if:

- **You're in a Wi-Fi hotspot.**

- **You have AT&T, T-Mobile, or Sprint in a VoLTE coverage area,** and you have VoLTE calling turned on (see page 490).

In other words, if you have Verizon (non-VoLTE) or Sprint (in a non-VoLTE area), and if you're not in a Wi-Fi hotspot, then you can't get online until the call is complete.

Not Answering Calls

Maybe you're in a meeting. Maybe you're driving. Maybe the call is from someone you *really* don't want to deal with. Fortunately, you have all kinds of ways to slam the cellular door in somebody's face.

Silencing the Ring

You might need a moment before you can answer the call, or you need to exit a meeting or put in the earbuds. In those cases, you can stop the ringing and vibrating by pressing one of the physical buttons on the edges (the side button or either volume key). The caller still hears the phone ringing, and you can still answer it within the first four rings, but at least the sound won't be annoying those around you.

(This assumes, of course, that you haven't just flipped the silencer switch.)

Ignore It—or Dump It to Voicemail

If you wait long enough (four rings), the call goes to voicemail (even if you silence the ringing as described already).

Or you can dump it to voicemail *immediately* (instead of waiting for the four rings). How you do that depends on the setup:

- **If the iPhone is asleep or locked,** tap the side button twice fast.

- **If you're using the iPhone,** tap the Decline button on the screen.

- **If you're wearing the earbuds,** squeeze the earbuds clicker for two seconds. You hear two low beeps, meaning: "OK, Master; dumped."

Of course, if your callers know you have an iPhone, they'll also know you've deliberately dumped them into voicemail—because they won't hear all four rings.

Auto-Dump to Voicemail

For the first time, Apple has provided you with a sliver of a weapon against robocallers and telemarketers. It's called Silence Unknown Callers, and it's described on page 636.

Respond with a Text Message

Whenever your phone rings, the screen bears a small white Message button (shown on page 136 at left). If you tap it, you get a choice of three canned text messages. Tapping one immediately dumps the caller to voicemail and sends the corresponding text message to the phone that's calling you. If you're driving or in a meeting, this feature is a lot more polite and responsive than just dumping the poor slob to voicemail.

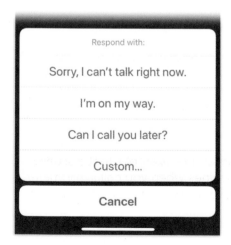

TIP: You can edit any of these three canned messages; they don't have to say, "Sorry, I can't talk right now," "I'm on my way," and "Can I call you later?" forever. To do that, open Settings→Phone, tap Respond with Text, and replace the text in the three placeholder boxes.

The fourth button, **Custom**, lets you type or dictate a new message on the spot. ("I'm in a meeting and, frankly, your call isn't worth getting fired for" comes to mind.)

Remind Me Later

The trouble with **Respond with Text**, of course, is that it sends a text message. What if the caller is using a landline that can't receive text messages? Fortunately, you have another option: **Remind Me**.

Tapping this button offers you one time-based option, **In 1 Hour** (which sets up a reminder to return the call an hour from now), and up to three location-based options (previous page, right): **When I leave**, **When I get home**, and **When I get to work**. (The home and work options appear only if the iPhone *knows* your home and work addresses—because you've entered them in your own card in Contacts.)

These options use the phone's GPS circuitry to detect when you've left your current inconvenient-to-take-the-call location, whether it's a job interview, a first date, or an outhouse.

Fun with Phone Calls

The iPhone makes it pitifully easy to perform stunts like turning on the speakerphone, putting someone on hold, taking a second call, and so on. Here are the options you get when you're on a call.

Mute

Tap this button to mute your own microphone, so the other guy can't hear you. (You can still hear him, though.) Now you have a chance to yell upstairs, to clear the phlegm from your throat, or to do anything else you'd rather the other party not hear. Tap again to unmute.

Keypad

Sometimes you have to input touch-tones. For example, that's usually how you operate home answering machines when you call in for messages, and it's often required by automated banking, reservations, and conference-call systems.

Tap **keypad** to produce the traditional iPhone dialing pad. Each digit you touch generates the proper touch-tone. When you're finished, tap **Hide** to return to the dialing-functions screen, or **End** if your conversation is complete.

Speaker (Audio)

For most people, tapping this button turns on the built-in speaker-phone—a great hands-free option.

But if the earbuds are plugged in, or a Bluetooth headset or speaker is connected, or you have a Mac associated with the phone (page 592), the button says **audio** instead of **speaker**. You get a little menu of audio sources for your call, including speakerphone and whatever other audio sources are available.

When you tap the button, it turns white. Now you can put the iPhone down on a table or a counter and have a conversation with both hands free. Tap **speaker** (or **audio**, and then **iPhone**) again to channel the sound back into the built-in earpiece.

Add Call (Conference Calling)

The iPhone is all about software, baby, and that's nowhere more apparent than in its facility at handling multiple calls at once.

The simplicity and reliability of this feature put other cellphones to shame. Never again, in attempting to answer a second call, will you have to tell the first person, "If I lose you, I'll call you back."

As you'll read, however, the details depend on whether you're using a GSM phone (AT&T or T-Mobile) or a CDMA phone (Verizon or Sprint).

Suppose you're on a call. Here are some of the tricks you can do:

- **Make an outgoing call.** Tap add call. The iPhone puts the first person on hold—neither of you can hear the other—and returns you to the Phone app and its various phone-number lists. You can now make a second call in any way you want. The top of the screen makes clear that the first person is still on hold as you talk to the second.

- **Receive an incoming call.** What happens when a second call comes in while you're already on a call?

  To answer on a GSM phone, tap **End Call + Answer**. On a CDMA phone, tap **End Current Call**; the new call makes the phone ring again, at which point you can answer it normally. Weird but true.

  You can also tap **End Current Call** (answer the incoming call, hang up on the first) or **Decline Incoming Call** (send it to voicemail).

When you're on two calls at once, the top of the screen identifies both other parties. Two new buttons appear, too:

- **swap** lets you flip between the two calls. At the top of the screen, you see the names or numbers of your callers. One says **Hold** (the one who's on hold, of course) and the other bears a time counter, which lets you know whom you're actually speaking to (next page, left).

  Think how many movie comedies have relied on the old "Whoops, I hit the wrong button and now I'm bad-mouthing somebody directly instead of behind his back!" gag. That can't happen on the iPhone.

  You can swap calls by tapping **swap** or by tapping the **Hold** person's name or number.

- **merge calls** combines your two calls so all three of you can converse at once. The top of the screen announces the names of your callers.

> **TIP:** On a GSM phone, you can tap ⓘ next to someone's name; at this point, you can drop someone from the call by tapping **End** or talk privately with someone by tapping **Private**. Tap **Merge Calls** to return to the group call.

This business of combining calls doesn't have to stop at two. At any time, you can tap **Add Call**, dial a third number, and then tap **Merge** to combine it with your first two. And then a fourth call, and a fifth. With you, that makes six people on the call.

Then your problem isn't technological; it's social, as you try to conduct a meaningful conversation without interrupting one another.

FaceTime

Tap this button to switch from your current phone call into a face-to-face video call, using the FaceTime app described starting on page 145.

(This feature requires that both you and the other guy have iPhones, iPads, iPod Touches, or Macs.)

Hold

The FaceTime button appears in place of what, on earlier iPhones, was the Hold button. But you can still trigger the Hold function—by holding down the **Mute** button for a couple of seconds. Now neither you nor the other guy can hear anything. Tap again to resume the conversation.

Contacts

This button opens the address book program so you can look up a number or place another call.

Call Waiting

What happens when you're on one phone call, and a second call comes in? On the iPhone, the phone rings (and/or vibrates) as usual, and the screen displays the name or number of the caller, as usual. Buttons on the screen offer you three choices (facing page, left):

- **End & Accept.** Hangs up on the first call and takes the second one.

- **Hold & Accept.** This is the traditional call-waiting effect. You say, "Can you hold on a sec? I've got another call," to the first caller. The iPhone puts her on hold, and you connect to the second caller.

  At this point, you can jump back and forth between the two calls, or you can merge them into a conference call.

- **Send to Voicemail.** The incoming call goes straight to voicemail. Your first caller has no idea anything has happened.

On AT&T phones, you can turn off call waiting (**Settings→Phone→Call Waiting**), so that additional incoming calls go straight to voicemail. If you have T-Mobile, Sprint, or Verizon, then you can turn off call waiting only one call at a time; just dial *70 before you dial the number. You won't be disturbed by call-waiting beeps while you're on that important call.

Call Forwarding

Here's a pretty cool feature you may not have known you had. It lets you route all calls made to your iPhone number to a *different* number. How is this useful? Let us count the ways:

- **When you're home.** You can have your cellphone's calls ring your home number so you can use any extension in the house, or so you don't miss any calls while the iPhone is turned off.

- **When you send your iPhone to Apple for repair.** You can forward the calls you would have missed to your home or work phone number.

- **When you're overseas.** You can forward the number to one of the web-based services that answers your voicemail and sends it to you as an email attachment (like Google Voice).

- **When you're going to be in a place with little or no cell coverage.** Let's say you're hiking in Alaska. You can have your calls forwarded to your hotel or to a friend's cellphone. (Forwarded calls eat up your allotment of minutes, though.)

You have to turn on call forwarding while you're still in an area with cell coverage. Here's how:

- **AT&T.** Tap Settings→Phone→Call Forwarding, turn call forwarding on, and then tap in the new phone number. That's all there is to it—your iPhone will no longer ring. At least not until you turn the same switch off again.

- **Verizon, Sprint, T-Mobile.** On the dialing pad, dial *72, plus the number you're forwarding calls to. Then tap 📞. (To turn off call forwarding, dial *73, and then tap 📞.)

Caller ID

Caller ID is another classic cellphone feature. It displays the phone number of the incoming call (and sometimes the name of the caller).

The only thing worth noting about the iPhone's implementation of caller ID is that you can prevent *your* number from appearing when you call *other* people's phones:

- **AT&T.** Tap Settings→Phone→Show My Caller ID, and then tap the on/off switch.

- **Verizon, Sprint, T-Mobile.** You can disable caller ID only for individual calls. For example, if you're calling your ex, you might not want your number to show up on his phone. Just dial *67 before you dial the number. (Caller ID turns on again for subsequent calls.)

Custom Ringtones

The iPhone comes with more than 50 creative and intriguing ringing sounds, from an old car horn to a peppy marimba lick (see page 606). You can also buy ready-made pop-music ringtones from Apple for $1.29 each. (On your iPhone, open the iTunes Store app. Tap More→Tones).

You can also make up *custom* ring sounds, either to use as your main iPhone ring or to assign to individual callers in your Contacts list. All kinds of free or cheap apps are available for doing that, with names like Ringtone Designer Pro 2.0 and Ringtones for iPhone; they let you make ringtones out of songs you already own, or even sounds you record yourself.

You can also use GarageBand, a free Apple program available for iOS or Mac. For instructions, see this chapter's free online appendix, "Making Custom Ringtones." It's a PDF available on this book's "Missing CD" page at *missingmanuals.com*.

> **TIP:** One feature blatantly missing on the iPhone is a "vibrate, *then* ring" option for incoming calls. That's where the phone first vibrates silently to get your attention—and begins to ring only if you haven't responded after, say, 10 seconds.
>
> GarageBand offers the solution: Create a ringtone that's silent for the first 10 seconds and only *then* plays a sound. Then set your iPhone to vibrate and ring. When a call comes in, the phone plays the ringtone immediately as it vibrates—but you won't hear anything until after the silent portion of the ringtone has been "played."

Get Your Ringtones Back

If you had custom ringtones in previous versions of iOS, but they no longer show up, you have two options:

- **If they came from the iTunes store, re-download them.** (On the phone, open Settings→Sounds & Haptics→Ringtones, and tap Download All Purchased Tones.)

- **If they're on your computer, reinstall them.** Connect your phone to your computer, open iTunes, and drag the ringtone files into the left-side sidebar, where your phone's name appears. (They're in your Music→iTunes→iTunes Media→Tones folder.) Details are at *support.apple.com/en-us/HT201593*.

FaceTime Video Calls

Your iPhone, as you're probably aware, has cameras both on the back and on the front. And that can mean only one thing: Video calling has arrived.

The picture and audio are generally rock-solid, with very little delay. Now Grandma can see the baby, or you can help someone shop from afar, or you can supervise brain surgery from thousands of miles away (some medical training recommended).

You can enjoy these *Jetsons* fantasies not just when calling other iPhones; you can also make video calls between iPhones and iPads, iPod Touches, and Macs. You can even place these calls when you're not in a Wi-Fi hotspot, over the cellular airwaves, when you're out and about.

FaceTime couldn't be easier to fire up—in many different ways:

- **From Siri.** The quickest way to start a video call may be simply to say, "FaceTime Mom," "FaceTime Chris Taylor," or whatever.

- **From Favorites.** Whenever you designate someone's FaceTime contact info as a favorite, a new entry appears in the Phone app's Favorites list (page 116).

- **When you're already on a phone call with someone.** This is a good technique when you want to ask first if the other guy *wants* to do video, or when you've been chatting and suddenly there's some *reason* to do video. In any case, there's nothing to it: Just tap the FaceTime button that's right on the screen when you pull the phone away from your face. (Your buddy can either accept or, if he just got out of the shower, decline.)

- **From the FaceTime app.** You can also start up a video chat without placing a phone call first. That's handy when you have Wi-Fi but no cell signal; FaceTime can make the call even when Verizon can't.

Of course, if you're not already on a call, the iPhone doesn't yet know whom you want to call. So you have to tell it. Open the FaceTime app. It presents a list of your recent FaceTime calls. Tap a name to place a new call to that person, or tap ⓘ to view a history of your calls with that person (and buttons for placing new ones).

Or, to find your callee from your own Contacts list, tap the + button. Find a name, tap it, and then tap 🎥 **Video** to place the call.

- **From Contacts.** In the Contacts app, if you tap a person's name, you'll find a **FaceTime** button. Or, in the Phone app, call up your Favorites or Recents list. Tap ⓘ next to a name to open the contact's card; tap **FaceTime**.

- **From Messages.** If you're chatting away with somebody by text and you realize that typing is no longer appropriate for the conversation, tap the name or photo at the top of the screen. Tap **FaceTime**.

At this point, the other guy receives an audio and video message inviting him to a FaceTime call. His screen shows what *he* looks like, so he can check for spinach in his teeth before accepting your call (facing page, left).

If he taps **Accept**, you're on. Your image now fills his screen (facing page, right), and you both see and hear each other in real time. You appear on your own screen, too, in a little inset window, so you can make sure your own lighting looks good.

Once the chat has begun, here's some of the fun you can have.

- **Rotate the screen.** FaceTime works in either portrait (upright) or landscape (widescreen) view; just turn your phone 90 degrees. Of course, if your calling partner doesn't *also* turn her gadget, she'll see your picture all squished and tiny, with big black areas filling the rest of the screen. (On the Mac, the picture rotates automatically when your partner's gadget rotates. You don't have to turn the monitor 90 degrees.)

TIP: The 🔒 (rotation lock) button described on page 45 works in FaceTime, too. That is, you can stop the picture from rotating when you turn the phone—as long as you're happy with full-time upright (portrait) orientation.

- **Show what's in front of you.** Sometimes you'll want to show your friend what you're looking at. That is, you'll want to turn on the camera on the *back* of the iPhone, the one pointing away from you, to show off the baby, the artwork, or the broken engine part.

Just tap the screen to make the buttons appear, and then tap flip (📷). Now you and your callee can both see what you're seeing. Tap 📷 again to return to the front camera.

- **Snap a commemorative Live Photo.** Within a FaceTime call, you can take a Live Photo (page 306)—three seconds of motion, with sound, deposited into your Photos app.

  Tap the screen to make the buttons appear, then tap ◎. That button appears only if *both* you and your pal have turned on FaceTime Live Photos in Settings→FaceTime. A message appears on *both* screens, so everybody knows what you've done and you can't act creepily.

  (Of course, you can also take a plain old screenshot; see page 357.)

- **Mute the audio.** Tap the screen to make the buttons appear; tap mute 🎤 to silence the audio you're sending. Great when you need to yell at the kids.

- **Mute the video.** When you leave the FaceTime app for any reason (open a different app), the other guy's screen shows just a blurry still photo of your face. He can't see what you're doing when you leave the FaceTime screen. He can still hear you, though.

  This feature was designed to let you check your calendar, look something up on the web, or whatever, while you're still chatting. But it's also a great trick when you need to adjust your clothing, pick at your teeth, or otherwise shield your activity from the person on the other end.

  In the meantime, the call is technically still in progress—and a green banner at the top of the Home screens reminds you of that. Tap there, on the green bar, to return to the video call.

You can mute the video even if you're not leaving the app. Tap the screen to make the buttons appear; swipe up to summon the Options screen, shown below; tap **Camera Off**. Now you're just transmitting a blurry photo of yourself.

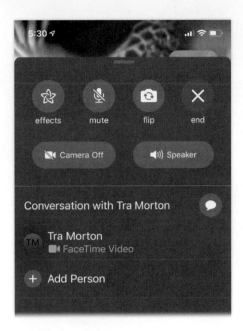

- **Change the audio source.** Ordinarily, the audio for a FaceTime call comes from your speakerphone, since your pal wouldn't see much if you were pressing the phone to your ear. But if you swipe upward to view the Options screen, you can use the **Speaker** button to switch to a different audio source (a Bluetooth headset, a Mac, or whatever you've got).

- **Apply a special effect.** If your conversation begins to lag during a FaceTime call, you can always spice things up with one of iOS's real-time, animated special effects. You can add speech balloons or fireworks around your head; you can substitute a cartoon animal—or cartoon Memoji version of yourself—for your actual head; you can apply an Instagram-type filter; you can slap "stickers" onto yourself; and much more.

Once your FaceTime call is under way, tap the screen to make the buttons appear, and then tap **effects** (✿) to reveal the row of available effects buttons. Tap one, dress yourself up, and revel in the admiration (or exasperation) of your video chat partners.

You're welcome to add more than one of these effects at once. (Animoji and Memoji are available only on Face ID phones.) Many of them, like the text effects, are designed to be used only when the phone is upright (in portrait orientation).

All these effects are described in depth on page 213.

Some of the special effects are rather impressive, arresting, and intriguing, at least at first. In practice, though, if you're over 13, you may find that the novelty wears off quickly.

To turn off all the effects you've applied so far, tap the white ✿ button to turn it off (gray). You now look normal to your callers once again.

When you and your buddy have had quite enough video chatting, tap the screen to make the buttons appear, and then tap ✖ to terminate the call. (Although it's easy to jump from phone call to video chat, there's no way to go the other direction.)

And marvel that you were alive to see the day.

Group FaceTime

Well, it took only eight years. But FaceTime, at last, can connect more than two people at once in a video chat. In fact, it can connect up to 32 people simultaneously, creating a video party line—as long as everyone concerned has iOS 12.1 or later, or macOS Mojave.

Begin the Call

Often, you'll want to dive into a group video call from within Messages, where a group chat is already under way. To do that, tap the participant-names strip at the top of the window, and then tap **FaceTime** (below, left). (Or, for a straight-up audio conference call, hit **audio**.)

Each participant gets a special group FaceTime message, complete with a **Join** button (below, right). Once you tap it, that special button in Messages changes to show how long the call has been going.

TIP: If you're in a group Messages session, that **Join** button remains yours to tap for as long as the group FaceTime call is still going. That is, you don't have to hop on instantly.

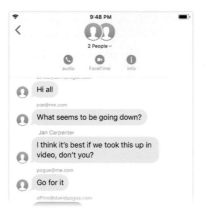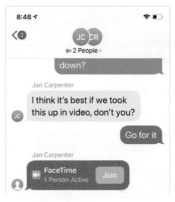

Or you can start in the FaceTime app. Tap the + at top right; in the To box, specify the names of the participants. Then tap **Audio** or **Video**.

The other people's phones start ringing, and when they tap **Accept**, the audio or video conference begins!

During the Call

In regular FaceTime calls, the other guy's image fills the screen. How are you supposed to conduct a call with dozens of people?

Each face occupies its own rectangle; the more people joining, the smaller the rectangles get.

When someone is talking, FaceTime brings that person's rectangle front and center (and makes it bigger) automatically. In a lively conversation, therefore, the four main boxes seem to be constantly inflating and deflating to reflect who's talking.

But even if someone is not speaking, you can bring him to the front on demand, with either of two degrees of prominence:

- **Tap his box once.** It comes to the front, gets slightly larger, and reveals his name or iCloud ID (below, left).

- **Double-tap his box.** Now it gets *much* bigger, shamelessly covering up everyone else's boxes. This is for when you really want to focus on this one person. (Tap again to enshrink the box again.)

> If you've tapped once, you can tap the little ↘ icon to zoom that slightly enlarged box into the fully enlarged version.

The Roster

The FaceTime app can't display big rectangles for more than four people at once. Starting with the fifth joiner, a horizontally scrolling row of faces appears at the bottom of the screen—Apple calls it the Roster (below, left). But the idea is the same: If one of them speaks, her box jumps into one of the larger four spots on the screen. And even if she's not speaking, you can tap or double-tap her square to give it one of the two zoom treatments described already.

Coming and Going

If someone is inviting you to a group call, a notification lets you know. You'll see an option called Join, Tap to Join, or ◼◀, depending on what you're doing on the phone. Or, if you're in Messages in a group chat, you'll see a Join button.

If you'd like to add someone to a call that's underway, tap the screen, tap ⬤, and tap Add Person.

If someone drops off the call (by tapping ✖), everyone else stays on the call, just as with a traditional conference phone call.

Effects

All the usual FaceTime fun is available during a group FaceTime call. You can flip your camera around, mute your audio or video, apply a sticker or two, add some floating text, or (on a Face ID phone) turn yourself into an Animoji or Memoji (page 218).

To see the options, tap the screen once to view the buttons (facing page, right). Then tap ✪ as usual for effects, or drag upward for the Camera Off, Speaker, and Add Person buttons.

FaceTime Audio Calls

Video calling is neat and all, but be honest: Don't you find yourself making *phone* calls more often? Video calling forces us to be "on," neatly dressed and well behaved, because we're on camera. Most of the time, we're perfectly content (in fact, *more* content) with audio only.

And FaceTime audio calls don't eat into your cellphone minutes and aren't transmitted over your cell carrier's voice network; instead, these are *internet* calls. (They use data, not minutes.) When you're in a Wi-Fi hotspot, they're free. When you're not, your carrier's data network carries your voice.

You start out exactly as you would when making a video call, as described already. That is, you can start from the FaceTime app, the Contacts app, the Phone app, Messages, and so on.

In each spot where FaceTime is available, you get a choice of two types of calls: Video (☐◀) and Audio (📞). (In Messages, if you tap the 📞, you get a choice of two voice options: Voice Call and FaceTime Audio. Unless you're in a group chat, in which case Audio automatically means "group FaceTime audio.")

When you place an audio FaceTime call, the other person's phone rings exactly as though you'd placed a regular call. All the usual buttons and options are available: **Remind Me**, **Message**, **Decline**, **Accept**, and so on.

Once you accept the call, it's just like being on a phone call, too: You have the options **Mute**, **Speaker**, **FaceTime** (that is, "Switch to video"), and **Contacts**. (What's missing? The **Keypad** button and the **Merge Calls** button. You can't combine FaceTime audio calls with each other, or with regular cellphone calls. If a cellphone call comes in, you'll be offered the chance to take it—but you'll have to hang up on FaceTime.)

You'll find that the audio quality is *amazing*—more like FM radio than cellular. It sounds like the other person is right next to your head; you hear every breath, sniff, and sweater rustle.

Try out FaceTime audio calls. Whenever you're calling another iPhone, iPad, iPod Touch, Mac, or even Apple Watch owner, you'll save money and minutes by placing these better-sounding free calls.

> **TIP:** iOS even offers FaceTime Call Waiting. If you're on a FaceTime audio or video call, and someone else FaceTime calls you, your phone rings—and you can either tap **Decline** or **End & Accept**.

Bluetooth Accessories

Bluetooth is a short-range *cable elimination* technology. It's designed to untether you from equipment that would ordinarily require a cord.

Most people use Bluetooth for two purposes: communicating with a smartwatch or fitness band, or transmitting audio to a wireless speaker, car stereo, or Bluetooth earpiece or headphones.

> **NOTE:** See page 274 for more on Bluetooth music.

Pairing with a Bluetooth Earpiece or Speaker

Pairing means "marrying" a phone to a Bluetooth accessory so that each works only with the other. If you didn't do this one-time pairing, then some other guy passing on the sidewalk might hear your conversation through *his* earpiece. And neither of you would be happy.

The pairing process is different for every cellphone and every Bluetooth earpiece. Usually it involves a sequence like this:

1. **On the earpiece, turn on Bluetooth. Make the earpiece or speaker discoverable.**

   Discoverable just means that your phone can "see" it. You'll have to consult the gadget's instructions to learn how to do so; it's usually a matter of holding down some button until a light blinks.

2. **On the iPhone, tap Settings→Bluetooth. Turn Bluetooth on.**

   The iPhone immediately begins searching for nearby Bluetooth equipment. If all goes well, you'll see the name of your earpiece or speaker show up on the screen.

3. **Tap the gadget's name. Type in the passcode, if necessary.**

   The *passcode* is a number, usually four or six digits, that must be typed into the phone within about a minute. You have to enter this only once, during the initial pairing. The idea is to prevent some evil-doer sitting nearby in the airport lounge, for example, to secretly pair *his* earpiece with *your* iPhone.

   The user's manual for your earpiece should tell you what the passcode is (if one is even required).

To make calls using a Bluetooth earpiece (or speaker as a speakerphone), you *dial* using the iPhone itself. You usually use the iPhone's own volume controls, too. You generally press a button on the earpiece or speaker to answer an incoming call, to swap call-waiting calls, or to end a call.

 NOTE: When you've got Bluetooth headphones or an earpiece successfully connected, the 🎧 symbol appears on your status bar (page 23) or, on Face ID phones, on the Control Center. The earpiece's battery gauge (🔋) may appear there, too.

If you're having problems making a particular gadget work, Google it. Type *pair Jabra Stealth with iPhone*, for example. Chances are good that you'll find a write-up by somebody who's successfully worked through the setup.

Bluetooth Car Systems

The iPhone works beautifully with Bluetooth car systems, too. The pairing procedure generally goes exactly as described previously: You make the car discoverable, enter the passcode on the iPhone, and then make the connection.

Once you're paired up, you can answer an incoming call by pressing a button on your steering wheel, for example. You hear the caller through the car's speakers, and a microphone for your own voice is hidden in the rearview mirror or dashboard. You make calls either from the iPhone or, in some cars, by dialing the number on the car's own touchscreen.

Of course, studies show that it's the act of driving while conversing that causes accidents—not actually holding a cellphone. So the hands-free system is less for safety than for convenience and compliance with laws.

Pairing with a Smartwatch or Fitness Band

The latest Bluetooth technology, called Bluetooth LE (for "low energy"), Bluetooth Smart, or Bluetooth 4.0 (or 5.0), turns on only when necessary and then turns off again to save power. Bluetooth LE has made possible a lot of smartwatches and fitness trackers.

As a handy bonus, you usually do the pairing right in the gadget's companion app, rather than fumbling around in Settings. That setup makes a lot more sense. For example, when you're setting up an Apple Watch, you use the Watch app to pair the watch; when you're setting up a Fitbit, you connect your band wirelessly in the Fitbit app.

5

Siri Voice Command

Siri, the iPhone's famous voice-recognition technology, is actually *two* features. First, there's *dictation*, where the phone types out everything you say. That's described in Chapter 3.

Second, there's Siri the *voice-controlled minion*. You can say, "Wake me up at 7:45 a.m.," or "What's Casey's work number?" or "How do I get to the airport?" or "What's the weather going to be like in San Francisco this weekend?"

You can also ask questions about movies, sports, and restaurants. Siri displays a beautifully formatted response and speaks in a calm voice—a voice that, in iOS 13, is much more natural-sounding.

You can even ask her, "What song is that?" or say, "Name that tune." She'll identify whatever song is playing in the background, just as the popular Shazam app does. It's creepy/amazing.

You can operate her hands-free, too. Instead of pressing the home button to get her attention, you just say, "Hey Siri." (The iPhone 6s and later models can respond even when unplugged and running on battery power.)

In the beginning, only Apple decided what Siri could understand. Now, though, the creators of certain apps can teach Siri new vocabulary, too. For example, you can say, "Send Nicki a message with WeChat," "Pay Dad 20 dollars with Square Cash," "Book a ride with Lyft," or "Order me an Uber." And thanks to the Shortcuts app (page 182), you can actually create your *own* Siri commands.

Voice Command

In 2010, Apple bought Siri, a company that made a voice-control app for the iPhone. Apple cleaned it up, beefed it up, integrated it with the iPhone's software, and wound up with Siri, your virtual servant.

Believe it or not, Siri is a spin-off from a Department of Defense project called CALO (Cognitive Agent that Learns and Organizes). In a very real way, therefore, Siri represents your tax dollars at work.

The spin-off was run by the Stanford Research Institute (SRI), but that's not where Siri's name came from. Siri, it turns out, is a Norwegian name meaning "beautiful woman who leads you to victory." (Co-creator Dag Kittlaus named her. He's Norwegian.)

In any case: Today, Siri is a crisply accurate, astonishingly understanding, uncomplaining, voice-commanded servant. No special syntax is required.

NOTE: Apple also keeps increasing the number of languages Siri understands. Already, she understands English (in nine varieties), Arabic, Cantonese, Danish, Dutch, Finnish, French, German, Hebrew, Italian, Japanese, Korean, Malay, Mandarin, Norwegian, Portuguese, Russian, Spanish, Swedish, Thai, and Turkish. You can change the language by visiting **Settings→Siri & Search**.

Many speech-recognition systems work only if you issue certain limited commands with predictable syntax, like "Call 445-2340" or "Open Microsoft Word." But Siri is different. She's been programmed to respond to casual speech. It doesn't matter if you say, "What's the weather going to be like in Tucson this weekend?" or "Give me the Tucson weather for this weekend" or "Will I need an umbrella in Tucson?" Siri understands almost any variation.

And she understands regular, everyday speaking. You don't have to separate your words or talk weirdly; you just speak normally.

It's not *Star Trek*. You can't ask Siri to clean your gutters or to teach you to knit. (Well, you can *ask*.)

But, as you'll soon discover, the number of things Siri *can* do for you is impressive. Furthermore, Apple continues to add to Siri's intelligence through software updates.

NOTE: In iOS 13, Siri is joined by Voice Control, another way to operate your phone hands-free that duplicates Siri's functions in some ways and expands them in others. See Chapter 7 for details.

How to Use Siri

To get Siri's attention, you have three choices:

- **Hold down the side button** until you see a wavy animation on the screen. (Home-button phones: Hold down the home button.) Siri gives a double-beep when you use CarPlay, your earbuds clicker, or "Hey Siri" (described next).

The phone doesn't have to be unlocked or awake, which is awesome. Just pull the phone out of your pocket and hold down the button.

TIP: Some people press the home or side button to trigger Siri, and then release the button and start talking. But you can also hold the button down *the entire time you're speaking*. That way you know Siri won't attempt to execute your command before you've finished saying it.

- **Hold down the clicker on your earbuds cord** or the Call button on your Bluetooth earpiece.

- **Say, "Hey Siri."** A double-beep plays. (See "How to Use 'Hey Siri' " on the next page.)

Now Siri is listening. Ask your question or say your command. You don't have to hold the phone up to your mouth; Siri works perfectly well at arm's length, on your desk in front of you, or on the car seat beside you.

NOTE: Apple insists that Siri is neither male nor female. In fact, if you ask Siri her gender, she'll demur with something like, "Animals and French nouns have genders. I do not." But that's just political correctness. Any baby-name website—or a Norwegian dictionary—will confirm that "Siri" is a girl's name.

When you're finished speaking, be quiet for a moment (or, if you've been pressing a button, release it). About a second after you stop speaking, Siri connects with her master brain online and processes your request. After a moment, she presents (and speaks) an attractively formatted response.

TIP: You generally see only the most recent question and response on the Siri screen. But you can drag downward to see all the previous exchanges you've had with Siri during this session.

And when you're completely finished talking to Siri, you can either press the home (side) button, hold down your earbuds clicker, or say something like "Goodbye," "See you later," or "Adios." You're taken back to whatever app you were using before.

NOTE: These days, Siri is much better at understanding follow-up questions, where the subject of the second question is the same as the first. ("Who coaches the Phillies? What's their win record?")

How to Use "Hey Siri"

Siri can also accept spoken commands without your touching the phone. It's ideal for the car, when your hands and eyes should be focused on driving. (Of course, it's safest not to interact with your phone *at all* when you're driving—and Apple has an answer for that, too [page 74].)

The phone won't respond to "Hey Siri" unless it's turned on in Settings→Siri & Search→Listen for "Hey Siri."

At that point, you're asked to do a quick training session to teach Siri what you sound like. Otherwise, a lot of people would be freaked out when they say things like "Jay's weary" or "Space? Eerie!" and the phone double-beeps in response.

As soon as you turn on **Listen for "Hey Siri"** the training screens appear. The screen prompts you to say several phrases to learn the sound of your voice.

At that point, whenever you want to ask Siri something, just say, "Hey Siri"; at the sound of the double-beep, say your thing. (iPhone models before the 6s don't respond to "Hey Siri" except when they're plugged in and charging.)

Thanks to "Hey Siri," you now have a front-seat conversationalist, a little software friend who's always happy to listen to what you have to say—and whose knowledge of the world, news, sports, and history can help make those cross-country drives a little less dull.

What to Say to Siri

Siri comes with a cheat sheet to help you learn her capabilities. To produce it, hold down the home or side button long enough to make the "Go ahead, I'm listening" screen appear. Then release the button.

Siri displays screen after screen of example command categories, under the heading "Some things you can ask me." Tap a category name (facing page, left) to see sample commands within that category (right).

> **TIP:** Or just trigger Siri and then say, "What can I say?" or "What can you do?" or "Help me!" The same cheat sheet appears.

Other Siri features include an ability to access your passwords, either for a specific app or your entire iCloud Keychain, and the ability to search through photos and memories based on people, places, events, time, and object keyword.

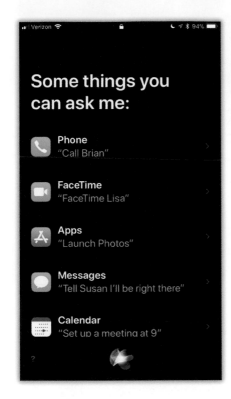

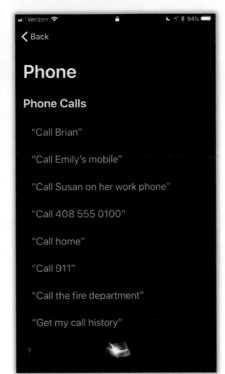

Here are the general categories of things you can say to Siri:

- **Opening apps.** If you don't learn to use Siri for anything else, for the love of Mike, learn this one. You can say, "Open Calendar" or "Play Angry Birds" or "Launch Calculator."

  Result: The corresponding app opens instantly. It's exactly the same as opening the Home screen, swiping across the screen until you find the app you're looking for, and then tapping its icon—but without opening the Home screen, swiping across the screen until you find the app you're looking for, and then tapping its icon.

TIP: You can *get* apps by voice, too, with commands like, "Get the Airbnb app" or "Search the App Store for crossword-puzzle apps."

- **Camera.** "Take a panorama" (or "selfie" or "photo" or "slo-mo video"). You can even say, "Scan a QR code"—a feature that saves you from having to download a QR app. (QR codes are those 1-inch-square bar codes that advertisers create as quick links to their websites.)

  Result: The Camera app opens, set to the mode you requested. If you asked for the QR code, when you aim the lens at the bar code, a notification banner appears, offering a link to the relevant site.

- **Flashlight.** You can turn the LED flashlight on by voice, which is handy when you're stumbling around in the dark. Say "Turn on the flashlight," and then, "Turn it off."

    Result: Siri turns the light on or off.

- **Change your settings.** You can change certain basic settings just by speaking your request. You can say, for example, "Turn on Bluetooth," "Turn off Wi-Fi," "Turn on Do Not Disturb," or "Turn on airplane mode." (You can't turn *off* airplane mode by voice, because Siri doesn't work without an internet connection.) You can also make screen adjustments: "Make the screen brighter." "Dim the screen."

    Result: Siri makes the requested adjustment, tells you so, and displays the corresponding switch in case she misunderstood your intention.

NOTE: If you've protected your phone with a fingerprint or Face ID, you may have to unlock it before you're allowed to change settings. Security and all that.

- **Open Settings panels.** When you need to make tweakier changes to Settings, you can open the most important panels by voice: "Open Wi-Fi settings," "Open Personal Hotspot settings," "Open Notification settings," "Open Sounds settings," "Open wallpaper settings," and so on. You can open your apps' settings this way, too: "Open Maps settings," "Open Netflix settings," "Open Delta settings," and so on.

    Siri is smart enough not to open security-related settings this way; remember that you can use Siri even from the Lock screen. She's protecting you from pranksters who might really mess up your phone.

    Result: Siri silently opens the corresponding page of Settings.

- **Calling.** Siri can place phone calls or FaceTime calls for you. "Call Harold." "Call Nicole on her mobile phone." "Call the office." "Phone home." "512-444-1212." "Start a FaceTime call with Sheila Withins." "FaceTime Alex."

    Result: Siri hands you off to the Phone or FaceTime app and places the call. It's just as though you'd initiated the call by tapping.

    Siri also responds to questions about your voicemail, like "Do I have any new voicemail messages?" and even "Play my voicemails." (After playing each message, Siri graciously offers to let you return the call—or to play the next one.)

- **Alarms.** You can say, "Wake me up at 7:35." "Change my 7:35 alarm to 8:00." "Wake me up in six hours." "Cancel my 6 a.m. alarm" (or "Delete my..." or "Turn off my..."). And, gloriously: "Turn off all my alarms."

This is *so* much quicker than setting the iPhone's alarm the usual way.

Result: When you set or change an alarm, you get a sleek digital alarm clock, right there beneath Siri's response, and Siri confirms what she understood.

- **Timer.** You can also control the Timer module of the phone's Clock app. It's like a stopwatch in reverse, in that it counts down to zero—handy when you're baking, limiting your kid's video-game time, and so on. For example: "Set the timer for 20 minutes." Or "Show the timer," "Pause the timer," "Resume," "Reset the timer," or "Stop it."

Result: A cool digital timer appears. A little stopwatch icon appears on the Lock screen to remind you that time is ticking down.

TIP: You can specify minutes and seconds: "Set the timer for 2 minutes, 30 seconds," for example.

- **Clock.** "What time is it?" "What time is it in San Francisco?" "What's today's date?" "What's the date a week from Friday?" Or just "Time."

Result: When you ask about the time, you see the clock identifying the time in question. (For dates, Siri just talks to you and writes out the date.)

- **Translations.** Siri can translate phrases to or from English, Mandarin Chinese, French, German, Italian, Spanish, Arabic, Japanese, Portuguese, or Russian. For example, you can say, "How do you say, 'Where's the bathroom?' in French?" Or "Say, 'This is delicious' in Mandarin." "Translate 'My toe hurts' into German."

Result: She displays the translated phrase. Tap ▶ to hear it spoken. She even nails the accents.

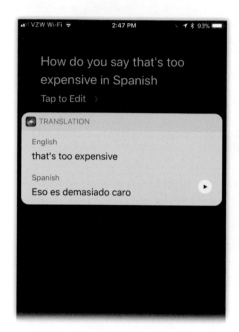

• **Contacts.** You can ask Siri to look up information in your address book (the Contacts app)—and not just addresses. For example, you can say, "What's Gary's work number?" "Give me Sheila Jenkins' office phone." "Show Tia's home email address." "What's my boss's home address?" "When is my husband's birthday?" "Show Larry Murgatroid." "Find everybody named Smith." "Who is P.J. Frankenberg?"

Result: A half "page" from your Contacts list. You can tap it to jump into that person's full card in Contacts. (If Siri finds multiple listings for the person you named—"Bob," for example—she lists all the matches and asks you to specify who you meant.)

You can even follow up. If you first asked, "What is Germaine's home address?" you can then say, "What's his cellphone number?"

TIP: In many of these examples, you'll see that you can identify people by their relationship to you. You can say, "Show my mom's work number," for example, or "Give me directions to my boss's house" or "Call my girlfriend." For details on teaching Siri about these relationships, see "Advanced Siri," starting on page 191.

- **Text messages.** "Send a text to Alex Rybeck." "Send a message to Peter saying, 'I no longer require your services.' " "Tell Cindy I'm running late." "Send a message to Janet's mobile asking her to pick me up at the train." "Send a text message to 212-561-2282." "Text Frank and Ralph: Did you pick up the pizza?"

Result: Siri prompts you for the body of the message, if you haven't specified it. Then you see a miniature outgoing text message. Siri asks if you want to send it; say, "Yes," "Send," or "Confirm" to proceed.

TIP: If you're using earbuds, headphones, or a Bluetooth speaker, then Siri reads the message back to you before asking if you want to send it. (You can ask her to read it again by saying something like, "Review that," "Read it again," or "Read it back to me.") The idea, of course, is that if you're wearing earbuds or using Bluetooth, you might be driving, so you should keep your eyes on the road.

If you need to edit the message before sending it, you have a couple of options. First, you can tap it; Siri hands you off to the Messages app for editing and sending.

Second, you can edit it by voice. You can say, "Change it to" to re-dictate the message; "Add" to add more to the message; "No, send it to Frank" to change the recipient; "No" to leave the message on the screen without sending it; or "Cancel" to forget the whole thing.

You can also ask Siri to read incoming text messages to you, which is great if you're driving. For example, you can say, "Read my new messages," and "Read that again." Or search for past messages: "Read my last message from Robin."

NOTE: If you've opted to conceal the actual contents of incoming texts so they don't appear on your Lock screen (page 67), then Siri can read you only the senders' names or numbers—not the messages themselves.

You can even have her reply to messages she's just read to you. "Reply, 'Congratulations (period). Can't wait to see your trophy (exclamation point)!' " "Call her." "Tell him I have a flat tire and I'm going to be late."

- **Email.** Siri can read your email to you. For example, if you say, "Read my latest email" or "Read my new email," Siri reads aloud your most recent email message. (She then offers you the chance to dictate a response.)

Or you can use the summary-listing commands. When you say, "Read my email," Siri starts walking backward through your inbox, telling you the subject of each, plus who sent it and when.

After a few listings, Siri says: "Shall I read the rest?" That's your opportunity to shut down what could be a very long recitation. If you say "Yes," though, she goes on to read the entire list of subject lines, dates, and senders.

Result: Siri reads aloud.

TIP: You can also use commands like "Any new mail from Chris today?" "Show new mail about the world premiere." "Show yesterday's email from Jan." All those commands produce a list of the messages, but Siri doesn't read them.

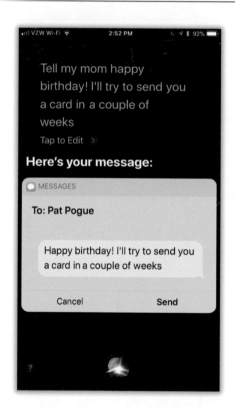
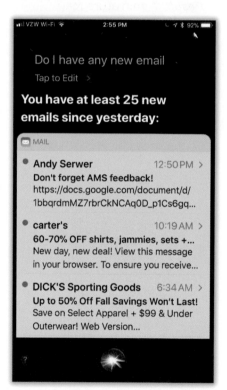

You can also compose a new message by voice. Anytime you use the phrase "about," that becomes the subject line for your new message. "Email Mom about the reunion." "Email my boyfriend about the dance on Friday." "New email to Freddie Gershon." "Mail Mom about Saturday's flight." "Email Frank and Cindy Vosshall and Peter Love about the picnic." "Email my assistant and say, 'Thanks for arranging the taxi!' " "Email Gertie and Eugene about their work on the surprise party, and say, 'I really value your friendship.' "

(If you've indicated only the subject and addressee, Siri prompts you for the body of the message.)

TIP: You can't send mail to canned groups of people using Siri—at least not without MailShot, an iPhone app that exists expressly for the purpose of letting you create email addressee groups.

You can reply to a message Siri has just described, too. "Reply, 'Dear Robin (comma), I'm so sorry about your dog (period). I'll be more careful next time (period).' " "Call her mobile number." "Send him a text message saying, 'I got your note.' "

Result: A miniature Mail message, showing you Siri's handiwork before you send it.

- **Calendar.** Siri can make appointments for you. Considering how many tedious finger taps it usually takes to schedule an appointment in the Calendar app, this is an enormous improvement. "Make an appointment with Patrick for October 17 at 3 p.m." "Set up a haircut at 9." "Set up a meeting with Charlize this Friday at noon." "Meet Danny Cooper at 6." "New appointment with Steve, next Sunday at 7." "Schedule a conference call at 5:30 tonight in my office."

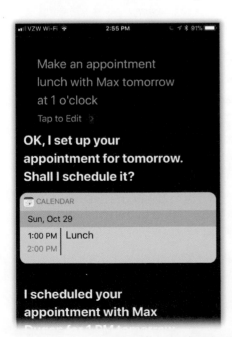
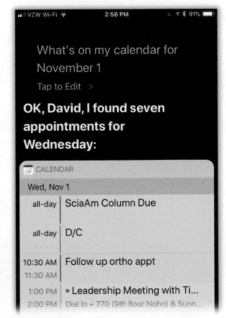

Result: A slice of that day's calendar appears, filled in the way you requested.

TIP: Siri may also alert you to a conflict, something like this: "Note that you already have an all-day appointment about 'Boston Trip' for this Thursday. Shall I schedule this anyway?" Amazing.

You can also move previously scheduled meetings by voice. For example, "Move my 2:00 meeting to 2:30." "Reschedule my meeting with Charlize to a week from Monday at noon." "Add Frank to my meeting with Harry." "Cancel the conference call on Sunday."

You can even *consult* your calendar by voice. You can say, "What's on my calendar today?" "What's on my calendar for September 23?" "When's my next appointment?" "When is my meeting with Charlize?" "Where is my next meeting?"

Result: Siri reads you your agenda and displays a tidy Day view of the specified date.

- **Directions.** By consulting the phone's GPS, Siri can set up the Maps app to answer requests like these: "How do I get to the airport?" "Show me 1500 Broadway, New York City." "Directions to my grandmother's house." "Take me home." "What's my next turn?" "Are we there yet?"

TIP: You can also say, "Stop navigation"—a great way to make Maps stop harassing you when you realize you know where you are.

You can ask for directions to the home or work address of anyone in your Contacts list—provided those addresses are *in* your Contacts list.

Result: Siri fires up the Maps app, with the start and end points of your driving directions already filled in.

- **Reminders.** Siri is a natural match for the Reminders app. She can add items to that list at your spoken command. For example: "Remind me to file my IRS tax extension." "Remind me to bring the science supplies to school." "Remind me to take my antibiotic tomorrow at 7 a.m." "Create a list called Packing List." "Add kissing to my Bucket list."

The *location-based* reminders are especially amazing. They rely on GPS to know where you are. So you can say, "Remind me to visit the drugstore when I leave the office." "Remind me to water the lawn when I get home." "Remind me to check in with Nancy when I leave here."

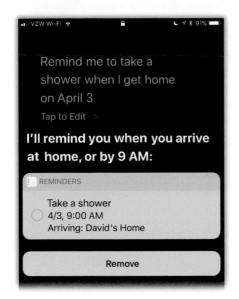

Siri can also understand the word "this" when you're looking at an email message, a web page, or a note. That is, you can say, "Remind me about this at 7 p.m." or "Remind me about this when I get home." Sure enough: Siri will flag you with a reminder notification at the appropriate time and add an entry—with a link to the original message, web page, or note—to the Reminders app.

Result: A miniature entry from the Reminders app, showing you that Siri has understood.

- **Notes.** You create a new note (in the Notes app) by saying things like, "Make a note that my shirt size is 15 and a half" or "Note: Dad will not be coming to the reunion after all." You can even name the note in your request: "Create a 'Movies to Watch' note."

  But you can also call up a certain note to the screen, like this: "Find my Frequent Flyer note." You can even summon a table-of-contents view of all your notes by saying, "Show all my notes."

  Result: A miniature Notes page appears, showing your newly dictated text (or the existing note that you've requested).

- **Restaurants.** Siri is happy to serve as your personal concierge. Try "Good Italian restaurants around here," "Find a good pizza joint in Cleveland," or "Show me the reviews for Olive Garden in Youngstown." Siri displays a list of matching restaurants—with ratings, reviews, hours, and so on.

  But she's ready to do more than that. She can actually book your reservations, thanks to her integration with the OpenTable website. You can say, "Table for two in Belmont tonight," or "Make a reservation at an inexpensive Mexican restaurant Saturday night at seven."

  Result: Siri complies by showing you the proposed reservation. Tap one of the offered alternative time slots, if you like, and then off you go. Everything else is tappable here, too—the ratings (tap to read customer reviews), phone number, web address, map, and so on.

- **Businesses.** Siri is a walking, talking (well, all right, not walking) Yellow Pages. Go ahead, try it: "Find coffee near me." "Where's the closest

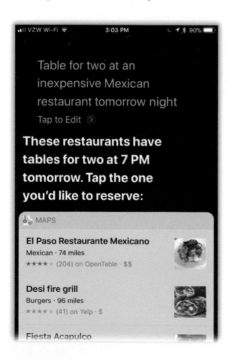

Walmart?" "Find some pizza places in Cincinnati." "Search for gas stations." "French restaurants nearby." "I'm in the mood for Chinese food." "Find me a hospital." "I want to buy a book."

Result: Siri displays a handsome list of businesses nearby that match your request.

- **Playing music.** Instead of fumbling around in your Music app, save yourself steps and time by speaking the name of any album, song, or band whose music you have on your phone: "Play some Beatles." "Play 'I'm a Barbie Girl.' " "Play some jazz." "Play my jogging play-list." "Play the party mix." "Shuffle my 'Dave's Faves' playlist." "Play." "Pause." "Resume." "Skip."

  Result: Siri plays (or skips, shuffles, or pauses) the music you asked for—without ever leaving the app you were using.

- **Apple Music.** If you subscribe to Apple's $10-a-month Apple Music service, Siri offers a huge range of even more useful voice controls. For example, you can call for any music in Apple's 30 million–song catalog by song name, album, or performer: "Play 'Mr. Blue Sky.' " "Show me some Elton John albums." "Play 'Yesterday' next" (or "...after this song"). Or ask to have a singer or album played in random order: "Shuffle Taylor Swift."

  When you hear a song you like, you can say, "Play more like this." Or "Add this song (or album) to my library." (Or, if you don't like it, "Skip this song.")

  If more than one person performed a song, be specific: "Play 'Smooth Criminal' by Glee." You can even ask for a song according to the movie it was in. "Play that song from *Frozen*."

  Or start one of your playlists by name ("Play 'Mellow Yoga' "). Or re-listen to a song: "Play previous." Or ask for one of Apple Music's radio stations: "Play Beats 1" or "Play Charting Now Radio."

  While music is playing, Siri is happy to tell you what you're listening to. ("What song is this?" "Who's the singer?" "What album is this from?") You can also tell her, "Like this song" or "Rate this song five stars."

You can ask her to play the top hits of any year or decade ("Play the top song from 1990"; "Play the top 35 songs of the 1960s").

Even if you're not an Apple Music subscriber, you're still welcome to say, "Buy 'Mr. Blue Sky' " or "Download the new Taylor Swift album." Apple welcomes your expenditures in any form.

Result: Just what you'd expect!

NOTE: In iOS 13, Apple has made its music-requesting feature available to other companies. Soon enough, in theory, you'll be able to say "Play Elton John on Spotify," or "Play '80s hits on Amazon Music." (Well, you've always been able to *say* those things, but now something will actually happen.)

- **Play radio.** Here's a neat new one in iOS 13: You can start listening to any of 100,000 radio stations, just by asking. "Play WCBS." "Play BBC Radio 1." "Play 98.1 The Breeze."

  If you've set up any *Apple* radio stations (Chapter 8), you can call for them by name, too: "Play Dolly Parton Radio." Or be more generic: Just say, "Play the radio" and be surprised. Or somewhere in between: Say, "Play some country music" (substitute your favorite genre).

  Result: Boom: Your phone instantly begins to play that station's internet stream. (Apple has teamed up with radio providers like TuneIn.com, Radio.com, and iHeartRadio.com.)

- **Identifying music.** Siri can listen to the music playing in the room and try to identify it (song name, singer, album, and so on). Whenever there's music playing, you can say things like, "What's that song?" "What's playing right now?" "What song is this?" or "Name that tune!"

  Result: Siri listens to the music playing at your home/office/bar/ restaurant/picnic—and identifies the song by name and performer. There is also, needless to say, a **Buy** button.

- **Weather.** "What's the weather going to be today?" "Show me the weather this week." "Will it snow in Dallas this weekend?" "Check the forecast for Memphis on Friday." "Can you give me the wind speed in Kansas City?" "Tell me the windchill in Chicago." "What's the humidity right now?" "Is it nighttime in Cairo?" "How's the weather in Paris?" "What's the high for Washington on Friday?" "When will Jupiter rise tomorrow?" "When's the moonrise?" "What's the temperature outside?" "Is it windy out there?" "When does the sun rise in London?" "When will the sun set today?" "Should I wear a jacket?"

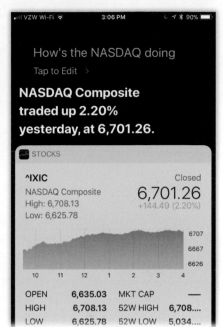

Result: A convenient miniature Weather display for the date and place you specified.

- **Stocks.** "What's Google's stock price?" "What did Ford close at today?" "How's the Dow doing?" "What's Microsoft's P/E ratio?" "What's Amazon's average volume?" "How are the markets doing?"

Result: A tidy little stock graph, bearing a wealth of statistics.

- **Find My.** "Where's Ferd?" "Is my dad home?" "Where are my friends?" "Who's here?" "Who is nearby?" "Is Mom at work?"

Result: Siri shows you a beautiful little map with the requested person's location clearly indicated by a blue pushpin. (She does, that is, if you've set up the Find My app [page 424], you've logged in, and your friends have made their locations available.)

- **Search the web.** "Search the web for a 2016 Ford Mustang." "Search for healthy smoothie recipes." "Search Wikipedia for the Thunderbirds." "Search for news about the Netflix-Amazon merger."

TIP: Siri uses Google to perform its web searches. If you prefer Microsoft's Bing search service, just say so. Say, "Bing Benjamin Franklin." (For that matter, you can also ask Siri to "Yahoo" something—for example, "Yahoo blueberry dessert recipes.")

Wikipedia is a search type all its own. You can say, "Look up Mariah Carey on Wikipedia." "Search Wikipedia for Tim Kaine" or "Tell me about Alexander Hamilton" or "Show me the Wikipedia page about Ruth Bader Ginsburg."

Pictures get special treatment, too: "Search the web for pictures of cows" to get an image search result. You can also say, "Find me…" or "Search for…"

Result: Siri displays the results of your search right on her screen. Tap one of the results to open the corresponding web page in Safari.

- **Sports scores.** At last you have a buddy who's just as obsessed with sports trivia as you are. Siri knows everything about everything when it comes to professional and college sports scores, schedules, standings, player details, and team stats.

  You can say things like, "How did the Indians do last night?" "What was the score of the last Yankees game?" "When's the next Cowboys game?" "What baseball games are on today?"

  You can also ask questions about individual players, like "Who has the best batting average?" "Who has scored the most runs against the Red Sox?" "Who has scored the most goals in British soccer?" "Which quarterback had the most sacks last year?"

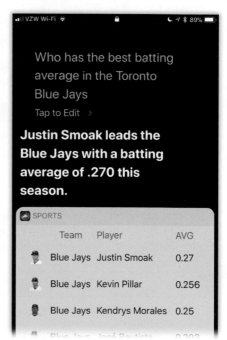

And, of course, team stats are fair game, like "Show me the roster for the Giants," "Who is pitching for Tampa this season?" and "Is anyone on the Marlins injured right now?"

Apple has, somewhat mystifyingly, also worked hard on motorsports answers: You can ask her for current standings, schedules, and stats.

Result: Neat little box scores or factoids, complete with team logos.

- **Movies in theaters.** Siri is also the virtual equivalent of an insufferable film buff. She knows *everything*. "Who was the star of *Groundhog Day*?" "Who directed *Chinatown*?" "What is *Doctor Strange* rated?" "What movie won Best Picture in 1952?"

  It's not just about old movies, either. Siri also knows everything about current showtimes in theaters. "What movies are opening this week?" "What's playing at the Watton Cineplex?" "Give me the reviews for *The Incredibles 3*." "What are today's showtimes for *Crazy Rich Norwegians*?"

  Result: Tidy tables of movies, theaters, or showtimes. (Tap one for details.) Sometimes you get a movie poster filled with facts. In the U.S., you can even buy tickets by voice: "Two tickets to see *Titanic 2*," for example, or "Four tickets to *Pelicans* at City Center at 7:30 p.m."

- **Facts, figures, famous people, food.** This is a huge category. It represents Siri's partnership with the Wolfram Alpha factual search engine (*wolframalpha.com*). The possibilities here could fill an entire chapter—or an entire encyclopedia.

  You can say things like, "How many days until Valentine's Day?" "When was Abraham Lincoln born?" "How many teaspoons are in a gallon?" "What's the exchange rate between dollars and euros?" "What's the capital of Belgium?" "What's a 17 percent tip on 62 dollars for three people?" "When is the next solar eclipse?" "Show me the Big Dipper." "What's the tallest mountain in the world?" "What's the price of gold?" "What's the definition of *schadenfreude*?" "How much is six dollars in pesos?" "Generate a random number." "Graph x equals 3y plus 12." "What flights are overhead?"

  Among other specialties, Siri offers good answers about celebrities ("Where was Jennifer Lawrence born?") and food and nutrition ("How much caffeine is in a cup of coffee?" or "How many calories in a hot dog?")

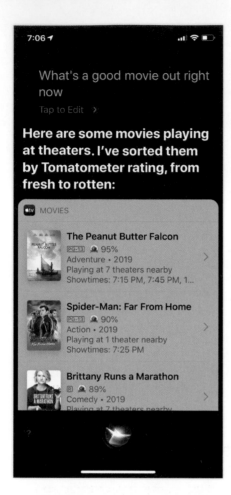

Result: For simple math and conversions, Siri just shows you the answer. For more complex questions, you get a specially formatted table, ripped right out of Wolfram Alpha's knowledge base.

- **Books.** Apple runs an ebook store, too, of course. Therefore, these commands are fair game: "Find books by Ian Fleming." "Buy the book *Purity*." "Show me Jonathan Franzen books."

   Result: The Books app opens, listing the book(s) you mentioned.

- **Podcasts.** While we're on the subject of entertainment: Apple's Podcasts app is Siri-controllable, too. "Play 'S-Town.' " "Play it twice as fast." "Skip ahead 30 seconds." "Pause." "Play." "Listen to the TED Radio Hour."

   Result: The app obeys.

- **Movies on iTunes.** Siri also helps you find flicks in online services (Netflix, Hulu, HBO Go, and so on) or on Apple's own movie store. You know: "Find movies about football." "Play *Jurassic World*." "Find new action movies on Netflix." "Get me documentaries on Hulu." "Find free movies for kids."

  Result: Thumbnails of the movies you seek.

TIP: Once you're playing a video, you can then ask Siri things like, "Who's in this?" or "Who directed this?" Kind of handy. And if you're binge watching, you can manage your Up Next queue verbally, too: "What's next on my Up Next?" "Add *Arrested Development* to my Up Next." "Remove *Big Little Lies* from my Up Next."

- **Search Twitter.** If you say something like, "What are people saying?" or "What's happening on Twitter?" you see a list of tweets on the trending topics on Twitter. (Tap a tweet in the list to open it into a new window that contains more information and a View in Twitter button.)

  Or ask, "What are people saying about the Chicago Bears?" to read tweets on that subject. Or, conversely, you can ask, "What is Samantha Bee saying on Twitter?" to see her most recent tweets. (You can substitute the names of other people or companies.) Or "Search Twitter for the hashtag 'FirstWorldProblems.' " (A *hashtag* is a searchable phrase like #toofunny or #iPhone11, which makes finding relevant tweets on Twitter much easier.)

  Result: Siri displays 10 or so tweets that match your query.

- **Round up photos or videos.** This trick can save you a lot of time and fussing. iOS can show you all photos and videos in your collection according to the time or place you shot them, the album name they're in, or even what they're pictures *of*. "Show me photos with dogs," you might say. Or "Show me pictures of Max from last year in San Francisco." Can you imagine how much time that might save you?

  More examples: "Show me the videos from Halloween last year," you can say. "Get me the videos from Utah." "Show me the Disney World album." "Open the Panoramas album." "Show me the Slo-mo videos from Oberlin College." "Give me the Austin pictures from last summer."

  Result: You get a screenful of square thumbnails of photos or videos that match your request. Tap one to open it, or tap Show All to see all the photos/videos in that batch.

- **Look up a password.** Siri can look up passwords for you, too. That's a godsend when you're trying to log into a website on a non-Apple (or non-yours) phone or laptop. "What's my Hulu password?" "Look up my Netflix password." "I need my Citibank password."

  Result: The iPhone requests proof that you're you—Face ID or Touch ID—and then displays the password! It's the greatest. (If you have several passwords for the same item, you must first tap the one you mean.)

Non-Apple Apps

These days, Apple permits Siri to control apps from other companies. Once you find out what these commands are, they can accelerate other apps just as much as Siri already accelerates Apple's. A few examples:

- **Lyft, Uber.** "Order a Lyft." "Call me an Uber." Siri asks you to tap the kind of car you want to order; one further tap orders the ride.

- **Pinterest.** "Find toddler bedroom idea pins on Pinterest." The Pinterest app opens, displaying pins that match your search query (from all of Pinterest, not just your pages).

- **Square Cash.** "Pay Casey two dollars with Square Cash." Boom: You've just sent money to lucky, lucky Casey.

- **LinkedIn.** "Send a LinkedIn message to Robin that says, 'Can you vouch for me?' "

- **WhatsApp, WeChat, Skype.** All of these chat apps work exactly like iOS's own Messages app, in that you can send "text messages" entirely by voice. Just say, "with [name of app]" at the end of your command, or use the messaging app's name.

  For example: "Tell Eric, 'I think I left my wallet in your car' with WhatsApp." "Send a WeChat to Phoebe saying, 'Are we still going out?'" "Let Marge know, 'I accidentally left your front door open this morning' in Skype."

Open **Settings→Siri & Search** to see all the Siri-compatible apps, each with an on/off switch for **Search, Suggestions & Shortcuts** (which includes responses to voice queries).

You may never find the end of the things Siri understands, or the ways she can help you. If her repertoire seems intimidating at first, start simple—use her to open apps, dial by voice, send text messages, and set alarms. You can build up your bag of tricks as your confidence grows.

NOTE: Remember that you can use Siri without even unlocking your phone—and therefore without any security, like your passcode. Among certain juvenile circles, therefore, Siri is the source of some interesting pranks. Someone who finds your phone lying on a table could change your calendar appointments, send texts or emails, or even change what Siri calls you ("Call me 'you idiot' "), without having to enter the phone's passcode!

The solution is simple. Open **Settings**→**Touch ID & Passcode** (or **Face ID & Passcode** on the iPhone Face ID). If you scroll way down, you can turn off **Siri**. Of course, you've now lost the convenience of using Siri when the phone is locked. But at least you've prevented having your own phone call you an idiot.

When Things Go Wrong

If Siri misrecognizes your instructions, you'll know it, because you can see her interpretation of what you said. And, as indicated by the little hint **tap to edit**, you can tap Siri's interpretation to open up an editing screen so you can make corrections by typing.

TIP: You can also correct a misheard command just by speaking the correct version, like this: "I meant Chicago." Siri gets what you mean.

If Siri recognizes what you said but it isn't within her world of comprehension, she offers you a **Search the web** button as a last resort.

Siri's Personality

Siri's understanding of casual spoken commands is so impressive that you might sometimes think she's almost human. And that, of course, is exactly what Apple wants.

You can say all kinds of off-kilter things to Siri. After you've encountered a few of her answers, you won't be surprised to learn that Apple actually employs a comedy-writing team exclusively for Siri-humor purposes.

For example, if you ask her, "What is the meaning of life?" she responds with one of more than a dozen different answers. She might say, "I can't answer that now, but give me some time to write a very long play in which nothing happens." Or: "It's nothing Nietzsche couldn't teach ya." Or: "All evidence to date suggests it's chocolate."

Siri is full of such comebacks, and there are whole websites dedicated to her snark. Here are a few examples (this list won't ruin the fun, because Siri actually has several different comebacks to most of these questions):

You: "Who's your daddy?" *Siri:* "You are. Can we get back to work now?"

You: "Open the pod bay doors, Hal." **Siri:** "I'm sorry, I'm afraid I can't do that." (Then: "Are you happy now?")

You: "What are you wearing?" **Siri:** "You have the wrong personal assistant, Carl."

You: "Who's the boss?" **Siri:** (Presents the vital statistics of Bruce Springsteen.)

You: "Beam me up, Siri!" **Siri:** "Please remove your belt, shoes, and jacket, and empty your pockets."

You: "Show me the money." **Siri:** "I've found 23 ATMs that are fairly close to you..."

You: You're boring. **Siri:** I'm juggling flaming swords right now. You just can't see it.

You: "How much wood would a woodchuck chuck if a woodchuck could chuck wood?" **Siri:** "42 cords of wood, to be exact. Everyone knows that."

You: "Guess what." **Siri:** "You won the lottery?"

You: "Talk dirty to me." **Siri:** "Humus. Compost. Pumice. Silt. Gravel."

You: "Why did the chicken cross the road?" **Siri:** "I am not perspicacious about the peregrinations of poultry."

You: How many Apple Store Geniuses does it take to screw in a light bulb? **Siri:** A thousand. One to screw it in, nine hundred ninety-nine to blog about it.

Here are a few other things to say to Siri when you get bored:

Sing a song.

Are you kidding me?

How much do you cost?

What's the best phone?

What are you doing later?

Do you believe in Santa Claus?

Do you believe in God?

LOL.

Knock knock.

Give me a kiss.

What are the three laws of robotics?

Read me a haiku.

Take me to your leader.

Can I borrow some money?

Siri, beatbox.

Testing 1, 2, 3

When will hell freeze over?

Which came first, the chicken or the egg?

Winter is coming.

Trick or treat!

What do you want?

What's your favorite animal?

Do you have children?

Do you have a boyfriend?

What are the lottery numbers going to be tomorrow?

Who are you voting for?

What are you doing this weekend?

What's your favorite movie (...TV show, song, color, book, computer, phone, Weird Al song, app)?

Are you smart?

Have you ever loved anyone?

Do you have any pets?

Flip a coin.

Roll a die.

Rock, paper, or scissors?

Yes or no?

Pick a card.

Tell me a riddle.

What's 0 divided by 0?

What's infinity times infinity?

How do I look?

When is the world going to end?

What should I have for dinner?

What's my horoscope?

Merry Christmas!

Where did I put my keys?

Is water wet?

Will pigs fly?

> **TIP:** Siri addresses you by name in her *typed* answers, but she doesn't always speak it when she reads those answers out loud.
>
> Ordinarily, she calls you whatever you're called in Contacts. But you can make her call you whatever you like. Say, "Call me Master" or "Call me Frank" or "Call me Ishmael." If you confirm when she asks, from now on, that's what Siri will call you in her typed responses.

Typing to Siri

You can type your questions and commands to Siri instead of speaking them. Every now and then, that silent method could be preferable to the talk-aloud method—when you're in church or a movie, for example, or when your query is of a delicate nature.

To set this up, open **Settings→Accessibility→Siri**. Turn on **Type to Siri**.

From now on, when you hold down the home or side button, you get a **Type to Siri** box and a keyboard. Tap out your query and then hit **Done**; Siri shows her response, exactly as though you had spoken.

Even with this feature turned on, your voice isn't completely useless. "Hey Siri" still works just as it always has, giving you the best of both worlds.

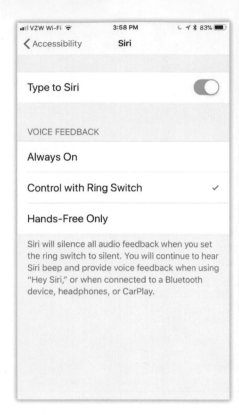
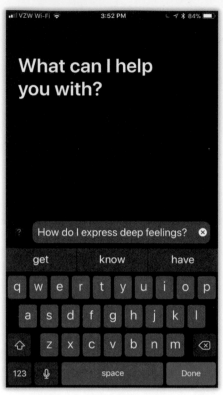

And even if you press the button and find yourself staring at the keyboard, you can still speak your request—by tapping the 🎤 and dictating. It's the best of all *three* worlds.

Siri Shortcuts

Shortcuts are what techies know as *macros*: multistep sequences of steps you can execute with a single command. In this case, it's a spoken command of your choice. Here's just a tiny tasting menu of what you can make iOS shortcuts do with one single spoken command:

- **"Head to work."** Siri speaks your estimated arrival time, lets you know what your first calendar appointment is for the day, starts your driving-to-work playlist, and gets directions based on current traffic conditions.

- **"Power nap."** Siri asks how many minutes you'll be asleep, says "Happy napping," turns on Do Not Disturb, and rings the alarm when the time comes.

- **"Running late."** Siri texts the participants of your next appointment that you're a little behind.

- **"Call in."** Siri checks your calendar for your first meeting's call-in number and then auto-dials it.

- **"Shut up for now."** Siri turns on Do Not Disturb until you leave your current location.

- **"Directions home."** Siri fires up Maps and begins navigation home.

- **"Log coffee."** Siri records a cup's worth of caffeine into the Health app.

- **"Top stories."** Siri displays the headlines from the News app.

- **"Back it up."** Siri turns on your Tesla car and backs it out of its parking place—great when some idiot has boxed you in too tightly to open your door.

In iOS 13, Apple took the original Shortcuts idea, cleaned it up, injected it with steroids, and readied it for a much bigger audience.

Now there's no more baffling Settings panel. You don't have to record a vocal trigger for each Shortcut. You can actually *converse* with a Shortcut, giving it more information as needed.

Most exciting of all (for the kind of person who gets excited by this kind of thing), shortcuts can be automated. They can fire off automatically based on new triggers: at certain times of day, when you arrive at certain places, when you get into your CarPlay car, when you change certain settings, when you open a certain app, when you snooze or shut off your alarm, when your phone connects to a certain Wi-Fi hotspot, or when you start or stop a workout on your Apple Watch.

Want your phone to detect when you've arrived home—and to turn on the lights, start up some Beethoven, and text your partner "I'm home"? One Shortcut can make it so.

My Shortcuts

To dive into the shortcuts world, open the Shortcuts app. It's now a standard iOS app—you don't have to go download it, as you once did.

Once you've accumulated (or built) some shortcuts, they appear on the My Shortcuts tab (next page, left). With a long-press, you can delete, edit, or rename them. The Edit button lets you drag them around. But that all comes later; first, you need some shortcuts to play with.

They're kind of like food: You can shop for ready-to-eat meals, or you can assemble them yourself from individual ingredients.

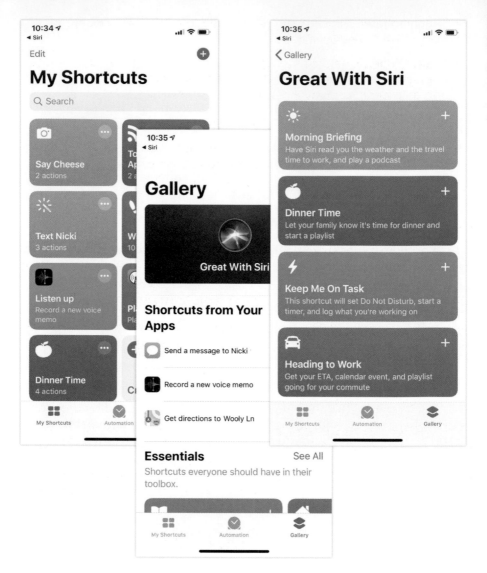

Built-In Shortcuts

Building custom shortcuts isn't as difficult as actual programming, but it's a thinkier process than just pushing a button. Fortunately, iOS comes with a bunch of canned, ready-to-use shortcuts. You can start using them instantly, without ever knowing how they were built.

To see them, open the Shortcuts app. Tap **Gallery**. Here they are: dozens or hundreds of commands, organized into categories like **Great With Siri**, **Share Sheet Shortcuts**, **Shortcuts for Accessibility**, and so on (above). Each is represented by a tile at the top of the screen; tap one to see the options within.

Here, for example, are some of the gems that lurk in the **Great With Siri** category (facing page, right):

- **Dinner Time.** Texts the message "Hey! It's time for dinner!" (or whatever similar message you want) to the family members you specify, and then begins to play a playlist you've chosen.

- **"Say Cheese."** Takes a photo, hands-free.

- **Share ETA.** Texts designated family members with the time Maps expects you'll arrive home, based on current commute conditions.

Scroll down to find **Shortcuts from Your Apps**. When you tap **Show All**, you see a long list of proposed shortcuts that reflect actions you've performed recently by hand.

Some of them might strike you as kind of useless—they're just things you've done on the phone recently, dumbly parroted back, even if they're obviously tasks you'll never use again, like "Text 'AUUUUGHH—my right contact lens fell out and landed deep in your hairbrush' to Casey Robin."

For Notes, you see the names of the three most recent notes you've read, so you can jump back into one with a quick voice command.

Note that this list includes *all* apps that have been equipped with shortcuts—Twitter, Overcast, Prime Video, and so on—not just the built-in apps from Apple. It's worth exploring them to see if any might save you time.

If something in the Gallery looks promising, tap it, and then tap **Get Shortcut**. The app asks you to tailor it—specifying what the texted message should be, for example, and which family members should receive it, and what its name should be (in the "When I say" box)—and then adds that shortcut onto the **My Shortcuts** tab. You've made Siri just a little bit smarter.

> **TIP:** The web is full of wider, crazier, more interesting assortments of ready-to-install shortcuts. Peruse *ShortcutsGallery.com*, for example, or maybe *reddit.com/r/shortcuts*. Read the shortcuts that your fellow citizens have created, and download the good ones.

Make Your Own Shortcuts

Now, using shortcuts *other* people have created may be plenty for your purposes. But you can also create your own shortcuts, step by step.

The internet is teeming with examples and tutorials; you could really go down a rabbit hole. But here's a quick, useful example that will introduce you to the shortcut-building process.

The one you're about to make grabs the most recent photo you've taken and texts it to somebody you've specified in advance—your parent, kid, boss, spouse, or whomever.

1. **In the Shortcuts app, tap +.**

    You arrive on the New Shortcut screen (below, top left).

2. **Tap Add Action.**

    In Shortcuts lingo, an Action is one step (out of several, usually).

    Now you're looking at the ingredients list: hundreds of possible steps you can string together (below, bottom left).

    At the top, there's a search box. At bottom, Suggestions (canned steps, like calling or texting specific people, that iOS has noticed you performing manually).

    But just below the top, you'll find categories like **Apps**, **Favorites**, **Scripting**, **Media**, and so on. Each is a fully stocked refrigerator of

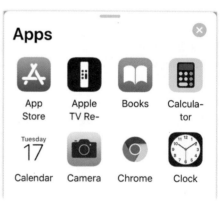

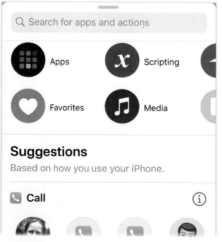

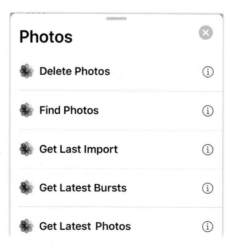

shortcut steps. **Apps**, for example, lists every Shortcuts-controllable app on your phone; tap an app to see all the commands it can take.

For this shortcut, you want to grab the most recent photo, so:

3. **Tap Apps.**

   You're now looking at the icons of every app you have that can be controlled by a Shortcut (facing page, top right).

4. **Tap Photos, and then Get Latest Photos (facing page, bottom right).**

   A new "step bubble" appears (below, left). This is the first step your shortcut will perform. You can tap to change the proposed number of pictures to send (it proposes "1 photo"), and you can tap **Show More** to specify whether or not you want screenshots to be ignored in the photo selection (so only photos get sent).

   Now you're ready to tack on the next step, which is sending that photo in Messages.

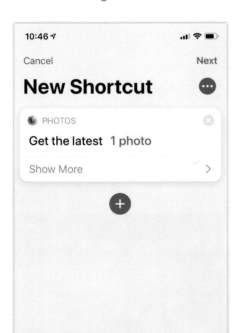
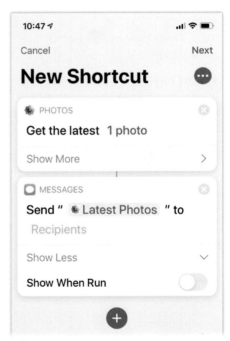

5. **Tap + to add the next step.**

   Because you just had the Photos app panel open, you'll have to tap its little ✕ to backtrack to the Apps panel. (If you hit the same ✕ again, you'd backtrack to the original master Actions starting list shown on page 184.)

6. **Tap Apps, and then Messages, and then Send Message.**

   This step's step bubble offers two options (previous page, right). Tap **Recipients** to specify who gets this text. If you hit **Show More**, you reveal the **Show When Run** switch. It means that before sending the photo, the Messages app will open to show you what it intends to send; you'll have to tap ⬆ to finish the job. It's a safety net. If you turn *off* Show When Run, then triggering this shortcut automatically and invisibly sends the photo without any further action on your part.

7. **Tap Next. Name your shortcut—this will also be its Siri command— and tap Done.**

And that's it! You've just created a new shortcut button on your My Shortcuts tab. More importantly, you've also created a new Siri voice command that will find the last photo you took, create an outgoing text message to the person you specified, and send it—all automatically.

But there are other ways to trigger a shortcut besides invoking its name with Siri.

On the My Shortcuts tab, tap the ⬤⬤⬤ in the tile's corner to open its list of steps. Then tap the ⬤⬤⬤ in *that* tile's corner to see the options pictured below at left:

- **Add to Home Screen** puts an icon for this shortcut on your Home screen, so you can trigger it with a tap. On the Preview screen, you have a chance to rename it or (by tapping its icon) to choose, or take, a new photo to serve as its icon. Tap **Add** when it all looks good.

- **Show in Widget** adds this shortcut's button to the Shortcuts widget (below, right) on your Today screen (page 76).

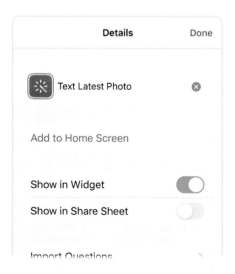
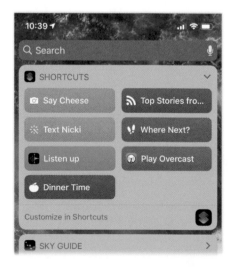

- **Show in Share Sheet** means this shortcut will show up in the list of sharing options that appears when you tap ⬆ in an app. (Yes, some shortcuts can actually process whatever text, graphic, or data you hand to it in this way.)

The list of available steps for building a shortcut includes some astonishingly complex and useful ingredients. The Scripting category, for example, contains steps that let you create "if...then" statements, branching menu options, and other programmery finery. The more comfortable you are with programming basics, the more elaborate your shortcuts can get.

Automated Shortcuts

Here's the part that has the nerdy and the lazy losing their minds with excitement: shortcuts that fire automatically based on where you are, what time it is, and what you're doing on your phone.

To build one, tap the Automation tab. On the next screen (below, left), you start out with two tiles:

- **Create Personal Automation.** These are shortcut triggers that affect only you.

- **Create Home Automation.** These shortcuts control Apple HomeKit-compatible automation stuff in your house, like door locks, security

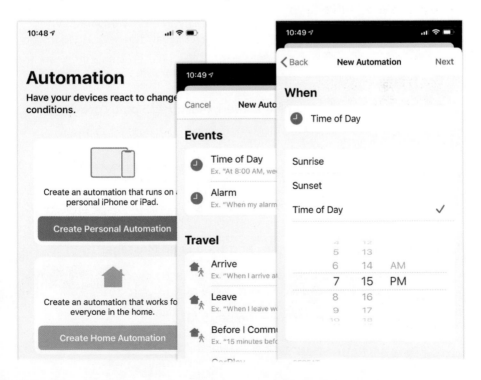

cameras, and lights. (These routines also appear in the Home app described on page 430.)

Suppose, as a tutorial project, you want to create a shortcut that texts your mom every night at 7:15 to take her pill. You'd proceed like this:

1. **Tap Create Personal Automation.**

    Here, on this screen, are all of the situations that can auto-trigger a shortcut (previous page, middle).

    A shortcut can run at a certain **Time of Day** (including intriguing options like **Sunrise** and **Sunset**), when you hear (or shut off or snooze) an **Alarm**, when you **Arrive** at a certain address (which you can limit to certain time ranges), just before you leave for your **Commute** to or from work, when your phone connects or disconnects to a **CarPlay** car, when you turn **Airplane Mode** on or off, when your phone connects to a certain **WiFi** network or **Bluetooth** gadget, when you turn **Do Not Disturb** on or off, when **Low Power Mode** kicks on or off, when you hold your phone up against an **NFC** sticker (which you can buy from Amazon), or when you open a specified **App**.

    The mind reels!

    When you come in range of your Bluetooth speaker, a certain playlist could begin automatically! When you enter Low Power Mode, your phone could text some underling to bring you a power bank! When your alarm goes off, the lights could come on and headbanger music could begin playing to make sure you're up!

    But for now:

2. **Tap Time of Day. On the next screen, dial up 7:15 p.m. (previous page, right).**

    Leave Repeat set to every day.

3. **Tap Next. Tap Add Action.**

    OK, you've said *when* you want this thing to happen. Now specify *what*.

4. **Tap Apps, and then Messages, and then Send Message.**

    (Of course, you might see an icon for messaging your mom already on the list of suggested icons, but this way works, too.)

    You arrive at the screen shown on page 187.

5. **Tap Message and type: "Mom! Time for your pill!" Then tap Recipients and enter her cell number or iCloud address. Tap Show More and make sure Show When Run is turned off. Tap Done.**

   You're back on the Actions screen, where you can look over your work.

6. **Tap Next and then Done.**

And that is it! Every night at 7:15 p.m., your phone will display a notification that offers to auto-text your mom with that reminder. There's nothing for you to do but tap **Run** and admire your own genius. (Sadly, there's no way to automate tasks without requiring this notification confirmation.)

Clearly, Apple has given you enough tools to keep you busy for months, thinking up shortcuts, building them, debugging them. You can learn this stuff really fast by downloading ready-made shortcuts and examining how they were built. There's a mini-manual built into the app, too (tap the ● on any shortcut's details screen, and then **Shortcuts Help**).

Yeah, that's all time you'll never get back. But you're spending it in the name of creating shortcuts you'll use over and over again, saving so much more time in the long run.

Advanced Siri

With a little setup, you can extend Siri's powers in some more intriguing ways.

Teach Siri About Your Relationships

When you say, "Text my mom" or "Call my fiancée," how does Siri know whom you're talking about? Sure, Siri is powerful artificial intelligence, but she's not actually *magic*.

You teach her by referring to somebody in your Contacts list. Say to her something like, "My assistant is Casey Robin" or "Tad Cooper is my boyfriend." When Siri asks for confirmation, say "Yes" or tap **Confirm**.

Or wait for Siri to ask you herself. If you say, "Email my dad," Siri asks, "What is your dad's name?" Just say his name; Siri remembers that relationship. (The available relationships include mother, father, grandmother, grandfather, brother, sister, child, son, daughter, spouse, wife, husband, boss, partner, manager, assistant, girlfriend, boyfriend, and friend.)

Behind the scenes, Siri lists these relationships on your card in Contacts. Now that you know that, you can figure out how to edit or delete these relationships as well. Which is handy—not all relationships, as we know, last forever.

Fix Siri's Name Comprehension

Siri easily understands common names—but if someone in your family, work, or social circle has an unusual name, you may quickly become frustrated. After all, you can't text, call, email, or get directions to someone's house unless Siri understands the person's name when you say it.

One workaround is to use a relationship, as described in the previous section. That way, you can say, "Call my brother" instead of "Call Ilyich" (or whatever). Another is to use Siri's pronunciation-learning feature. It fires up in several different situations:

- **When you're texting.** If Siri offers the wrong person's name when you try to text someone by voice, say, "Someone else." After you've sent the message, Siri apologetically says, "By the way, sorry I didn't recognize that name. Can you teach me how to say it?"

- **After Siri botches a pronunciation.** Tell her, "That's not how to pronounce his name."

- **Whenever it occurs to you.** You can start the process by saying, "Learn to pronounce Reagann Tsuki's name" or "Learn to pronounce my mom's name."

- **In Contacts.** Open somebody's "card" in Contacts; start Siri and say, "Learn to pronounce her name."

In each case, with tremendous courtesy, Siri walks you through the process of teaching her the correct pronunciation. She offers you several ▶ buttons; each triggers a different pronunciation. Tap **Select** next to the correct one (or tap **Tell Siri again** if none of the options is correct).

By the end of the process, Siri knows two things: how to say that person's name aloud, and how to recognize that name when *you* say it.

6

Texting & Messages

The term "iPhone" has never seemed especially appropriate for a gadget with so much power and flexibility. Statistics show, in fact, that making phone calls is one of the iPhone's least-used functions! In fact, 57 percent of us never use the iPhone to make phone calls at *all*.

But texting—now we're talking. Texting is the single most used function of the modern cellphone. In the U.S., we send 16 billion texts a day; on average, Americans send or receive 94 texts a day. Worldwide, we send 8.3 *trillion* texts a year. That's a lot of *LOL*s.

Apple—wary of losing customers to creative messaging apps like WhatsApp, Snapchat, and Facebook Messenger—is trying to compete via its Messages app. Its special effects and cool interactions match most offerings of rival apps—and, thanks to a Messages app *store*, even surpass them. Text-message conversations no longer look like a tidy screenplay. Now they can be overrun with graphics, cartoons, animations, and typographic fun.

Text Messages and iMessages

So why is texting so crazy popular? For reasons like these:

- **Like a phone call, a text message is immediate.** You get the message off your chest right now.

- **And yet, as with email, the recipient doesn't have to answer immediately.** The message waits for him even when his phone is turned off.

- **Unlike a phone call, a text is nondisruptive.** You can send someone a text without worrying that he's in a movie, a meeting, or anywhere else where holding a phone up to his head and talking would be frowned upon. (And the other person can answer nondisruptively, too, by sending a text message *back*.)

- **You have a written record of the exchange.** There's no mistaking what the person meant. (Well, at least not because of sound quality. Understanding the texting shorthand that's evolved—"C U 2mrO," and so on—is another matter entirely.)

Now, the first thing to learn about texting on the iPhone is that there are *two kinds* of messages. There are regular text messages (SMS), which any cellphone can send to any cellphone. And there are iMessages, which only Apple equipment (iPhones, iPads, Macs) can exchange.

The Messages app can send and receive both kinds of messages—but iMessages offer much greater creative freedom.

Standard Texting (SMS)

SMS stands for Short Message Service, but it's commonly just called texting. An SMS is a very short note (under 160 characters—a sentence or two) that you shoot from one cellphone to another. You can send pictures and videos, too.

iMessages

In many ways, iMessages and regular text messages work alike. You send and receive them in the same app (Messages). They show up in the same window. You can send the same kinds of things: text, photos, videos, contacts, map locations, whatever.

The big difference: iMessages go exclusively between Apple products. If your iPhone determines that the address belongs to any *other* kind of phone, it sends regular old text messages.

iMessages offer some huge advantages over regular text messages:

- **No 160-character limit.** A single message can be many pages long. (The actual limit is 18,996 characters per message, in case you're counting.)

- **iMessages don't count as text messages.** You don't have to pay for them. They look and work exactly like text messages, but they're transferred over the internet (Wi-Fi or cellular data) instead of your cell company's voice airwaves. You can send and receive an unlimited number of them and never have to pay a penny more.

- **You know when someone is typing.** When you're typing back and forth with somebody, you don't have to wonder whether, during a silence, they're typing a response to you or just ignoring you; when they're typing, you see an ellipsis (•••) in their speech bubble.

TIP: The ellipsis dots appear as soon as the other guy starts typing—and remain on your screen for 60 seconds, even if he *stopped* typing a long time ago. Conversely, they *disappear* from your screen after 60 seconds, even if he's still typing! Often you'll see the dots disappear shortly before you get a huge, long paragraph—because the other guy took longer than 60 seconds to write it.

- **You don't wonder if the other guy has received your message.** A tiny, light-gray word "delivered" appears under each message you send, briefly, to let you know the other device received it.

- **Read receipts.** You can even turn on a "read receipt" feature that lets the other person know when you've actually *seen* a message she sent. She'll see a notation that says, for example, "Read 2:34 PM." (See page 637.)

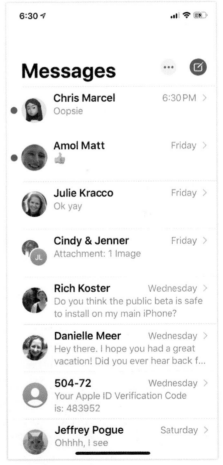

- **Your history of iMessages shows up on all your i-gadgets.** They're synchronized through your iCloud account. You can start a chat on your iPhone and later pick up your Mac laptop at home and carry right on from where you stopped (in *its* Messages program).

  As a result, you always have a record of your iMessages. You have a copyable, searchable transcript on your Mac.

- **iMessages can be more than text.** They can be audio recordings, video recordings, photos, sketches you make with your finger, games, "stickers," emoji symbols, animations, and much more.

iMessages happen automatically. All you do is open Messages and create a text message as usual. If your recipient is using a reasonably recent iPhone, iPad, iPod Touch, or Mac (and has an iCloud account), then your iPhone sends your message as an iMessage automatically. It somehow knows.

You'll know, too, because the light-gray text in the typing box says "iMessage" instead of "Text Message." There's also a color difference: Blue means iMessages, green means "everybody else." You'll see those colors on people's names when you search, in their speech bubbles, and even on the ⬆ button. (The gray names when you search—well, your iPhone doesn't know yet, maybe because they don't have phone numbers.)

Sending and receiving messages works mostly the same, whether it's SMS messages or iMessages. So the rest of this chapter applies equally well to both, with a few exceptions.

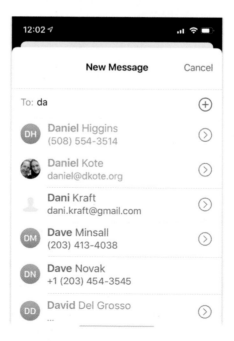

There's actually a third kind of message that Messages handles: Business Chat. It's a service Apple offers to corporate entities, where you can have a typed chat with a customer-service representative.

You can open one of these chats—which are denoted with dark-gray speech bubbles—only from a company's website or, more often, from its info pane when you've searched for it in Maps.

Only a few companies offer Business Chat, including Home Depot, Marriott, Discover, T-Mobile, and Hilton. But if you're ever unlucky enough to require customer-service attention, you'll know why your texts are suddenly showing up in dark gray.

Receiving Texts

When you get a text, the iPhone plays a sound. It's a shiny glockenspiel ding, unless you've changed it in Settings→Sounds & Haptics→Text Tone.

The phone also displays the name or number of the sender and the message—though if you have Face ID set up, you don't see the actual contents of the messages until the phone is sure it's really *you* looking at them (page 60). Unless you've fooled around with the Notifications settings, the message appears as a banner on your screen (page 69), disappearing momentarily on its own, so as not to interrupt what you're doing. (You can flick it up and away if it's blocking your screen.)

If the iPhone was asleep, it lights up long enough to display the message on its Lock screen. At that point, you have a few options:

- **Ignore it.** After a moment, the screen goes dark again. The incoming-text notification bubble will be there the next time you wake it.

- **Answer it.** Long-press the banner to expand it into a full keyboard, so you can respond without even unlocking the phone. (Or swipe to the *left* on the notification bubble to reveal the View button, which does the same thing.)

- **Open it.** If you tap a notification bubble, you're asked to unlock your phone; you wind up looking at the message in the Messages app.

On the Home screen, the Messages icon bears a circled number "badge" letting you know how many new text messages are waiting for you.

- **Shut it up.** Swipe left on the notification bubble to reveal the Manage button. It lets you make all future incoming message notifications silent—or prevents them from notifying you at all (page 65).

Once you tap a message notification to open it, you see the text-message conversation displayed as cartoon speech balloons.

To respond to the message, tap in the text box at the bottom of the screen. The iPhone keyboard appears. Type away, or dictate a response using the microphone (🎤), and then tap ⬆ —that's your Send button. As long as your phone has cellular or Wi-Fi coverage, the message goes out immediately.

If your buddy replies, then the balloon-chat continues, scrolling up.

And now, a selection of juicy Message tips:

- **The last 50 exchanges appear here.** If you want to see even older ones, scroll to the very top and then drag downward.

TIP: Having to scroll to the top, wait, and then drag downward can get old fast, especially when you're trying to dig up a message you exchanged a few weeks back. Fortunately, there's a glorious shortcut: *Tap the very top of the screen* (where the clock appears) or *the left ear* of a Face ID phone, over and over again. Each time you tap, you load another batch of older messages and scroll to the oldest one.

And by the way—if the keyboard is blocking your view of the conversation, swipe downward on the messages to hide it.

- **If someone sends you a web address,** it usually shows up as a little graphic of the website (below, left). Tap to open it in Safari. If it's a link to a video on YouTube or Vimeo, you can play it, at tiny size, right on that preview thumbnail. Just tap it (below, right). To open the video at full size, *on* YouTube or Vimeo, tap the thumbnail's *name*.

If someone sends a street address, tap it to open it in Maps. And if someone sends a phone number, tap it to dial.

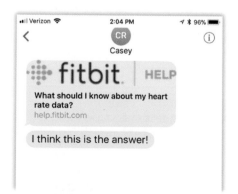
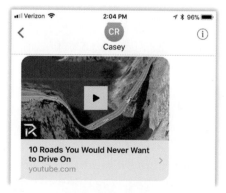

- **Once you've opened a text conversation,** you see that each flurry of messages is time-stamped when it begins. But at this point, you can also drag leftward anywhere on the screen to reveal the exact time stamps of every message *within* the chat.

The List of Conversations

The iPhone retains all your text exchanges. The Messages screen (of the Messages app) is a list of all your correspondents, like a table of contents. A blue dot indicates a conversation with new messages.

You can tap a person's listing to open the actual messages you've exchanged, going back in time to your very first texts. The iPhone saves you the administrative work of creating a new message, choosing a recipient, and so on.

In iOS 13, though, a new feature lets you shoot a canned response right from the conversation list. Just long-press that listing (below, left), and tap one of the short replies in the command panel that pops up (right).

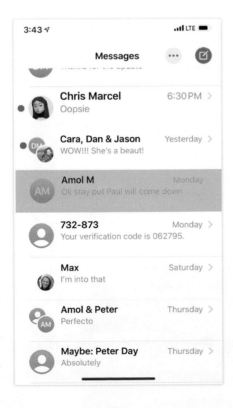

Your choices are usually along the lines of "Thanks," "Yes," "No," and "Talk later?" (**Custom** just opens the conversation as usual.)

To return to the Messages list from the actual chat view, tap ⟨ at top left—or swipe inward from the left edge of the screen.

If having these old exchanges hanging around presents a security (or marital) risk, you can delete them in several ways:

- **Delete just one text.** This technique is a little weird, but here goes: Open the conversation. *Hold down your finger* on the individual message you want to delete. When the options panel appears, tap **More**.

  Now you can delete all the exchanges simultaneously (tap **Delete All**) or vaporize only incriminating messages. To do that, tap the selection circles for the ones you want to nuke, putting checks (✅) by them; tap the 🗑 to delete them all at once. Tap **Delete Message** or **Delete Conversation** to confirm. (You can't delete a message from anyone *else's* phone; you're just deleting *your* copy of the conversation.)

- **Delete an entire conversation.** *Swipe* away the conversation. At the list of conversations, swipe your finger *leftward* across the conversation's name. The **Delete** button appears.

- **Delete multiple conversations.** Above the Messages list, tap ●●●; then **Manage Messages List**. Tap to select (✅) the conversations you want to ditch, and then tap **Delete**.

Mark All as Read

Here's a handy option: When you get off the plane, home from your honeymoon, you might see Messages bristling with notifications about texts you missed. Now you can mark them all as read at once, so the blue dots don't distract you anymore.

To do that, on the Messages screen, tap ●●●→Manage Messages List→ Read All.

The Details Screen

The Details screen offers six options that you may find handy in the midst of a chat. To see them, tap your correspondent's name at the top of the screen, and then tap info. Here's what you see now:

- **The map.** If your buddy has chosen to share her location with you, you'll see (after a few seconds) her little dot on a map.

- **Call.** If all this fussy typing is driving you nuts, you can jump onto a phone or video call. At the top of the Details screen, hit ■◀ (place a FaceTime video call) or ☎ (conclude the transaction by voice, with a phone call or FaceTime audio call). You can also tap this person's name to open the corresponding Contacts card, loaded with different ways to call, text, or email.

- **Send My Current Location.** Hit this button to transmit a map to the other person, showing exactly where you are, so that person can come and pick you up, meet you for drinks, or whatever.

   If your correspondent has an iPhone, iPad, or Mac, she can open the map you've sent in Maps, ready to guide her with driving directions. If

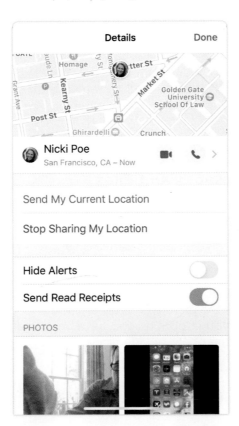

she's one of the unenlightened—she owns some non-Apple phone—then she gets what's called a Location vCard, which she *may* be able to open into a mapping app on her own phone.

- **Share My Location.** If you're moving around, you may prefer this option. It sends your whereabouts to your correspondent—and keeps that location updated as you meander, for a period of time you specify (**One Hour**, **Until End of Day**, or **Indefinitely**). That's great when you're club-hopping, say, and trying to help some buddies catch up with you. As your location changes, the map you sent to your recipient updates itself.

  At any time, you can stop broadcasting your location to this person; just open the Details screen again and tap **Stop Sharing My Location**.

- **Hide Alerts.** Otherwise known as "mute," "shush," or "enough already." It makes your phone stop ringing or vibrating with every new message from this person or group. Handy when you're trying to get work done, when you're being bombarded by silly group chitchat, or when someone's stalking you.

- **Send Read Receipts.** You can turn read receipts (page 637) on or off independently for each chat partner, using this switch.

- **Photos, Links, Locations, Attachments.** Crazy cool! Here are all the photos and non-textual goodies you've ever exchanged with this texting correspondent, going back to forever. You see the four or six most recent ones, but there's a **See All** button for each category.

  Tap one of these tiles to open it. Hold your finger down lightly to get some administrative options. For a photo, for example, your choices are **Save** (to your Photos app), **Copy**, **Share**, or **Delete**.

Capturing Messages and Files

In general, text messages are fleeting; most people have no idea how they might capture them and save them forever.

Some of the stuff *in* those text messages is easy to save, though. For example, if you're on the receiving end of a photo or video, tap the small preview in the speech bubble. It opens at full-screen size so you can have a better look at it—and if it's a video, there's a ▶ button so you can play it. Either way, if the picture or video is good enough to preserve, tap ⬆. Among a million other options, you get a **Save Image** or **Save Video** button; tap to add the photo or video to your iPhone's collection.

If someone sends you contact information (a phone number, for example), you can add it to your address book. Just tap inside that bubble and then tap either **Create New Contact** or **Add to Existing Contact**.

If you'd like to preserve the actual text messages, you have a few options:

- **Copy them individually.** Hold your finger down lightly on a text bubble, and then tap *Copy*. At this point, you can paste that message into, for example, an outgoing email.

- **Forward them.** Hold your finger down lightly on a text bubble; tap *More*, and then tap the selection checkmarks beside all the messages you want to pass on. Now you can tap the Forward (↗) button. All the selected messages go along for the ride in a single consolidated message to a new text-message addressee.

- **Save the iMessages.** If you have a Mac, then your iMessages show up in the Messages chat program. You can save them or copy them there.

> **TIP:** Behind the scenes, the Mac stores all your chat transcripts in a hidden folder as special text files. To get there, press the Option key as you open the *Go* menu in the Finder; choose *Go→Library*. The transcripts are in date-stamped folders in the *Messages→Archive* folder.

- **Use an app.** There's no built-in way to save regular text messages in bulk. There are, however, apps that can do this for you, like iMazing (for Windows) or iBackup Viewer (free for the Mac). They work from the invisible backup files you create when you sync your phone with iTunes.

Tapbacks (iMessages Only)

How many trillions of times a day do people respond to texts with repetitive reactions like "LOL" and "Awww" and "!!"? Many. It's how you demonstrate that you appreciate the import of the other person's text.

If you and your buddy are both using iOS 10 or later or macOS Sierra or later, though, you've now got a quicker, less cluttery, more visual way to indicate those sorts of standard reactions: what Apple calls tapbacks.

If you double-tap a message you've been sent, you're offered a tapback palette with six little reaction symbols: a heart, a thumbs-up, a thumbs-down, "Ha ha," two exclamation points, and a question mark. When you choose one, it appears instantly on your screen and your buddy's. You can use them to stamp your reaction onto the other person's text (or even one of your own, if you're weird).

In short, the tapback palette lets you react to a text without having to send a text back.

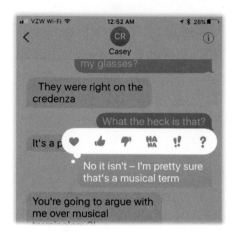 

Messages in the Cloud

For years, it was a real hassle of Messages: You'd pick up one Apple gadget after doing a lot of texting on another. Then you'd have to wait a very long time for your phone's copy of Messages to catch up—to download all the conversations you had on your Mac.

Today, an optional feature neatly solves that problem: Your message history can be saved *online*, in iCloud.

If you turn on this feature, here's what you get:

- **Your text messages and iMessages** (and all associated photos, videos, and attachments) are now stored online instead of on your iPhone, iPad, and Mac. Which means you save several gigabytes of storage, on every single device. That's storage that was duplicated on every machine—the same database stored in multiple places.

- **Your Mac, iPhone, and iPad backups** are much smaller, because they no longer include your Messages database.

- **All your messages are synced.** Delete a message or a conversation, and it's also deleted on all your other machines.

- **No more waiting for one device to "catch up."** That should sound like a pleasant development to anyone who, for example, uses Messages on the MacBook on a plane ride—and then upon landing can't use Messages on the phone for 10 minutes because it's still syncing.

- **If you get a new Apple device,** your entire history of text messages and attachments appear on it. (*Without* Messages in iCloud, your current and future messages appear, but you can't scroll to see past ones—at least not without restoring from a backup.)

There's one big downside of Messages in iCloud: Moving your database into your iCloud account online eats up space *there*. You're saving tons of space on all your Apple machines but losing space on your iCloud account online—and that may cost you money (page 578).

If you decide it's worth doing, here's how to set it up. First, you have to have two-factor authentication turned on, for security (page 662). Second, on each device, turn on Messages in iCloud:

- **On an iPhone or iPad,** open Settings. Tap your name at the top, tap iCloud, and then turn on Messages.

- **On the Mac,** open Messages→Preferences→Accounts, and turn on Enable Messages in iCloud.

It takes a few minutes for your devices to offload your entire Messages history; the phone/tablet must be plugged into power and on Wi-Fi before the process can begin.

Once that's done, you'll be treated to a technical but handy upgrade to your texting world.

Sending Messages

If you want to text somebody you've texted before, the quickest way is to resume one of the "conversations" already listed in the Messages list.

You can also tap a person's name in Contacts, or ⓘ next to a listing in the Phone app's Recents or Favorites, to open the Info screen; tap message.

Actually, options to fire off text messages lurk all over the iPhone—any-time you see the Share (⬆) button, which is frequently (page 378). Tapping Message sends you back to Messages, where the photo, video, page, or other item is ready to send. (More on multimedia messages shortly.)

In other words, sending a text message to anyone who lives in your iPhone is only a couple of taps away.

> **NOTE:** You can tap ⊕ to add *another* recipient for this same message (or tap the 123 button to type in a phone number). Repeat as necessary; they'll all get the same message.

Yet another way to start: Tap ✏️ at the top of the Messages screen. Or, easiest of all, use Siri. Say, "Text Casey" or whatever.

In any case, the text message composition screen is waiting for you now. You're ready to type (or dictate) and send!

Audio Texting

Sometimes an audio recording is just better than a typed message, especially when music, children, animals, or a lot of emotion are involved. You could probably argue that audio texting is also better than typed texting when you're driving, jogging, or operating industrial machinery.

If you and your friend are both Apple people, your phone can become a sort of walkie-talkie.

Hold down the 🎙️ button at the right end of the Messages text box. Once the sound-level meter appears, say something. When you're finished, release your finger. Now you can tap ⊗ to cancel, ▶ to play it back, or ⬆️ to send what you said to your buddy as an audio recording.

> **TIP:** If you're pretty confident that what you've said is correct, you can slide your thumb directly from the 🎙️ button straight up to the ⬆️ to send it.

The guy on the receiving end doesn't even have to touch the screen to listen. He just holds the phone up to his head! Your audio message plays automatically. (This works even if his phone is asleep and locked.)

And then get this: To reply, *he* doesn't have to touch anything or even look at the screen. He just holds the phone to his head again and speaks! Once he lowers the phone, his recording shoots back to you.

Throughout all this, you don't have to look at the phone, put your glasses on, or even touch the screen. It's a whole new form of quick

exchanges—something that combines the best of a walkie-talkie (instant audio) with the best of text messages (you can listen and reply at your leisure).

The off switch for the **Raise to Listen** feature is in **Settings→Messages**. But why would you want to disable such a cool feature?

> **TIP:** Audio eats up a lot more space on your phone than text. That's why iOS comes set to *delete* each audio message two minutes after you receive it. If that prospect worries you, then visit **Settings→ Messages**. Under Audio Messages, you can tap **Expire** and change that setting to **Never**.
>
> Even if you leave it set to two minutes, you're free to preserve especially good audio messages forever; just tap the tiny **Keep** button that appears below each one.

Help with Emoji and Info-Bits

Messages is a card-carrying fan of *emoji*—those little icons once known as smileys or emoticons. Now there are thousands of them, representing people, places, things, food, emotions, household objects, and on and on.

How easy is it to use emoji? Very:

- **Auto-emoji.** If iOS has an emoji symbol for a word you've just typed, it appears in the row of autocomplete suggestions (below, left). If you tap that emoji *before* tapping the space bar, you *replace* the typed word with the emoji. If you tap space and *then* the emoji, you get both the word *and* the emoji.

- **Jumbo emoji.** When you send *one, two, or three* emoji symbols as your entire response, they appear three times as large as normal, as shown above at right (at least if the recipient has iOS 10 or macOS Sierra or later).

- **Auto-info.** You know the QuickType word suggestions above the keyboard (page 87)? In Messages, those suggestions include *information* you might want to type.

  If you type "I'm available at," one of the suggestion buttons includes the next open slot on your calendar. If you say "Stacy's number is," the button offers her phone number (if she's in your Contacts). If someone texts you, "Where are you?" one of the buttons offers to send back a map showing your location.

  In fact, you may also see things like movie, song, and place names as auto-suggestions, based on stuff you've recently looked up on your phone. If you're driving somewhere, you might even see an estimated arrival time.

  Quite handy, actually.

The Finger-Sketch Pad

If you turn the phone 90 degrees and then tap the 𝒪 button that appears on the keyboard, the screen becomes a whiteboard. (In iOS 13, just turning the phone alone doesn't produce the whiteboard, much to the relief of people who were driven crazy when that happened accidentally.)

What you scribble with your finger looks like real ink on paper and gets sent as a graphic. (You also see your previous masterpieces displayed here for quick reuse.)

Tap the ⌨ button in the corner to bring the keyboard back without having to rotate the phone upright again.

Sending with Animated Fun

The Send button (⬆) is more than a button.

If you long-press that blue arrow, you get a palette of four sending styles (below, left).

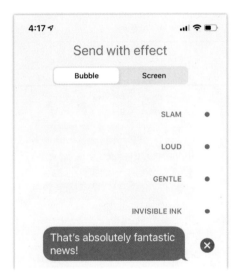

The first three—**Slam**, **Loud**, and **Gentle**—animate the typography of your text to make it bang down, swell up, and so on, at least when you're sending to fellow iOS or Mac fans. For example, **Slam** makes your text fly across the screen and then thud into the ground, making a shock wave ripple through the other messages.

The fourth special "Send with effect" is called **Invisible Ink**. It obscures your message with animated glitter dust until your recipient drags a finger across it (as shown above at right).

This idea is great for guessing games and revealing dramatic news, of course. But when you're sending, ahem, spicy text messages, it also prevents embarrassment if the recipient's phone is lying in public view.

When you long-press the ⬆ , the fifth option is **Screen**. It opens pages of *full-screen* animations. These, upon sending, fill the *entire background* of the Messages window to indicate your reaction to something: a swelling heart, ascending balloons, a laser show, fireworks, a shooting star, falling confetti, and so on. Swipe horizontally to preview each style before you commit to it.

If your text says "Congrats," "Happy birthday," or "Happy New Year," Messages fills the screen with a corresponding animation *automatically*. Which may or may not get old fast.

> **NOTE:** The full juiciness of these text and screen styles is available only if your recipient also has iOS 10 or later. So what if you're sending to an Android phone, an older iPhone, or a Mac?
>
> In that case, the animation you've so carefully picked out doesn't show up. Instead, the other person can only *read* about what you intended. She'll see the somewhat baffling written notation "sent with Slam effect," "sent with Balloons," or whatever.

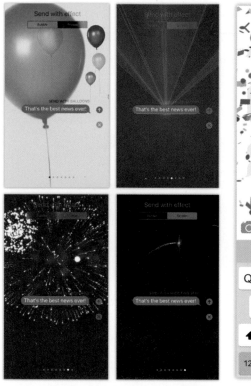

Photos and Videos

Depending on the age of your correspondents, typed text may be your *least*-used form of communication. As the saying goes, a picture is worth a thousand texts. And a video—well, you get it.

Taking a Photo

Next to the typing box, iOS presents the Photos button (📷). Tap it to open what looks like the full-blown Camera app (below, top left). Here are all the Camera modes—**Slo-mo**, **Video**, **Photo**, **Portrait**, **Square**, **Pano**—except Time Lapse). Here are the controls for the flash, filters, and flipping to the front camera. If you're going to take a photo to send as a message, you may as well have your full camera toolkit.

TIP: Here, too, at top left, is a 🖼 button. It opens the photo picker, so you can send an existing photo.

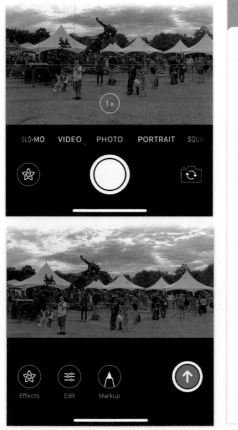 

There's only one button here that *isn't* in the Camera app: The 🌟 (Effects) button. It opens the Effects screen. Here you can dress up your video or photo with "stickers," text, arrows and squiggles, Animoji, and so on. Read on for details—for now, the point is that you can apply these effects either *before* or *after* snapping the picture:

- **Before.** Choose the filter (or pile up several of them), and then tap the ✕. (Don't hit Done, which sends you back to the Messages screen without accomplishing anything.) You wind up at the photo-taking screen (previous page, top left).

- **After.** Take a new photo or video as usual (see Chapter 9). After you snap it—but before you send it—you're treated to an intermediary screen that's full of options for processing the shot you've just taken.

In either case, you're now looking at the edit-before-sending screen (previous page, bottom left). Here are your options now:

- **Retake.** Try again.

- **Done.** Return to Messages, where the new photo or video is poised to go but hasn't been sent yet. You can type a text to go with it, or cancel the whole business by tapping the ✕ in the thumbnail's corner.

- **Effects (★).** Here again is the button that opens your "stickers," text, filters, shapes, Animoji, and so on. Tap it to apply some effects, unless you did so before taking the shot, in which case tapping it turns them *off*.

- **Edit.** Crop, rotate, filter, adjust the color and contrast, and otherwise improve the picture before you send it. See page 330.

- **Markup.** The Markup features (page 458) are super-useful in Messages. It can be amusing and educational to make notes on a photo, draw a little mustache on someone you don't like, or enlarge a certain detail for your chat partner's enlightenment.

- ⬆ fires off the new photo or video, at last, to your buddy.

NOTE: A copy of the photo also winds up in Photos, in your Camera Roll, in case you ever want to use it again.

Sending Existing Photos

You can also send a photo or video from your Camera Roll—something you've captured previously, something now in your Photos app. You get there using either of two somewhat hidden paths:

- **Tap the Camera button (📷),** and then the Photos button at top left (🖼).

- **Tap the colorful Photos button just above the keyboard.** If you don't see it, your Apps row must be hidden. Tap the Apps button (🅰) next to the message box to make it appear. Once you see the row of app buttons, tap the first one—the Photos button (✳).

In either case, the bottom part of your screen now fills with two scrolling rows of photos and videos you've taken recently. Tap one (or more) that you want to send. Its thumbnail pops into the message box. You can tap in the "Add comment or Send" box to type a little message (and put away the photo browser), or just hit ⬆ to send the picture on its way.

Or you can tap the ⊗ if you change your mind about sending this photo.

It's worth noting two useful features here:

- **All Photos.** If you tap **All Photos**, you open the regular Photos app, where you can find your albums, videos, and other organizational structures, for ease in finding an older picture or video to send.

- **Sharing Suggestions.** If you swipe up on this mini-browser to make it bigger, you reveal Sharing Suggestions. These are groups of photos from various recent events (page 352).

   The idea here is to make it easier to share photos with other people who were with you at some event: a party, a vacation, an outing, and so on. If you tap one of these suggestions, you open a screen where you can look over the individual photos inside this set. Tap a thumbnail to see it at full size, tap **Select** to choose which ones you want to send, or tap **Share All** to send the whole batch.

   If the recipients have iOS 12 or later, too, they can then *share* their photos of the same event with *you*. The whole cycle is described on page 351.

Effects

When you're about to take a photo in Messages (or have just taken one), tap the ✿ button. It makes another row of icons appear below the camera preview: **Animoji**, **Memoji**, **Filters**, **Text**, **Shapes**, **Activity**, and (if you've installed any) **Stickers**. They're hours of fun for the whole family (or at least for those under 14).

Each effect offers a dozen or so options—that is, graphic styles. (For Animoji, for example, they're various animated critters.) Only about three of them fit across your screen; you probably think you're supposed to scroll horizontally to see them all. And, yes, you can do that. But you can also swipe up to see a more complete palette of options on a single screen (next page, left). Swipe down from the top to collapse them back to a single row.

Here are the icons you may find there, depending on your phone model. Keep in mind that you can use as many of these as you want, stacking multiple effects (even multiple uses of the same effect) onto a single overwhelmed image:

- **Animoji.** If you have a Face ID phone, here are the monkey, robot, T. rex, and other animated cartoon heads that mimic your own expressions as you talk or emote (page 218).

- **Filters.** Each of these 14 Instagram-style filters fiddles with the color and style of your photo or video in a different way. The first ones—Comic Book (shown below at center), Ink, and Watercolor—are really extraordinary. They turn your photo or video into a living piece of artwork. (Ever seen rotoscoped movies like *Loving Vincent*, *A Scanner Darkly*, or *Yellow Submarine*? Then you'll recognize the effects immediately.)

- **Text.** You can stamp words or phrases onto your photo or video, too. The options here offer a range of colors and backgrounds, speech balloons and thought bubbles.

To plop one onto your image, tap it; a starter speech balloon appears. Type to replace the starter text ("Text"). Tap outside the balloon to finish typing. Now you can drag the balloon around the image; it will stay where you put it. (And if you're shooting video, it stays where you put it relative to your face. As you move, it moves.)

You can also two-finger spread to adjust its size, or two-finger rotate to adjust its angle. Tap the bubble to edit the text or (by tapping ❌) delete the whole thing.

- **Shapes.** Here are animated arrows, scribbles, checkmarks, circles, X's, and firework pops. All of them are intended to draw attention to something in your photo or video. (They're animated only in videos, of course.)

   Tap one to drop it onto your image. At this point, you can change its size or angle as described already. To remove it, tap the graphic overlay and then tap the ❌ that appears.

- **Activity.** These weird little animated badges all seem to have something to do with fitness or celebration—and, indeed, they derive from the Apple Watch. These are the little graphic awards you see on the watch for reaching certain activity goals. But now you can stick one onto your image or video even if all you did today was lie on the couch and shovel Doritos into your mouth.

- **Stickers.** If you've downloaded any "sticker packs" in the Messages App Store (read on), you'll find them here, too. You can move them, rotate them, enlarge them, or delete them, exactly the way you do shapes.

   If you open the Effects browser *before* taking a photo or video, a sticker you've stamped onto your image moves with your head. It becomes frozen in place when you snap the photo—or continues to move if you shoot a video.

- **Memoji Stickers**, new in iOS 13, are also stickers—but they're based on the Memoji cartoons you've made of yourself (page 219). Stamp one on your face, enlarge it (by spreading two fingers) to cover your whole head (facing page, right), and just try to contain your helpless laughter.

The Apps Drawer

Messages apps offer a universe of expressive possibilities even beyond these. Apple welcomes software companies to add their own modules—miniature apps—that let you text everything from movie schedules and restaurant reservations to cash.

If you don't see the row of tiny icons at the very bottom of the Messages screen—your apps—tap the 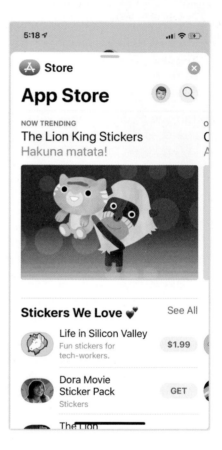 that hugs the left side of the typing box.

This app mechanism has a few basic guidelines:

- **To see the apps' names,** hold your finger down on them, or scroll them horizontally. The apps drawer grows taller—tall enough to show their names (below, left).

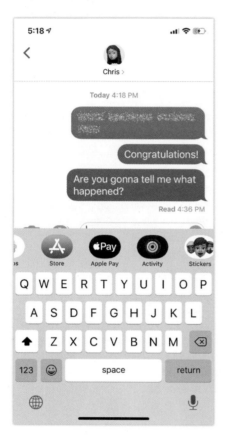

- **To use an app,** tap it. Now the bottom half of Messages presents you with the app's offerings. (Feeling claustrophobic? Swipe up. The app area expands to fill your screen.)

- **To delete an app,** scroll all the way to the right; tap **More**. Now you see the management screen. Swipe left across an app's name to reveal the **Delete** button. (If it's an Apple app, the button just says **Remove from Favorites**, so it won't be in your face anymore. And you're not allowed to remove the **Photos** or **App Store** apps from anything.)

- **To rearrange the apps,** tap **Edit** on the management screen; now you can drag the apps around with their grip handles (≡) or hide an app by turning off its switch.

  Here, too, you can manipulate the special list called Favorites; these are the apps that appear first, at the left end of the apps drawer. You can drag an app's grip handles up or down to rearrange its position among your favorites. Tap ⊖ to de-favorite an app, moving it into the list of also-rans. Or tap one of the ⊕ buttons to elevate an app into the Favorites list.

- **To hide the apps,** tap the Ⓐ again.

Here's what you'll find in the apps drawer on a new phone.

TIP: To move from one app to another, you can tap a different icon in the apps drawer—or you can swipe horizontally across the row.

Photos

Direct access to your Camera Roll, as described on page 212.

The App Store

The second icon (Ⓐ) takes you to the Messages App Store, a rabbit hole into a world of options beyond belief (facing page, right).

In this store, you can download all kinds of tiny apps that work within Messages. Some are free; some cost a couple of bucks.

Some are "stickers" or animations you can drag up onto other people's texts (or your own), thereby adding your own sarcastic or emotional commentary to it.

Others simply give you access, while you're chatting, to popular apps like Yelp or OpenTable (so you can research or book restaurants), Airbnb (to book lodging), Square Cash or Circle Pay or Venmo (to send money directly to friends), Fandango (to research and book movies), iTranslate (to convert your texts to or from another language), Kayak (to book flights), Doodle (to find a mutually free time to meet), hundreds of popular games, and on and on.

The idea is that you can do all of this right there in Messages, collaboratively with your buddy on the other end.

You can search or browse this store just as you do the regular App Store. For example, you can inspect the apps Apple is promoting today, or you can look through the best-seller lists.

When you find an app that looks appealing, tap **Get** (if it's free) or its price (if it's not), and then **Install** to install it, just as you would an App Store app (page 361). The new app appears in your apps drawer, ready to use. (It shows up first in line after your Favorites.)

Apple Pay

Once you've set up Apple Pay, you can send money to other iMessages folks directly from the Messages chat window. (If you've ever used Venmo, you get the idea.) See page 579.

Activity

Here's a strange assortment of cartoony stickers, some animated, that seem to have sports and celebration as themes. They're like the ones discussed on page 215.

Stickers

Here are your Memoji Stickers, as described on page 215. You can tap one to pop it into the message box, to send as a standalone graphic. Because they're basically *you* with different expressions, you can slap one in to indicate your delight or disgust with whatever your conversation partner just said. You can also drag one onto the actual chat bubble representing what she said.

#Images

This app is a searchable database of "reaction GIFs," which are very short, silent video loops, usually swiped from popular movies or TV shows. People (well, the young ones) use reaction GIFs to respond to things people say. For example, if you text your friend about a disastrous decision you made, you might get, in response, a two-second loop of Ben Stiller sarcastically slow-clapping.

Music

This mini-app lists songs you've recently played on your phone. Tap one to send a text saying, "I'm listening to [name of song]." That's it.

Animoji (Face ID Phones)

The TrueDepth camera (page 58) can create what Apple calls Animoji: animated cartoon faces whose expressions follow and mimic *your* expressions in real time, tracking the motion of 50 different muscles in your face. Smile, frown, wink, laugh, nod, shake, open your mouth, raise your eyebrows, stick out your tongue, whatever—your little cartoon-animal avatar does the same. Suddenly, you're Warner Bros. It's crazy fun.

Once you've tapped the Animoji icon, you get a choice of 28 Animoji. Most are cute animals (bunny, piggy, panda, unicorn, and so on), but you also get an alien, a robot, and—of course—an animated poop pile.

(Any *Memoji* you've created appear on the top row, too; read on.)

Look at your phone and start talking, moving, or expressing, and marvel as your onscreen doppelgänger impersonates you like a mirror.

TIP: A much larger, full-screen canvas awaits if you swipe upward on the app area. The app now expands to fill your screen.

Here are a few more things you can try:

- **Send a picture.** When you've got a great expression on your critter's face, tap it to paste it into the Messages text box, ready to send as a picture.

- **Stamp a sticker.** You can also use your critter as a sticker, stamping it onto something somebody has already said in your chat. Hold your finger down on the Animoji until it shrinks and sticks to your finger. Then, without lifting your finger, drag the image upward onto the appropriate text bubble.

- **Send a video.** If you tap ⬤, you can create a video recording of your little cartoon (up to 30 seconds long), complete with sound—so don't forget to talk! When you then hit ⬆, the phone sends your recording as a standard video file. In other words, your recipients can play it even if they don't have an iPhone.

TIP: Once you've made a recording, you can tap a different Animoji or Memoji character in the scrolling list. Without having to rerecord, you can now see what the effect is of *that* character speaking.

Memoji (Face ID Phones)

Those koalas and lions may follow the movements of your face muscles with expert precision, but they're not you. They don't look like you. But there's another kind of animation that can look a *lot* like you: *Memoji*.

At the far left end of the Animoji app's row of critters, tap the New Memoji button. Now the app offers you a bald, generic baby head. That's you. Or it will be, once you scroll through the various screens—Skin, Hairstyle, Brows, Eyes, Head, Nose, Mouth, Ears, Facial Hair, Eyewear, and Headware. On each screen, tap the variation you think resembles you most (or the one you *wish* resembled you most).

Don't forget to scroll down on each screen. In iOS 13, Apple has greatly expanded the number of decorative options. Now you can dress yourself up with more skin colors, hair designs, facial hair, and makeup, plus hats, glasses, AirPods, hearing aid, earrings, piercings, and teeth adornments like braces, a gap, a gold tooth, a missing tooth, or a metal grille.

By the end of the setup, you've created a little Fisher-Price, bubble-nosed, baby-headed version of your actual appearance (below, right).

NOTE: Of course, it doesn't have to look like you at all. You're welcome to design an alter ego, some kind of anti-you. You can create as many Memoji as you want and use them however you want.

When you tap **Done**, your new Memoji appears at the left end of the other Animoji characters. It works exactly the same way—it just looks more like a person than a critter. (Slightly.)

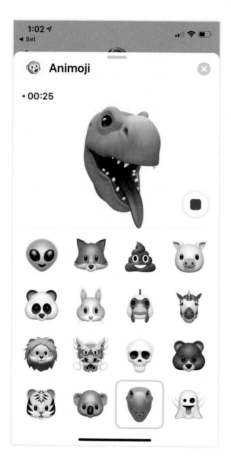
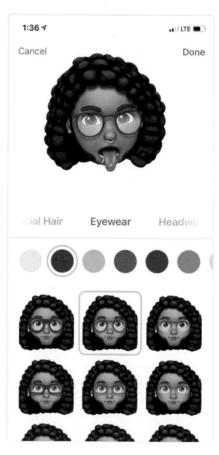

To edit or delete a Memoji, bring it to center in the Memoji picker and tap ●●●. You're offered options to **Edit**, **Duplicate**, or **Delete** it.

Digital Touch

This app opens a palette of crazy interactive art features, mostly inherited from the Apple Watch. Here's what all these controls do:

- **Color picker.** Tap to open a palette of seven colors, which will determine your "paint" color in the next step.

TIP: You're not limited to those seven colors. You can long-press one of the swatches to open a complete color wheel, from which you can dial up any shade you like. (Tap **Done** when done.)

- **Doodle with your finger.** Once you've got a color, you can start drawing. There's no eraser and no Undo, but it's fine for quick scrawls, comic exasperated faces, or technical blueprints.

  Tap ⬆ to send your sketch. What's cool is that if your recipient is an iMessages customer, she'll see the actual playback of your drawing, recreated before her eyes. (If you're corresponding with someone who doesn't have iOS 10 or later, she'll receive your doodle as a finished piece of artwork, without seeing its animated creation.)

- **Shoot a photo or video, and then deface it.** Tap ◼◀ to open a camera mode. (The app expands to full-screen height, if it wasn't already.) Here you'll find both a white "take a still" shutter button and a red "record a video" button. (The 🔄 button is here, too, in case you want to flip between the phone's front and back cameras.)

  You can draw on the photo after you've taken it; in fact, you can even draw on a video, or stamp a Digital Touch graphic onto it, *while* you're recording it. Your iMessages recipients will see the doodle "played back" on their screens, recreated line by line as you drew it. (Non-iMessages people simply receive the finished sketch superimposed on the video or photo.)

- **Send animated feelings.** There's not even a hint that you can create animated-feeling videos—you just have to know they're there.

  To generate one, you tap or press your fingers on the black canvas. You can generate any of these: a ring of fire (tap—as many times as you want); a flaming fireball (hold down your finger); a lip-kiss (do a two-finger tap); a red, beating heart (hold with two fingers); and an animated breaking heart (tap-and-hold/drag downward).

  No, the heart doesn't beat at the speed of your pulse, as it does on the Apple Watch; the iPhone doesn't have a heart-rate sensor.

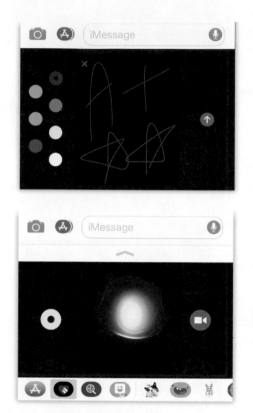

As you explore these Digital Touch options, you'll gradually become aware of how fluid and intermixable they are. You can draw or stamp fire/kiss/heart animations on top of a photo or video you're recording, for example. Or you can draw something—for example, a hand-sketched frame—and *then* take a photo or video that goes inside it.

As usual, fellow iMessages people will see all these glorious animations played back just as you made them—but non-Apple people receive only the finished image or video.

Sharing Your Headshot

Until this new iOS 13 feature came along, *you* didn't get to choose how you appeared to others in Messages. They picked whatever image they wanted, even if it was something you considered unflattering.

Now, the first time you message someone in iOS 13, the phone invites you to choose your own public avatar image. (Unless you've turned off Settings→Messages→Name and Photo Sharing.)

The phone walks you through the process of choosing a photo, an Animoji, Memoji, anything—and, if it's an Animoji or Memoji, making the funny face you want to represent you. (You can also do any of this later in Settings→Messages→Name and Photo Sharing.)

Along the way, you'll specify whether you want this new name/photo avatar to be offered automatically to anyone in your Contacts, or if you want to be asked on a person-by-person basis.

When it's all over, your chosen image (and name) now represent you not only in Messages and FaceTime, but also on information "cards" in Contacts.

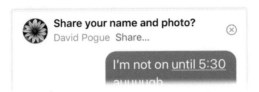

Of course, everything is optional on both ends. Your chat partner sees a message that "This person shared a new photo and name," along with an Update Contact button. (It offers the chance to update Name and Photo, Photo Only, or Name Only.)

If you later change your avatar, too bad; the ones you sent out earlier don't get updated on the other end.

Messages Prefs

You might not think something as simple as text messaging would involve a lot of fine print, but you'd be wrong.

Settings for Texts and iMessages

Tap Settings→Messages to find some intriguing options:

- **iMessage.** This is the on/off switch for the entire iMessages feature. It's hard to imagine why you would want to turn it off, but you know—whatever floats your boat.

- **Send & Receive.** Tap here to specify what cellphone numbers and email addresses you want to register with iMessages. (Your laptop, obviously, does not have a phone number, which is why iMessages gives you the option of using an email address.)

When people send iMessages to you, they can use any of the numbers or addresses you turn on here. That's the only time these numbers and addresses matter. *You* see the same messages exactly the same way on all your Apple gadgets, no matter what email address or phone number the sender used for you.

(If you scroll down on this Settings screen, you'll see the **Start new conversations from** options. This is where you specify which number or address others will see when you initiate the message. It really doesn't make much difference which one you choose.)

- **Share Name and Photo.** See the description on page 222.

- **Show Contact Photos.** If you turn this on, you'll see a little, round photo next to each texting correspondent in the chat list and at the top of a chat window—or the person's initials, if there's no photo available. If you turn this off, then you see the person's name at the top of Messages instead.

- **Text Message Forwarding.** This switch is the gateway to the cool Continuity feature described starting on page 591, in which you can use your Mac to send regular text messages to non-Apple phones.

- **Send Read Receipts.** When you turn this option on, your iMessage correspondents will know when you've seen their messages. The word "Read" will appear beneath each sent message that you've actually seen. Turn this off only if it deprives you of the excuse for not responding promptly ("Weird, I never even saw your message!").

> **TIP:** You can turn read receipts on or off independently for each chat partner; see page 202.

- **Send as SMS.** If iMessages is unavailable (meaning you have no internet connection at all), then your phone will send your message as a regular text message, via the regular cellphone voice network.

- **MMS Messaging.** MMS messages are like text messages—except they can also include audio clips, video clips, or photos, as already described. In the unlikely event that your cell company charges extra for these messages, you have an on/off switch here. If you turn it off, you can send only plain text messages.

- **Group Messaging.** Suppose you're sending a message to three friends. When they reply to your message, the responses will appear in a Messages thread dedicated to this particular group. It works only if *all* of you have turned on Group Messaging. (Note to the paranoid:

It also means everyone sees everyone else's phone numbers or email addresses.)

Messages tries to help you keep everybody straight by displaying their headshots (if you have them in Contacts), or their initials (if you don't).

- **Show Subject Field.** If email messages can have subject lines, why not text messages? Now, on certain newfangled phones (like yours), they can; the message arrives with a little dividing line between the subject and the body, offering your recipient a hint as to what it's about.

NOTE: It's OK to leave the subject line blank. But if you leave the *body* blank, the message won't send. (Incidentally, when you do fill in the subject line, what you're sending is an MMS message, rather than a plain old text message.)

- **Character Count.** If a text message (one sent to a non-Apple device) is longer than 160 characters, the iPhone breaks it up into multiple messages. That's convenient, sure. But if your cellphone plan permits only a fixed number of messages a month, you could wind up sending (and spending) more than you intended.

  The Character Count feature can help. When it's on, after your typing wraps to a second line, a little counter appears just above the Send button ("71/160," for example). It tracks how many characters remain within your 160-character limit for one message. (Of course, if you're sending an iMessage, you don't care how long it is.)

- **Blocked Contacts.** You can block people who are harassing or depressing you with their texts or calls. Tap here to view the list of people in your Contacts app you've decided to block; tap Add New to add new people to the list.

- **Keep Messages.** How long do you want your text messages to hang around on your phone? This is a question of privacy, of storage, and of your personality. In any case, here's where you get a choice of 30 Days, 1 Year, or Forever.

- **Filter Unknown Senders.** When you turn this on, the iPhone turns off notifications for senders not in your Contacts and sorts them into a separate list, which you can find in the "Unknown Senders" section of the Messages app.

- **Expire.** The iPhone ordinarily deletes audio and video messages a couple of minutes after they arrive, to avoid filling up your phone with old, no-longer-relevant audio and video files. The two Expire controls here let you turn off that automatic deletion (by choosing Never).

- **Raise to Listen.** Here's the on/off switch for the "raise to listen"/"raise to talk" features described starting on page 206, where the phone plays back audio messages, and sends your spoken replies, automatically when you hold it up to your head. You might want to turn that feature off if you discover the phone is playing back audio messages unexpectedly—or, worse, recording and sending them when you didn't mean to.

- **Low Quality Image Mode.** This feature is a gift to anyone who has to pay for cellular service. It automatically reduces the size (resolution) and quality (compression) of any photo you send to around 100 kilobytes. Sending *50* low-quality photos uses about the same amount of cellular data as *one* full-blown iPhone photo. Not only do you save a lot of money in the form of data, but you save a lot of time, too, because these photos are *fast* to send.

    And here's the best part: The photo looks exactly the same to the recipient at the other end (at least until she zooms in).

Apple has stashed a few additional text-messaging settings—the ones affecting how Messages gets your attention—in **Settings→ Notifications→Messages**.

7

Large Type, Accessibility & Voice Control

I f you were told the iPhone was one of the easiest phones in the world for a disabled person to use, you might spew your coffee. The thing has no physical keys! How would a blind person use it? It's a phone that rings! How would a deaf person use it?

But it's true. Apple has gone to *incredible* lengths to make the iPhone usable for people with vision, hearing, or other physical impairments. These features also can be fantastically useful to people whose only impairment is being under 10, over 40, or efficiency-crazed.

If you're deaf, you can have the LED flash get your attention. If you're blind, you can turn the screen off and operate everything by letting the phone speak what you're touching. It's pretty amazing.

You can also magnify the screen, reverse black for white (for better-contrast reading), set up custom vibrations for each person who might call you, and convert stereo music to mono (if you're deaf in one ear).

The kiosk mode is great for kids; it prevents them from exiting whatever app they're using. And if you have aging eyes, you might find the Large Text option handy. (You may also be interested in using the LED flash, custom vibrations, and zooming.)

And in iOS 13, Apple has introduced the astonishing Voice Control feature. It lets you do *everything* by voice, without touching any part of the phone: tap, swipe, drag, pinch, select text, correct errors, edit text, edit photos—everything.

To turn on any of the features described on these pages, open Settings→Accessibility.

And don't forget about Siri, described in Chapter 5. She may be the best friend a blind person's phone ever had. And, because you can *type* commands to her (page 181), she's also useful if you have trouble speaking.

TIP: You can turn many of the iPhone's accessibility features on and off with a triple-click of the home button or side button. See page 255 for details.

Voice Control

Voice Control, new in iOS 13, lets you operate the entire phone—every button, slider, app, physical control—by voice. It's absolutely amazing.

Apple's intention, of course, was to make life easier for people who can't use their hands and fingers to manipulate the iPhone. But when you see how fast, easy, and complete Voice Control is, you might decide it's worth adopting no matter what your physical abilities are.

(And yes, old-timer, your memory does serve you. There *was* once another iPhone feature called Voice Control, which debuted on the iPhone 4, before Siri came along. It let you speak to dial and speak to control music, but that was it. And *that* is not *this*.)

Voice Control comes turned off. To try it out, open **Settings→ Accessibility→Voice Control**. Turn it on (facing page, left). A tiny blue 🎤 appears on the status bar when the iPhone is listening.

You can immediately start to operate the phone by voice. Anything you say, Voice Control does with amazing speed.

The best part: When you're not talking to the phone, it's smart enough to ignore you. It executes commands only when you're *saying* commands. If you say, "Hey, buddy, could you toss me a napkin?" nothing happens (at least on the phone). If you say, "Open Photos," it opens Photos.

TIP: If you're still worried that the phone will accidentally interpret ordinary utterances as commands, scroll down on the Voice Control screen and turn on **Attention Aware**. Now Voice Control doesn't listen except when you're *looking* at the screen. (This is a feature of Face ID phones only.)

After each command, a tiny "hint" bubble appears at the top of the screen, confirming what Voice Control heard. And if you're fumbling or saying a command wrong, the same hint advises you about what you *could* be saying.

To see all the commands Voice Control understands, tap **Customize Commands**. You get a master list of command categories (facing page, middle); tap one to see the individual commands within (right).

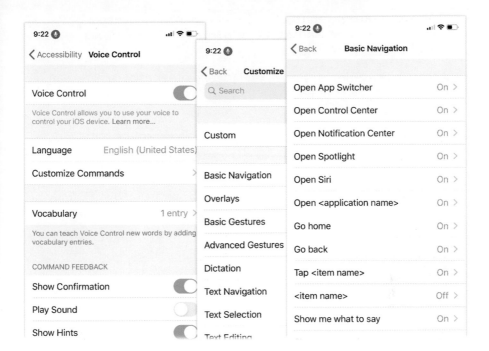

Here's a quick sampling of what you'll find there:

- **Tapping things.** "Tap Send." "Tap Reply." "Tap Done." "Long-press Mail." "Two-finger tap." "Two-finger swipe down" (or up, left, or right).

- **Opening things.** "Open Photos." "Open Facebook." "Go home." "Go back." "Open app switcher." "Open Control Center." "Open Notification Center." "Open Siri." "Open Spotlight" (that is, the search box at the Home screen).

- **Swiping and dragging.** "Scroll up" (or down, left, or right). "Swipe up" (or down, left, or right). "Swipe right three" (or whatever the number of items is—great for Photos). "Zoom in" (or out). "Increment brightness by two" (substitute whatever the name of the control is; you can say "increment" or "decrement"). "Rotate right" (or left). "Pan up" (or down, left, or right).

NOTE: Panning is usually the same thing as swiping, but not always. Panning shows up on the screen as a fingertip dot, as though you're performing the gesture manually.

"Repeat four times" is handy, too, especially when you've just used one of the Scroll or Zoom commands.

- **Hardware buttons.** "Turn volume up" (or down). "Mute sound" (or unmute). "Rotate to landscape" (or portrait). "Reboot device." "Lock screen." "Take screenshot."

- **Accessibility.** "Turn off VoiceOver" (or any other accessibility feature described in this chapter: Color Filters, Classic Invert Colors, Switch Control, Zoom, and so on).

- **Music and calling.** Voice Control still controls what its ancestor did: music and calls. The difference is that you no longer have to press any button when speaking!

  Examples: "Play artist 'Beatles' " (or album, song, or playlist). "Play music" (or pause). "Next track" (or previous). "Dial 'Mom' " (or FaceTime). "Dial Frank at the office."

- **Controlling Voice Control.** "Go to sleep" makes the iPhone stop listening for commands—except for the phrase "Wake up," which tells it to resume. "What can I say?" shows you a list of commands that will work right now.

Tapping Unlabeled Spots

This all works fast and beautifully. But not everything on the iPhone screen has a neat little textual label that you can refer to, as in "Tap Send." How are you supposed to tap some unlabeled tool in, say, Photos?

You can use one of two techniques:

- **"Show numbers."** Instantly, tiny number tags appear on every single tappable item on the screen (facing page, left). You don't need to know or care what their official names are. You can now just say "seven" to tap whatever is identified by the 7 tag.

- **"Show names."** Behind the scenes, iOS *does* have a name for everything on the screen. To see those internal labels, say, "Show names." Not only does everything appear with a labeled tag, but this is your chance to *learn* what things are called, so you won't need the labels next time (facing page, right).

And what if there are no identifiable graphic objects that are taggable? What if you're trying to edit a spot on a photo or tap a spot in Maps? Voice Control has you covered here, too.

When you say, "Show grid," the screen is overlaid with a grid of numbered squares; say the number of the one you'd like to tap. Or, if you anticipate that it will take a few consecutive attempts to home in on the spot you want, say, "Show grid continuously." Now when you speak a grid square's number, that square subdivides into an even smaller grid, giving you even more precision.

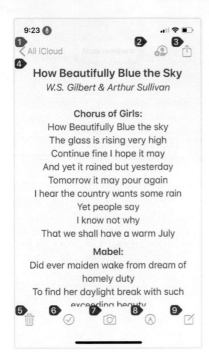 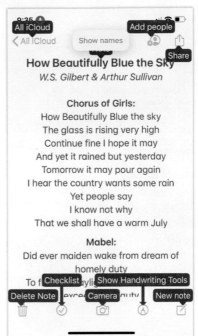

You can even specify the dimensions of the grid: "Show grid with three by five."

Editing Text

We all know the iPhone's dictation feature isn't perfect; you often have to manually correct some words you've dictated before you send that text or email.

No longer! Using Voice Control, you can perform stunts like these:

- **Deleting.** Say "Delete that" to backspace over the last word or utterance.

  You can say "Delete" in increments, too: "Delete previous two lines." (Or just "Delete 'stuck a feather in his cap.' ")

- **Moving the insertion point.** Say exactly where you want to move, using what you've already typed as a reference point: "Move after 'called it macaroni.' "

  You can also say, "Move to end" (or beginning) of whatever you've been writing—a text, for example.

  Or say, "Move to end of word" (or sentence, paragraph, line, or selection). Or "Move forward three characters" (or back—or words, lines, sentences, or paragraphs).

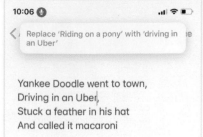

- **Selecting text.** "Select all." "Select 'Yankee Doodle Dandy.' " "Select next word" (or previous—or character, sentence, line, or paragraph). Or specify how many: "Select next four words," for example. And then you can do, "Extend selection back three words." And if you change your mind: "Deselect that."

  Once you've selected some text, you can say things like "Cut that," "Copy that," "Capitalize that" (or lowercase), "Bold that" (or italicize, or underline). Or say the words you want formatted: "Capitalize 'yankee doodle.' "

- **Editing text.** "Replace 'Riding on a pony' with 'Driving in an Uber.' "

  This feature, right there, is worth the upgrade to iOS 13. No more trying to move the tiny insertion point to a new tiny spot in the tiny paragraph with your huge fat finger; just say what you want to fix, and then say what you want it fixed with!

  If the mistake *just* happened, you can say, "Correct that" or "Correct 'went to town.' "

  You'll also get a lot of mileage out of "Delete that" (whatever you just said) or "Undo that."

TIP: Voice Control also makes it easy to teach your phone to recognize weird slang, names, or jargon when you're dictating. Just add them in advance to **Settings→Accessibility→Voice Control→ Vocabulary**.

Clearly, mastering Voice Control takes a little time. But you don't have to master it! Just learn a few commands. Even if all you ever use is the "Replace ___ with ___" command for editing texts before you send them, you'll save some frustration 30 times a day.

TIP: If you find yourself turning Voice Control on and off frequently, consider defining a triple-click of the side button or home button to be its on/off switch; see page 255.

VoiceOver

VoiceOver is a *screen reader*—software that makes the iPhone speak everything you touch. It's a fairly important feature if you're blind.

On the VoiceOver settings pane (**Settings→Accessibility**), tap the on/off switch to turn VoiceOver on. Because VoiceOver radically changes the way you control your phone, you get a warning to confirm that you know what you're doing. If you proceed, you hear a female voice begin reading the names of the controls she sees on the screen. You can adjust the **Speaking Rate** of the synthesized voice (read on).

> **NOTE:** A message appears to let you know that vibrations will help you navigate. As you swipe up from the bottom edge, the first vibration means "Stop here to go to the Home screen"; the second means "Stop here to open the app switcher" (page 373).

There's a lot to learn in VoiceOver mode, and practice makes perfect, but here's the overview:

- **Touch something to hear it.** Tap icons, words, even status icons at the top; as you go, the voice tells you what you're tapping. "Messages." "Calendar." "Mail—14 new items." "45 percent battery power." You can tap the dots on the Home screen, and you'll hear, "Page 3 of 9."

  Once you've tapped a screen element, you can also flick your finger left or right—anywhere on the screen—to "walk" through everything on the screen, left to right, top to bottom.

> **TIP:** A thin black rectangle appears around whatever the voice is identifying. That's for the benefit of sighted people who might be helping you.

- **Double-tap something to "tap" it.** Ordinarily, you tap something on the screen to open it. But since single-tapping now means "Speak this," you need a new way to open everything. So: To open something you've just heard identified, double-tap *anywhere on the screen*. (You don't have to wait for the voice to finish talking.)

> **TIP:** Or do a *split tap*. Tap something to hear what it is—and with that finger still down, tap somewhere else with a different finger to open it.

There are all kinds of other special gestures in VoiceOver. Make the voice stop speaking with a *two-finger tap*; read everything, in sequence, from the top of the screen with a *two-finger upward flick*; scroll one page at a time with a *three-finger flick up or down*; go to the next or previous screen (Home, Stocks, and so on) with a *three-finger flick left or right*; and more.

Or try turning on Screen Curtain with a *three-finger triple-tap*; it blacks out the screen, giving you visual privacy as well as a heck of a battery boost. (Repeat to turn the screen back on.)

TIP: VoiceOver is especially great at reading your Books titles out loud. Details are on page 400.

For more on VoiceOver, especially on customizing its behavior, see the free PDF appendix to this chapter, "More on VoiceOver," on this book's "Missing CD" at *missingmanuals.com*.

Zooming

Compared with a computer, an iPhone's screen is pretty tiny. Every now and then, you might need a little help reading small text or inspecting those tiny graphics.

The Zoom command is just the ticket; it lets you magnify the screen whenever it's convenient, up to 500 percent. Of course, at that point, the screen image is too big to fit the physical glass of the iPhone, so you need a way to scroll around.

To begin, you have to turn on the master Zoom switch in **Settings→Accessibility**. Immediately, the magnifying lens appears.

Scroll down and look at the **Zoom Region** control. If it's set to **Window Zoom**, then zooming produces a movable rectangular magnifying lens. If it's set to **Full Screen Zoom**, then zooming magnifies the entire screen.

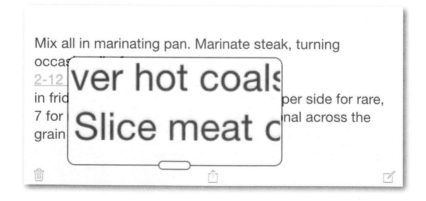

(And that, as many Apple Genius Bar employees can tell you, freaks out a lot of people who don't know what's happened.)

Now then. Next time you need to magnify things, do this:

- **Start zooming** by double-tapping the screen with three fingers. You've either opened up the magnifying lens or magnified the entire screen 200 percent. (Another method: Triple-press the home button—or side button on the Face ID phones—and tap **Zoom**.)

> **TIP:** You can move the rectangular lens around the screen by dragging the white oval handle on its lower edge.

- **Pan around inside the lens (or pan the entire virtual jumbo screen)** by dragging with three fingers.

- **Open the Zoom menu** by tapping the white handle on the magnifying lens. Up pops a black menu of choices like **Zoom Out** (puts away the lens and stops zooming), **Choose Region** (lets you switch between a full-screen zoom and the lens view), **Resize Lens** (adds handles so you can change the lens's shape), **Choose Filter** (lets you make the area inside the lens grayscale or inverted colors, to help people with poor vision), and **Show Controller** (gives you the little joystick described in a moment). There's also a slider that controls the degree of magnification—handy.

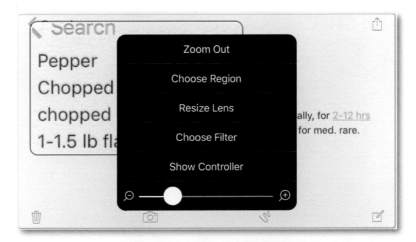

- **Zoom in more or less** by double-tap/dragging with three fingers. It's like double-tapping, except that you leave your fingers down on the second tap—and drag them upward to zoom in more (up to 500 percent) or down to zoom out again.

You can lift two of your three fingers after the dragging has begun. That way, it's easier to see what you're doing.

That's the big-picture description of Zoom. But back in Settings→ Accessibility→Zoom, a few more controls await:

- **Follow Focus.** When this option is turned on, the image inside the magnifying lens scrolls automatically when you're entering text. Your point of typing is always centered.

- **Smart Typing.** When this option is turned on, a couple of things happen whenever the onscreen keyboard appears. First, you get full-screen zooming (instead of just the magnifying lens); second, the keyboard itself isn't magnified, so you can see all the keys.

- **Keyboard Shortcuts** make it easier to control Zoom—if you've connected a full-size Bluetooth keyboard to your iPhone (page 98).

- **Zoom Controller** is this weird little onscreen joystick:

You use it to slide the magnifying lens, or the entire magnified screen, in any direction. The farther your finger moves from center dot, the faster the scrolling. It's an alternative to having to drag the magnified screen with three fingers, which isn't precise and also blocks your view.

You can tap the center dot of the Controller to open the Zoom menu described already. Or double-tap the center to stop or start zooming.

TIP: Long-press the controller for a pop-up magnifying lens. It remains open only as long as you're pressing.

- **Zoom Region** controls whether you're zooming the entire screen or just a window (that is, a magnifying lens).

- **Zoom Filter** gives you options for how you want the text in the zoom window to appear—for example, black on gray for viewing in low light.

- **Maximum Zoom Level.** This slider controls just how magnified that lens, or screen, can get.

NOTE: When VoiceOver is turned on, three-finger tapping has its own meaning—"Jump to top of screen." Originally, therefore, you couldn't use Zoom while VoiceOver was on.

You can these days, but you have to add an *extra* finger or tap for VoiceOver gestures. For example, ordinarily, double-tapping with three fingers makes VoiceOver stop talking, but since that's the "Zoom in" gesture, you must now *triple*-tap with three fingers to mute VoiceOver.

And what about VoiceOver's existing triple/three gesture, which turns the screen off? If Zoom is turned on, you must now triple-tap with *four* fingers to turn the screen off.

Magnifier

Oh man, this is great: You can triple-click the home button to turn the iPhone into the world's best electronic magnifying glass (on Face ID phones, you triple-click the side button). It's perfect for reading menus in dim restaurants, tiny type on pill bottles, and theater programs.

Once you've summoned the Magnifier, you can zoom in, turn on the flashlight, or tweak the contrast.

To set this up, open **Settings→Accessibility→Magnifier**. Turn on **Magnifier**. Turn on **Auto-Adjust Exposure**, too, for a better image.

Then, next time you need a magnifying glass, triple-click the home (or side) button. Instantly, the top part of the screen becomes a zoomed-in view of whatever is in front of the camera.

At this point, you gain a wealth of options for making that image even clearer (next page, left):

- **Zoom slider.** Adjusts the degree of magnification.

- **⚡.** Turns on the flashlight, to illuminate the subject.

or lower depending on your calorie n

Calories: 2,000

Total Fat	Less than	65g
Sat Fat	Less than	20g
Cholesterol	Less than	300mg
Sodium	Less than	2,400mg
Potassium		3,500mg
Total Carbohydrate		300g
Dietary Fiber		25g

NGREDIENTS: CASHEWS, CANO
EANUT AND/OR COTTONSEED OIL, S

ONTAINS: TREE NUTS (CASHEWS).

RODUCED IN A FACILITY THAT ALSO PROCE
HEAT, MILK, SOY AND OTHER TREE NUTS (A

at Fat	Less than	20g	25g
olesterol	Less than	300mg	300m
dium	Less than	2,400mg	2,400
assium		3,500mg	3,500
al Carbohydrate		300g	375g
ietary Fiber		25g	30g

REDIENTS: CASHEWS, CANOLA AND
NUT AND/OR COTTONSEED OIL, SEA SAL

TAINS: TREE NUTS (CASHEWS).

UCED IN A FACILITY THAT ALSO PROCESSES PE
T, MILK, SOY AND OTHER TREE NUTS (ALMONDS,
S, COCONUT, HAZELNUTS, MACADAMIA NUTS, P
CHIOS WALNUTS).

WHITE/BLUE   YELLOW/BLUE   GRAYSCALE

- 🔒. Locks the focus, so the phone quits trying to refocus as you move it around. (You can also tap the screen for this function.)

- ◎. Freezes the frame. That way, once you've finally focused on what you want to read, you can actually *read* it, without your hand jiggles ruining the view.

- ⊛. Opens the Filters screen.

The Filters screen offers even more tools for making things clear:

- **Filter.** Swipe horizontally across the screen (you don't have to aim for the little row of filter names) to cycle among the Magnifier's color filters: None, White/Blue, Yellow/Blue, Grayscale, Yellow/Black, Red/Black. Each may be helpful in a different circumstance to make your subject more legible (above, right).

- **☼ and ◑ sliders.** Adjust the brightness and contrast of the image.

- **⇄.** Swaps the two filter colors (black for white, blue for yellow, and so on).

To exit the Filters screen, tap ⊛ again; to exit the Magnifier, press the home button (or, on Face ID phones, swipe up from the bottom of the screen).

Display & Text Size

These options—found in **Settings**→**Accessibility**→**Display & Text Size**—affect the text size and boldness of all your apps, and the color schemes of the entire screen, in hopes of making it easier for you to see.

- **Bold Text.** The iOS system font is fairly light. Its strokes are very thin. But if you turn on **Bold Text**, the fonts everywhere are heavier: at the Home screen, in email, in every app. And much easier to read in low light or with aging eyesight.

  It's one of the most useful features in iOS—and something almost nobody knows about.

- **Larger Text.** This option is a game-changer if you, a person with several decades of life experience, often find type on the screen too small.

  Using the slider, you can choose a larger type size for all text the phone displays in apps like Mail, Books, Messages, and so on. (Turn on **Larger Accessibility Sizes** to make the slider reach *really* big sizes.)

  This slider doesn't affect all the world's *other* apps—at least until their software companies update them to be Dynamic Type–compatible. That day, when it comes, will be glorious. One slider to scale them all.

- **Button Shapes.** Among the criticisms of iOS's design: You can't tell what's a *button* anymore! Everything is just words floating on the screen, without border rectangles to tell you what's tappable!

  Well, despite the name of this setting, the button shapes of old are gone in iOS 13. But you can still spot the tappable buttons because

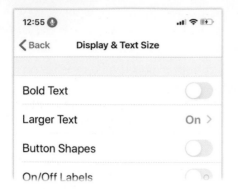
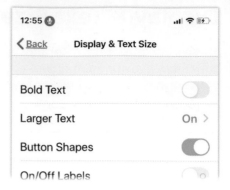

their text appears in blue type (above, left). And if *that's* not enough for you, iOS can also underline that blue text to emphasize its tappability (above, right). Just switch on **Button Shapes**.

- **On/Off Labels.** The Settings app teems with little tappable on/off switches, including this one. When something is turned on, the background of the switch is green; when it's off, the background is white. But if you're having trouble remembering that distinction, then turn on this option. Now the background of each switch sprouts a symbol to help you remember that green means On (you'll see a | marking) and white (o marking) means Off.

- **Reduce Transparency** adds opacity to screens like the Dock and the Notification Center. Their backgrounds become solid, rather than slightly see-through, so that text on them is much easier to read. You can see the before and after below.

- **Increase Contrast** makes type in some spots a little darker and heavier. You notice it in the fonts for buttons, in the Calendar, and in Safari, for example.

- **Differentiate Without Color** is supposed to help color-blind people by adding shapes to certain controls that currently use only color. You'll have a hard time finding any examples of this feature working, though.

- **Smart Invert, Classic Invert.** By reversing the screen's colors like a film negative (black for white, red for green, blue for yellow), you create a higher-contrast effect that some people find is easier on the eyes.

  Classic Invert inverts every single pixel (below, center), which can create some bizarre-looking photos and videos. Smart Invert doesn't touch photos, videos, app icons, or dark backgrounds (below, right). It inverts only light-colored iOS screen elements, making them dark.

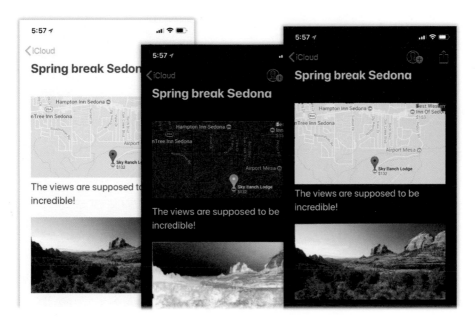

- **Color Filters.** The iPhone can help you if you're color-blind. The Color Filters option gives you screen modes that substitute colors you *can* see for colors you can't, everywhere on the screen. Tap the various color-blindness types in the list (Red/Green, Blue/Yellow, and so on) to see how each affects the crayons or color swatches at the top of the screen. Use the Intensity slider to govern the degree of the effect.

  The Color Tint option washes the entire screen with a certain shade (which you choose using the Hue slider that appears); it's designed to help people with Irlen syndrome (visual stress), who may have trouble reading. The Grayscale option removes all color from the screen. The Intensity slider lets you dial back (or dial up) the effect.

  The phone's colors may now look funny to *other* people, but you should have an easier time distinguishing colors when it counts. (You may even be able to pass some of those Ishihara dot-pattern color-blindness tests online.)

- **Reduce White Point** makes *all* colors *ever* depicted on the screen less intense—including the white of the background, which becomes a little yellowish. That might be nice if staring at your phone all day is causing you eyestrain.

- **Auto-Brightness** makes the screen brighten automatically when you're in bright light; in dim light, it darkens. That's because when you unlock the phone after waking it, it samples the ambient light and adjusts the brightness.

> **NOTE:** This works because of the ambient-light sensor near the earpiece. Apple says it experimented with having the light sensor active all the time, but it was weird to have the screen constantly dimming and brightening as you used it.

You can use this information to your advantage. By covering the sensor as you unlock the phone, you force it into a low-power, dim-screen setting (because the phone believes it's in a dark room). Or by holding it up to a light as you wake it, you get more brightness. In either case, you've saved the navigation it would have taken you to find the manual brightness slider in Settings or in the Control Center.

> **TIP:** You can set things up so that a triple-click of the home button (or the side button) instantly dims your screen, for use in the bedroom, movie theaters, or planetariums—without having to fuss with settings or sliders. See page 257 for this awesome trick.

Motion

Not everybody is a fan of all the animated special effects in iOS. If you're one of them, try these remedies:

- **Reduce Motion.** What kind of killjoy would want to turn off the subtle "parallax motion" of the Home screen background behind your icons, or the zooming-in animation when you open an app? In any case, you can if you want, thanks to this button.

- **Auto-Play Message Effects.** Remember those full-screen animations people can send you in Messages to celebrate big moments—fireworks, confetti, and so on? Here, you, the recipient, can turn them off.

- **Auto-Play Video Previews.** Here and there—Safari, App Store, iTunes Store—Apple apps include thumbnails of videos that play automatically. Turn this off to turn that off.

Spoken Content

Your phone can read to you aloud: an email message, a web page, a text message—anything. Open **Settings**→**Accessibility**→**Spoken Content**. Your choices here go like this:

- **Speak Selection** puts a **Speak** command into the button bar that appears whenever you highlight text in any app. Tap that button to make the phone read the selected text.

- **Speak Screen** reads everything on the screen, top to bottom, when you swipe down from the top of the screen with two fingers. Great for listening to an ebook page or having your email read to you.

- **Highlight Content.** Great for dyslexic or beginning readers. If you turn this on, then the phone underlines or uses a highlight color on each word or sentence as it's spoken, depending on your settings here.

- **Typing Feedback.** The phone can speak each **Character** as you type it ("T," "O," "P," and so on), with or without **Character Hints** ("T—Tango," "O—Oscar," "P—Papa"). Here you can also specify how much delay elapses before the spoken feedback plays; whether you want finished words and autocorrect suggestions spoken, too; and whether you want to hear QuickType suggestions (page 87) pronounced when you hold your finger down on them.

  This feature, of course, helps blind people know what they're typing. But it also lets sighted people type without taking their eyes off the keyboard, which is great for speed and concentration. And if you're zoomed in, you may not be able to see the suggested word appear under your typed text—but now you'll still know what the suggestion is.

- **Voices** gives you a choice of languages and accents for the spoken voice. Try Australian; it's really cute.

- **Speaking Rate** controls how fast the voice talks.

- **Pronunciations.** You can correct the phone's pronunciation of words it always gets wrong. Type the word into the Phrase box; tap 🎤 and speak how it *should* be pronounced; and then, from the list of weird phonetic symbol-written alternatives, tap the one that sounds correct. This technique corrects how your phone pronounces those words or names whenever it speaks, including Siri and the text-to-speech feature described on page 104.

Audio Descriptions

This option is for internet movies that come, or may someday come, with a narration track that describes the action for the blind. It's the on/off switch for playing that track.

Touch

Gotta admit: Using a phone that's all touchscreen might be a challenge if you have trouble touching things! For most people, Voice Control (page 228) is a superbly designed, powerful solution—but the features on the Touch page of the Accessibility settings were Apple's earlier attempt to help.

AssistiveTouch

When you turn AssistiveTouch on, you get a new, glowing white circle in a corner of the screen (below, top).

You can drag this magic white ball anywhere on the screen. (When you're not using it, it fades away almost to transparency—whatever amount you've dialed up using the Idle Opacity slider.)

When you tap it, it expands into the special palette shown below at left. It's offering six ways to trigger motions and gestures on the screen

without requiring hand or multiple-finger movement. All you have to be able to do is tap with a single finger—or even a stylus held in your teeth or toes.

You can add more buttons to this main menu, or switch around which buttons appear here. To do that, open Settings→Accessibility→ AssistiveTouch→Customize Top Level Menu.

Meanwhile, here are the starter icons:

- **Notifications, Control Center.** These buttons give you another way to open the Notifications pane and Control Center—one that doesn't require any hand movement. (Tap the same button again to *close* whichever center you opened.)

- **Siri.** Touch here when you want to speak to Siri, hands free. ("Hey Siri" works, too.)

- **Home.** You can tap here to get to your Home screen, instead of swiping or pressing the home button. (That's also handy if your home button gets sticky.)

- **Device.** Tap to open five functions that would otherwise require you to grasp the phone or push its physical buttons (facing page, right). There's **Lock Screen** (instead of pressing the side button), **Volume Up** and **Volume Down** (instead of pressing the volume keys), **Rotate Screen**, and **Mute/Unmute** (instead of flipping the silencer switch).

  If you tap **More**, you get some bonus buttons. They include **Shake** (does the same thing as shaking the phone to undo typing), **Screenshot** (page 357), **Multitasking** (brings up the app switcher, as described on page 373), **Apple Pay** (instead of using the home or side button), **Restart**, **SOS** (page 79), and **Gestures**.

  That **Gestures** button opens up a peculiar palette that depicts a hand holding up two, three, four, or five fingers. When you tap, for example, the three-finger icon, you get three blue circles on the screen. They move together. Drag one of them (with a stylus, for example), and the phone behaves as if you're dragging three fingers on its surface. Using this technique, you can operate apps that require multiple fingers dragging on the screen.

- **Custom.** Impressively enough, you can actually define your own gestures. On the AssistiveTouch screen, tap one of the + buttons, and then tap **Create New Gesture** to draw your own gesture right on the screen, using one, two, three, four, or five fingers.

  For example, suppose you're frustrated in Maps because you can't do the two-finger double-tap that means "Zoom out." On the Create

New Gesture screen, get somebody to do the two-finger double-tap for you. Tap **Save** and give the gesture a name—"2 double tap," say.

From now on, "2 double tap" shows up on the Custom screen, ready to trigger with a single tap by a single finger or stylus.

- **Custom Actions.** In iOS 13, you're allowed to assign functions to the floating AssistiveTouch white dot as though it were a button—without ever opening the button palette. One function fires when you tap it; another when you double-tap; a third when you long-press; a fourth when you hard-press (on 3D Touch phones). Tap the appropriate rows to program these functions. Maybe you want a double-tap to open the Control Center, a long-press to mute the phone, and so on.

 TIP: Apple starts you off with some useful predefined Custom Actions, each of which might be difficult for some people to trigger in the usual ways. There's **Single-Tap**, **Double-Tap**, **Long Press**, and **3D Touch**, for example. You can install any of these on the AssistiveTouch palette for quick access.

Pointer Devices

In iOS 13, you can, believe it or not, use a Bluetooth wireless mouse, trackpad, or full-sized keyboard with your iPhone.

Now, don't get all excited. It's not like you'll wind up with a full-blown laptop.

To get started, put your Bluetooth mouse or keyboard in pairing mode. On the phone, open **Settings→Accessibility→Touch→AssistiveTouch→ Devices→Bluetooth Devices**. Tap the name of the mouse or keyboard once it appears.

Once the mouse is paired, tap its name to open a screen where you can customize its buttons. **Single-Tap** is best for the left button; you can map the right button to, for example, **Open Menu** (meaning the AssistiveTouch white dot).

Your "cursor" is a fat circle, simulating your fingertip. You can drag and click as you'd expect, but you can't right-click for a shortcut menu; on a trackpad, you can't two-finger drag to scroll. Apple doesn't intend for this to be a mainstream setup. It's for people who can't use the phone any other way.

On the AssistiveTouch settings page, you can use **Pointer Style** to change the cursor's color, size, and speed of vanishing when you're not moving it. Turn off **Always Show Menu** if you'd prefer the AssistiveTouch white dot to hide itself when not in use (which is probably what you want if you've assigned the right mouse button to making it appear). Here, too, you can adjust the **Tracking Speed**.

If you've attached a keyboard, turn off **Show Onscreen Keyboard** so the onscreen keyboard never appears; why would you want it to take up screen space when you have an actual keyboard? Finally, **Mouse Keys** lets you use the keyboard's number pad (the keys surrounding the 5) to move the cursor; that may be useful if you have very limited motor skills. (Tap the Option key five times to turn this mode on and off.)

 TIP: If you have trouble clicking a mouse, you can use Dwell Control to do your clicking for you. Once you've turned on **Dwell Control** on the AssistiveTouch screen, you can point to something on the screen, without moving, and just wait; after two seconds (or whatever interval you set here), iOS performs the tap for you. Adjust what counts as "not moving" using the **Tolerance** slider.

Reachability

Starting with the iPhone 6, the standard iPhone got bigger—and the Plus, and Max models are even biggerer. Their screens are so big, in fact, that your dinky human thumb may be too short to reach the top portion of the screen (if you're gripping the phone near the bottom).

For that reason, Apple has built a feature called *Reachability* into these recent models. Turn it on or off in **Settings→Accessibility→Touch→ Reachability**. Then, whenever you want to reach something distant:

- **Face ID phones.** Tug downward at the bottom edge of the screen—for example, on the home indicator bar.

- **Home-button phones.** Touch the home button twice (don't click it— just touch it).

In each case, the entire screen image slides halfway down the glass so you can reach the upper parts of it with your thumb!

As soon as you touch anything on the screen—a link, a button, an empty area, anything—the screen snaps back to its usual, full-height position.

3D and Haptic Touch

Apple has mostly killed off the 3D Touch option (page 35). But on this screen, you can tweak what's left of it.

In **Settings→Accessibility→Touch**, you can turn the feature off, adjust the threshold of pressure (**Light**, **Medium**, **Firm**) required to trigger a "3D touch," and specify how quickly the shortcut menu pops open. (Apple even gives you a sample photo thumbnail to practice on, right on this screen, so you can gauge which degree of pressure you like best.)

Touch Accommodations

These options are intended to accommodate people who find it difficult to trigger precise taps on the touchscreen. **Touch Accommodations** is the master switch for all four of the following options:

- **Hold Duration** requires that you keep your finger on the screen for an amount of time that you specify (for example, one second—the seconds control appears when you turn **Hold Duration** on) before the iPhone registers a tap. That neatly eliminates accidental taps when your finger happens to bump the screen.

  When Hold Duration is on, a countdown cursor appears at your fingertip, showing with a circular graph how much longer you have to wait before your touch "counts."

- **Ignore Repeat** ignores multiple taps that the screen detects within a certain window—say, one second. If you have, for example, a tremor, this is a great way to screen out accidental repeated touches or repeated letter-presses on the onscreen keyboard.

- **Tap Assistance** lets you indicate whether the location of a tap should be the *first spot you touch* or the *last spot*. The **Use Final Touch Location** option means you can put your finger down in one spot and then fine-tune its position on the glass anytime within the countdown period indicated by the timer cursor. Feel free to adjust the timer window using the controls here.

  Once you turn Tap Assistance on, you can specify how quickly you have to lift your finger for its touch to register as a tap—and whether or not the same time limit applies to swipe gestures.

- **Swipe Gestures**, if you turn it on, means that you can swipe without having to wait for the Hold Duration.

Tap to Wake (Face ID phones)

The Face ID phones don't have a home button to press for waking them, so they offer a consolation prize: this option, which lets you tap *anywhere on the screen* to wake the phone.

Shake to Undo

In most of Apple's apps, you can undo your most recent typing or editing by giving the iPhone a quick shake. (You're always asked to confirm.) This is the on/off switch for that feature—handy if you find yourself triggering Undo accidentally.

Vibration

Here's a master off switch for all vibrations the phone makes. Alarms, notifications, confirmations—all of it. As Apple's lawyers cheerfully point out on this screen, turning off vibrations also means you won't get buzzy notifications of "earthquake, tsunami, and other emergency alerts."

Call Audio Routing

When a call comes in, where do you want it to go? To your headset? Directly to the speakerphone? Or the usual (headset unless there is no headset)? Here's where you make a choice that sticks, so you don't have to make it each time a call rings.

If you'd like to have the phone answer incoming calls automatically— when you're elbow-deep in garden mulch while wearing AirPods, for example—here's where you can turn on Auto-Answer Calls and tell the iPhone how long to wait before connecting.

Face ID & Attention

Phones with Face ID offer bonus features that have to do with your attention, which Apple defines as "looking at the phone"; see page 621.

Switch Control

Suppose your physical skills are limited to simple gestures: puffing on an air pipe, pressing a foot switch, blinking an eye, or turning your head, for example. A hardware accessory called a *switch* lets you operate certain gadgets this way.

When you turn on Switch Control on the Accessibility Screen, the phone sequentially highlights one object on the screen after another; you're supposed to puff, tap, or blink at the right moment to say, "Yes, *this* one."

If you don't have a physical switch apparatus, you can use the one nature gave you: your head. The iPhone's camera can detect when you turn your head left or right and can trigger various functions accordingly.

Switch Control is a broad (and specialized) feature. To read more about it, open the Accessibility chapter of Apple's iPhone User Guide: *help.apple.com/iphone*.

Side Button (or Home Button)

If you have motor-control problems of any kind, you might welcome this enhancement. It's an option to widen the time window for registering a double-press or triple-press of the home button (or, on the Face ID phones, the side button). If you choose **Slow** or **Slowest**, then the phone accepts double- and triple-presses spaced far and even farther apart, rather than interpreting them as individual presses a few seconds apart.

This is also a place where you can remove the triggering of **Siri** from the home button/side button's duties. If you choose **Off** here, then you can trigger Siri only by voice ("Hey Siri"). If you choose **Classic Voice Control**, then holding in the button lets you speak only the ancient, simple, 2010 music-control and phone-dialing commands.

If your phone has a home button, this screen lets you turn off the **Rest Finger to Open** feature (page 18).

Finally, **Use Passcode for Payments** means that, when buying something from Apple, you can type in your Apple Store password instead of double-clicking the side button—convenient if you find that double-clicking business difficult.

Apple TV Remote

So you have an Apple TV. You use the corresponding iPhone app as a remote control. And you find it hard to swipe to adjust, for example, the volume or the fast-forward functions. Turn on **Directional Buttons** to give you tappable arrow buttons instead.

Keyboards

These controls dictate what happens when you've hooked up a Bluetooth keyboard to your iPhone:

- **Key Repeat.** Ordinarily, holding down a key makes it repeat, so you can type things like "auuuugggggh!" or "zzzzzzzz." These two sliders govern how long you must hold down a key before it starts repeating (to prevent triggering repetitions accidentally), and how fast each key spits out characters once the spitting has begun.

- **Sticky Keys** lets you press multikey shortcuts (involving keys like Shift, Option, Control, and ⌘) one at a time instead of all together. (The **Sound** option ensures that you'll get an audio beep to confirm that the keyboard has understood.)

Toggle With Shift Key gives you the flexibility of turning Sticky Keys on and off at will. Whenever you want to turn on Sticky Keys, press the Shift key five times in succession. You'll hear a special clacking sound effect alerting you that you just turned on Sticky Keys. (Repeat the five presses to turn Sticky Keys off again.)

- With **Slow Keys** turned on, the phone doesn't register a key press at all until you've held down the key for more than a second or so—another feature designed to screen out accidental key presses.

- **Show Lowercase Keys** controls whether or not the onscreen keyboard's keys turn into CAPITALS when the Shift key is pressed; see page 84.

Hearing Devices

The next options in **Settings→Accessibility** are all dedicated to helping people with hearing loss. (Further details are at *apple.com/accessibility/ iphone/hearing*.)

Hearing aids with the "Made for iPhone" logo are designed to sound great without draining the battery. Better yet, you can triple-click the home button (or, on Face ID iPhones, the side button) to view the hearing aids' battery status, change the left and right volume, or switch to one of your audiologist's environmental presets—outdoors, restaurants, and so on. This page is where you pair the aids with the phone.

RTT/TTY

A TTY is a teletype or text telephone. It's a machine that lets deaf people make phone calls by typing instead of speaking. RTT (real-time text) is a newer, more reliable, more flexible service along the same lines.

iOS offers a built-in *software* TTY that requires no hardware to haul around. It resembles a chat app, and it works like this: When you place a phone call (using the standard Phone app), the iPhone gives you a choice of what kind of call you want to place:

- **Voice call.** Voice-to-voice, as usual.

- **TTY call.** You're calling another person who also has a TTY machine (or iOS 10 or later). You'll type back and forth.

- **TTY relay call.** This option means you can call a person who doesn't have a TTY setup. A human operator will speak (to the other guy) everything you type, and will type (to you) everything the other guy speaks. This, of course, requires a relay service, whose phone number you enter here on this Settings panel.

For more on using TTY on the iPhone, visit *support.apple.com/en-us/HT207033.*

Audio/Visual

On this page: handiness if you're hard of hearing.

- **Mono Audio.** If you're deaf in one ear, then listening to any music that's a stereo mix can be frustrating; you might be missing half the orchestration or the vocals. When you turn on Mono Audio, the iPhone mixes everything down to one monaural playback. Now you can hear the entire mix in one ear.

> **TIP:** This is also a great feature when you're sharing an earbud with a friend, or when one of your earbuds is broken, or when you're using only one AirPod.

- **Phone Noise Cancellation.** The iPhone's tiny, hidden microphones offer extremely good background-noise reduction when you're on a phone call. The microphones on the top and back, for example, listen to the wind, music, crowd noise, or other ambient sound and subtract that ambient noise from the sound going into the main phone mike.

  You can turn that feature off here—if, for example, you experience a "pressure" in your ear when it's operating.

- **Balance Slider.** The L/R slider lets you adjust the phone's stereo mix, in case one of your ears has better hearing than the other.

- **LED Flash for Alerts.** If you're deaf, you know when the phone is ring-ing—because it vibrates, of course. But what if it's sitting on the desk, or it's over there charging? This option lets you know when you're getting a call, text, or notification by blinking the flash on the back of the phone—the very bright LED light.

Subtitles & Captioning

These options govern internet videos that you play in the iPhone's TV app (primarily those from Apple's own iTunes Store).

- **Closed Captions + SDH.** The iPhone's TV app lets you tap the button to see a list of available subtitles and captions. Occasionally, a show also comes with specially written Subtitles for the Deaf and

Hard-of-Hearing (SDH). Turn this switch on if you want that 🗨 menu to show them whenever they're available.

- **Style** gives you control over the font, size, and background of those captions, complete with a preview. (Tap the ⬈ button to view the preview, and the sample caption, at full-screen size.) The **Custom** option even lets you dream up your own font, size, and color for the type; a new color and opacity of the caption background; and so on.

Guided Access (Kiosk Mode)

It's amazing how quickly even tiny tots can master the iPhone—and how easily they can muck things up with exploratory taps.

Guided Access solves that problem rather tidily. It's kiosk mode. That is, you can lock the phone into one app; the victim cannot switch out of it. You can even specify which *features* of that app are permitted. Never again will you find your Home screen icons rearranged or your text messages deleted.

Guided Access is also great for helping out people with motor-control difficulties—or tweens with self-control difficulties.

To turn on Guided Access, open **Settings**→**Accessibility**→**Guided Access**; turn the switch on. Now a **Passcode Settings** button appears. Here's where you protect Guided Access so the little scamp can't shut it off—at least not without a six-digit passcode (**Set Guided Access Passcode**) or your fingerprint or your face.

You can also set a time limit for your kid's Guided Access. Tap **Time Limit** to set up an alarm or a spoken warning when time is running out.

Finally, the moment of truth arrives: Your kid is screaming for your phone. Open whatever app you'll want to lock in place. Press the home or side button three times fast. The Guided Access screen appears (next page, left). At this point, you can proceed in any of three ways:

- **Declare some features off-limits.** With your finger, draw a circle around each button, slider, and control you want to deactivate. The phone converts your circle into a tidy rectangle; you can drag its corners to adjust its size, drag inside the rectangle to move it, or tap the ⊗ to remove it if you change your mind or want to start again.

  Once you enter Guided Access mode, the controls you've enclosed appear darkened (next page, right). They no longer respond—and your phone borrower can't get into trouble.

- **Change settings.** If you tap Options, you get additional controls. You can decide whether or not your little urchin is allowed to press the **Side Button** or the **Volume Buttons** when in Guided Access mode. If you want to hand the phone to your 3-year-old in the back seat to watch baby videos, you'll probably want to disable the touchscreen altogether (turn off **Touch**) and prevent the picture from rotating when the phone does (turn off **Motion**).

   Here, too, is the **Time Limit** switch. Turn it on to view hours/minutes dials. At the end of this time, it's no more fun for Junior.

- **Begin kiosk mode.** Tap Start.

Later, when you get the phone back, triple-press the side (or home) button again; enter your passcode or offer your fingerprint or face. At this point, you can tap Options to change them, Resume to go back into kiosk mode, or End to return to the iPhone as you know it.

Siri

You can *type* your questions and commands to Siri instead of speaking them, which can be a tremendous help if you have trouble speaking. (It's also a tremendous help if you're using Siri from the sidelines of a golf or chess tournament.) Here's the **Type to Siri** on/off switch; see page 181.

This is also where you control when Siri speaks to you with verbal responses: **Always**, **Control with Ring Switch** (in other words, she shuts up when you flip the side silencer switch), or **Hands-Free Only** (she speaks only when you use "Hey Siri" or have your phone connected to a car or headphones over Bluetooth).

Accessibility Shortcut

Burrowing all the way into **Settings→Accessibility** is quite a slog when all you want to do is turn some feature on or off. Therefore, Apple has

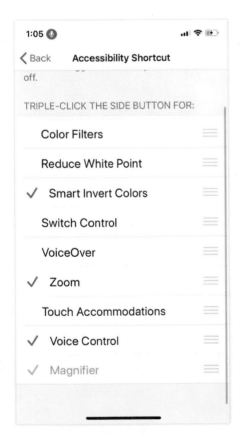 

blessed you with this handy shortcut: a fast triple-press of the side button (or the home button).

That action produces a little menu, in whatever app you're using, with options for the iPhone's various accessibility features (previous page, right). It's up to you, however, to indicate which ones you want on that menu in **Settings**→**Accessibility**→**Accessibility Shortcut** (previous page, left).

> **TIP:** If you've turned on Magnifier or Guided Access, as described earlier in this chapter, those two commands appear automatically in the Accessibility Shortcut menu. The only way to eliminate those commands from the Shortcut menu is to turn the features off entirely.

If you choose only one item here, then triple-pressing the home or side button doesn't produce the menu of choices. It just turns that one feature on or off.

Live Listen

Apple originally invented Live Listen for use with iPhone-compatible hearing aids. It's an ingenious feature that turns your iPhone into a remote microphone for your hearing aid.

In other words, if you're having trouble hearing across the restaurant table, you can hand your phone to whoever's talking—and now you hear them as though they were speaking directly into your ears. Or you can put your phone on the lectern at a lecture and hear the professor or speaker clearly from wherever you're sitting. Or put the phone by the TV, and now you can hear perfectly without having to crank the volume.

Apple eventually brought this feature to its wireless earbuds, the AirPods. Suddenly, Live Listen is available to a huge new audience—people who've spent $160 on AirPods, rather than $5,000 on a hearing aid.

To try it out, first add the Hearing button to your Control Center, as described on page 48. Now, when you're ready to Live Listen, put on your AirPods. (Putting them on ensures that they're awake and wirelessly connected to your phone.)

Then, on the phone, open the Control Center and tap **Hearing**. The Live Listen button is staring you in the face, but it's off. Tap it to turn on your "remote microphone"—the one on your iPhone. Place the phone where it will pick up the sound you want to hear, move to your seat (it can be more than 100 feet away), and marvel at the miracle of modern technology.

The Instant Screen-Dimming Trick

The Accessibility settings offer one of the greatest shortcuts of all time: the ability to dim your screen, instantly, with a triple-click. No Control Center, no Settings, no slider. It's a gift to people who go to movies, plays, or anywhere else where full-screen brightness isn't appropriate.

It's a bunch of steps to set up, but once that's done, the magic is yours whenever you want it.

1. **Open Settings→Accessibility. Turn on Zoom.**

   If the magnifying lens appears, tap the white handle at the bottom of it; in the shortcut menu, tap Zoom Out.

   Now the magnifying lens is gone.

2. **Scroll down to Zoom Region and set it to Full Screen Zoom. Tap Zoom (in the upper left) to return to the previous panel.**

3. **Tap Zoom Filter; tap Low Light. Tap Zoom (in the upper left) to return to the previous panel.**

   You've just set up the phone to dim the screen whenever zooming is turned on. Now all you have to do is teach the phone to enable zooming whenever you triple-click the home button (or side button).

4. **In the top-left corner, tap Accessibility.**

   You return to the main Accessibility screen. Scroll to the very bottom.

5. **Tap Accessibility Shortcut; make sure Zoom is the only selected item.**

   As noted in the previous Tip, this step may involve turning off Magnifier and Guided Access in Settings→Accessibility.

At this point, you can go back to the Home screen.

From now on, whenever you triple-click the home or side button, you turn on a gray filter that cuts the brightness of the screen by 30 percent. (Feel free to fine-tune the dimness of your new Insta-Dim setting at that point, using the Control Center; see page 42.) It doesn't save you any battery power, since the screen doesn't think it's putting out any less light. But it does give you instant darkening when you need it in a hurry—

like when a potentially important text comes in while you're in the movie theater.

(A "Zoom Enabled" or "Zoom Disabled" message appears briefly, but that's OK. The screen-dimming feature thinks it's part of the Zoom feature.)

Triple-click again to restore the original brightness, and be glad.

PART TWO

Pix, Flix & Apps

8

Music & Videos

No wonder Apple has almost completely given up making iPods; the iPhone's talents as a music and video player have supplanted it. Music gets impressive battery life (40 to 80 hours of playback, depending on the model), and there's enough room on your phone to store thousands of songs.

In the Music app, five tabs greet you across the bottom: Library, For You, Browse, Radio, and Search.

Some of the app's features are useful only if you've subscribed to Apple Music, Apple's $10-a-month music service—but not all of them. The internet radio stations, for example, mean you'll never run out of music to listen to—and you'll never pay a penny for it.

> **NOTE:** If you're not interested in paying for an Apple Music subscription, you can *hide* the two tabs you'll never use (**For You** and **Browse**). To do that, open **Settings→Music** and turn off **Show Apple Music** (page 264, top right).
>
> The **For You** and **Browse** tabs disappear.
>
> The bottom line: Your Music app might show you either of two different sets of tabs. Complicated? Yes. But this chapter is written as though you *haven't* hidden the Apple Music tabs.

This chapter also covers two other important audiovisual apps: the iTunes Store and TV.

Apple Music

The Apple Music service, which debuted in 2015, is a rich stew of components. For $10 a month (or $15 for a family of six), you get all the features described in this section.

- **Unlimited streaming music.** You can listen to any band, album, or song in the Apple Music library of 50 million songs—on demand, no ads. It's not like listening to a radio station, where someone else is programming the music; *you* program the music.

  On the other hand, this is not like Apple's traditional music store, where you pay $1 per download and then you *own* the song. If you ever stop paying, the music stops. You're left with nothing.

  If you do subscribe, you can tell Siri things like, "Play the top songs of 2010" or "Play some good running music" or "Play some Taylor Swift."

  But you're not obligated to do all your music programming manually. Apple Music comes equipped with ready-made playlists, prepared by human editors, in all kinds of categories. There are sets of starter songs by various singers ("Intro to Sarah McLachlan"), playlists by genre and era, and playlists for specific activities like Waking Up, Running, Getting It On, and even Breaking Up.

  You can freely mix the songs you're renting with the music you already own. You can even download songs for playback when you have no internet connection (as long as you're still paying your $10 a month).

- **Beats 1 radio.** Apple runs a "global, 24-hour internet radio station" called Beats 1. (It actually broadcasts live for 12 hours a day and then repeats.) Listening is free, even to nonsubscribers.

  Live DJs introduce songs and comment on the singers, just as on regular radio stations. Of course, you have no input on the style of music you hear on Beats 1, and you can't pause, rewind, fast-forward, or save anything you hear for later listening. It's old-style radio, offering the magic of serendipity.

- **iTunes Match.** iTunes Match, which dates back to 2011, is a cloud-based version of your iTunes library, available to any of your Apple devices. For $25 a year, you can stream Apple's copies of any song files you actually own—ripped from CDs or even acquired illegally. The advantages: First, you save a lot of space on your phone. Second, you can play them on any Apple gadget you own. Third, the versions Apple plays are often of higher quality than your originals.

iTunes Match continues as a separate service for non–Apple Music subscribers (the song limit is now 100,000 songs). But if you do subscribe to Apple Music, then in effect you get iTunes Match automatically.

- **iCloud Music Library.** This is a newer service, also part of Apple Music—a descendant of iTunes Match. This feature, too, matches all the songs on your phone with songs Apple has online, so you can play any of them on an Apple machine anywhere (once you've signed in). And if you have some songs Apple doesn't have, you can upload them to Apple and thereby add them to your locker.

NOTE: Apple's matching algorithms aren't flawless; sometimes they don't recognize and match a song that you and Apple both, in fact, have.

Another note: When you turn on iCloud Music Library, you're offered the opportunity to delete all the music on your phone and replace it with what's in your online locker. *Back up your phone's music before you do this* (page 564). There are occasional stories of people losing their entire music collections.

Library Tab

Here's all the music you've chosen yourself.

In the old days, this meant "music files actually on your phone." If you have an Apple Music membership, though, you'll also see *online* songs listed here that you've added to your personal catalog.

You can view them grouped in any of the lists you see here: **Playlists, Artists, Albums, Songs,** or (if you subscribe to Apple Music) **Downloaded Music.** Below all that, in the Recently Added section, you get thumbnails for albums and playlists you've recently downloaded or built.

TIP: There are other categories you could be seeing here, too, like Genres, Compilations, Composers, TV & Movies, and Music Videos. To add them to the list of headings—or to remove some of the ones that start out there—tap **Edit** next to the bold Library heading.

As you could probably guess, you operate the Music app by drilling down—by tapping from category to album to song or whatever. (Tap the top-left corner of the screen to backtrack.)

(As shown here, you may have either five or three tabs at the bottom, depending on whether or not you've turned off **Show Apple Music** in Settings→Music.)

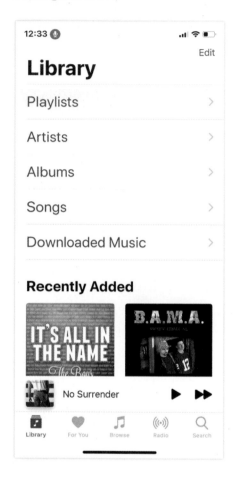
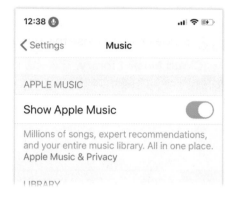
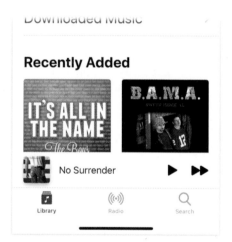

Playback Controls

When you tap the name of a song, album, playlist, or whatever, it plays. You can control playback—skip, rewind, and so on—in any of several ways.

Mini-Player

On almost every screen of the Music app, you get a miniature controller at the bottom of the screen, like the one shown above (near the bottom).

It identifies the current song, provides a "next song" button (▶▶), and offers the most important playback control of all: **II**.

Now Playing Screen

If you tap (or drag upward on) the mini-player, though, the Now Playing screen appears (below, left), showing info about the song. This time, there's room for *all* the controls you need to manipulate music playback:

TIP: Swipe down to close this screen.

- **Album art.** Sometimes the corresponding music video plays here as the song plays. The song and performer's name are here, too.

- **Options (•••).** This button is a shortcut menu of options that might apply at the moment, as described next.

- **Scrubber.** This slider reveals how much of the song you've heard, in minutes and seconds (at the left end) and how much time remains (at the right end). You can jump to any spot in the song by dragging the tiny round handle. (Tapping directly on the slider doesn't work.)

- **◄◄, ►► (Previous, Next).** Tap ◄◄ to skip to the beginning of this song. Tap ►► to skip to the next song.

TIP: If you're wearing Apple's earbuds, you can pinch the clicker *twice* to skip to the next song.

If you *hold down* one of these buttons, you rewind or fast-forward within the song. You hear the music speeding by (unless there's a music video, in which case the speeding is silent). The rewinding or fast-forwarding accelerates if you keep holding the button down.

- **►/II.** Your basic Play/Pause button.

TIP: If you're wearing the earbuds, pinching the microphone clicker serves the same purpose: It's a Play/Pause control.

Incidentally, when you plug in headphones, the iPhone's built-in speaker turns off, but when you unplug the headphones, your music pauses instead of switching abruptly back to the speaker.

- **Download (⬇).** If this song is on Apple Music (and not physically on your phone), you can tap to download it.

- **Add (+).** This button appears only when you're playing an Apple Music song; it adds the current song to your iCloud Music Library (page 263).

- **Volume.** You can use this slider to adjust the volume—or you can use the volume buttons on the left side of the phone.

- **Lyrics (💬).** Makes a screenful of lyrics appear (for most songs), scrolling to keep up with the playback (previous page, right). Slick.

- **AirPlay (◉).** Tap to send playback to an external speaker using AirPlay (page 285).

You can tap ☰ to see three more features:

- **Shuffle (⤨).** Shuffle, of course, plays the songs on your album or playlist in random order. (The ⤨ option also appears at the top of the Albums page.)

- **Repeat (⤸).** Tap this button to repeat the playlist or album you're listening to. Or, if you're really obsessed with the current song, tap Repeat so it displays a tiny 1. Now it will play the *same track* over and over until the end of time.

- **Up Next.** This queue shows which songs are coming up next for playback (page 271).

Options Panel

The ellipsis (•••) awaits on every Now Playing screen. Its choices depend on whether you've tapped some music you *own* (below, left) or some you've found in Apple Music's collection (right). But either way, this panel is the key to sharing a song with somebody (who also has Apple Music), creating a "radio station" full of music that sounds like this one (Apple Music only; see page 273), or adding this song to a playlist.

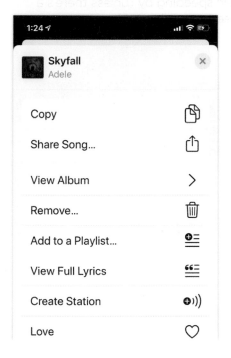
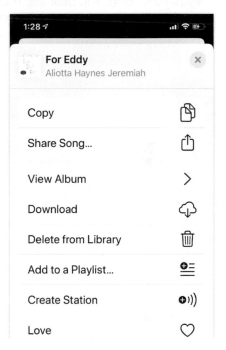

This screen also offers buttons to tell Apple when there's a song you particularly love or loathe (**Love**, **Suggest Less Like This**). Apple's magical computers take these hints into account when suggesting new music for you.

You can also rate a song on a five-star scale. Unfortunately, you can't *do* much with these ratings—you can't sort by rating, or make smart playlists by rating, or even use your ratings to affect the suggestions Apple Music makes. Ah, well.

TIP: You can *long-press* a song in a list (for example, a playlist) to open the same Options menu. That is, you don't have to burrow all the way to its Now Playing screen.

Control Center

The Control Center, of course, is the panel that appears when you swipe up from the bottom of the screen, or down from the top right of a Face ID phone (page 42). It includes playback controls, too. That means you never have to go to the Music app just to change tracks if you're busy doing something else on the phone.

Playback While Locked

Once you're playing music, it keeps right on playing, even if you change apps. After all, the only thing more fun than surfing the web is surfing it with a Beach Boys soundtrack.

If you've got something else to do—like jogging, driving, or performing surgery—tap the side button to turn off the screen. The music keeps playing, but you save battery power.

 TIP: Even with the screen off, you can adjust the music volume (use the volume buttons on the earbud clicker or the buttons on the side of the phone), pause the music (pinch the earbud clicker once), or advance to the next song (pinch it twice).

What's cool is that if you wake the phone, the Lock screen contains playback controls, so you can play, pause, skip, fast-forward, or adjust the volume without having to fully wake the phone.

If a call comes in, the music fades, and you hear your chosen ringtone—through your earbuds, if you're wearing them. Squeeze the clicker on the earbud cord or press one of the volume buttons on the side of the phone to answer the call. When the call ends, the music fades back in, right where it left off.

Voice Control

There's one more way to control your playback—a way that doesn't involve taking your eyes off the road or leaving whatever app you're using. You can control your music playback by voice, using Siri (see Chapter 5) or Voice Control (page 228).

Playlists

A *playlist* is a group of songs you've placed together, in a sequence that makes sense to you. You might make one consisting of party tunes, another with romantic dinnertime music, and a third featuring drum-heavy workout cuts.

Creating Playlists

To play with playlists, start on the **Library** tab. Tap **Playlists**. Here are all the playlists you've ever created—which might be zero (below, left).

Here's how to create one:

1. **Click the giant New Playlist button.**

    A screen appears, where you can name and set up your new playlist (below, middle).

2. **Tap Playlist Name; type a name for your playlist.**

    You can also, at this moment, tap the little 📷 button to take, or choose, a photo to represent this playlist, and type a description of it. This is also where you can decide whether to make your playlist *searchable* by others using Apple Music.

3. **Tap Add Music.**

    The Music screen appears, listing **Search**, **Library**, **For You**, and **Browse**—by now, familiar music-finding tools. If you hit Library, for example, you're offered the usual ways to view your collection: **Playlists** (that is, existing ones), **Artists**, **Albums**, **Songs**, **Videos**, **Genres**, **Compilations**, **Composers**, and **Downloaded Music** (previous page, right). (A *compilation* is one of those albums that's been put together from many different performers. You know: "Kazoo Classics," "Zither Hits of the Late 1600s," and so on.)

4. **Drill down until you find the music you want to add.**

   For example, if you first tap **Albums**, you see a list of your albums; tap + to add the entire album to the new playlist. Or tap the album's name to view the songs on it—and then + next to a song's name to add *it* to the list.

5. **Keep adding music to the playlist until you're satisfied.**

   You can keep tapping + buttons, without leaving this screen; each turns into a checkmark to indicate that you've added it (previous page, right). A playlist can be infinitely long; we're way past the days of worrying about how much will fit on a CD.

6. **Tap every Done button until you're back on the Playlists screen.**

   Your newly minted playlist is ready to play!

Using Playlists

To see what songs or videos are in a playlist, tap its name or picture. You arrive at a Playlist details screen, where your tracks are listed for your inspection. To start playing a song once you see it in the Playlist list, tap its name; you'll hear that song and all those that follow it, in order.

Or tap **Shuffle** (⋈) to start random-order playback.

> **TIP:** Here you can use a standard iOS convention: Anywhere you're asked to drill down from one list to another—from a playlist to the songs inside, for example—you can backtrack by *swiping from the left edge* of the phone into the screen.
>
> Or do it the long way: Tap ‹ at the upper-left corner of the screen. That button's name always tells you what screen you just came from (Library, for example).

Once you're here, you can have all kinds of fun:

- **To delete or rearrange songs:** Tap **Edit**. Use the ≡ handles to drag the songs into a new sequence. Hit ⊖ to make one disappear. (You're not deleting it from your phone—only from this playlist.) Tap **Done**.

- **To add more songs to the playlist:** Tap **Edit**. Tap **Add Music**.

- **To rename the open playlist:** Tap Edit. Tap the current title and edit away. (Tap Done.)

- **To delete the playlist:** Open the playlist; tap the ••• to open the Options panel; tap Delete from Library. Confirm by tapping Delete Playlist. (Scary though that wording may sound, no music is actually deleted from your library—only the playlist that contains it.)

Up Next

The Up Next playlist gives you a degree of song-ordering control without requiring the full project of programming a playlist.

The Up Next playlist always exists. If you tell Music to play an album, Up Next autofills with the songs on that album; if you're listening to all the music from a certain performer, Up Next displays what else you'll hear from that artist. And if you tap any song in your library, *everything after it* gets added to the Up Next queue automatically.

But you can also queue up music yourself, adding songs to Up Next on your own schedule. The playback will plow through them in order.

- **Add a song to Up Next.** Long-press a song, album, or playlist to open the Options panel. Tap Play Next to put this song at the beginning of the Up Next queue or Play Later to put it at the *end* of the queue. (Play Later is an option when you're playing a playlist.)

- **Play a song now.** Suppose you find some music you want to play right now. You don't care about the Up Next playlist.

  When you tap that item's name, the iPhone asks: "After playing this, do you want to keep playing your Up Next queue?" If you hit Keep Up Next, then you hear the new song without disturbing the Up Next list that will play afterward. If you hit Clear Up Next, then the new song plays and the music stops; you've nuked the current Up Next list.

View, Edit, or Clear the Up Next List

To see the Up Next playlist, tap the 🗐 button on any Now Playing screen.

When the list appears, you can remove a song from the queue by swiping left on it to reveal the Remove button; tap it. Rearrange the list by dragging the little "grip strip" handles up or down. (If you don't see them, it's because you've got your music on Repeat.)

Besides the Clear Up Next option mentioned above, the only way to clear the *entire* Up Next list at once is to force-quit the Music app (page 666) and then reopen it.

For You Tab

Fifty million is a lot of songs. You won't live long enough to hear them all. So Apple has supplied the **For You** tab of the Music app to present new songs, performers, and albums its algorithms think you'll like. (If you're not a paying subscriber, then this tab is just an ad for Apple Music.)

 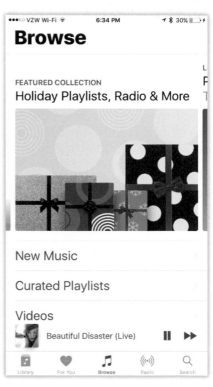

Scroll horizontally to see more tiles in a category; scroll vertically to see the playlists, albums, artists, and new releases Apple thinks you'll like.

And how does it guess what kind of music you'll like? When you sign up for the service, you're shown dancing red circles bearing music-genre names. You're supposed to tap the ones you like, double-tap the ones you *really* like, and hold your finger down on the ones you don't like.

Then, of course, as you go through your life listening to music, you can always turn the ♡ button on or off to further fine-tune Apple's understanding of your tastes.

Browse Tab

The Browse tab is also for paying subscribers only. It's lists of lists.

Scroll down long enough, and you'll find lists like New Music, Playlists (music lists created by Apple's editors for particular genres, activities, and moods), Music Videos, Top Charts, and Genres. Once again, the idea is to help you find new stuff you like.

Radio Tab

Your iPhone includes an amazing gift: your own radio station. Your own *empire* of radio stations, in fact.

They come in three categories: free, ready-made stations for subscribers, and subscriber-only custom stations based on a "seed" song.

Free Stations

What you see on the Radio screen depends on whether or not you've turned off Show Apple Music, as described on page 261.

If that's turned off, then you see only free stations here: Beats 1 (the Apple live station described on page 262) and—through Stations at the bottom of the screen—thousands of ready-to-play, software-curated "radio stations" in every conceivable category: Country, NPR, ESPN, Oldies, Soul/Funk, Chill, Indie, Classic Metal, Pop Workout, Kids & Family, Lullabies, Latin Pop, Classical, Reggae, and on and on.

These are free internet radio stations, the same ones you can now request with a simple Siri command (page 172).

Subscriber Stations

If Show Apple Music is turned on, then this screen offers ready-made "radio stations" Apple has supplied for you. If you're a subscriber, they play; if not, they give you an ad inviting you to sign up.

You can hit ▶▶ to skip a song you're not enjoying. And you don't hear any ads.

Custom Stations

If you're a paid subscriber, the Radio service offers more than canned stations; you can create a new "station" instantly, based on any song, artist, or genre you choose.

You don't get to choose the exact songs or singers you want to hear; you have to trust Radio to select songs *based* on your chosen song, singer, or music genre. For example, if you choose Billy Joel as your "seed," you'll hear a lot of Billy Joel, but also a lot of other music that sounds more or less like his.

To set up a new "radio station" of your own, find a song you like. Long-press its name to open the Options menu (page 33) and tap **Create Station**. You've just created a new station, and it begins playing instantly.

The idea of a radio service based on a seed song isn't new, of course. It's the same idea as Pandora, the website and app that's been around for years. But Radio is built-in, it's incorporated with Siri and the Control Center, and it's part of Apple's larger ecosystem; that is, you can see your same set of "radio stations" on your Mac or PC (in the iTunes app), iPad, and Apple TV.

Returning to a Custom Station

On the main Radio screen, the **Recently Played** list shows all the stations you've listened to. Tap to start playing.

Siri and Radio

Truth is, there's an easier way to create a custom radio station: Just let Siri do the work. No matter what you're doing on the iPhone, you can say, for example, "Start a station from Whitney Houston." Boom: The music begins.

Actually, Siri comes equipped to recognize a slew of commands pertaining to Radio. Here's a sampler; you don't have to use these precise wordings: "Play some Taylor Swift" (or any song, album, or artist). "Play the radio." "What song is this?" "Play more like this." "Don't play this song again." "Pause the music." "Resume the music." "Skip this song." "Add this song to my Wish List." "Stop the radio."

Speakers and Headphones

The iPhone's speakers are pretty darned good for such a tiny machine. But the world is full of better speakers—Bluetooth wireless speakers, car stereo systems, hi-fi TVs, and fancy earbuds and headphones. The iPhone is especially easy to use with them.

Bluetooth Wireless Speakers

You can buy amazingly small, powerful Bluetooth stereo speakers that receive your iPhone's music from as far as 20 or 30 feet away—made by JBL, Bose, and others. Oh, and Apple—with its HomePod speaker.

There are also wireless Bluetooth headphones and earbuds—an especially useful fact if your iPhone lacks a headphone jack (iPhone 7 and later).

Once you've bought your headphones or speakers, you have to introduce them to the iPhone—a process called *pairing*.

NOTE: Apple's AirPods—detached, entirely wireless earbuds—use their own, much simpler pairing process. Just bring the charging case near the phone and tap **Connect** on the phone's screen.

From the Home screen, tap **Settings→Bluetooth**. Turn Bluetooth on (below, left); you see the searching ✳ animation as the iPhone wirelessly hunts for your headphones or speakers.

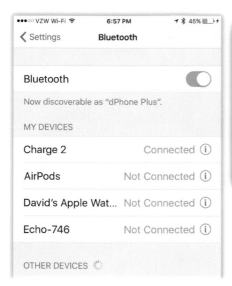

Grab them, turn them on, and start the pairing procedure, as described in the manual. Usually that means holding down a certain button until a tiny light starts flashing. At that point, the name of the headphones or speaker appears on the iPhone's screen.

TIP: If the headphones or speaker require a one-time passcode—it's usually 0000, but check the manual—the iPhone's keyboard appears, so you can type it in.

A few seconds later, it says Connected; now any sound the iPhone would ordinarily play through its speakers or earbuds instead plays through the wireless headphones or speakers. Not just music, but chirps, game sounds, and so on. Oh, and phone calls. If your headset has a micro-phone, too, then you can answer and make phone calls wirelessly. (There's an Answer button right on the headphones.)

Using Bluetooth wireless stereo does eat up your battery charge faster. But come on: Listening to your music without wires, with the iPhone still in your pocket or bag? How cool is that?

Switching Among Speakers

When your iPhone has a connection to a wireless sound source—Bluetooth speakers/earbuds or an AirPlay receiver, for example—you need some way to direct the music playback to it.

The answer is the ⊚ button. It's in the Control Center (page 42), but it's hidden: You have to long-press the music-playback controls to see it.

When you tap ⊚, the iPhone offers a button for each speaker or set of earbuds or headphones (previous page, right). Tap the one you want.

Instantly, the sound begins flowing from your other source. Use the same method to switch back to the iPhone's speakers when the time comes.

AirPods

Ever since Apple ditched the headphone jack (page 28), it's offered for sale the wireless, detached AirPods as an alternative.

When you're listening to music over AirPods, you can control music play-back by double-tapping the device in your ear; each one (right and left) can have a different effect. In **Settings→Bluetooth**, tap the ⓘ next to the AirPods' name; you'll see that double-tapping the left one can trigger **Siri**, **Play/Pause**, **Next Track**, **Previous Track**, or do nothing (**Off**)—and you have the same choices, independently, for the right one.

Unfortunately, changing the volume, or performing any control function other than the two you've assigned to double-taps, still requires a Siri command (or pulling out your phone).

AirPlay

There's another way to transmit audio wirelessly from the iPhone (and video, too): the Apple technology called AirPlay. You can buy AirPlay speakers, amplifiers, and TV sets. The Apple TV, of course, is the best-known AirPlay machine; Apple's HomePod is another one.

AirPlay is described on page 285, because most people use it to trans-mit video, not just audio. But the steps for transmitting to an AirPlay audio gadget are the same.

Music Settings

The iPhone has a long list of traditional iPod features for music playback. Most of these options await in **Settings→Music**. (Shortcut: Tell Siri, "Open Music settings.") A few worth noticing:

- **EQ (Equalization).** Like any good music player, the iPhone offers an EQ function: a long list of presets, each of which affects your music by boosting or throttling various frequencies. One might bring out the bass; another might emphasize the midrange for clearer vocals; and so on. ("Late Night" is especially handy; it lowers the bass so it thuds less. Your downstairs neighbors will love it.)

- **Volume Limit.** Listening to a lot of loud music through earphones can damage your hearing. Pump it up today, pay for it tomorrow.

  Portable music players can be sinister that way, because in noisy places like planes and city streets, people turn up the volume much louder than they would in a quiet place, and they don't even realize how high they've cranked it. That's why Apple created this volume slider. It lets you limit the maximum volume level of the music.

  Find the slider in **Settings→Music→Volume Limit**.

  If you're a parent, you can lock down this setting so your kid can't override it. But it's a slog: Open **Settings→Screen Time→Content & Privacy Restrictions**; turn on **Content & Privacy Restrictions**; scroll down to **Media & Apple Music**; turn on **Don't Allow Changes**.

  Finally, you can add the passcode. Return to the main Screen Time settings. Scroll down and tap **Use Screen Time Passcode**; set a passcode for it.

- **Sound Check.** This feature smooths out the master volume levels of tracks from different albums, compensating for differences in their recording levels. It doesn't deprive you of peaks and valleys in the music volume, of course—it affects only the baseline level.

TIP: Here's a trick you weren't expecting: You can store many terabytes of music on your Mac or PC upstairs—and play it on your phone in the kitchen downstairs. Or anywhere on the same Wi-Fi network, actually. This nifty bit of wireless magic is brought to you by Home Sharing, a feature of the iTunes program. For details, see the free "Home Sharing Music" PDF on this book's "Missing CD" page at *missingmanuals.com*.

iTunes Store

Just as you can buy apps using the App Store app, you can browse, buy, and download songs, TV shows, and movies using the iTunes Store app. Anything you buy gets autosynced back to your computer's copy of iTunes when you get home. Whenever you hear somebody mention a buy-worthy song, you can have it within a minute.

To begin, open the iTunes Store *app*. The store you see here (below, left) is modeled on the App Store described in Chapter 10. This time, the buttons at the bottom of the screen include **Music**, **Movies**, **TV Shows**, **Search**, and **More**.

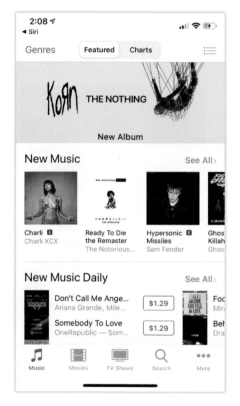 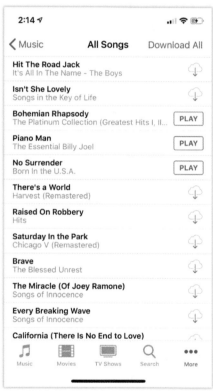

When you tap **Music**, **Movies**, or **TV Shows**, the screen offers further buttons. In Music, for example, the scrolling horizontal rows of options might include **New Releases**, **Recent Releases**, **Singles**, and **Pre-Orders**.

(At the bottom of the screen is a **Redeem** button, which you can tap if you've been given an iTunes gift certificate or a promo code; a **Send Gift** button, which lets you buy a gift card for someone else; and an **Apple ID** button, which can show you your current credit balance.)

You can't buy TV shows or movies on the cellular network—just in Wi-Fi hotspots. That's your cell company's way of saying, "We don't want you jamming up our precious cellular network with your hefty video downloads, bucko."

Note, by the way, that you can *rent* movies from the store instead of buying them. You pay only $3 to $6 to rent (instead of $10 to $16 to buy). But once you start watching, you have just 48 hours to finish; after that, the movie deletes itself from your phone. (If you like, you can sync it to your Mac or PC to continue watching in iTunes—but still within 48 hours.)

To search for something in particular, tap **Search**. The keyboard appears. Type what you're looking for: the name of a song, movie, show, performer, or album, for example. At any time, you can stop typing and tap the name of a match to see its details. You can use the buttons across the top to restrict the search to one category (just songs or movies, for example).

Sometimes it's quicker to search directly from the main iOS search bar (page 111), which can search the iTunes Store directly.

All these tools eventually take you to the details page of an album, song, or movie. For a song, tap its name to hear an instant 90-second preview (tap again to stop). For a TV show or movie, tap ▶ to watch an ad or the sneak preview.

If you're sold, then tap the price button to buy the song, show, or album (and tap **Buy** to confirm). For movies, you can choose either **Buy** or **Rent**, priced accordingly. At this point, your iPhone downloads the music or video you bought.

Purchased Items

Anything you buy from the iTunes Store winds up in the appropriate app on your iPhone: the TV app for TV shows and movies, the Music app for songs. (Within the Music app, everything you've bought that isn't on the phone shows up with a ☁ icon next to its name.)

In the iTunes Store app, you can tap **More** and then **Purchased** to see what you've bought. Once you tap a category (**Music**, **Movies**, **TV Shows**), you get a list of everything you've bought from iTunes—on your iPhone or on any other Apple machine. When you tap the name of something that you own but isn't on your phone, you can download it now (tap ☁). No extra charge.

More in "More"

Tapping More at the bottom of the screen offers these options:

- **Tones.** You can buy ready-made ringtones here—30-second slices of pop songs. (Don't ask what sense it makes to pay $1.29 for 30 seconds of a song when the whole song is the same price.)

- **Genius.** Apple offers a list of music, movies, and TV shows for sale that it thinks you'll like, based on stuff you already have.

- **Purchased.** Here's another way to examine the goodies you've bought on all your devices. If you've turned on Apple's Family Sharing feature (page 586), you can also examine everything your family members have bought.

- **Downloads.** A progress bar for anything you've started to download.

So you've downloaded one of the store's millions of songs, podcasts, TV shows, music videos, ringtones, or movies directly to your phone. Next time you sync, that song will swim *upstream* to your Mac or PC, where it will be safely backed up in iTunes. (And if you lost your connection before the iPhone was finished downloading, your Mac or PC will finish the job automatically. Cool.)

TV App

This weird hybrid app is intended to serve as a single repository for *paid* TV shows and movies online, in these three categories:

- **Videos you've bought or rented from Apple's iTunes Store.** In this regard, the TV app takes over the functions of the dearly departed Videos app.

- **Paid video-service apps like Showtime, Hulu, and HBO Go.** A few of these apps work with the TV app's "single sign-on" feature, meaning you can enter the name and password for your cable account *once*, and thereafter you're spared having to enter it into each individual app. (Most of the time, the TV app hands you off to the corresponding app—HBO Go or whatever—to watch whatever show you've tapped.)

- **Channels your cable package provides.** Or at least those that have apps: ABC, A&E, AMC, TBS, and so on. Each one requires that you provide your cable or satellite TV account name and password. (Here again, a few may work with the single sign-on feature, meaning you don't have to sign in individually.)

NOTE: Some channel apps are free to watch without a subscription, including PBS, PBS Kids, CBS Sports, ABC News, and The Weather Channel.

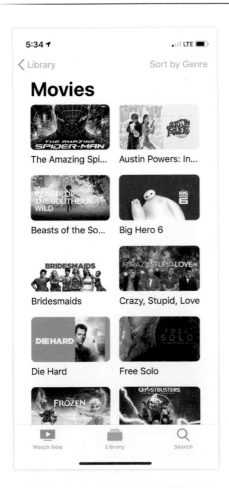

The TV app works with over 100 video services—but Netflix and Amazon Prime Video, alas, are not among them. (Although, if you have the Netflix app or the Amazon Prime app, the TV app offers to redirect you there to watch something you've searched for.)

Until more players join the party, here's how to use the TV app.

Three Tabs

The buttons across the bottom clearly exhibit the TV app's split personality (split between iTunes purchases and cable-channel apps):

- **Watch Now.** An App Store–ish page of suggestions for shows and movies available to watch. The Up Next row at top is especially handy; it lists new episodes of shows you've already been watching.

  At the top are category buttons like **Movies**, **TV Shows**, **Kids**—and **Sports**. The **Sports** tab lists, among other sports shows, any sporting events that are on TV *right now*. Unfortunately, it lists all of them, even from channels you don't subscribe to. Still, pretty cool.

- **Library.** TV and movies you've bought or rented from Apple.

- **Search.** If you know what you're looking for, the search box is the best way to find it.

How to Play a Video

When you tap a video's thumbnail, it either opens up in the corresponding channel app—or, if it came from Apple, it opens a Details screen (plot summary, year of release, and so on).

NOTE: If you see a ☁ on the Details screen, it means that this bought or rented movie is not actually on your phone. If you have a good Wi-Fi signal, you can watch it right now by streaming it (instead of downloading it to your phone).

If you don't see that icon, then the video file is actually on your phone. You can tap the **Edit** button (and then ⊗) to delete the video.

Tap your way to the ▶ button to begin watching.

When you're playing an Apple video, anything else on the screen is distracting, so Apple hides the video playback controls. Tap the screen once to make them appear and again to make them disappear.

Here's what they do:

- ✕. Tap to stop playback and return to the master list of videos.

- ▭ or ⬍ Zooms or unzooms the video (read on).

- **Volume.** Use this slider (top of the screen) to adjust the volume—or use the volume buttons on the left side of the phone.

- **Scroll slider.** This progress indicator (bottom of the screen) shows the elapsed time, the remaining time, and a round handle that you can drag to jump forward or back in the video.

> **TIP:** Drag your finger farther (up or down) from the handle to choose a faster or slower scrubbing speed.

- ⟲15 or 15⟳. Skips 15 seconds back (great if the actor mumbled) or forward (great if the next shot looks too grisly).

- **Play/Pause (▶/II).** These buttons (and the earbud clicker) do the same thing to video as they do to music: alternate playing and pausing.

- **Previous, Next (◀◀, ▶▶).** Hold down your finger to rewind or fast-forward the video. The longer you hold, the faster the zipping. (When you fast-forward, you even get to hear the sped-up audio.)

If you're watching a movie from the iTunes Store, you may be surprised to discover that it comes with what were once called DVD Extras: chapter markers, deleted scenes, and so on. To see the **Extras** buttons for these goodies, tap the screen.

> **TIP:** If you're wearing earbuds, you can pinch the clicker *twice* to skip to the next chapter or *three times* to go back a chapter.

- **AirPlay (⊡).** This symbol appears if you have an Apple TV (or another AirPlay-compatible device). Tap it to send your video playback to the TV, as described on the next page.

- **Language (⊟)** summons subtitle and alternate-language soundtrack options.

TIP: To delete a video from the library, swipe leftward across its name in the Videos list; tap **Delete** to confirm. (You can always re-download it, of course.)

Zoom/Unzoom

Before HDTV, television shows were squarish, not rectangular. So when you watch them on a rectangular screen, you get black letterbox columns on either side of the picture.

Movies have the opposite problem. They're usually too wide for the iPhone screen. So when you watch movies, you may wind up with *horizontal* letterbox bars above and below the picture.

Some people can't stand letterboxing. You're already watching on a small screen; why sacrifice some of that precious area to black bars?

Fortunately, the iPhone gives you a choice. If you double-tap the video as it plays, you zoom in, magnifying the image so it fills the entire screen. Or, if the playback controls are visible, you can tap ▭ or ⊡ .

Of course, now you're not seeing the entire original composition. You lose the top and bottom of old TV scenes, or the left and right edges of movie scenes.

Fortunately, if this effect chops off something important—some text, for example—the original letterbox view is just another double-tap away. (No zooming happens if the source material is already a perfect fit for the iPhone's screen shape.)

Ordinarily, videos don't extend into the area occupied by the notch (page 22). When you double-tap to zoom a video, though, playback fills the entire screen—and part of it is now obscured by the notch. You get used to it.

TV Output

When you crave a screen bigger than a few inches, you can play your iPhone's videos on a regular TV. All you need is a cable: the Apple Digital AV Adapter. It carries both audio and video over a single HDMI cable.

It *mirrors* what's on the phone: your Home screen, email, Safari, and everything else. (Photos and presentations appear on your TV in pure, "video outputted" form, without any controls or other window clutter.)

AirPlay

Your iPhone also offers wireless projection. AirPlay transmits music or high-def video, with audio, from your iPhone to an Apple TV (or another AirPlay-equipped receiver) across the room. It's a fantastic way to send video, slideshows, presentations, games, FaceTime calls, and web-sites to your TV for a larger audience. Whatever is on the screen gets transmitted.

AirPlay receivers include the Apple TV (version 2 or later) and speakers, stereos, and receivers from Denon, Marantz, JBL, iHome, and so on.

When you're playing a video or music, open up the Control Center (page 42), and tap ⏏ to see a list of available AirPlay receivers. If you have an Apple TV, tap its name. (If this is your first time, enter the four-digit code you see on the TV.)

> **TIP:** If you're playing a TV show or movie from within the TV app, use the ⏏ button there instead of the one on the Control Center. That way, the video continues to play on your TV—but on your phone, you can duck out of the TV app and do other things.

Everything on the iPhone screen now appears on the TV or sound system. (The ⏏ icon appears on the playback controls and in the Control Center, so you don't forget that every move you make is visible to everyone in the living room.)

How to Project or Record the iPhone's Screen

If you're a teacher, trainer, or product demonstrator, you might find it useful to be able to project the iPhone's activity on a much larger screen, or to record it as a QuickTime movie to use in presentations or to post online. Here are three ways to go about it:

- **The built-in way.** You can create video recordings of your iPhone's screen, using the Control Center (see page 42). Once captured, you can move the movie to a computer and project it from there, or display it directly from your iPhone to a large video screen using AirPlay or the Apple Digital AV Adapter.

- **The Mac way.** If your Mac has OS X Yosemite or later, connect the phone to the Mac with its white USB charging cable. Open the Mac app called QuickTime Player. Choose **File→New Movie Recording**. From the little ∨ menu next to the ⏺ button, choose **iPhone**.

  Now you're seeing the iPhone's screen on your Mac—and you can record it, project it, or screen-capture it for future generations!

- **The wireless way.** A $15 program called Reflector (*reflectorapp.com*) lets you view the iPhone's live image on the Mac's screen—and hear its sound. (It actually turns the Mac into an AirPlay receiver.) There's also a **Record** command, so you can create a movie of whatever you're doing on the phone.

9

The Camera

Why is it even called the iPhone? What most people do with it, most of the time, is take photos. In fact, the iPhone is the most popular camera in the world. More photos are posted online from this phone than from any other machine in existence. It *should* be called the iCamera.

With each new version of the iPhone, Apple improves its cameras—and on the 2019 models, they're unbelievably good. The videos look amazing, too. They're auto-stabilized. They shoot in 4K (four times the resolution of high-def video), and the Face ID phones can even play back *high dynamic range* videos (incredibly dark darks and bright brights).

This chapter is all about the iPhone's ability to display photos, take new ones with its camera, and capture videos.

The Camera App

The cameras on the latest iPhones are pretty impressive. The iPhone 7 and later, for example, have four LED flashes, manual exposure controls, optical stabilization, and phase-detection autofocus (the same kind of very fast refocusing found in professional SLR cameras). These phones can manage 10 shots a second and do amazingly well in low light.

And then there's the iPhone 11 Pro: three lenses and enough artificial-intelligence photographic smarts to make it almost impossible to muff a shot.

Now that you know what you're in for, here's how it works.

Firing Up the Camera

Photographic opportunities are frequently fleeting; by the time you fish the phone from your pocket, wake it, unlock it, find the Camera app, and wait for it to load, the magic moment may be gone forever.

Fortunately, there's a much quicker way to get to the Camera app: Once the phone is awake, at the Lock screen, *swipe to the left*. (Drag the background—not one of the notification banners.)

The Camera app opens directly. Over time, the wake-and-swipe ritual becomes natural, fluid—and fast.

> **NOTE:** On Face ID phones, as an alternative to swiping, you can long-press the 📷 at lower right on the Lock screen.

By the way: This shortcut bypasses the Lock screen. Any random stranger who picks up your phone can, therefore, jump directly into picture-taking mode, without your password, fingerprint, or Face ID.

That stranger can't do much damage, though. She can take new photos, or delete the new photos taken during her session—but the photos you've *already* taken are off-limits, and all the features that could damage your reputation (editing, emailing, and posting) are unavailable. She would have to be able to open the Photos app to get to those.

> **TIP:** Of course, there's a hands-free way to fire up the camera, too: Tell Siri, "Open camera."

Camera Modes

The Camera app can capture six or seven kinds of photos and videos, depending on your phone model. By swiping your finger horizontally *anywhere* on the screen (not just on the mode labels), you switch among its modes. Here they are, from left to right:

- **Time-Lapse** speeds up your video yet somehow keeps it stable. You can reduce a two-hour bike ride into 20 seconds of superfast playback.

- **Slo-Mo.** You get a video filmed at 120 or 240 frames a second—so it plays back at one-quarter or one-eighth speed, incredibly smoothly. Fantastic for sports, tender smiles, and cannonballs into the pool.

- **Video** is your camcorder mode: 4K video on the 6s and later models, high definition on earlier ones.

- **Photo** is the primary mode for taking pictures.

- **Portrait.** This mode is available only on the 7 Plus, 8 Plus, and Face ID iPhone models, whose two camera lenses create a softly blurred background that looks super-professional. (The iPhone XR has only one lens on the back, but it simulates the same effect using clever software.)

- **Square.** Why would Apple go to the trouble of creating a whole camera mode devoted to taking square, not rectangular, pictures? Answer: Instagram, which prefers square images. (On the iPhone 11 Pro, Square mode is hiding in the proportion picker described on page 335.)

- **Pano.** Captures super-wide-angle panoramic photos.

TIP: If you tend to stick to one of these modes (like Square because you're an Instagram junkie, for example), you can make the iPhone's camera stay in your favorite mode, rather than resetting itself to Photo mode every time you reopen it. That switch is in Settings→Camera→Preserve Settings→Camera Mode.

All these modes are described in this chapter, but in a more logical order: still photos first, and then video modes.

Photo Mode

Most people, most of the time, use the Camera app to take still photos. It's a pretty great experience. The iPhone's screen is a huge digital-camera viewfinder. You can turn it 90 degrees for a wider or taller shot.

Tap to Focus

All right: You've opened the Camera app, and the mode is set to Photo. You may see a yellow box appear briefly on the screen.

It's telling you where the iPhone will focus, the area it examines to calculate the overall brightness of the photo (exposure), and the portion that will determine the overall *white balance* of the scene (the color cast).

If you're taking a picture of people, the iPhone tries to lock in on a face—up to 10 faces, actually—and calculate the focus and exposure so that *they* look right.

But sometimes there are no faces—and dead center may not be the most important part of the photo. The cool thing is that you can *tap* somewhere else in the scene to move that yellow square—to recalculate the focus, exposure, and white balance.

Here's when you might want to do this tapping:

- **When the whole image looks too dark or too bright.** If you tap a *dark* part of the scene, the photo brightens up; if you tap a *bright* part, it darkens a bit. You're telling the camera, "Redo your calculations so *this* part has the best exposure; I don't care if the rest of the picture gets brighter or darker." At that point, you can override the phone's exposure decision.

Tap the sky to make it correctly exposed, even if the beach is now too dark.   *Tap the dark beach to brighten it up, although that also brightens up the sky.*

- **When the scene has a color cast.** If the photo looks, for example, a little bluish or yellowish, tap a different spot—the one you care most about. The iPhone recomputes its assessment of the white balance.

- **When you're in macro mode.** If the foreground object is very close to the lens—4 to 8 inches away—the iPhone automatically goes into *macro* (super close-up) mode. In this mode, you can do something really cool: You can *defocus the background.* The background goes soft, slightly blurry, just like the professional photos you see in magazines. No, not as well or as flexibly as in Portrait mode (page 308), but it works on all iPhones.

Adjust Exposure

When you tap the screen to set the focus point, a new control appears: a little yellow sun slider. That's your exposure control. Slide it up to brighten the whole photo or down to make things darker. Often, just a small adjustment is all it takes to add a splash of light to a dim scene, or to dial the details back into a photo that's bright white.

To reset the slider to the iPhone's original proposed setting, tap somewhere else, or just aim the phone at something different for a second.

The point is that the Camera app lets you fuss with the focus point and the exposure level independently.

Focus Lock/Exposure Lock

The iPhone likes to focus and calculate the exposure before it shoots. Cameras are funny that way.

That tendency, however, can get in your way when you're shooting something that moves fast. Horse races, divers. Pets. Kids on merry-go-rounds, kids on slides, kids eating breakfast. By the time the camera has calculated the focus and exposure, which takes about a second, you've lost the shot.

Therefore, Apple provides auto-exposure lock and autofocus lock. They let you set up the focus and exposure in advance, so there's zero lag when you finally snap the shot.

To use this feature, point the camera at something that has the *same distance and lighting* as the subject-to-be. For example, focus at the base of the merry-go-round, directly below where your daughter's horse will appear. Or point at the bottom of the waterslide before your son is ready to go.

Now hold your finger down on that spot on the iPhone's screen until you see the yellow square blink twice. When you lift your finger, the phrase "AE/AF Lock" tells you that you've now locked in exposure and autofocus. (You can tap again to unlock it if you change your mind.)

At this point, you can drag the yellow sun slider to adjust that locked exposure, if you like.

Now you can snap photos, rapid-fire, without ever having to wait while your iPhone rethinks focus and exposure.

The LED Flash

As on most phones, the iPhone's "flash" is a very bright LED light on the back. You can make it turn on momentarily, providing a small boost of illumination when the lights are low. (That's a *small* boost—it won't do anything for subjects more than a few feet away.)

The iPhone SE, 6, and 6s models, in fact, have two LED flashes: one white, one amber. The 7 and later models take that a step further, with *four* flashes, together producing 50 percent more light.

The flashes go off simultaneously, with their strengths mixed so that their light matches the color temperature of the scene. (You might notice that the phone flashes once *before* it captures the shot. That's the camera's opportunity to *measure* the light color of the scene.)

This multi-flash trick makes a huge difference in the quality of your flash photos. Especially in skin tones, which may be why Apple calls the feature "True Tone." Here's the before and after:

To adjust the flash's behavior, tap the ⚡ in the upper-left corner of the screen. You can choose **On** (the flash will fire no matter what the lighting conditions), **Off** (the flash won't fire), or **Auto**. That means the flash will turn on automatically when, in the iPhone's opinion, the scene is too dark. In all cases, you get a warning if the flash will go off for the next shot: a ⚡ in a yellow box above the preview.

The Screen Flash

The iPhone 6s and later models offer a "flash" on the *front*, too, for selfies. But it's not an LED like the one on the back.

Instead, at the moment you take the shot, the *screen* lights up to illuminate your face. Better yet: It adjusts the color of the screen's "flash" to give your face the best flesh tones, based on a check of the ambient light color.

Of course, the normal iPhone screen is too tiny to supply much light, even at full brightness. So Apple developed a custom chip with a single purpose: to overclock the screen. In selfie situations, the screen blasts at *three times* its usual full brightness for a fraction of a second. It is crazy bright.

And it works fantastically well. Here you can see the nuked-looking result from a traditional back LED "flash" (left) side by side with the more nuanced screen flash (right).

Night Mode (iPhone 11 Family)

If you have an iPhone 11, 11 Pro, or 11 Pro Max, you may not need any flash at all. As long as your subject isn't moving, you're in for a treat.

When there's not much light where you are—even when *you* perceive pitch darkness—these cameras switch automatically into Night mode. A small 🌓 indicator appears in the top or bottom left corner (facing page, left).

When you take the shot, the iPhone captures many photos over several seconds; cumulatively, the camera soaks up far more faint light than it could with the usual exposure time. The result: absolutely astonishing low-light photos that seem to have been photographed in much brighter light, revealing color and detail not even visible to your eyes (facing page, right).

Professional cameras can do this trick, too, with long exposures—when they're on tripods. What's amazing is that the iPhone can do it even when you're holding the phone in your hand.

Here's the routine:

1. **When the light is low, open the Camera app.**

    The 🌓 icon may be either gray (meaning, "Night mode is available if you tap me, but it's not absolutely necessary in this light") or yellow

("You need Night mode in this light"). When it's yellow, it also shows you how many seconds long the exposure will be.

TIP: At this point, you can tap the 🌐 icon to make a time slider appear above the ◎ button, shown above at left. It lets you override the iPhone's time estimate (Auto), so the exposure is longer or shorter. Experiment! (By dragging this slider all the way to 0, you can actually turn Night mode off.)

If you do, in fact, put the phone on a tripod or otherwise prop it up, the slider offers much longer time options—30 seconds, for example. That's for you, stargazers.

Note that Night mode is available only when you're using the standard lens (iPhone 11 and Pro) and the zoomed-in lens (11 Pro only)—not the ultra-wide lens.

2. **Tap the Shutter button (◎).**

The time slider becomes a countdown. During this time, hold the phone as still as you can.

It's best to avoid trying Night mode for the first time in a place where sudden vocal outbursts might be undesirable. You're going to exclaim something the first time you see the results.

Fake Zoom

Every iPhone has a zoom, which can bring you "closer" to the subject. On any iPhone with only one lens on the back, it's a *digital* zoom. It doesn't work like a real camera's optical zoom, which actually moves lenses to blow up the scene. Instead, it basically just blows up the image, making everything bigger, and slightly degrading the picture quality in the process. Sometimes getting closer to the action is worth the subtle image-quality sacrifice.

To zoom in like this, *spread two fingers* on the screen. As you spread, a zoom slider appears; you can also drag the handle in the slider, or tap **+** or **–**, for more precise zooming.

True Optical Zoom

On the fancier iPhones—iPhone 7 Plus, 8 Plus, XS, 11, and 11 Pro—Apple had enough room to install *two* lenses, right next to each other. (The 11 Pro has a third lens, described in a moment.)

They include one standard lens (Apple calls it wide-angle) and one telephoto. With one tap on the little **1x** button (facing page, left), you can zoom in 2x (middle). This is true *optical* zoom, not the fake zoom on most previous phones.

2x zoom isn't a huge amount, but it's incredibly useful incredibly often.

You can also dial up any amount of zoom *between* 1x and 2x, again without losing quality. The iPhone performs that stunt by seamlessly

combining the zoom lens's image (in the center of the photo) with a margin provided by the wide lens. Just plant your finger on the **1x** and drag it to the left. The circular scale of zooming appears (above, right).

You can even zoom while shooting a video, which is very cool.

You can also keep dragging your finger to the left, *past* 2x—all the way up to a really blotchy 10x (or 6x for video). Beyond 2x, of course, you're invoking *digital* zoom. But sometimes it's just what you need.

TIP: Once you've dragged your finger to open the zooming scale, you can tap the current magnification button ("2.5x" or whatever) to reset the zooming to 1x. (On the iPhone 11 Pro, tapping resets the scale to the closest lens preset: **0.5**, **1**, or **2x**.)

iPhone 11 Family: Wide-Angle Lens

The iPhone 11, 11 Pro, and 11 Pro Max, introduced in 2019, introduce an "ultra-wide angle" lens, great for capturing a big group of people, a tall monument, or a whole building facade at close range.

The iPhone 11 therefore has two lenses on the back: ultra-wide and standard. The iPhone 11 Pro models have *three* lenses: ultra-wide, standard, and telephoto (zoom), giving you a total zoom range of 4x.

Apple made no attempt to play down the design prominence of these lenses; they stick out, big and black, leading internet wags to mock up future iPhones with squadrons of lenses cluttering up the back like the dots on dice.

To accommodate all this zoominess, Apple had to redesign the Camera mode. On the Pro, you see three buttons: **0.5x** (the ultra-wide angle), **1x** (standard), and **2x** (zoomed in). You can tap these buttons, or you can drag across them to produce a zoom dial (below, right). It lets you dial up any zoom level between 0.5x and 2x—and even higher, all the way to 10x. Once again, though, anything over 2x is a digital zoom that degrades the quality.

TIP: When you're at 1x or a higher zoom level, the outer edges of the screen—which are usually black—become translucent previews of a wider view (below, bottom left). That's to remind you that you have wider lenses available—that you *could* be capturing all that extra image, if you chose to zoom out.

You can use these lenses in any of the modes—Video, Time Lapse, and so on—although in Panorama mode, the ultra wide-angle lens distorts the

picture quite a bit. Note, too, that the ultra-wide lens isn't stabilized, like the others, and isn't as good in low light.

TIP: Now, this is just Apple's camera engineers geeking out: If you like, when you take a photo with the standard or zoom lens, the iPhone can secretly take a second shot with the *next wider lens* on your phone. Later, when you're editing the photo, you'll therefore be able to crop *outward*—to widen your shot beyond what you thought you captured. (Or, when adjusting the angle of the shot, you'll have a safety margin of image to fill in the blank corners.) See page 336.

To turn this feature on, visit **Settings→Camera**; turn on **Capture Outside the Frame**. You can turn it on independently for photos and videos.

Now every picture you take with the zoom or standard lens—well, those you take in bright light, and in HEIF format (page 648)—will be marked with a **⁅⁎** badge. They'll also take up twice the storage space, thanks to that secretly piggybacking wider-angle photo. (If you don't edit the photo to take advantage of your extra canvas within 30 days, the iPhone deletes the wider photo forever.)

iPhone 11 and 11 Pro: Changing the Proportions

The 11 and 11 Pro Camera app hides the ⟳ and ⊛ buttons (Self-Timer and Filter) until you swipe up on the screen (or tap ∧ at the top).

That action opens a new row of controls—including one not available on other models: the one directly over the ◎ button, usually labeled **4:3**.

When you tap it, you're offered a choice of three *aspect ratios*, meaning proportions (below, left). **4:3** is the standard iPhone dimensions, the

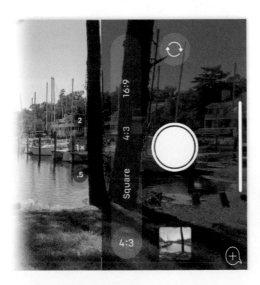

proportions of old TV sets (previous page, top right). **16:9** is a wide rect-angle, matching the screen shape of high-def videos (bottom right). And **Square** is—well, you know.

The "Rule of Thirds" Grid

The rule of thirds, long held as gospel by certain painters and photog-raphers, suggests that you imagine a tic-tac-toe grid superimposed on your frame. As you frame the shot, position the important parts of the photo on those lines or, better yet, at their intersections. Supposedly, this setup creates a stronger composition than putting everything in dead center.

Now, it's really a *consideration* of thirds; plenty of photographs are, in fact, strongest when the subject is centered.

But if you want to know where those magic intersections are, duck into **Settings→Camera**. Turn on **Grid**. Now the phone displays the tic-tac-toe grid, for your composition pleasure (it's not part of the photo). You turn it off the same way.

> **TIP:** This grid also features a carpenter's level, which is handy if you're using your phone to scan a document on the table. If you hold the phone parallel to the floor, a special + indicator floats around the center of the screen. Once it's aligned with the *nonmoving* +, you'll know you're holding it perfectly flat.

High Dynamic Range (HDR) and Deep Fusion

In one regard, digital cameras are still pathetic: Compared with the human eye, they have terrible *dynamic range*.

That's the range from the brightest to darkest spots in a single scene. If you photograph someone standing in front of a bright window, you'll just get a black silhouette. The camera doesn't have enough dynamic range to handle both the bright background and the person in front of it.

You *could* brighten up the exposure so that the person's face is lit—but then you'd brighten the background to a nuclear-white rectangle.

A partial solution: *HDR* (high dynamic range) photography. That's when the camera takes three (or more) photos—at dark, medium, and light exposure settings. Its software combines the best parts of all three, bringing details to both the shadows and the highlights.

Your iPhone has a built-in HDR feature. It's not as amazing as what an HDR guru can do in Photoshop—for one thing, you have zero control over how the images are combined. But, often, an HDR photo does show more detail in both bright and dark areas than a regular shot would. In the photo below, the sky is blown out in the left image—pure white. On the right, the HDR feature brings back streaks of color.

Out of the box, the iPhone applies HDR automatically when it thinks the lighting is right. If you'd rather have manual control, open Settings→Camera→Smart HDR (or Auto HDR). Now there's an HDR button right in the Camera app, which you can tap to turn HDR off or on.

> **TIP:** Should the phone save a standard shot in addition to the HDR shot? On phone models before the 11, that's up to you. In Settings→Camera, you'll find the on/off switch for **Keep Normal Photo**.

And what's the difference between **Smart HDR** and **Auto HDR**? They both work by combining multiple exposures. But Smart HDR also performs dozens of other analysis and adjustment steps in the process. For example, its artificial intelligence has been taught to recognize common elements like faces, hair, beards, and sky. It then examines each of the multiple frames it shot to find the best grab of each of those elements. Smart HDR might light a face more evenly, sharpen the hair, and remove noise (grain) from the sky—all in a fraction of a second.

Furthermore, on these models, Smart HDR affects types of shots that regular HDR does not, like panoramas, shots in dim light, and action photos. Welcome to the world of computational photography.

On iPhone 11 and 11 Pro models, Apple takes this basic concept and runs a marathon with it. These cameras take *nine shots* every time you tap the ◎ button, analyze all 24 million captured pixels, and assemble the finished photo from only the finest, clearest, and best-focused among them. The process is called Deep Fusion, and it's responsible for some of the most impressive phone photography yet.

There's no Deep Fusion on/off switch; it happens automatically every time the phone thinks you need it. It works only on the standard and telephoto lens, not the ultra-wide angle one, and requires that **Settings→ Camera→Capture Outside of Frame** be turned off.

Filters

The success of Instagram made it clear to Apple that the masses want *filters*, special effects that tweak the color of your photo in artsy ways. You, too, can make your pictures look old, washed-out, or oversaturated. In fact, you have nine options at your disposal.

- **Filter before you shoot.** Tap ⚭ to view your options (below, left). You see a scrolling strip of color and black-and-white filters. The first one always represents "no filter."

NOTE: On the iPhone 11 and 11 Pro, swipe up on the screen to reveal the filters button.

Tap a filter thumbnail to try it. Each turns your photo into a variation of black-and-white or plays with its saturation (color intensity), as

shown on the facing page at right. When you've decided what you want, take the shot as usual. (To turn off the filters, tap ⊛ again, and then select the **Original** tile.)

- **Filter after you shoot.** You can also apply a filter to any photo you've already taken; see page 334.

TIP: If you love a certain filter, you can keep it turned on all the time. Open **Settings→Camera→Preserve Settings** and turn on **Creative Controls**.

Taking the Shot

All right. You've opened the Camera app. You've set up the focus, exposure, flash, grid, HDR, and zoom. If, in fact, your subject hasn't already left the scene, you can now take the picture. You do that in any of four ways:

- **Tap** ◎.

- **Press either of the physical volume buttons** on the left edge of the phone.

  This option is fantastic. If you hold the phone with the volume buttons at the top, they're right where the shutter would be on a real camera. Pressing one feels more natural than—and doesn't shake the camera as much as—tapping the screen.

- **Press a volume button on your earbuds clicker**—a great way to trigger the shutter without jiggling the phone at all, and a more convenient way to take selfies when the phone is at arm's length.

- **Say "Hey Siri, say cheese."** Yes, you can snap a shot by voice control—if you've set up the "Say Cheese" shortcut (page 184). With this trick, you can set the phone down 5 feet away and take a photo of yourself with only your voice as the shutter button.

Either way, if the phone isn't muted, you hear the *snap!* sound of a picture successfully taken.

You get to admire your work for only about half a second—and then the photo slurps itself into the thumbnail icon at the lower-left corner of the screen. To review the photo you just took, tap that icon.

At this point, you can look at other pictures you've taken (if the phone is unlocked) by tapping the screen and then **All Photos**.

This is your opportunity to choose a photo (or many) for emailing, texting, posting to Facebook, and so on; tap **Select**, tap the photos you want, and then tap the Share button (⬆). See page 378.

TIP: For details on copying your iPhone photos and videos back to your Mac or PC, see page 562.

Burst Mode

The iPhone can snap *many* photos in a burst—10 shots a second—which is great when you're trying to capture a moment that will be over in a blink: a golf swing, a pet trick, a toddler sitting still.

- **iPhone 11 family.** Drag the ◎ button to the left and hold it there. (You can no longer shoot a burst by holding down a volume key.)

- **Older models.** Hold down the ◎ button or a volume key.

As you hold down your finger, a counter rapidly ticks off how many shots you've fired.

TIP: The front-facing camera can capture bursts, too.

Better yet, the phone helps you *clean up the mess* afterward—the hassle of inspecting all 130 photos you shot, to find the ones worth keeping.

Tap the lower-left thumbnail. To keep you sane, the iPhone depicts your burst as a single photo, with the phrase "Burst (72 photos)" (or whatever) in the corner of the screen. (Its thumbnail bears multiple frames, as though it were a stack of slides.)

Here's where it gets cool. If you tap Select, you see all frames of the burst in a horizontally scrolling row. Underneath, you see an even smaller "filmstrip" of them—and a few are marked with dots.

These are the ones the iPhone has decided are the keepers. It does that by studying the clarity or blur of each shot, examining how much one frame is different from those around it, and even skipping past shots where somebody's eyes are closed. Tap the marked thumbnails to see if you approve of the iPhone's selections.

Whether you do or not, you should work through the larger thumbnails in the burst, tapping each one you want to keep. (The circle in the corner sprouts a blue checkmark.)

When you tap Done, the phone asks: "Would you like to keep the other photos in this burst?" Tap Keep Everything to preserve all the shots in the burst, so you can return later to extract a different set of frames; tap Keep Only 2 Favorites (or whatever number you checked off) to discard the ones you skipped.

Self-Portraits (the Front Camera)

The iPhone has a second camera on the front, above the screen. It lets you use the screen itself as a viewfinder to frame yourself, experiment with your expression, and check your teeth.

To activate the front camera, tap the ⬜ or ⊙. Suddenly, you see yourself on the screen. Frame the shot, and then tap ◯ to take the photo.

Now, the front camera is not the back camera. Unless you're using one of the new iPhone 11 family phones, its resolution, light sensitivity, and focusing ability aren't as good.

But when your goal is a well-framed selfie that you'll use on the screen— email or the web, for example, where resolution isn't very important— then having the front-camera option is better than not having it.

TIP: On an iPhone 11 or 11 Pro, when you hold the phone upright, you get a vertical, 7-megapixel selfie. But if you tap the ⬉ button (or rotate the phone to landscape), the front camera zooms in a tiny bit. Now you'll get a full, 12-megapixel (landscape) photo.

The Self-Timer

A self-timer is essential when you want to be in the picture yourself; you can prop the phone on something and then run into the scene. It's also a great way to prevent camera shake (which produces blurry photos), because your finger doesn't touch the phone. Just tap the ⏱, and then **3s** (a 3-second countdown) or **10s** (10 seconds).

NOTE: On the iPhone 11 and 11 Pro, swipe up on the screen to reveal the self-timer button.

Now, when you tap ◎ or press a volume key, you get a countdown: huge digits on the screen if you're using the front camera, a blinking flash if you're using the rear camera. After the countdown, the phone takes the picture all by itself. (If the sound is on, you'll hear the shutter noise.)

Correction: In its regular, non-Live modes, the phone takes *10* pictures, in burst mode. The phone assumes that if you're using the self-timer, then you won't be able to see when everybody's eyes are open. So it takes 10 shots in a row; you can weed through them later to find the best one.

TIP: The self-timer is available for both the front and back cameras. In other words, it's also handy for selfies.

Live Photos

A Live Photo is a weird hybrid entity: a still photo with a three-second video attached (with sound). You can play it back on any iPhone or Mac.

What you're getting is 1.5 seconds before the moment you snapped the photo, plus 1.5 seconds after. In the Camera app, the ◉ icon lets you know whether or not you're about to capture the three-second video portion when you take a still. (The factory setting, yellow, means it's on.)

TIP: When you take a Live Photo, hold the phone still both before and after you tap the ◉ button. That's when you're recording video.

A yellow "Live" label appears while the video is being captured. That's a warning to keep the phone still longer than you ordinarily would. (If you forget, and you drop your hand too soon, iOS is smart enough to auto-delete the blurry garbage that results at the end of the shot.)

Now, your obvious concern might be file size. "The iPhone takes 12-megapixel photos," you might say. "But video has 30 frames a second! One Live Photo must take up 90 times as much storage as a still image!"

Fortunately, no. The actual photo *is* a full 12-megapixel shot. But the other frames of the Live Photo are video with much lower resolution. (And a Live Photo stores only 15 frames a second, not 30.) Overall, an entire Live Photo takes up about *twice* as much space as a still photo.

That's still from 2 to 4 megabytes a shot, though, so be careful about leaving Live Photos turned on for everyday shooting. To prevent Live Photos from turning itself back on again every time you open the Camera app, open **Settings→Camera→Preserve Settings** and turn on **Live Photo**.

Reviewing Live Photos

As you flick through the photos in the Photos app, you'll know when a photo is a Live Photo; you'll see it animate for a half-second.

To play the full three-second video with sound, long-press it.

Editing Live Photos

You can edit Live Photos in all kinds of interesting ways; see page 336.

Sharing Live Photos

What happens if you try to send a Live Photo to some other device? Well, first of all, you'll know you're about to share a Live Photo. After you tap ⬆, a special ⊙ LIVE icon reminds you. You can tap to turn off that logo before you send, so you're sharing only the still photo.

If you proceed with Live Photos turned on, what happens next depends on what kind of device receives it.

If it's running recent Apple software (iOS 9 or later, OS X El Capitan or later), the Live Photo plays on that gadget, too. On the Mac, in Photos, click **Live Photo** to play it. On an iPad or older iPhone, long-press to play it back.

What if it's a device or software program that doesn't know about Live Photos—if you send it as a text message, for example, or open it in Photoshop? Behind the scenes, a Live Photo has two elements: a 12-megapixel JPEG still image and a three-second QuickTime movie. In these situations, only the JPEG image arrives at the other end.

Portrait Mode

Any iPhone with two or more lenses on the back does more than just zoom in or out. These phones can also tell the foreground subject apart from its background. And with that knowledge, the phone can create a soft, blurry-background look. Shown at left, the original shot; at right, the blurred one:

Ordinarily, you see that look only in professional photos, or at least photos taken with big black SLR cameras using high-aperture lenses (f/1.8, for example). But now you can do it with your phone.

The blur in this case is not optically created, the way an SLR makes it. This is a glorified Photoshop filter; it's done with software. Still, the effect generally looks fantastic, even when the outline of the subject is complex (like frizzy hair).

Once you've scrolled through the Camera app's modes to **Portrait**, point the camera at someone between 15 inches and 8 feet away. You see the background blur right in the preview image. Take the shot. If a second person is standing within the range, you can tap the screen to make *that* person the subject.

NOTE: Portrait mode also works on the one-lens iPhone XR, using software alone. Alas, it can focus only on *people*. Two- or three-lens iPhones can focus on pets, objects, people, or anything.

Now, Portrait mode occasionally gets confused when the light is dim; when the subject is covered with a repeating pattern; or when the subject is not in that 15-inches-to-8-feet range. In those instances, you may get *blur bleed*, where the blurriness leaks into the subject like some kind of hideous, detail-eating virus.

As long as the light and the distance are right, though, the results are surprisingly good. Already, the Flickrs and Facebooks of the world are teeming with great-looking, blurry-background photos—taken by iPhones.

 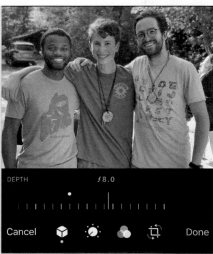

Adjusting the Blur

On the iPhone XS, XS Max, and 11 family, you can dial in how *much* blur you get, either before or after taking the shot. This feature is super-useful, especially when the phone's instinct is to blur out a detail you'd rather remain sharp (like a companion in your group).

To view the **Depth** (blur) slider *before* you take the shot, tap ⓕ in the corner. To adjust the blur later, in Photos, tap **Edit**, and then tap **f4.5** (or whatever the number is) in the corner of the screen.

Neither adjustment is permanent; you can increase or decrease the blur months or years later, without ever affecting the quality of the photo. (You can edit the blur on the Mac, too.)

Studio Lighting

On the iPhone 8 Plus and Face ID models, a further refinement to Portrait mode awaits, something Apple calls *studio lighting*. It's a set of five lighting effects that scroll by as though on a disc. **Natural Light** is the original shot. **Studio Light** brightens your subjects as though they were lit

from the front with pro studio lighting (facing page, top). **Contour Light** deepens shadows.

Stage Light, incredibly, *cuts out the background*, making it black (facing page, bottom left). **Stage Light Mono** does the same, but in black-and-white. And **High-Key Light Mono**, new in iOS 13, is black-and-white with a *white* background (bottom right).

In iOS 13, for the first time, you're allowed to adjust how much of those lighting modes you're applying. After choosing the effect you want to apply, just drag the Amount-O-Meter, the little ruler by the studio-lighting icons.

You can try these lighting modes out either before you snap or after (in Photos, when you tap **Edit**).

Square Mode

Square mode is exactly like Photo mode, except that the photos are square instead of rectangular.

Pano Mode

The iPhone lets you capture a 240-degree, ultra-wide-angle photo (63 megapixels!) by swinging the phone around you in an arc. The phone creates the panorama in real time, smoothly adjusting the exposure of the scene as you pan. You don't have to line up the sections yourself.

Next time you're standing at the edge of the Grand Canyon—or anything else that requires a *really* wide or tall angle—keep this feature in mind.

> **TIP:** The big white arrow tells you which way to move the phone. But you can reverse it (the direction) just by tapping it (the arrow) before you begin.

Tap ◎ (or press a volume key). Now, as instructed by the screen, swing the phone around you—smoothly and slowly, please, especially in low light. You can pan either horizontally or (to capture something very tall) vertically.

As you go, the screen gives you feedback. It may say "Slow down" if you're swinging too fast, or "Keep the arrow on the center line" if you're not keeping the phone level. Use the big white arrow itself like a level; you'll leave the center line if you're moving your arm up and down.

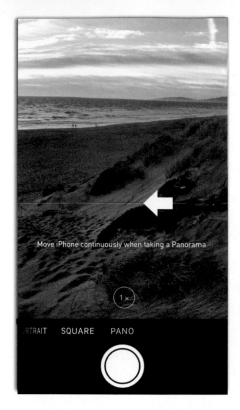

The preview of your panorama builds itself as you move. That is, you're seeing the final product, in miniature, while you're still taking it.

You'll soon learn that 240 degrees—the maximum—is a *really* wide angle. You'll feel twisted at the waist. But you can end the panorama at any stage, by tapping the ⊙ button.

At that point, you'll find that the iPhone has taken a very wide, amazingly seamless photograph at very high resolution (over 16,000 pixels wide). If a panorama is *too* wide, you can crop it, as described later in this chapter.

If you take a real winner, you can print it out at a local or online graphics shop, frame it, and hang it above the entire length of your living-room couch.

Video Mode

The iPhone can record sharp, colorful video. It's at the best flavor of high definition (1080p), or even 4K (four times the resolution of high-def)—and it's stabilized to prevent hand jerkiness. You can shoot in gorgeous, 120- or even 240-frames-per-second *slow-motion* that turns even frenzied action into graceful, liquidy visual ballet.

Shooting video is almost exactly like taking stills. Open the Camera app. Swipe over to, or tap, Video. You *can* hold the iPhone either vertically or horizontally while you film. But if you hold it upright, people on the internet will spit on you; tall-and-thin videos don't fit the world's horizontal screens, including YouTube, laptops, and TVs.

> **TIP:** When you switch from still-photo mode to video, you may notice that the video image on the screen suddenly jumps bigger, as though it's zooming in. And it's true: The iPhone is oddly more "zoomed in" in camcorder mode than in camera mode.

Tap to compute focus, exposure, and white balance, as described for still photos. (You can even long-press to trigger the exposure and focus locks, or drag the tiny yellow sun to adjust exposure manually, as described earlier.)

Then tap Record (⏺)—or press a volume key—and you're rolling! As you film, a time counter ticks away at the top.

iPhone 11 Family: QuickTake Video

If you have an iPhone 11 or 11 Pro, a special treat awaits, which Apple calls QuickTake: You can now shoot videos even in Photo mode! No mode-switching necessary, which can be a time-saving, fumble-reducing blessing.

Instead, just *hold down* the regular shutter button (◎), or single-press either volume key on the side of the phone. You're recording video as long as you're pressing. (A new ◎ button appears, too, in case you want to snap a still photo while you're rolling.)

NOTE: Unfortunately, your video will have whatever aspect ratio (proportions) your *still photo* would have had. Usually, that's 4:3, which is standard for photos but awfully squarish for a video.

Now you understand why Apple granted you a quick way to switch to standard video dimensions, 16:9, as described starting on page 299.

Love that tip? Then here's something even tippier: If your finger gets tired holding down the ◎ button while recording, slide it to the right and then let go. You've just triggered Record Lock (below). Now you'll keep on filming until you tap ⦿ to stop.

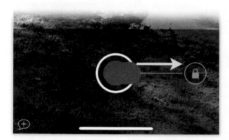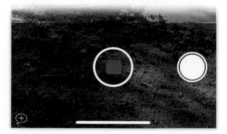

A Note About Resolution—and 4K Video

Video generally plays back at 30 frames a second. But the iPhone 6 and later can record and play back *60* frames a second. Video you shoot this way has a smoothness and clarity that's almost surreal. (It also takes up twice as much space on your phone.) You choose the video quality you want in **Settings→Camera→Record Video**. Experiment with 60 frames per second; see if you feel the result is worth the storage space.

This is also, by the way, where you turn on 4K recording on the 6s and later models. 4K televisions, also called Ultra HD, are TV sets with four times as many tiny pixels as an HDTV, for four times the clarity.

4K shooting is *not* the factory setting, and that's a good thing; it takes up a huge amount of storage space (375 megabytes a minute). Furthermore, you probably don't have anywhere to *play back* recorded 4K video! Paradoxically, no iPhone has enough pixels to play 4K video. To see the difference, you need a 4K television or 4K computer screen, and you still have to sit very close. (You can post 4K video to YouTube—but even then, few people have screens capable of playing it back in 4K.)

TIP: On the iPhone 11 and 11 Pro, tiny readouts at the top of the screen indicate the resolution and frame rate for the video you're *about* to shoot (for example, **4K • 30**). Niftily enough, you can now tap these numbers to change them. The first number cycles among **720p**, **HD**, and **4K**; the frame rate cycles among **24**, **30**, **60**. In other words, you can now change video settings before each shot, without visiting Settings.

Things to Do While You're Rolling

Once you've begun capturing video, don't think your work is done. You can have all kinds of fun during the recording. For example:

- **Change focus.** You can change focus while you're filming, which is great when you're panning from a nearby object to a distant one. Refocusing is automatic. But you can also force a refocusing (for example, when the phone is focusing on the wrong thing) by tapping to specify a new focus point. The iPhone recalculates the focus, white balance, and exposure at the point where you tapped, just as it does when you're taking stills.

- **Change exposure.** While you're recording, you can drag your finger up or down to make the scene brighter or dimmer.

- **Zoom in.** You can zoom in or out while you're rolling. Just spread or pinch two fingers on the screen, like you would to magnify a photo. Pinch two fingers to zoom out again. (This option is not available if you're shooting in 4K mode at 60 frames a second, however.)

  On two- or three-lens phones, you can either do that two-finger spreading *or* drag across the zoom buttons (**0.5**, **1x**, **2x**), as described on page 298. Or *tap* the zoom buttons to jump between zoom levels while you're recording. On the iPhone 11 and 11 Pro, the phone adds a graceful animated zoom effect when you do that, so that the jump isn't quite so sudden.

TIP: On single-lens phones, once you start to zoom, a zoom *slider* appears on the screen. It's much easier to zoom smoothly by dragging its handle than it is to use a two-finger pinch or spread.

So here's a smart idea: Zoom in slightly before you start recording, so the zoom slider appears on the screen. Then, during the shot, drag its handle to zoom in, as smoothly as you like.

- **Take a still photo.** Yes, you can snap still photos *while* you're capturing video. Just tap the ◎ that appears while you're filming. Awesome.

The pictures you take while filming have the same aspect ratio (proportions) you're using for your video. Videos are usually 16:9—wider and squatter than 4:3 photos—so you may be in for a surprise.

When you're finished recording, tap ⏺. The iPhone stops recording and plays a chime; it's ready to record another shot.

There's no easier-to-use camcorder on earth. And what a lot of capacity! Each individual shot can be an hour long—and on the 512-gigabyte iPhones, you can record *272 hours* of video. Enough to capture the entire elementary-school talent show.

The Front Camera

You can film yourself, too. Just tap ⬚ or ⟳ before you film to make the iPhone use its front-mounted camera. The resolution isn't as high as what the back camera captures—except on the iPhone 11 and 11 Pro—but it's still high definition.

The Video Light

You know the LED "flash" on the back of the phone? You can use it as a video light, too, supplying some illumination to subjects within about 5 feet or so. Just tap the ⚡ and then tap **On** before you start recording. (Alas, you have to turn the light on before you start rolling. You can't turn it on or off in the middle of a shot.)

Slow Motion

The Camera app's Slo-Mo mode is exactly like its video mode—but, behind the scenes, the phone is recording 120 or 240 frames a second instead of the usual 30.

Here are some of the settings involved:

- **Adjust the frame rate.** The iPhone can record at *either* 120 frames per second (slow motion) or 240 (even slower motion). You make your choice in **Settings→Camera →Record Slo-mo**.

- **Shoot front or back.** Most iPhones can shoot slo-mo only using the back camera. The iPhone 11 family, however, can even shoot slow-motion from the *front* camera, creating an effect Apple hopes people will call "slowfies." (Dream on, Apple.)

When you open the captured movie to watch it, you see something startling and beautiful: The clip plays at full speed for one second, slows down to one-quarter or one-eighth speed, and, for the final second, accelerates back to full speed.

What you may not realize, however, is that you can adjust *where* the slow-motion effect begins and ends in the clip. When you open the video for playback and then hit **Edit**, a strange kind of tick-marked ruler track appears below it. Drag the vertical handles inward or outward to change the spot where the slow motion begins and ends.

Just above those tick marks is a second, taller strip with yellow handles; you use this one to trim the ends off the video (see below) or to scroll quickly through the clip to see where you are.

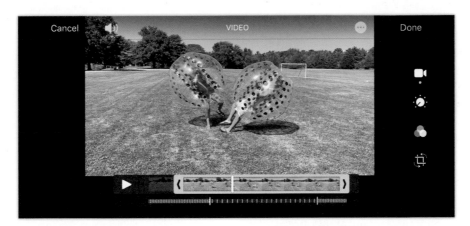

Time-Lapse Mode

Whereas Slo-Mo mode is great for slowing down *fast* scenes, the Time-Lapse mode speeds up *slow* scenes: flowers growing, ice melting, candles burning, and so on.

Actually, this mode might better be called *hyperlapse*. Time-lapse implies that the camera is locked down while recording. But in a hyperlapse video, the camera is moving. This mode works great for bike rides, hikes, drives, and so on; it compresses even multihour events down to under a minute of playback, with impressive smoothness.

The longer you shoot, the greater the speed-up. The app accelerates every recording enough to play back in 20 to 40 seconds, whether you film for 1 minute, 100 minutes, or 1,000 minutes.

If you film for less than 20 seconds, your video plays back at 15 times original speed. But you can film for much, much longer, like 30 hours or more. Time-Lapse mode speeds up the result from 15x, 240x, 960x—whatever it takes to produce a 20- to 40-second playback.

Viewing Your Photos

Once you've got some photos, the Photos app has another job: presenting them, sharing them, and slideshowing them for all your fans. In iOS 13, Apple has dramatically upgraded this aspect of Photos.

At the bottom of the Photos app screen, four tabs lie in wait: **Photos**, **For You**, **Albums**, and **Search**. The following pages crawl through them in sequence.

TIP: The Photos app is fully rotational. That is, you can turn the phone 90 degrees. Whether you're viewing a list, a screen full of thumbnails, or an individual photo, the image on the screen rotates, too, for easier admiring. (Unless, of course, you've turned on rotation lock, as described on page 45.)

The Photos Tab

On the Photos tab, iOS groups your photos intelligently into sets that are easy to navigate.

The **Years**, **Months**, and **Days** views are extraordinary displays. Each presents representative photos chosen by artificial intelligence. These displays aren't cluttered up by screenshots, receipts, or duplicate photos, and the AI crops each thumbnail to show only the important part of the photo it represents.

You can switch among the views by tapping the buttons at the bottom of the Photos tab, of course. But it's much more fun to pinch or zoom with two fingers to move from **Years** to **Months** to **Days**—or the other direction.

What's cool is that as you zoom into finer time increments, you remain on the same key photo. For example, if a photo of you doing a belly flop is the sample photo for 2019, zooming into **Months** reveals the same photo in the context of July of that year, and zooming into **Days** reveals the same photo on July 15. (If you zoom in still more, you actually open that photo and start enlarging it.)

- **Years view** presents one handsome photo for each year (facing page, left); it starts out showing you a photo from *this time of year* each year. Scrolling through them is like a photographic time machine.

- **Month view** (above, middle) *isn't* one photo per month. There *are* month headings, but the photo thumbnails are grouped by Moments—that is, taken in one place at one time (all the shots at the picnic by the lake one weekend, for example). The phone even uses its GPS to give each cluster a name: "San Francisco, California (Union Square)," for example.

- **Days view** is a grid of beautiful photos (above, right). You can, of course, tap one of the pictures or videos to open it full-screen, but the photo grid is almost as good as a slideshow right there.

NOTE: As you scroll through these displays, videos and Live Photos play silently in place. It's a lovely effect.

- **All Photos** (next page, left) carries over from previous iOS versions. It's a massive, chronological, endlessly scrolling sheet of tiny photo thumbnails.

  Long-press any image within the batch to see a larger version of it, complete with **Copy**, **Share**, **Favorite**, and **Delete** buttons.

The "For You" Tab

The more Apple invests in machine learning (a form of AI), the better Photos gets at figuring out which are your best shots and how to present them to you!

This tab offers groupings like this:

- **Shared Album Activity.** Here are the latest photos in your Shared albums (page 351).

- **Recently Shared** are photos and videos you've sent to somebody (or somebodies) as Messages.

- **Memories.** What Apple calls *Memories* are automatically selected groups of pix and videos from certain time periods or trips, which, with a tap, become gorgeous, musical slideshows (below, right). Most people are pleasantly surprised at how coherent and well-created these are, even though they're totally automated. Photos, short pieces of your videos, and even scrolling panoramas are all first-class citizens in these slideshows.

Right off the bat, you see a few of Photos' suggestions, represented as labeled billboards ("Cape Cod Summer," "Best of Last Week," "Casey and Me"). Tap to open a Memory. Tap ▶ to start an instant slideshow, with music, with photos changing to the beat. They're usually fantastic.

During the slideshow, you can tap for some quick editing options (below, left). You can change the animation/music style (**Dreamy, Sentimental, Gentle, Chill,** and so on) or the slideshow length (**Short, Medium, Long**).

For more detailed editing at this point, tap **Edit**. Now you can edit the Memory's **Title** (name), **Title Image** (the main photo representing this Memory), **Photos & Videos** (tap + to add one, 🗑 to delete one), **Music** (either the app's selections or anything from your music library), or **Duration** (dial up any length you want).

> **TIP:** When you tap +, the Select Photos screen shows all candidate shots; checkmarks appear on the ones Photos has chosen to include. Now you can adjust which shots appear in the Memory— and also admire how clever Photos has been in the first place.

When playback (and editing) are all over, you can scroll down to see the photos, people, and places that make up this Memory.

At the very top, the ⚫ button offers options like **Share Photos** (uses the same sharing mechanism described on page 378—even suggests, as shares, people it recognizes in the photos); **Delete Memory**; and **Add to Favorite Memories** (adds this slideshow to a new folder on the Albums tab called Favorite Memories, for quick access later).

Once you've got a killer Memory on your hands, don't miss the option to send it to other people as a video. While a Memory slideshow is playing, tap it to reveal the 📤 button at the bottom.

• **Featured Photos.** Apple is coy about which photos show up in this row, other than to say its AI considers them your "best photos." They're usually in focus and well-lit, and occasionally you'll see one that was taken "On This Day" in an earlier year. Think of it as Photos' version of the Facebook feature that digs up old photos it thinks you might like to be reminded of.

• **Effects Suggestions** are photos that Photos, in all its modesty, thinks could be improved with one of its effects. If you take a lot of Live Photos (page 306), that may mean applying something like Loop, Bounce, or Long Exposure—see page 336. If you've taken some Portrait-mode shots, you may see a proposal to add one of the studio-lighting effects (page 310).

• **Sharing Suggestions** are pictures that were all taken at the same time and place. Photos does its best to recognize who's *in* the pictures— and to propose sharing with those people. Details on page 351.

The Albums Tab

The third tab of your Photos app, **Albums**, presents another set of roads into your photo collection. Each category presents a few example albums to get you started—and then offers a **See All** button to expand that category.

The primary headings are these:

- **My Albums.** Here you get a list of albums *you've* created (or copied to the phone from your Mac or PC). The first one is always **Recents**—everything on your phone, including videos.

  Favorites is here, too. This folder gives you quick access to your favorite photos. And how does the phone know which photos are your favorites? Easy: You've told it. You've tapped the ♡ icon under a photo, anywhere within the Photos app.

- **Shared Albums** lists the most recent clusters of pictures you've electronically shared with other people—or that they've shared with you, as described on page 351. Each thumbnail shows tiny headshots of the people you've sent them to.

- **People & Places.** Impressively enough, Photos can auto-group your photos according to which people are in them (using facial recognition) and the places where you shot them (using GPS). You get one icon here for People, and one for Places.

  People: Once you've given the software a running start, it can find those people in the rest of your photo collection automatically. That's handy every now and then—when you need several photos of your kid for a school project, for example.

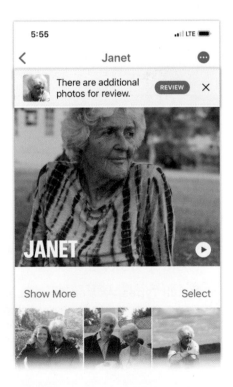

On the People screen, you get thumbnails representing the faces Photos has found and grouped, complete with a tally of how many photos it's found. At the top, you see people you've designated as favorites (previous page, left).

Tap a thumbnail to see all the photos of this person (previous page, right). If you see "There are additional photos for review" at the top, tap **Review**; Photos shows you other photos it thinks are the same person. Select the ones it got right, and then hit **Done**; hit **Add Name** to name the person (if you haven't already), so Photos will more correctly identify her from now on.

TIP: If Photos has created two "people" icons for the same person, here's how to fix it: Tap one of her thumbnails to open it; tap **Select**; tap each duplicate, and then hit **Merge**.

If there's a photographed person in your life whom Photos doesn't offer on the People screen, by all means add that person yourself. Open the photo, swipe up to see a tiny round headshot of each person in it, tap a person, tap **Add Name**, enter the name, tap **Next**, and then tap **Done**.

And if there's someone Photos is misidentifying—an Aunt Gertie wound up as an Uncle Eugene—you can fix her, although you'll have to tap this sequence very carefully:

In the People album, tap the **Uncle Eugene** thumbnail. Tap **Show More**→**Select**→**Show Faces** and select each misidentified face. Then tap ⬆ to open the Share sheet, and finally tap **Not This Person**.

TIP: That weird Share-sheet method is also how you choose a different *key photo*—the one headshot that represents this person on the main People screen. In the People album, tap the person's tile, and then tap **Select**. Tap the preferred photo, tap ⬆ to open the Share sheet, and then finally tap **Make Key Photo**.

Places: Every photo you take with a smartphone (and a few very fancy cameras) gets *geotagged*—stamped, behind the scenes, with its geographic coordinates. When you tap **Places**, you see a map, dotted with clusters of photos you took in each place. Tap one to see the photos you took there.

- **Media Types.** As a convenience to you, these categories give you one-tap shopping for everything you've captured using the Camera app's specialized picture and video modes: **Videos**, **Selfies**, **Live Photos**, **Portrait** (if you have a Plus or Face ID phone), **Long Exposure**,

Panoramas, Time-Lapse, Slo-Mo, Bursts, Screenshots, Screen Recordings, and Animated. (Long Exposure and Animated are Live Photos to which you've applied the effects described on page 337.)

Super-handy when you're trying to show someone your latest time-lapse masterpiece, for example; now you know where to look for it.

- **Imports.** This "album" is incredibly useful, if you can remember it exists. It lists all the photos you've taken with *other cameras*—actual cameras, drones, GoPros, and so on—that you imported into the iPhone, a Mac, or any other Apple gadget associated with your iCloud account.

- **Hidden.** Here are photos you've hidden, as described on page 329.

- **Recently Deleted.** Even after you think you've deleted a photo or video from your phone, you have 30 days to change your mind. Deleted pictures and videos sit in this folder, quietly counting down to their own doomsdays.

  If you wind up changing your mind, you can open Recently Deleted, tap the photo you'd condemned, and tap Recover. It pops back into its rightful place in the Photos app, saved from termination.

  On the other hand, you can also zap a photo into oblivion immediately. Tap to open one of your recently deleted photos, tap Delete, and then confirm with Delete Photo. If you tap Select, you can also hit Delete All or Recover All.

As you'd guess, you can drill down from any of these groupings to a screen full of thumbnails, and from there to an individual photo.

You can manually add selected photos into new albums—a great way to organize a huge batch you've shot on vacation.

To do that, open a set of photos (for example, your All Photos album). Tap Select; and then tap (or drag through) all the photos you want to move to a new or different album. Tap ⬆ to open the Share sheet; scroll down, and hit Add to Album. From here, you can either choose an existing album or hit New Album.

NOTE: These buttons don't actually move photos around. You're creating *aliases* of them—pointers to the original photos. If you edit a photo from one album, it's edited in all of them.

To delete an album you created on the phone, start on the main Albums tab. Tap See All, and then Edit, and then tap the ⊖ button on the album you want to delete.

The Search Tab

A search tab in Photos might seem odd. How can you search for a blob of pixels? How does the phone know what's *in* a picture?

Artificial intelligence, people. Apple has given Photos the ability to recognize what's *in* your pictures and videos. You can search for "dog," or "beach," or whatever. You can search by who's in the pictures, what the event was (concerts, festivals), by month or season or year, by business or museum, and so on. Or combine all of those into one search.

When you tap Q, the phone offers some one-tap canned searches based on dates (like **One Year Ago** and **Trips**), people's faces, locations (like **Massachusetts** and **San Francisco Airport**), and categories (like **Animals**, **Sports**, and **Performances**). Tap to see the photos and videos that match.

To search for something more specific, you can type things like these:

- **Place or event names.** *Tucson, bay area, detroit, daleford road, sundance film festival, superbowl, home, lincoln high school, museum...*

- **Times.** *Last year, 2018, summer, night, morning, last week, march 2016, yesterday...*

- **People.** *Casey, dad, me, sherwood atkinson...*

- **Captions or album names.** *Chess club, corp offsite, robin's first jalapeño, mom bday...*

- **Nouns.** *Forest, girl, plane, piano, fence, field, food truck, restaurant, party, citrus fruit, storefront, pizza, graffiti, money, mountain, cats, skiing, hat, dancing, music...*

As you type, Photos builds a list of search terms it thinks you might intend. (If you've typed *Fi*, it might list **Fish**, **Fish Tank**, **Fig Tree**, and so on.) Each shows how many pictures match that term.

Tap one of these autocomplete terms to see all the matching photos. (The best matches appear in clusters: photo thumbnails, Moments, Albums, Dates, Memories. To see all the matching photos, tap **See All**.)

You can also *combine* search terms. The instant you tap one of the search results, you're offered two ways to refine your search:

- **The search-results list changes** to reveal subcategories. If you just searched for *2015*, for example, the options may now include **Fall**, **Winter**, **United States**, **Sports**, and **Mom**—all from 2015.

- **The result you tapped becomes** a *token* in the search box—a blue rectangle with an icon, as shown below.

  In this example, if you tap **Musical Instruments** in the first results list, that term becomes a token (middle).

  The results list now offers subcategories *within* that token. In the example, suppose you tap **Jeffrey** as the person (middle). Now *Jeffrey* becomes a token.

By the time you're finished, the tokens might include **Musical Instruments Jeffrey Summer**—the perfect way to pull up that hilarious picture you remember taken of your nephew struggling to carry a string bass that one July.

Apple's image recognition software is pretty amazing. It makes occasional mistakes—you may find a truck in your **Cars** category or something—but in general, it's an amazing way to find a pixel in a haystack.

TIP: For simple queries, it's usually faster to request such photos by voice, using Siri: "Show me all the photos from Texas in 2017." See page 177.

Working with Photos

What do the **Photos**, **For You**, **Albums**, and **Search** tabs all have in common? They all permit you to drill down, eventually, to an individual photo or video. Once you're there, here's what you can do.

Flicking, Rotating, Zooming, Panning

Once a photo is open at full size, you have your chance to perform the four most famous and dazzling tricks of the iPhone: flicking, rotating, zooming, and panning a photo.

- **Flicking** horizontally is how you move to the next/previous photo or movie. As you flip through your collection in iOS 13, videos start playing automatically—but silently. If you tap ◤, the audio plays, too, even if your silencer switch is on. (If you prefer the old way, where videos didn't play automatically at all—and played with sound when they did—turn off **Settings→Photos→Autoplay Videos and Live Photos**.)

- **Zooming** a photo means magnifying it. Double-tapping it is one way, but the two-finger spread gives you more control over what gets magnified and by how much. Once you've spread a photo bigger, you can then pinch to scale it down again. Or just double-tap to restore the original size. (You don't have to restore a photo to original size before advancing to the next one, though; if you flick enough times, you'll pull the next photo onto the screen.)

- **Panning** is moving a photo around on the screen after you've zoomed in. Just drag your finger; no scroll bars are necessary.

- **Rotating** is what you do when a horizontal photo or video appears on the upright iPhone, which makes the photo look small and fills most of the screen with blackness.

  Just turn the iPhone 90 degrees in either direction. The photo rotates and enlarges to fill its new, wider canvas. (This doesn't work when the phone is flat on its back—on a table, for example. It has to be more or less upright. It also doesn't work when portrait orientation is locked.)

  When the iPhone is rotated, all the controls and gestures reorient themselves. For example, flicking right to left still brings on the next photo, even if you're now holding the iPhone the wide way.

Hide a Photo

Here's a quirky little feature: It's possible to hide a photo from the Photos tab so it appears only in a special Hidden folder.

Apple noticed that lots of people use their phones to take screenshots of apps, pictures of whiteboards, shots of package labels or parking-garage signs, and so on. These images aren't scenic or lovely; they're not memories; you don't want a slideshow of them; and they don't look good when they appear nestled in with your shots-to-remember.

Open the photo and then tap 🔼; in the Sharing options that appear, tap **Hide**. To confirm, tap **Hide Photo**.

Whatever photos you hide go to the **Hidden** folder on the Albums tab, so you can find them easily. From here, you can unhide a shot the same way: Hit 🔼 and then **Unhide**.

Deleting Photos

If some photo no longer meets your exacting standards, you can delete it. Open the photo; tap 🗑. When you tap **Delete Photo**, that picture is gone. Or, rather, it's moved to the **Recently Deleted** folder described on page 325; you have 30 days to change your mind.

The exception: If you use iCloud Photos (page 354), you're warned that you're about to delete the photo from all your devices—and that's what happens.

Photo Controls

When you first open a photo, some useful controls appear, in blue against the white background (next page). They show up either at the top or bottom of the screen, depending on how you're holding the phone. (Tap the photo to hide them and summon a black background, for a more impressive photo presentation.)

- **Where and When.** The top of the screen shows where and when this photo was taken ("Dallas, September 13," for example).

- **Edit** is the gateway to the iPhone's photo-editing features, described starting on page 330.

- **Favorite (♡).** When you find a picture you love—enough that you might want to call it up later to show people—tap ♡. This photo or

video now appears in the Favorites folder (in the Albums tab of the Photos app), so it's easy to find with your other prize-winners.

- **Share (⬆) opens the Share sheet,** described starting on page 341. This is where you can *do* something with this photo besides just staring at it. You can use it as your iPhone's wallpaper, print it, copy it, text it, send it by email, use it as somebody's headshot in your Contacts list, post it on Twitter or Facebook, and so on.

- **Delete (🗑).** Gets rid of this photo, as described already.

- **Related photos.** There's one more element of the photo screen that you might miss. To see it, drag upward. You may see a map of where it was taken (and the address) or the headshots of people Photos has recognized.

The New Photo Editor

In iOS 13, Apple blessed the Photos app with a huge makeover of its editing tools. You can crop, edit, and adjust the color of your photos in more ways than ever before, with much greater flexibility—and for the first time, you can crop, edit, and adjust the color of your *videos* with the same controls.

> **TIP:** Whenever you're in editing mode, *tap the screen* for a momentary flashback to the original image. Great for A/B comparisons.

To edit a photo, tap its thumbnail (anywhere in the Photos app) to open it. Tap **Edit**. (Almost everything you read here applies equally well to videos, but see page 339 for details.)

Once you've entered Edit mode, you're in a realm of three principal adjustment types. They're represented by the three icons against the bottom of the phone: Adjust Color (⦿), Filters (⊛), and Crop/Straighten (⌗).

> **NOTE:** For the first time in iPhone history, you can zoom in on a photo while editing!

(A fourth icon appears when you're editing a Live Photo, a Portrait photo, or a video; details later.)

In the following pages, you can read about each of these icons.

> **TIP:** You can hold the phone either horizontally or vertically. The control rows jump to the side or the bottom of the screen.

Adjust Color (⦿)

Just beneath or beside the photo, a scrolling line of 16 circular buttons awaits. These are the adjustment buttons. They control **Exposure**, **Contrast**, and so on.

For each picture adjustment, you can dial in how *much* of each effect (**Exposure, Contrast**, and so on) you want to apply. For your convenience, you feel a little click when you return to the original zero-adjustment point.

As you drag this intensity ruler, you can see its effect on the photo. As you drag, for your reference, two other wonderful things happen: The adjustment button itself sprouts a yellow intensity ring that grows as you approach 100 percent, and a number inside the button shows the exact amount you've applied (on a scale up to 100).

> **TIP:** At any time, you can tap the adjustment button to turn its effect off completely—a great way to compare it with the original. Tap again to restore what you'd just dialed in.

Now that you have the lay of the land, here's a tour of the 17 controls.

NOTE: All the changes described on these pages are *nondestructive*. That is, the Photos app never forgets the original photo. At any time, hours or years later, you can return to the Edit screen and undo the changes you've made (tap **Revert**). You can recrop the photo back to its original size, for example, or turn off the Auto-Enhance button. In other words, your changes are never really permanent.

- **Auto-Enhance** (✨). When you tap this magical button, Photos analyzes the relative brightness of all the pixels in your photo and attempts to "balance" it. After a moment, the app adjusts the brightness and contrast and intensifies dull or grayish-looking areas. Usually, the pictures look richer and more vivid as a result.

  You may find that Auto-Enhance has little effect on some photos, only minimally improves others, and totally rescues a few. In any case, if you don't care for the result, you can drag the intensity ruler to dial back the effect, or tap the ✨ button again to turn Auto-Enhance off.

- **Exposure** adjusts the brightness of all pixels.

- **Brilliance** brightens dark areas and dials back the brightest spots to reveal hidden detail.

- **Highlights** recovers lost details out of very bright areas.

- **Shadows** pulls lost details out of very dark areas.

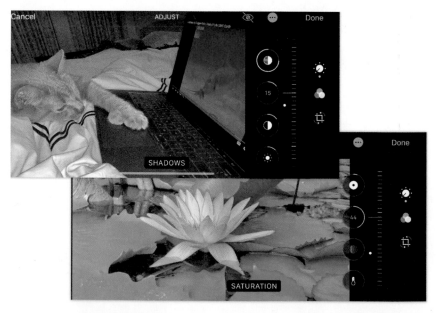

- **Contrast** deepens the most saturated colors.

- **Brightness** is like Exposure, but it doesn't brighten parts that are already bright.

- **Black Point** determines what is "black," shifting the entire dark/light range upward or downward.

- **Saturation** affects the intensity of the colors—from vivid fake-looking Disney all the way down to black and white. Often, just a nudge can liven a dull photo or make blue skies "pop" a little more.

- **Vibrance,** new in iOS 13, intensifies colors, much like Saturation—but without altering skin tones.

- **Warmth** adjusts the color tint of the photo, making it warmer or cooler overall by shifting all colors along the yellow-to-blue spectrum.

- **Tint** is similar to Warmth but affects colors on the green-to-magenta spectrum.

- **Sharpness,** new in iOS 13, applies a subtle crispness to the photo by emphasizing the brightness differential of adjacent color areas.

- **Definition** (also new) adds clarity by adjusting the contrast of the photo's midtones.

- **Noise Reduction** attempts to remove the tiny colored speckles (digital "noise") that sometimes appear in low-light photos, making them look grainy.

- **Vignette** is new in iOS 13. It darkens or brightens the four corners of the photo. When applied subtly, the result draws the viewer's eyes to the center of the picture; when applied heavily, the whole thing looks like an 1850s daguerreotype image.

- **Remove Red Eye (⊘).** This button appears at the top of the editing screen only if Photos does, in fact, find red-eye—devilish, glowing-red pupils—in your subjects' eyes.

  Red-eye is caused when the light of your flash illuminates the blood-red retinal tissue at the back of the eyes. That's why red-eye problems are worse when you shoot pictures in a dim room: Your subjects' pupils are dilated, allowing even *more* light from your flash to reach their retinas.

  When you tap this button, a message says, "Tap each red-eye." Do what it says: Tap with your finger inside each eye that has the problem. A little white ring appears around the pupil, and the app turns the red in each eye to black.

At any point, you can tap **Cancel** to abandon your editing altogether, or **Done** to save the edited photo and close the editing controls.

Filters (⊗)

Filters are effects that make a photo black and white, oversaturated, or washed out. You can apply a filter either as you take the picture (page 302) or afterward.

Tap ⊗ to view a scrolling row of filter buttons. Tap each to see what it looks like on your photo. As with picture adjustments, you can then dial back the intensity of the filter by dragging the effects ruler. And you can temporarily remove the filter (to compare with the original photo) by tapping the photo itself.

(Don't these filters more or less duplicate the effects of the color adjustments described already? Yes. But filters produce canned, instant changes that don't require as much tweaking.)

Crop/Straighten (⛶)

This button opens a crazy editing screen where you can adjust the proportions, angle, or perspective of the photo, and even make a mirror image of it.

Here's the fun you can have in this mode:

- **Auto.** When you first tap ⛶, iOS analyzes whatever horizontal lines it finds in the photo—the horizon, for example—and uses them as a guide to straightening the photo *automatically*. You see the whole thing rotate, tilting and enlarging slightly to fill the frame without leaving gaps at the corners.

  You can reject the iPhone's proposal (tap **Auto** to turn it off). Or you can tilt the photo more or less (drag your finger across the ruler scale).

- **Flip Horizontal (▲).** Creates a mirror image of the photo or video—something you've never been able to do before in the Photos app. The effect is shown on the facing page at right.

- **Rotate ().** Tap as many times as necessary to turn the picture 90 degrees or even upside-down.

- **Straighten (⊖).** This slider lets you tilt the photo manually, to compensate for bad framing when you took the shot.

- **Vertical, Horizontal Perspective (▲, ◀).** As a little gift to you in iOS 13, Apple has now given you perspective-correction tools. Drag the slider to "tip" the photo in space, either vertically or horizontally, as though you're changing your viewing angle. Below at right, the lower edge is being expanded to emphasize the dog's size.

- **Constrain Cropping (▢).** The other work you can do in this mode is *cropping* (below, left).

Cropping means shaving off unnecessary portions of a photo. Usually, you crop a photo to improve its composition—adjusting where the subject appears within the frame of the picture. Often, a photo has more impact if it's cropped tightly around the subject, especially in portraits. Or maybe you want to crop out wasted space, like big

expanses of background sky. If necessary, you can even chop a former romantic interest out of an otherwise perfect family portrait.

To crop a photo you've opened, drag inward on any edge of the white border. The part of the photo the iPhone will eventually trim away is dimmed. You can recenter the photo within your cropping frame by dragging any part of the photo, inside or outside the white box. Adjust and drag until everything looks just right.

TIP: Remember the **Capture Outside the Frame** option described on page 299 (iPhone 11 and 11 Pro)? This is the big payoff.

A tiny ⌜⁺⌟ symbol on an open photo or video indicates that it was captured with that extra margin of image. Tap **Edit**, then tap ⌑. Now you can not only crop into the photo or video—you can crop *outward*, bringing previously hidden portions into view.

If you've turned on **Settings→Camera→Apply Auto Adjustments**, the app may use that extra image area automatically, for the purposes of straightening the photo or video and improving its composition. If you're not a fan of its work, tap **⌐⌐AUTO** to turn it off.

Ordinarily, you can create a cropping rectangle of any proportions, freehand. But if you tap ◧, you get a choice of nine canned proportions: **Original**, **Freeform**, **Square**, **16:9**, **7:5**, **4:3**, and so on. They force the cropping frame to preset proportions as you drag.

NOTE: The **Original** option here maintains the proportions of the original photo even as you make the grid smaller.

This aspect-ratio feature is important if you plan to order prints of your photos at standard photo sizes: 4 × 6, 5 × 7, 8 × 10, and so on. (The iPhone's standard photos are 4 × 3, which doesn't divide evenly into most of those standard print sizes.)

When you tap one of the preset sizes, the cropping frame *stays* in those proportions as you drag its edges.

Marking Up Your Photos

Here's a feature nobody saw coming: You can draw or type on your photos, right from within the Photos app. Once you're in editing mode, tap ⊙ and then **Markup**. iOS 13 presents its new, improved standard drawing kit, which is described on page 458.

Editing Live Photos

When you tap **Edit** on a Live Photo, you get a bonus button at the bottom that looks like this: ◎.

When you tap it, you get a ◀)) button, which lets you turn off the sound; a ⊙LIVE button, which eliminates the three-second video and creates a plain old photo; and a sort of filmstrip along the bottom. You can use it for two things:

- **Drag the (and) markers** (currently at the outer ends of the little filmstrip) inward, exactly as shown on page 317. You're trimming the Live Photo so that it's shorter.

- **Tap a different "frame" of the filmstrip,** and then tap Make Key Photo, to designate that frame as the new face of this Live Photo—the one that shows up as its thumbnail in, for example, the Photos app.

NOTE: If you change the key photo and then export the Live Photo, remember that you're sending what used to be a frame of video. It may be blurrier than the actual photo, and it has somewhat lower resolution. Still, sometimes it may be just what you need.

But there's even more fun to be had with Live Photos—and not in the Edit mode, either. (Hit Done or Cancel to get out of there, if necessary.)

On the Live Photo's normal viewing page, the one with the ‹ and Edit buttons, you can *swipe upward* to reveal a choice of four special video-playback effects, which used to require separate apps to achieve:

- **Live.** That's the normal Live Photo as you know it.

- **Loop** makes the three-second video play over and over again, with a crossfade to conceal the seam. Great for funny expressions, cat yawns, pratfalls.

- **Bounce** plays start→finish→start→finish, and so on, playing forward and then backward. Use it on a Live Photo of a kid doing a cannonball into a pool. Pure comedy.

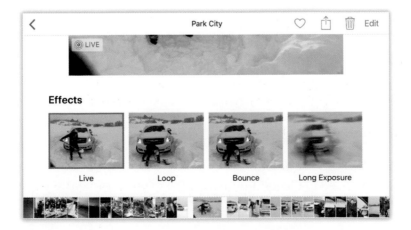

- **Long Exposure** simulates the effect of leaving the camera on a tripod with the lens open for a long time. In "real" photography, the result might produce the milky, softly blurred surface of a babbling brook, or cool-looking red streaks of taillights.

Realistically, this effect works only on scenes where the background *doesn't* move, but the subject *does*. Classic examples include moving water, moving traffic, and moving people—in crowds or on teams.

Unlike the other effects, the result of this one is a still image; the effect more or less *superimposes* all the frames in the Live Photo. (The video element is still there, looking like a standard Live Photo—long-press the screen to see it.) But the goal here is to export the finished still image. Every now and then, the result is surprising and delightful.

Original Live Photo

Long Exposure effect

Handing Off to Other Editing Apps

OK, Apple: Who are you, and what have you done with the company that used to believe in closed systems?

Camera+, Fragment, and other photo apps now work so well with the Photos app that it can seem as though their tools are built right into it.

Here's the drill: Open a photo in Photos. Tap **Edit**. Tap ⦿. Now you see the icons of all apps on your phone that have been updated to work with this feature, which Apple calls Extensibility.

The photo opens immediately in the app you choose, with all its editing features available. You can freely bounce back and forth between Apple's editor and its competitors'.

Saving Your Changes

Once you've rotated, cropped, auto-enhanced, or color-tweaked a photo, tap **Done**. You've just made your changes permanent.

Or, rather, *temporarily* permanent. Remember: You can return to an edited photo at any time to undo the changes you've made (tap **Revert**). When you send the photo off the phone (by email, to your computer, whatever), *that* copy freezes the edits in place—but the copy on your phone is still revertable.

> **NOTE:** If you sync your photos to Photos on the Mac (over a cable or via iCloud Photos), they show up in their edited condition. Yet, amazingly, you can undo or modify the edits there! The original photo is still lurking behind the edited version. You can use your Mac's Crop tool to adjust the crop, for example. Or you can use Photos' **Revert to Original** command to throw away *all* the edits you made to the photo while it was on the iPhone.
>
> (If you transfer the photos using email, AirDrop, or Messages, however, you get only the finished JPEG image; you *can't* rewind the changes.)

Editing Videos

The miracle of the Photos app in iOS 13 is that it's perfectly happy editing videos in all the same ways it can edit photos.

There, against the bottom of the phone, are four modes, three of which are now familiar:

- **Color Adjustments (☀).** Here are your color adjustments. You can now apply them to entire videos! Brighten them up, goose their saturation, sharpen them a little, bring out detail from the murky blacks, and so on.

- **Filters (⊗).** Yep. You can now apply these canned color filters to videos, too.

- **Crop/Straighten (⛶).** This is amazing. In iOS 13, for the first time, you can rotate, flip, and straighten videos right in Photos! (You know all those times the phone got confused about which way was right-side-up during filming? Now you can fix it.)

You can also crop in on your videos. If you shot in 4K, for example, you can effectively zoom in on a subject by cropping away the outer margins of the shot, and still have plenty of resolution left for hi-def playback. It's a classic video-editing cheat, and now it's yours.

Even the two perspective buttons work on videos.

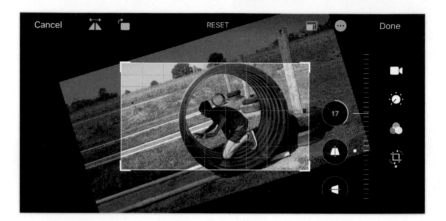

- **Video (▢◁).** This first icon lets you trim off the dead air at the beginning and the end of your video. To do that, drag the **(** and **)** markers (currently at the outer ends of the little filmstrip) inward so they turn yellow. (It helps to pause with your finger down before dragging.) Adjust them, hitting ▶ to see the effect as you go.

TIP: You can drag the playback cursor—the vertical white bar that indicates your position in the clip—with your finger. That's the closest thing you get to Rewind and Fast-Forward buttons. (In fact, you may have to move it out of the way before you can move the end handles for trimming.)

When the handles properly isolate the good stuff, tap **Done**.

This operation is no more destructive to the original video than cropping is to a still photo. That is, at any time later, you can return to Edit mode and reposition those **(** and **)** markers. Restore all the dead air, if you're so inclined.

iMovie for iPhone

You still can't do real video editing in Photos. You still can't string clips together, split them in half, add titles, create crossfades, drop in music, and so on. For that, there's iMovie or Clips for iPhone. Both are free from the App Store.

753 Ways to Share Photos and Videos

It's great that the iPhone has a superb camera. But what you may have forgotten is that it's also a cellphone! That is, it's online. So once you've taken a picture, you can *do* something with it right away. Mail it, text it, post it to Facebook, use it as wallpaper—right from the iPhone.

Step 1: Choose the Photos

Before you can send or post a photo or video, you have to tell iOS which one (or ones) you want to work with. To send just *one*, well, no big mystery; tap its thumbnail and then tap 📤.

But you can also send a bunch of them in a group—whenever you see a Select button (in an album or the Photos tab, for example).

Tap it and then tap the photos you want to send—or drag through several in a row. With each tap, a ✅ appears, meaning, "OK, this one will be included." (Tap again to remove the checkmark.)

Note that, in iOS 13, you can make the thumbnails bigger, making it easier to see what you're dealing with. Tap the ⊘ button, and then either **+** or **−** to enlarge or enshrink them (below, right).

Step 2: Preparing to Send

Once you've opened a photo (or selected a few), tap 📤.

The Share Sheet appears (page 378). At top, a scrolling row of other photos appears. It lets you add more photos to the one(s) you've already selected, or deselect some of them. That's a lot less crazymaking than having to back out of the Share screen to change your selection.

TIP: If you're holding the phone horizontally, select the photos first and then tap **Next** to see the sharing icons.

Below the photos: a row of icons for people (and sharing methods) you use a lot, as described on page 378.

Below that: icons for channels like **AirDrop** (page 380), **Messages**, **Mail**, **Notes**, and other apps you've installed that can accept photos or videos.

TIP: You can hand off a photo to other apps and services—beyond the set Apple provides. Tap **More** to see a setup headquarters for the row of "where you can send photos" icons. They may include **Facebook**, **Twitter**, **WhatsApp**, **Snapchat**, **Instagram**, and so on.

Tap the one you want to use right now—or hit **Edit**. Now you can rearrange them (put the ones you use most often at the top by dragging the ≡ handle); add to the list (turn on the switches for new, non-Apple photo-sharing apps you've installed); hide the services you don't use (turn off the switches); or designate some as Favorites (which appear first in the row of options) by tapping their ⊕ buttons.

Sadly, YouTube and Vimeo aren't listed here. To post videos to those services, use their apps, or iMovie for iPhone.

If you're sending a longish video by Messages, the iPhone compresses it first so it's small enough to send as a text-message attachment (smaller dimensions, lower picture quality). Then it attaches the clip to an outgoing text message; it's your job to address it.

If you're sending a photo by Mail, you may be asked how much you want the photo *scaled down* from its original size. Tap **Small**, **Medium**, **Large**, or **Actual Size**, using the megabyte indicator as a guide. (Some email systems don't accept attachments larger than 5 megabytes.) Any video clip you send by email gets compressed—smaller, lower quality—for the same reason.

Scroll down far enough, and you find a list of commands for further photo sharing. They vary depending on what you've selected (photo or video) and how many, but you might see any combination of these:

- **Copy Photos** puts the photo(s) onto the Clipboard, ready for pasting into another app (an outgoing Mail message, for example). Once you've opened an app that can accept pasted graphics, double-tap to make the **Paste** button appear.

- **Save Image** appears only when you're looking at a photo somebody has texted or emailed to you. It saves the picture to your own photo collection, so you'll be able to cherish it for years.

- **Shared Albums.** You can share batches of photos or videos with other people, either directly to their Apple gadgets or to a private web page. What's more, they can (with your permission) contribute their *own* pictures to the album.

  This is a big topic, though, so it gets its own write-up on page 347.

- **Add to Album.** If this is a photo you've taken with the phone, you're now free to file it away into one of the albums you've made (page 322).

- **Duplicate.** Makes a copy of the photo, which you can doctor beyond all recognition.

- **Hide.** Here's the option to hide a photo, as described on page 329.

- **Slideshow** instantly generates a gorgeous, musically accompanied, animated slideshow. The slideshow incorporates both photos and videos—and when there's sound, the background music actually gets softer so you can hear the audio.

  After the slideshow has begun, tap the screen and then tap Options to see some adjustment controls. For example, a Theme is a canned presentation style, incorporating animations, crossfades, and music. Each makes the photos appear, interact, overlap, and flow away in a different way. You're offered five choices, some of which display more than one photo at a time.)

  You can also choose among the five pieces of background Music here, opt for None, or tap Music Library to choose a song from your music collection.

  There's a Repeat option, too, which makes the slideshow play over and over again until you stop it manually, and a speed slider that controls how much time each photo gets.

  While the show is playing, you can tap the screen to produce the Pause (❙❙) button, or swipe leftward to blow past a photo or video that's taking too long.

- **Copy iCloud Link.** With one tap here, you can copy a link to your invisible Clipboard, ready for texting or emailing to someone: a link that lets your recipient add the selected photos to his own copy of Photos! World's simplest sharing method—and least secure, because he can share that link with anyone.

- **Create Watch Face.** This one's for you, Apple Watch owners! Now a picture you took can become the background for a watch-face design.

- **Save to Files.** Here you can plop some selected photos into one of your iPhone "desktop folders" (see page 421). You may also have a **Save to Dropbox** command, if you use that service.

- **Assign to Contact.** You can use any photo—or part of one—as the headshot for somebody in your Contacts. After that, her photo appears on your screen every time she calls.

  When you tap **Assign to Contact**, your address book list pops up. Tap the name of the person who goes with this photo.

  Now you see a preview of what the photo will look like when that person calls. This is the **Move and Scale** screen described on page 125. You want to crop the photo and shift it in the frame so only *that person* is visible (if it's a group shot)—in fact, probably just the face.

  When you've got the person centered, tap **Choose**.

- **Print.** You can print a photo easily enough, provided that you've hooked up your iPhone to a compatible printer. Once you've opened the photo, tap the ⬆️ button and then tap **Print**. The rest goes down as described on page 377.

- **AirPlay.** This button offers a list of nearby AirPlay gadgets—the only one you've probably heard of is Apple TV—so you can display the current photo on your TV or another screen.

- **Use as Wallpaper.** *Wallpaper* is the background photo that appears in either of two places: the Home screens (plastered behind your app icons) or the Lock screen (which appears every time you wake the iPhone).

  This button lets you replace Apple's standard photos with one of *your* photos. It opens the Move and Scale screen, which lets you fit your photo within the wallpaper "frame." Pinch or spread to enlarge the shot; drag your finger on the screen to scroll and center it.

  Finally, tap **Set**. You now specify where you want to use this wallpaper; tap **Set Lock Screen**, **Set Home Screen**, or **Set Both** (if you want the same picture in both places).

  You can also change your wallpaper within Settings, as described on page 617.

- **Save as Video.** Here's the new option mentioned on page 308. It turns a Live Video into a regular old three-second video clip, which is easier to share with non-Apple people (yes, there are a few left).

- **Edit Actions.** Once again, iOS offers a way to rearrange the Share options—this time, the list of commands—or to add new buttons. If you don't have an Apple Watch, for example, you may as well turn off the Create Watch Face option.

- **Shortcuts.** If you've created any Shortcuts (page 185) that involve photos or videos, you'll see their names in this list too.

Step 3: Options for Messages or AirDrop

In iOS 13, a new strip appears at the top of the screen when you're about to share some pix or vids. It says "9 Photos Selected" (or whatever) and offers an Options button.

Options appears no matter which sending method you're about to choose, but it affects only two sharing methods: Messages and AirDrop.

- **Send As.** When you're sending a big video or a bunch of photos in Messages, do you really want to force your recipients to burn up all that data downloading your stuff? If so, choose Individual Photos.

  But what may be a better option awaits: iCloud Link. It makes Photos post your photos and videos to a private web page and sends only the *link* to them to your recipients. (Automatic means Photos will use the iCloud Link option automatically if you're sending four or more photos, or a really big video.) This way, the recipients can view the photos on a web page, with the option to download only the ones they really want. On the other hand, your link expires in 30 days.

- **Location.** Ordinarily, every photo you take remembers where you took it. Here you're given the option to strip away that information as you share, which could be important if you're a cheater or a spy.

- **All Photos Data.** When you're sending photos and videos *using* AirDrop (page 380), you might want to send only the finished, edited, polished product. They'll receive exactly what they'd get if you used Messages or Mail. If that's how you want it, turn off All Photos Data.

  But if you turn that switch on, your recipients get the original-quality photos and videos, complete with descriptions and keywords you may have applied. Even more amazingly, they get the *editing history*; on their own phones or Macs; they can undo or change any edits you've applied! All Photos Data means "These photos will be every bit as editable on my recipients' machines as pictures and videos they've taken themselves."

My Photo Stream

The concept of My Photo Stream is simple: Every time a new photo enters your life—when you take a picture with your iPhone or import one onto your computer—it gets added to your Photo Stream. From there, it appears automatically on all your *other* iCloud machines.

> **NOTE:** My Photo Stream doesn't sync over the cellular airwaves. It sends photos around only when you're in a Wi-Fi hotspot.

Using My Photo Stream means all kinds of good things:

- **Your photos are always backed up.** Lose your iPhone? No biggie—when you buy a new one, your latest 1,000 photos appear on it automatically.

- **Any pictures you take with your iPhone** appear automatically on your computer. You don't have to sync anything yourself.

> **NOTE:** There's one exception. If you delete a fresh photo while it's still in the Camera app, that photo won't enter your Photo Stream.
>
> A similar rule holds true with edits: If you edit a photo you've just taken, those edits become part of the My Photo Stream copy. But if you take a photo, leave the Camera app, and *later* edit it, My Photo Stream gets the original copy only.

Truth is, My Photo Stream is a very old feature, one Apple has long since expanded and replaced with iCloud Photos (page 354). It works only with photos, not videos, and they're not available on the web (as they are with iCloud Photos). But since Photo Stream is free, a lot of people still use it—as follows.

To turn *on* My Photo Stream, go to **Settings→Photos→My Photo Stream**. (You should also turn it on using the iCloud control panel on your computers. That's in System Preferences on your Mac, or in the Control Panel of Windows.) Give your phone some time in a Wi-Fi hotspot to form its initial slurping-in of all your most recent photos.

Once My Photo Stream is up and running, your **All Photos** folder appears in the Photos app on every iOS device, Mac, or Apple TV you own (or have signed into using iCloud). Inside are the photos that have entered your life most recently.

Now, your iPhone doesn't have nearly as much space as your Mac or PC; you can't yet buy an iPhone with 4 terabytes of storage. That's why, on your phone, your Photo Stream consists of just the last 1,000 photos.

(There's another limitation, too: The iCloud servers store your photos for 30 days. As long as your gadgets go online at least once a month, they'll remain current with My Photo Stream.)

TIP: Ordinarily, the oldest of the 1,000 photos in your Photo Stream scroll away forever as new photos come in. But you can rescue the best ones from that fate—by saving them onto your phone, where they're free from the risk of automatic deletion. Use the **Save Images** button.

Deleting Photos from My Photo Stream

Here's the thing about My Photo Stream: You might think you're taking a private picture with your phone, forgetting that your spouse or parent will see it seconds later on the family iPad.

Fortunately, you can delete incriminating photos from My Photo Stream. Just select the thumbnail of the photo you want to delete, and then tap 🗑. The confirmation box warns you that you're about to delete the photo from all your iCloud machines (and, for shared streams, the machines of everyone who's subscribed to your photographic output).

If you haven't saved it to a different album or roll, it's gone for good when you tap **Delete Photo**.

TIP: My Photo Stream is an older, less capable feature than iCloud Photos (page 354). Yet there are situations where you might want to use both.

Suppose, for example, you own an iPhone, an iPad, and a Mac. You could turn on iCloud Photos, so all your phone pictures automatically appear on the Mac and at *icloud.com*. But maybe, on the iPad, you leave iCloud Photos turned off, so you don't fill up your storage—but then you turn *on* My Photo Stream, so you'll always have access to your latest pictures.

Shared Albums

Shared Albums (formerly iCloud Photo Sharing) is like a tiny Instagram network of your very own, consisting solely of people you invite. You send photos or videos to *other* people's gadgets. After a party or some other get-together, you could send your best shots to everyone who attended; after a trip, you could post your photographic memories for anyone who might care.

The lucky recipients can post comments about your photos, click a "like" button, or even submit pictures and videos of their own.

In designing this feature, Apple had quite a challenge. There's a lot of back-and-forth among multiple people, sharing multiple photos, so Shared Albums can get complicated. Stay calm and keep your hands and feet inside the tram at all times. Here's how it works.

> **NOTE:** On a new iPhone, the feature is already turned on (in Settings→Photos→Shared Albums). On the Mac, open **System Preferences→iCloud**. Make sure **Photos** is turned on; click **Options** and confirm that **Shared Albums** is on, too. On a Windows PC, it's in the iCloud Control Panel for Windows (a free download from Apple's website).

Share Some Photos

To share some of your masterpieces with your adoring fans, do this:

1. **Choose the photos.**

   Open the Photos app. You can open just one photo, open an album, or use the **Select** button to select any bunch of pictures.

2. **Choose the album.**

   Tap ⬆. On the Share sheet, tap **Add to Shared Album** (facing page, top left). Photos proposes putting the photo into whatever shared album you used last, but by tapping its name, you can choose either a different shared album or **New Shared Album** (bottom left).

3. **Specify the audience.**

   You're asked for the iCloud phone number or email addresses of your audience members. Hit ⊕ and choose their addresses just as you would address an outgoing email. For your convenience, a list of recent sharees appears below the To box.

4. **Tap Next.**

   You return to the original sharing windoid, where you can type a comment, if you like ("Here are my best pix of the reunion!"). In theory, you and other people can add to this album later. That's why you're offered the chance to caption each new batch.

5. **Tap Post.**

   Your recipients' phones now get a notification that you've shared some pictures with them!

At any time, you can look over the Shared Album Activity at the top of the **For You** tab in the Photos app. Here, for your amusement, is a visual record of everything that's gone on in Shared Photo Album Land: photos you've posted, photos other people have posted, comments back and forth, likes, and so on. It's your personal photographic Facebook.

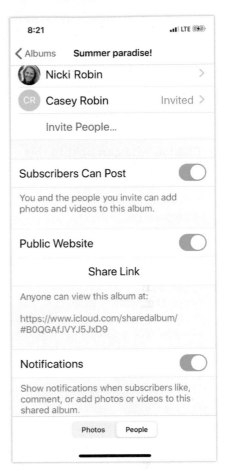

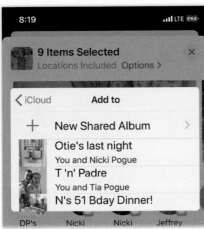

Shared-Photo Management

Once you've shared some pictures like this, here's how you can keep track or change your settings:

- **Look over your shared albums** by tapping the **Albums** tab and scrolling down to Shared Albums. (They also show up on the For You tab, under Shared Album Activity.) Then tap **See All**.

- **Add more photos to an album.** Tap the shared album's thumbnail, and then +. Find the additional photos or videos (use the **All Photos** or **Albums** tabs at the bottom), choose them, tap **Done**, add a comment if you like, and then tap **Post**. (You can also go the other way—by selecting the photos first, anywhere in the Photos app. Then hit 🔄, then **Shared Albums**, then the name of the album you've already shared, and then **Post**.)

- **Delete some.** Tap the shared album, then **Select**; choose the photos to delete, and then hit 🗑. Confirm with a tap on **Delete Photo(s)**.

(You're not deleting photos from your collection—you're just unsharing them.)

- **Change who can see this album.** Tap Albums, then the shared album, and then People (previous page, right). At top, the list identifies everyone with whom you've shared the album. To add a new subscriber, tap Invite People. To delete a subscriber, tap the name and then (at the bottom of the contact card) tap Remove Subscriber.

- **Change who can post to this album.** Your subscribers can contribute photos and videos to your album. That's a fantastic feature when it contains pictures of an event where there was a crowd: a wedding, show, political rally, picnic, badminton tournament. Everyone who was there can enhance the gallery with shots taken from their own points of view with their own phones or cameras.

  Subscribers Can Post, on the same People screen, is the on/off switch for this feature.

- **Make the photos public.** If you turn on Public Website (on the People screen), then even people who aren't members of the Apple cult will be able to see these photos. The invitees will get an email containing a web address. It links to a hidden page on the iCloud website that contains your published photos.

  When you turn this switch on, the web address of your new gallery appears in light-gray type. Tap Share Link for a selection of methods for sending the link to people: by Message, Mail, Twitter, Facebook, AirDrop, and so on.

  What they'll see is a mosaic of pictures, laid out in a grid on a single sort of web poster. Your fans can download their favorites by clicking the ⬇ button. (You can't add comments or "like" photos on the web, however.)

> **TIP:** If you click one of these medium-sized photos, you enter slideshow mode, in which one photo at a time fills your web browser window. Click the arrow buttons to move through them.

- **Adjust notifications.** If the Notifications switch is on (also on the People screen), your phone will notify you each time someone adds photos or videos to your album, clicks the "Like" button for a photo, or leaves a comment.

- **Delete the Shared Album.** If the whole thing gets out of hand, you can slam the door in your subscribers' faces by making the entire album disappear. On the shared album's People screen, hit Delete Shared Album.

Receiving a Photo Album on Your Gadget

When other people share photo albums with *you*, your phone makes a little warble, and a notification banner appears: "[Your buddy's name] invited you to join '[name of shared photo batch]'."

Simultaneously, a badge like (**2**) appears on the Photos app icon and on the **For You** tab within Photos, letting you know how many albums have come your way.

> **NOTE:** If you have Photos or Aperture on a Mac, an invitation to accept the album appears there, too.

You can tap the new album's name to see what's inside it; tap **Accept**.

Once you're subscribed, you view the photos and movies as you would any album—with a couple of differences. First, you can tap **Comment** to make worshipful or snarky remarks, or tap **Like** to offer your silent support.

> **TIP:** Either you or the photo's owner can delete one of your comments. To do that, long-press on the comment itself and then tap the **Delete** button that appears.

You can also snag a copy of somebody's published photo or video for yourself. With the photo before you, tap the 🗋 button to see the usual sharing options—and tap **Save Image**. Now the picture or video isn't some virtual online wisp—it's a solid, tangible electronic copy in your own photo pool.

If your buddy has turned on **Subscribers Can Post** for this album, you can send your own photos and clips into it; everybody who's subscribed to it (and, of course, its owner) will see them.

To do that, tap the + on the album's page of thumbnails; choose your photos and movies; tap **Done**; add a comment; and tap **Post**.

Sharing Suggestions

If you're using iCloud Photos (page 354), then the **For You** tab contains pictures and videos that Apple's artificial-intelligence bot thinks might interest you (next page, left). These tiles appear when the app notices two things about a clump of pictures:

- **There are *people* in the shots**—especially people whose faces it recognizes, because you've tagged them in the People mode (page 323).

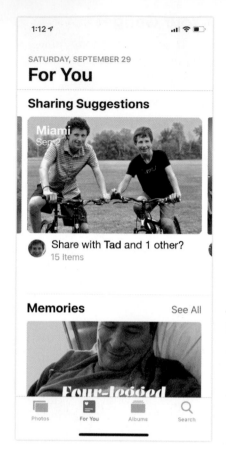

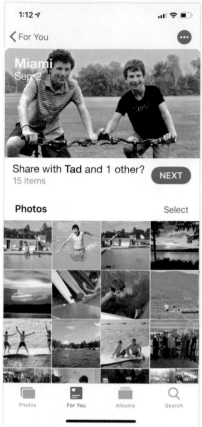

- **They seem to be clustered around a certain time or place,** suggesting that this was an outing, a vacation, an event, a party, or whatever.

iOS is attempting to solve the age-old problem of different attendees having different photos of the same event. It lets all of you share all your photos of the same event with everybody.

If Photos knows who's in these photos, it says, "Share with Casey Robin?" (above, left). If not, it just says, "Share with friends?" Here's how to proceed:

1. **Tap the preview photo to open the details page for this batch.**

   Here's where you can see thumbnails of the photos that Photos intends to send (above, right).

2. **Tap Select, and choose the photos you want to send.**

   If you want to send *most* of them, tap the rejects to turn off their blue checkmarks. If you want to send only a few, tap **Deselect All** and then tap to turn *on* the blue checkmarks.

3. Tap Next. Choose the recipients.

Now you're on the Choose People to Share With screen. If Photos recognizes any faces, you'll see their names.

If you'd like to share these photos with somebody *not* already identified, tap **Add People**; on the next screen, tap ⊕ to choose the person's name from Contacts (or type enough of the name until it's recognized). Repeat until you've added everyone. Tap **Done**.

4. Tap Share in Messages.

Now Messages opens, with your photo set represented as a link, all ready to send. Add a note, if you like, and then tap ⬆.

Let's say you just shared some family-reunion photos with your Aunt Gertie. When she taps your link, she sees a screen almost identical to the one shown on the facing page at left—except that she sees an **Add All** button (meaning she can add all those photos to her own photo library). Of course, she can also tap **Select** and choose only the winners.

Ah, but here's the cool part. If Gertie *also* took some pictures at the reunion, she sees, on the same screen, a Share Back notice, so she can send *her* photos back to *you*. That way, you each wind up with a full collection (or as full as you choose). These are full-resolution original photos. (When she taps **View**, she sees her own set of Family Reunion photos, complete with a **Select** button, so she can choose which photos to send to you.)

A few additional elements to Sharing Suggestions:

• **The Sharing Suggestions** are just another form of the Shared Albums feature described on page 347. For example, once you've shared

7 Photos

From Casey Robin
iCloud link available until Feb 13

Share Back

Share your photos
from San Francisco

VIEW

an album, its thumbnail appears at the top of the **For You** tab, under the heading Shared Album Activity. It lets you monitor who's got your pictures. You can also leave comments, or read other people's comments, exactly as with the Shared Albums feature.

• **If you want to withdraw** your invitation, tap the thumbnail of the shared set (under Recently Shared); tap ●●●; tap **Stop Sharing**. Incredibly, those photos now vanish from your friends' collections.

• **Sharing Suggestions works** by sending a link (via Messages). Keep in mind that anyone who has this link can see those photos. Aunt Gertie is capable of sharing that link with total strangers.

• **You can also see** the identical Sharing Suggestions within the Messages app, which makes sense, since you may well be chatting with the person in those photos. Tap the Photos app button (✳), and then swipe up to see them.

• **Sharing Suggestions aren't available** immediately. It takes the phone a day or so to process all your pictures and choose which ones are worth grouping.

iCloud Photos

If distinguishing among My Photo Stream, Shared Suggestions, and Shared Albums wasn't hard enough, well, hold onto your lens cap. Apple offers yet *another* online photo feature: iCloud Photos (formerly iCloud Photo Library).

The idea this time is that *all* your Apple gadgets will keep *all* your photos and videos backed up online and synced. The advantages:

• **All your photos and videos** are always backed up—not just the last 1,000.

- **All your photos and videos** appear identically on all your Apple machines.

- **You can access** all your photos and videos at *icloud.com*, from any computer or phone.

- **You can reclaim** a lot of storage space. There's an option to offload the original photos and videos to iCloud but leave small, phone-sized copies on your phone.

There's a sizable downside to iCloud Photos, too:

- **Your entire iCloud account** comes with only 5 gigabytes of free storage. If you start backing up your photo library to it, you'll almost certainly have to pay to expand your iCloud storage. Photos and videos eat up a lot of storage space.

If you decide to dive in, turn on **Settings→Photos→iCloud Photos**.

Once iCloud Photos is on, you won't be able to copy pictures from your computer to your phone using iTunes anymore; iTunes will be completely removed from the loop. That's why, at this point, you may be warned that your phone is about to *delete* any photos and videos you've synced to it from iTunes (Chapter 15). Don't worry—they'll be safe in iCloud.

And, of course, you might be warned that you need to buy more iCloud storage space.

Now the Settings panel expands and offers this important choice:

- **Optimize iPhone Storage.** If you turn this on, your original photos and videos get backed up to iCloud—but on your phone, you'll be left with much smaller versions that are just right for viewing on the phone's screen (but not high enough resolution to, for example, print). This arrangement saves you a *ton* of space on your phone.

- **Download and Keep Originals** leaves the big originals on your phone.

Finally, the uploading process begins. If you have a lot of photos and videos, it can take a very long time. But when it's all over, you'll have instant access to all your photos and videos in any of these places:

- **On the iPhone (or other iOS gadgets).** In the Photos app, on the Albums tab, the "album" called **All Photos** represents your new online photo library. Add to, delete from, or edit pictures in this set, and you'll find the same changes made on all your other Apple gear.

- **On the web.** You can sign into *icloud.com* and click **Photos** to view your photos and videos, no matter what machine you're using. Click a photo to open it full size, whereupon the icons at the top of the screen let you delete, download, or favorite it.

- **On the Mac.** Everything appears in the All Photos heading in the Photos program. (There's no way to see your iCloud Photos contents in the older iPhoto and Aperture programs, alas.)

Geotagging

Mention to a geek that a gadget has both GPS and a camera, and there's only one possible reaction: "Does it do *geotagging*?"

Geotagging means "embedding your latitude and longitude information into a photo or video when you take it." After all, every digital picture you've ever taken comes with its time and date embedded in its file; why not its location?

The good news is that the iPhone can geotag every photo and video you take. How you use this information, however, is a bit trickier. The iPhone doesn't geotag unless the following conditions are true:

- **The location feature on your phone is turned on.** On the Home screen, tap **Settings→Privacy→Location Services**. Make sure Camera is set to **While Using the App**. (The rest of the time, the camera does not record your location.)

- **You've given permission.** The first time you use the iPhone's camera, a message appears, asking if it's allowed to use your location information. It's asking, "Do you want to geotag your pictures?" If you tap **OK**, the iPhone's geographic coordinates will be embedded in each photo.

OK, so suppose the geotagging feature is working. How will you know? Well, the Moments feature can put geotagging to work right on the

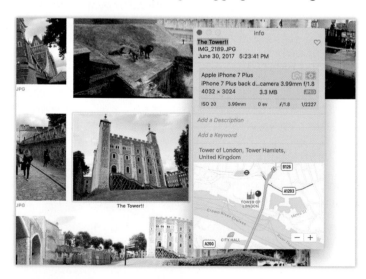

phone. You can open a map and see all the photos you took in that spot. You can also transfer the photos to your computer, where your likelihood of being able to see the geotag information depends on what photo-viewing software you're using. For example:

- **When you've selected a photo in Photos** (on the Mac), you can press ⌘-I for the Info panel. It shows the photo's spot on a map.

- **Once you've posted your geotagged photos on Flickr.com** (the world's largest photo-sharing site), people can use the Explore menu to find them by location or even see them clustered on a world map.

- **If you use Google Photos** (*photos.google.com*), you can open any photo and click the ❶ button to see a picture's location on the map.

Capturing the Screen

Let's say you want to write a book about the iPhone (hey, it could happen). How are you supposed to illustrate that book? How can you take pictures of what's on the screen?

The trick is very simple: Get the screen just the way you want it, even if that means holding your finger down on an onscreen button or a keyboard key. Now hold down the screenshot buttons:

- **Face ID phones:** Simultaneously press the side button and volume-up button. They're directly across from each other.

- **Home-button models:** Press the home button, and while it's down, press the side button (which may be on the top). You might need to invite some friends over to help you execute this multifinger move.

> **TIP:** If you've turned on Voice Control (page 228), you can just say, "Take a screenshot."

The screen flashes—and now the screenshot you just took appears as a miniature at the lower-left corner of the screen, and waits for six seconds (next page, left). If you do nothing (or if you swipe it away to the left), the thumbnail slides away. The screenshot winds up in Photos, in the Screenshots album: a perfect image of whatever was on the screen. (Its resolution matches the screen's.) Send it, share it, study it, whatever.

But if you *tap the miniature* before it slides away, you get a screenshot-editing window (next page, right).

You can drag the corners or edges to crop the shot, or use the Markup tools (page 458) to draw on it.

New in iOS 13: If you've captured something scrollable—a web page, map, long note, or email message, for example—a **Full Page** button lets you keep it all as one very tall graphic. It's a PDF document, too, complete with active, clickable links and text that you can select and search.

When you're finished cropping or annotating your shot, tap ⬆ to send it, or **Done** to close it—at which point the phone asks if you want to save the screenshot or, having made your point by sending it to someone, just delete it.

TIP: After you've shared a screenshot, closing and deleting it takes three fussy taps. When you just want to get on with your life, here's a quick exit: After you've shared a screenshot, *swipe down* on the Share sheet. It closes *and* the markup screen closes *and* nobody asks you "Are you sure?" Swiping down just means, "Exit, and no, I don't want to save my screenshot."

Recording Screen Video

There's no way to take a screenshot of some corners of iOS. For example, when the phone is ringing, pressing the screenshot button combination sends the call to voicemail instead of capturing the screen image. In those situations, you may have to rely on a backup trick: the iPhone's screen-*recording* feature.

Yes, for the first time in cellphone history, you can create *video* recordings of the screen—with narration, if you like. It's fantastic as a teaching tool, when you want to capture some anomaly to show tech support, or to demo an app. There's no app for that, no Settings page that even mentions it; the only way to record the screen is with the Control Center.

Install the Record Screen (◉) button onto the Control Center, as described on page 48. Tap it.

If you'd like to record narration, long-press the button instead, and then tap ◉ to turn the microphone on. Here, too, you can specify where you

want the finished video to go. That's usually **Photos**, but some video apps may list themselves here, too. Then hit **Start Recording**.

You see a 3-2-1 countdown, which is intended to give you time to get out of the Control Center and into whatever app you're trying to record.

Now do whatever it is you want to capture. (The phone's status bar or left ear turns red to remind you that you're rolling; unfortunately, that red patch will be part of the finished video.) To stop recording, tap that red bar, or open the Control Center and tap the ⏺ button again.

A notification appears: "Screen Recording video saved to Photos." If you do nothing, the finished video lands in your Photos app with all your other videos—with pristine quality and smooth motion, ready to share as you see fit. If you tap it, you jump into Photos to view your video.

> **TIP:** If, on the other hand, you long-press or swipe down on the notification bubble, you get two options: **View** or **Delete**. The latter gives you a chance to vaporize a bad take without wasting time and space saving it to Photos.

All About Apps

App is short for *application*, meaning software program, and the App Store is a single, centralized catalog of every authorized iPhone app in the world. In fact, it's the *only* place where you can get new programs (at least without hacking your phone).

You hear people talk about the downsides to this approach: Apple is stifling the competition; Apple is taking a 30 percent cut of every program sold; Apple is maintaining veto power over apps it doesn't like.

But there are some huge benefits, too. First, there's one central place to look for apps. Second, Apple checks out every program to make sure it's decent and runs decently. Third, the store is beautifully integrated with the iPhone itself.

There's an incredible wealth of software in the App Store. These programs can turn the iPhone into a pocket internet radio, a medical reference, a musical keyboard, a time and expense tracker, a TV remote control, a photo editor, a recipe box, a tip calculator, a restaurant finder, a teleprompter, and on and on. And games—thousands of dazzling handheld games, some with smooth 3D graphics and tilt control.

It's so much stuff—3.5 million apps, hundreds of billions of downloads—that the challenge is just finding your way through it. Thank goodness for those Most Popular lists.

Getting New Apps

To check out the App Store, tap the **App Store** icon on your phone. You arrive at the colorful, scrolling wonder of the store itself.

NOTE: Until 2017, you could shop the App Store, and organize your apps into folders, on your computer, using the iTunes program. As of iTunes 12.7, however, Apple has removed all app-management tools. Now your phone is the only way to get to the App Store.

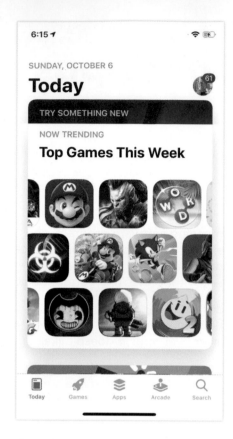

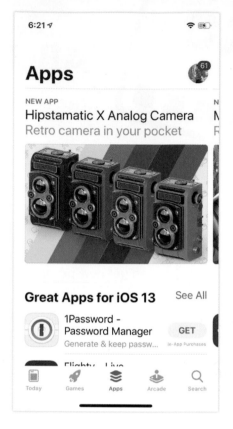

The App Store app has five tabs at the bottom. Here they are, in order:

- **Today.** The big problem with the App Store has always been finding the good stuff among the millions of apps. On this tab, Apple starts you off with a kind of blog, featuring mini-profiles of apps that Apple finds interesting. Tap and read. Needless to say, downloading the app that's being described is always just a tap away.

- **Games.** Games! Listed by category, by best-selling status, by Apple promotion.

- **Apps.** Here's everything else—again, listed by category, best-selling status, and Apple promotion.

- **Arcade** is Apple's $5-a-month, all-the-games-you-can-play subscription service. You (and five family members) can download and play hundreds of games that have been made part of the program. There are no ads or extra charges.

- **Search.** As the number of apps grows into the many millions, viewing by scrolling through lists begins to get awfully unwieldy.

Fortunately, you can also *search* the catalog, which is efficient if you know what you're looking for (either the name of a program, the kind of program it is, or the software company that made it).

Before you even begin to type, this screen shows you a list of trending searches—that is, the most popular searches right now. Odds are pretty good that if you want to download the latest hot app you keep hearing about, you'll see its name here.

Or tap in the search box to make the keyboard appear. As you type, the list shrinks so that it's showing you only the matches. You might type *tetris*, or *piano*, or *Disney*, or whatever.

Tap anything in the results list to see matching apps. You can swipe vertically to scroll through them. Tap one to view its details screen, as described in the next section.

About a third of the App Store's programs are free; the rest are usually under $5. A few, intended for professionals, can cost a lot more.

The App Details Screen

No matter which button was your starting point, eventually you wind up at an app's *details screen*. There's a description, a scrolling set of screenshots, info about the author, the date posted, the version number, a page of related and similar apps, the all-important reviews from fellow iPhoners, and so on.

Why are the ratings so important? Because the App Store's goodies aren't equally good. Remember, these programs come from a huge variety of people—professional firms in Silicon Valley, college students goofing around on weekends, teenagers in Hungary—and just because they made it into the store doesn't mean they're worth the time to download.

If you decide something is worth getting, you're ready to download and install it. You may see any of these buttons:

- **Get.** Good news: This is a free app! Download away, conscience-free.

- **$0.99** (or whatever). This app costs money. If you proceed, your Apple account will be charged automatically.

- ⬇. This button means you've previously bought an app, either on this iPhone or on another Apple touchscreen gadget. You don't have to pay for it again. Just tap to re-download.

- **Open.** This app is *already* on your iPhone! Tap to open it.

TIP: A little **+** sign on the price button means the app works well on both the iPad and the iPhone.

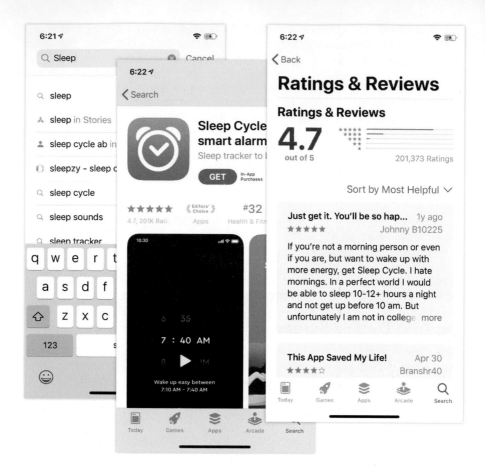

Once you tap **Get** or the price, you've committed to downloading the program.

The first time you access the App Store, and periodically thereafter, you have to enter your Apple ID and password. That's Apple's way of making sure some marauding child in your household isn't trying to run up your bill without your knowledge. (Mercifully, you don't have to enter your Apple ID just to download an *update* to an app you already own.) If you've allowed the App Store to accept your fingerprint on the home button or your face in Face ID, you can skip the name-and-password business. (You set this up in **Settings→Face ID & Passcode** [or **Touch ID & Passcode**]→**iTunes & App Store**.)

> **NOTE:** In iOS 13, there's no longer a size limit for apps you download over the cellular airwaves. Yay! In **Settings→iTunes & App Store→App Downloads**, though, you can specify whether or not you at least want to be *warned* when an app is especially big (over 200 MB).

Once you begin downloading an app, a pie chart on its Home screen icon fills in to indicate the download's progress. Tap the icon to pause or unpause the download. You can long-press the icon for a short-cut menu offering buttons for **Cancel Download, Pause Download,** and **Prioritize Download**—in other words, finish ahead of any other down-loading apps.

> **NOTE:** You don't have to sit there and stare at the progress bar. You can go on using the iPhone. In fact, you can even go back to the App Store and start downloading something else simultaneously.

If you're still on the app's App Store page when the downloading is done, tap **Open** to launch it and try it out.

A Welcome Note About App Backups

You don't have to worry about losing your apps if something happens to your phone. The App Store remembers everything you've bought. You can re-download a purchased app at any time, on any of your iPhones, iPads, or iPod Touches, without having to pay for it again.

Organizing Your Apps

As you add new apps to your iPhone, it sprouts new Home screens as necessary to accommodate them all, up to a grand total of 15 screens. That's 364 icons (and yet you can actually go all the way up to many thousands of apps, thanks to the miracle of *folders*—see page 367).

That multiple–Home screen business can get a little unwieldy, but a cou-ple of tools can help you manage. First, you can use Siri or Voice Control to open an app, without even knowing where it is. Just say, "Open Minecraft" (or whatever).

Second, a search can pluck the program you want out of your app hay-stack, as described on page 111.

Third, you can organize your apps into folders, which greatly alleviates the agony of TMHSS (Too Many Home Screens Syndrome).

It's worth taking the time to arrange the icons on your Home screens into logical categories, tidy folders, or at least a sensible sequence.

Rearranging Apps on the Home Screen

In iOS 13.2, Apple radically changed the way you move or delete your app icons. Now you long-press any icon; from the shortcut menu, choose **Edit Home Screen** (next page, left). The icons begin to—what's the cor-rect term?—*wiggle*.

TIP: Do you miss the old way of entering app-wiggle mode, where one long press did the trick? It still works. Long-press *long* enough, and the shortcut menu goes away—and your apps are wiggling.

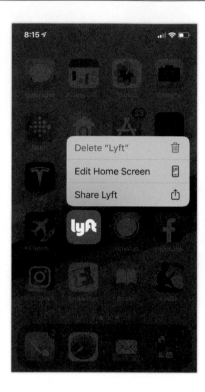

At this point, you can drag your icons into a new order (above, right); other icons scoot aside to make room. You can even move an icon onto the Dock (page 19). Just make room for it first, if necessary, by dragging an *existing* Dock icon to another spot on the screen.

TIP: You can drag multiple icons simultaneously. That's a time-saver—but you'd never in a million years guess how to do it.

Once you're in wiggle mode, start dragging icon #1, just far enough for its ⊗ to disappear. Now, with another finger, tap icon #2; it flies over to become part of a "stack" bearing a tally, like ❷. You can keep tapping to add apps, all the while keeping that first finger down. When you finally drag your first finger, you can drop the stack onto a folder, onto another app to create a folder, or onto a new page, where they'll land in reverse order of your tapping.

If you drag an icon to the edge of the screen, you "turn the page." That's how you put an app onto a different Home-page screen—or, if you drag it to the right edge of the rightmost Home screen, you create a new, blank Home screen, where you can deposit the icon.

When you've finished your interior app decoration, tap **Done**, or press the home button, or (on Face ID phones) swipe up from the bottom edge.

NOTE: You can no longer organize your Home screens on the computer, in the iTunes program. You must do this on the phone itself.

Deleting Apps

To delete an app, long-press it and then tap **Delete "[app's name]."**

Or do it the old-fashioned way: Enter app-wiggling mode as described, and then tap the ⊗ on the undesired app. You're asked if you're sure; if so, it says bye-bye.

NOTE: You can even use this technique to nuke preinstalled apps you never use, like Stocks and Watch. You're not *actually* deleting them—only hiding them. They still occupy, all told, 150 megabytes. (To "reinstall" them to your phone, download them from the App Store as usual.)

When everything looks good, press the home button—or, on Face ID phones, the **Done** button on the right ear—to stop all the wiggling.

Restoring the Home Screen

If you ever need to undo all the damage you've done, tap **Settings→ General→Reset→Reset Home Screen Layout**. That function preserves any new programs you've installed, but it consolidates them. If you'd put 10 apps on each of four Home screens, you'll wind up with only two screens, each packed with 20 icons. Leftover blank pages are eliminated. This function also places your downloaded apps in alphabetical order.

Folders

Just as on a computer, folders let you organize your apps, deemphasize the ones you rarely use, and restore order to that dizzying display of icons.

Each folder can have many pages of its own, each displaying nine icons. A single folder, in other words, can contain as many apps as you want. Only memory limits how many apps you can fit onto your phone.

To create and edit folders, begin by entering Home screen editing mode. That is, hold your finger down on any app icon (lightly) until the shortcut menu appears; tap **Edit Home Screen**.

Now, to create a folder, *drag one app's icon on top of another* (below, left). iOS puts both of them into a new folder—and, if they're the same kind of app, even tries to figure out what category they both belong to and names the new folder accordingly ("Music," "Photos," "Kid Games," or whatever). You can type in your own preferred name at this point (right).

You're welcome to add more apps to this folder. Tap the Home screen background to close the folder, and then (while the icons are still wiggling) drag another app onto the folder's icon. Lather, rinse, repeat.

If one of your folders has more than nine apps in it, iOS creates a second "page" for the folder—and a third, a fourth, and so on. You can move apps around within the pages and otherwise master your new multipage folder domain.

You can scroll the folder "pages" by swiping sideways, just as you scroll the full-size Home pages. The only limit to how many icons a folder can hold is your tolerance for absurdity.

Once you've created a folder or two, they're easy to rename, move, delete, and so on. (Again, you can do the following *only in icon-wiggling editing mode*.) Like this:

- **Take an app out of a folder** by dragging its icon anywhere else on the Home screen. The other icons scoot aside to make room, just as they do when you move them from one Home screen to another.

- **Move a folder around** by dragging, as you would any other icon.

> **TIP:** You can drag a folder icon onto the Dock, too, just as you would any app. Now you've got a pop-up subfolder full of your favorite apps on the Dock, which is present on every Home screen. That's a useful feature; it multiplies the handiness of the Dock.

- **Rename a folder** by opening it (tapping it). At this point, the folder's name box is ready for editing.

> **TIP:** On an iPhone 6s or later, you can long-press a folder icon—even when you're not in wiggling-icon mode—to reveal the Rename command.

- **Move an icon from one folder "page" to another** by dragging it to the edge of the folder, waiting with your finger down until the page "changes," and then releasing your finger in the right spot.

- **Delete a folder** by removing all its contents. The folder disappears automatically.

When you're ready to stop the wiggling madness:

- **Home-button phones.** Press the home button.

- **Face ID phones.** Swipe up from the bottom of the screen, or tap Done at top right.

App Preferences

If you're wondering where you can change an iPhone app's settings, consider backing out to the Home screen and then tapping Settings. Apple encourages programmers to add their programs' settings *here*, way down below the bottom of the iPhone's own settings.

Some programmers ignore the advice and build the settings right into their apps, where they're a little easier to find. But if you don't see them there, now you know where else to look.

App Updates

When a circled number (like ❷) appears on the App Store's icon on the Home screen, or on the Updates icon within the App Store program, that's Apple's way of letting you know an app you already own has been updated. Apple knows which programs you've bought—and notifies you when new, improved versions are released. (Which is remarkably often; software companies are constantly fixing bugs and adding new features.)

Manual Updates

There's no more Updates tab in the App Store app. Instead, to find a list of updates for your apps, tap your account icon at top right. On this screen, you're shown a list of the programs with waiting updates; a little description lets you know what the changes are—new features, perhaps, or some bug fixes. And when you tap a program's name, you go to its details screen, where you can remind yourself of what the app does and read other people's reviews of the new version.

You can download one app's update or, with a tap on the **Update All** button, all of them...no charge.

Automatic Updates

If you have a lot of apps, you may come to feel as though you're spending your whole life downloading updates. They descend like locusts, every single day, demanding your attention. Fortunately, your phone can install updated versions of your apps quietly and automatically in the background.

To turn on this feature, open **Settings→iTunes & App Store**. Under **Automatic Downloads**, turn on **App Updates**. (If you'd prefer the phone wait to do this downloading until it's in a Wi-Fi hotspot—to avoid eating up your monthly cellular data allotment—then, under "Cellular Data," turn off **Automatic Downloads**.)

From now on, the task of manually approving each app's update is off your to-do list forever.

> **NOTE:** Fortunately, the iPhone also keeps a tidy record of every app it's updated and what that update gives you. Open the App Store app; tap your account icon at top right. There's your list, sorted chronologically.

How to Find Good Apps

If the best-seller lists and editorial promotions in the App Store aren't inspiring you, there are all kinds of websites dedicated to reviewing iPhone apps. There are *appadvice.com* and *whatsoniphone.com* and many others.

But if you've never dug into iPhone apps before, you should at least try out some of the superstars, the big dogs almost everybody has.

Many of the most popular apps are designed to deliver big-name websites in the best-looking way possible. That's why there are apps for Facebook, Twitter, LinkedIn, Spotify, Pandora, Flickr, Yelp, Netflix, YouTube, Wikipedia, and so on.

Here are a very few more examples—a drop in the bucket at the tip of the iceberg of the infinite app variety beyond those basics:

- **Apple Apps (free).** Apple offers all kinds of free apps that aren't preinstalled on the phone: Clips, Podcasts, and so on. You can find them by searching the App Store for *Apple apps*.

- **Google Maps (free).** Google Maps is a replacement for the built-in Maps app. It's *much* better than Maps—even Apple has admitted that. Among other things, it incorporates restaurant reviews, and it's unbelievably smart about knowing what you're trying to type into the search box. Usually, about three letters is all you need to type before the app guesses what you mean.

- **Waze (free).** Here's another driving-directions app, also owned by Google. The genius here is that fellow drivers take note when they pass an accident, a police car, construction, a broken-down vehicle, and so on; all these anomalies show up on your Waze screen. As a result, Waze is better than Google Maps at working the back roads when the main route is compromised.

- **Flight Update Pro ($6).** Shows every detail of every flight: gate, time delayed, airline phone number, where the flight is on the map, and more. Knows more—and knows it sooner—than the actual airlines do. (For hardcore fliers, a rival app, Flighty, is more beautiful and includes even more features—including tracking your plane in the 24 hours before it reaches your departure city—the primary cause of delays— but it costs $9 a month.)

Other essentials: Uber and Lyft. Skype. Hipmunk (finds flights). *The New York Times*. The Amazon Kindle book reader. Dictionary. TED. Mint.com. Scrabble. Facebook Messenger. Dark Sky (hyper-local weather for the spot where you're standing). Snapchat (the millennials' go-to app for sending selfies that self-destruct after viewing). OpenTable. Apple TV Remote (if you own an Apple TV). HQ (a live trivia game show). Fandango or Ticketmaster. Movies Anywhere. Gas Buddy. TripAdvisor. Plus, of course, apps from your own favorite restaurants, stores, movie theaters, airlines, and banks.

Augmented Reality (AR) Apps

Apple has embraced AR in a big way, and some of the results are thrilling.

AR is where you use your phone as a viewer for the world around you—and the computer superimposes graphics on it. As you move the phone, the sizes, angles, and distances of the simulated objects smoothly change in real time as though they really existed. (Pokémon GO is an AR app. So is Snapchat, when it adds goofy glasses and antennas to your live image.)

The Measure app (page 447), is one example. But the App Store is full of other people's AR masterpieces:

- **IKEA Place (free).** You inspect a catalog of living-room furniture. You tap the item you want, choose a color for it, and then tap the iPhone screen to plop it down on the floor. Now you can walk around the room, checking out how it looks from various angles and in various positions. The idea, of course, is to let you try out furniture at home before hauling it in from a store. (Houzz, Overstock, Amazon, and other companies have similar apps.)

- **Porsche Mission E (free).** As a sales tool, this app is pure genius: It lets you see exactly what a $71,000 red Porsche Boxster convertible would look like in your driveway. Or garage. Or bedroom, for that matter.

- **Hair Color by ModiFace (free).** Use your phone like a magic mirror. Tap a new hair color from the scrolling palette at the bottom of the screen, and see how you'd look with that dye job.

- **Sky Guide ($3).** Point your phone at the sky, and see the stars—labeled and, in the case of constellations, conveniently connected by line segments. Works in the daytime or the nighttime. It's a perfect use of AR, because it provides ordinarily invisible information about whatever you're looking at. (The free Night Sky is a similar app.)

The world is full of people, places, and things with a story to tell. Imagine an app that identifies the repair history of a used car you're considering. Or an app you can hold up to your airplane window that labels the cities below. Or an app that shows how you'll look after plastic surgery. Or one for house hunters that shows your furniture in a candidate house.

The mind reels.

Re-Downloading Apps

The App Store remembers what apps you've downloaded, even years later. Next time you're having one of those "What was that crazy app that, you know, had the frog in a grocery store, and you were supposed to make it eat its way through produce and stuff?" moments, this feature can save you a lot of hunting.

Open the App Store app. Tap [your icon at top right]→Purchased→ My Purchases. Here you're offered two tabs: All (every app you've ever grabbed) and Not on this iPhone (apps you've grabbed but don't currently have installed). Tap ⬇ to reinstall the app you want.

> **TIP:** What if that My Purchases list is full of apps you tried once in 2009, and now they're just cluttering up the list?
>
> In the modern App Store app, you can *hide* them. Swipe left across any name and tap **Hide**. You can always search the App Store if you want that app again, but in the meantime, it's not polluting the list of apps you *do* want to see.

The App Switcher

Often, it's useful to switch among open apps. Maybe you want to copy something from Safari (on the web) into Mail (in a message you're writing). Maybe you want to refer to your frequent-flier number (in Notes) as you're using an airline's check-in app. Maybe you want to adjust something in Settings and then get back to whatever you were doing. Here's how to call up the app switcher:

- **Face ID phones.** Swipe up from the bottom of the screen (it doesn't have to be far), and stop with your finger still touching.

- **Home-button phones.** The key to switching apps is to *double-click the home button*.

(In either case, if you're using Voice Control, you can just say, "Open App Switcher" instead.)

In any case, whatever is on the screen gets replaced by the app switcher (shown below at left as it appears on a Face ID iPhone).

You see a scrolling row of "cards" that represent the open apps, in chronological order. They're big enough that you can actually see what's going on in each open app. In fact, sometimes, that's all you need; you can refer to another app's screen in this view, without actually having to switch *into* that app.

The app switcher always puts the *previous app* front and center when you first open it. For example, if you're in Safari but you were using Mail a minute ago, Mail appears centered in the app switcher. That makes life easier if you're doing a lot of jumping back and forth between two apps; one tap takes you into the previous app.

When you tap an app's card in the app switcher, that app opens.

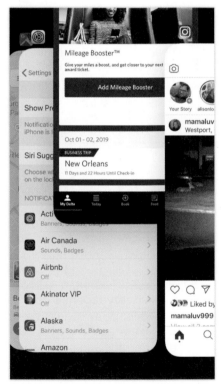

Force-Quitting an App

The app switcher lets you manually exit an app, closing it down. To do that, flick the unwanted app's card upward, so it flies up off the top of the screen (above, right).

You'll need this gesture only rarely. You're not *supposed* to quit every app when you're finished. Force-quit an app only if it's frozen or acting glitchy and needs to be restarted.

NOTE: There may be one more element on the app switcher: a small bubble, naming an app, at the bottom of the screen. That's a document, email, or web page being sent to your phone by your Mac, using Handoff (see page 595).

A Word About Background Apps

Switching out of an app doesn't actually close it; all apps continue running in the background.

Of course, if every app ran at full-tilt simultaneously, your phone would guzzle down battery power. To solve that problem, Apple has put two kinds of limits in place:

- **iOS's limits.** Not all apps run full speed in the background. Apps that really need constant updating, like Facebook or Twitter, get refreshed every few seconds; apps that don't rely on constant internet updates get to nap in the background when they're not in use.

- **Your own limits.** You can't control which apps *run* in the background, but you can control which ones *download new data* in the background. In Settings→General→Background App Refresh, you'll find a list of every app that may want to update itself in the background. To make your battery last longer, you can turn off background updating for apps you don't really care about; you can even turn off *all* background updating using the master switch at the top.

The bottom line: There's no need to quit apps you're not using, ever. Contrary to certain internet rumors, they generally don't use enough battery power to matter. You may see dozens of apps in the app switcher, but you'll never sense that your phone is bogging down as a result.

Face ID Phones: Bypass the App Switcher

If you have a Face ID phone, a delightful surprise awaits. You can switch apps directly, without a layover at the app switcher.

All you have to do is swipe horizontally on the *home indicator bar*, the black or white horizontal line at the bottom of almost every app screen (next page, left). Your first swipe should generally be to the *right*, because the app you're using now is always at the far right of the lineup.

There's one exception. If you're in App A, and you swipe right to check App B (your second-to-last app), you have *six seconds* to swipe left, *back* to App A. After that, App B becomes the new rightmost app. Apple always wants the most recent app to be at far right, but it doesn't want to confuse you if you're hopping back and forth between two apps.

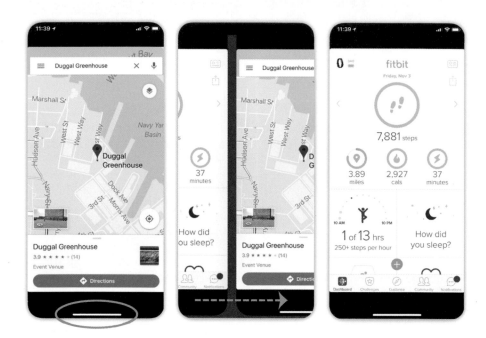

As you do so, the next-most-recent app heaves into view—full size, already running. No need to tap it or select it from among some cards: You're there.

Keep swiping that bar to the right to summon older and older open apps; swipe to the left to return to the ones you've used more recently.

Back to App (<)

This is a Back button that appears when you've tapped a link of some kind that takes you into a different app. For example:

- **You're in Messages,** and you tap a web link (facing page, left) that takes you into Safari. A < **Messages** button appears at top left (right).

- **You're on Twitter or Facebook,** and you tap a link that opens a web page. The top-left button says < **Twitter** or < **Facebook**.

- **You're in Mail,** and you tap an underlined date or time that takes you into the Calendar app. A < **Mail** button appears in the corner.

- **You're in Safari,** and you tap a link that opens in YouTube. Sure enough: The button says ◀ **Safari**.

And so on. This tiny enhancement can save you *minutes* a week.

 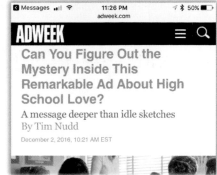

AirPrint: Printing from the Phone

How do you print from a gadget that's smaller than a Hershey bar—a gadget without any jacks for connecting a printer? Wirelessly, of course.

You can send printouts from your phone to any printer that's connected to your Mac or PC on the same Wi-Fi network if you have a piece of software like Printopia ($20).

Or you can use the iPhone's built-in AirPrint technology, which can send printouts directly to a Wi-Fi printer without requiring a Mac or a PC.

Not just any Wi-Fi printer, though—only those that recognize AirPrint. Most recent Brother, Canon, Epson, HP, and Lexmark printers work with AirPrint; you can see a list of them on Apple's website: *support.apple.com/kb/HT4356*.

Not all apps can print. Of the built-in Apple programs, only Books, Mail, Photos, Notes, and Safari offer **Print** commands. Those apps contain what most people want to print most of the time: PDF documents, email messages, driving directions, and so on. Plenty of non-Apple apps work with AirPrint, too.

> **TIP:** Of course, you can always take a screenshot of what you want to print (see page 357) and then print *that* from the Photos app.

To use AirPrint, start by tapping ⬆; tap **Print**. You're offered a **Select Printer** option. Tap it to introduce the phone to your printer, whose name should appear automatically. Now you can adjust the printing options

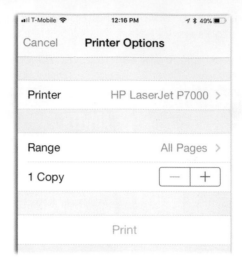

(number of copies, page range)—and when you finally tap **Print**, your printout shoots to the printer, exactly as though your phone and printer were wired together.

The Share Sheet

Every app is different, but they all have certain things in common; otherwise, you'd go out of your mind.

One of those things is the Share sheet. It's the headquarters for sending stuff from your phone to other people, other apps, the internet, a printer, and so on. Using this screen, you can share your "card" in Contacts with a colleague, a picture in Photos with your best friend, a Maps location with your boss, a Notes page with a collaborator, and so on.

In all those apps and many others, the Share button (⬆️) appears. Tap it to view the Share sheet (facing page, left).

The buttons in the Share sheet depend on the app; you may see only two options here or dozens. Starting on page 341, for example, you can read descriptions of the icons that appear when you're sending a photo: AirDrop, Message, Mail, Twitter, Facebook, Copy, AirPlay, Print, and so on.

In general, the newly redesigned iOS 13 Share sheet offers three sections—two rows of icons and a tall list of commands:

- **First row: Frequent shares.** This row right here may be one of the most welcome, time-saving, tap-saving features in all of iOS 13.

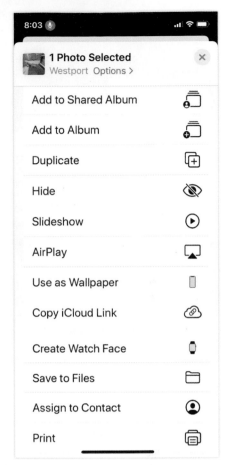

This row displays icons not just for *how* you most often share things, but *with whom*. There might be a Messages icon for Casey, a Mail icon for Chris, an AirDrop icon for your own laptop, and so on.

The idea, of course, is to let you share something with one tap. No longer must you choose a sharing method first, and then type out the recipient's name in Contacts. If you frequently send photos by Messages to your sister, then you'll see her name with a Messages icon—and a single tap does the share.

- **Second row: Ways to share.** The second row of icons lists **AirDrop** (read on) and apps that can receive what you're sharing: **Messages**, **Mail**, **Reminders**, **Notes**, and so on.

There's a **More** button at the end of this row. That's an invitation for other, non-Apple apps to install their own "send to" options into the Share sheet—and an invitation for you to *edit* this second row of

Share icons, so it shows the app names you want in the order you want them.

Once you tap More, you can see the full list of apps that have inserted themselves here.

If you tap Edit, you can edit this row of the Share sheet in all kinds of ways. You can tap ⊕ to promote an app's name to the Favorites section (the leftmost icons on the Share sheet); tap ⊖ to remove an app from that favored section; turn off the switch for items in the Suggestions list to hide them; or drag the grip handles up or down to rearrange the Favorites row's icon order.

- **Menu of commands.** Below that second row of icons, you get a tall list of things you can do with whatever you're sharing (previous page, right). These may not strike you so much as sharing options as miscellaneous commands for each app that have nowhere else to go.

For Photos, these commands include **Add to Album**, **Slideshow**, **Use as Wallpaper**, **Print**, and so on. In Notes, they include **Lock Note**, **Find in Note**, and **Pin Note**. In Safari, this is where you'll find **Add Bookmark**, **Add to Favorites**, **Add to Reading List**, and so on.

Some of your apps' most useful features are hiding here.

AirDrop

It's a headline feature: AirDrop, a way to shoot things from one Apple phone, tablet, or Mac to another—wirelessly, instantly, easily, encryptedly, without requiring names, passwords, or setup. It's much faster than emailing or text messaging, since you don't have to type (or know) the other person's address.

NOTE: If the Mac is running OS X Yosemite or later, you can shoot files between it and your phone, too.

You can transmit pictures and videos from the Photos app, people's info cards from Contacts, directions (or your current location) from Maps, pages from Notes, web addresses from Safari, electronic tickets from Wallet, apps you like in the App Store, song listings from the iTunes app, and so on. Because AirDrop can send big things fast, it's great for sharing videos. Many non-Apple apps offer AirDrop, too.

Behind the scenes, AirDrop uses Bluetooth (to find nearby gadgets within about 30 feet) and a private, temporary Wi-Fi mini-network (to transfer the file). Sender and receiver must have Bluetooth and Wi-Fi on.

Here's how to do it:

1. **Tell the recipients to wake their phones.**

   You can't send by AirDrop unless the receiving machine is *awake*.

2. **Make sure the other phone can receive AirDrop shipments from you.**

   This step always feels technical and annoying, but it's a must.

   Apple wanted to make sure obnoxious strangers couldn't bombard you with unsolicited AirDrops whenever you were in public. That's why, unless you've fiddled with settings, you can accept AirDrop data sent only from people who are *already in your Contacts*.

   If the sender isn't in your Contacts list, you won't show up as a potential recipient, and you'll never get whatever they're sending.

   Fortunately, you can change this setting. You can do it in **Settings→ General→ AirDrop**, but the quicker way is to open the Control Center (page 42) and long-press the upper-left control cluster, as shown below (left). Boom: The cluster expands to reveal the hidden AirDrop button (middle). Tap it to view your three security choices (right):

   Receiving Off: Nobody can send you anything by AirDrop.

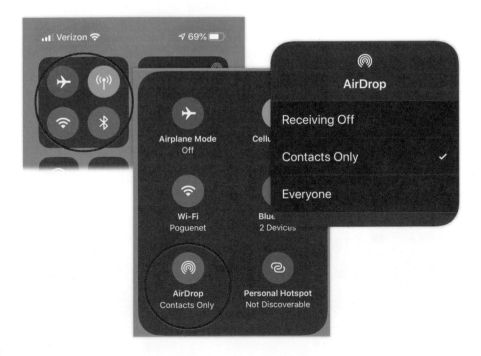

Contacts Only: Only people in your address book can AirDrop things to you. Your phone is invisible to strangers. (Your Contacts card for the other guy must include his iCloud address.)

Everyone: Anyone, even strangers, can try to send you things. Of course, you can still accept or decline each shipment.

3. **Open the item you want to share. Tap Share (⬆).**

   If only one person nearby can accept AirDrop, you see that iPhone's icon in the Share sheet.

TIP: When you send a *photo*, the top row of the Share sheet shows your other photos and videos so you can select additional items to go along for the ride. A blue checkmark identifies each item you've selected to send.

If there are several sendable iPhones (or iPads, or Macs), the AirDrop icon shows how many—for example, ❸—as shown below at left; tap AirDrop to see all of them (middle).

If you have an iPhone 11 or 11 Pro, and so does the other person, you can *point the top of your phone* at hers. You'll see her AirDrop icon big and centered at the top of the AirDrop-icons screen, making it quicker to choose.

4. **Tap the icon of the device you want to share with.**

   Actually, you can select *more than one* person's icon. In that case, you'll send this item to everyone at once.

   In about a second, a message appears on the recipient's screen, conveying your offer to transmit something good—and, when it makes sense, showing a picture of it (facing page, right).

   At this point, it's up to your recipients. If they tap **Accept**, then the transfer begins (and ends); whatever you sent them opens automatically in the relevant app. You'll know AirDrop was successful because the word "Sent" appears on your screen.

   If they tap **Decline**, then you must have misunderstood their willingness to accept your item (or they tapped the wrong button). In that case, you'll see the word "Declined" on your screen.

There's one other AirDrop setting to fiddle with: In **Settings→ Sounds & Haptics**, you can specify the sound effect that means "AirDrop file received."

Screen Time

It might seem strange that Apple, whose primary business is persuading you to consume more of its goods and services, is concerned that you might be spending *too much* time on your phone. But it's true: iOS contains a feature designed to help you set reasonable limits on your screen time.

Or at least on your *kids'* screen time.

In **Settings→Screen Time**, you'll find a vast suite of tools that help you keep track of how much time you're spending on your iPhones and iPads; monitor which apps you're using during that time; and set daily limits for how much time you're allowed to spend in each category of app.

Four hours a day of social-network apps like Facebook and Twitter, tops? That's a good start.

Of course, Apple is not about to lock you out of your own phone; these limits are more like friendly reminders. You can choose to ignore the "Time's up!" message when it appears.

But for your kids, it's another story. You can require a parental password to keep using the phone after time is up.

Here's a tour of what's on this Settings page.

Screen Time

This big, bold graph shows how much time you've spent on your phone today so far, color-coded by app type (Social Networking, Entertainment, and so on). You get to see whether today you've been more or less addicted than usual (below, left).

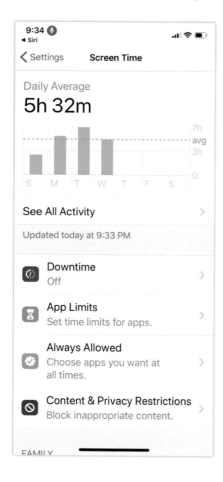
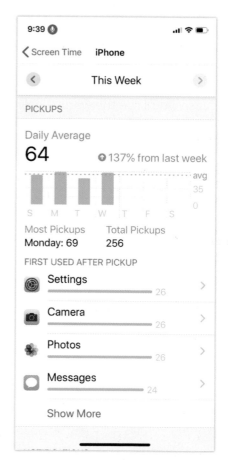

If you have more than one iOS 12 or 13 gadget—say, a phone and an iPad—then Screen Time is only too happy to add their totals. If this feature is turned on (**Share Across Devices** at the bottom of the main screen) on *each* of these devices, then the graph at the top is the grand tally. You can tap the names of the devices to see their individual breakdowns.

If you tap **See All Activity**, you open up a much more detailed, much more frightening page. Now you see how much time you've spent in each of those categories *per hour* today, including a record of your longest session. You can see the data either by **Day** (today) or **Week**; if you scroll down, you make arrows appear that let you rewind into *past* days or weeks.

Then comes a list of the apps you've been using, sorted by most time eaten.

Below that, the horrifying Pickups graph, showing how many times you've awakened your phone per hour; the average amount of time between pickups (aka your willpower grade); and which time of day saw the most pickups.

Below that, how many notifications you get, by hour or by day, and which apps are sending you the most.

If most of the controls in Screen Time are dimmed, it's because your family is using Family Sharing (page 586), and you're not a designated parent. Sorry, kid!

Every Sunday, a Screen Time notification appears, announcing that your weekly report is available. Open the notification to see a colorful report, full of bar graphs and stats that show how much you, and your other family members, rotted their brains on their devices, and on which apps, and how many times you lost your will and went over your limits.

Downtime

For some people, just seeing those startling graphs may be enough to produce a change in behavior—like looking up from your phone now and then. But if you need a little reminder to help curb your addiction, tap **Downtime**, and then turn on the Downtime switch.

Here you're supposed to indicate a slice of the day when you're willing to quit using your phone—during dinner, maybe, or the couple of hours before bed.

Five minutes before the beginning of the Downtime, you'll get a notification that warns you to wrap it up. Then, at the witching hour, most of your apps' icons on the Home screens become dimmed and un-tappable. The only exceptions: You can still make or take phone calls, and you can use whatever apps you've chosen by tapping **Always Allowed**, described next. (And if you deem Instagram to be essential—well, you do you.)

Of course, it's not so hard to bypass your own Downtime limits. You can always just open **Settings→Screen Time** and turn Downtime *off*. So what's the point? First, even a thin obstacle is, psychologically speaking, better than nothing. Second, you can put a password on Downtime so that you *can't* turn it off. This, of course, isn't intended for *you* as much as it is for your kids (see page 387).

There may be some deep conversations at dinner tonight.

Always Allowed

When Downtime is on, your phone isn't completely bricked. It's still a phone—and you can designate certain apps as exceptions that you can use. It's probably smart to block Facebook, Twitter, and Mail before bed. But maybe Spotify is OK, so you can relax with some music, or maybe Books, so you can read. Or maybe Maps, so you can find your hotel.

To choose the permitted apps, tap **Always Allowed** (on the main Screen Time screen). As you can see, Apple proposes that communication hubs like Phone, Messages, and FaceTime be kept legal, along with Maps. To add to this list, tap the ⊕ next to the apps you want. (To remove an app from the permitted list, of course, hit ⊖ and then **Remove**.)

App Limits

You can also set daily time limits for individual app *categories*. Maybe you want to cut back your social-networking habit to an hour a day. Maybe you think three hours a day watching videos is plenty (well, at least for your kid).

When you tap **App Limits→Add Limit**, iOS doesn't show you a list of apps; it presents app *categories*, like Social Networking, Games, Entertainment, Education, and Health & Fitness. (Actually, who on earth would limit Health & Fitness?)

In iOS 13, you can limit either an entire category—or tap the ⟩ to see the names of the apps *in* that category, so that you can limit them individually (facing page, left). When you tap **Next**, you can dial up the number of hours and minutes you want as the maximum per day (right). If you want the limit to vary on different days (to be less strict on weekends, say), hit **Customize Days**, change the time by day, and then hit ⟨ **Back**. When everything looks good, hit **Add**.

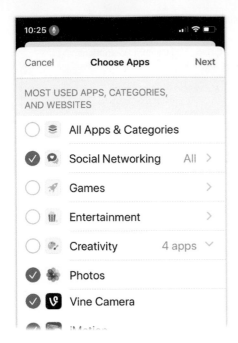
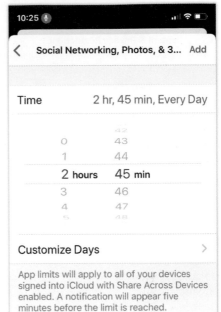

At this point, you can tap **Add Limit** to set up another app-category time limit, repeating the process.

Content & Privacy Restrictions

This section is probably better known as "parental controls."

If you're issuing an iPhone to a child, or someone who acts like one, you'll be gratified to discover that iOS offers a good deal of protection. That's protection of your offspring's delicate sensibilities (it can block pornography and dirty words) and protection of your bank account (it can block purchases of music, movies, and apps without your permission).

The setup is here, in **Settings→Screen Time→Content & Privacy Restrictions**. The master switch at the top is there in case you ever want to shut off all restrictions in a hurry.

NOTE: Before you dive in, note that the parental controls don't start out with a password. You can declare certain websites or apps off-limits, but to get around those limits, all someone has to do is return to this screen and turn off the restrictions.

That's why, on the main Screen Time page, you're offered a **Use Screen Time Passcode** button. When you tap it, you're asked to make up a passcode that permits only you, the all-knowing parent, to make changes to these settings. (Or you, the corporate IT administrator who's doling out iPhones to employees.)

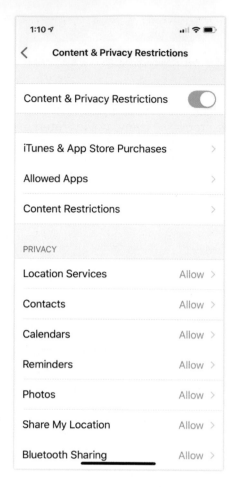

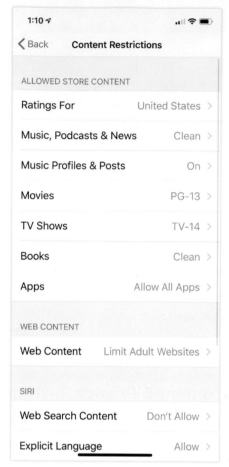

All right. Once Restrictions is turned on, you can put up data blockades in a number of categories:

- **iTunes & App Store Purchases.** Is your kid allowed to install apps? Delete them? Buy new levels, weapons, and features within apps? And is your Apple ID required to make a *second* purchase once you've made the first one?

- **Allowed Apps.** Here you can specify exactly which apps your kid is allowed to use.

- **Content Restrictions.** This is where you can spare your child's sensitive eyes and ears by blocking inappropriate material.

  Ratings determine the effectiveness of the parental controls described in this section. Since every country has its own ratings schemes (for movies, TV shows, games, song lyrics, and so on), you use the **Ratings For** control to tell the iPhone which country's rating system you want to use.

Once that's done, you can use the **Music, Podcasts & News** control, plus **Music Profiles & Posts** (the news and discussion within Apple's defunct music service), **Movies**, **TV Shows**, **Books**, and **Apps**, to specify what your kid is allowed to watch, play, read, or listen to. For example, you can tap **Movies** and then tap **PG-13**; any movies rated "higher," like R or NC-17, won't play on the iPhone. (And if your sneaky offspring try to buy these naughty songs, movies, or TV shows wirelessly from the iTunes Store, they'll discover that the Buy button is dimmed and unavailable.)

For some categories, like **Music, Podcasts & News**, you can turn off Explicit to prevent the iPhone from playing iTunes Store songs that contain naughty language.

Web Content lets you shield impressionable young eyes from pornography online. **Unrestricted Access** means no protection at all; **Limit Adult Websites** means Apple will apply its own judgment in blocking dirty websites, using a blocked-site list it has compiled; and **Allowed Websites Only** is a "whitelist" feature. It means the entire web is blocked except for the sites listed here: safe bets like Disney, PBS Kids, Smithsonian Institution, and so on. You can add your own sites to this list, but the point is clear: This is the web with training wheels.

That doesn't mean you can't override Apple's wisdom, however. Within the Limit Adult Websites options, **Always Allow** and **Never Allow** controls let you add the addresses of websites you think should be OK (or should not be OK).

Under **Siri**, **Web Search Content** lets you turn off your youngsters' ability to say to Siri, "Look up naked ladies" (or whatever naughty searches they dream up), and **Explicit Language** lets you plug Siri's ears when your little monster says unspeakable things to her.

The last categories here have to do with games that work with Apple's Game Center technology. These controls let you stop your kid from playing multiplayer games (against strangers online), screen recording in games, or adding game-playing friends to the center.

- **Privacy.** These switches can prohibit your kids from making changes to the phone's privacy settings, which are described on page 623.

- **Allow Changes.** In this category, you'll find **Allow/Don't Allow** options for a whole bunch of features that locked-down corporations might not want their employees—or parents might not want their children—to use, because they're considered either security holes, time drains, or places to spend your money.

They include **Passcode Changes**, **Account Changes** (meaning the email and social-media accounts you've set up in Settings), **Cellular Data Use** (limits you've set up for various apps), **Background App Activities** (which apps are allowed to run when they're not the frontmost), and Volume Limit (page 277). **Do Not Disturb While Driving** ensures that your underling can't simply *turn off* that important safety feature (page 74), thereby defeating the entire purpose. **TV Provider** makes sure the rapscallion won't attempt to change your cable-TV company (page 281).

Family

Here are the names of any underage family members, as you've set them up in Family Sharing (page 586). Tap a kid's name to see a replica of *your* Screen Time screen—but this time, you're changing the settings only for that kid. And, yes, that means you can also see the *kid's* graph.

Use Screen Time Passcode

Unless you add this four-digit password, your underlings can simply bypass whatever screen-time limits you've set up by opening **Settings** and turning off Screen Time (or the individual features within).

Share Across Devices

Here's the "Tally up the screen time from *all* my Apple devices" switch described on page 385.

Turn Off Screen Time

If you're offended by the entire notion of iOS as a nanny, always harassing you about your phone addiction and sending you judgy reports about your progress, just tap to turn it all off.

The Built-In Apps

Eventually, of course, you'll fill your iPhone with apps you choose yourself, but Apple starts you off with about 25 essential ones. They include gateways to the internet (Safari), communications tools (Phone, Messages, Mail, Contacts), visual records of your life (Photos, Camera), shopping centers (iTunes Store, App Store), entertainment (Music), and so on.

Those core apps get special treatment in the other chapters. *This* chapter covers the secondary programs, in alphabetical order: Books (formerly iBooks), Calculator, Calendar, Clock, Compass, Files, Find My, Health, Home, Maps, Measure, News, Notes, Podcasts, Reminders, Stocks, Tips, Voice Memos, Wallet, Watch, and Weather.

> You can open any of these apps by hunting it down and tapping its icon. But it's usually much faster to tell Siri to do it. Say, "Open Compass," for example.

Books

Books (formerly called iBooks) is Apple's ebook reading program. It turns the iPhone into a sort of tiny Kindle. You can carry around dozens or hundreds of books in your pocket, which, in the pre-ebook days, would have drawn some funny looks in public.

Most people think of Books as a reader for books that Apple sells on its iTunes bookstore—best sellers and current fiction, for example—and it does that very well. But you can also load it up with your own PDF documents, as well as thousands of free, older, out-of-copyright books.

> Books is very cool and all. But, in the interest of fairness, it's worth noting that Amazon's free Kindle app, and Barnes & Noble's free B&N Nook app, are much the same thing—but offer bigger book libraries at lower prices.

Across the bottom of the app are five tabs; they're as good a tour guide as any.

Reading Now

This tab prominently displays whatever book you've been reading most recently—and below that, a row of books you've been reading slightly less recently. The idea is to make it easier, if you're reading multiple things at once, to get back into them.

Well, and also to sell you more books. Below those rows are suggestions of more books to buy, based on books you've already bought (or indicated, with the **Suggest More Like This** button, that you loved). Additional "books we'd love for you to buy" thumbnails appear even farther down.

Then, at the bottom: Reading Goals. In iOS 13, Apple is trying to encourage you to read more (and, of course, to buy more books) by gamifying

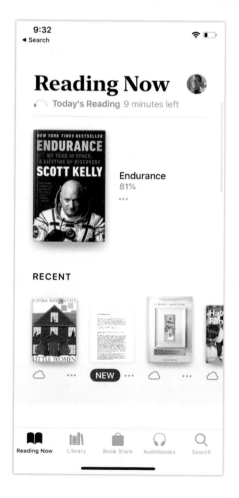

the process. You can set goals for minutes a day and books a year—and then the app keeps track for you.

To see the minutes-a-day goal, tap the **Today's Reading** timer and then **Adjust Goal**. To adjust the books-a-year goal, tap one of the book images under Books Read This Year.

Library

Once you've supplied Books with some reading material, the fun begins. The **Library** tab represents all your reading material as little book covers; books by the same author, or that are part of the same series, appear as little *stacks* of books.

NOTE: When you first start using a new iPhone, iPad, or Mac, your book covers bear the ☁ symbol. It means: "You've bought this book, but it's still online. Tap to download it to your phone."

Mostly what you'll do here is tap a book to open it. But there are other activities waiting for you:

- **Collections.** You can create subfolders for your books called *collections*. You might have one for school and one for work, or one for you and one for somebody who shares your phone, for example. Categories of books can also be collections, like Finished, Want to Read, Audiobooks, PDFs, and so on.

  To see what's in a collection, tap it. (The Finished collection is especially cool—it shows the date you finished each book.)

  To create a new collection, hit **New Collection** and type a name for it.

  And to move a book into a different collection: On the Library tab, tap ••• just below a book's thumbnail to see the options; tap **Add to Collection**.

TIP: You can reorganize your bookshelf in a collection. Long-press on a book until it swells with pride, and then drag it into a new spot.

- **Sort by** Recent (what you've been reading lately), Title, Author, or Manually (drag them around with your finger—hold for a second before moving).

- **Switch to list view.** Tap ☰, which switches the book-cover view to a much more boring (but more compact) list view.

- **Rename, Remove, Mark.** There's a whole menu's worth of manipulations you can perform on a book. Tap ••• just below a book's thumbnail to see the options.

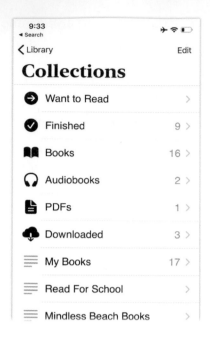

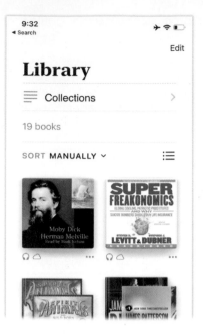

They may include **Download** (books you haven't read in a while may be stored in your iCloud "locker," ready for actual downloading to your phone), **Remove** (from the phone; you can always re-download it at no charge), **Rename**, **Add to Want to Read** (that is, a wish list), **Add to Collection** (read on), **Mark as Finished**, **Share PDF** (if it's a PDF file), **Share Book** (send a link to buy it), **Rate and Review**, and **Suggest More Like This** or **Suggest Less Like This**.

- **Tap Edit if you want to delete a book,** or a bunch of them. To do that, tap each book thumbnail you want to target for termination; observe how they sprout ✅ marks. Then tap 🗑. Of course, deleting a book from the phone doesn't delete your safety copy online.

Book Store, Audiobooks, Search

These tabs are the literary equivalents of the App Store. Here are **New & Trending** books or audiobooks, **Top Charts** (this week's best sellers, including what's on *The New York Times* Best Sellers list), **Books We Love** ("We" being Apple), and so on. Scroll all the way down for the list of genres like **Fiction**, **Mysteries**, **Romance**, and so on.

Once you find a book that looks good, you can tap **Sample** to download a free chapter (or **Preview** to download a free audiobook teaser), read reviews, or tap **Buy** to download the book straight to the phone.

TIP: Once you've bought a book, you can download it again on other iPhones, iPod Touches, iPads, and Macs. Buy once, read many times.

PDFs and ePub Files

You can also load up your ebook reader from your computer, feeding it with PDF documents and ePub files.

Your Mac or PC is the most convenient loading dock for files bound for your iPhone. If you have a Mac, open the Books program. If not, open iTunes, click your iPhone's icon at the top (when it's connected), and then click **Books**.

Either way, you now see all the books, PDF documents, and ePub files you've slated for transfer. To add to this set, just drag files off your desktop and directly into this window.

And where are you supposed to get all these files? Well, PDFs are everywhere—people send them as attachments, and you can turn any document into a PDF file. (For example, on the Mac, in any program, choose **File→Print**; in the resulting dialog box, click **PDF→Save as PDF**.)

TIP: If you get a PDF document as an email attachment on the phone, adding it to Books is even easier. Tap the attachment to open it; now tap **Open in Books** in the corner of the page.

But free ebooks in ePub format are everywhere, too. There are 33,000 books at *gutenberg.org*, for example, and over a million at *books.google.com*—classic oldies, with lots of Mark Twain, Agatha Christie, Herman Melville, H.G. Wells, and so on. (Lots of these are available in the Free pages of Apple's own Book Store, too.)

TIP: These freebie books usually come with generic covers. But once you've dragged them into iTunes on your computer, it's easy to add good-looking ones. Use *images.google.com* to search for the book's title. Right-click (or Control-click) the cover image in your web browser; from the shortcut menu, choose **Copy Image**. In iTunes, in Library mode, choose **Books** from the top-left pop-up menu. Right-click (or Control-click) the generic book; choose **Get Info**; click **Artwork**; and paste the cover you copied. Now that cover will sync over to the iPhone along with the book.

Once you've got books in iTunes, connect the iPhone, choose its name at top right, click the **Books** tab at top, and turn on the checkboxes of the books you want to transfer.

Reading

Open a book or PDF by tapping the book cover. The book opens, ready for you to read. Looks great, doesn't it? (If you're returning to a book you've been reading, Books remembers your place.)

If the phone detects that it's nighttime (or just dark), the screen appears with white text against a black background. That's to prevent the bright-white light of your phone from disturbing other people in, for example, the movie theater. (This is the Night theme, and you can turn it off.)

> **TIP:** Turn the phone 90 degrees for a wider column of text.

In general, reading is simple: Just read. Turn the page by tapping the edge of the page—or swiping your finger across the page. (If you swipe slowly, you can actually see the "paper" bending over, as shown on page 392—in fact, you can see through to the "ink" on the other side of the page! Amaze your friends.) You can tap or swipe the left edge (to go back a page) or the right edge (to go forward).

> **TIP:** This is rotation lock's big moment. When you want to read lying down, you can prevent the text from rotating by locking the phone into portrait orientation (page 45).

But if you tap a page, a row of additional controls appears:

- < **takes you back** to the bookshelf view.

- :≡ **opens the table of contents.** The chapter or page names are "live"—you can tap one to jump there.

- ₐA **lets you change the look of the page.** For example, this panel offers a screen-brightness slider for the whole phone. (This is the same control you'd find in the Control Center or in Settings.)

  The A **and** A **buttons** control the type size—a huge feature for people with tired or over-40 eyes. Tap the larger one repeatedly to enlarge the text; tap the smaller one to shrink it.

  The same panel offers a Fonts button, where you can choose from eight typefaces for your book, as well as a Themes button, which lets you specify whether the page itself is White, Sepia (off-white), Dark Gray, or Night (black page, white text, for nighttime reading). And there's an Auto-Night Theme button; if you don't care for the white-on-black theme, then turn this switch off. Finally, there's a Scrolling View switch. In scrolling view, you don't turn book "pages."

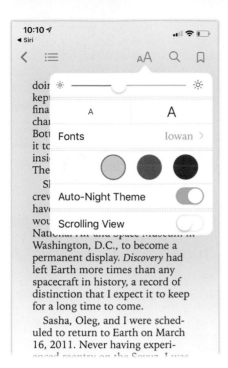

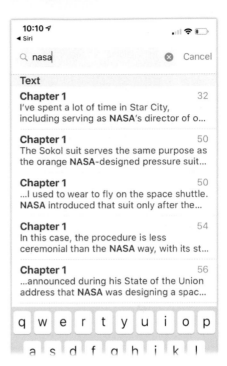

Instead, the book scrolls vertically, as though printed on an infinite roll of Charmin.

- **Q lets you search for text** within the book you're reading, which can be extremely useful. As a bonus, there are also **Search Web** and **Search Wikipedia** buttons so you can hop online to learn more about something you've just read.

- **⧠ adds a bookmark** to the current page. You can flag as many pages, for as many reasons, as you like.

- **Chapter slider.** At the bottom of the screen, a slider represents the pages of your book. Tap or drag it to jump around in the book; as you drag, a pop-up indicator shows what chapter and page number you're scrolling to. (If you've magnified the font size, of course, then your book consumes more pages.)

TIP: A Books ebook can include pictures and even videos. Double-tap a picture in a book to zoom in on it.

When you're reading a PDF document, by the way, you can do something you can't do when reading regular Books titles: zoom in and out using the usual two-finger pinch-and-spread gestures. Very handy indeed.

> **NOTE:** On the other hand, here are some features that *don't* work in PDF files (only in ebooks): font and type-size changes; page-turn animations; sepia, gray, or black backgrounds; and notes.
>
> And if you want highlights, you'll have to draw them on manually with the Markup tools (page 458).

Notes, Bookmarks, Highlighting, Dictionary

Here are some more stunts you'd have trouble pulling off in a printed book. If you *hold your finger down* on a word, you get a black editing bar (below, top) that offers these options:

- **Speak** reads the highlighted passage aloud. (This button appears only if you've turned on **Speak Selection** in **Settings→Accessibility→ Spoken Content**.) Thank you, Siri!

- **Copy.** You can probably guess this one.

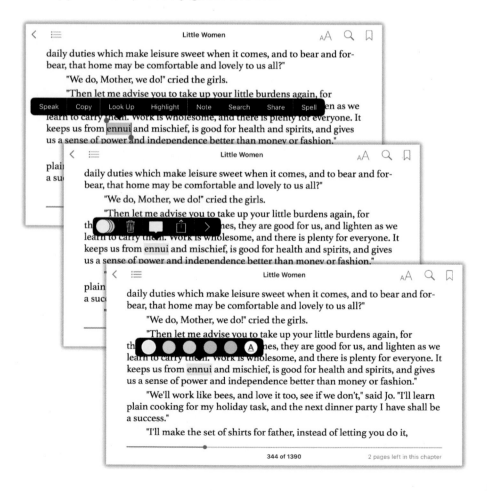

- **Look Up.** Opens a page from Books' built-in dictionary. You know—in the unlikely event you encounter a word you don't know.

- **Highlight.** Adds tinted, transparent highlighting, or underlining, to the word you tapped. For best results, don't tap the Highlight button until you've first grabbed the blue-dot handles and dragged them to enclose the entire passage you want highlighted.

  Once you tap Highlight, the buttons change into a special Highlight bar (facing page, middle). The first button (⬤))) opens a *third* row of buttons (bottom), so you can specify which highlight color you want. (The final button in this row designates underlining.)

  To remove highlighting, tap 🗑. The ■ button adds a note, as described next. The ⬆ button opens the Share sheet, also described momentarily.

- **Note (■)** creates highlighting *and* opens an empty, colored sticky note so you can type in your own annotations. When you tap Done, your note collapses down to a tiny yellow Post-it peeking out from the right edge of the margin. Tap to reopen it.

  To delete a note, tap the highlighted text. Tap 🗑.

- **Search** opens the same search box you'd get by tapping the Q icon— except this time the highlighted word is already filled in, saving you a bit of typing.

- **Share** opens the Share sheet (page 378) so you can send the highlighted material to somebody else, post it to Facebook or Twitter, or copy it to your Clipboard for pasting into another app.

NOTE: If you've highlighted a single word, and if you have Speak Selection turned on in Settings→Accessibility→Spoken Content, then there's one more option: Spell. It spells the word aloud for you, one letter at a time.

There are a couple of cool things going on with your bookmarks, notes, and highlighting, by the way. Once you've added them to your book, they're magically and wirelessly synced to any other copies of that book—on your other gadgets, like the iPad or iPod Touch, your other iPhones, or even Mac computers running OS X Mavericks or later. You can read the same material seamlessly on any of your devices.

Furthermore, if you tap the ☰ to open the Table of Contents, you'll see the Bookmarks and Notes tabs. Each presents a tidy list of all your bookmarked pages, notes, and highlighted passages. You can tap ⬆ (and then Share Notes) to print or email your notes, or tap one of the listings to jump to the relevant page.

Books That Read to You

Books can actually read to you! It's a great feature when you're driving or jogging, when someone's learning to read, or when you're having trouble falling asleep. There's even a special control panel just for managing your free audiobook reader.

To get started, open **Settings→Accessibility→Spoken Content**. Turn on **Speak Screen**.

Now open a book in Books. Swipe down from the top of the page with two fingers to make the iPhone start reading the book to you, out loud, with a computer-generated—but fairly natural-sounding—voice. At the same time, a palette appears, offering the speech controls shown here.

Collapse controls   *Close controls*

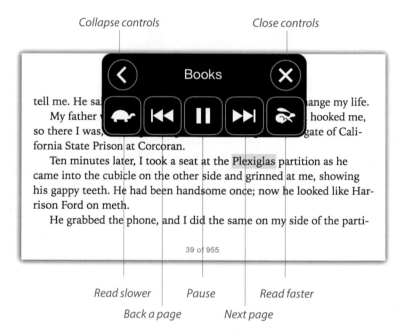

Read slower | *Pause* | *Read faster*
Back a page   *Next page*

After a few seconds, the palette shrinks into a ∨ button at the edge of the screen—and, after that, it becomes transparent, as though trying to make itself as invisible as possible. You can, of course, tap it to reopen it.

NOTE: Yes, this is exactly the feature that debuted in the Amazon Kindle and was then removed when publishers screamed bloody murder—but, somehow, so far, Apple has gotten away with it.

Books Settings

If you've embraced the simple joy of reading electronic books the size of a chalkboard eraser, then you deserve to know where to make settings changes: in Settings→Books. The options include the usual Siri & Search (Chapter 5); Notifications (page 62); Background App Refresh (page 375); and Cellular Data (do you want Books to be able to download books over a cellular connection when you're away from Wi-Fi?).

But here's what else you'll find:

- **Online Content.** A few books contain links to video or audio clips online. This option comes set to Off, because video and audio can eat up your monthly cellular data allotment like a hungry teenager.

- **Update Other Devices.** Tap to open a list of other Apple products you own that *haven't* been updated to iOS 12 or macOS Mojave or later. Your Books library won't sync to them until they're up-to-date.

- **Reading Now.** Do you want your choice of current reading material synced to other gadgets? (That'd be a big *no* if you like to read one book on your iPhone and a different one on your iPad.)

- **iCloud Drive.** If you've added PDF files to your library (page 395), is it OK to use your precious iCloud Drive storage space (page 576) to make them available to all your Apple devices? If not, they won't sync.

- **Full Justification.** Ordinarily, Books presents text with fully justified margins (even margins on both sides—an effect created by adding tiny bits of space between the words on each line). Turn this off if you prefer ragged-right margins (uneven on the right margin).

- **Auto-hyphenation.** Sometimes, typesetting looks better if hyphens allow partial words to appear at the right edge of each line. Especially if you've also turned on Full Justification.

- **Both Margins Advance.** Usually, tapping the right edge of the screen turns to the next page, and tapping the left edge turns *back* a page. If you turn on this option, then tapping *either* edge of the screen opens the next page. That can be nice if you're a lefty, for example.

- **Reading Goals** turns on or off that whole goal business (page 392). Include PDFs counts the time reading PDF documents toward your goal. And why not?

- **Book Store.** Turn this off if you want the Search tab to search only the books you already own.

- **Skip Forward, Skip Back.** The little jump back/jump forward buttons that appear when you're listening to an audiobook: How many seconds should they skip?

- **External Controls.** If you're listening to an audiobook in your car or with earbuds, what should happen when you press the ◀◀ or ▶▶

buttons or controls? Should playback jump to the **Next/Previous** chapter, or just **Skip Forward/Back** 15 seconds (or whatever interval you set)?

- **Reset Identifier.** Apple collects data about what books people are reading. But it doesn't know you as *you*; it considers you to be user 195827349205. That's your Identifier. You can throw Apple off your scent at any time, though, by *resetting* your Identifier, so your data seems to come from a whole new person.

Calculator

In Calculator's basic four-function mode, you can tap out equations (like *15.4 × 300 =*) to see the answer at the top. (You can *paste* things you've copied into here, too; just hold your finger down until the **Paste** button appears.) There's no memory function in the basic calculator, but you do get a +/– button; its function is to change the currently displayed number from positive to negative, or vice versa.

TIP: When you tap one of the operators (like ×, +, -, or ÷) it turns from orange to white to help you remember which operation is in progress. Let's see an ordinary calculator do *that*!

Now here's the twist: If you rotate the iPhone 90 degrees in either direction, the Calculator morphs into a full-blown HP *scientific* calculator, complete with trigonometry, logarithmic functions, a memory function, exponents, and roots beyond the square root. Go wild, ye engineers and physicists!

If you make a mistake while entering a number, swipe horizontally across the numerical display (either direction). Each swipe backspaces over the rightmost digit. And if you mistakenly touch the wrong operator (× when you meant -, for example), there's no need to start over. Just tap the *correct* operator before tapping the number. The app ignores the errant tap.

TIP: You can use the Calculator instantly, at any time, even without waking or unlocking the phone—from the Control Center (page 42). And you can make a calculation without opening the Calculator app at all—by asking Siri to do it for you (page 175).

Calendar

The iPhone's calendar syncs, automatically and wirelessly, with whatever online calendar you keep: iCloud, Google Calendar, a corporate Exchange calendar, and so on. Everything is kept in sync with your computers and tablets, too. Make a change in one place, and it changes everywhere else. Then again, you can also use Calendar all by itself.

NOTE: The Calendar icon on the Home screen shows what looks like one of those paper Page-a-Day calendar pads. But if you look closely, you'll see a sweet touch: It actually shows today's day and date.

Day View

When you open Calendar, you see today's schedule, broken down by time slot (next page, right). You can navigate to other days' schedules in any of three ways: Swipe horizontally across the Day screen to see the previous or next day. Tap a date at the top to see another day this week. Swipe across the dates at the top to jump to another week. If the date you want to check is further away than a week or two, though, it might make more sense to pop into Month view, described next.

Month View

Month view, of course, shows an entire month at a glance (above, center). You can scroll the months vertically, thereby scanning the entire year in a few seconds. To get there from Day view, tap the name of the month at the top left.

Of course, your little phone screen is too small to show you what's written on each calendar square; all you get is a gray dot on any date when you've scheduled an appointment. Tap that dot to jump back into Day view and read your schedule.

Year View

If you're in Month view, you can "zoom out" yet another level—to Year view (above, left). It's a simple, vertically scrolling map of the year's months. Tap the name of the year to see it. From there, tap a month block to open it back into Month view.

> **TIP:** In all three of these views—Day, Month, Year—you can tap **Today** (bottom left) to return to today's date.

The Rotated Calendar

Some cool things happen when you turn the phone into landscape view (below, top). You get an interactive slice of the week: Swipe sideways to move to earlier or later dates. Swipe up or down to move through the hours of the day.

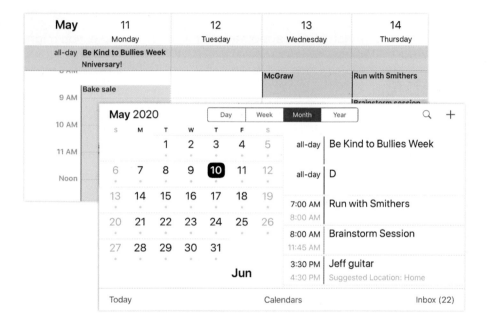

Plus and Max Model Views

If you have a Plus or Max model—one with the Jumbotron screen—then there's room for extra information (above, bottom). On those models, the Day and Month views offer a split screen, showing the calendar on the left and details on the right. You also get a row of view buttons (**Day**, **Week**, **Month**, **Year**)—something the owners of puny regular iPhones never see.

Subscribing to Your Online Calendars

To set up real-time, wireless connections to your calendars online, tap your way to **Settings→Passwords & Accounts→Add Account**. Here you can tap **iCloud**, **Exchange**, **Google**, **Yahoo**, **AOL**, or **Outlook.com** to set up your account. (You can also tap Other→Add CalDAV Account to fill in the details of a less well-known calendar server, or Other→Add Subscribed Calendar to connect to an online calendar subscription service—from TripIt or your favorite sports team, for example.

Making an Appointment (Day or Month View)

Recording an event on this calendar is more complex than entering one on, say, one of those "Midwest Police Stations Hunks" paper calendars.

Start by tapping + (top-right corner of the screen). The New Event screen pops up, filled with tappable lines of information. Tap one (like Starts or Repeat) to open a configuration screen for that element.

For example:

- **Title/Location.** Name your appointment here. For example, you might type *Fly to Phoenix*.

  The second line, called **Location**, makes a lot of sense. If you think about it, almost everyone needs to record *where* a meeting is to take place. You might type a reminder for yourself like *My place*, a specific address like *212 East 23rd*, a contact phone, or a flight number.

- **Starts/Ends.** Tap **Starts**, and then indicate the starting time for this appointment, using the four spinning dials that appear at the bottom of the screen (facing page, right). The first sets the date; the second, the hour; the third, the minute; the fourth, AM or PM.

  Then tap **Ends**, and repeat the process to schedule the ending time. (The iPhone helpfully presets the Ends time to one hour later.)

  An **All-day** event, of course, has no specific time of day: a holiday, a birthday. When you turn this option on, the Starts and Ends times disappear. The event appears at the top of the list for that day.

> **TIP:** Calendar can handle multiday appointments, like trips. Turn on All-day—and use the **Starts** and **Ends** controls to specify beginning and ending *dates*. The appointment appears as either a list item that repeats on every day's square or as a banner across the days, depending on the iPhone model and screen space available.

- **Repeat.** The screen here contains common options for recurring events: every day, every week, and so on. It starts out saying **Never**. And if you click **Custom**, you'll see an infinitely customizable range of *less*-common options—every seven years on the third Tuesday in February, say.

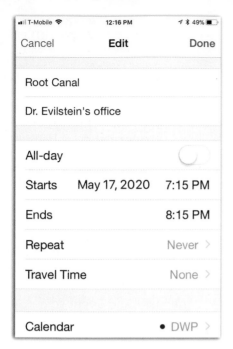

Once you tap a selection, you return to the Edit screen. Now you can tap the **End Repeat** button to specify when this event should *stop* repeating. If you leave the setting at **Never**, you're stuck seeing this event repeating on your calendar until the end of time (a good choice for recording your anniversary, especially if your spouse might be consulting the same calendar).

In other situations, you may prefer to tap **On Date** and spin the three dials (month, day, year) to specify an ending date, which is useful for car payments or a season's worth of soccer games.

Tap **New Event** to return to the editing screen.

- **Travel Time.** If you turn on this switch, you can indicate how long it'll take you to get to this appointment. You get six canned choices, from five minutes to two hours. Or you can tap **Starting Location** and specify your starting point, and marvel as the iPhone calculates the driving time automatically. (Walking time, too, if it's close enough.)

  Two things then happen. First, the travel time is blocked off on your calendar, so you don't accidentally schedule things during your driving time. (The travel time is depicted as a dotted extension of the appointment.)

  Second, if you've set up an alarm reminder, it will go off that much earlier, so you have time to get where you're going.

- **Calendar.** Tap to specify which color-coded *calendar* (category, like Home, Kids, or Work) this appointment belongs to (see page 410).

- **Invitees.** If you have an iCloud, Exchange, or CalDAV account, you can invite people to an event—a meeting, a party, whatever—and track their responses, right there on your phone (or any iCloud gadget). See page 412.

- **Alert.** This screen tells Calendar how to notify you when a certain appointment is about to begin. Calendar can send any of four kinds of flags to get your attention. Tap how much notice you want: 5, 15, or 30 minutes before the big moment; an hour or two before; a day or two before; a week before; or on the day of the event.

> **NOTE:** For all-day events like birthdays, you get a smaller but very useful list of choices: **On day of event (9 AM)**, **1 day before (9 AM)**, **2 days before (9 AM)**, and **1 week before**.

When you tap **Add Event** and return to the main Add Event screen, a new line, called **Second Alert**, has sprouted up beneath the first alert line. This line lets you schedule a *second* warning for your appointment, which can occur either before or after the first one. Think of it as a backup alarm for events of extra urgency.

Once you've scheduled these alerts, you'll see a message appear on the screen at the appointed time(s). (Even if the phone was asleep, it appears briefly.) You'll also hear a chirpy alarm sound.

> **NOTE:** The iPhone doesn't play the sound if you've turned off Calendar Alerts in **Settings→Sounds** or **Settings→Sounds & Haptics**. It also doesn't play if you've silenced the phone with the silencer switch on the side.

- **Show as.** If you work in the business world, it's courteous to mark your new appointments as either **Busy** or **Free**. That way, other people who see your calendar, trying to schedule a meeting when you can attend, will know which events on your calendar are movable and which are nonnegotiable. If you're just indicating "*Keeping Up with the Kardashians* TV marathon," maybe that one should be marked as **Free**.

- **Add attachment.** This option, new in iOS 13, opens your iCloud Drive (page 568). You can now choose a photo, PDF document, Word document, or some other file to attach to this appointment for reference later. It's great for attaching an itinerary or a business document to review for a meeting.

- **URL.** Here's a spot where you can record the web address of some online site that provides more information about this event.

- **Notes.** You can type any text you want in the Notes area—driving directions, contact phone numbers, a call history, or whatever.

When you're done filling in all these blanks, tap Add. Your newly scheduled event shows up on the calendar.

Making an Appointment (Day View, Week View)

As noted earlier, turning the phone 90 degrees opens up a widescreen, scrolling Week view of your life.

In both Day view and Week view, you can *hold your finger down on a time slot* to add a new, one-hour appointment right there. You're asked to enter a name and, if you like, location for this new appointment. Tap Add. You can always edit this appointment's details or duration later, as described next—but this quick-and-dirty technique saves the effort of tapping in Starts and Ends times.

Editing and Rescheduling Events (Fun Way)

In Day or Week views, you can *drag an appointment's block* to another time slot or even another day. Just hold your finger down on the appointment's bubble for about a second—until it darkens—before you start to drag. It's a lot quicker and more fluid than having to edit in a dialog box.

You can also change the *duration* of an appointment in Day and Week views. Hold your finger down on its colored block for about a second; when you let go, round handles appear.

You can drag those tiny handles up or down to make the block taller or shorter, in effect making it start or end at a different time.

Whether you drag the whole block, the top edge, or the bottom edge, the iPhone thoughtfully displays ":15," ":30," or ":45" on the left-side time ruler to let you know where you'll be when you let go.

Editing, Rescheduling, Deleting Events (Long Way)

To examine the details of an appointment in the calendar, tap it once. The Event Details screen appears, showing the details you previously established. At bottom: a red **Delete Event** button. That's the only way to erase an appointment from your calendar. (You can't erase events created by other people—Facebook birthdays, meetings on shared calendars, and so on—only appointments *you* created.)

To edit any of the details, tap **Edit**. You return to what looks like a clone of the New Event screen.

The Calendar (Category) Concept

A *calendar*, in Apple's somewhat confusing terminology, is a color-coded subset—a category, really—into which you can place various appointments. One person might make calendars called Home, Work, and TV Reminders. Another might have Me, Spouse 'n' Me, and The Kidz. A small business could have categories called Deductible Travel, R&D, and R&R.

You can create and edit calendar categories right on the iPhone, in your desktop calendar program, or (if you're an iCloud member) at *icloud.com* when you're at your computer; all your categories and color-codings show up on the iPhone automatically.

At any time, on the iPhone, you can choose which subset of categories you want to see. Just tap **Calendars** at the bottom of Day, Month, or Year view. You arrive at the big color-coded list of your categories (facing page, left). As you can see, it's subdivided according to your accounts: your Gmail categories, your Yahoo categories, your iCloud categories, and so on.

> **NOTE:** iOS no longer gives you the option to hide or show your Facebook friends' birthdays. So if you give Facebook access to your Contacts app, they *all* show up on your calendar. If that's not contributing to your productivity, you'll have to delete those events one at a time in Contacts.

This screen exists partly as a reference, a cheat sheet to help you remember what color goes with which category, and partly as a tappable subset chooser. That is, you can tap a category's name to hide or show its appointments on the calendar. A checkmark means you're seeing its appointments. (The **Show All/Hide All [account name]** button turns on or off all that account's categories at once.)

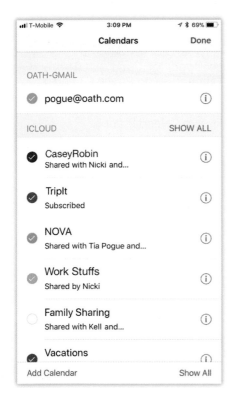
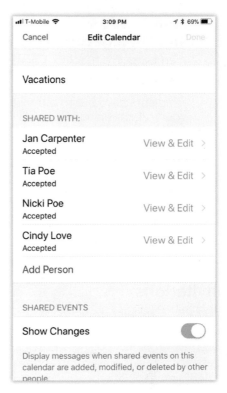

If you tap ⓘ next to a calendar's name, you're offered a screen where you can change the calendar's name; the list of people who can see it ("Shared With:"); whether or not you get notified when one of those people changes events in this category (**Show Changes**); what color you want this category's events to have ("Color"); whether you want to get notifications of items in this calendar (**Event Alerts**); and if you want other people to be able to see (but not edit) this category (**Public Calendar**, described in the Tip on the next page).

Or scroll all the way down to see the **Delete Calendar** button.

The Edit Calendars screen also offers an **Add Calendar** button. It's the key to creating, naming, and colorizing a *new* calendar on the phone. (Whatever changes you make to your calendar categories on the phone will be synced back to your Mac or PC.)

You can share an iCloud calendar with other iCloud members (previous page, right), which is fantastic for families and small-business employees who need to coordinate. Tap **Calendars**, and then tap ⓘ next to the calendar's name. Tap **Add Person** and enter the person's name. Your invitees get invitations by email; with one click, they've added your appointments to their calendars. They can make changes, too.

You can also share a calendar with anyone (not just iCloud members) in a "Look but don't touch" condition. Tap **Calendars**, and then tap ⓘ next to the calendar's name. Turn on **Public Calendar**; tap **Share Link** to open the Share sheet for sending the link. The recipients have but to tap that link and then tap **Subscribe** to see your Public calendar's events in their own Calendar apps.

Search

If you tap Q and type into the search box, you pare down the list of calendar events; only events whose names match what you've typed show up. Tap one to jump to its block on the corresponding Day view.

Next time you're sure you made an appointment with Robin but you can't remember the date, keep this search feature in mind.

Invitations

Invitations are electronic invitations that co-workers send you from Calendar, Outlook, or other calendar apps. If you click **Accept**, the meeting gets dropped onto the proper date in your calendar, and your name gets added to the list of attendees maintained by the person who invited you. If you click **Maybe**, the meeting is flagged *that* way, on both your calendar and the sender's.

You'll know when you have an invite. You get a standard notification, a numbered "badge" on Calendar's icon on the Home screen, and a similar badge on the **Inbox** at the lower-right corner. Tapping **Inbox** shows the Invitations list, which summarizes all invitations you've accepted, maybe'd, or not responded to yet.

Invitations you haven't dealt with also show up on the Calendar's List view or Day view with dotted shading. That's the iPhone's clever way of showing you just how severely your workday will be ruined.

You can also *generate* invitations. When you're filling out the Info form for a new appointment, tap the field called **Invitees**; you get an Add Invitees screen, where you can type in the email addresses of your desired guests. (Or tap ➕ to choose them from your Contacts list.)

Later, when you tap **Done**, the phone fires off email invitations to those guests. It contains buttons for them to click: **Accept**, **Decline**, and **Maybe**. You get to see their responses right here in the details of your calendar event.

As icing on the cake, your guests will see a pop-up reminder on their phones when the time comes for the party to get started.

TIP: The iOS calendar is pretty basic. For more features and power, consider calendar apps like Fantastical 2 or BusyCal.

Clock

It's not just a clock—it's more like a time factory. Hiding behind this icon on the Home screen are five programs: a world clock, an alarm clock, a stopwatch, a countdown timer, and a bedtime-management module.

NOTE: The app icon on the Home screen shows the current time! Isn't that cute?

World Clock

When you tap **World Clock** on the Clock screen, you start out with only one clock, showing the current time in Apple's own Cupertino, California.

You can open up *several* of these clocks and set each one to show the time in a different city. Now you'll know what time it is in some remote city, so you don't wake somebody up at what turns out to be 3 a.m.

To specify which city's time appears on the clock, tap + at the upper-right corner. Scroll to the city you want, or tap its first letter in the index at the right side to save scrolling, or tap in the search box at the top and type the name of a major city. As you type, matching city names appear; tap the one whose time you want to track.

As soon as you tap a city name, you return to the World Clock display.

You can scroll the list of clocks. You're not limited by the number that fit on your screen at once.

> **TIP:** Only the world's major cities are in the iPhone's database. If you're trying to track the time in Squirrel Cheeks, New Mexico, add a major city in the same time zone instead—like Albuquerque.

To edit the list of clocks, tap **Edit**. Delete a city clock by tapping ⊖ and then **Delete**, or drag clocks up and down using the ≡ as a handle. Then tap **Done**.

Alarm

If you travel much, this feature could turn out to be one of your iPhone's most useful functions. It's reliable, it's programmable, and it even wakes *the phone* first, if necessary, to wake *you*.

To set an alarm, tap **Alarm** at the bottom of the Clock screen. You're shown the list of alarms you've already created (facing page, left), even if none are currently set to go off. You could create a 6:30 a.m. alarm for weekdays and an 11:30 a.m. alarm for weekends.

To create a new alarm, tap + to open the **Add Alarm** screen.

> **TIP:** Really, you *should not bother* setting alarms using this manual technique. Instead, you'll save a lot of time and steps by using Siri. Just say, "Set my alarm for 7:30 a.m." (or whatever time you want).
>
> And while we're at it: You can also say, "Change my 7:30 a.m. alarm to 8 a.m." And if you get really lucky with your life karma, you may even have the opportunity to say the greatest thing you can possibly say to Siri: "Turn off my alarm."

You have several options here:

- **Time dials.** Spin these three vertical wheels—hour, minute, AM/PM—to specify the time you want the alarm to go off.

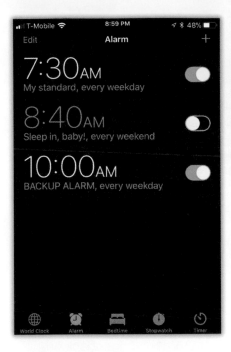

- **Repeat.** Tap to specify what days this alarm rings. You can specify, for example, Mondays, Wednesdays, and Fridays by tapping those three buttons. (Tap a day-of-the-week button again to turn off its checkmark.) Tap **Back** when you're done. (If you choose Saturdays and Sundays, iOS is smart enough to call that "Weekends." And it knows that Monday, Tuesday, Wednesday, Thursday, and Friday are "Weekdays.")

- **Label.** Tap to give this alarm a description, like "Get dressed for wedding." That message appears on the screen when the alarm goes off.

- **Sound.** Choose what sound you want to ring. You can choose from any of the iPhone's ringtone sounds, any you've added yourself—or, best of all, **Pick a Song**. That's right—you can wake to the music of your choice.

- **Snooze.** If this option is on, then at the appointed time the alarm message on the screen offers you a **Snooze** button. Tap it for nine more minutes of sleep, at which point the iPhone tries again. (If your phone was in Sleep mode, it gives you a countdown to the next rude awakening.)

When you finally tap **Save**, you return to the Alarm screen, which lists your new alarm. Just tap the on/off switch to cancel an alarm. It stays in the list, though, so you can quickly reactivate it another day, without having to redo the whole thing. You can tap + to set another alarm, if you like.

Now ⌚ appears in the status bar at the top of the iPhone screen (or, on Face ID phones, just in the Control Center). The alarm is set.

To delete an alarm, swipe left across its name and then tap **Delete**. To change the time, name, sound, and so on, tap **Edit**, and then the alarm.

> **TIP:** The iPhone never deletes an alarm; over time, therefore, your list of alarms may grow alarmingly large. Fortunately, you can tell Siri to clean them up for you in one fell swoop. Just say, "Delete all my alarms."

So what happens when the alarm goes off? The iPhone wakes itself up, if it was asleep. A message appears, identifying the alarm label and the time.

And, of course, the sound rings. This alarm is one of the only iPhone sounds that you'll hear *even if the silencer switch is turned on*. Apple figures that if you've gone to the trouble of setting an alarm, you probably want to know about it, even if you forget to turn the ringer back on.

To stop the alarm, tap **Stop**. To snooze it, tap the **Snooze** button or press the side button or a volume key. (In other words, in your sleepy haze, just grab the phone with your whole hand and squeeze. You'll hit *something* that shuts the thing off.)

Bedtime

Medical research tells us that sleep deprivation and inconsistent sleep schedules take a terrible toll on our health, mood, and productivity. So iOS's Clock app offers a **Bedtime** tab, newly redesigned in iOS 13. The app will attempt to keep your sleep regular—prompting you when it's time to get ready for bed, waking you at a consistent time, and keeping a graph of your sleep consistency.

The first time you open this panel, the interview begins: What time would you like to wake up? Which days of the week should the alarm go off? How many hours of sleep do you need each night? When would you like a bedtime reminder? What ringtone or sound do you want to hear when you wake up?

> **TIP:** You can change your answers to any of these questions later by tapping **Options** at top left.

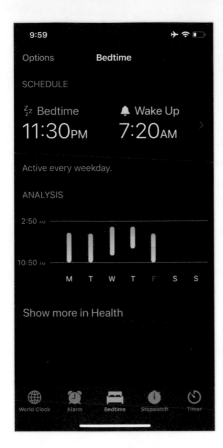

Once that's done, you see the master **Bedtime** screen shown above at left. At top, it shows your target start and stop points for sleep tonight; below that, the all-important Analysis graph. Your goal is to keep the bars consistent over time—both in length and vertical position. It's not enough to get enough sleep; you should also try to sleep during the same period each night.

Tap **Options** to set up a **Bedtime Reminder** (say, half an hour before sleepytime); turn **Track Time in Bed** on or off (measures how much time you use your phone while in bed); turn **Do Not Disturb During Bedtime** on or off (page 72); and choose an alarm sound and volume.

If you tap the Bedtime/Wake Up strip, you open the screen shown above at right—a handy visualization of the mental math millions of people perform every night anyway: "If I go to bed now, I'll get five hours of sleep!"

You can drag either end of the round graph to adjust it, specify which days of the week you want this Bedtime to be active, or turn the whole Bedtime Schedule feature off entirely.

TIP: The **Show more in Health** button opens the Health app described starting on page 427. Behind the scenes, the Health app is doing the actual work for the Bedtime module.

Stopwatch

You've never met a more beautiful stopwatch than this one. Tap **Start** to begin timing something: a runner, a train, a person who's arguing with you.

While the digits are flying by, you can tap **Lap** as often as you like. Each time, the list at the bottom identifies how much time elapsed since the *last* time you tapped **Lap**. It's a way for you to compare, for example, how much time a runner is spending on each lap around a track. You see the numbered laps and the time for each.

TIP: If you prefer an old-timey analog stopwatch display, slide the digital readout to the left. Swipe right to bring back the digital stopwatch.

You can work in other apps while the stopwatch is counting. In fact, the timer keeps ticking away even when the iPhone is asleep! As a result, you can time long-term events, like how long it takes an ice sculpture to melt, the time it takes for a bean seed to sprout, or the length of a Michael Bay movie.

Tap **Stop** to freeze the counter; tap **Start** to resume it. If you tap **Reset**, you reset the counter to zero and erase all the lap times.

Timer

The fifth Clock mini-app is a countdown timer. You input a starting time, and it counts down to zero. (Now with a cool circular countdown graph!)

Countdown timers are everywhere in life. They measure the periods in sports and games, cooking times in the kitchen, time limits for auditions. But on the iPhone, the timer has an especially handy function: It can turn off the music or video playback after a specified amount of time. In short, it's a sleep timer that plays you to sleep and then shuts off to save power.

To set the timer, open the Clock app and then tap **Timer**. Spin the three dials to specify the number of hours, minutes, and seconds you want to count down.

Then tap **When Timer Ends** to set up what happens when the timer reaches 0:00. Most of the options here are ringtone sounds, so you'll have an audible cue that the time is up. The last one, though, **Stop Playing**, is that sleep timer. It stops audio and video playback at the appointed time, so you (and the iPhone) can sleep. Tap **Set**.

Finally, tap **Start**. Big clock digits count down toward zero. While it's in progress, you can do other things on the iPhone, change the **When Timer Ends** settings, or just hit **Cancel** to forget the whole thing.

> **TIP:** It's much faster and simpler to use Siri to start, pause, and resume the Timer. See page 163.
>
> You can also open the Control Center (page 42) and long-press the Timer icon. Its shortcut menu offers instant options for 12 increments, from one minute to two hours.

Compass

The iPhone offers a magnetic-field sensor known as a magnetometer— even better known as a *compass*.

When you open the Compass app (it begins life in your Extras folder), you get exactly what you'd expect: a classic Boy Scout wilderness compass that always points north.

Except it does a few things the Boy Scout compasses never did. Like displaying a digital readout of your heading, altitude, city name, and precise geographic coordinates at the bottom. And offering a choice of *true* north (the "top" point of the Earth's rotational axis) or *magnetic* north. (In the U.S., the spot where traditional compasses point is as much as 23 degrees away from true north, depending where you are.) You choose in **Settings→Compass**.

To use the compass, hold it roughly parallel to the ground, and then read it like...a compass. Tap the center of the compass to lock in your current heading; a red strip shows how far you are off course. Tap again to unlock the heading.

> **TIP:** For many people, the real power of the compass is in the Maps app. (You can jump directly from Compass to Maps by tapping the coordinates below the compass dial.)
>
> The compass lets Maps know which way you're *facing*. That's a critical detail when you're lost in a strange city, trying to find a new address, or emerging from the subway with no idea which way to walk.

Incidentally: If you're looking for the Compass's traditional second personality, where it impersonates a carpenter's level—that's moved to a new address. It's now part of the Measure app, described starting on page 447.

Files

Files is a fantastically useful app. But explaining it might take a few paragraphs.

Meet iCloud Drive...

When you switch on iCloud Drive (in **Settings**→**[your name]**→**iCloud**), your phone has a magic folder. Whatever you put into it appears, almost instantly, in the iCloud Drive folders on all your *other* machines: Macs, iPhones, iPads, and even Windows PCs. In fact, your files are even available at *icloud.com*, so you can grab them when you're stranded on a desert island with nothing but somebody else's computer. (And internet access.)

This is an incredibly handy feature. No more emailing files to yourself. No more carrying things around on a flash drive. After working on some document at the office, you can go home and resume from right where you stopped; the same file is waiting for you, exactly as you left it.

The iCloud Drive is a great backup, too, because of its automatic duplication on multiple machines. Even if your phone is stolen or burned to aluminum dust, your iCloud Drive files are safe.

...And Its Rivals

Ah, but iCloud Drive is not the only magic folder-syncing service. There's also Dropbox, Google Drive, OneDrive (Microsoft), Creative Cloud (Adobe), and Box. They all work essentially alike.

> **NOTE:** For example, they all offer a certain amount of free storage— 5 GB, in Apple's case—and if you outgrow that, you can pay monthly for more room.

So Apple thought it might be cool to create one single app that can access *all* these services. You can search them all at once, too!

Working with Files

On the Browse tab, tap **Locations** to hook up your various accounts (Google Drive, Dropbox, and so on). Tap **Edit**, and then turn on the services you use. Each will require you to log in with your name and password for that service. You can also drag the ☰ handle to rearrange them in the list. Tap **Done**.

To see your actual files, tap one of the services' names—say, iCloud Drive. And boom: You're looking at a tidy list of all the files and folders on that "drive" (above, right). Here's what you can do with them:

- **To download a file to your phone,** tap its name (or the ☁ button).

- **To open a file, tap it.** Now, iOS is not macOS or Windows; still, it can open many kinds of documents right on the phone. Graphics, music and video files, Microsoft Office documents, and PDFs all open right up—at least once they've been downloaded. Other kinds of computer files may open in their associated apps on the phone—or not at all. In those cases, Files is still useful, though, because it lets you forward those documents by email to a machine that *can* open them.

In iOS 13, in fact, you can even create or open .zip files, compressing or decompressing a file on the fly. The trick is to long-press the file and, from the shortcut menu, choose **Compress** (or **Decompress**).

TIP: If you've opened a photo or PDF file, you can annotate it using the Markup tools described on page 458. Tap the Ⓐ.

- **To delete, move, or manipulate a file or folder,** long-press it. Buttons appear for Copy, Duplicate, Move (into a different folder), Delete, Info, Quick Look, Tags (or Favorite), Rename, and Share.

  Those are fairly self-explanatory, but don't miss the Share feature. It lets you send anyone in the world a copy of anything on any of your virtual drives, just by sending a link to it.

  Quick Look is pretty awesome, too; it lets you see what's in a file without fully opening it.

- **To operate on multiple files simultaneously,** tap Select, and then tap the files you want. Now you can use the ⬆️ (Share), ⊞ (Duplicate), 🗀 (Move to different folder), and 🗑 (Delete) buttons at the bottom.

TIP: There's a second way to select multiple files, in readiness for moving into a folder. It's tricky but faster once you get it. Start dragging one file or folder, and then pause. Without releasing your finger, use other fingers to tap other icons. You'll see those additional icons jump to your original finger, ready to complete the drag into a folder's icon.

If you tug downward on the display of files and folders, you reveal three new blue controls at the top:

- **To create a new folder,** tap 🗀➕ at the top-left corner.

- **To change the sorting order,** tap Sorted by at the top; choose Name, Date, Size, or Tags.

- **To switch from list view to icon view,** tap the ☰ icon at top right.

Tagging Files

The Browse tab also lets you round up all files with a particular tag (a color-coded label that you make up, like *Important* or *Smithers Project*). What's especially powerful is that your tagged files can come from all different services—one from Dropbox, a few from Google Drive, and so on. They all appear in one unified, harmonious "tagged" list, without reference to creed, color, or place of origin.

To apply a tag, select a file, or several. Now tap ⬆️ (or tap the Share button that appears in the scrollable black command bar when you long-press the icon). Tap +Tag, and then tap the tag name(s) that you want to apply. This, by the way, is your only chance to create a *new* tag (Add New Tag).

Thereafter, you can see all the files bearing a certain tag in either of two ways:

- **On the main Browse screen,** tap a tag name to see all the files you've tagged that way.

- **On the Recents screen,** scroll down to the tag headings; there are your tagged files. (As you could probably figure out, the Recents screen's other purpose is to display the icons of files you've opened recently.)

(To remove a tag, long-press to select the file or files, and then tap **Tags** in the black command bar. Tap the tag name to remove the checkmark.)

Favorites Folders

Tags work only on files. What about folders?

For those, Apple has supplied a Favorites feature. Select a folder (or several); then, from the command bar that appears when you long-press an icon, tap **Favorite**. Those folders now appear beneath the Favorites heading on the main Browse tab, for quick access.

Here again, your Favorites folders can come from all different syncing services. They're just happy to be your favorites.

> **TIP:** Your iCloud Drive folder contains inner folders named for Apple apps like Pages, Numbers, and so on. Yes, these folders hold the corresponding kinds of documents, for ease of finding later.
>
> But Pages, Keynote, and Numbers offer a cool feature: *real-time, simultaneous editing* across the internet. You and your colleagues can collaborate on one of these kinds of documents live. (If you've ever used Google Docs, you're familiar with the process.)
>
> There's a lot of fine print to making this work; fortunately, Apple has created a guide here: *support.apple.com/en-us/HT206181*.

In all these apps, there's an **Open** button or icon that presents the iCloud Drive's contents. In Pages, for example, when you're viewing your list of documents on the **Browse** tab, you can tap **iCloud Drive** to see all the folders on your iCloud Drive, corresponding perfectly to what you would have seen on a Mac or a PC. Tap a folder to open it.

Find My

No, that's not a typo. The app's name really is missing a direct object. Find My what?

The name makes a little more sense when you realize that it combines what used to be two apps: Find My iPhone and Find My Friends. The purpose of both apps was the same—to show where things are on a map. This new uni-app has three tabs: Friends, Devices, and Me.

People

Find My People is great for keeping tabs on your very young or very old loved ones, for arranging meet-up points in a crowded city, or for making sure nobody's cheating on you.

This feature requires transparency and approval on both sides; you can't track people without their permission and awareness.

It may seem backward, but to start tracking someone, you're supposed to first show goodwill by letting them track *you*. They then have the option of letting you track them back.

Suppose, for example, that Juliet wants to monitor Romeo's position. In the app, Juliet taps **Share My Location**. She starts typing *romeo* into the **To** box; she taps his name in the list and then taps **Send**.

Her phone asks how she wants to broadcast her position to Romeo: **Share for One Hour** (good for locating a friend downtown), **Share Until End of Day** (good for finding your colleague at the company off-site), or **Share Indefinitely** (good for finding your spouse).

At this moment, Romeo sees a notification that says, "Juliet Capulet started sharing location with you. Do you want to share yours?" Romeo, too, can choose either **One Hour**, **End of Day**, or **Indefinitely** (or, if he's still hung up on someone else, **Don't Share**).

Now Juliet sees a note that Romeo has shared his location, and his name shows up in the People list. She can tap his name to see his position on a map.

At that point, the info panel on the bottom half of the screen (which she can drag upward to expand) offers her buttons to **Contact** Romeo, get **Directions** to his location, set up **Notifications** (described next), add or remove him from the Favorites list, edit his location's name (to, for example, "Montague House"), stop sharing her location with him, or remove him altogether from this app's list.

Under Notifications, if Juliet taps **Add**, the app offers to **Notify Me** or **Notify Romeo**. Answering this question is a little baffling for her, since she doesn't yet know what she's asking to be notified *about*—but here's how it shakes down:

- **Notify Me.** Juliet will get notified when Romeo either arrives at, or departs from, a certain place—either his **Current Location** or another one that she specifies. Yes, it's super-creepy in the wrong hands—but, again, this doesn't work unless he has invited her to know where he is. Also, Romeo will be notified that Juliet has turned this notification feature on.

- **Notify Romeo.** In this case, *Romeo* will get notified when *Juliet* arrives at, or departs from, her **Current Location** or another address that she sets up here.

In each case, she can also choose how often to get these notification bubbles: either **Only Once** (meaning today only), or **Every Time** (meaning, every time, every day, that this person arrives or leaves).

Once you've finished checking out somebody's location, tap anywhere on the map to return to the original Find People screen, with the full list of trackees.

Devices

This tab is the new incarnation of the old Find My iPhone app. It lists the Apple gadgets you own (signed into your iCloud account). Tap one to see where it is on a map (below, left). The expandable panel at the

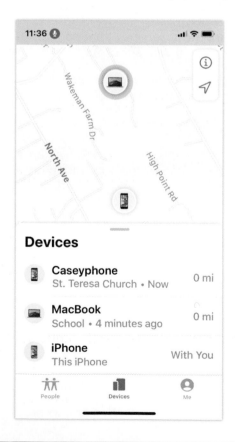
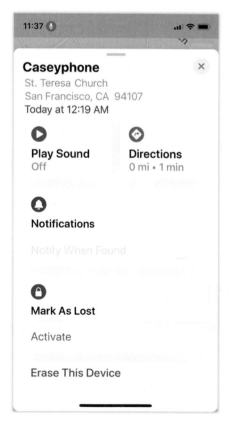

bottom of the screen offers five powerful tools for the panicking gadget owner: **Play Sound**, **Notifications**, **Mark As Lost**, and **Erase This Device** are described on page 572. **Directions** opens Maps to guide you to the location of your lost thing.

TIP: When you first open the app, it asks if you want to turn on "Send Last Location." That's a fantastic idea. It means you'll get to see where your phone was the last time it had a charge, just in case you don't realize it's missing until after it's dead. Tap **Turn On**, for heaven's sake.

Me

On this tab, you can see where you are, and turn off **Share My Location**—crucial if you're about to do something shady. Other fun to have here:

- **Allow Friend Requests.** Are other people even allowed to *ask* if they can track you?

- **Receive Location Updates.** Remember that business about getting notified when someone arrives at or departs from a location? If you have a lot of friends, that feature could wind up bombarding your phone with notifications. This item lets you limit those incoming notifications to people you've shared *your* location with (instead of getting them from **Everyone**).

- **Use This Phone as My Location** is important if you own multiple Apple devices. Which one, for locating purposes, is you?

- **Edit Location Name** lets you label your current location, as other people will see it ("My pad," for example, or "Secret nook").

- **Help a Friend.** At last, Apple has recognized the towering logical fallacy of the Find My iPhone feature. If you *can't find your iPhone*, what good is an app, on your phone, that helps you find it?

  The idea here is that you can use somebody *else's* phone to find your lost one. That good Samaritan taps **Help a Friend**; you log in with your Apple ID; and you get to see where your phone is hiding!

Health

This app is a dashboard for all the health data—activity, sleep, nutrition, relaxation—generated by your fitness apps. But even if you don't have an app or a band, you have the iPhone itself; unbeknownst to you, it's been quietly tracking the steps you've been taking and the flights of stairs you've been climbing, just by measuring the jostling of the phone in your pocket or bag! (If that creeps you out just a bit, you can turn it off in Settings→Privacy→Motion & Fitness.)

Lots of apps and fitness bands share their data with Health: the Apple Watch, MyFitnessPal, Strava, MapMyRun, WebMD, 7 Minute Workout, Garmin Connect, Lark, Lose It!, Sleepio, Weight Watchers, and so on. Fitness tracking is a big, big deal these days, now that your phone and/or your fitness band can measure your steps, exercise, and sleep.

> **TIP:** Screamingly missing from this list: Fitbit. A Fitbit band can't share its data with the Health app—at least not without the help of a $5 app called Sync Solver or a free one called Power Sync for Fitbit.

If you have one of those bands or apps, you'll have to fish around in its settings until you find the option to connect with Health. At that point, you turn on the kinds of data you want it to share with Health.

Now open the Health app. The setup screens invite you to set up a Medical ID, to become an organ donor, or to share your health data (anonymously) with Apple.

The Summary

In iOS 13, Apple redesigned the Health app, making it far simpler. Now the app opens to a Summary screen (facing page, left). Here's some of what it includes:

- **Steps you've taken today.** Tap to see a details screen that lists your total steps by day, week, months, or year (facing page, center); Highlights (observations about how many more or fewer steps you're taking than usual); a list of apps that can also count your steps and track your runs; Add to Favorites (brings the Steps tile to the top of the Summary screen, where it probably is already); Show All Data (breaks down your step totals by day); and Data Sources & Access (shows a list of apps you've allowed to see your step count; also lists all your step-counting gadgets, and lets you drag them into priority order—tap Edit).

- **Highlights** are artificially intelligent observations that the app makes about your fitness. It might say, for example, "Last week, you were taking more steps a day than you are this week."

- **Get More From Health** cards offer health-related actions you can take (for example, Register as an Organ Donor or Access Your Records), along with cheerful health-related articles.

- **Apps** is a list of diet, exercise, and health-related apps that Apple thinks might interest you. Tap one to open the App Store to read more.

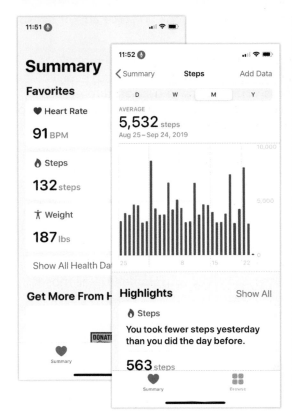
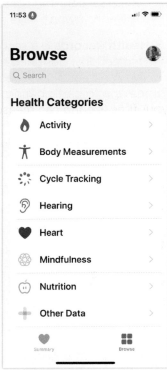

You're welcome to customize the "tiles" on this screen, by the way. Tap **Edit**. The **Existing Data** list shows everything on the Summary screen now; tap the ★ to make it a Favorite (shown at the top of the Summary screen). The **All** list shows everything Health can track, whether it's got any data on you or not.

Browse

Hey, it's a list of lists! Two of them, in fact (above, right):

- **Health Categories.** These are all the health-data types the Health app can store: **Activity** (steps, flights of stairs, workouts), **Body Measurements** (height and weight, body fat percentage), **Cycle Tracking**, **Hearing**, **Heart** (rate, blood pressure, ECG), **Mindfulness** (minutes meditating), **Nutrition** (calcium, cholesterol), **Other Data** (blood glucose, inhaler usage, sexual activity, tooth brushing), **Respiratory** (oxygen saturation, VO_2 max, rate), **Sleep**, and **Vitals** (heart rate, blood pressure).

    For most of these items, you'll see No Data Available. Remember, Health is supposed to be the database for numbers sent to it by fitness sensors and other apps. Until you hook up some app or sensor to Health, it won't have much to show you.

- **Health Records** is a second list (Allergies, Immunizations, Medications) designed to store your medical history and records. You can't enter these records yourself; you're supposed to hook up the app to participating labs, hospitals, and medical networks. Tap **Get Started** to get started; along the way, you'll need the login details for each institution, which may mean some phone calls.

Once you're hooked up, though, your medical records update automatically in the Health app whenever they change at the medical center.

Home

HomeKit is Apple's home-automation standard. The Home app lets you control any product whose box says "Works with HomeKit"—all those "smart" or "connected" door locks, security cameras, power outlets, thermostats, doorbells, light bulbs, leak/freeze/temperature/humidity/air-quality sensors, and so on.

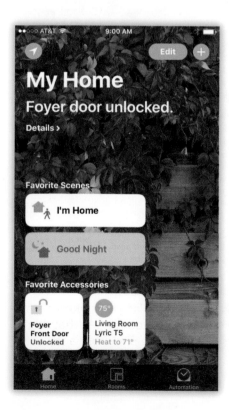
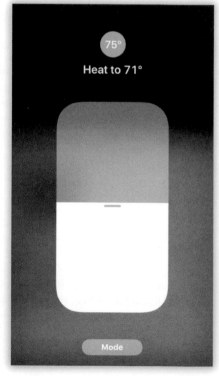

Introducing your new smart-home doodad to the app is simple. In the app, hit + and then **Add Accessory**. The top half of the screen becomes a camera; you're supposed to aim it at the squarish bar code (or eight-digit number) on the product's box or sticker.

> **TIP:** If you're really lucky, your smart-home gizmo bears a little Wi-Fi-looking icon. That means that, instead of scanning the bar code, you can just *hold your phone near that label* to introduce the app to the device.

Now you're asked to enter the product's name and location. If you also turn on **Include in Favorites**, you'll be able to control this gadget from the Control Center (page 42) or an Apple Watch, without even having to fire up the Home app. Tap **Done**.

Once you've installed the gadget, you can use this app to turn it on and off, monitor its readouts, or adjust its settings (a thermostat is shown on the facing page at right). You can do all that from the Home app, from the Control Center, or by using Siri voice commands ("Lock the front door," "Turn on the downstairs lights," and so on).

This isn't really a book about smart-home accessories, but here's some of the fun you can have once you've bought a few (and then read the instructions at *support.apple.com/en-us/HT204893*):

- **Set up rooms.** If you've got a lot of HomeKit accessories—you lucky duck—you may find it easier to keep track of them all by putting their icons on different screens, named for different rooms of your house. You'll also be able to tell Siri, "Turn off the lights in the living room."

> **TIP:** You can take this concept one step further by putting your rooms into *zones*, which are usually "upstairs" or "downstairs." To get started: On the Rooms tab, tap ☰ and then **Room Settings**. Now tap a room's name and then **Zone**. And voilà: You can say, "Turn off the lights upstairs"!

- **Automate your gadgets.** You can automate many actions based on the time or your location, or hand off control of certain devices to other people's iPhones.

- **Create a scene.** A "scene" is a bunch of accessories you switch on and off simultaneously. You might have one called "Goodnight" that turns off all the lights and locks the doors with a single Siri command.

- **Set up notifications.** The Home app can alert you when a door was opened or closed, or when a light was left on. Those doggone kids!

- **Control your home by remote control.** It's possible to set things up so you can operate your gadgets from across the internet when you're not even there. This does, however, require that you also own an Apple *home hub*, which can take the form of a recent Apple TV, a HomePod speaker, or an iPad.

- **Automate the whole works.** If you do, in fact, have a home hub, then you can really smartify your home. You can set things up so that all the lights turn off when you leave the house, or that a certain scene happens at a certain time, or that the temperature goes up when your teenager gets home.

  It can get really complicated. But imagine the magic once you get it all figured out!

Maps

The first version of Maps, Apple's competitor to the navigation app Google Maps, was a disaster. Its databases had serious errors, often guiding drivers to nonexistent roads or over what appeared to be melting bridges. Apple promised to keep working on Maps, but in the meantime, in a remarkable apology letter, CEO Tim Cook advised his customers to use one of Maps' rivals—like Google Maps.

It's taken many years, but Apple's Maps is closing the gap. Instead of cobbling together data from a bunch of different mapping companies, Apple undertook a massive, multiyear project: driving millions of miles of roads in camera vans, building its own database—and images—of the world's roads.

The result: By the end of 2019, the entire U.S. will appear in Maps with much more detailed ground maps (like foliage, pedestrian routes, individual buildings, and so on).

Because Apple now maintains its own database, you'll get quicker updates to reflect construction and new roads, much better traffic information, and real-time road conditions. (Apple intends to roll out the new maps in other countries in 2020.)

Meet Maps

Maps lets you type in any address or point of interest and see it plotted on a map, with turn-by-turn driving directions. It also gives you a live national Yellow Pages business directory and real-time traffic-jam alerts. You can get bus and train schedules for some U.S. cities. You have a choice of a street-map diagram or actual aerial photos, taken by satellite.

Maps Basics

In iOS 13, Maps generally displays two halves: The map itself at top and an info panel at the bottom (below, left). Tap or drag that info panel to see more of it; tap again to collapse it.

A blue dot on the map always represents your current location. Tap ⌃ to center the map on your current spot. To zoom in, double-tap, "pinch out" with two fingers, or double-tap/drag with a single finger. (That is, double-tap and, with your finger still down, drag up or down.) Eventually, you zoom in enough to see actual city blocks.

To zoom *out* again, you can use the rare *two-finger double-tap*.

To scroll around the map, drag or flick; twist two fingers to rotate it. (A compass icon at top right helps you keep your bearings; you can tap it to restore the map's usual north-is-up orientation.) And if you drag two fingers up the screen, you tilt the map into 3D view, which makes it look like you're surveying the map at an angle instead of straight down.

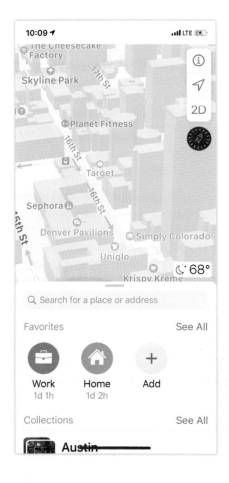

At any time, you can tap (i) to open a secret panel. Here's how you switch among Maps' three views of the world: Map, Transit, or Satellite (which is shown on the previous page at right).

You can set up some preferences here, too. Tap **Map** to decide if you want to see color-coded roads that show the current traffic situation. Tap **Satellite** to tell Maps whether you want street names and/or traffic colors superimposed on the aerial views.

Each of these tabs offers buttons that let you **Mark My Location** (drop a pin in your current spot, add it to your Favorites, add it to your Contacts, and so on), **Add a Place** (record the address and other details of a business, thereby adding it to Apple's database), and **Report an Issue** (tell Apple about a bug).

Finding Yourself

If any phone can tell you where you are, it's the iPhone. It has not one, not two, but *three* ways to determine your location:

- **GPS.** First, the iPhone contains a traditional GPS chip, of the sort that was found in windshield navigation units of old.

- **Wi-Fi Positioning System.** Metropolitan areas today are blanketed by Wi-Fi signals. At a typical Manhattan intersection, you might be in range of 30 base stations. Each one broadcasts its own name and unique network address (its *MAC address*—nothing to do with Mac computers) once every second. A laptop or phone can detect this beacon signal from up to 1,500 feet away.

  Imagine if you could correlate all those beacon signals with their physical locations. Why, you'd be able to simulate GPS!

  For years, millions of iPhones have been quietly logging all those Wi-Fi signals, noting their network addresses and locations. (The phones never *connect* to these base stations—they just read the one-way beacon signals.) At this point, Apple's database knows about millions of hotspots—and the precise longitude and latitude of each.

  So, if the iPhone can't get a fix on GPS, it sniffs for Wi-Fi base stations. If it finds any, it looks up those network addresses and learns the coordinates. This system fails once you're out of populated areas. On the other hand, it works indoors, which GPS definitely doesn't.

- **The cellular triangulation system.** As a last resort, the iPhone can check its proximity to the cellphone towers around you. The software works a lot like the Wi-Fi location system, but it relies upon its knowledge of cellular towers' locations rather than Wi-Fi base stations.

The first Maps trick is to show you where you are: Tap the ⌁ at the top of the Maps screen. The button turns solid blue, indicating that the iPhone is consulting its various references to figure out where you are. You show up as a blue dot that moves with you. It keeps tracking you until you tap the ⌁ enough times to turn it off.

Orienting Maps

It's great to see a blue pin on the map and all—but how do you know which way you're facing? Just tap the ⌁ until it points straight up. The map spins so that the direction you're facing is upward, and a "flashlight beam" emanates from your blue dot; its width indicates the iPhone's degree of confidence. (The narrower the beam, the surer it is.)

Searching Maps

The following paragraphs guide you through using the search box in Maps. But it's *much* quicker to use Siri.

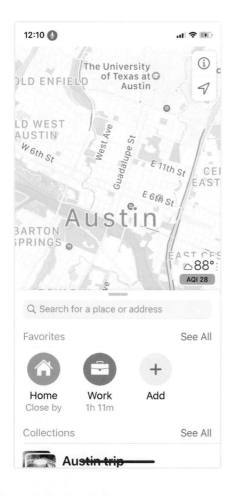

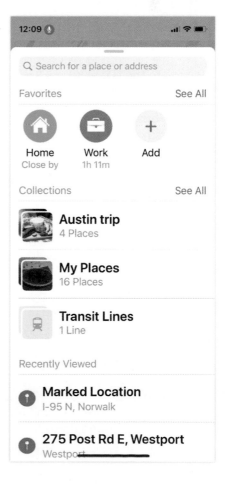

You can say, for example, "Show me the map of Detroit" or "Show me the closest Starbucks" or "Directions to 200 West 79th Street in New York." Siri shows you that spot on a map; tap to jump into the Maps app.

If you *must* use the search box, here's how it works. It shouldn't be hard to find, since it opens when you open Maps (previous page, left).

- **Siri Suggestions.** One nice thing about Maps is the way it tries to eliminate typing at every step. This first row, new in iOS 13, is a great example. It appears when Siri finds something on your calendar that involves travel. It might be details for a flight, for example, or the name of a restaurant where you're supposed to arrive soon. Places you've recently looked up appear here, too.

  Tap to open a details screen, whose prominent feature is a Go button, to start your navigation there.

- **Favorites** are addresses, like Home and Work, that you use often. Tap Add to enter a new one, or tap Add to Favorites on a place's Location card (page 438). (If you're not seeing Favorites, tap the lower info panel to expand it, as shown on the previous page at right.)

  Tap one to jump to its spot on the map, or tap Show All and then swipe to the left to reveal Share and Remove buttons. (This screen's Edit button lets you reorder the Favorites, too.)

  Each Favorite shows, at this moment, how long it will take you to get there. To get going, tap the Favorite's icon and then tap Go. Two taps!

- **Business Categories.** When you tap into an empty search box, you get icons for Restaurants, Gas Stations, Groceries, and so on. Each expands into a list of nearby options.

TIP: Don't miss the scrollable list of subcategories or establishments at the very bottom of some of these screens. When you tap Bars, for example, this ticker may list Sports Bars, Cocktail Bars, Pubs, and so on. Oh—and see the little temperature indicator on the map? If you long-press, it sprouts an hourly weather forecast; tap to open the Weather app for that place.

- **Collections,** new in iOS 13, are lists of places you intend to use on a trip, for example. A collection might include your hotel, the conference venue, the restaurants you've booked, and the local airport.

  To create one, tap New Collection (or See All and then +). Name the new collection ("Austin," for example), hit Create, tap the newly created Collection's name, hit Add a Place, and go to town, searching and tapping addresses to add. Hit Done.

- **Recently Viewed.** Next on this scrolling screen: a list of searches you've recently conducted. You'd be surprised at how often you want to call up the same spot again later.

TIP: If you swipe a listing to the left, you reveal two buttons: **Share** (send the location info to someone) and **Remove** (if you intend to elope and don't want your parents to find out).

All that appears *before* you tap into the search box itself. Often, though, you'll wind up *typing* what you want to find. You can type all kinds of things into the search box:

- **An address.** You can skip the periods (and usually the commas, too). And you can use abbreviations. Typing *710 w end ave ny ny* will find 710 West End Avenue, New York, New York. (In this and any of the other examples, you can type a zip code instead of a city and state.)

- **An intersection.** Type *57th and lexington, ny ny*. Maps finds the spot where East 57th Street crosses Lexington Avenue in New York City.

- **A city.** Type *chicago il* to see that city. You can zoom in from there.

- **A zip code or a neighborhood.** Type *10014* or *greenwich village*.

- **Latitude and longitude coordinates.** Type *40.7484° N, 73.9857° W*.

- **A point of interest.** Type *washington monument* or *niagara falls*.

- **A business type.** Type *drugstores in albany ny* or *hospitals in roanoke va*.

- **A contact's name.** Maps is tied into Contacts, your master address book (page 121). Start typing a person's name to see the matches.

- **A business category.** Maps is a glorified national Yellow Pages. If you type, for example, *pharmacy 60609*, then red bubbles show you all the drugstores in that Chicago zip code. It's a great way to find a gas station, a cash machine, or a hospital in a pinch. Tap a pushpin to see the name of the corresponding business.

The resulting map shows little pushpins, as well as a scrolling list of search results. Tap either one to open a details screen (the Location card, described on page 438).

TIP: You can also create a pin by holding your finger down on the spot.

The Location Card

Whenever you've tapped a pin, or the name of some place in a Maps list (like a store, restaurant, or point of interest), the bottom part of the screen lists its information screen—its location "card." Tap it or swipe up to expand it to full screen.

The location card shows the all-important **Directions** button. If this is the location for a restaurant or a business, you may get several screens full of useful information, courtesy of Yelp: hours of operation, one-tap links for placing a phone call to the place or visiting its website, customer reviews, photos, delivery and reservation information, and so on.

Links here let you add the place to Favorites, add it to Contacts, share it with other people (via AirDrop, email, text message, Facebook, or Twitter), or **Report an Issue** (tell Apple about a problem with Maps' information).

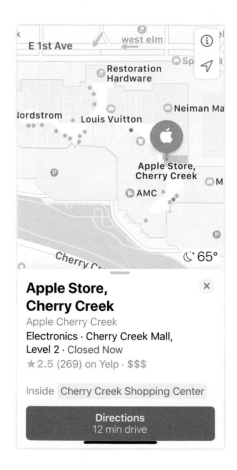

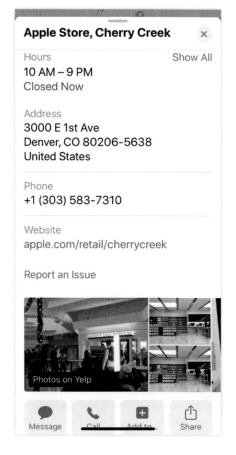

The location card for a restaurant may even offer a **Reservations** button, so that you can book a table on the spot—if, that is, that eatery participates in OpenTable's online booking system.

TIP: As you burrow deeper into the screens of the information panel (bottom part of the Maps screen), eventually, you'll want to get back to the opening Search page. To do that, tap the ✖ over and over until you're there.

Directions

Suppose you've just searched for a place. Its location card is open. At this point, you can tap **Directions** for instant directions, using four modes of transportation (below, left):

- **Drive.** You'll get the traditional turn-by-turn driving directions.

- **Walk.** The app will guide you to this place by foot. You get an estimate of the time it'll take, too.

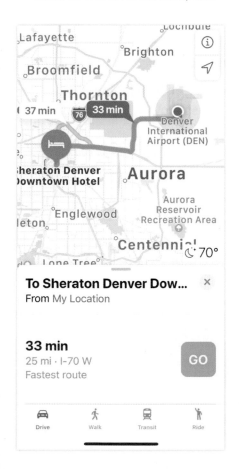

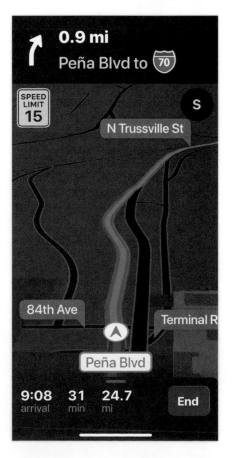

- **Transit.** This button applies if you're in one of the 60-plus cities, states, and countries for which Apple has public-transportation schedules: buses, subways, and trains. More cities are coming, Apple says.

  If you're lucky enough to be in one of those places, you'll discover the public-transport directions are surprisingly clear and detailed. You even see the color, letter, and number schemes of that city's bus or rail system right there in the app. In iOS 13, you get arrival times, station stops, and connections, as well as news about outages, delays, and cancellations.

  And if you're *not* in one of those cities, Maps helpfully offers a list of other apps in the App Store that do have your transit information. Click **View Routing Apps**.

- **Ride** means calling an Uber or Lyft driver. (This feature requires that you have the Uber or Lyft app installed and set up.) One tap on **Ride** shows you the time and price estimates—and offers you a **Request** button.

In each case, Maps displays an overview of the route you're about to drive. In fact, it may propose several different routes, each labeled by journey time: **3 hrs 37 min**, **4 hrs 11 min**, and **4 hrs 33 min**, for example.

If you tap one of these tags, the app lets you know the distance and estimated time for that option and identifies the main roads you'll be on (previous page, left).

In each case, tap **Go** to see the first instruction. The map zooms in, and Navigation mode begins.

Navigation Mode

When the iPhone is guiding you to a location, you see a simplified map of the world around you, complete with the outlines of buildings, with huge banners that tell you how to turn next, and onto what street (previous page, right). Siri's familiar voice speaks the same information at the right times ("Turn right at the next light"), so you don't even have to look at the screen.

Even if you hit the side button to lock the phone, the voice guidance continues. (It continues even if you switch to another app; return to Maps by tapping the banner at the top of the screen—or, on Face ID phones, the blue button on the left ear.)

The bottom bar shows your projected arrival time, plus the remaining time and distance. It also offers the **End** button, which ends guidance.

While Maps is guiding you, you can zoom in and out; you can also pan the map to look ahead at upcoming turns or to inspect alternate routes. You can twist two fingers to turn the map, too. Once you've shifted the view in these ways, a ↗ button appears. Tap it to restore Maps' usual centered view.

At any time, you can tap the top instruction banner to see an overview map of your entire route.

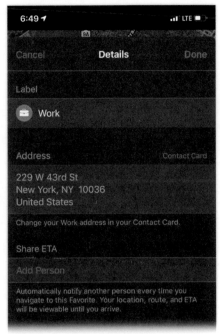

While you're navigating, you can also tap (or swipe up on) the bottom bar to reveal quick-tap buttons like these:

- **Details.** Tap to get a written list of turn-by-turn instructions.

- **Share ETA.** Whenever you begin navigating in Maps, a little Share ETA button appears for a few seconds (above, top left). If you don't tap it in time, you can swipe up on the lower panel to reveal it (bottom left).

  If you tap it, and then tap the icon of a frequent correspondent (or tap Contacts), you trigger one of iOS 13's finest new features: You share your estimated time of arrival.

  Suppose you've shared your ETA with your sister. If she's running iOS 13 or later, she gets a notification on her phone, announcing your ETA. By tapping it, she opens Maps, where she can track your progress.

If she has something inferior, like an Android phone or iOS 12, she gets only a normal text message containing your ETA. She'll get additional texts if traffic and other variables change your ETA by more than five minutes.

What's really cool, though, is that you can also set up *automatic* Share ETAs—a perfect setup if you commute home each day and want to keep your partner posted without any additional effort.

You can set this up before you start traveling. It requires that you've created a Favorite place, as described on page 436. (The **Home** and **Work** icons work nicely.)

In the Favorites section, tap **See All**. Then tap the ⓘ next to your destination. Tap **Add Person** (previous page, right); choose contact info for each person you want to add; and hit **Done**.

From now on, that person will get Share ETA notifications every time that location is your destination. No more 11-second phone calls saying "Hi, honey, I should be home around eight." Honey already knows.

Tap the screen (or just wait) to hide these additional controls once again.

Directions Between Two Other Points

The design of Maps seems to suggest that you'll always want to navigate somewhere from your current location. But sometimes, you might want directions between two points—when you're not currently at either one.

First, select your starting point. For example, add a pushpin (page 434), or tap a point-of-interest icon. Tap **Directions**, and then **My Location**.

Now you can change the From box (where it currently says **My Location**), using the same address-searching tactics described on page 435. (At this point, you can also swap your start and end points by tapping the ↑↓ double arrow.) Finally, tap **Route** to see the fastest route.

Night Mode

If the phone's light sensor notices that it's dark in your car, it switches to a dimmer, grayer version of the map. It wouldn't want to distract you, after all. When there's enough light, it brightens back up again.

Where You Parked

Maps automatically remembers where you parked, and can guide you back to your car.

How does the phone know when you've parked? Because it connects wirelessly to your car over Bluetooth or CarPlay. (So if your car doesn't have Bluetooth or CarPlay, you don't get this feature.)

When you turn off the car, the phone assumes you've parked it, checks its GPS location, and shows a notification to let you know it's memorized the spot. (If, that is, this feature is turned on in **Settings→ Maps→Show Parked Location**.)

TIP: If you tap the notification, you get a chance to take a photo of the parking spot or to record notes about it. You also see how long you've been parked—handy if you have to feed a meter.

When the time comes to return to your car, the phone makes life as easy as possible. Wake the phone and swipe to the right to view the Maps widget or the Maps Destinations widget. Once you know where you parked, a swipe gets you started finding your way back. (See page 76 for more on widgets.)

TIP: You can also ask Siri, "Where's my parked car?" or even, "Dude, where's my car?"

The car's location also appears in the Maps app itself, right there in the list of recent locations, and as a reminder in the Today tab of the Notification Center. Tap to begin your journey home.

Traffic

How's this for a cool feature? Free, real-time traffic reporting. Just tap the ⓘ (visible in map or satellite view whenever you're *not* in Navigation mode), and then turn on **Traffic**. Now traffic jams appear as red lines on the relevant roads, for your stressing pleasure; less-severe slowdowns show up in orange.

Better yet, tiny icons appear, representing accidents, closures, and construction. Tap to see a description bar at the bottom of the screen (like "Accident, Park Ave at State St"); tap that bar to read the details.

If you don't see any colored lines, it's either because traffic is moving fine or because Apple doesn't have any information for those roads. Usually, you get traffic info only for highways, and only in metropolitan areas.

3D Mode

Apple spent two years filming cities in helicopters to create 3D models of major cities and landmarks: San Francisco, New York, Tokyo, London, Paris, Rome, Madrid, Vancouver, San Jose, Cape Town, and Stockholm, for example. Or places like Yosemite National Park, Sydney Opera House, Stonehenge, St. Peter's Basilica, or the Brooklyn Bridge. These city models are responsible for three cool Maps features: 3D view, Flyover, and Flyover Tours.

When you've called up one of these chosen places (and zoomed in enough to see buildings), a **3D** button appears. Tap it to tilt into a more 3D view. Now you can conduct your own virtual chopper tour of the city. You can look over and around buildings to see what's behind them, using the usual techniques:

- **Drag with one finger** to move around the map.

- **Pinch or spread two fingers** to zoom out or in.

- **Drag two fingers up or down** to change your camera angle relative to the ground.

- **Twist two fingers** to turn the world before you.

When you've had enough, tap the **2D** button in the upper-right corner.

Flyover (iPhone 8 and later)

Flyover is a 3D, augmented-reality, aerial view of the cities and places Apple has scanned as described already. You can use your phone like a viewer, turning your body and moving the phone around in space to change your view.

To begin, tap **Flyover** (a button that appears on the location card of major cities). Wait for a moment as the phone downloads the photographic models. It's immersing, completely amazing, and very unlikely to make you airsick.

At this point, you get a **Start City Tour** button. It starts a crazy treat: a fully automated video tour of that city or place. The San Francisco tour shows you the baseball park, the famous Transamerica Pyramid, the

Alcatraz prison island, and so on. It's slow, soothing, cool, and definitely something paper maps never did. Tap the screen to open the Pause Tour button; tap the ⓧ to end the tour.

Look Around

Google Maps may have Street View, which lets you view a 360-degree photographic representation of any address. But in iOS 13, Apple has its own rival feature, called Look Around. It's much better than Google's thing—faster, smoother, higher resolution, almost video-like as you move from one spot to another—but at the outset it works in very few places. (Google's Street View covers almost every place on earth, including underwater, on mountains, on hiking trails, in the interiors of museums and other important buildings, and even on the International Space Station.)

To try it out, call up a major U.S. city (Honolulu, Las Vegas, San Francisco, and San Jose all have Look Around). Tap **Look Around** on the location card, or tap the 👓 button at top right (once you've zoomed in enough to see street names).

And behold: You're practically in that city, standing in the middle of the street. Drag to "look around." Pinch or spread two fingers to zoom out or in. Tap any spot to fly there; in this way, you can tour an entire neighborhood without ever leaving the comfort of your couch. It's a fantastic way to get a feeling for a place before you actually go there, meet someone there, or buy a house there.

You can tap ⤢ to fill the screen with the image (next page, bottom). In this view, you can tap labels (street names, place names) to jump there or open the corresponding location cards. (Too cluttery? When you're not reading about a place of interest, you can tap the place label to view the **Hide Labels** button.)

Alternatively, you can tap 🔭 to view the image as an inset on the map (below, top). In this latter view, you can tap or drag the map to jump around the city. (Any street shaded in blue has Look Around.)

When you've completed your tour, tap **Done**. And hope that Apple hurries up with the next-largest 4,000 U.S. cities.

Extensions

There's one more goody in Maps: Extensions. These are add-on features made by other companies—auto-installed into Maps by their full-blown apps—like Uber, Lyft, Yelp, and OpenTable. The point, of course, is to let you order cars, read restaurant reviews, reserve tables, or buy tickets right from within Maps.

Extensions, for example, are responsible for adding the Ride button described on page 440.

You'll probably find them quite handy, but maybe not all of them. Fortunately, you can turn off individual extensions in **Settings→Maps→ Extensions**.

Measure

Apple has been putting a lot of engineering (and marketing) effort into making the iPhone a great machine for *augmented reality* apps (page 372).

You can find thousands of AR apps on the App Store. But to jump-start things, Apple offers Measure: a virtual tape measure, handy for measuring real-world objects (posters, windows, doors, furniture, staplers), using only the camera on the back.

When you first open Measure, a message says, "Move iPhone to start." It wants you to move your phone through the air in a squarish pattern. You're helping it gain its bearings, to calibrate.

Now you're ready to measure stuff!

- **If there's a very obvious square or rectangular object in view,** like a mirror/poster/window, the app auto-recognizes it and highlights it in yellow (below, top). Tap that rectangle (or the ⊕ button) to say "Yes, that's what I want to measure—give me the dimensions!"

- **If it's not completely obvious what you want to measure,** aim the tiny white dot so that it's near the starting point—the spot where you'd hold the end of a traditional measuring tape. (The dot tries to detect potential corners and snap into position.) When it's lined up,

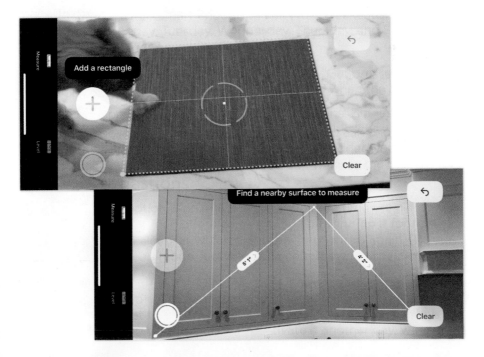

tap ⊕ to "plant" the tape there. Now aim the tiny white dot at the far end of the object or space, and tap ⊕ again. Voilà: There's your measurement (previous page, bottom).

Feel free, at this point, to move the white dot to a third position to repeat the process. In other words, you can create as many additional measurements as you like on the same screen.

The measurement readout appears on a tiny tab in the middle of the straight measurement line. But if you tap that little tab, you open a pop-up bubble that offers not only a big-type version of the same measurement (below, left), but also the equivalent in metric units (or imperial units, if you were using metric). And if you've measured a rectangular shape, then this bubble also gives you the area and the diagonal distance! You'll never have to do math again.

At any point, you can tap ◎ to capture the screen image with the measurements in place. You can send the resulting photo to your builder, interior designer, or orthodontist.

You'll discover fairly quickly that Measure's measurements aren't always perfectly precise; you are, after all, just pointing your phone at things. It's

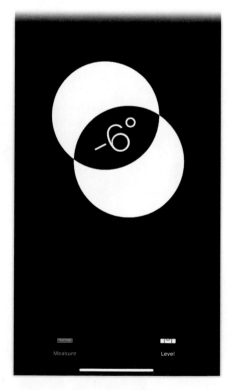

fantastic for measuring the space where you're considering putting a bed or a chair, but don't rely on it if you're building a Mars lander.

The Level

Measure has another trick up its sleeve, too: It can also act as a carpenter's level! The next time you need to hang a picture, prop up a wobbly table, or raise a barn, you'll now know when you've got things perfectly horizontal or vertical.

This isn't a new feature in iOS—it was part of the Compass app for years—but it *is* in a new place. In the Measure app, tap Level to get to it.

> **TIP:** On the Home screen, you can also long-press the Measure app's icon. The shortcut menu offers you direct access into the two modes: Measure and Level.

You can measure things' levelness in two dimensions:

- **Right/left.** Hold the iPhone upright (against a picture you're hanging, say), and tilt it left and right. When it's perfectly upright, the readout says 0 degrees and the bottom half of the screen turns green.

- **Forward/back.** Hold the phone upright and tip it away from or toward you. Once again, "0 degrees" and green mean "level."

- **Perfectly flat.** Hold the phone on its back, screen facing the sky. When the two circles merge (facing page, right), you'll know you've got it perfectly level. You could, for example, put the iPhone on a table you're trying to adjust, using its gauge to know how close you're getting as you wedge something under its short leg.

  Level doesn't have to be the zero point, either. You can tilt the phone to any angle and declare *that* to be the zero point—by tapping the screen.

News

The News app does just what Apple promises: It "collects all the stories you want to read, from top news sources, based on topics you're most interested in." Apple employs human editors—rather than software robots—to choose the stories in the Top Stories and Top Videos sections. Everybody sees the same stories here, no matter what their political leanings; in theory, this approach minimizes the triumph of fake news and clickbait.

If you see a bunch of news headlines right off the bat, well, sweet; you're the beneficiary of iCloud syncing (page 569). News has inherited your taste in news from iOS 12 or some other Apple gadget.

If this is the very first time you've ever opened News, though, tap **Continue** on the welcome screen. You're hit with today's headlines, beautifully laid out. It's like a specialized newspaper that's been lovingly cobbled together from all sorts of websites, magazines, and *real* newspapers.

This is the **Today** tab (below, left). Scroll down far enough, and you'll discover that your "front page" is broken up into sections like **Top Stories** (chosen by those human editors), **Trending Stories** (chosen by algorithm based on popularity), **For You** (stories that match your interests—described in a moment), **Top Videos**, and so on. Eventually, you

scroll down into topic areas like Politics, Sports, and Movies, plus any super-specialized topics you choose yourself.

Once you've tapped to open a story (facing page, right), using News is simplicity itself. Swipe vertically to scroll through an article, or horizontally to pull the next article into view.

The middle tab, **News+**, is the home for Apple's $10-a-month "Netflix for magazines" service. It gives you full access to current and past issues of 300 magazines and newspapers: *The Atlantic*, *Better Homes & Gardens*, *Entertainment Weekly*, *Esquire*, *GQ*, *National Geographic*, *New York Magazine*, *The New Yorker*, *Parents*, *People*, *Runner's World*, *Sports Illustrated*, *Vanity Fair*, *Vogue*, *Wired*, *The Wall Street Journal*, and many others.

The **Following** tab (facing page, middle), though, is where you make News your own. Here's where you specify which publications, websites, and topics (tech, business, politics, fashion, and so on) you want to follow in your News app. It boils down to these sections:

- **Saved Stories** is where you find articles you've seen and bookmarked.

- **History** lists every story you've seen recently.

- **Channels & Topics** offers a *very* tall scrolling list of favorite online publications (*The New York Times, Wired, The New Yorker,* and hundreds more). Tap to dive into that publication's latest stuff. You can search for topics, too.

- **Suggested by Siri** offers a few starter categories, based on iOS's observations about the kinds of news you like to read; tap ☺ to open that category, or ⊕ to add this category to your For Your collections. Swipe left and tap **Ignore** if that topic doesn't interest you.

- **Notifications** lets you set things up so that only certain kinds of news stories grab your attention with an iPhone notification (page 62).

- **Discover Channels and Topics** brings you to the setup screen: a massive, nearly endless list of magazine, newspaper, and website thumbnails. Tap to say "Yes, please include stories from these pubs in what you show me."

News no longer offers a list of *topics* that may interest you—the Cleveland Cavaliers, say, or Tesla cars, or seafood recipes. But you can still let News know your preferences—in a couple of ways:

- **Use the search box.** At the top of the Channels screen, a search box lets you search for topics, stories, or publications. In the search results, tap ⊕ for each item you want News to find for you.

- **Just use News.** As you use the News app, it notices which kinds of headlines you tap, read, or "favorite" (by tapping 📤→**Suggest More Like This**). It will, in other words, learn your interests—and tailor its reporting accordingly.

These operations make new story categories appear on the Today tab.

And that's it: Suddenly, you have a beautiful, infinite, constantly updated, free magazine stand, teeming with stories that have been collated according to your tastes. It's all free, although you're not getting the listed publications in full—usually you're offered just a few selected stories.

TIP: If you anticipate that you'll be spending time in the living hell known as Offline mode (like on a subway, sailboat, or airplane), you can save some stories for reading later. To do that, tap 📤 and then **Save Story**. You'll find your saved stories on the **Following** tab, under **Saved Stories**.

Notes

The Notes app is great for jotting down (or dictating) lists, reminders, brainstorms, recipes, directions, serial numbers, and so on.

These days, a Notes page can include checklists of to-dos, photos, maps, web links, or sketches you draw with your finger. You can even share notes wirelessly with another iPhone fan, so you can collaborate.

The modern-day Notes app offers full font and paragraph formatting. You can create tables. You can scan documents and then annotate them, right from within a note. And, of course, the powerful **Access Notes from Lock Screen** option means your phone is now ready, at a finger-tap's notice, to receive your jotted or scanned wisdom—without even having to unlock the phone first. See page 49.

As always, any changes you make in Notes are automatically synchronized to all your other Apple gadgets.

To get started, tap 📝 to start a new blank note. The keyboard appears so you can begin typing.

TIP: You can also send text from other apps *into* Notes. For example, in Mail, select some text you've typed into an outgoing message; in the command bar, tap **Share**. Similarly, you can tap a Mail attachment's icon; tap **Add to Notes** in the Share sheet. In each case, your selection magically appears on a new Notes page.

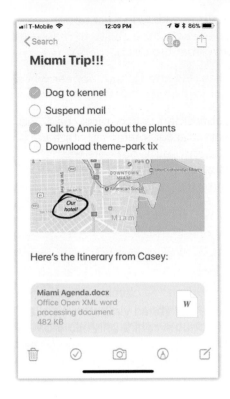

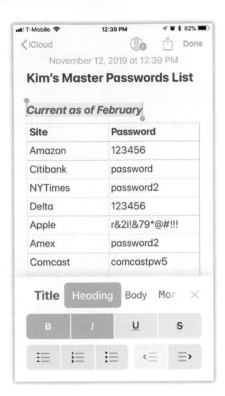

When you tap **Done**, the keyboard goes away, and a handy row of icons appears at the bottom of your Notes page. You can trash the note (🗑); add a checklist to it (⊘); add a graphic to it—photo, video, or scanned document (📷); add a sketch (Ⓐ); or start a new note (✐).

The Share 🖯 button is always available too, at the upper right. Tap it to print your note, copy it, or send it to someone by email, text message, AirDrop, and so on. For example, if you tap **Mail**, the iPhone creates a new outgoing message, pastes the first line of the note into the subject line, and pastes the note's text into the body. Address the note, edit if necessary, and hit **Send**. The iPhone returns you to Notes. (See page 378 for more on the sharing options.)

Herewith: A tour of the five buttons that appear above the keyboard. They're your gateway to everything you can put on a note: tables, text and paragraph formatting, lists, photos, sketches, and scanned documents.

Tables

When you tap ▦, you get a table with two columns and two rows. Tap in a cell and then start typing. To move to the next cell, tap **Next** on the keyboard (or tap with your finger).

Poke around long enough, and you can find controls for just about every formatting tool you'd ever need in a table (except the ability to manually adjust column widths and the ability to format the cell borders).

The keys to most of it are the tiny handles (⬚ and ⬚) that appear when you tap inside a cell:

- **Add or delete columns and rows.** Tap inside a cell to make the ⬚ and ⬚ buttons appear. Tap ⬚ to make the command bar appear, including **Add Column** and **Delete Column**; tap ⬚ to make the **Add Row** and **Delete Row** buttons appear. (If you're typing in the lower-right cell, tapping **Return** also makes a new row.)

- **Move a row or column.** Tap ⬚ or ⬚ to highlight the corresponding row or column; now you can drag it to a new spot.

- **Copy or paste cells.** Double-tap (or hold your finger down on) a cell to make the **Select** button appear. Once you've tapped it, you can drag the selection handles to expand the highlighting. The **Cut**, **Copy**, and **Paste** buttons appear in the command bar, along with the **B***I*U (bold, italic, underline) controls, **Look Up**, **Spell**, and other controls.

- **Convert text into a table.** Select the text, and then tap the table (▦) button. The selected text winds up in the first column—one cell per paragraph.

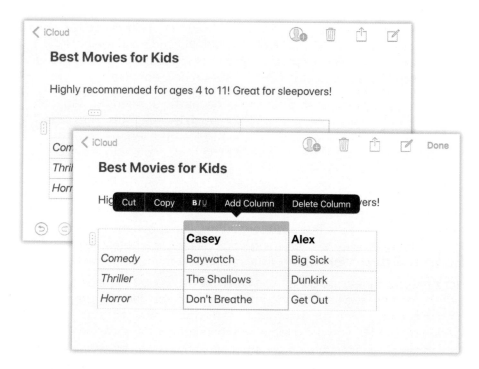

- **Convert table into text.** Tap inside a cell, and then tap the ⊞ button. Choose Convert to Text. (This menu also includes Copy Table, Delete Table, and Share Table.)

Text and Paragraph Formatting

A wide array of text-formatting options await in the Notes app. Once you've tapped **Aa** to open the formatting panel, you can try out any of these options:

- **Paragraph styles.** Hey, there are style sheets! You can create a Title (big and bold type), a Heading (bold), Body text (normal), and Monospaced (every character is the same width, even I and W—useful when you're trying to line up characters on different rows).

- **Character formatting.** The B, I, U, and S refer to **bold**, *italic*, underline, and ~~strikethrough~~ styles.

- **Lists.** The first buttons on the bottom row create dashed lists, auto-numbered lists, and automatically bulleted lists.

- **Paragraph indentation.** The final two buttons move the entire selected paragraph to the right or to the left, indenting or outdenting it.

Checklists

The ⊘ button creates a checklist (page 453, left). Every paragraph sprouts a circle—which is actually a checkbox. Tap it to place a check-mark in there. (Should completed items sort to the bottom? See page 635.)

This feature is fantastic for lists: to-do lists, packing lists, movies to see, gift tracking, party planning, job hunting, homework management, and so on.

Each time you press Return, you create a new checklist item. But you can also select existing paragraphs and then tap ⊘, turning them into a checklist after the fact. And in iOS 13, you can swipe right or left to indent or outdent a line, or drag one into a new list position using its circle as a handle.

Scan a Document

Here's where things get good. You can now use your iPhone as a high-resolution, supersmart document scanner. You can capture a letter, an article, a receipt. If you scan a contract, you can add your signature to it and send it back. The fun begins when, on any Notes page, you tap 📷. Then:

1. **From the pop-up menu, tap Scan Documents.**

   The camera springs into action, with the instruction that you should "Position the document in view."

2. **Tap the ⊛, and choose the type of scan you want.**

   Your options are **Color**, **Grayscale** (shades of gray), **Black & White** (no shades of gray), and **Photo** (a regular snapshot, without any document features). For most printed documents, Grayscale is the cleanest, most space-efficient choice.

3. **Hold the phone up high enough that you can see the entire page.**

   The document scanner can snap pages of any size, from little receipts to whole newspaper sheets that would be tough to feed into a scanner.

   Using yellow highlighting (below, left), the iPhone tries to find the edges of the page. Take a moment to marvel as it automatically

straightens the image and fixes any perspective errors. In other words, even if you're shooting the page at an angle (to avoid shadows, for example), the app is smart enough to produce a perfectly crisp, rectangular page image.

When you're holding the phone steady, the camera snaps *automatically*. (If you're impatient, tap the ∨ button or press one of the volume keys. The app displays the cropping screen, so you can adjust the page boundaries yourself.)

The captured image appears briefly and then shrinks down to the lower-left thumbnail corner—and you're instantly ready to snap another page. Thanks to the automatic snapping, you can chug through a multipage document pretty quickly.

When you've scanned enough, tap **Save**. Your work here is done.

Or, if you'd like to fine-tune the results, read on:

4. **Tap the thumbnail (lower-left corner of the screen).**

   The scanned image opens so you can make adjustments. For example, the ⊗ button lets you change your mind about the decision you made in step 2 (facing page, center). If you tap ⛶, you can use the four round handles to adjust the page boundaries, cropping out more or less background (facing page, right). If you snapped the page at a slight angle, this is your chance to correct the perspective.

   Here, too, you can tap ↻■ to rotate the scan 90 degrees—or 🗑 to delete it. Or tap Retake to reshoot just this page.

   Tap Done and then Save. You return to the Note that now contains the scanned images.

If you tap a scanned page thumbnail to open it, you can have endless fun:

- **Use the ⛶, ⊗, ↻■, and 🗑 icons** to revisit the choices you made in step 4.

- **Tap + to scan a new page** to add to the existing ones.

- **Tap ⬆ and then Markup** to annotate the scan (adding your signature or highlighting, for example), using the tools described on page 458.

- **Tap ⬆ and then Create PDF** to convert the finished scan into a PDF page, ready to send (by tapping ⬆ again).

Once you've given the Scan feature a try, you may well consider it one of iOS's finest achievements.

Add a Photo to a Note

There are more goodies hiding behind the ⓞ button on every Notes page, above the keyboard. The pop-up menu offers **Take Photo or Video**, which opens the Camera app, and **Photo Library**, which opens your Photos app. Either way, the resulting photo or video lands right there in the Notes page you're working on. Incredibly handy. (Try inserting labeled face shots of people whose names you keep forgetting at work!)

TIP: Should new photos and videos you take also wind up in your Photos app? That's up to you, thanks to the **Settings→Notes→Save to Photos** option.

Add a Sketch

Sometimes, only a freehand drawing will do—and in Notes, you can draw with your finger! If you tap the Ⓐ icon, you summon the new, improved iOS 13 artist's kit (below, left).

In the following tour, note that you can tap a tool to produce a pop-up palette of potentially pleasing possibilities. For the Pen, Highlighter, and

Pencil, for example, the pop-up panel offers five line thicknesses, plus a slider that controls the opacity of the lines you draw (facing page, right).

You can use the Undo button (↶) as often as you mess up. It's an infinite Undo; tap it enough times, and you go all the way back to the blank, untouched image.

To choose a color for the next line you draw, tap ●. You get a palette of 144 shades. Each drawing tool remembers its color from note to note; that way, you'll always have a yellow highlighter or a red pencil handy.

TIP: If you have a 3D Touch iPhone (page 35), the lines you draw get thicker as you press harder—just as with real pens, highlighters, and pencils!

- **Pen.** Drag on the image to create lines in the color you've chosen from the ● panel.

- **Highlighter** creates translucent lines, just like a high-school highlighting marker.

- **Pencil.** Just like the Pen, except that the edges of the lines have a rougher, more graphite-looking texture.

- **Eraser.** The pop-up panel offers two choices: **Pixel Eraser** (drag with your finger to erase *pieces* of lines) or **Object Eraser** (tap to delete entire lines).

- **Selection Pen.** Drag your finger around lines or shapes you've made to enclose them with animated dotted-line selection boundaries. At this point, you can drag the whole selected mass into a new position on the screen.

- **Ruler.** This is a surprisingly sophisticated tool. To use it, put two fingers on the ruler itself on the screen, and twist them to the angle you want. (As you twist, the app shows you the current angle off the horizontal.) Then you can "draw against" it for perfect straight lines.

- **Text or objects.** The ⊕ is part of iOS 13's standard drawing kit, but you don't see it when you're sketching; only when you're annotating a photo or graphic (in Notes, Mail, Messages, and so on). It produces a choice of canned goodies you can add to the image:

   Text: A text box appears on the photo, saying "Text." Drag the tiny blue handles to adjust the shape of the box; drag inside to move the box; or twist two fingers to rotate it. Double-tap it (or tap it and then tap **Edit**) to open the keyboard; type what you want it to say. Tap the photo to put away the keyboard. Tap the text box and then tap ᴀA to choose font, size, and paragraph justification options.

Signature: Tap to insert a handwritten signature. (And where do these stored signatures come from? You've tapped **Add or Remove Signature** and then +, and then used your finger to write your name.)

Magnifier: Tap to slap a magnified circular area onto your photo—great for calling out a detail. Drag the blue handle to adjust the circle's size; drag the green one to adjust the degree of magnification inside it. And drag inside the circle to move it.

NOTE: You're not enlarging this for your own editing purposes; this magnified area will *stay* magnified when you send the photo. It's for calling your correspondent's attention to some detail.

Square, circle, speech bubble, arrow: Tap one to place it on your photo. Then tap 🔲 to see some choices for line thickness and filled-in-ness. Drag blue dots to change size, or green ones to change shape—for example, the angle and direction of the speech balloon's "where it's coming from" angle, or the curvature of the arrow.

TIP: In Notes, you can set up a lined background for new sketches. Choose 🗂, scroll up, and then **Lines & Grids**. You can have your notes start out with lines (three different spacings) or graph-paper grids (three grid sizes).

If you want your selection to apply to every new note you create, make your decision in **Settings→Notes→Lines & Grids**.

Sharing Notes

You and a buddy (or several) can edit a page in Notes *simultaneously*, over the internet. It's great when you and your friends are planning a party and brainstorming about guests and the menu, for example. Also great for adding items to the grocery or to-do list even after your spouse has left the house to get them taken care of.

In iOS 13, in fact, you can share an entire folder of notes—a handy way to get started with a project's worth of info:

- **Share one open note.** Tap 👤₊ at the top of the screen. On the Add People screen, specify how you want to send the invitation: by message, email, Facebook, Twitter, or whatever.

- **Share a folder full.** On the folder list (page 464), tap the folder name to open it. Tap ⊙ at the top of the screen; then **Add People**.

In either case, the Add People screen appears. Tap **Share Options** to indicate whether the people you're inviting are allowed to *see* these notes or *see and edit* them. Then specify how you want to send the invitation: by message, email, Facebook, Twitter, or whatever.

Once your collaborators receive and accept the invite, they can begin reading the note(s), or editing them (if you gave permission), right alongside their own notes in Notes.

The live editing isn't as animated as it is in, for example, Google Docs—you don't see letter-by-letter typing—but other people's edits do appear briefly in yellow highlighting.

Once you've shared a note, the icon at the top changes to ▣, and a matching icon appears next to the note's name in the master list. At any time, you can stop sharing the note—or add more people to its collaboration—by tapping that ▣ icon again and editing the sharing panel that appears.

Locking Notes

You can password-protect individual notes—a great feature, suitable for listing birthday presents you intend to get for your nosy kid, the formula for your top-secret invisibility potion, or your illicit lovers' names.

Note that you generally hide and show all your locked notes with a *single* password. You don't have to make up a different password for every note.

> **TIP:** You *can* make up multiple passwords, though. Each time you want to start using a new password, open **Settings→Notes→Password** and tap **Reset Password**. After supplying your iCloud password, you're offered the chance to make up a password for any *new* notes you lock. All *existing* locked notes are still protected by the previous password.
>
> And if you've forgotten the password? Unless you've turned on Touch ID or Face ID (you're asked the first time you try to open a locked note), all those old notes are locked forever. But you can still make up a new password to protect your latest secrets.

To lock a note, tap 🔼; on the Share screen, scroll down and tap **Lock Note**. (Why is locking a note sharing it? Never mind.) Make up a password for locking/unlocking all your notes (or, if you've done this before, *enter* the password).

Once your locked notes are all unlocked, you can still see and edit them. But when there's any risk of somebody else coming along and seeing them (on your Mac, iPhone, iPad, or any other synced gadget), click the ⊓ to lock all your notes. (They also all lock when the phone goes to sleep.)

Now all you see of the locked notes are their titles. Everything on them is replaced by a "This note is locked" message. Tap **View Note** to unlock them with your fingerprint or password.

TIP: To remove the padlock from a note, tap ⬆ and then tap **Remove Lock**.

Use your power wisely.

The Notes List

As you create more pages, the ⟨ button (top left of the screen) becomes more useful. (It bears the name of whatever online account stores your notes: Gmail, Exchange, or whatever. Or, if your notes exist only on the phone, you see the name of the folder they're in.)

It opens your table of contents for the Notes app (facing page, left). It's the only way to jump from one note to another.

TIP: You can swipe rightward to jump from an open note back to the list.

Here's what's on this screen:

- ☺→**View Attachments** brings up a tidy display of every photo, sketch, website, audio recording, and document that's ever been inserted into any of your notes. All in one place (facing page, right).

  The beauty is that you don't have to remember what you called a note; just tap one of these items to open it. (At that point, you can tap **Show in Note** to open the note that contains it.)

NOTE: Attachments in locked notes (whether or not they're locked right now) don't show up here.

- ☺→**Select Notes.** When you enter Select mode, you can tap a bunch of notes and then **Move To** (a different folder) or **Delete** them. (Or *don't* tap to select any, and use **Move All** or **Delete All**.

- **A search box.** Tug down on the list to bring the search box into view. Tap it to open the keyboard. You can now search all your notes instantly—not just their titles, but also the text inside them.

NOTE: Don't worry about your locked notes. iOS can search their titles, but never their contents—even if the notes are currently *unlocked*.

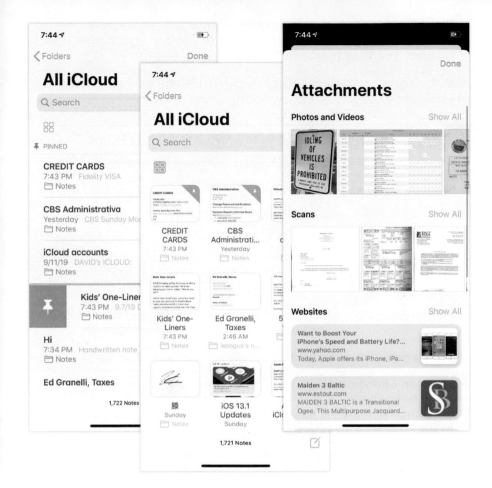

- . This button, too, is hidden until you tug down on the Notes list. Tap it to switch your entire notes collection from a list view to an icon view, revealing miniatures of every single note (above, middle).

- **The first lines of your notes,** along with the time or date you last edited them. If there's a photo or sketch on a note—an unlocked one, anyway—you see its thumbnail, too. Tiny icons denote locked or shared notes.

  To open a note, tap its name. To delete a note, swipe across its name in the list, right to left, and then confirm by tapping 🗑.

NOTE: On iPhone Plus and Max models, rotating the phone produces a whole new two-column layout. The left column shows your table of contents (first line of every note); the right column shows the selected note itself.

- **Pinned notes.** Ordinarily, your notes appear chronologically, most recent at the top. But in **Settings→Notes**, you can specify that they be sorted by **Date Edited** or **Title** instead.

  But you may have a couple of notes—things you refer to a lot—that you want to appear at the top all the time. Passwords, credit card numbers, or frequent-flyer numbers, for example.

  That's why you can *pin* notes to the top of the list, where they won't move. To pin one, swipe to the right (previous page, left); tap 📌.

Notes Folders

For your organizational and sharing pleasure, Notes lets you create folders to contain batches of notes.

To set them up, tap the ❮ at top left until you arrive at the Folders screen, which displays both your list of accounts (read on) and any folders you've created.

New Folder does just what you'd think; enter a name and then hit **Save**. The new folder appears in the list of accounts and other folders.

Whenever you want to move a note into a folder, you have these options:

- **From an open note,** tap 📤; on the Share screen, scroll down and tap **Move to Folder**.

- **In the notes list,** swipe left on a note; tap 🗂.

- **To move a batch of notes at once,** begin on the Notes list. Tap ⊙→**Select Notes**. Select the notes you want to move, and then hit **Move All**.

In each case, Notes now shows you your list of folders; tap the one you want to be the new destination for your note or notes.

Notes Accounts

Your notes can sync wirelessly and automatically not only to your other Apple gadgets, but also with the Notes modules on Google, Yahoo, AOL, Exchange, or another IMAP email account. To set this up, open **Settings→Passwords & Accounts**. Tap the account you want (iCloud, Gmail, AOL, or whatever); turn the Notes switch **On**.

Now your notes are synced nearly instantly, wirelessly, both directions.

One catch: Notes that you create at *gmail.com*, *aol.com*, or *yahoo.com* don't wind up on the phone. Those accounts sync wirelessly in one direction only: *from* the iPhone to the website, where the notes arrive in a Notes folder. (There's no problem, however, if you get your AOL or Gmail mail in an email program like Outlook, Entourage, or Apple Mail. Then it's two-way syncing as usual.)

At this point, a ⟨ bracket appears at the top-left corner of the table of contents screen. Tap it to see your note sets from various accounts.

If you've created Notes *folders* on your Mac (Mountain Lion or later), then you see those folders here, too.

 In Settings→Notes, you can specify which Notes account you want to be the main, default one for new notes.

All of this makes life a little more complex, of course. For example, when you create a note, you have to worry about which account it's about to go into. To do that, be sure to specify an account name (and a folder within it, if necessary) *before* you create the new note.

In Settings→Notes, you can turn on the **"On My Phone" Account**. Any notes you add to this "folder" are super-private. They don't get synced or sent online, ever.

Podcasts

A podcast is a "radio" show that's distributed online. Lots of podcasts begin life as *actual* radio and TV shows; most of NPR's shows are available as podcasts, for example, so you can listen to them whenever and wherever you like.

But thousands more are recorded just for downloading. Some have millions of listeners and make huge money from ads; some have only a handful of fans. One thing's for sure: There's a podcast out there that precisely matches whatever weird, narrow interests *you* have.

The Podcasts app helps you find, subscribe to, organize, and listen to podcasts. It's designed just like Apple's online stores for apps, music, movies, and so on. Tap **Browse** to see recommended podcasts and **Top Charts** to see what the rest of the world is listening to these days (next page, right). Or use **Search** to look for something specific.

There are video podcasts, too, although they're much less common. The most popular are clips from network or cable TV shows, but there are plenty of quirky, offbeat, funny video podcasts that will never be seen except on pocket screens.

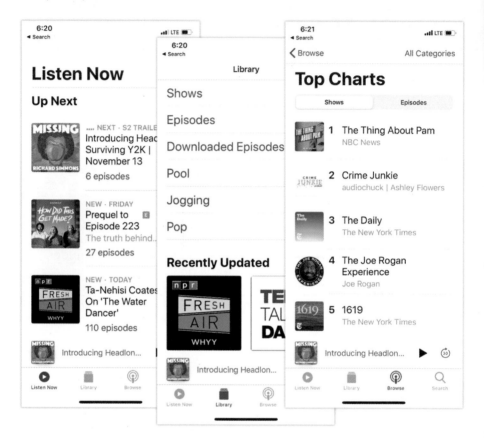

In any case, once you've drilled down to a particular episode that seems worthy, you can listen to it in either of two ways:

- **Stream it.** Tap ▶ to play it directly from the internet. It's never stored on your iPhone and doesn't take up any space, but it does require an internet connection. Generally not what you want for plane rides.

- **Download it.** If you tap + and then ⬇ instead, you download the podcast to your phone. It takes up space there (and podcasts can be big)—but you can play it back anytime, anywhere. And, of course, you can delete it when you're done.

Subscribing

Most podcasts are series. Their creators crank them out every week or whatever. If you find one you love, subscribe to it so that your phone downloads each new episode automatically. Just tap **Subscribe** on its details page.

The episodes wind up on the **Library** screen (facing page, middle), under **Shows**. Tap a podcast's icon to open the Episodes screen, where you can find listings for further episodes; controls for deleting an episode or adding it to the playback queue; and links to share this podcast by Messages, Mail, Twitter, Facebook, and so on.

Settings

There's a lot to control when it comes to podcasts. Do you want new episodes downloaded automatically? Do you want them auto-deleted when you're finished?

You make these choices in **Settings→Podcasts**. Those are the global settings for podcasts.

But you can also override them for *individual* shows. On any podcast's details screen, tap ⬤ and then **Settings** to see those options and many more. You can limit how many episodes of this show are stored on your phone, specify the playback order—oldest first or newest first, and much more.

Listening

The Podcasts app offers two ways to dive in. The **Listen Now** tab shows you the *next* episode of each podcast series—the one you're up to. The **Library** tab offers icons for each podcast, so that you can drill down to a particular episode. Tap the playback strip at the bottom to reveal all the usual audio-playback controls (page 264)—with the handy addition of a button to toggle the talking speed (½x, 1x, 1½x, or 2x regular speed).

TIP: There are skip-forward and skip-backward buttons here, too. Handy for jumping through ads! The factory setting is 15-second skips per button press, but you can change the interval in Settings→Podcasts→Skip Buttons.

If you press the side button to turn off the screen, the podcast continues playing. And even if the phone is locked, you can open the Control Center (page 42) to access the playback controls.

TIP: Don't forget to use Siri! You can say things like "Play 'Fresh Air' podcast," "Play my latest podcasts," "Play my podcast" (to resume your last podcast), "Play the latest TED podcast," and so on.

Reminders

Reminders not only records your life's little tasks, but it also reminds you about them at the right time or right place. For example, it can remind you to water the plants as soon as you get home.

Thanks to iCloud, your reminders sync across all your gadgets. Create or check off a task on your iPhone, and you'll also find it created or checked off on your iPad, iPod Touch, Mac, PC, and so on.

> **TIP:** Reminders sync wirelessly with anything your iCloud account knows about: Calendar or BusyCal on your Mac, Outlook on the PC, and so on.

Siri and Reminders are a match made in heaven. "Remind me to file the Jenkins report when I get to work." "Remind me to set the TiVo for tonight at 8." "Remind me about Timmy's soccer game a week from Saturday." "When I get home, remind me to take a shower."

Now, Reminders in iOS 13 does all of that and more—and better, because Apple rewrote the app from scratch, with juicy new features. Unfortunately, you can't have the new features without upgrading your reminders to the new data format.

And once you convert to the new format, you won't be able to open them on any other gadgets unless they, too, have iOS 13 (or, on the Mac, macOS Catalina). And you won't be able to open them in Windows at all (except by logging in to *icloud.com*). The new Shared Lists feature, too, is available only to people who have likewise upgraded.

When you first open Reminders in iOS 13, you can tap **Upgrade Now** or **Upgrade Later**. In the latter case, you can still use Reminders, but without all the cool new features. (You can always upgrade by tapping the big **UPGRADE** button next to My Lists.)

The Four Smart Lists

The new Reminders app offers four "smart lists" at the top (facing page): one-tap bubbles that show you all the reminders due **Today**, all the ones you've **Scheduled** for later, all the ones you've **Flagged** as significant, and **All**. Tap one to open the corresponding list.

My Lists

Below the smart list buttons, it should be clear that you can create *more than one* to-do list, each with its own name: a groceries list, kids' chores, a running tally of expenses, and so on. It's a great way to log what you eat, or to keep a list of movies that people recommend.

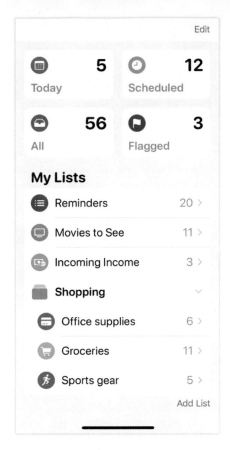

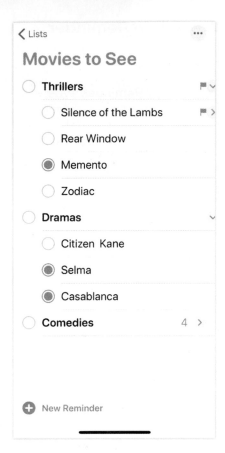

Tap a list's name to open the to-do list within. Tap ‹ **Lists** (or swipe right) to return to the master page.

To create a new list, begin at the list of lists (above, left). Tap **Add List**. You're asked to enter a name, choose a color (for the list's title font and also of the "checked-off" circles once the list is underway), and pick a graphic icon symbol for your new list; then hit **Done**.

(To delete a list, swipe left across it and then tap 🗑.)

When you're viewing the list of lists, you can rearrange them by dragging their title bars up or down.

You can also, in iOS 13, *group* them by dragging one list's name on top of another; iOS asks you to name the new group. You might, for example, create a group called Shopping (above, left), which contains lists for Groceries, Sports Gear, and Office Supplies. You can expand or collapse the sublist by tapping the little ∨ next to the group's name.

Creating a Reminder

Once you've tapped to open a list, you create a new reminder in any of these ways:

- **Tap New Reminder.** Type your reminder (or dictate it). Feel free to specify dates, times, locations, and repeat schedules: "Remind me to feed the cats every day at 8:30 a.m." "Print the Wiggins report when I get to work." "Work out Tuesday and Thursday." As you can see by the colored text, Reminders correctly recognizes and interprets those where/when phrases.

  Tap Done (or tap Return to add another item to the same list).

- **Use Siri's "Add" command.** You can say, "Add avocados to my Groceries list." "Add *Titanic 2* to my Movies list." This trick is awesome, because it works no matter what app you're using on the phone.

> **TIP:** Siri can also *find* these reminders, saving you a lot of navigation. You can say, "Find my reminder about dosage instructions," for example.

- **Use "Remind me about this."** When you're looking at something in one of Apple's apps, you can tell Siri, "Remind me about this later." That might be a text message in Messages, a web page in Safari, an email in Mail, a document in Pages, or whatever. (This command works in Calendar, Clock, Contacts, Books, Health, Mail, Maps, Messages, Notes, Numbers, Pages, Phone, Podcasts, Reminders, and Safari. Software companies can upgrade their apps to work with "Remind me about this," too.)

  Instantly, Siri creates a new item on your main Reminders list—named for the precise message, location, web page, document, or thing you were looking at—complete with the icon of the app you were using.

  Later, you can tap that icon to open the original app—to the exact spot you were when you issued the command.

  You can also say things like, "Remind me about this tomorrow night at seven" or, "Remind me about this when I get home."

  Put it all together, and you've got an effective system for bookmarking your life. Maybe this feature will, once and for all, end the practice of people emailing stuff to themselves just so they'll remember it.

- **Create a reminder from another app.** You can create a new Reminder from within Messages, Mail, Photos, Maps, and other apps. Once you've selected some text (or a photo, or a location, or whatever), hit ⬆ and then tap Reminders. You're invited to name this new reminder, tap Details to specify a list for it (and assign times, places,

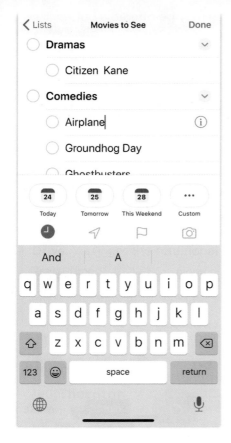

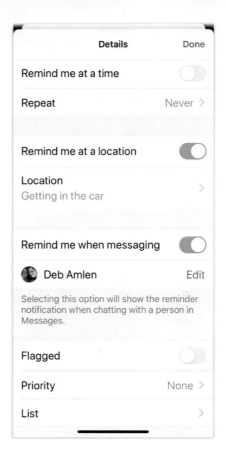

priority, and other niceties), and then hit **Done**. Behind the scenes, you've just added that material to a new Reminder.

Typing into the Reminders app itself, though, gives a reminder far more power, thanks to the four shortcuts above the keyboard:

- 🕐 summons buttons (**Today**, **Tomorrow**, **This Weekend**) that schedule this reminder to pop up on a certain date (above, left).

  If you tap **Custom**, you open the Details screen, where you can dial up far more precise date-and-time options. Because **Remind me on a day** is turned on, you can now specify a date when you'll be reminded; **Remind me at a time** adds a time-of-day control. Tap **Repeat** if you want this reminder to appear every day, week, two weeks, month, or year—great for reminding you about things that recur, like quarterly tax payments, haircuts, and anniversaries.

  Tap **Done** when it's all set up.

- ◤ lets you schedule this item to nag you when your phone's GPS detects that you have reached (or departed from) a certain *place*, which is a rather amazing feature. You may be offered a button like **Getting in Car**, but the real magic happens when you hit **Custom**.

The Location page opens, where you can tap **Current Location**—wherever you are at the moment. That's handy if, for example, you're dropping off your dry cleaning and want to remember to pick it up the next time you're driving by. But you can also choose **Home** or **Work** (as you've set them up in Contacts). Or you can use the search box at the top, either to enter a street address, or to search your own Contacts list.

> **NOTE:** If you use Bluetooth to pair your phone to your car, you have a couple of other helpful choices: **Getting in the car** (to get a reminder when the iPhone connects to your car) and **Getting out of the car** (to get one when it disconnects).

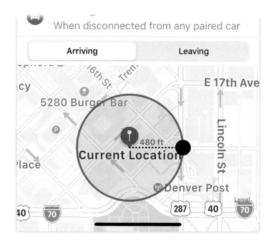

Once you've specified an address, the Location screen shows a map. The diameter of the circle shows the area where your presence will trigger the appearance of the reminder on your screen.

> **TIP:** You can adjust the size of this "geofence" by dragging the black handle to adjust the circle. In effect, you're telling the iPhone how close you have to be to the specified address for the reminder to pop up. You can adjust the circle's radius anywhere from 328 feet ("Remind me when I'm in that store") to 1,500 miles ("Remind me when I'm in that country").

The final step here is to tap either **Arriving** or **Leaving**. Later, the phone will remind you as you approach (or leave) the address, which is fairly mind-blowing the first few times it happens.

- ⚑ **lets you flag this reminder.** A flag can mean anything you want. It can mean "Front-burner item." It can mean "I've procrastinated on these too long." It can mean "Items I'm gathering up to put into a single new list for the McGillicuddy project." All of the flagged Reminders appear, of course, in the Flagged smart list described already.

- 📷 **offers three buttons,** each of which creates an attachment to this reminder: Take Photo, Photo Library, or Scan Document. Chapter 9 offers details about navigating your photo library; page 455 describes the scanning operation. What's cool is that a thumbnail image of whatever photo or document you've attached appears right in the Reminders list for quick reference—and you can tap to open it full-size.

The Details Screen

The four icons above the keyboard are only shortcuts to the more complete Details screen, which appears when you tap ⓘ next to an item's name (page 471, left). These offer the same options as those four icons, but with more detailed details. For example:

- **Notes.** Here's a handy box where you can record freehand notes about this item: an address, a phone number, details of any kind.

- **URL** stores any web address you want to associate with this item.

- **Remind me on a day.** You already know how this works—but on the Details screen, you can also choose an Alarm sound for this reminder's appearance.

- **Remind me at a location.** You've read about this one, too; tap Location to specify where you want to be reminded.

- **Remind me when messaging** is new in iOS 13, and super-useful. Turn it on, hit Choose Person, and select somebody's name from Contacts. The idea is that when you next begin chatting with this person in Messages, a reminder will pop up right there.

  Think of this option every time you're turning out the light and say to yourself something like, "Dang, I forgot to remind Casey to pay me back that $75."

- **Flagged.** As described already.

- **Priority.** Tap to specify whether this item has low, medium, or high priority—or **None**. In some of the calendar programs that sync with Reminders, you can sort your task list by priority.

- **List.** Tap to assign this to-do to a different reminder list, if necessary.

- **Subtasks,** new in iOS 13, are to-do items within a to-do item. The main Reminder might be "Prep for the in-laws' visit," and the indented subtasks might be "Mow lawn," "Paint house," and "Retile roof."

  One way to create a subtask is to tap **Subtask**, tap **Add Reminder**, and then enter the new to-do item. When you return to the list, you'll see that the main reminder ("Prep for in-laws' visit") bears a little collapse-o-button (⊘) that hides or shows the subtasks.

  When you're looking at a list of reminders, though, there's a much faster way to nest items: Hold your finger down on item B for half a second, and then drag it down under item A's name. It indents itself nicely.

> **TIP:** You can also drag a list item to the right and then tap **Indent**.

To exit the Details screen, tap **Done**.

Checking Off Reminders

As you go through life being productive, you're supposed to tap the little circle next to each item in Reminders that you've completed. A checked-off to-do remains in place until the next time you visit its list. At that point, it disappears to a separate list called Completed.

If you ever want to take pride in how much you've accomplished, tap ☺→**Show Completed** to bring your checked-off tasks back into view. (The same menu then offers a **Hide Completed** command.)

Other stuff you can do:

- **Delete a to-do item altogether, as though it never existed.** Swipe leftward across its name; tap **Delete** to confirm.

- **Delete a bunch of items in a row.** Tap ☺→**Select Reminders**. Tap each little circle, and then tap **Delete** to eliminate them all at once.

- **Rearrange the list items.** Hold down your finger on an item briefly, and then drag it up or down the list.

Sharing Lists

You can share your to-do lists with other people electronically, just as you can with notes—a great way for you to share a list of chores with your kids, a wedding-gift registry with your guests, a shopping list with your partner, and so on.

Tap ☺→**Add People**. On the Add People screen, specify how you want to share the list (by Messages, Mail, or whatever). Address the invitation, and off you go.

Once the recipient receives your invitation, you'll both see the progress as you edit and check off To Do items on the shared list.

Stocks

This one's for you, big-time day trader. The Stocks app tracks the rise and fall of your portfolio by downloading the very latest stock prices.

(All right, maybe not the *very* latest. The price data may be delayed as much as 20 minutes, which is typical of free stock-info services.)

When you first fire it up (and hit **Continue** to pass the welcome screen), Stocks shows you a handful of sample securities and indexes—the Dow Jones Industrial Average, the NASDAQ Composite Index, the S&P 500 Index, Apple, Google, and Facebook, for example (previous page, left).

Next to each, you see a tiny spark graph (a miniature of today's price fluctuations), its current share price, and beneath *that*, how much that price has gone up or down today. As a handy visual gauge to how elated or depressed you should be, this final number appears on a *green* background if it's gone up or a *red* one if it's gone down. Tap this number to cycle the display from a percentage to a dollar amount to current market capitalization ("120.3B," meaning $120.3 billion in total corporate value).

When you tap a stock, the bottom part of the screen zooms in for the details on that company (previous page, right). Drag up or down to make this details pane bigger, smaller, or scrolled. Here's what it contains:

- **A table of statistics.** A capsule summary of today's price and volume statistics for this stock.

- **A graph of the stock's price.** It starts out showing you the graph of today's fluctuations. But by tapping the scrolling list of headings above the chart, you can zoom in or out, from one day (**1D**) to ten years (**1OY**) or even **ALL** the years in its existence, with many other increments in between.

> **TIP:** Drag a finger across the graph to see the readout for a certain day. Or pinch with two fingers (or two thumbs) to isolate a certain time period; a pop-up label shows you how much of a bath you took (or how much of a windfall you received) during the interval you highlighted (previous page, right). Cool!

- **An assortment of relevant headlines,** brought to you by the News app (page 449) and, if you subscribe, the News+ service (page 451). Tap a headline to read the article. (If you have a 3D Touch phone [page 35], you can peek at the underlying story without leaving the main screen by long-pressing the headline.)

Tap the ⊗ at the top right of the details panel to close it.

> **NOTE:** The Stocks app no longer displays a different view when you rotate the phone 90 degrees. It's all upright, all the time.

Customizing Your Portfolio

It's fairly unlikely that *your* stock portfolio contains just Apple, Google, and Facebook. Fortunately, you can customize the list of stocks to reflect the companies you *do* own (or want to track).

To edit the list, tap **Edit**. You arrive at the editing screen, where these choices await:

- **Delete a stock** by tapping ⊖ and then **Remove**.

- **Rearrange the list** by dragging the grip strips (≡) on the right side.

- **Add a stock** by tapping ⊕; the Add Stock screen and the keyboard appear.

  You're not expected to know every stock-symbol abbreviation. Type the company's *name* into the search bar at top. The iPhone shows a list of company-name matches. Tap one you want to track and then its **Add** button. Tap ⊗ to return to the stocks-list editing screen.

When you're finished setting up your stock list, tap **Done**.

Tips

This app (in your Extras folder) is designed to show you tips and tricks for getting the most from your iPhone. Each Collection (**What's New**, **Genius Picks**, and so on) screen offers a set of tips—a paragraph of text apiece—explaining one of iOS's marvels. Swipe leftward to see the next tip, and the next, and the next.

It's not exactly, you know, a handsome, printed book. But it's something.

Voice Memos

This audio app (probably in your Extras folder) is ideal for recording lectures, musical performances, notes to self, and cute child utterances (next page, left). The microphone is incredibly good, even from a distance. You can edit the recordings, and even sync them to your Mac.

> **NOTE:** If your Mac doesn't have macOS Mojave or later, then it doesn't have the Mac version of Voice Memos. In that case, you'll have to sync your recordings to the Mac as described on page 555. You'll find them in the iTunes folder called Voice Memos.

Making the Recording

Tap ◎ (or click your earbud clicker) to start recording. A little ding signals the start (and stop) of the session—unless you've flipped the phone's silencer switch (you sneak!).

You get to watch the actual sound waves as the recording proceeds.

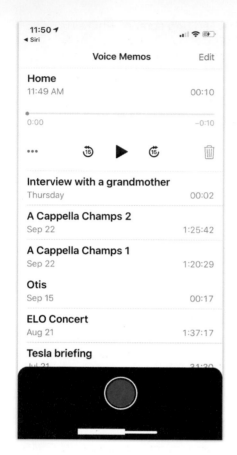

You can switch out of the app to do other work, if you like; a red banner across the top of the screen (or, on the Face ID phones, the left ear) reminds you that you're still recording. You can even *switch the screen off*; the recording goes on!

You can make *very* long recordings with this thing. Let it run all day, if you like. Even your most long-winded friends can be immortalized.

To pause the recording, *swipe up* on the recording panel; tap **II**.

At this point, Voice Memos offers you the ability to listen to what you've got so far, and even record over sections of it! In essence, you've just entered Edit mode. It's described on page 480.

> **TIP:** The built-in mike records in mono. But you can record in stereo if you connect a stereo mike (to the headphone jack or charging jack).

Press Stop (⦿) when the recording session is over. The phone names your recording after your location (if Location Services is turned on for

Voice Memos in **Settings→Privacy**), but you can rename it easily enough: Double-tap the temporary name and then type something better: "Baby's First Words," "Orch Concert," whatever. Tap **return** on the keyboard or anywhere on the screen to finish.

Playback

When you tap a recording in the list, a convenient set of controls appears. (They look a lot like the ones that appear when you tap a voicemail message in the Phone app.)

> **TIP:** If you have a large enough iPhone model, you can turn the screen 90 degrees—and see both the list of recordings *and* the editing screen, in two columns.

Here's what you can do here:

- **[Recording name].** Double-tap the name to edit or rename it.

- **▶.** Tap to play the recording. You can pause with the **II** button.

- **Rewind, Fast Forward.** Drag the little dot in the scrubber bar to skip backward or forward in the recording. It's a great way to skip over the boring pleasantries. Or tap the ⟲₁₅ or ₁₅⟳ buttons to jump back or forward by 15 seconds.

- **•••.** The three dots here open a pop-up menu containing some useful commands. They include **Edit Recording** (described in the next section), **Duplicate** (makes a copy), **Share** (opens the standard Share sheet, for sending this recording to someone else), and **Save to Dropbox** and **Save to Files** (for transferring the full-quality recording into an internet transfer bucket that you can later access on your computer).

- **🗑.** Tap to get rid of a recording. You're not asked for confirmation, but a message appears, letting you know that the deleted recording will sit in the Recently Deleted folder for 30 days.

  To see these recordings-on-death-row, tap **Recently Deleted**. When you tap a recording in that list, you can choose to **Recover** it or **Erase** it before the 30 days is up.

> **TIP:** In **Settings→Voice Memos→Clear Deleted**, you can specify how quickly these deleted recordings disappear. Your choices are **Immediately**, **After 1 Day**, **After 7 Days**, **After 30 Days**, or **Never**.

- **⬆.** Tap to open the standard Share sheet. It gives you the chance to send your recording to someone else by AirDrop, email, or MMS.

Editing Your Recording

You might not guess that such a tiny, self-effacing app actually offers some basic editing functions, but it does. Tap a recording, then the ••• button, and then tap **Edit Recording**.

Here you have these options:

- **Navigate** by dragging the sound-wave map horizontally, or tap the ⟳ or ⟲ buttons to jump in 15-second increments.

- **Record over it.** When the blue playhead line is parked at the beginning or middle of the audio, the big red button says **Replace**. Tap it to record over part (or all) of your original recording. If you recorded a brilliant speech, but stumbled on the opening line (or any line, actually), you can replace it without having to redo the whole thing. Be nimble with the **Replace** and **‖** buttons; you can "punch in," replacing certain parts of the recording without disturbing the rest.

- **Add onto it.** You can also add on more audio to your existing recording. Just park the blue playhead line at the end of the current sound waves, and then hit **Resume**. Hit **‖** to stop.

- **Trim it.** You can trim off the beginning or end of your audio clip—which is great, since that's where you'll usually find "dead air" or microphone fumbling before the good stuff starts playing.

  To do that, tap the Crop button (⌐). At this point, the "map" of the entire sound recording (at the bottom of the screen) sprouts yellow crop handles. Drag them inward to isolate the part you want to keep. When you're close, use the magnified area at top to fine-tune the trip points, using the vertical yellow lines. Play the sound as necessary to guide you (▶).

  Tap **Trim** to shave away everything outside your selected area. If you like the results, tap **Save**. If you'd rather try again, *shake the phone*; in the Undo Trim box, tap **Undo**. Or hit **Cancel** to forget the whole thing.

- **Cut out a chunk.** To cut something out of the middle, isolate the undesired audio using the crop and trim handles as described already. This time, though, hit the **Delete** button. You've just chopped the selection out of the middle.

Here again, you can hit **Save** (to preserve the edit), shake the phone and hit **Undo Delete** (to try again), or **Cancel** to back out of the entire operation.

TIP: In iOS 13, you can spread or pinch two fingers to zoom in or out of your waveforms as you edit. Slick!

The beauty of all this, by the way, is that your audio recordings can now magically and wirelessly appear on all your other Apple machinery, just as though they were calendar appointments or Safari bookmarks. The on/off switch for this syncing is in **Settings→[your name]→iCloud→ Voice Memos**.

Wallet

This app is designed to store, in one place, every form of ticket that uses a bar code. For most people, that means airline boarding passes, but Wallet also works with apps like Fandango (movie tickets), Starbucks, Walgreens, Ticketmaster, and Major League Baseball. Wallet holds down a second job, too: It's the key to Apple Pay, described on page 579.

TIP: You can rearrange the items in Wallet; just hold still briefly before you start moving your finger up or down. (That order syncs to your other iOS gadgets, for what it's worth.)

What's cool is that Wallet uses both its own clock and GPS to know when the time and place are right. For example, when you arrive at the airport, a notification appears on your Lock screen. Each time you have to show your boarding pass as you work through the stages of airport security, you can wake your phone and swipe across that notification; your boarding-pass bar code appears instantly. You're spared having to unlock your phone (enter its password), hunt for the airline app, log in, and fiddle your way to the boarding pass.

TIP: At the very bottom of the Wallet screen, the **Edit Passes** button awaits. It gives you a list of tickets for quick deletion—a good way to purge boarding passes you've already used—as well as a **Find Apps for Wallet** button.

In some Wallet-compatible apps, you're supposed to open the app to view the bar code first and put it into Wallet from there. For example, in most airline apps, you call up the boarding pass and then tap **Add**.

Wallet can also accommodate the student IDs from a few lucky colleges. The phone can provide access to the dorm, library, parties, and so on—or pay for laundry, snacks, and dinners.

Once your bar codes have successfully landed in Wallet, the rest is pure fun. When you arrive at the theater or stadium or airport, the Lock screen displays an alert. Swipe it to open the bar code in Wallet. You can put the entire phone under the ticket-taker's scanner.

Tap ● in the corner to read the details—and to delete a ticket after you've used it (tap **Remove Pass**). That details screen also offers a **Show On Lock Screen** on/off switch, in case you *don't* want Wallet to hand you your ticket as you arrive.

Finally, Wallet is one of the two places you can enter your credit card information for Apple Pay on an iPhone 6 or later model, as described on page 579. (Settings is the other.)

Watch

If you own an Apple Watch, you use this little app to set up its settings. (OK, *big* app—there are *90 screens* of settings!) So why do you have the Watch app on your phone even if you *don't* have an Apple Watch? You'll have to ask someone in Marketing.

If it bugs you, you can get rid of it (page 367).

Weather

This app shows current conditions for your city (or any other city). The weather display is animated: Clouds drift by, rain falls gently. If it's night-time in the city you're looking up, you might see a beautiful starscape.

The current temperature is shown nice and big; the table below it shows the cloud-versus-sun forecast, as well as the high and low temperatures. In major cities, you even see an alert about today's air quality—handy if you have asthma or just aren't a fan of pollution.

You don't even have to tell the app what city you want; it uses your location and assumes you want the *local* weather forecast.

There are three places you can tap or swipe:

- **Swipe up** to see a table of stats: humidity, chance of rain, sunrise time, wind speed, "feels like" (chill or heat index), and so on.

- **Swipe horizontally** across the hourly forecast to scroll later in the day.

- **Swipe horizontally anywhere else** to view the weather for other cities (if you've set them up). The tiny dots beneath the display correspond to the cities you've set up—and the white bold one indicates where you are in the sequence.

> **TIP:** The dots are *really* tiny. Don't try to aim for a specific one—it's a lot easier to tap the row of dots on either the right or left side to move backward or forward among the cities.

The first city—the screen at far left—is always the city you're *in now*.

The City List

It's easy to get the weather for other cities—great if you're going to be traveling, or if you're wondering how life is for distant relations.

When you tap ☰ at lower right (or pinch with two fingers), the screen collapses into a list of your preprogrammed cities (above, right).

You can tap one to open its weather screen. You can delete one by swiping leftward across it (and then tapping **Delete**). You can drag them into a new order (long-press before dragging).

Or you can tap ⊕ to enter a new city, using its name, zip code, or airport abbreviation (like JFK for John F. Kennedy airport). Tap **Search**, and then tap the city. When you return to the configuration screen, you can choose degrees Celsius or Fahrenheit.

The Weather Channel icon at the bottom opens Safari browser, which loads itself with an information page about that city from *weather.com*.

If you've added more than one city to the list, by the way, just swipe to flip through the weather screens for the cities.

More Standard Apps

This book describes every app that comes on every iPhone. But Apple has another suite of useful programs for you. And they're free.

To find them, search the App Store app for these goodies:

- **Pages, Numbers, and Keynote** are, believe it or not, phone-sized versions of Apple's word-processing, spreadsheet, and slideshow apps.

- **iMovie for iPhone** is, yes, a video-editing program on your phone, with all the basics: rearranging clips; adding music, crossfades, and credits.

- **Clips** is an ingenious video-recording app. It records when you're pressing the Record button, and stops when you're not—so you can make videos composed of multiple shots. It can replace your background, green-screen style, in real time with (for example) an artsy linescape or the bridge of the Millennium Falcon, and so on.

- **GarageBand** is a pocket music studio.

- **iTunes U** is a catalog of 600,000 free courses by professors at colleges, museums, and libraries all over the world. The app lets you browse the catalog, and watch and read the course materials.

PART THREE
The iPhone Online

Getting Online

Making actual *phone calls* with the iPhone is fading in importance. Today, Americans send texts five times more often than they make calls. Among teenagers, 92 percent *never* make calls with their smartphones.

What do they do with them, then? Go online—and use apps that go online.

The iPhone can get onto the internet using either of two kinds of wireless networks: *cellular* or *Wi-Fi*. Which kind you're on makes a huge difference to your iPhone experience.

Cellular Networks

Once you've accepted the miracle that a cellphone can transmit your voice wirelessly, it's not much of a stretch to realize that it can also transmit your data. Cellphone carriers (Verizon, AT&T, and so on) maintain separate networks for voice and internet data—and they spend billions of dollars trying to make those networks faster. Over the years, they've come up with data networks like these:

- **Old, slow cellular network.** The earliest, slowest cellular internet connections were called things like EDGE (AT&T) or 1xRTT (Verizon and Sprint). You'll know when you're on one of these networks because your status bar bears a symbol like **E** or **o**. It's slow. *Dog* slow—dial-up slow. You can't be on a phone call while you're online using EDGE or 1xRTT, either.

- **3G cellular networks.** 3G stands for "third generation." (The ancient analog cellphones were the first generation; EDGE-type networks were the second.) Geeks refer to the 3G network standard by its official name: HSDPA, for High-Speed Downlink Packet Access.

Web pages that take two minutes to appear using EDGE or 1xRTT show up in about 20 seconds on 3G. Voice calls sound better, too, even when the signal strength is very low, since the iPhone's 3G radio can communicate with multiple towers at once.

Oh, and on AT&T and T-Mobile, you can talk on the phone and use the internet simultaneously, which can be very handy indeed.

- **4G networks.** AT&T enhanced HSDPA, making it faster using a technology called HSPA+ (High-Speed Packet Access), and now calls it 4G. (You'll know when you're on a 4G network; your status bar says **4G**.) But nobody else recognizes HSPA+ as real 4G, which is why AT&T feels justified in advertising "the nation's largest 4G network." The other carriers aren't even measuring that network type.

- **4G LTE networks.** Now *this* is 4G. An LTE network (Long-Term Evolution) gives you amazing speeds—in some cases, faster than your broadband internet at home. When your status bar says **LTE**, it's *fantastic*.

  But LTE has two huge downsides. First: coverage. LTE is available in hundreds of U.S. cities, which is a good start. But that still leaves much of the country, including huge chunks of several entire states, without any 4G coverage at all (hi there, Montana!). In those places, your iPhone falls back to the slower speeds.

  The second big problem with LTE is that, to receive its signal, a phone's circuitry uses a lot of power. That's why the latest iPhones are bigger than their predecessors; they need beefier batteries.

NOTE: Yes, there's something called 5G, too. It's slowly appearing as a network offering in major cities, but phones that can hop onto this superfast cellular network won't appear until 2020.

A Word About VoLTE

If you have an iPhone 6 or later, the dawn of LTE cellphone networks brings another benefit: You can use Voice over LTE, or *VoLTE* ("volty"). That's a delightful cellular feature that promises amazing voice quality—sounds more like FM radio than cellphone—*and* simultaneous calling/internetting, even on Verizon. (Behind the scenes, it sends your voice over the carrier's *internet* network instead of the voice network. That's why it's called "Voice over LTE.")

To make this work, every link in the chain has to be compatible with VoLTE: your phone and your cellphone network, *and* (for that great sound quality) the phone and network of the person you're *calling*.

All four big U.S. carriers offer VoLTE, but you may not get the high-quality sound if the person you're calling has a different cell carrier. VoLTE calls between Verizon and AT&T work well, but may not if, for example, you have Verizon and the other guy has T-Mobile.

> **TIP:** You can turn on Low Data Mode: a massive cellular-data diet. Very handy when you're approaching your monthly data cap. See page 603.

Wi-Fi Hotspots

Wi-Fi, known to geeks as 802.11, is wireless networking, and your phone uses the same technology that gets laptops online at high speed at Wi-Fi hotspots.

When you're in a Wi-Fi hotspot—like the ones in homes, offices, coffee shops, hotels, airports, and thousands of other places—your iPhone usually gets a fast connection to the internet. When you're online this way, you can make phone calls and surf the internet simultaneously. And why not? Your iPhone's Wi-Fi and cellular antennas are independent.

(Over cellular connections, only the AT&T and T-Mobile iPhones let you talk and get online simultaneously. Verizon and Sprint can do that only when you're on a VoLTE call, as described previously.)

The iPhone always looks for a Wi-Fi connection first. It considers connecting to a cellular network only if there's no Wi-Fi. You always know which kind of network you're on, thanks to the icons on the status bar: You'll see either 📶 for Wi-Fi, or one of the cellular icons (**E**, °, **3G**, **4G**, **LTE**, or **5G E**.

If there's nothing available at all, you see "No service" or five square periods (▪▪▪▪▪).

Sequence of Connections

The iPhone isn't online all the time. To save battery power, it opens the connection only on demand: when you check email, request a web page, and so on. At that point, the iPhone tries to get online following this sequence:

- **First, it sniffs around for a Wi-Fi network** you've used before. If it finds one, it connects automatically. You're not asked for permission, a password, or anything else.

- **If the iPhone can't find a previous hotspot** but it detects a *new* hotspot, a message appears (below, left). It displays any new hotspots' names; tap the one you want. (If you see a 🔒 icon, that hotspot is password-protected.)

TIP: If you're feeling bombarded by those "Select a Wireless Network" messages, open **Settings→Wi-Fi** (or tell Siri, "Open Wi-Fi settings"). Here you have three options under **Ask to Join Networks**.

Off means you'll never be told about Wi-Fi hotspots nearby; you must connect manually, using one of the techniques described below. **Notify**, a new option in iOS 13, means you'll see an ignorable notification that Wi-Fi networks are available; tap to see the list of them. **Ask** is the traditional annoying interrupting box shown below at left.

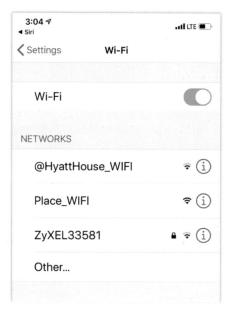

- **If the iPhone can't find any Wi-Fi hotspots to join,** or if you don't join any, it connects to the cellular network, like LTE.

The List of Hotspots

To see the complete list of available hotspots, iOS 13 offers two procedures.

- **Open Settings**. The full list appears in **Settings→Wi-Fi**. Tap the one you want to join, as shown above at right.

- **Use the Control Center.** In iOS 13, at long last, you can choose a Wi-Fi network without having to open Settings. Just open the Control Center (page 42); long-press the Wi-Fi cluster (below, left); and then long-press the Wi-Fi icon (middle). You get the full list of Wi-Fi hotspots, plus a link to jump into Settings (right).

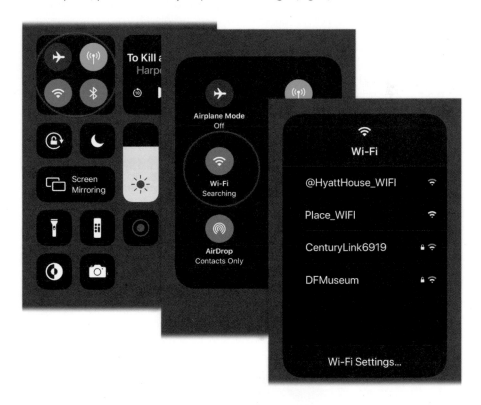

Commercial Hotspots

Tapping the name of the hotspot you want to join is generally all you have to do—if it's a *home* Wi-Fi network. Unfortunately, joining a *commercial* Wi-Fi hotspot—one that requires a credit card number (in a hotel room or an airport, for example)—requires more than just connecting to it. You also have to *sign into* it, exactly as you'd do if you were using a laptop.

In general, the iPhone prompts you to do that automatically. A login screen pops up on its own, interrupting whatever else you're doing; that's where you supply your credit card information or (if you have a membership to this Wi-Fi chain, like Boingo or T-Mobile) your name and password. Tap **Submit** or **Proceed** and enjoy your surfing.

Mercifully, the iPhone memorizes your password. The next time you use this hotspot, you won't have to enter it again.

Airplane Mode and Wi-Fi Off Mode

When battery power is precious, you can turn off all three of the iPhone's network connections in one fell swoop. You can also turn off Wi-Fi alone.

- **To turn all radios off.** In airplane mode, you turn off *all* wireless circuitry: Bluetooth, Wi-Fi, and cellular. Now you can't make calls or get onto the internet. You're saving an amazing amount of power, however, and also complying with regulations that ban cellphones in flight.

  The short way: Open the Control Center (page 42); tap ✈ so it turns orange. (The long way: Open **Settings**; turn on **Airplane Mode**.)

- **To turn Wi-Fi on or off.** Open the Control Center; tap 📶. (When it's blue, it's on.) You can also switch it on or off in **Settings→Wi-Fi**.

TIP: Once you've turned on airplane mode, you can turn **Wi-Fi** back *on* again. Why? To use it on a flight. This is how you turn Wi-Fi *on*, but your cellular circuitry *off*.

Conversely, you sometimes might want to do the opposite: turn *off* Wi-Fi, but leave cellular *on*. Why? Because, sometimes, the iPhone bizarrely won't get online at all. It's struggling to use a Wi-Fi network that, for one reason or another, isn't connecting to the internet. By turning Wi-Fi off, you force the iPhone to use its cellular connection—which may be slower, but at least it works!

In airplane mode, anything that requires voice or internet access—text messages, web, email, and so on—triggers a message: "Turn Off Airplane Mode or Use Wi-Fi to Access Data." Tap either OK (to back out of your decision) or Settings (to turn off airplane mode and get online).

You can, however, enjoy all the offline iPhone features: Music, Camera, and so on. You can also work with stuff you've *already* downloaded to the phone, like email, voicemail messages, and web pages you've saved in the Reading List.

Personal Hotspot (Tethering)

Tethering means using your iPhone as an internet antenna, so your laptops, iPads, game consoles, and other internet-connectables can get online. (The other gadgets can connect to the phone over a Wi-Fi connection, a Bluetooth connection, or a USB cable.) In fact, several laptops and other gadgets can all share the iPhone's connection simultaneously. Your phone becomes a personal cellular router.

That's incredibly convenient, and Apple's execution is especially nice. For example, the hotspot shuts itself off 90 seconds after the last laptop disconnects. That's hugely important, because a personal hotspot is a merciless battery drain.

The hotspot feature may be included with your data plan, or it may cost something like $20 a month extra.

To get this feature, you have to sign up for it by calling your cellular company or visiting its website.

 TIP: If you have a Mac running OS X Yosemite or later, you're in for a real treat: a much more streamlined way to set up Personal Hotspot called *Instant* Hotspot. Skip the instructions below and jump immediately to page 595.

Turning On the Hotspot

On the phone, open Settings→Cellular→Set Up Personal Hotspot (or tell Siri, "Open cellular settings").

 TIP: Once you've turned on Personal Hotspot for the first time, you won't have to drill down as far to get to it. A new Personal Hotspot item appears right there on the main Settings screen from now on.

The Personal Hotspot screen contains details on connecting other computers. It also has the master on/off switch—which, in iOS 13, is called **Allow Others to Join** (even though "Others" includes you). Turn this on.

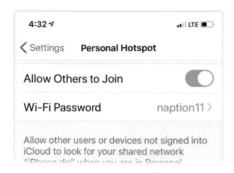 

(If you see a button that says **Set Up Personal Hotspot**, it means you haven't yet added the monthly tethering fee to your cellular plan. Contact your wireless carrier to get that change made to your account.)

You have to use a password for your personal hotspot; it's to ensure that people sitting nearby can't surf using your connection and run up your cell bill. The software proposes a password, but you can edit it and make up one of your own.

Personal Hotspot has received lots of love from Apple in iOS 13. For example, your laptop can stay connected even when you close the lid, so it still gets incoming messages and notifications. Your laptop also connects to your phone's hotspot automatically when it can't find any other internet network.

If you've set up Family Sharing (page 586), this screen also lets you bestow your Wi-Fi generosity upon your family members. You can allow each person's gadgets to connect **Automatically**—or require your permission.

Your laptops and other gadgets can connect to the internet using any of three connections to the iPhone: Wi-Fi, Bluetooth, or a USB cable.

Connecting via Wi-Fi

After about 15 seconds, the iPhone shows up on your laptop or other gadget as though it were a Wi-Fi network. Just choose the iPhone's name from your computer's Wi-Fi hotspot menu (on the Mac, it's the 📶 menu). Enter the password, and bam—your laptop is now online, using the iPhone as an antenna. On the Mac or an iPad, the 📶 changes to look like this: ⊕.

You can leave the iPhone asleep in your pocket or purse while connected. Your laptop can now use email, the web, chat programs—anything it could do in a real Wi-Fi hotspot (just a little slower).

Connecting via Bluetooth

There's no compelling reason to use Bluetooth instead of Wi-Fi, especially since Bluetooth slows your internet connection. But if you're interested, see the free downloadable PDF appendix "Bluetooth Tethering" on this book's "Missing CD" page at *missingmanuals.com*.

Connecting via USB Cable

If you can connect your laptop to your iPhone using the white charging cable, you should. Tethering eats up a lot of the phone's battery power, so keeping it plugged into the laptop means you won't wind up with a dead phone when you're finished surfing.

Once You're Connected

On the iPhone, a blue bar or (on Face ID phones) a blue oval on the left "ear" appears to make you aware that the laptop is connected (facing page, right). You can tap that blue patch to open the Personal Hotspot screen in Settings. In general, five gadgets connected at once is the maximum.

Turning Off Personal Hotspot

Personal Hotspot is a battery hog. It'll cut your iPhone's battery longevity in half. That's why, if no laptops are connected for 90 seconds, the iPhone turns the hotspot off automatically.

You can also turn off the hotspot manually, just the way you'd expect: In Settings→Personal Hotspot, tap Allow Others to Join off.

Turning Personal Hotspot Back On

To fire Personal Hotspot back up again, open Settings and tap Personal Hotspot. That's it—just visit the Personal Hotspot screen to make the iPhone resume broadcasting its Wi-Fi or Bluetooth network to your laptops and other gadgets.

Share Your Wi-Fi Password

It happens in homes and apartments all over the world. A friend comes over and asks: "Hey, what's your Wi-Fi password?"

And then you crawl behind the water heater to find the password sticker on the router. Or the evening grinds to a halt as you try to dictate it: "Capital P, lowercase u, capital M, number 1...."

This feature eases that everyday pain point. You can allow a buddy to hop onto your network without having to spell out your password—or even reveal it! It works like this:

1. **The buddy opens Settings→Wi-Fi and taps your network name.**

    He's staring at the box where he's supposed to enter the password. He brings his phone near your iPhone (or your iPad, or your Mac).

NOTE: This trick requires that you both have Bluetooth and Wi-Fi turned on, and that your buddy is someone in your Contacts.

2. **You see a Wi-Fi Password screen. You tap Share Password.**

3. **Your buddy marvels as the password appears in the Password box before his eyes.**

    He can tap Join and dive right in, ready to enjoy the internet instead of paying attention to you.

Safari

The iPhone's web browser is Safari, a lite version of the same one that comes on the Mac. It's fast, simple to use, and very pretty. On the web pages you visit, you see the real deal—the actual fonts, graphics, and layouts—not the stripped-down mini-web on cellphones of years gone by.

Safari has most of the features of a desktop web browser: bookmarks, autocomplete (for web addresses), scrolling shortcuts, cookies, a pop-up ad blocker, password memorization, and so on. About all it's missing is Java, Flash, and other plug-ins.

Safari Tour

Don't be freaked out: *The main screen elements disappear* shortly after you start reading a page. That's supposed to give you more screen space to do your surfing. To bring them back, scroll to the top, scroll to the bottom, or just scroll up a little. At that point, you see the controls again. Here they are, as they appear from the top left:

- **The website menu (ᴀA).** This menu is new in iOS 13, and it's a real winner. Tap it to open a panel of options that will apply just to this website (next page, left).

  For example, there are the A and A buttons, which make all the text bigger or smaller—a blessing in times of tiny type. (Tap the percentage number between them to jump back to original "100%" size.)

  Show Reader View makes all the ads, boxes, banners, and other junk disappear. Only text and pictures remain, for your sanity-in-reading pleasure. See page 520.

  As noted, when you scroll down a page, Safari automatically hides the search/address bar and the bottom-of-screen controls; they reappear every time you start to scroll up again. Sometimes, when

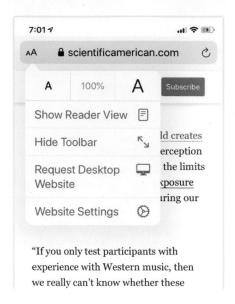

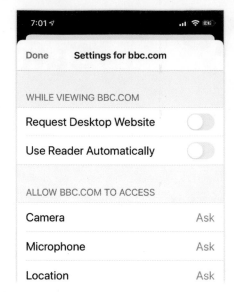

you're moving up and down a page, it gets annoying to see those controls popping in and out—so in iOS 13, you can now **Hide Toolbar**. It keeps those elements hidden even when you scroll up—even when you open a new link from this window. (To bring them back and turn off **Hide Toolbar**, tap the tiny web address at the very top.)

In an effort to conserve time and bandwidth (yours and theirs), many websites supply *mobile* versions to your iPhone—smaller, stripped-down sites that transfer faster than (but lack some features of) the full-blown sites. You generally have no control over which version you're sent. But if you tap **Request Desktop Website**, the full-blown desktop version of that site now appears. (At that point, the command changes to say **Request Mobile Website**.)

If you're using an ad blocker, this is also where you'll see the **Turn off Content Blocker** command, to allow those ads through just this time.

Finally, the **Website Settings** opens the screen shown above at right. Here, you can specify that Reader View or Desktop Site always appears when you visit this site. (This is also where you can allow or deny the site access to your camera, microphone, and location.)

- **Address/search bar.** A single, unified box serves as both the address bar and the search bar at the top of the screen.

  This box (visible above at left) is where you enter the *URL* (web address) for a page you want to visit. ("URL" is short for the even-less-self-explanatory *Uniform Resource Locator*.) For example, if you type *amazon.com*, tapping **Go** takes you to that website.

But this is also where you search the web. If you type anything else, like *cashmere sweaters* or just *amazon*, then tapping **Go** gives you the Google search results for that phrase.

TIP: If you have a URL already copied to your Clipboard, just tap once in the address/search bar. From the options that appear, tap **Paste and Go** to *paste* the link and *go* to that site.

You can jump directly to the address bar, no matter how far down a page you've scrolled, just by tapping the very top edge of the screen (the status bar, or the ears of the Face ID phones). That "tap the top" trick is timely, too, when a website is designed to *hide* the address bar.

- **Stop, Reload (✕, ↻).** Tap ✕ to interrupt the downloading of a web page you've just requested (if you've made a mistake, for instance).

TIP: You don't have to wait for a web page to load entirely. You can zoom in, scroll, and begin reading the text even when only part of the page has appeared.

Once a page has finished loading, the ✕ button turns into a ↻ (reload) button. Click it if a page doesn't look or work quite right. Safari re-downloads the web page and reinterprets its text and graphics.

- **Download (⊕).** This button, new in iOS 13, appears only when you're downloading a file; it's a full-on download manager. A tiny progress bar appears beneath the icon—or you can tap it to view the file's name and progress, along with a Cancel button (✕), a list of previous downloads, and even a **Q** that lets you find it on your phone.

- **Back, Forward (‹, ›).** Tap ‹ to revisit the page you were just on. Once you've tapped ‹, you can then tap › to return to the page you were on *before* you tapped the ‹ button. You can also *hold down* these buttons to see the complete history list of this tab.

TIP: Since these buttons disappear as soon as you scroll down a page, how are you supposed to move back and forward among pages?

By *swiping in* from outside the screen. Start your swipe on the edge of the phone's front glass and whisk inward. Swiping rightward like this means "back"; leftward means "forward again." Do it slowly, and you can actually see the page sliding in.

- **Share/Bookmark (⬆).** When you're on an especially useful page, tap this button. It offers every conceivable choice for commemorating or sharing the page, including bookmarking it. See page 508 for details.

- **View Bookmarks ( )** brings up your list of saved bookmarks—plus your History list, Favorites, Reading List, and links recommended by the people you follow on Twitter. You can read about these elements later in this chapter.

- **Page Juggler ( ).** Safari can keep multiple web pages open, just like any other browser. Page 518 has the details.

Zooming and Scrolling

If a web page is too small, the next step is to magnify the part of the page you want to read. The iPhone offers four ways to do that:

- **Enlarge the text,** as described on page 239.

- **Double-tap.** Safari can recognize different *chunks* of a web page—each block of text, each photo. When you double-tap a chunk, Safari magnifies *just that chunk* to fill the whole screen. It's smart and useful.

 Double-tap again to zoom back out.

Double-tap

- **Rotate the iPhone.** Turn the device 90 degrees in either direction. The iPhone rotates and magnifies the image to fill the wider view. Often, this simple act is enough to make tiny type big enough to read.

- **Do the two-finger spread.** Put two fingers on the glass and slide them apart. The Safari page stretches before your very eyes. Then you can pinch to shrink the page back down again. (Most people do several spreads or pinches in a row to achieve the degree of zoom they want.)

Once you've zoomed to the proper degree, you can then scroll around the page by dragging or flicking with a finger. You don't have to worry about "clicking a link" by accident; if your finger is in motion, Safari ignores the tapping action, even if you happen to land on a link.

 TIP: Once you've double-tapped to zoom in on a page, you can use this little-known trick: Double-tap anywhere on the *upper* half of the screen to scroll up or the *lower* half to scroll down. The closer you are to the top or bottom of the screen, the more you scroll.

Typing a Web Address

Some of the iPhone's greatest tips and shortcuts all have to do with the address/search bar at the top of the screen:

- **The Start page.** When you tap in the address bar but haven't yet typed anything, iOS 13's new Start page appears (next page, left). It's also the page you see when you tap the + button, or close all open pages. It's like a page of visual bookmarks.

  At top, it shows a few of your **Favorites** (your very favorite book-marked sites; see page 509).

 TIP: You don't have to use the Favorites folder of bookmarks as the one whose contents appear here. In **Settings→Safari→Favorites**, a list of all your Bookmarks folders appears. Whichever one you select there becomes your new Favorites folder, even if its name isn't "Favorites."

Next on this screen, icons appear for some of your **Frequently Visited** sites.

At bottom are **Siri Suggestions**—links to sites that iOS found in your Messages chats, recent Mail email, and stories you've read in the News app.

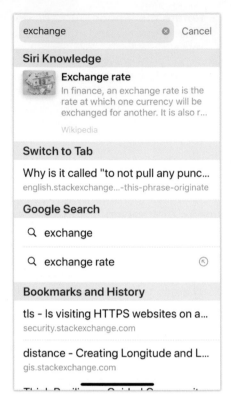

If you long-press on any of these icons, you get a command panel, new in iOS 13, offering options like **Copy**, **Open in New Tab**, **Edit**, and **Delete**. If you long-press a *folder* of Favorites (page 509), the panel offers the new **Open in New Tabs** command, which opens all the sites in this folder at once.

- **Don't type http://www.** You can leave that stuff out; Safari will supply it automatically. Instead of *http://www.cnn.com*, for example, just type *cnn.com* (or tap its name in the suggestions list) and hit **Go**.

- **Don't delete.** There *is* a ❌ button at the right end of the address bar whose purpose is to erase the current address so you can type another one. (Tap inside the address bar to make it, and the keyboard, appear.) But the ❌ button is for suckers.

  Instead, whenever the address bar is open for typing, *just type*. Forget that there's already a URL there. The iPhone is smart enough to figure out that you want to *replace* that web address with a new one.

- **Type .com, .net, .org, or .edu the easy way.** Safari's canned URL choices can save you four keyboard taps apiece. To see their secret menu, hold your finger down on the *period key* on the keyboard. Then tap the common suffix you want. (Or, if you want .com, just release your finger without moving it.)

Otherwise, this address bar works just like the one in any other web browser. Tap inside it to make the keyboard appear.

Tap the blue Go key when you're finished typing the address. That's your Enter key. (Or tap Cancel to hide the keyboard *without* "pressing Enter.")

Searching in Safari

The address bar is also the search box. Just tap into it and type your search phrase (or speak it, using the 🎤 button).

Safari produces a menu filled with suggestions that could spare you some typing—things it guesses you might be looking for (facing page, right). The result categories vary, but here are the kinds of tappable results you may get:

- **Siri Knowledge.** If your search term is something Siri knows about—a sports team, a famous person, an app, a movie or book name, an important concept—you may see a single, special, graphically rich listing right at the top. One tap takes you directly to the main page for that entity; sometimes it shows enough of the answer that you don't even need to tap (see "ambulance" on the next page).

- **Switch to Tab.** If your search term appears on a page that you've already got open, it's listed here for your convenience—a new iOS 13 nicety.

- **Top Hits.** The Top Hits are Safari's best guesses at the websites you're looking for. They're the sites on your bookmarks and History lists that you've visited most often (and that match what you've typed so far).

  If you tap a Top Hit, you'll find that the site appears almost instantly. It doesn't seem to have to load. That's because, as a favor to you, Safari quietly downloads the Top Hits in the background, while you're still entering your search term, all to save you time.

NOTE: If you're concerned that this feature is sucking down some of your monthly cellular data allowance unnecessarily, you can turn it off in Settings→Safari→Preload Top Hit.

- **Google Search.** The next category of suggestions: a list of search terms you *might* be typing, based on how popular those searches are on Google (or whatever search service you're using). For example, if you type *chick*, then this section proposes things like *chicken* *recipes, chick fil a,* and *chicken pox.* It's just trying to save you a little typing; if none of these tappable choices is the one you want, then ignore them.

- **Bookmarks and History.** Here Safari offers matching selections from websites you've bookmarked or recently visited. Again, it's trying to save you typing.

- **On This Page.** Here's how you search for certain text *on the page you're reading.*

    Scroll to the very bottom of the results list to find the **On This Page** heading. It lists one result, called **Find "ambu" (32 matches)** (or whatever you've typed so far). Tap that line to jump to the first appearance of that text on the page. (There's a less hidden way to start this process, too: Tap ⬆ and then **Find on Page**.)

    Use the ⌄ and ⌃ buttons to jump from one match to the next (below, right). Tap **Done** (or anywhere on the web page) to return to your regularly scheduled browsing.

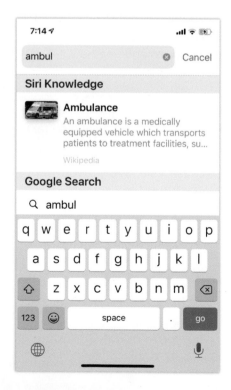

Suppose you've started typing a search term. Safari pipes up with its usual list of suggestions. At this point, you can drag up or down the screen to hide the keyboard—so you can see the suggestions that were hidden behind it.

You can tell the iPhone to use a Yahoo, Bing, or DuckDuckGo search instead of Google, if you like, in **Settings→Safari→Search Engine**. (DuckDuckGo is a search service dedicated to privacy. It doesn't store your searches or tailor the results to you. On the other hand, it's not nearly as good at searching the web.)

If you've set your search options to use Google, then there are all kinds of cool things you can type here—special terms that tell Google, "I want *information*, not web page matches."

You can type a movie name and zip code or city/state (*Titanic Returns 10024*) to get a list of today's showtimes in theaters near you. Get the forecast by typing *weather chicago* or *weather 60609*. Stock quotes: Type the symbol (*AMZN*). Dictionary definitions: *define schadenfreude*. Unit conversions: *liters in 5 gallons*. Currency conversions: *25 usd in euros*. Then tap **Go** to get instant results.

Quick Website Search

This crazy feature lets you search *within* a certain site (like Amazon or Reddit or Wikipedia) using Safari's regular search bar. For example, typing *wiki mollusk* can search Wikipedia for its entry on mollusks. Typing *amazon ipad* can offer links to buy an iPad from Amazon. Typing *reddit sitcoms* opens *reddit.com* to its search results for sitcoms.

None of this will work, however, until (a) you've turned the feature on (**Settings→Safari→Quick Website Search**), and (b) you've manually *taught* Safari how to search those sites one time each.

To do that, pull up the site you'll want to search (let's say it's *reddit.com*) and use its regular search bar. Search for anything.

That site's name now appears in the list at **Settings→Safari→Quick Website Search**. (Usually. Many sites don't work with Quick Website Search.) From now on, you can search that site by typing, for example, *reddit sitcoms*. You'll jump directly to that site's search results.

Bookmarks (▢)

Bookmarks, of course, are links to websites you might want to visit again without having to remember and type their URLs.

To see the list of bookmarks on your phone, tap 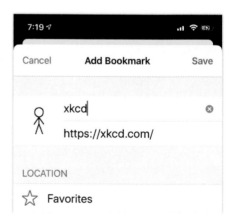 at the bottom of the screen. You see the master list of bookmarks. They're organized in folders, or even folders *within* folders.

Tapping a folder shows you what's inside, and tapping a bookmark begins opening the corresponding website.

> **NOTE:** Actually, what you see when you tap ⊓ are *three* tabs at the top: ⊓ (Bookmarks), ⊙⊙ (Reading List), and ⊙ (History). The latter two are described later in this chapter.

You may be surprised to discover that Safari already seems to be pre-stocked with bookmarks—that, amazingly, are interesting and useful to *you* in particular! How did it know?

Easy—it copied your existing desktop computer's browser bookmarks from Safari on the Mac, thanks to Safari syncing through iCloud (page 569). Sneaky, eh?

Creating New Bookmarks

When you find a web page you might like to visit again, long-press the ⊓ icon; from the shortcut menu, choose **Add Bookmark** (below, left). The Add Bookmark screen appears (right).

> **TIP:** In iOS 13, if you have multiple tabs open, you even get the chance to create a single bookmark that opens all of them.

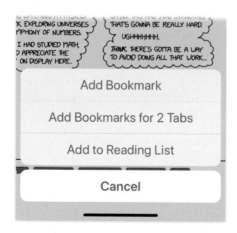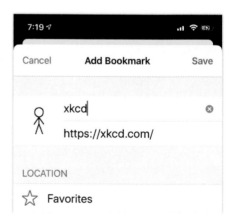

You have two tasks here:

- **Type a better name.** In the top box, you can type a shorter or clearer name for the page. Instead of "Bass, Trout & Tackle—the web's

Premier Resource for the Avid Outdoorsman," you can just call it "Fish."

Below that: The page's underlying URL, which is independent of what you've *named* your bookmark. You can't edit this one.

- **Specify where to file this bookmark.** If you tap Favorites, then you open Safari's hierarchical list of bookmark folders, which organize your bookmarked sites. Tap the folder where you want to file the new bookmark so you'll know where to find it later.

Editing Bookmarks and Folders

It's easy enough to massage your Bookmarks list within Safari—to delete favorites that aren't so favorite anymore, to make new folders, to rearrange the list, to rename a folder or a bookmark, and so on.

To begin, tap 📖 to see the list of bookmarks (below, left). What you'll probably do most on this screen, of course, is to tap one to visit that site.

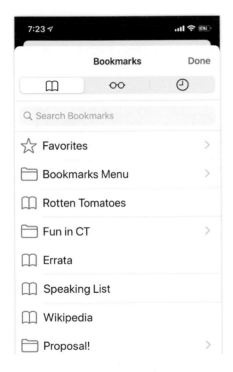
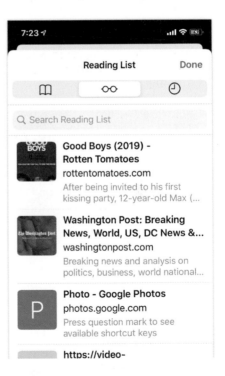

But you can also delete a bookmark or folder by swiping leftward and tapping Delete. Or, for more surgical operations, tap Edit. Now you can get organized:

- **Delete something.** Yes, another way to nuke a bookmark. Tap ⊖ next to a folder or a bookmark, and then tap Delete to confirm.

- **Rearrange the list.** Drag the grip strip (≡) up or down in the list to move the folders or bookmarks around. (You can't move or delete the top folder, Favorites.)

- **Edit a name and location.** Tap a folder or a bookmark name. If you tap a folder, you arrive at the Edit Folder screen, where you can edit the folder's name and which folder it's inside of. If you tap a bookmark, you arrive at the Edit Bookmark screen, where you can edit the bookmark's name, the URL it points to, and its location folder.

  Tap **Done** when you're finished.

- **Create a folder.** Tap **New Folder**. You're offered the chance to type a name for it and to specify where you want to file it (that is, in which *other* folder).

Tap **Done** when you're finished.

> **TIP:** As you've read, preserving a bookmark requires quite a few taps. That's why it's extra important for you to remember iOS's gift to busy people: the "Remind me about this later" command to Siri (page 470). You've just added a new item in your Reminders list, complete with a link to whatever page you're looking at now. (Feel free to be more specific, as in "Remind me about this when I get home.")

The History List (🕐)

Behind the scenes, Safari keeps track of the websites you've visited in the past week or so, neatly organized into sections like This Evening and Yesterday. It's a great feature when you can't recall the address for a website you visited recently—or when you remember it had a long, complicated address and you get the psychiatric condition known as iPhone Keyboard Dread.

To see the list of recent sites, tap 📖, and then 🕐. Once the History list appears, just tap a bookmark to revisit that web page.

Erasing the History List

Some people find it creepy that Safari maintains a History list, right there in plain view of any family member or co-worker who wanders by. They'd just as soon their wife/husband/boss/parent/kid not know what websites they've been visiting.

You can delete one History listing easily enough; swipe left across its name and then tap **Delete**. You can also delete the *entire* History menu, erasing all your tracks. To do that, tap **Clear**; confirm by tapping **The last hour**, **Today**, **Today and yesterday**, or **All time**. You've just rewritten History.

Long Press on a Link

Link tapping, of course, is the primary activity of the web. But in Safari, *long*-pressing a link (below, left) harbors special powers.

That operation shows you, in advance, a preview of the page that it intends to bring up, along with a handy panel of commands (right). Drag upward to pull the whole menu into view: **Open**, **Open in New Tab**, **Download Linked File**, **Add to Reading List**, **Copy** (meaning "copy the link address"), and **Share**.

global temperatures could alter the ratio of sexes produced, making it harder for these animals to find mates.

Eastern three-lined skink females can partially compensate for temperature increases by digging deeper nests and laying earlier in the season. Nevertheless, **according to a study published in 2009**, their nests still warmed by 1.5C over 10 years. This shifted the sex ratio towards females.

Not every species is as badly affected. **Australian water dragon** females have been shown to **buffer temperature differences of 4C** by nesting in sunnier or shadier locations. When it comes to climate change, behavioural flexibility is often a big advantage.

Warmer temperatures are quietly spoiling the mood, making it harder for plants and animals to reproduce

In the plant world, temperature can influence sex ratios in more subtle ways. For example, the **tobacco root plant**, which lives in alpine meadows

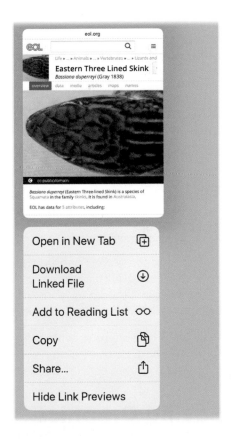

There's also **Hide Link Previews**, which makes the preview image of the page-to-be vanish from this link-preview screen (you see only the address). To back out of this screen, tap anywhere on the background.

The Reading List (◯◯)

The Reading List, the center tab of the Bookmarks ▢ screen, is a handy list of web pages you want to read later. Unlike a bookmark, it stores entire pages, so you can read them even when you don't have an internet connection (on the subway or on a plane, for example).

The Reading List also keeps track of what you've read. You can use the **Show All/Show Unread** button at the bottom of the screen to view everything—or just what you haven't yet read.

> **TIP:** To make matters even sweeter, iCloud synchronizes your Reading Lists on your Mac, iPhone, iPad, and so on—as long as you've turned on bookmark syncing. It's as though the web always keeps your place.

To add a page to the Reading List, tap 🔲, scroll up a little, and tap **Add to Reading List** (previous page, right). Or just hold your finger down on a link until a set of buttons appears, including **Add to Reading List**. (At this point, iOS may politely ask if you want all future Reading List stories to be downloaded to your phone, rather than simply bookmarked.)

Once you've added a page to the Reading List, you can get to it by tapping ▢ and then ◯◯ . Tap an item on your list to open and read it.

> **TIP:** When you get to the bottom of a Reading List item you've just read, keep scrolling down. The phone is nice enough to offer up the *next* article in your Reading List, as though they were all vertically connected.

By the way, some web pages require a hefty amount of data to download, what with photos and all. If you're worried about Reading List downloads eating up your monthly data allotment, you can visit **Settings→Safari** and turn off **Automatically Save Offline**.

Now you'll be able to download Reading List pages only when you're on Wi-Fi, but at least there's no risk of your Wikipedia addiction pushing you over your monthly cellular-data allotment.

Saving Graphics

If you find a picture online that you wish you could keep forever, you have two choices: You could stare at it until you've memorized it, or you could save it.

To do that, long-press the image. This time, the panel of commands includes **Add to Photos**; the iPhone thoughtfully deposits a copy of the image in Photos so it will be copied back to your Mac or PC at the next sync opportunity. If you tap **Copy**, then you nab a copy of that graphic, which you can now paste into another program.

Passwords and Credit Cards

You're probably familiar with password hell. You're supposed to create a long, complex, unguessable password—capital and lowercase letters, numbers, and symbols, with a few Hindi characters thrown in if possible. For each site. And you can't reuse a password. Oh, and you have to change them all every month.

It's not possible. Not even security experts have that kind of memory.

Fortunately, Apple has come up with a system that comes very close to the ideal: complex, secure passwords—without your having to remember any of them!

And since typing on glass isn't fun for anyone, iOS can also autofill your name, address, and credit card information on websites, too.

Memorized Passwords

When you're signing up for a new account on some website, and you tap inside the box where you're supposed to enter a password, Safari announces, "iPhone created a strong password for this website."

And sure enough: The suggested password is a doozy, along the lines of *23k2k4-29cs8-58384-ckk3322* (next page, left).

You don't have to use it; you can tap **Choose My Own Password** and make up one of your own. (In iOS 13, Safari will object if you use something dumb like "password" or "123456.")

If you tap **Use Strong Password**, though, you won't have to remember it. Safari automatically memorizes it for you (and syncs it to your other Apple computers, if they're on the same iCloud account). Next time you're logging in, Safari's AutoFill offers to enter that password with one tap on the QuickType bar.

If you have several accounts for the same site, you'll see two buttons on the QuickType bar (next page, top right). And if you have even more, you can tap the little 🔑 button to open the Passwords screen described in a moment.

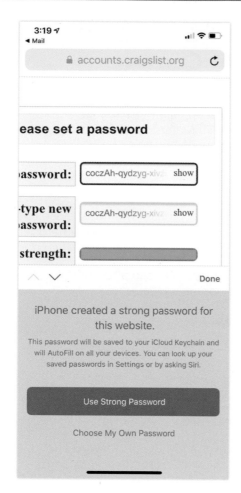
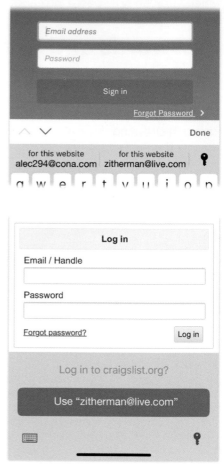

Safari may even offer to log you in *completely*, filling in your email address and password (above, bottom right). It's a miracle.

The Master Password List

You can view a master list of the actual memorized names and passwords. It waits for you at **Settings→Passwords & Accounts→Website & App Passwords** (next page, left). You have to prove your identity with Face ID or Touch ID before you're allowed to see them.

On this screen, you can change any saved password, too; tap it and tap **Edit**. To add a password manually, tap +. Or, if a login no longer pleases you, swipe leftward across it, and then tap **Delete**.

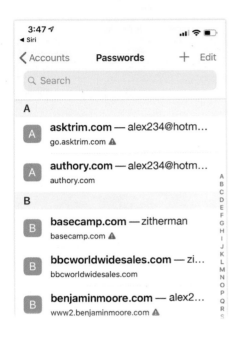

This list might display the occasional ⚠ symbol. That's flagging passwords you've used more than once, for different sites. Almost everyone does that, because who's really going to memorize 300 different passwords? But security experts frown on the practice, because it means that once a hacker gets the password for one of your accounts (from some corporate data breach, for example), he's got access to your other accounts, too. Since iOS can remember and fill in your passwords all by itself, you might as well avoid that fate.

Automatic Text-Code Entry

You know how, when you try to log onto certain websites, they first send your phone a text message to prove that you're you (next page, left)? (It's called two-factor authentication. Security experts like it. People hate it.)

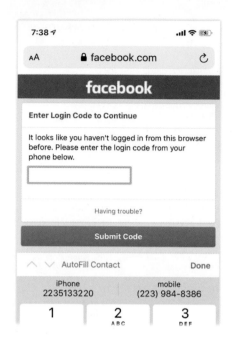
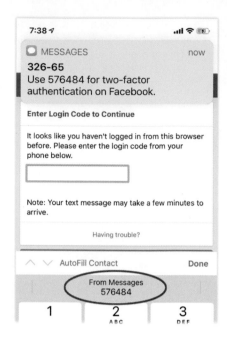

Yeah, you get the notification that a text has come in (above, right). But then you have to either memorize the six-digit code they just sent you, or switch into Messages, find the text they sent you, and copy the code to your Clipboard. And then go back to Safari, tap in the "Enter code here" box, and paste it. Augh.

Not anymore. Now, whenever one of these sites sends a code by text, iOS finds it in the text message, identifies it, and offers to paste it directly into the site (or the app). It's fantastic.

Name, Address, Credit Card Autofill

Safari can fill in your name, address, and credit card details automatically, too, when you're ordering something online.

And thanks to iCloud syncing, all those passwords and credit cards can auto-store themselves on all your other Apple gadgetry.

To turn on AutoFill, visit Settings→Safari→AutoFill. Here's what you find:

- **Use Contact Info.** Turn this On. Then tap **My Info**. From the address book, find your own listing. You've just told Safari *which* name, address, city, state, zip code, and phone number belong to you.

  From now on, whenever you're asked to input your address, phone number, and so on, you'll see an AutoFill button at the top of the keyboard. Tap it to make Safari auto-enter all those details, saving you no end of typing. (It works on *most* sites.) If there are extra blanks that AutoFill doesn't fill, you can tap ∨ and ∧ to move your cursor from one to the next instead of tapping and scrolling manually.

TIP: If your contact card contains a secondary address (like a work address), or even a third, then tapping AutoFill produces a pop-up panel listing both (or all three). Just tap the one you want.

- **Credit Cards.** Turn on Credit Cards, of course, if you'd like Safari to memorize your charge card info. To enter your card details, tap Saved Credit Cards (where you see a list of them) and then Add Credit Card. You can type in your name, card number, expiration date, and a description—or you can save yourself a little tedium by tapping Use Camera. Aim the camera at your credit card; the phone magically recognizes your name, the card number, and the expiration date, and proposes a description of the card.

When you buy something online, iOS offers an AutoFill Credit Card button. When you tap it, Safari asks you first which credit card you want to use, if you've stored more than one (it displays the last four digits for your reference). Tap it, and boom: Safari cheerfully fills in the credit card information, saving you time and hassle.

Unfortunately, Safari makes no attempt to fill in the little three- or four-digit security code, sometimes called the CSC, CVV, or CV2 code. You always have to enter it manually. That's one last safeguard against a kid, a spouse, a parent, or a thief using your phone for an online shopping spree when you're not around.

TIP: You don't have to enter all your stored passwords and credit cards into other Apple gadgets. They sync via iCloud (page 569).

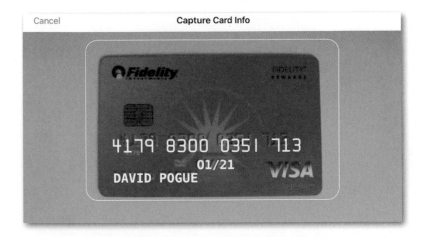

Manipulating Multiple Pages

Like any other self-respecting browser, Safari can keep multiple pages open at once, making it easy for you to switch among them. You can think of it as a miniature version of tabbed browsing, a feature of browsers like Safari Senior, Firefox, Chrome, and Microsoft Edge. Tabbed browsing keeps a bunch of web pages open simultaneously.

One advantage of this arrangement is that you can start reading one web page while the others load into their own tabs in the background.

To Switch Among Windows (Vertical)

If you're holding your iPhone upright, you can tap 🗗 to see something like the 3D floating pages shown on the facing page. These are all your open tabs (windows). Here's how you can proceed:

- **Open a new tab.** If you tap ＋, you open a brand-new window—the Start page (see page 503). Tap an icon, enter an address, or use a bookmark.

- **Close a tab** by tapping the ✕ in the corner—or by swiping a page away horizontally. It slides away into the void.

- **Close all the tabs** by long-pressing the **Done** button (or the 🗗 button). Tap **Close All 488 Tabs** (or whatever the number is), as shown on the facing page at right.

> **NOTE:** At this point, Safari offers to continue closing all the tabs you leave in your wake—after a day, week, or month. That's a new feature in iOS 13, intended to solve the inevitable problem of building up 500 open tabs (the maximum) that you never intend to revisit. (You can also set up auto-tab closing in **Settings→Safari→Close Tabs**.)

- **Rearrange these windows** by dragging them up or down.

- **Open a window** to full screen by tapping it.

You can open a third window, and a fourth, and so on, and jump among them, using these techniques.

> **TIP:** Although not one person in a thousand realizes it, you can search your open Safari tabs' website titles and URLs. Tap the 🗗 button and either drag down the topmost tab—or hold the phone horizontally (landscape mode). There's your secret search box.

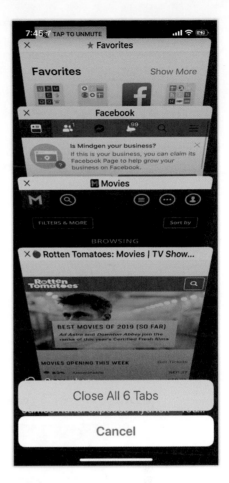

To Switch Among Windows (Horizontal)

If you turn the iPhone 90 degrees, into landscape orientation, you get a treat: tab thumbnails. Now you can pop between sites by tapping their little previews. (That's *if* **Settings→Safari→Show Tab Bar** is turned on.)

iCloud Tabs

Thanks to the miracle of iCloud syncing, the last windows and tabs you had open on your other Apple gadgets (even if they're currently turned off) show up here, at the bottom of the page-juggling screen (above, left).

They're sorted into headings that correspond to your other Apple gadgets.

The concept is to unify your Macs and i-gadgets. You're reading three browser windows and tabs on your phone—why not resume on the big screen when you get home and sit down in front of your Mac?

You won't see these tabs unless the Macs have OS X Mountain Lion or later. And, of course, Safari syncing has to be turned on in **System Preferences→iCloud** on the Mac, and **Settings→[your name]** → **iCloud** on the phone or tablet.

Reader View

How can people read web articles when there's Times Square blinking all around them? Fortunately, you'll never have to put up with that again.

The A**A** button in the address bar offers the **Show Reader View** command, which is amazing. With one tap, it eliminates *everything* from the page you're reading except the text and photos. No ads, toolbars, blinking, links, banners, or anything else.

The text is also changed to a clean, clear font and size, and the background is made plain white. Basically, it makes any web page look like a printed book page, and it's glorious. Shown below: the before and after of the identical article. Which looks easier to read?

To exit Reader, tap ᴀA and then **Hide Reader View**. Best. Feature. Ever.

The fine print: Reader doesn't appear until the page has fully loaded. It doesn't appear on "front page" pages, like the *nytimes.com* home page— only when you've opened an article within. (You see a blinking "Reader View Available" when Reader View's available.) And it may not appear on sites that are already specially designed for access by cellphones.

Web Security

Safari on the iPhone isn't meant to be a full-blown web browser like the one on your desktop computer, but it comes surprisingly close—especially when it comes to privacy and security. Cookies, pop-up blockers, parental controls: They're all here, for your paranoid pleasure.

Pop-Up Blocker

The world's smarmiest advertisers inundate us with pop-up and pop-under ads—nasty little windows that appear in front of the browser window or, worse, behind it, waiting to jump out the moment you close your window. Fortunately, Safari comes set to block those pop-ups so you don't see them.

The thing is, though, pop-ups are sometimes useful (and not ads)— notices of new banking features, seating charts on ticket-sales sites, and so on. Safari can't tell these from ads—and it stifles them, too. So if a site you trust says "Please turn off pop-up blockers and reload this page," then you know you're probably missing out on a *useful* pop-up message.

In those situations, you can turn off the pop-up blocker. The on/off switch is in **Settings→Safari**.

Cookies

Cookies are something like preference files. Most websites deposit them on your hard drive so they'll remember you the next time you visit. That's how Amazon is able to greet you with "Welcome, Chris" (or whatever your name is). It's reading its own cookie.

Most cookies are perfectly innocuous—and, in fact, useful. But fear is widespread, and the media fan the flames with tales of sinister cookies that track your movement on the web. If you're worried about invasions of privacy, Safari is ready to protect you.

If you turn on **Settings→Safari→Block All Cookies** (and confirm in the "Are you sure" box), then you create an acrylic shield around your iPhone. No cookies can come in, and no cookie information can go out. You'll probably find the web a very inconvenient place; you'll have to reenter your information upon every visit, and some sites may not work at all.

When this option is off, Safari accepts cookies from sites you *want* to visit, but blocks cookies deposited by sites you're not actually visiting—cookies an especially evil banner ad gives you, for example.

The **Settings→Safari** screen offers a slew of additional privacy and security settings; see page 642, right.

Private Browsing

Private browsing lets you surf without adding any pages to your History list, searches to your Google search suggestions, passwords to Safari's saved password list, or AutoFill entries to Safari's memory. You might want to turn on private browsing before you visit websites that would raise interesting questions with your spouse, parents, or boss.

To begin, tap ⬚ to open the page-juggler screen; tap **Private** at the bottom-left corner. When you tap ＋ to open a new page, a huge new warning appears to let you know that Safari will record nothing while you surf.

When you're ready to browse "publicly" again, turn private browsing off once more (tap ⬚, and then tap **Private**). Safari resumes taking note of the pages you visit—but it never remembers the ones you opened while in Private mode. In other words, what happens in private browsing stays in private browsing.

Parental Controls

If your child (or employee) is old enough to have an iPhone but not old enough for the seedier side of the web, then don't miss the Restrictions feature in Settings. The iPhone can remove the Safari icon from the iPhone altogether so that no web browsing is possible at all. See page 387 for instructions.

Happy Surprises in the 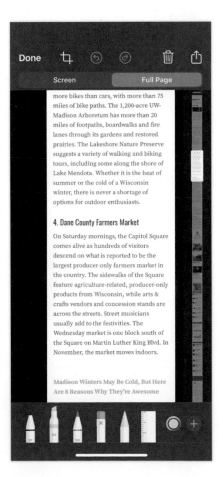 Panel

The Share sheet (tap ⬆️) is especially useful in Safari. When you drag upward to see it all, you'll find an amazing wealth of options for setting a web page aside for use later (**Add Bookmark**, **Add to Favorites**)—but also some equally useful buttons that nobody ever talks about; here are a few highlights (below, left):

- **AirDrop, Message, Mail, Twitter, and Facebook.** Pretty obvious; they share the link of your current page with other people.

- **Reminders.** Remember how you can say to Siri, about a web page you're on, "Remind me about this later?" (If not, see page 470.) There's a button for that here on the Share sheet. Great for when speaking to your phone would be socially awkward.

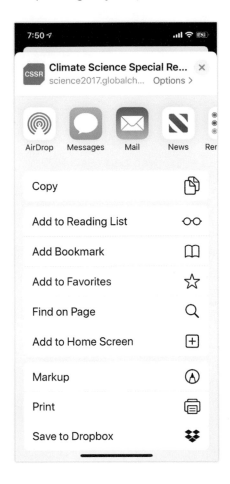

- **Add to Notes.** You can send a link to a web article (complete with opening sentences and an image) directly to a note in the Notes app—no copy and paste required. You're invited to annotate the note before hitting **Save**, or even add it to an existing Notes page.

- **Copy.** Copies the page's address, to paste it into some other app.

- **Open in News.** Turns the article you're reading into a nicely formatted "magazine" page in the News app (page 449). If it's not an article-style post, you just get an error message.

- **Add to Home Screen.** Is there a certain website you visit every day? This button adds that page's icon right to your Home screen. It's a shortcut that Apple calls a web clip. You're offered the chance to edit the icon's name; tap **Add**. When you return to your Home screen, you'll see the icon; you can move or delete it as you would any app.

- **Find on Page.** Here's your search command.

> **TIP:** You can rearrange the icon buttons, if you like. Tap **More** and then drag their "grip strips" up or down in the list. You can also adjust which commands appear in the written half of the list by tapping **Edit Actions**.

The PDF Trick

In iOS versions of old, you could export an entire web page as a PDF document, for reading offline or sharing with any computer or phone on earth. In iOS 13, you still can—in fact, more flexibly than ever—but the command is hidden.

The trick is to take a screenshot, as described on page 357. In the resulting preview, tap **Full Page**. Now you can use the right-side scroll bar to look over the very tall, multipage document (previous page, right). Mark it up as you like (page 458), tap , and then hit **Save to Files**. Your new PDF-ized web page awaits in the Files app (page 421).

14

Email

Email on your iPhone offers full formatting, fonts, graphics, and choice of type size; the use of attachments like photos, PDFs, .zip compressed files, and Word, Excel, PowerPoint, Pages, Numbers, and other documents; and compatibility with Yahoo Mail, Gmail, AOL Mail, iCloud mail, Microsoft Outlook, corporate Exchange mail, and any standard email account.

Dude, if you want a more satisfying portable email machine than this one, buy a laptop.

This chapter covers the basic email experience. If you've gotten yourself hooked up with iCloud, see Chapter 16 for details.

Setting Up Your Account

If you have a free email account from Google, AOL, Outlook, or Yahoo; an iCloud account (Chapter 16); or a Microsoft Exchange account run by your employer, then setup on the iPhone is easy.

From the Home screen, tap **Settings**→**Passwords & Accounts**→**Add Account**. Tap the appropriate corporate colorful logo (Google, Yahoo, or whatever).

On the page that appears, sign into your account. Tap **Next**.

Now you may see the list of non-email data the iPhone can show you (from iCloud, Google, Yahoo, Exchange, and so on): contacts, calendars, reminders, and notes. Turn off the ones you don't want synced to your phone, and then tap **Save**.

Your email account is ready to go!

TIP: Jump to page 548 for a look at some of the new settings you can adjust for the way Mail handles and displays your correspondence.

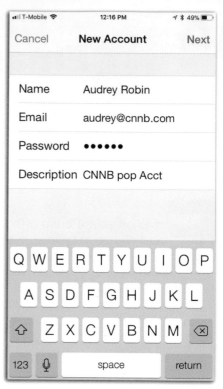

POP and IMAP Accounts

Those freebie, brand-name, web-based accounts are super-easy to set up. But millions of people have more generic email accounts, perhaps supplied by their employers or internet providers. They're generally one of two types:

- **POP accounts** are the oldest type on the internet. (POP stands for Post Office Protocol, but this won't be on the test.)

  A POP server transfers incoming mail to your computer or phone before you read it, which works fine as long as you're using *only that machine* to access your email.

- **IMAP accounts** (Internet Message Access Protocol) are newer and have more features than POP servers, and they're quickly putting POP out to pasture. IMAP servers keep all your mail online, rather than making you store it on your computer; as a result, you can access the same mail from any computer (or phone). IMAP servers remember which messages you've read and sent, and they even keep track of how you've filed messages into mail folders. (Yahoo, Gmail, iCloud, and corporate Exchange accounts are all IMAP. Gmail accounts *can* be POP, too.)

The iPhone copies your IMAP messages onto the phone itself, so you can work on your email even when you're not online. You can, in fact, control where these messages are stored (in which mail folder). To see this, open Settings→Passwords & Accounts→[your IMAP account name]→[your IMAP account name again]→Advanced. See? You can specify where your drafts, sent messages, and deleted messages wind up on the phone.

The iPhone can communicate with both kinds of accounts.

Tap your way to Settings→Passwords & Accounts→Add Account. Tap Other, tap Add Mail Account, and then enter your name, email address, password, and an optional description. Tap Next.

Apple's software attempts to figure out which kind of account you have (POP or IMAP) by the email address. If it can't decide, then you arrive at a second screen, where you're asked for such juicy details as the host name for incoming and outgoing mail servers. (This is also where you tap either IMAP or POP, to tell the iPhone what it's dealing with.)

If you don't know this stuff offhand, you'll have to ask your internet provider, corporate tech-support person, or next-door teenager to help you. When you're finished, tap Save.

To delete an account, open Settings→Passwords & Accounts→[account name]. At the bottom of the screen, you'll find the Delete Account button.

You can make, rename, or delete IMAP or Exchange mailboxes (mail folders) right on the phone.

In the Mail app, view the mailbox list for the account and then tap Edit. Tap New Mailbox to create a new folder. To edit an existing mailbox, tap its name; you can then rename it, tap the Mailbox Location folder to move it, or tap Delete Mailbox. Tap Save to finish up.

Downloading Mail

If you have "push" email (Yahoo, iCloud, or Exchange), then your iPhone doesn't have to *check* for messages; new messages show up on your iPhone *as they arrive*, around the clock.

If you have any other kind of account, then the iPhone checks for new messages automatically on a schedule—every 15, 30, or 60 minutes. It also checks for new messages each time you open the Mail program, or whenever you *drag downward* on the Inbox list.

You can adjust the frequency of these automatic checks or turn off the "push" feature (because it uses up your battery faster) in **Settings**; see page 628.

When new mail arrives, you'll know it. You hear the iPhone's little "You've got mail" sound, unless you've turned that off in Settings (or have the phone silenced).

A notification appears, too, even on the Lock screen. As you can read on page 17, it's perfectly possible to process a message right from its notification banner—**Trash**, **Mark as Read**, **View**, **Open**, and **Manage** commands are all one swipe away.

At the Home screen, Mail's icon sprouts a circled number that tells you how many new messages are waiting. If you have more than one email account, it shows you the *total* number of new messages, from all accounts.

If you routinely leave a lot of unread messages in your inbox, and you don't really care about this "badge," you can turn it off. In fact, you can turn it off on a per-account basis, which is great if one of your accounts is sort of a junk account that you keep as a spare. Tap **Settings→ Notifications→Mail→[account name]→Badges**.

In any case, once you know you have mail, tap the Mail icon on the Home screen to start reading it.

> **TIP:** The Mail app, more than any other app, is designed to be a series of nested lists. You start out seeing a list of accounts; tap one to see a list of folders; tap one for a list of messages; tap one to open the actual message.
>
> To *backtrack* through these lists, you can tap the button in the upper-left corner over and over again—or you can *swipe rightward* across the screen. That's a bigger target and more fun.

The Unified Inbox

If you have more than one email address, you're in luck. The iPhone offers a *unified inbox*—an option that displays all the incoming messages from all your accounts in a single place. (If you don't see it—if Mail opened up to some other screen—keep swiping rightward, backing up one screen at a time, until you do.)

This Mailboxes page has two sections:

- **Unified inboxes (and other unified folders).** All the incoming messages are consolidated into one unified box called **All Inboxes**. Below that, you see the inboxes for each of the individual accounts (facing page, left).

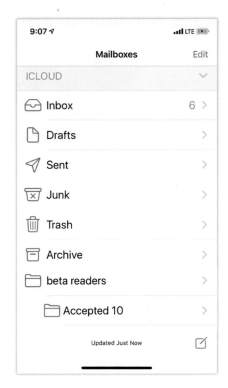

This part of the main Mail list also offers unified folders for **VIP** and **Flagged** messages, which are described later in this chapter.

But what you may not realize is that you can add *other* unified folders to this section. You can, for example, add a folder called **Unread**, which contains only new messages from *all* accounts. (That's not the same thing as **All Inboxes**, because that inbox can contain messages you *have* read but haven't deleted or filed. Maybe a lot of them.)

You can also add a unified folder showing all messages where you were either the To or Cc addressee; this folder won't include any mail where your name appeared on the Bcc (blind carbon copy) line, like mailing lists and, often, spam.

You can also add an **Attachments** folder here (messages with files attached), a **Today** folder, or unified folders that contain **All Drafts**, **All Sent**, or **All Trash**. ("All" means "from all accounts.")

To hide or show these special uni-folders, tap **Edit**, and then tap the selection circles beside the names of the folders you want to appear. (You can also take this opportunity to drag them up or down into a pleasing sequence.) Tap **Done**.

- **Accounts.** Farther down the Mailboxes screen, you see your accounts listed again. You can tap an account's name to expand or collapse its list of traditional mail folders: Inbox, Drafts (emails written but not sent), Sent, Junk, Trash, and any folders you've created yourself (Family, Little League, Old Stuff, whatever). If you have a Yahoo, iCloud, Exchange, or other IMAP account, then the iPhone automatically creates these folders to match what you've set up online, as shown on the previous page at right.

NOTE: Not all kinds of email accounts permit the creation of your own filing folders, so you might not see anything but Inbox, Sent, and Trash.

The Message List—and Threading

If you tap an inbox's name, you wind up face-to-face with the list of incoming messages. (To return to the Mailboxes list, tap ‹ **Mailboxes**, or swipe to the right.)

At first, you see only the subject lines of your messages, plus, in gray type, the first few lines of their contents; that way you can scan through new messages to see if there's anything important. You can flick upward to scroll this list. Blue dots indicate messages you haven't yet opened.

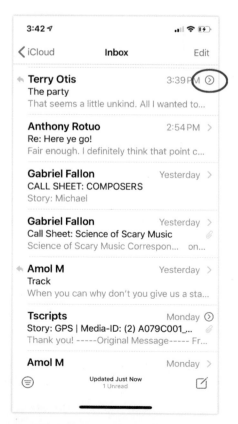
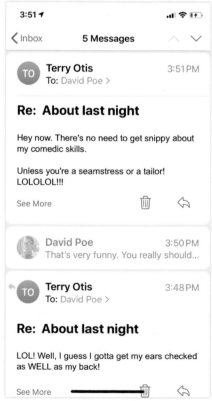

Each message bears a gray > at the right side. That means "Tap this message's row to read it in all its formatted glory."

Here and there, though, you may spot a circled arrow at the right side of the message list, like this: ⊘. That means you're looking at some *threaded* messages.

That's where several related messages—back-and-forths on the same subject—appear only once, in a single, consolidated entry. The idea is to reduce inbox clutter and to help you remember what the heck people have been talking about.

When you tap a threaded message, you open what appears to be all the messages in this topic, scrolling and attached vertically as though they're sheets of paper towel. Messages you've already seen appear collapsed, as shown at right on the previous page, to help you keep your bearings.

In general, threading is a nice feature. But if it bugs you, you can turn it off. Open **Settings**→**Mail**, scroll down, and turn off **Organize By Thread**. (While you're there, notice the option called **Collapse Read Messages**. It's responsible for the collapsing effect just described.)

TIP: If you have an iPhone Plus or Max model, you can turn the phone 90 degrees to see a mini-tablet-like view, with the message list on the left and open message on the right, visible simultaneously.

Filters

The iPhone offers one-click filters that hide or show all messages of a certain kind in the list—like ones you haven't yet read.

See the button below the list of messages? When you tap it, you automatically turn on the first filter: Unread. All the messages in the list that you've read are hidden—until you hit ⊜ again to turn the filter off.

When the filter is on, you can click the word **Unread** to see a list of other ways to filter the list. You can tell Mail to show you only messages you've flagged; only messages to you (or that you were copied on); only the ones with attachments; only the ones from people in your VIP list, or only messages you've sent today. You can also combine filters, if you want.

VIPs and Flagged Messages

You might notice, on the Mailboxes screen, two "email accounts" you didn't set up: **VIP** and **Flagged**. They're both intended to help you round up important messages from the thousands that flood you every day.

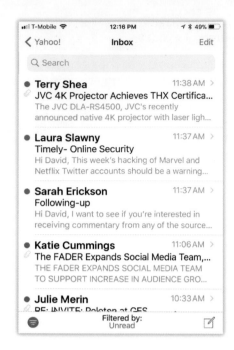
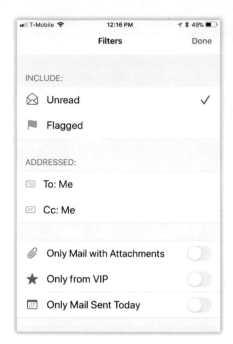

Each one magically rounds up messages from *all* your account inboxes, so you don't have to go wading through lots of accounts to find the really important mail. (Note: That's *inboxes*. Messages in other mail folders don't wind up in these special inboxes, even if they're flagged or are from VIPs.)

VIPs

In the real world, VIPs are people who get backstage passes to concerts or special treatment at business functions (it stands for "very important person"). In iOS, it means "somebody whose mail is important enough that I want it brought to my attention immediately when it arrives."

So who should your VIPs be? That's up to you. Your spouse, your boss, and your oncologist come to mind.

To designate someone as a VIP, proceed in either of these two ways:

- **On the accounts screen,** tap the ⓘ next to the VIP item. Your master list of all VIPs appears (next page, left). Tap **Add VIP** to choose a lucky new member from Contacts.

  This is also where you *delete* people from your VIP list when they've annoyed you. Swipe leftward across a name, and then tap **Delete**. Or tap **Edit** and then tap each ⊖ button; tap **Delete** to confirm.

TIP: You can set things up so that when a new message from a VIP comes in, the iPhone lets you know with a sound, a banner, an alert bubble, a vibration, and so on. Tap **VIP Alerts** to set them up. (That's a shortcut to the **Settings→Notifications→Mail→VIP** screen.)

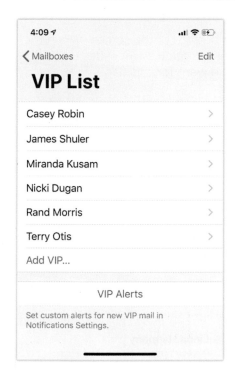

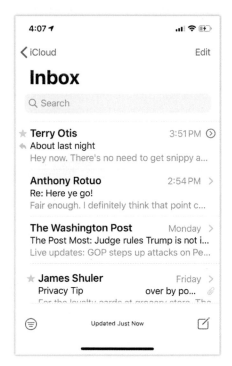

- **In a message from the lucky individual,** tap his name in the From, To, or Cc/Bcc box; tap again. His Contact screen appears; tap **Add to VIP**.

Once you've established who's important, interesting things happen:

- **The VIP inbox automatically collects** messages from your VIPs.

- **VIP names in every mail list** sprout a gold star (above, right).

- **If you use iCloud,** the same person is now a VIP on all your other iPhones and iPads (iOS 6 or later) and Macs (Mountain Lion or later).

TIP: You can hide the VIP inbox on the main Mailboxes screen—handy if you don't really use this feature. Tap **Edit,** and then . Tap **Done.**

Flag It

Sometimes you receive email that prompts you to take some sort of action, but you may not have the time (or the fortitude) to face the task at the moment. ("Hi there, it's me, your accountant. Please round up your expenses for 2007 through 2017 and sending me a list by email.")

That's why Mail lets you *flag* a message, summoning a little colored ⚑ symbol in a new column next to the message's name. Each color can mean anything you like—they simply call attention to certain messages.

To flag an open message, tap ↩ at the bottom of the screen. When the new Reply menu slides into view, the confirmation sheet slides up (below, left), tap **Flag**, and then tap the color you want for this flag.

You can also rapidly flag messages directly in a *list* (the inbox, for example). Just swipe left across the message—half an inch of finger sliding does the trick—to reveal the set of buttons shown below at right.

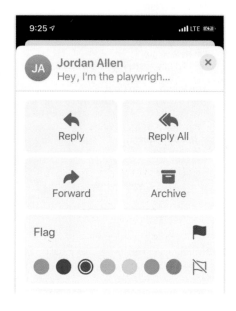
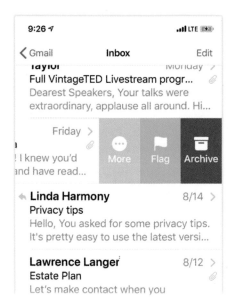

Tap **Flag**. (You get a flag of whatever color you last used. To change the color, or unflag the message, you'll have to tap ↩ at the bottom of the screen to open the full Flag panel.)

The ⚑ icon appears in the body of the message and next to the message's name in your inbox. The flag appears even on the corresponding message in your Mac or PC email program, thanks to the miracle of wireless syncing.

The Flagged mailbox appears in your list of accounts, making it easy to work with all flagged messages, from all accounts, in one place.

TIP: If you don't use this feature, you can hide the Flagged folder. Tap **Edit**, and then tap the ⊘ to turn it off. Tap **Done**.

This might be a good time to point out another, newer way to draw attention to a message: Tell Siri to "Remind me about this later." See page 470 for details.

What to Do with a Message

Once you've opened a message, you can respond to it, delete it, file it, and so on. In iOS 13, every conceivable one of these options appears in the new Reply panel shown on the facing page at left. Here's the drill.

 TIP: If you have an iPhone 6s or later, the *first* thing to learn is that you can see what's in a message without ever leaving the Inbox list—just by long-pressing it.

List View: Preview, Flag, Trash, Mark as Unread

It's easy to plow through a teeming Inbox, processing messages as you go, without ever having to open them. All you have to do is swipe or touch:

- **Full left-swipe delete.** Swipe your finger leftward *all the way* across the message to delete it. No confirmation tap required.

- **Partial left-swipe options.** If you swipe leftward only halfway, you reveal a set of three buttons on the right (shown on the facing page at right). They're: Trash or Archive (same as before, but now you have to tap again to confirm); Flag (described in the previous section); and More (opens up a raft of other options, like Reply, Forward, Flag, Mute, and so on).

- **Full right-swipe.** Swipe your finger to the *right* all the way across the message to mark it as new (unread). Great for reminding yourself to look at this message again later. Or, if it's already unread, that swipe marks it as *read*.

- **Preview.** If you long-press a message in a list, you get a sneak preview of its contents (next page, right), along with a panel of buttons for processing it (Reply, Forward, Move Message, Delete, and so on). Drag upward on the commands panel to expand it for easier access. Tap anywhere on the background to return to the message list.

  This technique is great for spot-checking a few important-looking messages in the list without committing to fully opening any email.

To a certain extent, you can *customize* these gestures. You can turn off the right-swipe gesture. Or swap the positions of the Flag and Read options, for example, so that you flag a message when you swipe fully to

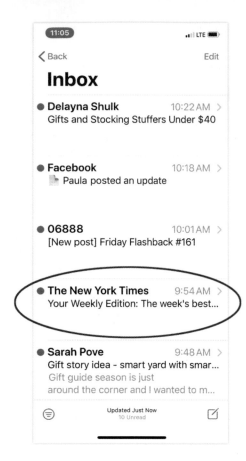

the right and **Read** appears as a button when you swipe to the left. Or you can put the **Archive** button into the place of **Flag** when you swipe to the left. **Mute** (page 540) and **Move Message** (page 538) are here, too.

To check out your options, open **Settings→Mail→Swipe Options**.

Tap **Swipe Left** to specify which button appears in the center of the three when you swipe partway leftward: **None**, **Mark as Read**, **Flag**, or **Move Message**. Tap **Swipe Right** to choose which function you want to trigger with a full rightward swipe (**None**, **Mark as Read**, **Flag**, **Move Message**, or **Archive**).

Read It

The type size in email messages can be pretty small. Fortunately, you have some great iPhone-y enlargement tricks at your disposal. For example:

- **Spread two fingers** to enlarge the entire email message.

- **Double-tap a narrow block of text** to make it fill the screen, if it doesn't already.

- **Drag or flick your finger** to scroll through or around the message.

- **Choose a larger type size for all messages.** See page 616.

Links are "live" in email messages. Tap a phone number to call it, a web address to open it, a YouTube link to watch the video, an email address to write to it, a time and date to add it to your calendar, and so on.

Reply to It

To answer a message you've opened by tapping its name in the list, tap at the bottom of the screen; in the Reply panel (page 534, left), tap Reply. If the message was originally addressed to multiple recipients, then you can choose Reply All to send your reply to everyone simultaneously.

A new message window opens, already addressed. As a courtesy to your correspondents, Mail pastes the original message at the bottom of the window.

If you'd like to splice your own comments into the paragraphs of the original message, replying point by point, then use the Return key to create blank lines in the original message.

The brackets by each line of the original message help your correspondents keep straight what's yours and what's theirs.

> **TIP:** If you select some text before you tap Reply or Reply All, then the iPhone pastes only that selected bit into the new, outgoing message. In other words, you're quoting back only a portion.

Before you tap Send, you can add or delete recipients, edit the subject line or the original message, and so on.

Forward It

Instead of replying to the sender, you may sometimes want to pass the note on to a third person. To do so, tap . This time, tap Forward.

> **TIP:** If there's a file attached to the inbound message, the iPhone says, "Include attachments from original message?" and offers Include and Don't Include buttons. Rather thoughtful, actually—the phone can forward files it can't even open.

A new message opens, looking like the one that appears when you reply. You can precede the original message with a comment of your own, like, "Frank: I thought you'd be interested in this joke about your mom." Finally, address and send it as usual.

Follow It

Your phone can notify you when anyone responds to a certain email conversation.

If you're composing or replying to a message, tap in the subject line to make the 🔔 appear; tap it. If you're *reading* a message, tap ⤺, scroll down, and tap **Notify Me**. In a list, swipe leftward, partly across a message; tap **More**; tap **Notify Me**. In each case, a 🔔 icon appears beside the message (or thread) in the list.

When anybody replies, a notification banner appears on your screen, ready for swiping and reading.

File or Delete One Message

Once you've opened a message that's worth keeping, you can file it into one of your account's folders ("mailboxes"). Tap ⤺, scroll down, and tap **Move Message**. Up pops the list of your folders; tap the one you want.

It's a snap to delete a message you no longer want, too. If it's open in front of you, tap 🗑 or 🗃 at the bottom of the screen. The message rapidly shrinks into the icon and disappears.

> **NOTE:** If that one-touch deletion method makes you a little nervous, by the way, you can ask the iPhone to display a confirmation box before trashing the message forever. Visit **Settings→Mail→Ask Before Deleting**.

You can also delete a message from the message *list*—the inbox, for example—by swiping left.

> **TIP:** Gmail doesn't want you to throw anything away. That's why swiping like this produces a button that says **Archive**, not **Delete**, and why the usual 🗑 button in a message looks like a filing box. If you prefer to delete a message for good, hold down the 🗃 until the **Trash Message** and **Archive Message** buttons appear.

There's a long way to delete messages from the list, too, as described next. But for single messages, the finger-swipe method is *much* more fun.

> **TIP:** There's a handy Undo shortcut, too: Shake the phone lightly. Tap **Undo Trash**. The deleted message jumps back to the folder it just came from. (You can then shake again to undo the Undo!)

File or Delete Batches of Messages

You can also file or delete a bunch of messages at once. In the message list, tap **Edit**. A circle appears beside each message title. You can tap as many of these circles as you like, scrolling as necessary, adding a ✓ with each touch.

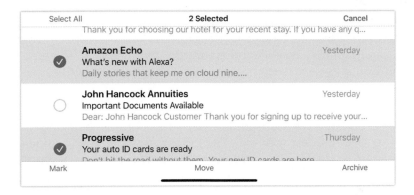

Finally, when you've selected all the messages in question, you can tap Mark (you'll be offered to **Flag**, **Mark as Unread**, or **Move to Junk**), **Move** (to a different folder), or **Trash** (or **Archive**).

If you decide you've made a mistake, just shake the phone lightly. Tap **Undo Move** to put the filed messages back where they just came from.

By the way: When you delete a message, it goes into the Trash folder. In other words, it works like the Mac Trash or the Windows Recycle Bin. You have a safety net.

NOTE: You can ask the iPhone to empty the Trash folder every day, week, or month. From the Home screen, tap **Settings→Passwords & Accounts**. Tap the account name of one of your accounts, and then tap it again on the next screen. Then choose **Advanced→ Remove**. You can change the setting from **Never** to **After one day** (or **one week**, or **one month**).

Add the Sender to Contacts

When you get a message from someone new who's worth adding to your iPhone's Contacts address book, tap that person's name (in black, at the top) to make it turn blue; tap it again. You're offered buttons for **Create New Contact** and **Add to Existing Contact**. Use the second button to add an email address to an existing person's "card."

Mute a Conversation

If the notifications for a certain back-and-forth discussion are getting on your nerves, you can, in iOS 13, silence them. Tap , scroll down, and then tap **Mute**.

Block Someone

Is that disastrous bad date not getting the message? Are you feeling harassed? The iPhone's **Block this Caller** already let you block nuisance phone calls—but now it works on email, too. Tap the person's name to view his Contacts card, and then choose **Block this Contact**.

Open an Attachment

The Mail program downloads and displays the icons for *any* kind of attachment—but it can *open* only documents from Microsoft Office (Word, Excel, PowerPoint), those from Apple iWork (Pages, Keynote, Numbers), PDFs, text, RTFs, VCFs, graphics, .zip files, and un-copy-protected audio and video files.

Just scroll down, tap the attachment's icon, wait a moment for downloading, and then marvel as the document opens up, full screen. You can zoom in and out, flick, rotate the phone 90 degrees, and scroll just as though it were a web page or a photo.

Save or Share an Attachment

If you long-press the attachment's name, you get something that looks something like the picture on page 536: at top, a preview of the attachment; beneath, a list of ways you can process this attachment.

For a picture or PDF file, for example, you might get **Save Image**, **Markup and Reply**, **Copy**, or **Share** to someone else (by AirDrop, Messages, or Mail).

> **TIP:** For a graphic, tapping **Share** at this point produces the standard Save sheet, filled with lesserly useful options like **Print**, **Create Watch Face** (for Apple Watches), and **Assign to Contact** (as a person's face photo). All the usual sending methods are represented here, too, so you can fire off this photo via AirDrop, Messages, Mail, Twitter, and Facebook.

If you tap a Word document, you may be offered buttons for **Mail**, **Dropbox**, **Evernote**, and other apps that can open Word docs. (**Quick Look** means the same non-editable preview as you'd get with a quick tap.)

Tap the background to return to the original email message.

Snag a Contact or a Date

Mail can recognize contact information or calendar information from an incoming email message—and can dump it directly into Contacts or Calendar for you.

You'll know when it's found something—the block of contact information below somebody's signature, for example—because you see a special gray banner at the top of the screen (below, left).

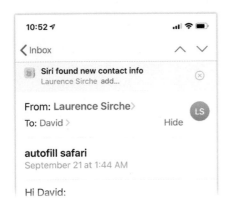 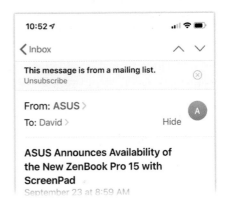

If it's somebody worth tracking, tap **add...**. A new Contacts screen appears, ready to save.

Similarly, if the message contains a reference to a date and time, the same sort of banner appears, offering to pop the appointment onto your calendar. (This banner appears only when it's *really sure* you're being offered a date and time: e-invitations and airline-ticket confirmations, for example.)

iOS: saving you time since 2016.

Unsubscribe

Every now and then, when you open a piece of junk mail, Mail offers you an **Unsubscribe** button at the top (above, right). And sure enough: Tapping it (and then tapping **Unsubscribe** to confirm) gets you off that mailing list.

Now, before you uncork the champagne, keep in mind that this button appears only on some pieces of spam—from only the kind-hearted, legitimate senders who include an **Unsubscribe** link at the bottom of their messages. All Mail does is automate that process (and move the **Unsubscribe** button to the top).

View the To/From Details

When your computer's screen is only a few inches tall, there's not a lot of extra space. So Apple designed Mail to conceal header details (To, From, and so on) that you might need only occasionally. And if there's a long list of addresses, you may see only "Michael & 15 more"—not the actual list of names.

To see all that hidden stuff—the complete list of addressees, for example, or the full set of Cc, Bcc, and From lines—just tap the abbreviated header to make it expand.

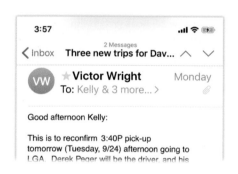 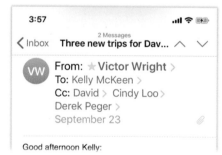

Mark as Unread

In the inbox, any message you haven't yet read is marked by a blue dot (●). Once you've opened the message, the blue dot goes away.

If you slide your finger to the right across a message in the list, you trigger the Unread command—you make that blue dot *reappear*. It's a great way to flag a message for later, to call it to your own attention. The blue dot can mean not so much "unread" as "un-dealt with."

Move On

Once you've had a good look at a message and processed it to your satisfaction, you can move on to the next (or previous) message in the list by tapping ⌄ or ⌃ in the upper-right corner. Or you can swipe rightward to return to the inbox (or whatever mailbox you're in).

Search

Praise be—there's a search box in Mail. The search box is hiding *above* the top of every mail list, like your inbox. To see it, swipe down or just tap the status strip at the top of the screen.

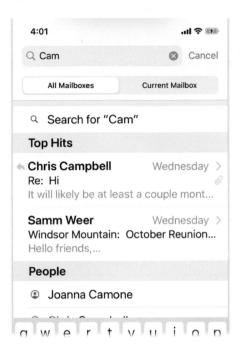

Tap inside the search box to make the keyboard appear, along with helpful canned searches like **Flagged Messages** and **Messages with Attachments**. As you type, Mail hides all but the matching messages; tap any one of the results to open it.

You don't have to specify *which fields* to search (From, To, Subject, Body), or which folder. You're searching everywhere.

> **TIP:** If you *want* to restrict the search to just the folder you're in, you can. After the search results begin to appear, two new buttons appear: **All Mailboxes** and **Current Mailbox**.

Wait long enough, and the search continues with messages that are still out there on the internet but are so old that they've scrolled off your phone.

> **TIP:** If, after typing a few letters, you tap **Search**, the keyboard goes away and an **Edit** button appears. Tapping it lets you select a whole bunch of the search results—and then **Mark**, **Move**, or **Trash** them simultaneously.

Writing Messages

To compose a new piece of outgoing mail, open the Mail app, and then tap 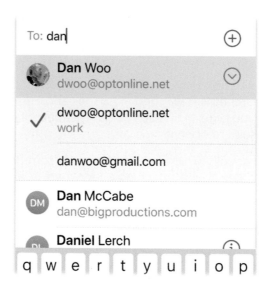 in the lower-right corner. A blank, new outgoing message appears, and the iPhone keyboard pops up.

Here's how you go about writing a message:

1. **In the To field, type the recipient's email address—or grab it from Contacts.**

   Often, you won't have to type much more than the first couple of letters of the name *or* email address. As you type, Mail displays all matching names and addresses so you can tap one instead of typing. (It thoughtfully derives these suggestions by analyzing both your Contacts *and* people you've recently exchanged email with.)

> **TIP:** The ones bearing (i) buttons are the people you've recently corresponded with but who are not in your Contacts. Tap the (i) to open a screen where you can add them to Contacts—or *remove* them from the list of recent correspondents, so Mail's autocomplete suggestions will no longer include those lowlifes.

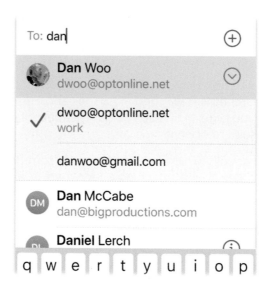

When you address an email message, Mail even suggests *clusters* of people you tend to email together—"Erin and Sam," "Erin and Andy," and so on—to save you the trouble of reassembling these teams.

Similarly, if you type a subject you've used before, Mail suggests the names of people who've received this subject line. (For example, if you send "This month's traffic stats" every month to three co-workers, then their names appear automatically when you type out that subject line.) You'll get to go home from work that much quicker.

Finally—new in iOS 13—when you've started addressing a message, you can tap the ⓘ beside someone's name to see all their email addresses. Tap the one you really want.

If you long-press the period (.) key, you get a pop-up palette of email-address suffixes, like .com, .edu, .org, and so on, just as in Safari.

Alternatively, tap ⊕ to open your Contacts list. Tap the name of the person you want. You can add as many addressees as you like; just repeat the procedure.

> **TIP:** You can address an email to an existing Group, so you can send one message to a predefined set of friends—but there's no way to *create* groups on the phone. Fortunately, you can create address groups at *icloud.com*. Tap **Contacts**, and then + (lower left), and then **New Group**.

2. **To send a copy to other recipients, enter the address(es) in the Cc or Bcc fields.**

   If you tap **Cc/Bcc, From**, the screen expands to reveal two new lines beneath the To line: Cc and Bcc.

   Cc stands for *carbon copy*. An email message where your name is in the Cc line implies: "I sent you a copy because I thought you'd want to know about this correspondence, but I'm not expecting you to reply."

   Bcc stands for *blind carbon copy*. It's a copy that goes to a third party secretly—the primary addressee never knows who else you sent it to. For example, if you send your co-worker a message that says, "Chris, it bothers me that you've been cheating the customers," you could Bcc your supervisor without getting into trouble with Chris.

   Each of these lines behaves exactly like the To line. You fill each one up with email addresses in the same way.

> **TIP:** You can drag people's names around—from the To line to the Cc line, for example. Just hold your finger down briefly on the name before dragging it. (It puffs and darkens once it's ready for transit.)

3. **Change the email account you're using, if you like.** If you have more than one email account set up, you can tap **Cc/Bcc, From** to expand the form and then tap **From** to open up a spinning list of your accounts. Tap the one you want to use for sending this message.

4. **Type the topic of the message in the subject field.**

Leaving it blank only annoys your recipient.

5. **Type your message in the message box.**

All the usual iPhone keyboard and dictation tricks apply (Chapter 3). Don't forget that you can use Copy and Paste. Both text and graphics can appear in your message.

And here's a fantastic trick: As you're composing a message, you can refer to *another* email—maybe the one you're responding to—without losing your place.

To do that, drag downward on the title bar, where it says **New Message** or whatever the reply's title is; your message in progress collapses to the bottom of the screen. Now you can scroll through the message behind it—or you can navigate to *any* message in any Mail account or folder. This is great when, for example, you want to copy some text out of an earlier message.

Swipe down to reveal what's behind your reply.

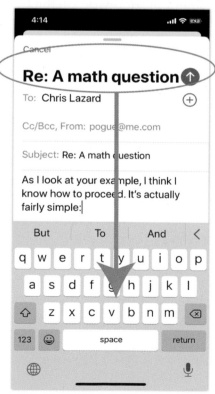

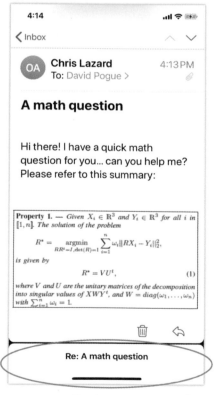

Tap to reopen your reply.

When you're ready to resume writing, tap the title bar at the bottom of the screen; your composition window opens right back up.

6. **Format the text, if you like.**

    In iOS 13, you can dress up your email with every bit as much over-the-top flexibility as you can on your Mac or PC. We're talking fonts, styles, sizes, paragraph indenting and justification...and you can insert a drawing or photo, take a picture, scan a document, or attach a file. Just tap ⟨ at the right end of the QuickType suggestions bar (or select some text) to see your options. Read on for all the details.

7. **Attach a photo, video, scan, or drawing, if you like.**

8. **Tap Send (to send the message) or Cancel (to back out of it).**

    If you tap **Cancel**, the iPhone asks if you want to save the message. If you tap **Save Draft**, then the message lands in your Drafts folder.

    Later you can open the **Drafts** folder, tap the aborted message, finish it up, and send it.

> **TIP:** If you *long-press* the ✍ button, the iPhone presents a list of your saved drafts. Clever stuff—if you remember it!

Oh, and by the way: You can begin composing a message on your phone, and then continue writing it on your Mac, without ever having to save it as a draft. Or go the other way. See page 595 for details on Handoff.

Signatures

A *signature* is a bit of text that gets stamped at the bottom of your outgoing messages. It can be your name, a postal address, or a pithy quote.

Unless you intervene, the iPhone stamps "Sent from my iPhone" at the bottom of every message. You may be just fine with that, or you may consider it the equivalent of free advertising for Apple—or it may just feel like gloating. In any case, you can change the signature if you want to.

From the Home screen, tap **Settings→Mail→Signature**. You can make up one signature for **All Accounts**, or a different one for each account (tap **Per Account**). A Signature text area appears, complete with a keyboard, so you can compose the signature you want. It can even include emoji!

> **TIP:** You can use bold, italic, or underline formatting in your signature, too. Just follow the steps on the previous page for formatting a message: Select the text, tap the ▶ to bring the **B**_I_U button into view, and so on.

Finish with a Phone Call

If you're typing out some reply, and you realize it'd be faster to wrap this up by phone, hold down the home button or side button to trigger Siri and just say, "Call him" or "Call her."

If the addressee has a phone number in Contacts, Siri knows who you mean; she dials the number for you, right from the Mail app!

The New Formatting Bar

In iOS 13, you have "desktop-class" freedom to decorate your outgoing email with fonts, styles, formatting, attachments, and photos.

It all lives in the new formatting bar, which appears when you tap the ‹ at the right end of the QuickType suggestions bar—or whenever you've selected some text.

The formatting bar is shown on the facing page at left. Here's what its buttons do, from left to right:

Text Formatting (Aa)

This first button opens up a veritable Microsoft Word of formatting buttons (facing page, bottom left) including these:

- **Typographic styles.** The first row offers buttons for **Bold**, *Italic*, Underline, and ~~Strikethrough~~ styles.

- **Fonts.** The second row lets you change the font, size, and color (facing page, middle) of the text.

- **Paragraph styles.** Third row: Buttons that automatically turn selected paragraphs into numbered or bulleted lists, and buttons that control the justification of the selected paragraphs (left-justified, centered, or right-justified).

- **Quoting and indentation.** Last row: Buttons that quote or unquote the selected text.

  The second button, for example, indents the text and adds a colored vertical stripe beside it, indicating that it's a quote from a previous email, for example.

  The pair of buttons at lower right adjust the indentation of the selected paragraph(s): outdent or indent.

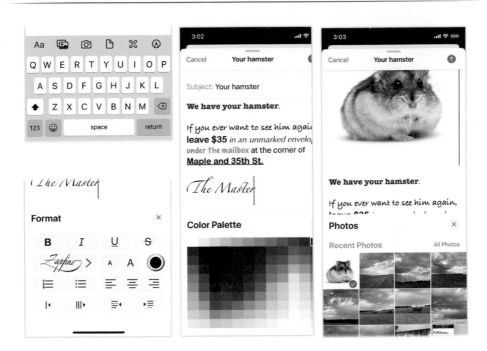

Insert (or Take) Photos or Videos

The 🖼 button on the new formatting bar reveals your 96 most recent photos and videos (above, right). (Drag up to make the panel bigger.) Tap to insert a photo into your email. Tap another, and another, until you're photographically satisfied; tap ✕ to close the panel.

Alternatively, tap 📷 to take a new picture or video; tap **Use Photo** to insert it.

Later, when you tap **Send**, you're offered the opportunity to scale down the photo to a more reasonable (emailable) size.

Attach a File (⧉)

The next button opens your Files browser (page 422), so you can hunt down, for example, a Word or PDF document to attach.

Scan a Document (⧉)

Lawyers, rejoice! The next button opens iOS's "scan a document" mode, as described on page 455. The idea is that you can use your phone to capture (and auto-straighten) a document that's before you in the real world.

Make a Drawing (Ⓐ)

The last button lets you create a freehand drawing (or maybe the term is free*finger*). It opens a blank canvas and the standard set of drawing tools (page 458). The ⊕ button even lets you add text; drop in your signature; magnify a spot; or add arrows, squares, ovals, or speech bubbles.

The same editing bar offers buttons for **Add Document**, **Scan Document**, and **Insert Drawing**. The latter opens the standard Markup tools, as described on page 458.

PART FOUR

Connections

Syncing with Computers

15

I n the olden days, you needed a Mac or PC to load an iPhone with music, videos, apps, calendar data, and contacts info. Nowadays, all that stuff is wireless. It's perfectly possible to use an iPhone without even owning a computer.

There are still at least two reasons to sync the phone with a Mac or PC, though, and both involve saving money.

First, syncing is a great way to get music files onto your phone if you don't want to pay for Apple's $10-a-month Apple Music service. Second, syncing is a free way to back up everything on your phone. (You can back up the phone to iCloud, but that costs money, and furthermore, the data is no longer within your sole control.)

The Death of iTunes

On Windows PCs and Macs running macOS versions that came along before 2019, you can use Apple's iTunes program on your Mac or PC to load up your phone with music, movies, TV shows, podcasts, and audiobooks.

But in macOS 10.15 Catalina, iTunes no longer exists. Apple broke it into three separate apps, called Music, Podcasts, and TV. None of them syncs with an iPhone.

Instead, when you connect an iPhone to your Mac with a cable, its icon and contents show up right at the desktop, in every Finder window.

NOTE: If your iPhone's icon doesn't seem to show up in the left-side Sidebar, confirm that the Sidebar heading Locations is expanded (click the **Show** button, if it's present). Also open **Finder→Preferences→General**; turn on **External disks** and **CDs, DVDs, and iPods**.

As you can see here, the iPhone window in Catalina (bottom) looks almost identical to iTunes (top). The biggest difference is that the tabs (**Music**, **Movies**, **TV Shows**, and so on) appear across the top instead of down the left side.

This chapter covers both setups.

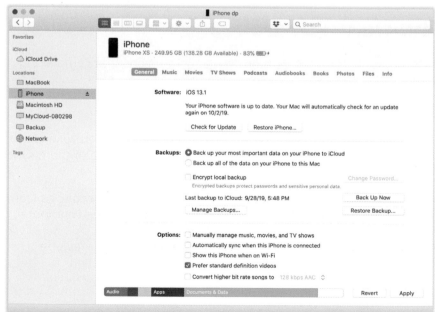

Connecting the iPhone

You can connect the phone to your computer either wirelessly (over Wi-Fi) or wirefully (with the white USB cable that came with the iPhone).

- **Connecting the phone with a cable.** Plug one end of the iPhone's white charging cable into your computer's USB jack. Connect the other end to the phone.

> **NOTE:** Recent Apple laptops don't have any standard USB jacks—only newfangled USB-C jacks. To connect your phone, then, you'll need either a USB-C adapter or a USB-C–to–Lightning cable.

- **Connecting over Wi-Fi.** The iPhone can be charging on your bedside table, happily and automatically syncing with your laptop somewhere else in the house. It transfers all the same stuff to and from your computer—apps, music, books, contacts, calendars, movies, photos, ringtones—but through the air instead of a cable.

  Your computer has to be on and running iTunes (unless, of course, you're on macOS Catalina). The phone and the computer have to be on the same Wi-Fi network.

  To set up wireless sync, connect the phone using the white USB cable, one last time. Ironic, but true.

  Open iTunes and click the ☐ (iPhone) button near the top-left corner of the iTunes screen, or in Catalina's Finder window. Now you can look over the iPhone's contents or sync it (read on).

> **NOTE:** If you have more than one iPhone, and they're all connected, then this button is a pop-up menu. Choose the name of the one you want to manipulate.

On the Summary tab, scroll down; turn on **Sync with this iPhone over Wi-Fi** (or, in macOS Catalina, **Show this iPhone when on Wi-Fi**). Click **Apply**. You can now detach the phone.

From now on, whenever the phone is on the Wi-Fi network and plugged into power, it's automatically connected to your computer, wirelessly. You don't even have to think about it. (Well, OK—you have to think about leaving the computer turned on with iTunes open, which is something of a buzzkill.)

All About Syncing

Truth is, most people these days don't bother with iTunes for syncing; they let the phone sync with their computer wirelessly, via iCloud.

If you're a little queasy about letting a third party (Apple) store your personal data, though, you can let the iPhone and computer sync directly—no internet involved.

Ordinarily, the iPhone–iTunes relationship is automatic. All of these things happen when you sync:

- **Bidirectional copying (iPhone ↔ computer).** Contacts, calendars, and web bookmarks get copied in both directions. After a sync, your computer and phone contain exactly the same information.

  Music, TV, movies, ringtones, and ebooks flow automatically from the computer to the iPhone—but if you've bought that stuff on the phone, you're offered a Transfer button to bring it over to the computer.

- **One-way sync (computer→iPhone).** Photos from your computer, and email account information.

- **One-way sync (iPhone→computer).** Photos and videos taken with the iPhone's camera; music, videos, apps, ringtones, and ebooks you bought right from the phone—it all gets copied the other way, from the phone to the computer.

- **A complete backup.** iTunes/Catalina also backs up *everything else* on your iPhone: settings, text messages, call history, and so on. See page 564.

Manual Syncing

OK, but what if you don't *want* iTunes to start syncing every time you connect your iPhone? What if, for example, you want to change the assortment of music and video that gets copied to it? Or what if you just want to connect the USB cable to *charge* the phone, not to sync it?

You can stop the autosyncing in any of these ways:

- **Interrupt a sync in progress.** Click ⊗ in the iTunes status window or (in macOS Catalina) next to the iPhone's name.

- **Stop syncing with the iPhone just this time (iTunes only).** As you plug in the iPhone's cable, hold down the Shift+Ctrl keys (Windows) or the Option-⌘ keys (Mac) until the iPhone pops up in the iTunes window. Now you can see what's on the iPhone and change what will be synced to it—but no syncing takes place until you command it.

- **Stop autosyncing with this iPhone.** Connect the iPhone. Click ☐ in the upper-left corner of iTunes, or in the Sidebar of a Catalina Finder window. On the **Summary** or **General** tab, turn off **Automatically sync when this iPhone is connected**.

- **Stop autosyncing any iPhone, ever (iTunes only).** In iTunes, choose **Edit→Preferences** (Windows) or **iTunes→Preferences** (Mac). Click the **Devices** tab and turn on **Prevent iPods, iPhones, and iPads from syncing automatically**. You can still trigger a sync on command when the iPhone is wired up—by clicking the **Sync** button.

In any case, here are the two ways you can sync manually:

- **Use the tabs.** With the iPhone connected, you can specify exactly what you want copied to it—which songs, which TV shows, and so on—using the various tabs in iTunes/Catalina, as described on the following pages. Once you've made your selections, click **Apply** or **Sync**. (In iTunes, that button is on the Summary tab.)

- **Drag files onto the iPhone icon.** Once your iPhone is connected to your computer, you can click its icon and then turn on **Manually manage music and videos** (on the Summary or General screen). Click **Apply**.

  Now you can drag songs and videos directly onto the iPhone's icon (or the appropriate tab, in Catalina) to copy them there. Wilder yet, you can bypass iTunes *entirely* by dragging music and video files *from your computer's desktop* onto the iPhone's icon.

  Just two notes of warning here. First, the iPhone accommodates dragged material from a *single* computer only. Second, if you ever turn this option off, then all those manually dragged songs and videos will disappear from your iPhone at the next sync.

TIP: On the iTunes Summary tab, you'll find the baffling little option called **Sync only checked songs and videos**. This is a global override—a last-ditch "Keep the embarrassing songs off my iPhone" option.

When this option is turned on, iTunes consults the tiny checkboxes next to every single song and video in your iTunes library. If you turn off a song's checkbox, it won't get synced to your iPhone, no matter what—even if you use the Music tab to sync **All songs or playlists**, or explicitly turn on a playlist that contains this song. If the song's or video's checkbox isn't checked in your Library list, then it will be left behind on your computer.

The Tabs

Once your iPhone is connected to the computer, and you've clicked its icon in the upper-left corner of iTunes (or the Sidebar in Catalina), then the left side of the iTunes window reveals a column of word buttons (page 554, top): **Summary (General)**, **Music**, **Movies**, **TV Shows**, **Podcasts**, **Books**, **Photos**, **Files**, and **Info**. In iTunes, below all that is a second, duplicate listing, labeled **On My Device**. For the most part, these represent the categories of stuff you can sync to your iPhone.

In Catalina, these tabs go across the top of the window instead of down the side. And there's an **Audiobooks** tab as well.

The following pages cover each of these tabs, in sequence, and detail how to sync each kind of iPhone-friendly material.

> **TIP:** At the bottom of the screen, a colorful graph shows you the number and types of files: Audio, Video, Photos, Apps, Books, Documents & Data, and Other (for your personal data). More importantly, it also shows you how much room you have left, so you won't get overzealous in trying to load the thing up.
>
> Point to each color block without clicking to see how much space they take up.

Summary (General) Tab

This screen gives basic stats on your iPhone, like its serial number, capacity, and phone number. Buttons in the middle control how and where the iPhone gets backed up. Checkboxes at the bottom of the screen let you set up manual syncing, as described previously.

Serial Number, UDID

If you click your phone's serial number, it changes to reveal the *unique device identifier* (UDID). That's Apple's behind-the-scenes ID for your exact product, used primarily by software companies (developers). You may, during times of beta testing a new app or troubleshooting an existing one, be asked to supply your phone's UDID.

You can click the same label again to see your phone's Product Type and *ECID* (exclusive chip ID). Or click your phone number to see your various cellular identifiers, like the MEID, IMEI, and ICCID. Or click the iOS version to see your iOS version's build number.

In Catalina, click the line beneath your iPhone's name repeatedly to see all of these gruesome details.

Right-click (on the Mac, Control-click) any of these numbers to get the Copy command. It copies those long strings of letters and numbers onto your computer's Clipboard, ready to paste into an email or a text.

Music Tab

Turn on Sync Music. Now decide *what* music to put on your phone.

> **NOTE:** If you're using iCloud Music Library (page 263), this Music tab is empty except for a note that you can play all your music wirelessly from the internet. Since all your music is online, there's no point in choosing some subset of it to sync to your phone.

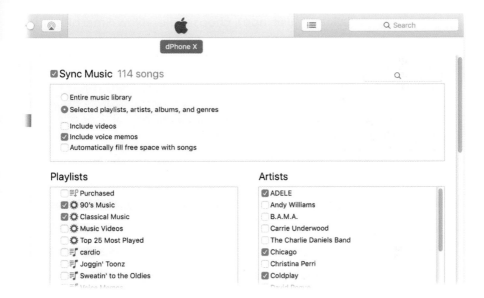

- **If you have a big iPhone** and a small music collection, you can opt to sync the Entire music library.

- **If you have a big music collection** and a small iPhone, you'll have to take only *some* of it along for the iPhone ride. In that case, click Selected playlists, artists, albums, and genres. In the lists below, turn on the checkboxes for the playlists, artists, albums, and music genres you want to transfer. (These are cumulative. If there's no Electric Light Orchestra in any of your selected playlists, but you turn on ELO in the Artists list, you'll get all your ELO anyway.)

Music videos and voice memos (recorded by the iPhone and now residing on your computer) get their own checkboxes.

Making It All Fit

An iPhone holds a finite amount of music and video. If you turn on **Sync All** checkboxes, a message may say that it won't all fit on the iPhone. One solution: Tiptoe through the tabs, turning off checkboxes and trying to sync until the "too much" error message goes away.

If you don't have quite so much time, turn on **Automatically fill free space with songs**. It uses artificial intelligence to load up your phone automatically, using your most played and most recent music as a guide. (It does not, in fact, fill the phone completely; it leaves a few hundred megabytes for safety—so you can download more stuff on the road, for example.)

Another approach is to use the *smart playlist*, a playlist that assembles itself based on criteria you supply. Once you're on the Music tab, do this:

1. **In iTunes (or Catalina's Music app), choose File→New Smart Playlist.**

   The Smart Playlist dialog box appears.

2. **Specify the category.**

   Use the pop-up menus to choose, for example, a musical genre, songs you've played recently, songs you *haven't* played recently, or ones you've rated highly.

3. **Turn on the "Limit to" checkbox, and set up the constraints.**

   You could limit the amount of music in this playlist to 2 gigabytes, chosen at random. That way, every time you sync, you'll get a fresh, random supply of songs on your iPhone.

4. **Click OK.**

   The new smart playlist appears in the list of playlists at left; you can rename it. Click it to look it over, if you like. Then, on the Music tab, choose this playlist for syncing to the iPhone.

Movies and TV Shows Tabs

TV shows and movies you've bought or rented from the iTunes Store look great on the iPhone. (And if you start watching a movie on your computer, the iPhone can begin playing it from right where you left off.)

Syncing TV shows and movies works just like syncing music or podcasts. Once again, you can turn on the checkboxes of just the individual movies or shows (either seasons or episodes) you want—or, using the **Automatically include** pop-up menu, request only the most recent, or the most recent ones you haven't seen yet.

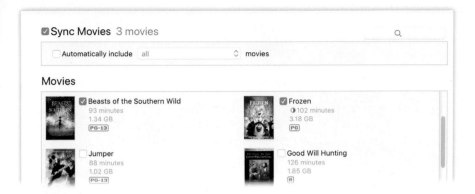

Podcasts Tab

The iTunes Store lists thousands of free amateur and professional podcasts (page 465). On this tab, you can choose to sync all episodes, selected shows, all unplayed episodes—or just a certain number of episodes per sync. This tab also includes your iTunes U recordings (educational seminars that used to get their own tab).

Books, Audiobooks Tabs

Here are thumbnails of your audiobooks and your ebooks—those you've bought from Apple, downloaded from the web, or dragged into iTunes from your desktop (PDF files, for example). You can ask iTunes to send them all to your phone—or only the ones whose checkboxes you turn on.

Photos Tab

If you've turned on iCloud Photos (page 354), this tab appears blank, except for a note that "iCloud Photos is On." After all, your photos are *already* syncing. If not...read on.

Syncing Photos and Videos (Computer→iPhone)

iTunes and Catalina can sync the photos from your hard drive onto your iPhone. You can even select individual albums of images that you've already assembled on your computer.

Here are your photo-filling options for the iPhone:

- **Windows:** You can sync with Photoshop Elements, Photoshop Album, or any folder of photos, like Pictures.

- **Mac:** You can sync with Photos, iPhoto, or Aperture.

When you're ready to sync your photos, click the **Photos** tab in iTunes/Catalina. Turn on **Sync photos from**, and then indicate *where* you'd like to sync them from (Photoshop Elements, the Mac's program Photos, or whatever).

If you've chosen a photo-shoebox program's name (and not a folder's name), you can then click **Selected Albums, Events, and Faces**. Turn on the checkboxes of the albums, events, and faces you want synced. (The "faces" option is available only if you're syncing from Photos or Aperture on the Mac, and only if you've used the Faces feature, which groups your photos according to who's in them.)

This option also offers to tack on recent Events (photos taken the same day). Indicate whether or not you want videos included (**Include videos**).

Once you make your selections and click **Apply**, the program computes for a time, "optimizing" copies of your photos to make them look great on the iPhone (for example, downsizing them from 20-megapixel over-kill to something more appropriate for a 0.6-megapixel screen), and then ports them over.

After the sync is complete, you'll be able to wave your iPhone around, and people will *beg* to see your photos.

Syncing Photos and Videos (iPhone→Computer)

You can go the opposite direction, too: You can send photos and videos you took with the iPhone's camera *to* the computer.

In this case, *iTunes is not involved* in this process. It doesn't know anything about photos or videos *from* the iPhone.

So what's handling the iPhone-to-computer transfer? Your operating system. It treats the iPhone as though it's a digital camera and suggests importing your photos just as it would from a camera's memory card.

Here's how it goes: Plug the iPhone into the computer with the USB cable. What you'll see is probably something like this:

- **On the Mac.** Photos (the Mac version) opens and goes into Import mode. Click **Import All**, or select some thumbnails from the iPhone and then click **Import Selected**.

- **In Windows.** When you attach a camera (or an iPhone), a dialog box asks how you want its contents handled. It lists any photo-management program you might have installed (Photoshop Elements, Photoshop Album, and so on), as well as Windows' own camera-management software. Click the program you want to handle importing the iPhone pictures and videos.

You'll probably also want to turn on **Always do this for this device**, so it'll happen automatically the next time.

Info Tab

This tab is unnecessary if you're using iCloud (Chapter 16) to sync your phone's contacts, calendar, email settings, and web bookmarks with your computer. Instead, this tab is exclusively for the six people who still use iTunes to sync these data types with a Windows program like Outlook, Outlook Express, or Windows Mail; a Mac program like Contacts or Entourage/Outlook for Mac; or an online address book like Google Contacts or Yahoo Address Book.

Similarly, you can sync the phone's calendar with a program like Outlook (for Windows) or Calendar or Outlook (on the Mac).

File Sharing (Files) Tab

A few iPhone apps create documents you can open in similar apps on your computer—and vice versa. You can edit the same iMovie videos on both the Mac and the iPhone, for example. Similarly, scanning apps can share their scanned image files.

This tab lists all iOS apps that can share their documents, and lets you copy them to or from your computer.

> **NOTE:** Actually, though, using the Files app—and a virtual disk like iCloud Drive or Dropbox—is a far simpler, more useful way to move these files back and forth. Why? Because you don't *have* to move them back and forth. They're always available, in their latest versions, to all your machines. See page 421.

If you still decide to use this clunky method, here's how it goes:

- **From phone to computer.** Click the app's name to see the files that belong to it. Drag the files you want out of the iTunes window onto your desktop.

- **From computer to phone.** Click the app's name. Drag the files you want out of a desktop window into the rightmost iTunes column. (Or click **Add** and choose the files manually.)

Next time you sync, those files will move the way you've specified.

On My Device (iTunes)

At the left side of the iTunes window, there's a second, similar set labeled On My Device. It's a tidy list of everything that is, in fact, on your device, organized by type (Music, Movies, and so on). There's not really much you can *do* here—you can get more information about some items by pointing to them—but just seeing your multimedia empire arrayed before you can be very satisfying.

The Purchased category, in particular, can be handy; it shows everything on your phone that you've bought *with* the phone.

Backing Up the iPhone

Your computer can back up everything it doesn't already have a copy of: stuff you downloaded straight to the phone (music, ebooks, apps, and so on), plus less visible things, like your iPhone's mail and network settings, call history, contact favorites, notes, text messages, and so on.

> **TIP:** If you turn on Encrypt iPhone Backup or (in Catalina) Encrypt Local Backup, you'll be asked to make up a password for the backup itself. Don't forget it! The beauty of an encrypted backup is that it includes all your *passwords*: for Wi-Fi hotspots, websites, email accounts, and so on. That can save you tons of time when you have to restore the phone from the backup.

On the Summary (General) tab, specify where you want the backup stored:

- **On your computer.** On the Summary tab of iTunes, choose This Computer. In Catalina, on the General tab, choose Back up all of the data on your iPhone to this Mac.

- **In iCloud.** You can instead back up your phone wirelessly and automatically—to iCloud. That kind of backup will be available even if your computer croaks. On the other hand, since your free iCloud storage holds only 5 gigabytes, and your phone holds 16 gigabytes or more, the free iCloud account usually isn't enough. See the next chapter for details.

  To make this choice in iTunes, choose iCloud (on the Summary tab); in Catalina, on the General tab, choose Back up your most important data to iCloud.

Using That Backup

Maybe you lost your phone, or maybe you've upgraded to a new phone.

To restore your data and settings, connect the iPhone to the computer you normally use to sync with. Click the ▯ (iPhone) icon; click the **Summary** or **General** tab; click **Restore iPhone**.

A message announces that you can't erase the phone without first turning off Find My iPhone. This is a security measure to stop a thief from erasing a stolen phone, which requires your iCloud password. Go to the phone to do that (in **Settings→[your name]→iCloud**).

Let iTunes/Catalina restore all your settings and stuff from the backup.

If you see multiple backup files listed from other iPhones (or an iPod Touch), be sure to pick the backup file for *your* phone.

> **NOTE:** An iPhone backup doesn't include your apps. Instead, the backup remembers *which* apps you had, and where their icons were on your Home screens—but the actual multi-gigabyte wad of the apps themselves is not part of the backup. That trick saves a lot of time and space on your computer.
>
> It does mean, though, that after a restore, you see only dimmed copies of your apps. It takes some time in a Wi-Fi hotspot for iOS to re-download them all. Little pie charts on the icons let you know how it's doing.

Deleting a Backup File

To save disk space, you can delete old backups (especially for i-gadgets you no longer own). In iTunes, choose **Edit→Preferences** (Windows) or **iTunes→Preferences** on the Mac) and click the **Devices** tab.

Click the dated backup file you don't want and hit **Delete Backup**.

16

iCloud &
Apple Pay

The free iCloud service stems from Apple's brainstorm that, since it controls both ends of the connection between a Mac and the Apple website, it should be able to create some pretty clever internet-based features.

This chapter concerns what iCloud can do for you, the iPhone owner.

NOTE: To get a free iCloud account if you don't already have one, sign up in **Settings→iCloud**.

What iCloud Giveth

So what is iCloud? It's the suite of services available to anyone who signs up for a free Apple account. Mainly, it's these things:

- **iCloud Sync** keeps your calendar, address book, reminders, notes, messages, passwords, web bookmarks, credit card numbers, and documents updated and identical on all your gadgets: Mac, PC, iPhone, iPad, iPod Touch. Also your settings and preferences: for AirPods (wireless earbuds), News, Stocks, Home, Books, Health, Wallet, Siri, and so on. It's a huge convenience—almost magical.

- **Find My iPhone.** Find My iPhone pinpoints the current location of your iPhone (or iPad, or Mac, or AirPods) on a map. It's great for helping you find your gadgets if they've been stolen or lost.

  You can also make a lost device make a loud pinging sound for a couple of minutes by remote control—even if it was silenced. That's a blessing when your phone has slipped between the couch cushions.

- **Automatic backup.** iCloud can back up your iPhone—automatically and wirelessly (over Wi-Fi, not over cellular connections). It's a quick backup, since iCloud backs up only the changed data.

If you ever want to set up a new i-gadget, or if you want to restore everything to an existing one, life is sweet. Once you're in a Wi-Fi hotspot, all you have to do is re-enter your Apple ID and password in the setup assistant that appears when you turn the thing on. Magically, your gadget is refilled with everything that used to be on it.

Well, *almost* everything. An iCloud backup stores everything you've bought from Apple (music, books); photos and videos in your Photos app; settings, including the layout of your Home screens; text messages; and ringtones. You'll have to reestablish your passwords (for hotspots, websites, and so on) and anything that came from your computer (like music/ringtones/videos from iTunes and photos from the Photos app).

> **NOTE:** A backup doesn't store—or take up space for—your apps. Instead, to make the backup faster and smaller, it stores only *references* to your apps—bookmarks, basically. See page 576 for details.

- **iCloud Drive** is Apple's version of Dropbox. It's a folder, present on every Mac, iPhone, iPad, and iPod Touch, that lists whatever you've put into it—an online "disk" that holds 5 gigabytes (more, if you pay for it).

  The iCloud Drive is a perfect place to put stuff you want to be able to access from any Apple gadget, wherever you go. It's a great backup, too.

- **An email account.** Handy, really: An iCloud account gives you a new email address, ending with *@icloud.com* or *@me.com*. If you already have an email address, great! This new one can be a backup account, one you never enter on websites so that it never gets overrun with spam. Or vice versa: Let *this* be your junk account, the address you use for online forms. Either way, it's nice to have a second account.

- **An online locker.** Anything you buy from Apple—music, TV shows, ebooks, apps—is stored online for easy access at any time. For example, whenever you buy a song or a TV show from the online iTunes Store, it appears automatically on your iPhone and computers. Your photos are stored online, too.

- **Apple Pay** is the feature that lets you pay for things just by waving your phone at them, or send money to friends and family, phone-to-phone. No wallet, no credit card needed.

- **Family Sharing** is a broad category of features intended for families (up to six people).

First, everyone can share Apple subscriptions (News+, TV+, Apple Arcade) and stuff bought from Apple's online stores (music, movies, apps, books, and so on). It's all on a single credit card, but you, the all-knowing parent, can approve each person's purchases—without having to share your account password. That's a great solution to a long-standing problem.

There's also a shared family photo album, shared Reminders list, and an auto-shared Family category on the calendar. Any family member can see the location of any other family member, and they can find one another's lost iPhones or iPads using Find My iPhone.

- **Continuity.** The Continuity features (Chapter 17) turn the iPhone into a part of the Mac. They let you make calls from your Mac as though it were a speakerphone. They let you send and receive text messages from your Mac—to any cellphone on earth. They let you AirDrop files between computer and phone, wirelessly. And more.

That was the quick overview. The rest of this chapter covers each of these iCloud-related features in greater depth, in the same order—except for Continuity, which gets its own chapter right after this one.

iCloud Sync

For many people, this is the killer app for iCloud: The iCloud website, acting as the master control center, can keep multiple Macs, Windows PCs, and iPhones/iPads/iPod Touches synchronized. That offers both a huge convenience factor—all your stuff is always on all your gadgets—and a safety/backup factor, since you have duplicates everywhere.

It works by storing the master copies of your stuff—email, notes, contacts, calendars, web bookmarks, documents, and settings—on Apple's servers online. (Or "in the cloud," as the product managers would say.)

Whenever your Macs, PCs, or i-gadgets are online—over Wi-Fi or cellular—they connect to the mother ship and update themselves. Edit an address on your iPhone, and you'll find the same change in Contacts (on your Mac) and Outlook (on your PC). Send an email reply from your PC at the office, and you'll find it in your Sent Mail folder on the Mac at home. Add a web bookmark anywhere and find it everywhere else. Edit a spreadsheet in Numbers on your iPad and find the same numbers updated on your Mac.

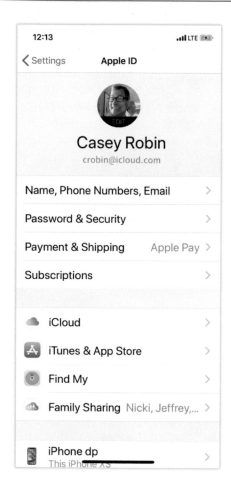

To control the syncing, tap **Settings→[your name]→iCloud** on your iPhone. Turn on the switches for the stuff you want to be synchronized all the way around:

- **Photos.** Tap to see the controls that control iCloud's photo features. They're described starting on page 354.

- **Mail.** "Mail" refers to your actual email messages, plus your account settings and preferences from iOS's Mail program.

- **Contacts, Calendars.** This option keeps all your address books and calendars synchronized. Delete a phone number on your computer at home, and you'll find it gone from your phone. Enter an appointment on your iPhone, and you'll find the calendar updated everywhere else.

- **Reminders** refers to the to-do items you create in the phone's Reminders app; those reminders magically show up on your Mac (in Reminders, Calendar, or BusyCal) or PC (in Outlook). How great to make a reminder for yourself in one place and have it reminding you later in another one!

- **Notes** syncs the notes from your phone's Notes app into the Notes app on the Mac, the email program on your PC, your other i-gadgets, and, of course, the iCloud website.

- **Messages** means everything you've texted as an iMessage. See page 204 for the pros and cons of storing them all in iCloud.

- **Safari.** If a website is important enough to merit bookmarking on your phone, why shouldn't it also show up in the Bookmarks menu on your desktop PC at home, your Mac laptop, or your iPad? This option syncs your Safari Reading List (page 512), too.

- **News** refers to the sources and topics you've set up in the News app (page 449).

- **Stocks** is your investment portfolio from the Stocks app (page 475).

- **Home** refers to the setups for any home-automation gear you've installed (page 430).

- **Health** can sync via iCloud. It includes all the fitness and medical stats.

- **Wallet.** If you've bought tickets for a movie, show, game, or flight, you sure as heck don't want to be stuck without them because you left the bar code on your other gadget.

- **Game Center.** Your gamer name, scores, and progress.

- **Siri** means iCloud will store your custom commands (page 182).

- **Keychain.** The login information for your websites (names and passwords), and even your credit card information, can be stored right on your phone—and synced to your other iPhones, iPads, and Macs (running OS X Mavericks or later).

  Having your passwords and credit cards synced across your computers and mobile gadgets saves you unending headaches. This is a truly great feature, and it's worth enduring the setup.

- **Books** stores your list of books, notes, highlighting, and "where I stopped reading" across devices.

- **Other apps' data.** If you've turned on iCloud Drive, you also see two lists of apps that would like permission to save their data onto it—so that your *apps'* data is synced across devices, too. The first list is all Apple apps (**Pages, Numbers, Keynote,** and so on); the second is other companies' apps.

Find My iPhone

Did you leave your iPhone somewhere? Did it get stolen? Has that mischievous 5-year-old left it somewhere in the house again? Sounds like you're ready to use one of Apple's finest creations: Find My iPhone.

Log into *icloud.com* and click **Find iPhone**. Immediately, the website updates to show you, on a map, the current location of your phone—and Macs, iPod Touches, iPads, and even AirPods earbuds. (If they're not online, or if they're turned all the way off, you won't see their current locations.)

TIP: Don't forget that you have a Find My *app*, too; see page 424.

If you own more than one, click **All Devices** and, from the list, choose the one you're looking for.

If just knowing where the thing *is* isn't enough to satisfy you, then click the dot representing your phone, click the ⓘ next to its name, and then marvel at the appearance of these three buttons:

- **Play Sound.** When you click this button, the phone starts dinging and vibrating loudly for two minutes, wherever it is, so you can figure out which jacket pocket you left it in. It beeps even if the ringer switch is off, and even if the phone is asleep. Once you find the phone, just wake it to make the dinging stop.

- **Lost Mode.** When you lose your phone for real, proceed immediately to Lost Mode. Its first step: prompting you to password-protect it, if you haven't already. Without the password, a sleazy crook can't get into your phone without erasing it. (If your phone is already password-protected, you don't see this step.)

  The passcode you dream up here works just as though you'd created one yourself on the phone. That is, it remains in place until you, with the phone in hand, manually turn it off in Settings.

  Next, the website asks for a phone number where you can be reached and (when you click **Next**) a message you want displayed on the iPhone's Lock screen. If you left the thing in a taxi or on some restaurant table, you can use this feature to plead for its return.

When you click **Done**, your message appears on the phone's screen, wherever it is, no matter what app was running, and the phone locks.

Whoever finds it can't miss the message, can't miss the **Call** button that's right there on the Lock screen, and can't do anything without dismissing the message first.

If the finder of your phone really isn't such a nice person, at least you'll get an automatic email every time the phone moves from place to place, so you can track the thief's whereabouts. (Apple sends these messages to your iCloud email address.)

- **Erase iPhone.** This is the last-ditch security option, for when your immediate concern isn't so much the phone as all the private stuff on it. Click this button, confirm the dire warning box, enter your Apple ID password, and click **Erase**. By remote control, you've just erased everything from your phone, wherever it may be. (If it's ever returned, you can restore it from your backup.)

Once you've wiped the phone, you can no longer find it or send messages to it using Find My iPhone.

Enable Offline Finding

This feature, new in iOS 13, is insane. It lets the Find My iPhone feature work *even if your lost phone is offline*! Incredibly, this feature turns the world's 1.4 billion *other* iPhones, iPads, and Macs into remote detectors for your lost phone.

Suppose you left your phone in an Upper Peninsula restaurant where there's no Wi-Fi and no cell service. It's lying there, asleep, at the end of the booth seat where you sat.

Fortunately, your phone is still broadcasting an ever-changing ID number by Bluetooth, silently and invisibly.

The next day, a total stranger carrying another Apple device eats in the same restaurant. Unbeknownst to her, the sleeping iPhone in her purse picks up that Bluetooth signal, relays it and its location to Apple's servers, and from there back to you. You're at home in Madison, Wisconsin, using your Mac. You use Find My iPhone on the iCloud website, and boom: You've found your iPhone!

To make all this work privately and securely, Apple had to do some astonishing engineering. How can the feature transmit the location of your lost phone without anyone else—not even Apple—finding out? How could Apple design this feature so that nobody could use it to track somebody or intercept your lost phone's location before you get it?

Answer: That anonymous, constantly changing serial number broadcast by your phone is of no value to anyone except you, because only another Apple device *owned by you* can decrypt it.

The downside of this system is that it doesn't work unless you own two Apple devices. The upside is that it keeps your lost phone's location utterly hidden from anyone in the world but you.

The on/off switch for this feature is in **Settings**→**[your name]**→**Find My**→ **Find My iPhone**.

Send Last Location

Find My iPhone works great—as long as your lost phone has power. Often, though, it's lying dead somewhere. In that situation, you might assume that Find My iPhone can't help you.

But, thanks to **Send Last Location**, you still have a prayer of finding your phone again. Before it dies, your phone will send Apple its location. You have 24 hours to log into *icloud.com* and use the Find My iPhone feature to see where it was at the time of death. (After that, Apple deletes the location information.)

You definitely want to turn this switch on.

Activation Lock

Thousands of people have found their lost or stolen iPhones using Find My iPhone. Yay!

But until recently, Find My iPhone had a back door the size of Montana: The thief could simply erase the phone and sell it on the black market, which was his goal all along. Suddenly, your phone was lost in the wilderness, and you had no way to track or recover it.

That's why Apple offers the ingenious Activation Lock feature. It's very simple: Nobody can erase your phone, or even turn off Find My iPhone, without entering your Apple ID password. This isn't a switch you can turn on or off; it's always on.

So even if the bad guy has your phone and tries to sell it, the thing is useless. It's still registered to you, you can still track it, and it still displays your message and phone number on the Lock screen. Without your iCloud password, your iPhone is just a worthless brick. Suddenly, stealing iPhones is a much less attractive prospect. (Fun fact: In New York City, reported iPhone thefts are down 90 percent since Activation Lock came along.)

iCloud Backup

Your phone can back itself up online, automatically, so that you'll never worry about losing your files along with your phone.

Of course, most of the important stuff is *already* backed up by iCloud, in the process of syncing it (calendar, contacts—all the stuff described on these pages). So this option (in **Settings→[your name]→iCloud→iCloud Backup**) just backs up everything else: all your settings, your documents, your account settings, and your photo library.

There are some footnotes. The wireless backing-up happens only when your phone is charging and in a Wi-Fi hotspot (because in a cellular area all that data would eat up your data limit each month). And a free iCloud account includes only 5 gigabytes of storage; your phone may require a lot more space than that. Using iCloud Backup generally means paying for more iCloud storage.

iCloud Drive

iCloud Drive is a single folder whose contents are replicated on every Apple machine you own—Mac, iPhone, iPad—*icloud.com*, and even Windows PCs. See page 421 for details.

Email

Apple offers an email address as part of each iCloud account. Of course, you already *have* an email account. So why bother? The first advantage is the simple address: *YourName@me.com* or *YourName@icloud.com*.

Second, you can read your me.com email from any computer anywhere in the world, via the iCloud website, or on your iPhone/Mac/iPad.

To make things even sweeter, your me.com or icloud.com mail is completely synced. Delete a message on one gadget, and you'll find it in the Deleted Mail folder on another. Send a message from your iPhone, and you'll find it in the Sent Mail folder on your Mac. And so on.

Video, Music, Apps: Locker in the Sky

Once you buy a song, movie, app, or book from Apple, you can download it again as often as you like—no charge. In fact, you can download it to your *other* Apple equipment, too. If you're using Family Sharing

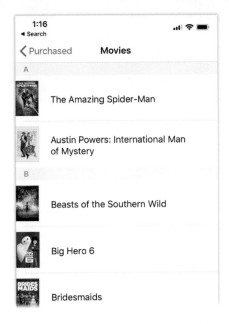
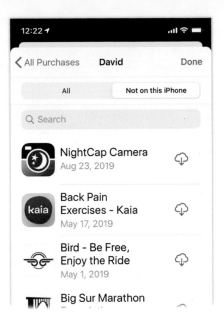

(page 586), you can even see what the other family members have bought.

iCloud automates, or at least formalizes, that process. Once you buy something, it's added to a list of items you can download to all your *other* machines. Here's how to grab them:

- **iPhone, iPad, iPod Touch.** *For apps:* Open the App Store icon. Tap your icon at top right. Tap **Purchased**→**My Purchases**→**Not on This iPhone**.

    For music, movies, and TV shows: Open the iTunes Store app. Tap **More** and then **Purchased**.

    There they are: all the items you've ever bought, even on your *other* machines using the same Apple ID. To download anything listed here onto *this* machine, tap the ☁ button. Or tap an album name to see the list of songs on it so you can download just *some* of those songs.

    You can save yourself all that tapping by opening **Settings**→**iTunes & App Store** and turning on **Automatic Downloads** (for music, apps, books, and audiobooks). From now on, whenever you're on Wi-Fi, stuff you've bought on other Apple machines gets downloaded to this one *automatically*.

- **Mac or PC.** Open the App Store program (for Mac apps) and click your icon (lower left). Use the **Purchased By** pop-up menu to view other family members' downloads, if you like.

Or open the iTunes app (for songs, TV shows, books, and movies). Click **Store** and then, under Music Quick Links, click **Purchased**, then **Not in My Library**. Here again, you can see what family members have bought; use the pop-up menu at top left.

> **TIP:** To make this automatic, open iTunes. Choose **iTunes→ Preferences→Downloads**. Under **Automatic Downloads**, turn on **Music, Movies**, or **TV Shows**, as you see fit. Click **OK**. From now on, iTunes will auto-import any of those items that you buy on any of your other machines.

If your Mac is running macOS Catalina or later, well, Apple has chopped up iTunes into four new programs: Music, TV, Podcasts, and Books. All your purchased digital goodies show up, except those bought by Family Sharing members. To see those purchases in TV or Music, choose **Account→Family Purchases**. In Books, click **Book Store**, and then **Purchased**. (Podcasts are free; you can see the ones you've subscribed to in the Library section.) Finish by clicking the name of the family member.

Any bookmark you set in an Apple Books book is synced to your other gadgets, too. The idea, of course, is that you can read a few pages on your phone in the doctor's waiting room and then continue from the same page on your iPad on the train ride home.

The Price of Free

A free iCloud account gives you 5 gigabytes of online storage. That may not sound like much, especially when you consider how big some music, photo, and video files are. Fortunately, anything you buy from Apple—like music, apps, books, and TV shows—doesn't count against that 5-gigabyte limit. Neither do the photos in your Photo Stream.

So what's left? Some things that don't take up much space, like settings and documents—and some things that take up a lot of it, like photos and videos, backups, email, and Messages in the Cloud. Anything you put on your iCloud Drive eats up your allotment, too.

When you open **Settings→[your name]→iCloud**, you get a colorful graph showing how full your iCloud storage is, and what's filling it (page 570, right).

Tap **Manage Storage** to open a comprehensive screen that shows where all your iCloud space is going. For example, you'll see how much of it your **Photos** library occupies (tap for the option to turn it off); how much space your entire Messages history consumes; how much each phone/tablet's **Backups** are eating up (tap a device's name to view the size and date of the last backup—and, if you like, to delete them); how much space your iCloud **Mail** account is eating up; and how much space the data from other apps—both Apple's and other companies'—are consuming.

If you've turned on Family Sharing (page 586), then your family members can share your iCloud storage plan with you. **Family Usage** shows how much *they're* gobbling up.

Change Storage Plan lets you upgrade or downgrade your iCloud storage. For example, if you find 5 gigs constricting, you can expand it to 50 GB, 200 GB, or 2 TB—for $1, $3, or $10 a month.

Apple Pay

You were alive to see the day: You can pay for things without cash, without cards, without signing anything, without your wallet: Just *pick up the phone*. You don't have to open some app, don't have to enter a code, don't even have to wake the phone up. Touch ID or Face ID confirms that it's really you making the purchase; you've just paid.

You can't pay for things everywhere; the merchant has to have a wireless terminal attached to the register. You'll know, because you'll see one of two logos nearby, as shown here.

Apple says that 65 percent of all U.S. stores, gas stations, and restaurants now accept Apple Pay, including chains like McDonald's, Walgreens, Starbucks, Macy's, Subway, Panera Bread, Best Buy, Duane Reade, Bloomingdale's, Staples, Chevron, Whole Foods, and the New York City subway system. The list grows all the time.

Apple Pay depends on a special chip in the phone: the NFC chip (near-field communication), and models before the iPhone 6 don't have it. Stores whose terminals don't speak NFC—like Walmart—don't work with Apple Pay, either.

The Setup

To set up Apple Pay, you have to teach your phone about your credit card. To do that, open the Wallet app. You can also start this process in Settings→Wallet & Apple Pay.

Tap Add Card. Tap Continue.

Now, on the Add Card screen, you're asked to aim the phone's camera at whatever Visa, Mastercard, or American Express card you use most often. Hold steady until the digits of your card, your name, and the expiration date blink onto the screen, autorecognized. Cool! The phone even suggests a card description. You can manually edit any of those four fields before tapping Done.

> **NOTE:** If you don't have the card with you, you can also choose Enter Card Details Manually and type in the numbers yourself.

Check over the phone's interpretation of the card's information, and then hit Next. Proceed through whatever red-tape or legalese screens now appear.

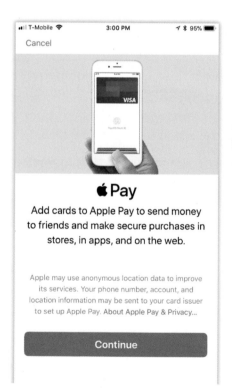

Next, your bank has to verify that all systems are go for Apple Pay. That may involve responding to an email or a text, or typing in a verification code. In any case, it's generally instantaneous.

You can record your store loyalty and rewards cards, too—and when you're in that store, the phone chooses the correct card automatically. When you're in Jamba Juice, it automatically uses your Jamba Juice card to pay.

The Shopping

Once the cashier has rung up your total, here comes the magic. The exact steps depend on whether or not your phone has a home button:

- **With a Face ID iPhone.** Begin by double-clicking the side button to make the Apple Pay screen appear. (At this point, you can tap the picture of your default card to choose a different one.)

   Authenticate by looking at the phone (Face ID). Now bring the top of the phone within an inch of the terminal. The phone buzzes, beeps, and says "Done"; it's all over.

- **With a home button.** Rest your finger on the home button—no need to wake the phone—and bring it within an inch of the terminal. The phone buzzes, beeps, and says "Done"; it's all over.

   If you've stored more than one card, and you want to use one that's not your primary card, the procedure is slightly different: Bring the phone near the terminal (*without* involving the home button). When your main card appears, tap it, choose a different card, and *then* touch the home button.

When you're rushing through the turnstile to catch the subway, the last thing you want is to fuss with double-pressing a button, bending over to look at your Face ID camera, and so on. Fortunately, iOS offers an ingenious Express setting. It lets you pay for your subway or bus ride by holding the phone near the reader—without pressing any buttons, without authenticating, without even waking it up!

To turn this on, open **Settings→Wallet & Apple Pay**; tap **Express Transit Card** and specify which card you'll want to use for paying.

An Apple Pay purchase is just a regular credit card purchase. So you still get your rewards points, frequent-flyer miles, and so on. (Returning something works the same way: At the moment when you'd swipe your card, you bring the phone near the reader until it beeps. Slick.)

Apple points out that Apple Pay is much more secure than using a credit card, because the store never sees, receives, or stores your card number, or even your name. Instead, the phone transmits a temporary, one-time, encoded number that means nothing to the merchant. It incorporates verification codes that only the card issuer (your bank) can translate and verify.

Apple never sees what you've bought or where, either. You can open Wallet and tap a card's picture to see the last few transactions, but that info exists only on your iPhone.

And what if your phone gets stolen? Too bad—for the thief. He can't buy anything without your fingerprint or face. If you're still worried, you can always visit *icloud.com*, click **Settings**, tap your phone's name, and click **Remove All** to de-register your cards from the phone by remote control.

Apple Pay Online

You can buy things online, too, using iPhone apps that have been upgraded to work with Apple Pay. The time savings: no typing your name, address, and phone number every time you buy something.

Instead, when you're staring at the checkout screen for some app, just tap **Buy with Apple Pay**.

There's Apple Pay on websites, too. For example, if you're shopping on a Mac (and it doesn't have its own fingerprint reader), you can authenticate with your *phone's* fingerprint reader or Face ID. The "OK, all clear" signal gets sent to your Mac automatically.

Apple Pay Cash

You can send cash to other members of the great, global Apple family with just a couple of taps, directly from your phone. Pay the piano teacher. Pay your share of the bill at a restaurant. Send money to your kid at college. It's like writing a check or handing over cash—without the checks or the cash. It's just like Venmo, Square Cash, or PayPal Cash, only...it's Apple's.

To use Apple Pay Cash, you need two-factor authentication turned on (page 662). Then:

- **Set up Apple Pay Cash.** The Apple Pay Cash card is, of course, an electronic fiction—there's no actual plastic card you slip into your physical purse or wallet. (That didn't stop Apple from trying to make it *look* like a real card, in the Wallet app, complete with anti-piracy features—try shifting your phone around, and marvel at the iridescent, color-changing "anti-piracy" design!)

  So you can't use Cash until you've first set up Apple Pay, which requires a *real* credit or debit card. Whenever you pay somebody, your Cash card draws money from that actual card. (If you link to a *debit* card, then using Apple Pay cash is always free—nobody takes a cut. If you link it to a *credit* card, you get hit with a 3 percent fee each time.)

  Once that's done, open **Settings→Wallet & Apple Pay**. Tap the little Apple Pay Cash card to begin the activation process, which mostly involves reading legalese. (Along the way, you're prompted to tap **Add Debit Card**; if you've already got a card set up, you can skip this step.)

One more thing: If you tap **Verify Identity** and supply your contact info and driver's license, you raise your maximum balance from $500 to $20,000.

You have the option of tapping **Add Money** to preload money (between $10 and $3,000) onto the Cash card—but there's no good reason to do so. The card automatically pulls money from your linked debit or credit card as needed.

NOTE: In **Settings→Wallet & Apple Pay**, a master **Apple Pay Cash** on/off switch awaits. It's a quick way to shut down the whole thing if your sending-money addiction starts becoming a problem.

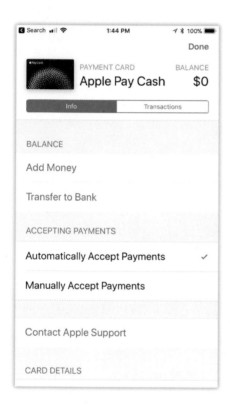
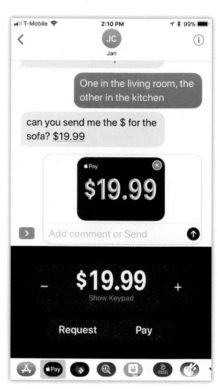

- **Pay someone.** Open Messages; open a chat with the lucky recipient (somebody who also has Apple Pay Cash set up). In the apps drawer (page 215), tap **Apple Pay**.

Or—here's that old Apple magic at work—tap any underlined dollar amount *in a text message* you've recently exchanged. The Apple Pay app opens automatically in the bottom part of the screen, with that amount already entered.

Similarly, if somebody writes in text a request for money ("Hey, do you want to split the bill? It's $30"), the QuickType bar above the keyboard offers the **Pay** button. Tap for insta-prep of the payment.

Enter an amount from $1 to $3,000, either by tapping the **+** and **−** buttons or by tapping the large dollar amount—or tapping **Show Keypad** and entering an amount.

When the amount looks good, tap **Pay**, and then ⬆. (That Send button, usually blue, appears in black as a visual reminder that you are about to spend money.)

A confirmation screen appears, showing which real card will be funding this amount. (Tap ▶ to change to a different card, if you like.) You're asked to confirm that you're really you, either by fingerprint or, on a Face ID phone, face recognition (and a double-click of the side button).

If, at this point, you return to the Wallet app, you'll see a screen full of details—time and date, amount, payee, and so on.

You don't have to bother with Messages. You can just tell Siri, "Send 35 bucks to Robin," or "Ask Casey for 80 dollars," or whatever. Siri shows you what she's about to do; say "Send" to confirm.

You can also tap the Ⓢ next to somebody's name in Contacts to begin the process, but it's not as much fun.

- **Request payment.** You can also operate Apple Pay Cash in reverse. That is, you can generate what amounts to an invoice for the person who owes you money.

  To do that, in a Messages thread with the ower, tap an underlined dollar amount in a text message—or open the Apple Pay app. Here's the **Request** button; enter the amount and hit ⬆. Of course, there's no guarantee you're actually going to *get* that money; the Request function mainly saves the other person the effort of (a) entering the amount, and (b) remembering.

For some reason, Apple gives you a choice of whether or not to receive these incoming amounts automatically. Open the Wallet settings, tap the Apple Pay Cash card, and then tap (i).

Here you can select **Manually Accept Payments**, which means that when someone sends you money, you don't get it unless you tap **Accept** in the notification. If you wait seven days without doing that (or if you tap the **Transactions** tab and tap **Reject Payment**), then you never get the money. What's wrong with you?

- **Track the payment.** If you open your Wallet and tap the Apple Pay card, you'll see that the amount you sent is "Pending"; the other guy hasn't yet accepted your generous gift. Until he does, you can cancel the payment on the Transactions tab. When he accepts, you'll get a notification letting you know. The transaction, in the Wallet app, appears with all the others you've made on the Transactions tab. Here you can also request a statement by email.

- **Cash out.** At any point, you can dump money (up to $3,000 at a time, up to $20,000 a week) from the Cash card into your bank account with just a couple of taps. On the Cash info screen, tap **Transfer to Bank**. (You'll be asked to enter your bank's tracking number the first time you try.) The funds will show up in your bank account in "one to three business days," says Apple.

Incidentally, AP Cash goes beyond person-to-person payments. You can treat your new Cash card as just another credit card for use with regular Apple Pay, and you can also send and receive person-to-person cash with an Apple Watch.

Family Sharing

It used to be a hassle to manage your Apple life with kids. What if they wanted to buy a book, movie, or app? They had to use your credit card—and you had to reveal your iCloud password to them. Or what if they wanted to see a movie you bought? Did they really have to buy it again?

Not anymore. Once you've turned on Family Sharing and invited your family members, here's how your life will be different:

- **One credit card to rule them all.** Up to six of you can buy books, movies, apps, and music on your master credit card.

- **Buying permissions.** When your kids try to buy stuff, your phone pops up a permission request. You have to approve each purchase.

- **Younger Appleheads.** You can create Apple accounts for tiny tots. (For regular Apple accounts, 13 is the age minimum.)

- **Shared purchases.** All of you get instant access to one another's music, video, Books books, and app purchases—again, without having to know one another's Apple passwords.

- **Shared Subscriptions.** You can all share a single subscription to Apple Arcade ($5 a month for hundreds of games), Apple News+ ($10 a month for hundreds of magazines), and Apple TV+ ($5 a month for Apple-produced TV shows).

- **Shared storage.** You can share any extra iCloud storage you've bought (page 578) with your fellow family members.

- **Find one another.** You can use your phone to see where your kids are, and vice versa (with permission, of course).

- **Find one another's phones.** The miraculous Find My iPhone feature (page 572) works for every phone in the family. If your daughter can't find her phone, you can find it for her with *your* phone.

- **Mutual photo album, mutual calendar, and mutual reminders.** When you turn on Family Sharing, your Photos, Calendar, and Reminders apps each sprout a new category that's preconfigured to permit access by everyone in your family.

Setting Up Family Sharing

The setup process means wading through a lot of screens, but at least you'll have to do it only once. Before you begin, ensure that each family member already has an Apple account (an Apple ID).

Tap **Settings**→**[your name]**→**Set Up Family Sharing**. Click **Get Started**. Work through the settings screens, like **Get Started** (tap the first feature you'd like to share— probably **iTunes & App Store Purchases**); **Confirm Account**; and **Shared Payment** (choose the credit card to share).

Finally, you're ready to introduce your family to the Family Sharing software circle. Tap **Invite Family Members**. Once you confirm the security code from your master credit card, an outgoing Messages message appears, with the invitation to join the family ready to send. Send it.

Once the lucky family member accepts the invite, they're in!

All of that describes only the introduction of the first family member. For additional members, return to **Settings**→**[your name]**→**Family Sharing**, and hit **Add Family Member**.

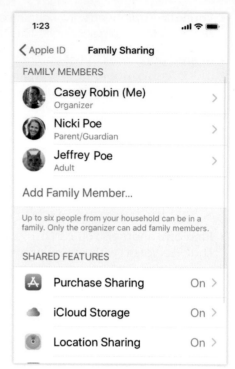

This time, you get three ways to add a person:

- **Invite via iMessage** sends the invite just the way you did that first time.

- **Invite in Person.** If the kid is standing right there with you, you can skip that iMessage business. Just type in the person's Apple ID and account password.

  Once you've confirmed a two-factor authentication request (page 662), the lucky recipient gets a notification on his gadget. If he accepts the invite, he can read a screen outlining all the benefits of joining your family. And voilà: The family grows.

- **If the kid is under 13.** Ordinarily, you have to be 13 or older to create an Apple ID account. That would put something of a damper on the whole Family Sharing idea.

  For that reason, this option lets you create special Family Sharing accounts for preteens.

NOTE: Once you create an account for someone under 13, *you won't be able to remove that person from your family until he turns 13!* You can transfer him to someone else's Family Sharing setup, but you can't ever delete him.

On the screens that follow, you'll enter the kid's birth date; agree to a Parent Privacy Disclosure screen; type the kid's name; set up an iCloud account (name, password, three security questions); decide whether or not to turn on Ask To Buy (each time your youngster tries to buy something online from Apple, you'll be asked for permission in a notification on your phone); and accept a bunch of legalese.

When it's all over, the lucky kid's name appears on the Family screen.

You can repeat this cycle to add additional family members, up to a maximum of six. Their names and ages appear on the Family screen.

From here, you can tap someone's name to perform stunts like these:

- **Designate a Parent/Guardian.** You, the family organizer, aren't the only person who can approve the kiddies' purchases. Anyone you designate (partner, spouse, nanny, super-smart teenager) can become a Parent/Guardian with this switch.

- **Delete a family member.** Man, you guys really don't get along, do you? Anyway, tap Remove.

- **Turn Ask To Buy on or off.** This option appears when you've tapped a child's name on your phone. If you decide your kid is responsible enough not to need your permission for each purchase, you can turn this option off.

> **NOTE:** If you turn off Ask To Buy for someone after she turns 18, you can't turn it on again.

Once kids turn 13, by the way, Apple automatically gives them more control over their digital lives. They can, for example, turn off Ask To Buy themselves, on their own phones. They can even express their disgust for you by leaving the Family Sharing group. (On her own phone, for example, your daughter can visit Settings→[her name]Cloud→Family, tap her name, and then tap Leave Family. Harsh!)

Life in Family Sharing

Once everything is set up, here's how you and your kids will get along:

- **Purchases.** Whenever one of your kids (for whom you've turned on Ask To Buy) tries to buy music, videos, apps, or books from Apple—even free items—he has to ask you (next page, left). On your phone, you're notified about the purchase—and you can decline it or tap Review to read about it on its Store page. If it seems OK, you can tap Approve. You also have to enter your Apple ID password, or supply your face or fingerprint, to prevent your kid from finding your phone and approving his own request.

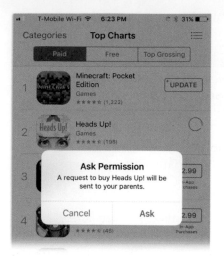

(If you don't respond within 24 hours, the request expires. Your kid has to ask again.)

Furthermore, each of you can see and download everything that everyone else has bought, as described on page 587.

- **Where are you?** Open the Find My app to see where your posse is right now. Use the same app if one of them has lost his phone (or use the web page; see page 572).

see page 587; see page 572

NOTE: If one of you needs secrecy for the afternoon (Apple sweetly gives, as an example, shopping for a gift for your spouse), open the Find My app, tap **Me**, and turn off **Share My Location**. Now you're untrackable until you turn the switch on again.

- **Photos, appointments, and reminders.** In Calendar, Photos, and Reminders, each of you will find a new category, called Family, that's auto-shared among you all. (In Photos, it's on the Shared tab.) You're all free to make and edit appointments in this calendar, to set up reminders in Reminders ("Flu shots after school!"), or to add photos or videos (or comments) to this album; everyone else will see the changes instantly.

Continuity: iPhone Meets Mac

Apple products have always been designed to work together. Macs, phones, tablets, watches: They all have similar software, design, wording, and philosophy. That's nice for you, of course, because you have less to learn and to troubleshoot. But it's also nice for Apple, because it keeps you in velvet handcuffs; pretty soon, you've got too much invested in its product "ecosystem" to consider wandering over to a rival.

Apple has taken this gadget symbiosis to an astonishing extreme. Today, your Mac can be an *accessory* to your iPhone. The Mac can be a speakerphone, using the iPhone as a wireless antenna. The Mac can send and receive regular text messages. AirDrop lets you drag files back and forth, wirelessly, from phone to computer. You can copy material on the phone and paste it on the Mac (or vice versa).

Apple's name for this suite of symbiosis is *Continuity*. And once you've got it set up, the game changes in a big way.

Continuity Setup

For many people, this all just works. For many others, there's a certain degree of setting up and troubleshooting. These are the primary rules:

- **You need a Mac running OS X Yosemite or later.**

- **The Mac and the phone have to be signed into the same iCloud account.** (That's a security thing—it proves you're the owner of both machines and therefore unlikely to pose a risk.) On the Mac, you do that in **System Preferences→iCloud**. On the phone, you do it in **Settings→[your name]→iCloud**. But you should also make sure you've entered the same iCloud address in **Settings→Messages→Send & Receive** and **Settings→FaceTime**.

- **For some of these features, Bluetooth must be turned on.** On the Mac, you can do that in System Preferences→Bluetooth. On the phone, it's Settings→Bluetooth.

  Modern Bluetooth doesn't drain your battery the way it once did, so it's fine to leave it on. But older Macs don't have Bluetooth LE, so most Continuity features work only on 2012 and later Macs.

All right. Setup ready? Time to experience some integration!

Mac as Speakerphone

You can make and take phone calls on your Mac. The iPhone, anywhere in your house, can be the cellular module for your Mac—even if that iPhone is asleep and locked. The Mac and the phone must be on the same network.

> **NOTE:** Actually, there's a mind-blowing exception to that statement: Continuity over *cellular*. In this scenario, your Mac and iPhone *don't* have to be on the same Wi-Fi network. Even if you left your phone at home, you can still make calls and send texts from your Mac, wherever you are in the country!
>
> This amazing feature requires participation by the cellular carrier. (How do you know? Open Settings→Phone→Wi-Fi Calling; if you see an option called Allow Calls on Other Devices, you're golden.)

Here's the setup:

- **On the phone,** turn on Settings→Phone→Calls on Other Devices→ Allow Calls on Other Devices.
- **On the Mac,** open the FaceTime program, weird as that sounds. Turn on FaceTime→Preferences→Settings→Calls from iPhone.

Once you've set things up as described, it just works. When a call comes in to your iPhone's number, your *Mac* plays whatever ringtone your phone is playing. A notice appears on your Mac's screen, as shown on the facing page. You can click Accept to answer it (or Decline it); your Mac's microphone and speaker become your speakerphone.

You can *place* a call the same way. Just click any phone number you find on the Mac: in Contacts, in Safari, in an email message, and so on.

Even call waiting works—if a second call comes in, your Mac notifies you and offers you the chance to put the first one on hold. And on the Mac,

the Contacts app offers Ringtone and Texttone menus, so you can assign custom sounds that play when your *Mac* rings. Crazy.

Texting from the Mac

You can send and receive text messages (as well as picture, audio, and video messages) on your Mac, too.

We're not talking about sending texts to other *Apple* people, using the Apple-only iMessages format (page 194). We're talking about something much better: You can type *any* cellphone number and send a regular SMS text message to *anyone*. Or receive them at your iPhone number.

Or you can initiate the text conversation by clicking a phone number in Contacts, Calendar, or Safari to send an SMS message. Once again, your iPhone acts as a relay station between the cellular world and your Mac.

First, as usual, Mac and phone must be on the same Wi-Fi network. Then:

- **On the phone,** open Settings→Messages→Send & Receive; make sure both your phone number and email address are turned on. Back on Settings→Messages, tap Text Message Forwarding. Your Mac's name appears. Turn on the switch. (If you're using two-factor authentication—see page 662—you'll have to type in a six-digit code.)

- **On the Mac,** open Messages; choose Messages→Preferences→ iMessage. Confirm that the Apple ID shown matches what you saw on the phone.

All this is to prove you're the owner of both devices. You wouldn't want some bad guy reading your text messages, would you?

That's it—your gadgets are paired. You can now use Messages to send standard text messages to *any* cellphone. You can also click and hold on a phone number wherever it appears—in Contacts, in a search result, in Safari, in Mail—and choose **Send Message** from there. And when a text message comes in, a standard Mac notification bubble appears in the top-right corner of the screen.

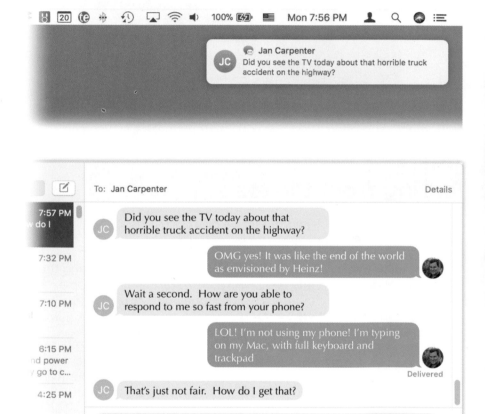

The beauty of this is that your back-and-forths are kept in sync between the Mac and the phone. You can jump to the other machine and continue the texting conversation. (You'll note that, as usual, the bubbles containing your utterances are green. Blue is reserved for iMessages—that is, messages to other people with iCloud accounts.)

Instant Hotspot

As you know from page 495, the Personal Hotspot feature turns the iPhone into a portable Wi-Fi hotspot, so your laptop (or any other devices) can get online almost anywhere.

Continuity makes life especially easy on your Mac. The phone can stay in your pocket. Its name appears in your Mac's 🛜 menu, ready for choosing at any time—even if the phone is asleep and locked, and even if Personal Hotspot is turned off! Handily enough, the 🛜 menu also shows the phone's battery and signal status.

Once your Mac is online through your iPhone's cellular connection, it tries to save you money by suspending data-intensive jobs like full backups and software updates. And it closes down the connection when you no longer need it, to save your iPhone's battery. Sweet.

Handoff

Handoff passes half-finished documents between the phone and the Mac, wirelessly and automatically.

For example, suppose you've been writing an email message on your iPhone (next page, left). When you arrive at home and sit down at the Mac, a new icon appears at the left end of the Mac's Dock (top right). When you click it, the Mac's Mail program opens, and the half-finished message is there for you to complete (lower right).

It doesn't have to be an email message, either. If you were reading a web page or a map on your phone, then that icon on the Mac opens the same web page or map. If you were working on a Reminder; a Calendar entry; a Contacts entry; a note in Notes; or a document in Keynote, Numbers, or Pages; you can open the same in-progress item on the Mac.

It works in the other direction, too. If you're working on something on the Mac, but you're called away, an icon that opens the same item appears on the lower-left corner of your iPhone's Lock screen.

TIP: There's another way to find the Handoff icon: It's in the app switcher on both devices. On the phone, swipe up from the bottom of the screen or (on home-button phones) double-press the home button. The new strip at the bottom identifies the document you're handing off from the Mac. (The illustration below shows the app switcher from both a home-button phone and an iPhone X.) On the Mac, press ⌘-Tab to open the app switcher; there's the icon for the app being handed off.

Here's the setup: Once again, your gadgets must have Bluetooth turned on and be within Bluetooth range of each other (about 30 feet).

On the Mac, open **System Preferences→General**; turn on **Allow Handoff between this Mac and your iCloud devices**.

On the iPhone, the on/off switch is in **Settings→General→AirPlay & Handoff**.

Now try it out. Start an email message on your iPhone. Have a look at the Dock on your Mac: There, at the left end, pops up the little icon of whatever program can finish the job.

AirDrop

AirDrop is pretty great. As described on page 380, it lets you shoot photos, videos, maps, Contacts cards, PDF files, Word documents, and other stuff between iPhones. Wirelessly. Without names, passwords, permissions, or even an internet connection. What page 380 doesn't cover, though, is how you can use AirDrop *between a phone and a Mac*.

From iPhone to Mac

Open whatever it is you want to send to the Mac: a photo, a map, a website, a contact...anything with a ⬆ button. Tap the AirDrop icon on the second row, exactly as described on page 382.

If the Mac's icon doesn't show up, it's probably because its owner hasn't made the Mac discoverable by AirDrop. Instruct him to open the AirDrop *window* on his Mac. (Click AirDrop in the sidebar of any Finder window.) See the small blue control at the bottom? It governs who can "see" this Mac for AirDrop purposes: **No One**, **Contacts Only** (that is, people in the Mac's address book), or **Everyone**.

Once that's set up right, that Mac shows up in the iPhone's AirDrop panel. Send away.

The receiving Mac displays a notification. Click **Accept** to download the incoming item to your Mac's Downloads folder (or **Decline** to reject it).

TIP: If the phone and the Mac are both signed into the same iCloud account, you don't encounter that **Accept/Decline** thing. The file goes directly into your Downloads folder without asking. You do get a notification on the Mac that lets you know how many files arrived, and it offers an **Open** button (shown below).

Since you own both the phone and the Mac, the usual permission routine isn't necessary.

Universal Clipboard

Now this is magic. You can copy some text, a picture, or a video on your phone—and then, without any further steps, turn to your Mac and paste it. Or go the other way. Somehow the contents of the Clipboard transfer themselves wirelessly between the two machines.

In this example, you copy something on the iPhone, in Safari (below, top)—and then paste it instantly in Mail on the Mac. There's no on/off switch, no extra steps, and no sign of this feature in Settings. It just works. (Provided, of course, that you've obeyed the Three Laws of Continuity Setup: same Wi-Fi network, Bluetooth turned on, both signed into the same iCloud account.) If you don't paste within two minutes of copying, then whatever was already on the Clipboard gets restored, so you don't get confused later.

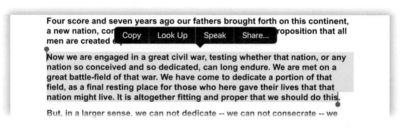

18

Settings

The Settings app is like the Control Panel in Windows or System Preferences on the Mac. It houses hundreds of settings for every aspect of the iPhone and its apps. Almost everything in the list of Settings is a doorway to another screen, where you make the actual changes.

In this book, you can read about the iPhone's preference settings in the appropriate spots—wherever they're relevant. And the Control Center, of course, is designed to *eliminate* trips into Settings. But so you'll have it all in one place, here's an item-by-item walk-through of the Settings app and its structure in iOS 13.

TIP: Settings has a search box at the top! Tug down to see it. You don't need a great memory (or this chapter) to find a certain setting.

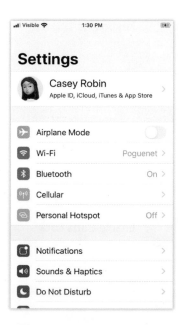

Three Important Settings Tricks

The Settings app is many screens deep. You might "drill down" by tapping, for example, **General**, then **Keyboard**, and then **Text Replacement**. It's a lot of tapping, a lot of navigation. Fortunately, you have three kinds of shortcuts.

First, you can jump directly to a particular Settings screen using Siri (Chapter 5). You can say, for example, "Open Sound settings," "Open Notifications settings," "Open Wi-Fi settings," and so on. Siri promptly takes you to the corresponding screen—no tapping required.

NOTE: Unless Siri thinks you are driving (see page 74).

Second, you can jump directly to the four most frequently adjusted panels—Bluetooth, Wi-Fi, Cellular Data, and Battery—by *long-pressing* the Settings app icon on the Home screen. The shortcut menu offers direct access to those panes.

Finally, you can *swipe to go back*. Once you've drilled down to, say, **General→Keyboard→Text Replacement**, you can "drill up" again by swiping across the screen to the right (start from the *edge*).

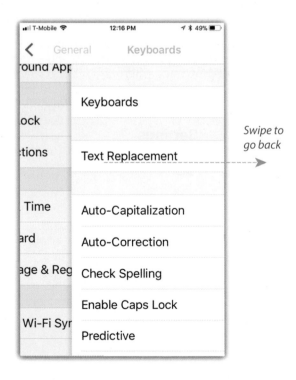

[Your Name]

At the top of the Settings screen, a tappable banner displaying your name and photo appears. Tap it to open a screen that summarizes everything Apple knows about you: your phone numbers; email addresses; passwords; credit card information; iCloud account info; and even the list of iPhones, iPads, iPod Touches, and Macs you own. Tap one of these items to edit it.

Airplane Mode

As you're probably aware, you're not allowed to make cellphone calls on U.S. airplanes. According to legend (if not science), a cellphone's radio can interfere with a plane's navigation equipment.

But the iPhone does a lot more than make calls. Are you supposed to deprive yourself of all the music, videos, movies, and email that you could be using in flight, just because calling is forbidden?

Nope. When you turn on airplane mode, the word **Cellular** dims in Settings (you've turned off your cellular circuitry), but the **Wi-Fi** and **Bluetooth** switches are still available, though turned off; you're now welcome to switch them back *on*, even in airplane mode.

Now it's safe (and permitted) to use the iPhone in flight, even with Wi-Fi on, because its cellular features are turned off completely. You can't make calls, but you can do anything else in the iPhone's bag of tricks.

 TIP: Turning airplane mode on and off is faster if you use the Control Center (page 42) or Siri ("Turn on airplane mode"). Same for Wi-Fi, described next.

Wi-Fi

This item in Settings opens the Wi-Fi networks screen:

- **Wi-Fi On/Off.** If you don't plan to use Wi-Fi, then turning it off gets you a lot more life out of each battery charge. Tap anywhere on this switch to change its status.

- **Choose a Network.** Here's a list of all nearby Wi-Fi networks. See page 491 for details on using Wi-Fi with the iPhone.

- **Ask to Join Networks.** See page 492.

- **Auto-Join Hotspot,** new in iOS 13, offers you the option to have your phone connect to somebody else's Personal Hotspot (page 495) **Automatically** (assuming it has ever connected before). Or **Never**. Or you can make it **Ask to Join**.

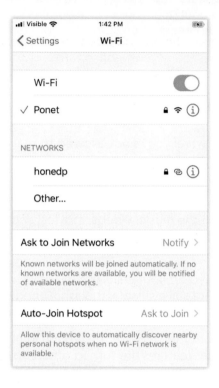

Bluetooth

Here's the on/off switch for the iPhone's Bluetooth transmitter, which is required to communicate with a Bluetooth fitness band, earpiece, keyboard, or hands-free system in a car. When the switch is on, you're offered the chance to pair the iPhone with other Bluetooth equipment; the paired gadgets are listed here for ease of connecting and disconnecting.

TIP: The Control Center (page 42) has a Bluetooth button. It's faster to use that than to visit Settings.

Cellular

These days, all major cell carriers are pushing their unlimited data plans. (They're not actually *unlimitedly* unlimited; after you've used a certain amount of data, your internet speed slows way down until the end of the month.) But most people still have capped plans, where, for example, you pay $50 a month for 8 gigabytes of internet data use.

That's why iOS offers so many settings to help you control how much internet data your phone uses:

- **Cellular Data.** This is the on/off switch for internet data. If you're traveling overseas, you might want to turn this off to avoid racking up insanely high roaming charges. Your smartphone becomes a dumb-phone, suitable for making calls but not for getting online. (You can still get online in Wi-Fi hotspots.)

- **Cellular Data Options.** These controls can prevent staggering interna-tional roaming fees. **Enable LTE** lets you turn off LTE—just for data, or for both voice and data—for situations when LTE costs extra.

> **TIP:** Every now and then, you'll be in some area where you can't connect to the internet even though you seem to have an LTE signal; forcing your phone to the 4G or 3G network often gives you at least some connection. Turning LTE off does just that.

On AT&T or T-Mobile, you can turn off **Data Roaming** (so when you're out of the country, you won't get slapped with those outrageous internet fees). On Verizon and Sprint, once you tap **Roaming**, you have separate controls for **Data Roaming** and **Voice Roaming**. Turning off the last item, **International CDMA**, forces the phone to use only the more common GSM networks while roaming; sometimes you get better call and data quality that way, and you may save money.

One of iOS 13's most helpful features is buried in here: **Low Data Mode**. It's something like Low Power Mode—but instead of throttling back *battery* usage when you're desperate, it throttles back use of cellular data when you're approaching your monthly limit.

Knowing when you need it is left to you; that may mean using a data-plan measuring app like DataMan or My Data Manager.

When you turn this mode on, your phone stops backing up photos to iCloud, no longer auto-downloads updates, turns off automatic playback of video previews in the App Store, lowers video and audio playback quality, and stops background apps from using the inter-net for nonessential purposes. (This option is also available for Wi-Fi networks—open **Settings→Wi-Fi**, and tap the ⓘ next to a certain network's name—although it's rarely as essential there.)

- **Personal Hotspot.** Here's the setup and on/off switch for Personal Hotspot (page 495). Once you've turned it on, a new Personal

Hotspot on/off switch appears on the main Settings screen, so you won't have to dig this deep in the future.

- **Default Voice Line, Cellular Plans.** These settings govern the two different phone numbers your XS, XR, 11, or 11 Pro phone can have once you set up the eSIM feature. Once you've got it set up, you can use one phone number for business and another for personal calls. Or you can use the second line as a local data plan when you're overseas. Both numbers can make and receive voice calls, FaceTime calls, and text messages.

  There's a lot of complexity to the two-line feature; see Apple's write-up at *support.apple.com/en-us/HT209044*.

- **Wi-Fi calling.** How would you like crisp, solid phone calls even indoors, even where the cell signal barely reaches? That's what Wi-Fi Calling can do for you.

  You can also turn on **Prefer Wi-Fi While Roaming**—and you should. When you're traveling abroad, calls will use Wi-Fi, if you're in a hotspot, instead of the outrageously priced cellular network.

NOTE: When you call 911 in an emergency on a cellphone, the operator sees your location. That's why, when you call from your iPhone, it uses a cellular connection *even if* you've turned on Wi-Fi Calling.

Unless there is no cellular signal, that is. In that case, the phone tries a Wi-Fi call. But Wi-Fi doesn't supply your location! That's why you're supposed to specify your location here, in **Update Emergency Address**—and then *change it every time you go anywhere*. Nobody will bother. Moral of the story: When you call 911, say where you are.

Add Wi-Fi Calling For Other Devices means, "When you're using Continuity (Chapter 17) to make calls through this iPhone from non-cellular Apple machines like Macs and iPads, give me the rich sound of Wi-Fi Calling."

- **Calls on Other Devices** is part of Continuity; see page 592.

- **Carrier Services** is just a bunch of stuff inserted here by your cellphone carrier. For Verizon, it's a list of phone numbers (411 for directory assistance and so on); for T-Mobile, it's links to customer service and apps. You get the idea.

- **SIM PIN.** Carriers use this code to lock your iPhone to their service (page 26). Once you're paid up, they can give you a code to put in here, which unlocks the iPhone so you can use it with another company's service.

TIP: If an evildoer guesses wrong three times—or if you do—then the words "PIN LOCKED" appear on the screen, and the SIM card is locked forever. You'll have to get another one from your carrier. So don't forget the code.

- **Add Cellular Plan** is your ticket to creating a second line on your XR, XS, or 11-family phone, as described above. You can either scan a QR bar code, if your cell company provided one, or enter the details manually.

- **Cellular Data.** The phone tracks how much internet data you've used this month, expressed in megabytes: from email messages, web page material, iMessages, Facebook updates, and so on. You may have a capped data plan—8 gigabytes a month, for example. If you exceed your monthly maximum, then you're instantly charged $15 or $20 for another chunk of data. So keeping an eye on these statistics is a very good idea.

  (Current Period means so far this month; Current Period Roaming means overseas or in places where your carrier doesn't have service.)

  Next, you see every internet-using app on your phone and how much data it's used. Better yet, the list offers individual on/off switches for every app. Each could consume data without your awareness. You can find out where the heck all your data is going and shut off the data hogs you really don't feel like spending megabytes on.

- **Wi-Fi Assist.** Thousands of iPhone fans know about The Old Flaky Wi-Fi Trick. If the phone is struggling and struggling to load a web page or download an email message on a Wi-Fi network, it often helps to *turn off Wi-Fi*. The phone hops over to the cellular network, where it's usually got a better connection.

  Wi-Fi Assist is supposed to do all that automatically. If the phone is having trouble with its Wi-Fi connection, it just hops over to cellular data. (You'll know when that's happened because of the cellular-network indicator on your status bar, which will show **4G**, **LTE**, or **5G E** instead of the 🛜 Wi-Fi symbol.)

  If you're worried about this feature eating up your data allowance, you can, of course, turn Wi-Fi Assist off. Apple notes, however, that Wi-Fi Assist doesn't kick in (a) when you're data roaming, (b) for background apps (it helps only the app that's in front), or (c) if large amounts of data would be consumed. For example, it doesn't kick in for audio or video streaming or email attachments.

  A little readout shows you how much cellular data this feature has gobbled up in the last month.

- **iCloud Drive.** Is the phone allowed to use data (if no Wi-Fi is available) for syncing with your iCloud Drive (page 576)?

- **Call Time.** These statistics break down how much time you've spent talking on the iPhone, both in the Current Period (that is, this billing month) and in the iPhone's entire Lifetime. Yes, your cellphone helps you keep track of your minutes, so you can avoid exceeding the number you've signed up for (and therefore racking up overage charges).

- **Reset Statistics** resets the call time and data usage counters to zero.

Personal Hotspot

Once you've turned this feature on (page 495) in Cellular, the switch appears here, too—on the main Settings screen for your convenience.

Notifications

This panel lists all the apps that think they have the right to nag for your attention. On this panel, you can tailor, to an almost ridiculous degree, how you want to be nagged. See page 62 for a complete description.

Sounds & Haptics

Here's a more traditional cellphone-settings screen: the place where you choose a ringtone sound for incoming calls.

- **Vibrate on Ring, Vibrate on Silent.** Like any self-respecting cellphone, the iPhone has a Vibrate mode—a little shudder in your pocket that might get your attention when you can't hear the ringing. There are two on/off controls for the vibration: one for when the phone is in Silent mode and one for when the ringer is on.

- **Ringer and Alerts.** The slider here controls the volume of the phone's ringing.

  Of course, it's usually faster to adjust the ring volume by pressing the up/down buttons on the left edge of your phone whenever you're not on a call or playing music or a video. But if you find that your volume buttons are getting pressed accidentally in your pocket, you can also turn off Change with Buttons. Now you can adjust the volume *only* with this slider, here in Settings, or with the Control Center slider.

- **Sounds and Vibration Patterns.** The iPhone is, of course, a cellphone—and therefore it sometimes rings. The sound it makes when it rings is up to you; by tapping **Ringtone**, you can view the iPhone's list of 27 built-in ringtones, 25 more ringtones from iOS versions past (tap **Classic** to see them), 40 "alert tones," plus any you've added yourself. You can use any of them as a ringtone or an alert tone, no matter how it's listed.

Tap a ring sound to hear it. After you've tapped one you like, confirm your choice by tapping ‹ **Back** to return to the Sounds (or Sounds & Haptics) screen.

NOTE: Remember, you can choose a different ringtone for each listing in your address book (page 126).

But why stop with a ringtone? The iPhone can make all kinds of other sounds to alert you: to the arrival of a voicemail, text, or email; to the sending of an email message, tweet, or Facebook post; to Calendar or Reminders alarms; to the arrival of AirDrop files; and so on.

This is a big deal—not just because you can express your individuality through your choice of ringtones, text tones, reminder tones, and so on, but also because you can distinguish *your* iPhone's blips and bleeps from somebody else's in the same family or workplace.

For each of these events, tap the text that identifies the current sound (**Tri-tone** or **Ding**, for example). On the next screen, tap the sound options to find one you like; tap ‹ **Sounds** to return to the main screen.

On that Sounds screen, you can also turn on or off **Lock Sound** (the sound you get when you tap the side button) and the **Keyboard Clicks** that play when you type on the virtual keyboard.

Meet Haptics

If you have an iPhone 7 or later, there's one more switch at the very bottom: **System Haptics**. *Haptics* are the tiny, click-like vibrations that Apple has scattered throughout iOS to accentuate the animations that make the iPhone fun to use.

These little bumps mark the maximum positions for things like pinch zooming, sliders, and panels that slide onto the screen (Control Center, search, Notification Center). You'll also feel these clicks when you spin the "dials" that specify times and dates (in Calendar, Clock, and so on), when you turn a Settings switch on or off, when your icons start wiggling on the Home screens (page 365), and when you send or receive iMessage screen effects like lasers and fireworks (page 209).

Haptics are subtle yet effective—but if you disagree, here's where you turn them off.

Do Not Disturb

This is one of iOS's most brilliant and useful features. See page 70.

Screen Time

See page 383 for this addiction-curbing feature.

General

The General pages offer a *huge* assortment of settings.

- **About** tells you how many songs, videos, and photos your iPhone holds; how much storage your iPhone has; techie details like the iPhone's software and firmware versions, serial number, model, Wi-Fi and Bluetooth addresses; and so on. (It's kind of cool to see how many apps you've installed.)

  At the very top, you can tap **Name** to rename your phone.

- **Software Update.** When Apple releases a new operating system update, you can download it directly to the phone.

  You'll know when an update is waiting for you, because you'll see a little number badge on the Settings icon, as well as on the word **General** in Settings. Tap it, and then tap **Software Update**, to see and install the update (below). If no number badge is waiting, then tapping **Software Update** just shows you your current iOS version.

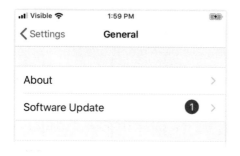 

- **AirDrop.** Who's allowed to AirDrop photos and files to you? (See page 380.)

- **AirPlay & Handoff.** In iOS 13.2, three switches appear here. **Automatically AirPlay to TVs** means: "If I, Apple's all-knowing artificial intelligence, notice that, in a certain app, you always AirPlay-send it to a certain Apple TV to watch on your big screen, I can start doing that handoff for you." If you worry that you might broadcast something to your TV that you wouldn't want your family seeing, choose **Ask** or **Never**.

Transfer to HomePod is similar. It means that, if you walk into the room playing music on your iPhone, you can hold the phone near your HomePod (Apple's Siri speaker) to make the music playback jump to that much nicer speaker.

Finally, **Handoff** is for people who own both a Mac and an iPhone; it automatically passes half-finished documents between them, as described on page 595. This is the on/off switch.

- **Home Button** appears on the iPhone 7 and 8 models. The home button on these phones, believe it or not, doesn't actually move. It doesn't actually click. Instead, a tiny speaker makes the button feel as though you've clicked it by producing a little twitch vibration. That helps with the iPhone's water resistance, of course, but it also permits features like this one: You can actually specify how big the phony click feels, using the settings Apple calls 1, 2, or 3 (and then try it out, right on this screen).

- **CarPlay.** Many car models come equipped with a technology called CarPlay, which displays whatever app icons won't distract you while you're driving—Phone, Music, Maps, Messages, Podcasts, Audiobooks,

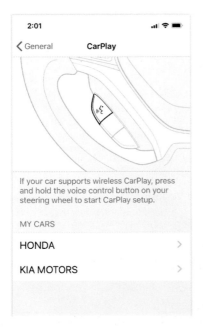
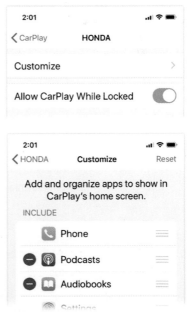

Waze, Spotify, and so on—on the car's dashboard touchscreen. The idea is to make them big and simple and limited to things you'll need while you're driving.

Tap your car model (previous page, left); on the second screen, you can turn off Allow CarPlay While Locked (so the phone will have to be awake to work—why would you want that?). Tap **Customize** to hide or rearrange the apps as they'll appear on the CarPlay screen (lower right).

- **iPhone Storage.** Here's a clean graph showing how full your phone is—and some recommendations. One suggests deleting all text messages and attachments older than one year. Another proposes offloading apps you don't use much. (That is, their dimmed icons remain on your Home screen, but they're just bookmarks that download the real apps when tapped.)

Then comes a list of all your apps, complete with the dates you last used them and how much storage they (and their documents) are eating up on your phone. (Biggest apps are at the top.) Tap an app's name to review more details, along with **Offload App** and **Delete App**

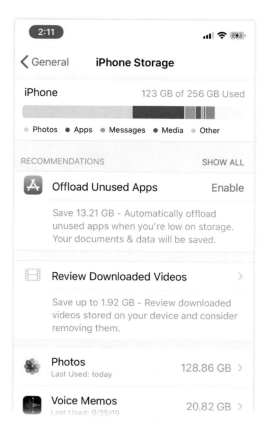

buttons. This is an amazing tool if you're constantly running out of space.

- **Background App Refresh.** The list that appears here identifies apps that try to access the internet, even when they're in the background. Since such apps can drain your battery, you have the option here to block their background updating.

  You can also turn off the master **Background App Refresh** switch. Now the only apps that can get online in the background are a standard limited suite (music playback and GPS, for example).

- **Date & Time.** Here you can turn on **24-Hour Time**, also known as military time, in which you see "1700" instead of "5:00 PM." (You'll see this change everywhere times appear, including at the top of the screen.)

  Set Automatically refers to the iPhone's clock. If this item is turned on, then the iPhone finds out what time it is from an atomic clock out on the internet. If not, then you have to set the clock yourself.

- **Keyboard.** Here you can turn off—or expand upon—some of the very best features of the iPhone's virtual keyboard. (All these shortcuts are described in Chapter 3.)

  Keyboards lets you add keyboards suited to all the different languages you speak. **Text Replacement** is where you set up auto-expanding abbreviations for longer words and phrases you type often. **One Handed Keyboard** is described on page 95.

  Auto-Capitalization is where the iPhone thoughtfully capitalizes the first letter of every new sentence for you. **Auto-Correction** is where the iPhone suggests spelling corrections as you type. **Check Spelling** refers to the pop-up spelling suggestions. **Enable Caps Lock** is the on/off switch for the Caps Lock feature, in which a fast double-tap on the Shift key turns on Caps Lock.

  Predictive refers to QuickType, the row of three word candidates that appears above the keyboard when you're typing.

  Smart Punctuation automatically replaces two hyphens (--) with an em dash (—), and straight quotes ("like this") with typographically proper curly ones ("like this") as you type. (This feature can interfere if you're a programmer typing code; you've been warned.)

Slide to Type is the new swipe-typing feature described on page 88; **Delete Slide-to-Type by Word** is covered on page 90.

Character Preview is the little bubble that pops up, showing the letter, when you tap a key. The **"."** **Shortcut** switch turns on or off the "type two spaces to make a period" shortcut for the ends of sentences.

Enable Dictation is the on/off switch for the ability to dictate text. (If you never use dictation, turning this switch off hides the 🎤 button on the keyboard, giving the space bar more room to breathe. Use **Dictation Languages** to specify which languages the phone will understand when you speak. This option appears only if you've installed additional keyboards, as described already.

- **Fonts.** For the first time in iPhone history, in iOS 13, you can install new typefaces! Well, in theory.

  In practice, you must first download a font-installation app like AnyFont, iFont, or Fonteer; each also adds a bunch of fonts. Keep in mind, though, that only certain text-editing apps will make your new fonts available, including Microsoft Word and Apple's own Pages.

- **Language & Region.** The iPhone: It's not just for Americans anymore. The **iPhone Language** screen lets you choose a language for the iPhone's menus and messages. **Region Format** controls how the iPhone displays dates, times, and numbers. (For example, in the U.S., Christmas is on 12/25; in Europe, it's 25/12.) **Calendar** lets you choose which kind of calendar system you want to use: Gregorian (that is, "normal"), Japanese, or Buddhist. **Temperature unit**—well, you know.

- **Dictionary.** Which dictionaries (which languages) should the phone use when looking up definitions and checking your spelling?

- **Profile.** You'll probably see this item only if your company issued you this phone. It shows what *profile* the system administrators have installed on it—the set of restrictions that govern what you're allowed to change without the company's permission.

- **VPN.** The typical corporate network is guarded by a team of steely-eyed administrators for whom Job One is preventing access by unauthorized visitors. They perform this job primarily with the aid of a super-secure firewall that seals off the company's network from the internet.

  So how can you tap into the network from the road? Only one solution is both secure and cheap: the *virtual private network*, or VPN. Running a VPN lets you create a super-secure, encrypted "tunnel" from your iPhone straight into your corporate network. Your company's tech staff can tell you whether or not there's a VPN server set up for you to use.

If so, they'll tell you what settings to plug in here. (If this is a company phone, you may see that your overlords have already set up some VPN connections; tap the one you want to use.)

Once everything is in place, the iPhone can connect to the corporate network and fetch your corporate mail. You don't have to do anything special on your end when you try to access your corporate email or calendar; the VPN is automatic. When your iPhone goes to sleep, it terminates the VPN connection, both for security purposes and to save battery power.

> **NOTE:** Once you've set up a VPN connection, it appears on the main Settings page, too—the "front door" of Settings—to save you having to burrow into General.

- **Legal & Regulatory.** A bunch of legal logos you don't care about.
- **Reset.** On the all-powerful Reset screen, you'll find six ways to erase your phone:

Reset All Settings takes all the iPhone's settings back to the way they were when it came from Apple. Your data, music, and videos remain in place, but the settings all go back to their factory settings.

Erase All Content and Settings is the one you want when you sell your iPhone, or when you're captured by the enemy and want to make sure they will learn nothing from it.

> **NOTE:** This feature takes a while to complete—and that's a good thing. The iPhone doesn't just delete your data; it also overwrites the newly erased memory with gibberish to make sure the bad guys can't see any of your deleted info, even with special hacking tools.

Reset Network Settings makes the iPhone forget all the memorized Wi-Fi networks it currently autorecognizes.

Reset Keyboard Dictionary has to do with the iPhone's autocorrection feature, which kicks in whenever you're trying to input text. Ordinarily, every time you type something the iPhone doesn't recognize— some name or foreign word, for example—and you don't accept the iPhone's suggestion, it adds the word you typed to its dictionary so it doesn't bother you with a suggestion again the next time. If you think you've entered too many misspellings into it, you can delete from its little brain all the new "words" you've taught it.

Reset Home Screen Layout undoes any icon moving you've done on the Home screen. It also consolidates your Home screen icons, fitting them onto as few screens as possible.

Finally, **Reset Location & Privacy** refers to the "OK to use location services?" warning that appears whenever an iPhone program, like Maps or Camera, tries to figure out where you are. This button makes the iPhone forget all your responses to those permission prompts. In other words, you'll be asked for permission all over again the next time you use each of those programs.

- **Shut Down.** This item offers a visual button for turning off the phone—just in case you don't know or can't remember the holding-in-the-buttons trick described on page 20. (You still have to swipe the "slide to power off" message to confirm.)

Control Center

The Control Center is written up on page 42. There are two settings to change here. If you turn off **Access Within Apps**, then you won't land in the Control Center by accident when you're playing some game that involves a lot of swiping; you'll be able to open it only from the Home screen. And **Customize Controls**, of course, is where *you* decide which buttons appear on the Control Center, and in which order.

Display & Brightness

Ordinarily, the iPhone controls its own screen brightness. An ambient-light sensor hidden behind the glass at the top of the iPhone's face samples the room brightness each time you wake the phone and adjusts the screen: brighter in bright rooms, dimmer in darker ones.

When you prefer more manual control, here's what you can do:

- **Light/Dark.** Here it is, folks: the Big New Feature in iOS 13—the option to turn on Dark mode, as described on page 5. Here, too, is the **Automatic** switch, meaning that Dark mode will kick in unbidden when the ambient light around you gets low. (When you turn on **Automatic**, you can tap the **Options** line to specify when, exactly, you'd like to see automatic Dark mode. Your options are **Sunset to Sunrise**, or **Custom Schedule**, meaning whenever you want it.)

TIP: The Control Center (page 42) lets you turn on Dark mode, too. And, of course, you can also tell Siri, "Turn on Dark Mode."

- **Brightness slider.** Drag the handle on this slider to control the screen brightness manually, keeping in mind that more brightness means shorter battery life.

  If True Tone (read on) or Auto-Brightness is turned on, then the changes you make here are *relative* to the iPhone's self-chosen brightness. In other words, if you goose the brightness by 20 percent, then the screen will always be 20 percent brighter than the iPhone would have chosen for itself.

TIP: The Control Center (page 42) gives you a much quicker road to the brightness slider. And, here again, you can also tell Siri, "Make the screen brighter" (or "dimmer"). This version in Settings is just for old-timers.

- **True Tone** (iPhone 8 models and later): This on/off switch goes beyond the old Auto-Brightness setting. Now it's Auto-Brightness *and* Auto-Tint. That is, the screen colors actually shift, based on the lighting color of the room or place you're in. The idea is to make colors on the screen seem consistent from one lighting condition to another.

  If you find the result off-putting, you can always turn True Tone off. Now the brightness of the screen is under complete manual control, and the tint never shifts.

- **Night Shift.** "Many studies have shown that exposure to blue light in the evening can affect your circadian rhythms and make it harder to fall asleep," Apple says. You can therefore use this function to give your screen a warmer, less blue tint, either automatically (**Sunset to Sunrise**), on a bedtime schedule (for example, from 11 p.m. to 6 a.m.), or right now (**Manually Enable Until Tomorrow**). You can also tweak the slider to adjust the color temperature (yellowness) of the screen when Night Shift kicks in.

  You can also turn on Night Shift by telling Siri, "Turn on Night Shift." Or you can long-press the brightness slider on the Control Center to find the on/off switch.

NOTE: Truth is, there's not much research indicating that blue light from *screens* affects your circadian rhythm, let alone little screens like your phone. (If using a gadget before bed makes it hard to sleep, it's more likely from the brain stimulation of what you're doing or reading.) Sleep scientists have a more universally effective suggestion: Turn off all your screens a couple of hours before bedtime.

- **Auto-Lock.** As you may have noticed, the iPhone locks itself (goes to sleep) after a few minutes of inactivity on your part, to save battery power and to prevent accidental screen taps in your pocket.

  On the **Auto-Lock** screen, you can change the interval of inactivity before the auto-lock occurs, or you can tap **Never**. In that case, the iPhone locks only when you click it to sleep.

- **Raise to Wake.** This on/off switch makes the phone light up when you *pick it up*—no button-pressing required. The ramifications are huge, because the Lock screen now has many more functions than it did before. There's a lot you can accomplish on the iPhone *before* you enter your password to unlock it; see Chapter 2.

- **Lock/Unlock,** new in iOS 13, means the phone will auto-unlock when you open its cover, and auto-lock when you close it. Cool, right? The fine print: This feature works only with a "compatible cover," which includes Apple's own Leather Folio covers ($100) and not much else.

- **Text Size.** As you age, small type becomes harder to read. This universal text-size slider can boost the text size in every app on your phone.

  Technically, what you're seeing is the front end for Apple's *Dynamic Type* feature. And, even more technically, not all apps work with Dynamic Type. But most of the built-in Apple apps do—Contacts, Mail, Maps, Messages, Notes, Phone, Reminders, and Safari Reader—and many other software companies follow suit.

- **Bold Text.** If the spindly fonts of iOS are a little too light for your reading tastes, you can flip this switch on (see page 239).

- **Display Zoom.** The iPhone 6, 6s, 7, Plus, and Max models have bigger screens than the iPhones that came before them. The question here is: How do you want to use that extra space? If you tap **View** and choose **Standard**, then icons and controls remain the size they always were; the bigger screen fits more on a page. If you choose **Zoomed**, then those elements appear slightly larger, for the benefit of people who don't have bionic eyes.

NOTE: The iPhone X, XS, XR, 11, and 11 Pro models don't offer Display Zoom; they're too skinny.

Accessibility

These options are intended for people with visual, hearing, and motor impairments, but they might come in handy now and then for almost anyone. All these features are described in Chapter 7.

Wallpaper

Wallpaper can mean either the photo on the Lock screen (what you see when you wake the iPhone up), or the background picture on your Home screen. On this panel, you can change the image used for either one.

It shows miniatures of the two places you can install wallpaper—the Lock screen and the Home screen. Each shows what you've got installed there as wallpaper at the moment. You can tap either screen miniature to open a Set screen, where you can adjust the current photo's size and positioning.

 TIP: This screen also offers **Dark Appearance Dims Wallpaper**, a reference to Dark mode (page 5). This feature makes the wallpaper dimmer when Dark mode is on.

When you tap **Choose a New Wallpaper**, you're shown a list of photo sources you can use as backgrounds. At the top, you get three categories:

- **Dynamic** wallpapers look like soft-focus bubbles against solid backgrounds. Once you've installed the wallpaper, these bubbles actually *move*, rising and falling on your Lock screen or Home screens behind your icons. Yes, animated wallpaper has come to the iPhone.

- **Stills** are lovely nature photographs. They don't move.

- **Live wallpapers,** once installed, behave like the Live Photos described on page 306: When you long-press the screen hard, they play as three-second movies. (It's not immediately clear what that gains you.) Note that live wallpapers play back only on the Lock screen (not the Home screen).

 TIP: You can install your *own* Live Photos as Lock screen backgrounds. They, too, will play their little three-second loops when you long-press the Lock screen.

Scroll down a little, and you'll find your own photos, nestled in categories like **All Photos** (or **Camera Roll**), **Favorites**, **Selfies**, **My Panoramas**, and so on. Tap one to see what it looks like at full size.

TIP: Complicated, "busy" photos make it harder to read icons and icon names on the Home screen.

Once you've spotted a worthy wallpaper, tap it. The little ⊙ icon is the on/off switch for Perspective mode, which means that the photo will *shift* slightly when you tilt the phone, as though it's several inches under the

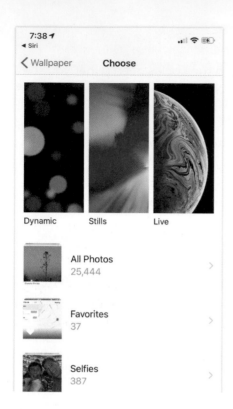

glass. (If you've chosen a Live Photo, you'll see another icon, ⊚, meaning it will "play" when it's on the Lock screen and you long-press the glass.)

Finally, tap **Set**. Now the iPhone wants to know which of the two places you want to use this wallpaper; tap **Set Lock Screen**, **Set Home Screen**, or **Set Both** (if you want the same picture in both places).

Siri & Search

Here are the on/off switches for Siri (Chapter 5) and a whole slew of options for her behavior, including Shortcuts (page 182). For example:

- **Listen for "Hey Siri."** If you don't want Siri to respond to "Hey Siri," (see page 160), you can turn her listening off here. Now Siri works only when you hold down the home (or side) button.

- **Press Home for Siri/Press Side Button for Siri.** If you turn this off, then holding down the home (or side) button no longer summons Siri. (If **Listen for "Hey Siri"** is *also* turned off, then you can't use Siri at all. In essence, you've just turned your modern iPhone into an iPhone 4.

NOTE: Why would anyone turn off Siri? One reason: Using Siri involves transmitting a lot of data to Apple, which gives some people the privacy willies. Apple collects everything you say to Siri, your song and playlist names, plus all the names in Contacts (so that Siri can recognize them when you refer to them)—but stresses that all of this information is anonymized.

- **Allow Siri When Locked.** Lets you turn off Siri at the Lock screen.

- **Language.** What language do you want Siri to speak and recognize? The options here include dozens of languages and dialects, including English in nine flavors (Australian, Canadian, Indian, and so on).

- **Siri Voice.** Siri can have either a man's voice or a woman's voice—in a choice of accents. Even if you're American, it's fun to give Siri a cute Australian accent.

- **Voice Feedback** asks: Do you want to hear Siri's "I'm listening!" beep and her spoken responses even if the ringer switch is off? How about when you're going hands-free (using "Hey Siri" or a Bluetooth ear-piece, car, or headphones)?

  Always On: Siri always replies to queries with a synthesized voice (in addition to a text response).

  Control with Ring Switch: Siri speaks her answers only when the phone isn't silenced.

  Hands-Free Only: You're telling Siri not to bother speaking when you're looking at the screen and can read the responses for yourself. She'll speak only if you're on speakerphone, using a headset, listening through your car's Bluetooth system, and so on.

- **My Information.** Siri needs to know which card in Contacts contains your information and lists your relationships. That's how she's able to respond to queries like "Call my mom," "Remind me to shower when I get home," and so on.

- **Announce Messages.** This option appears only if you have second-generation AirPods or Powerbeats Pro wireless headphones. The idea is that if a text message comes in while you're wearing your 'buds or 'phones, Siri reads it to you out loud and lets you reply by voice—all without ever putting down your packages or taking your hands off the bike handlebars.

  The first time you use your AirPods after installing iOS 13.2, you're invited to turn this feature on. You can also turn it on (or off) in Settings→Siri & Search→Announce Messages. If you also turn on

Reply without Confirmation, Siri won't bother to read its transcription of your reply back to you before sending it.

- **Siri & Dictation History.** With one tap on Delete Siri & Dictation History, you delete, from Apple's computers, any (anonymous) recordings of your voice that Apple may have collected for quality-assurance purposes.

- **Suggestions in Search, Suggestions in Look Up, Suggestions on Lock Screen.** You get to control when iOS provides outside results it considers helpful when you Search (page 111), when you use the Look Up button (page 110), and when you're looking at the Lock screen (page 17).

- **Apps list.** Finally, this screen contains a scrolling list of Siri-compatible apps. Turn them on or off at will.

Face ID (Touch ID) & Passcode

Here's where you set up a password for your phone, or where you teach the phone to recognize your fingerprints or (on the Face ID phones) your face. Details on training the phone start on page 59. The rest of the settings—which you can't see until after you enter your passcode—include controls like these:

- **Use Face ID (Touch ID) For:** As it turns out, your fingerprint or face can do more than unlock the phone (iPhone Unlock). You can also use them to authenticate your identity when using Apple Pay (page 579) or buying songs, movies, and apps (iTunes & App Store).

  Your finger or face can also unlock the auto-typing of memorized website and app passwords (Password AutoFill).

  On the Face ID phones, Other Apps reveals a list of other apps that can use Face ID as authentication, including Notes (to unlock notes you've password-protected), Dropbox, Apple Store, and so on. In those situations, you'll see the little Face ID icon on the screen, and a message will instruct you to double-click the side button to seal the deal.

- **Turn Passcode Off, Change Passcode.** You can't use Touch ID or Face ID without a traditional passcode as a backup; that's why these tools are here.

- **Require Passcode.** How soon after your last phone-unlocking does it require your phone passcode again? If you're using Touch ID or Face ID, you don't have a choice: You'll have to unlock it every single time.

- **Voice Dial, Allow Access When Locked.** This is a list of iPhone features you can use at the Lock screen (Chapter 2), *before* you've unlocked the phone (**Notification Center**, **Siri**, **Return Missed Calls**, and so on). You may not be comfortable with the notion that somebody picking your phone up from your desk could dive into some of these things—so you can turn them off here.

- **Erase Data.** The note says it all: "Erase all data on this iPhone after 10 failed passcode attempts." (That's *passcode*, not fingerprint or Face ID attempts.) Clearly, if somebody needs that many guesses, he's not you. Useful if you work for the CIA, NSA, or DMV.

The Face ID iPhones offer a few important additional settings:

- **Set Up an Alternate Appearance.** You can now store a second memorized face; see page 60.

- **Reset Face ID.** Start from scratch.

- **Require Attention for Face ID.** Ordinarily, the face recognition system on the Face ID iPhones unlocks the phone only when you're *looking* at the phone. That way, no evildoing relative can unlock your phone when you're asleep by holding it in front of your snoozing face.

  But if you're blind, wear opaque sunglasses all day, or have no eyes, what then? In that case, you can turn off this option. Now the phone will unlock whenever it recognizes you, even if your eyes aren't open and looking at it.

- **Attention Aware Features.** Apple hasn't said much about this option, but it's very cool. The TrueDepth camera will prevent the screen from turning off after 30 seconds (or whatever your auto-sleep setting is) while you're looking at it—and it will make your morning alarm quieter if you're looking at it.

Emergency SOS

This is the beating heart of iOS's emergency-calling feature, which is described on page 79.

Battery

This panel is a full-on 747 cockpit of battery information:

- **Battery Percentage.** Instead of just a "filling-up-battery" fuel-gauge icon at the top of your screen, how would you like a digital percentage readout, too ("75%")?

This option isn't available on Face ID phones, because there's no room for the percentage on the right ear. But if you ever do want to see the battery percentage, just swipe down on that ear to see the Control Center; there it is.

- **Low Power Mode.** See page 37.

- **Insights & Suggestions.** You may see these personalized tips for better battery life, like turning on automatic brightness adjustment.

- **Battery Health.** Lithium-ion batteries like the one in your phone have limited lifespans. Over time, they hold less charge. After about 500 chargings, for example, your phone may store only 80 percent as much juice as it did when it was new. This screen (iPhone 6 and later), shows you just how far along that death spiral your battery is. It might say, for example, Maximum Capacity 83%.

You may also see Peak Performance Capability. You may recall that, in 2017, Apple was caught deliberately slowing down some iPhones. Skeptics assumed it was to boost sales of new phones, but Apple gave a different explanation.

As batteries age, Apple explained, they become too weak to handle sudden spikes in energy demand from your apps. Worst case, the whole phone suddenly shuts off. Apple had been slowing down those processors to prevent the crashes. Well, OK—but why didn't they tell anyone?

Now they do. The explanatory text here starts out saying, "Your battery is supporting normal peak performance" (no slowdown, no crashes). But if the battery ever gets so weak that the phone shuts down, then iOS turns on the slowdown features (euphemistically called "Performance Management"). You'll know, because this screen now says, "This iPhone has experienced an unexpected shutdown... Performance management has been applied to help prevent this from happening again."

At this point, you have three options: live with the slower phone, replace the battery, or tap Disable and accept the possibility of an occasional sudden shutdown.

One more control appears on the Battery Health screen, a new one in iOS 13: Optimized Battery Charging. As any chemistry student can tell you, you get the best life from a lithium-ion battery if you avoid charging it to 100 percent every day.

When you turn Optimized Battery Charging on, the iPhone stops charging at 80 percent *except* when it thinks you'll need the extra oomph, which it tries to figure out by observing your daily charging patterns. You can turn it off—but your battery will hold more charge for more years if you leave it on.

- **Battery Usage.** Here's the readout for all your apps, showing their battery appetite over the past day or 10 days; see page 41.

TIP: Tap Show Activity to see exactly how much time you wasted using that app over the given time period—either the past 24 hours or the past 10 days.

- **Screen On, Screen Off.** These stats show you how many hours and minutes of life you've gotten from your current battery charge. (Screen On = you using the phone. Screen Off = phone asleep.)

Privacy

By "privacy," Apple means "the ability of apps and Apple to access your data."

Many an app works better, or claims to, when it has access to your address book, calendar, photos, and so on. Generally, when you run such an app for the first time, it explicitly asks you for permission to access each kind of data. But here, on this panel, you have a central dashboard— and on/off switches—for each data type and the apps that want it.

Location Services

Suppose, for example, that you tap Location Services. At the top of the next screen, you'll find the master on/off switch for all location services. If you turn it off, then the iPhone can no longer determine where you are on a map, geotag your photos, find the closest ATM, tell your friends where you're hanging out, and so on. Below this master switch, you'll find these options:

- **Location Alerts.** Once you started using iOS 13, you may have noticed that the phone keeps asking you about one app after another that's been using your location in the background. For each one, you're offered the chance to shut down the app's access to your location, to allow it just this once, or to Allow While Using App.

  It's all part of Apple's never-ending effort to give you control and awareness of which apps are using your personal data. But if those frequent pop-up messages are getting on your nerves, here's your off switch. (You can always change each app's access to your location elsewhere on this screen, as described next.)

- **Share My Location.** Apple has designed plenty of ways for you to broadcast your phone's location—and, by extension, your own. For example, Find My, Messages, and Family Sharing all have features that let certain other people see (with your permission) where you are right now.

  Here's the on/off switch for the whole feature. If it's off, nobody can find you right now. If **Share My Location** is on, then you can tap **From** to see every iPhone you've ever owned, so you can specify which one should be transmitting its location (the one you're carrying now). This is the **Find My iPhone** master switch, too (page 572).

  The **Family** section lists any members of your family with whom you're sharing your location; similarly, the **Friends** list identifies anyone else who has permission to track you. These are handy reminders—and you can tap a name to reveal its **Stop Sharing My Location** button.

- **List of apps.** Here's every single app that uses your location information, so that you can turn off this feature on a by-app basis. You might want to do that for privacy's sake—or you might want to do that to save battery power, since the location searches sap away a little juice every time.

  Tap an app's name to see when it wants access to your location. You might see **Always, Never, Ask Next Time** (meaning, "next time the app wants to see your location") or **While Using the App** (the app can't use your location when it's in the background). On the same screen, you may see a description of why the app thinks it needs your location. Why does the Calendar need it, for example? "To estimate travel times to events."

  The little ➚ icon indicates which apps have actually *used* your location data. If it's gray, that app has checked your location in the past 24 hours; if it's purple, it's locating you right now; if it's hollow, that app is using a *geofence*—it's waiting for you to enter or leave a certain location, like home or work. The Reminders app uses the geofencing feature, for example.

- **System Services.** Here are the on/off switches for the iPhone's own features that use your location.

  For example, there's **Apple Pay Merchant Identification** (tells Apple Pay what store you were in); **Cell Network Search** (lets your phone tap into Apple's database of cellular frequencies by location, which speeds up connections); **Compass Calibration** (lets the Compass app know where you are, so it can accurately tell you which way is north); **Emergency SOS** (finds the nearest police station if you've turned off the 911 feature, as described on page 79); **Location-Based**

Apple Ads (advertisements that Apple slaps at the bottom of certain apps—or, rather, their ability to self-customize based on your current location); Setting Time Zone (permits the iPhone to set its own clock when you arrive in a new time zone); and so on.

Under the Product Improvement heading, you also get iPhone Analytics (sends location information back to Apple, along with diagnostic information so that, for example, Apple can see where calls are being dropped); Popular Near Me (the section of the App Store that lists apps downloaded by people around your current spot); Routing & Traffic (sends anonymous speed/location data from your phone, which is how Maps knows where there are traffic tie-ups); and Improve Maps (sends Apple details of your driving, so it can improve its Maps database).

Finally, here's where you choose whether or not the little ➚ Status Bar Icon is allowed to appear in your menu bar when one of the System Services is using your location, as opposed to an app.

Contacts, Calendars, Reminders...

This list (on the main Privacy screen) identifies the kinds of data your apps might wish to access; we're going way beyond location here. For example, your apps might want to access your address book or your calendar.

Tap a category—Contacts, for example—to see a list of the apps that are merrily tapping into its data. And to see the on/off switch, which you can use to block that app's access.

Analytics & Improvements

Do you give Apple permission to collect information about how you're using your phone and how well the phone is behaving each day? On this screen, you can turn Share iPhone Analytics off or on. (You can even tap Analytics Data to *see* the data your phone has sent, although it's gibberish unless you're a programmer.)

Share With App Developers gives the phone permission to send non-Apple app writers the details of any crashes you experience while using their apps, so that, presumably, they can get busy analyzing and fixing those bugs. Improve Siri & Dictation, new in iOS 13.2, lets you opt out of letting Apple engineers listen to anonymous voice recordings of your Siri and dictation commands.

Share iCloud Analytics—same deal, but about your iCloud activity. Improve Health & Activity and Improve Wheelchair Mode share your activity and—if you have an Apple Watch—wheelchair-motion data with

Apple, for similar reasons. Deciding whether to share this data all boils down to where you land on the great paranoia-to-generosity scale.

Advertising

The final Privacy option gives you a **Limit Ad Tracking** switch. Turning it on doesn't affect how many ads you see within your apps—but it does prevent advertisers from delivering ads *based on your interests*. You'll just get generic ads.

There's a **Reset Advertising Identifier** button here, too. You may not realize that, behind the scenes, you have an Ad Identifier number. It's "a non-permanent, non-personal device identifier" that advertisers can associate with you and your habits—the things you buy, the apps you use, and so on. That way, advertisers can insert ads into your apps that pertain to your interests—without ever knowing your name.

But suppose you've been getting a lot of ads that seem to mischaracterize your interests. Maybe you're a shepherd, and you keep seeing ads for hyperviolent games. Or you're a nun, and you keep getting ads for marital aids. In those cases, you might want to reset your Ad ID with this button, thus starting from scratch as a brand-new person about whom the advertisers know nothing.

iTunes & App Store

If you've indulged in a few downloads (or a few hundred) from the App Store or iTunes music store, then you may well find some settings of use here. For example, when you tap your **Apple ID** at the top of the panel, you get these buttons:

- **View Apple ID.** This takes you to the web, where you can look over your Apple account information, including credit card details.

- **Sign Out.** Tap when, for example, a friend wants to use her own iTunes account to buy something on your iPhone. As a gift, maybe.

- **iForgot.** If you've forgotten your password, tap here. You'll be offered a couple of different ways of establishing your identity—and you'll be given the chance to make up a new password.

Automatic Downloads

If you have an iCloud account, then a very convenient option is available to you: automatic downloads of music, apps, audiobooks, and ebooks you've bought on *other* iOS gadgets. For example, if you buy a new album on your iPad, then turning on **Music** here means your iPhone will download the same album automatically next time it's in a Wi-Fi hotspot.

App Updates means that if you accept an updated version of an app on one of your other Apple gadgets, it will be auto-updated on this phone, too.

Those downloads are, however, big. They can eat up your phone's monthly data allotment right quick and send you deep into Surcharge Land. That's why the iPhone does that automatic downloading only when you're in a Wi-Fi hotspot—unless you turn on **Automatic Downloads** (under the Cellular Data heading).

There's also an **App Downloads** control here that lets you block auto-downloads of apps if they're over 200 megabytes (or to ask you every time it encounters one that large). Hope you know what you're doing.

Video Autoplay

On the App Store, many apps offer little videos as part of their description. You may object to their tendency to start playing automatically— either because video eats up cellular data, or because they're annoying.

Your choices are **On** (videos play), **Off** (they don't play until you tap), or **Wi-Fi Only** (they won't play when you're on a cellular-only connection).

In-App Ratings & Reviews

Don't you hate it when you're happily using some app—and then it ruins everything by interrupting you, begging you to rate it on the App Store? If you turn off **In-App Ratings & Reviews**, those groveling little messages won't appear.

Offload Unused Apps

Finally, hiding way down here is the powerful **Offload Unused Apps** master switch. It's a great way to fight "my iPhone is always full" syndrome. If you turn it on, then iOS will automatically delete apps you never use to make space (but not their settings and data). Their icons remain on your Home screen as dimmed ghosts. If you ever need that app again, just tap to re-download it.

Wallet & Apple Pay

This panel, available on the iPhone 6 and later, sets all the preferences for Apple Pay (page 579), including the master switch for **Apple Pay Cash** (page 583). You see any credit cards you've enrolled, plus **Add Card** to enroll another.

Double-Click Home Button or **Side Button** is the on/off switch for using Apple Pay when the phone is locked.

Express Transit Card is a fantastic time-saver for subway riders, described on page 582. **Transaction Defaults** set up the card, address, email account, and phone number you prefer to use when buying stuff online.

Allow Payments on Mac is the on/off switch for the option to use your iPhone's fingerprint reader (or iPhone Face ID face recognition) to approve purchases you make on the web using your *Mac* (an option on sites that offer Apple Pay online).

Passwords & Accounts

This screen is a central clearinghouse for your email accounts—and the associated calendar, contacts, notes, and reminder accounts. (Yahoo, Google, iCloud, Microsoft, and others all offer such unified suites of services.)

At the top, **Website & App Passwords** (after requiring Touch ID, Face ID, or your passcode) shows a complete list of every password your iPhone has memorized for you (page 513). And **AutoFill Passwords** is the master switch for automatically entering your passwords, which it's hard to imagine anyone wanting to turn off.

Accounts

Your email accounts are listed here; this is also where you set up new ones. Page 525 covers most of the options, but one important item is worth noting: **Fetch New Data**.

The beauty of "push" email is that new email appears on your phone immediately. You get push email if you have, for example, a Yahoo Mail account, iCloud account (Chapter 16), or Microsoft Exchange account.

Having an iPhone that's updated with these critical life details in real time is amazingly useful, but there are several reasons why you might want to turn off the **Push** feature. You'll save battery power, save money when you're traveling abroad (where every "roaming" internet use can run up your cellular bill), and avoid the constant "new mail" jingle when you're trying to concentrate.

And what if you don't have a push email service, or if you turn it off? In that case, your iPhone can still do a pretty decent job of keeping you up to date. It can check your email every 15 minutes, every half-hour, every hour, or only on command (**Manually**). That's the decision you make in the **Fetch New Data** panel. (Keep in mind that more frequent checking means shorter battery life.)

> **TIP:** The iPhone *always* checks email each time you open the Mail app, regardless of your setting here. If you have a push service like iCloud or Exchange, it also checks for changes to your schedule or address book each time you open Calendar or Contacts—again, no matter what your setting is here.

Standard App Settings

Almost all the remaining options in Settings—and in this chapter—are names of apps. Here's where you set up your preferences for every single app on your phone.

As you investigate each app's settings, you'll discover that they often begin with identical standard options:

- **Location.** When is this app allowed to know your location (page 623)?

- **Siri & Search** opens a screen that offers **Show in Search** and **Suggest Shortcuts** switches. They let this app's data snippets show up in search results (page 114), the definition boxes when you look up words (page 110), and in QuickType suggestions above the keyboard (page 87). **Show Siri Suggestions** allows this app's data to show up on the Lock screen as time-and-place suggestions (page 77).

- **Background App Refresh.** Is this app allowed to access the internet when it's not the frontmost app (page 375)?

- **Cellular Data.** Is this app allowed to get online over the cellular data network, or only when you're in Wi-Fi (page 491)?

- **Preferred Language.** If you've set up multiple languages on your phone (page 96), which one would you like this app to favor?

Mail

The settings here on the Mail screen govern how often you want your Mail app to look for new messages, and more:

- **Allow Mail to Access**. Is Mail information allowed to show up in searches and QuickType suggestions? Is it allowed to display

Notifications? Is it allowed to use **Cellular Data**, or must it wait until you're in a Wi-Fi hotspot?

- **Preview.** Messages in your inbox are listed with the subject line in bold type *and* a couple of lines, in light-gray text, that preview the message itself. You can control how many lines of the preview show up here, from **None** (you see more message titles on each screen without scrolling) to **5 Lines**. More lines means you can skim your inbound messages without having to open many of them; fewer lines means more messages fit without scrolling.

- **Show To/Cc Labels.** The iPhone can display a **To** or **Cc** logo on each message. At a glance, it helps you identify which messages are actually intended for *you*. Messages without those logos are probably spam, newsletters, mailing lists, or other messages that weren't specifically addressed to you.

  If there's no logo at all, then the message is in some other category. Maybe it came from a mailing list, or it's an email blast (with your name in Bcc), or the message is from you, or it's a bounced message.

- **Swipe Options.** Which colorful insta-tap buttons would you like to appear when you swipe across a message in a list? See page 535 for details.

- **Ask Before Deleting.** Ordinarily, you can delete an open message quickly and easily, just by tapping the 🗑 icon. But if you'd prefer to encounter an additional confirmation step before the email message disappears, then turn this option on.

NOTE: The confirmation box appears only when you're deleting an open message—not when you delete a message from the inbox list.

- **Load Remote Images.** Spammers, the vile undercrust of lowlife society, have a trick. When they send you email that includes a picture, they don't actually paste the picture into the message. Instead, they include a "bug"—a piece of code that instructs your email program to *fetch* the missing graphic from the internet. Why? Because that lets the spammer track who has actually opened the junk mail, making those email addresses much more valuable for reselling.

  If you turn this option off, then the iPhone does not fetch "bug" image files at all. You're not flagged as a sucker by the spammers. You'll see empty squares in the email where the images ought to be. (Graphics sent by normal people and legitimate companies are generally pasted right into the email, so they'll still show up just fine.)

- **Organize by Thread.** This is the on/off switch for the feature that clumps related back-and-forths into individual items in your Mail inbox.

- **Collapse Read Messages.** See page 531 for details.

- **Most Recent Message on Top.** The messages in a conversation usually appear chronologically, newest at the top. (The latest message still appears when you click the thread's name.) If you prefer oldest at the top, then turn off this setting.

- **Complete Threads.** What if, during a particular back-and-forth, you've filed away certain messages into other folders? Should they still show up in a conversation thread? They will, if this switch is on. (The moved messages are *actually* sitting in those other folders; they just *appear* here for your convenience.) Now your conversations seamlessly combine related messages from all mailboxes.

- **Muted Thread Action.** When you've muted a conversation thread, as described on page 202, what do you want to happen to those messages? Mark as Read leaves them in your inbox, no longer flagged as new; Archive or Delete gets rid of them entirely.

- **Blocked Sender Options** is similar. When you block a contact, do you want that person's messages to stay in your inbox, get dumped into the trash, or neither?

- **Blocked** opens the list of phone numbers you've blocked. (You can unblock one by swiping to the left and tapping Unblock.) Take that, robocallers!

- **Always Bcc Myself.** If this option is on, then you'll get a secret copy of any message you send. Some people use this feature to make sure their computers have records of replies sent from the phone.

- **Mark Addresses.** Your phone can warn you when you're addressing an email to somebody outside your company—just type in its email suffix here (@widgets.com). Whenever you address a message to anyone else, it appears in red in the To line.

- **Increase Quote Level.** Each time you reply to a reply, it gets indented more, so you and your correspondents can easily distinguish one reply from the next.

- **Include Attachments with Replies.** Let's say you receive a message with a file attached. When you reply, do you want the attachment to come along, too? Your choices are Never, Ask, Always, or When adding recipients, which is pretty smart.

- **Signature.** A signature is a bit of text that gets stamped at the bottom of your outgoing messages. Here's where you can change yours.

- **Default Account.** Your iPhone can manage an unlimited number of email accounts. Here you can tap the account you want to be your *default*—the one that's used when you create a new message from another program, like a Safari link, or when you're on the All Inboxes screen of Mail.

Contacts

Contacts gets its own little set of options in Settings:

- **Sort Order, Display Order.** How do you want the names in your Contacts list sorted—in alphabetical order by first name or by last name? Note that you can have the names *sorted* one way but *displayed* another way. Also note that not all those combinations make sense.

- **Short Name.** When this switch is on, the Mail app may fit more email addressees' names into its narrow To box by shortening them. It may display "M. Mouse," for example, or "Mickey M."—whatever you select here. **Prefer Nicknames**, on the same screen, is similar. It instructs Mail to display the *nicknames* for your friends (as determined in Contacts) instead of their real names.

- **My Info.** Tap here to tell the phone which card in Contacts represents *you*. Knowing who you are is useful to the phone in a number of places: For example, it's how Siri knows what you mean when you say, "Give me directions home."

- **Default Account.** If you have several accounts, which one does the iPhone use when you send mail from other apps—like when you email a photo from Photos or a link from Safari?

  It uses the *default* account, of course, which you choose here..

- **Import SIM Contacts.** If you came to the iPhone from another, lesser GSM phone, your phone book may be stored on its little SIM card instead of in the phone itself. In that case, you don't have to retype all those names and numbers to bring them into your iPhone. This button can do the job for you. (The results may not be pretty. For example, some phones store all address book data in CAPITAL LETTERS.)

Calendar

Your iPhone's calendar, wirelessly synced as it is, is a miracle of effortless technology (page 403). Here are its settings:

- **Time Zone Override.** Whenever you arrive in a new city, the iPhone actually learns (from the local cell towers) what time zone it's in and changes its own clock automatically.

  So here's a mind-teaser: Suppose there's a big meeting in California at 2 p.m. tomorrow—but you're in New York right now. How should that event appear on your calendar? Should it appear as 2 p.m. (that is, its local time)? Or should it appear as 5 p.m. (your East Coast time)?

  It's not an idle question, because it also affects reminders and alarms.

  Out of the box, Time Zone Override is turned off. The phone slides appointments around on your calendar as you travel to different time zones. If you're in California, that 2 p.m. meeting appears at 2 p.m. When you return to New York, it says 5 p.m. Handy—but dangerous if you forget what you've done.

  If you turn on the Override, though, the iPhone leaves all your appointments at the hours you record them—in the time zone you specify with the pop-up menu here. This option is great if you like to record events at the times you'll be experiencing them; they'll never slosh around as you travel. If you, a New Yorker, will travel to San Francisco next week for a 2 p.m. meeting, write it down as 2 p.m.; it will still say 2 p.m. when you land there.

- **Alternate Calendars.** If you prefer to use the Chinese, Hebrew, or Islamic calendar system, go nuts here.

- **Week Numbers.** This option makes Calendar display a little gray notation that identifies which week you're in (out of the 52 this year). It might say, for example, "W42." Because, you know, some people aren't aware enough of time racing by.

- **Show Invitee Declines.** You can invite someone to a meeting, as described on page 412. If they click Decline (they can't make it), maybe you don't need your phone to alert you. In that case, turn this switch off.

- **Sync.** If you're like most people, you refer to your calendar more often to see what events are *coming up* than to see the ones you've already lived through. Ordinarily, therefore, the iPhone saves you some syncing time and storage space by updating only relatively recent events on your iPhone calendar. It doesn't bother with events that are older than two weeks, or six months, or whatever you choose here. (Or you can turn on **All Events** if you want your entire life, past and future, synced each time—storage and wait time be damned.)

- **Default Alert Times.** This is where you tell the iPhone how much warning you need in advance of birthdays and events you've put on your calendar. Tailor it to your level of absentmindedness.

- **Start Week On.** This option specifies which day of the week appears at the *left edge of the screen* in the calendar's Week and Month views. For most people, that's Sunday, or maybe Monday—but, for all iOS cares, your week could start on a Thursday.

- **Default Calendar.** This option lets you answer the question: "When I add a new appointment to my calendar on the iPhone, which *calendar* (category) should it belong to?" You can choose Home, Work, Kids, or whatever category you use most often.

- **Location Suggestions.** You may have noticed that if you enter the location for a calendar appointment, the phone proposes a list of full street addresses that match what you're typing. That's to save you data entry, and also to calculate travel times. Here's the on/off switch.

Notes

Notes can sync with various online services: iCloud, Gmail, Yahoo, and so on. Tap **Default Account** to indicate which account you use *mainly*—the one that should contain any new note. **Password** is the command center for the locked notes feature (page 461). You can change your password here, or create an additional one—or allow your fingerprint or face to unlock your locked notes.

You can also turn on an **"On My iPhone" Account**—a completely private one that's not synced to *any* online service, or even your Mac. That data lives only on your phone—handy if you have deeply personal information, or if you just don't trust those online services.

Your notes start out sorted with the most recently edited ones at the top. Now, using **Sort Notes By**, you can specify that you want them listed alphabetically by title, or chronologically by date *created*.

Notes comes with ready-to-use type styles like Title, Heading, and Body. So you can use the **New Notes Start With** option to choose which of those is the first line when you create a new note. If you usually start with a title for your note "card," then choose **Title**, for example.

Sort Checked Items—talk about tweaky!—governs the order of checklist items. **Automatically** puts checked-off items at the bottom of the list.

Lines & Grids lets you choose "lined paper" or "graph paper"; see page 460.

You can take photos, scans, and videos right from within Notes. If you turn on **Save to Photos**, then you'll also get a copy of them in your Photos app, just as though you'd taken them with the Camera app.

Finally, here are all the options for creating Notes from the Lock screen (on the Control Center); they're described on page 49.

Reminders

Hey, it's the preference settings for the Reminders app!

- **Default List.** Suppose you've created multiple Reminder lists (Groceries, Movies to Rent, To Do, and so on). When you create a new item—for example, by telling Siri, "Remind me to fix the sink"—which list should it go on? Here's where you specify.

- **All-Day Reminders.** When you create a reminder assigned to a certain day (but not a certain time), do you want it to pop up on your screen that day? And at what time?

- **Show as Overdue.** What if you fail to check off those all-day Reminders tasks? If you turn this item on, the same reminder will pop up tomorrow, and tomorrow, and tomorrow, until you finally get it done.

Voice Memos

Voice Memos gets its own little Settings page.

- **Clear Deleted** refers to the app's own self-emptying Trash: How long should it hold onto memos you delete?

- **Audio Quality** offers a choice between amazing but space-eating quality (**Lossless**) or pretty good quality that takes up less space (**Compressed**).

- **Location-based naming** means "How should I name new recordings? Just 'New Recording 3' or whatever? Or named after where I am when I record?"

Phone

These settings have to do with your address book, call management, and other phone-related preferences:

- **My Number.** Here's where you can see your iPhone's own phone number. You can even edit it, if necessary (just how it appears—you're not actually changing your phone number).

- **Announce Calls.** Cool—the iPhone can speak the name or number of whoever is calling you. Here you can turn that feature on or off, or specify when you want it to happen.

- **SMS/Call Reporting.** Apple now makes it possible for software companies to write apps that report spammy calls and text messages. If you've installed one, it appears here. Apple wants to be sure you know that means you're forwarding some of your messages to the spam-reporting company.

- **Wi-Fi Calling, Calls on Other Devices.** Duplicates of the controls described on page 604.

- **Respond with Text.** This feature is described on page 138; here's where you can edit the canned "Can't talk right now" text messages.

- **Silence Unknown Callers.** There's no easy, complete way to muzzle obnoxious robocallers and telemarketers. But in iOS 13, Apple offers a start. When you turn on Silence Unknown Callers, the only calls that will make your phone ring are those from people in your Contacts, as well as people you've actually called. Everything else goes straight to voicemail without making your phone ring, buzz, or display a notification.

- **Blocked Contacts** shows the list of phone numbers you've blocked, like harassing ex-lovers, jerky siblings you're not speaking to, and collection agencies. Swipe left on a number to unblock it. (You can also see and edit this list in the Messages and FaceTime panels of Settings.)

- **Change Voicemail Password.** Yep, pretty much just what it says.

- **Call Forwarding, Call Waiting** (AT&T and T-Mobile only). Here are the on/off switches for Call Forwarding and Call Waiting, which are described in Chapter 4.

- **Show My Caller ID** (AT&T and T-Mobile only). If you don't want your number to show up on the screen of the person you're calling, then turn this off.

- **Dial Assist.** When this option is turned on, and when you're calling from another country, the iPhone automatically adds the proper country codes when dialing numbers in your contacts. Pretty handy, actually.

Messages

These options govern text messages (SMS) and iMessages, both of which are described in Chapter 6:

- **iMessage.** This is the on/off switch for iMessages. If it's off, then your phone never sends or receives these handy, free messages—only regular text messages.

- **Send & Receive.** Here you can enter additional email addresses that people can use to send your phone iMessages.

  This screen also offers a Start New Conversations From item that lets you indicate what you want to appear on the other guy's phone when you send a text: your phone number or email address.

- **Share Name and Photo** is described on page 222.

- **Show Contact Photos.** Do you want to see the tiny headshots of your conversation partners in the chat window?

- **Text Message Forwarding** is the text-message element of Continuity; it's described on page 593. You get an on/off switch for each gadget that you might want to display your phone's text messages.

- **Send Read Receipts.** If this is on, then people who send you iMessages will know when you've seen their texts. They'll see a tiny gray text notification beneath the iMessage bubble that contains their message. If you're creeped out by them being able to know when you're ignoring them, then turn this item off.

- **Send as SMS.** If you try to send an iMessage to somebody when there's no internet service, what happens? If this item is on, then the message goes to that person as a regular text message, using your cell carrier's network. If it's off, then the message won't go out at all.

- **MMS Messaging.** This is the on/off switch for picture and video messages (as opposed to text-only ones).

- **Group Messaging, Show Subject Field, Character Count.** These options are described starting on page 224.

- **Blocked Contacts.** Here's another way to build up a list of people you don't want to hear from, as described on page 225.

- **Keep Messages.** You can specify how long you want Messages to retain a record of your exchanges: 30 days, a year, or forever.

- **Filter Unknown Senders.** This feature gives you a sliver of protection from bombardment by strangers. It prevents you from getting notifications of iMessages from anyone who's not in your Contacts. In fact, you'll also see two tabs in Messages—one that lists chats for people you know (and regular non-Apple text messages), and the other labeled Unknown Senders.

- **Audio Messages.** You can now shoot audio utterances to other people just as easily as you can type them. And, under Expire, you can set them to auto-delete after two minutes. Why? First, because audio files take up space on your phone. Second, because you may consider them *spoken text messages*—not *recordings* to preserve for future generations. This is also where you turn on Raise to Listen.

  The audio-texting feature lets you send and receive audio messages without looking at the screen or touching it; see page 206.

- **Low Quality Image Mode.** This option can save a huge amount of cellular data when you send photos. See page 226.

FaceTime

These options pertain to FaceTime, the video-calling feature described on page 145. Here, for example, is the on/off switch for the entire feature; a place to enter your Apple ID, so people can make FaceTime calls to you; and a place to enter email addresses and a phone number, which can also be used to reach you.

The Caller ID section lets you specify how you want to be identified when you place a call to somebody else: either as a phone number or an email address. FaceTime Live Photos lets you take a Live Photo during a FaceTime call—a three-second video slice of your conversation.

Finally, here yet again is the Blocked Contacts option—yet another way to edit the list of people you don't want to hear from.

Maps

The expanded Maps app has an expanded set of settings. At the top are several controls that also appear elsewhere in Settings, but are here again because they're so important: Location (page 623), Siri & Search (page 618), **Notifications** (do you want turn-by-turn instructions to pop up when you're driving?), **Background App Refresh** (page 375), and **Cellular Data** (do you want Maps to be able to eat up your cellular internet allotment?).

Then there's:

- **Preferred Transportation Type.** Do you mainly drive, walk, or take public transit? By specifying here, you save yourself a tap every time you plot directions.

- **Driving & Navigation.** Here's where you tell Maps that you want your plotted courses to avoid **Tolls** or **Highways**, turn a **Compass** display on or off on the map, specify the **Navigation Voice Volume**, ask to be shown the **Speed Limit** of the roads you're on, and direct the playback of any spoken entertainment (like podcasts or audiobooks) to **Pause** whenever the Maps voice is giving you an instruction.

  Also on this screen: **Share ETA**. It's the on/off switch for the new iOS 13 feature described on page 441.

- **Walking.** Maps' ability to orient the map correctly when you're on foot has always been iffy. The **Optical Heading** feature gives it a fighting chance by using your camera and motion sensors to determine which way you're heading.

- **Transit.** Which modes do you want Maps to show you when proposing routes? **Bus**, **Subway & Light Rail**, **Commuter Rail**, **Ferry**?

- **Distances.** Measured in miles or kilometers, sir/madam?

- **Climate.** Would you like the map to show you the current **Air Quality Index** and **Weather Conditions** for the city you're exploring?

- **Map Labels.** Should names of streets and things be in English, even when you're in Tokyo or Hong Kong?

- **Ride Booking Extensions.** Now that Maps *can* incorporate other apps (see page 446), which ones *should* it show you? Lyft and Uber are the obvious ones here, so Maps can incorporate those ride-sharing services into its proposals for your travel.

- **Show Rides From New Apps.** Lyft and Uber aren't the only ride-sharing apps in town. But when you install new ones, you might want Maps to include their options automatically, so you don't have to remember to burrow in here and turn on their Extensions switches.

- **Table Booking Extensions.** If you turn on OpenTable and/or Yelp here, then whenever you search for a restaurant in Maps, you'll see whether it has tables available, courtesy of these apps.

- **Show Parked Location.** You wouldn't turn off this cool Maps feature, would you (page 443)?

- **Follow up by Email.** When you report a problem with Maps' still-buggy database of the world, may Apple technicians get back to you by email?

Compass

You wouldn't think that something as simple as the Compass app would need a Settings page, but here it is: an on/off switch called **Use True North**. (*True* north is the "top" point of the earth's rotational axis. If you turn it off, then Compass uses *magnetic* north, the spot traditional compasses point to; it's about 11 degrees away from true north.)

Measure

Here's where you specify whether you want to use metric or imperial units in this app, which is described on page 447.

Safari

Here's everything you ever wanted to adjust in the web browser but didn't know how to ask. (At the top: the usual **Siri & Search** options, as described on page 618.)

Search

- **Search Engine.** Your choice here determines who does your searching from the search bar: Google, Bing, Yahoo, or others.

- **Search Engine Suggestions.** As you type into Safari's search box, it tries to save you time in two ways. First, it sprouts a list of common search requests, based on what millions of other people have sought. This list changes with each letter you type. Second, Safari may autocomplete the address based on what you've typed so far, using suggestions from your History and bookmarks list. This switch shuts off those suggestions. (It's here primarily for the benefit of privacy hounds, who object to the fact that Apple processes their search queries in order to show the suggestions.)

- **Safari Suggestions.** Safari searches (Chapter 3) can find matches from the iTunes, Books, and App stores; from databases of local businesses, restaurants, and theaters; and from the web. Unless you turn this off.

- **Quick Website Search.** You can search *within* a site (like Amazon or Reddit or Wikipedia) using only Safari's regular search bar, as described on page 507. If, that is, this switch is on.

- **Preload Top Hit.** As you type into the search box, Safari lists websites that match. The first one is the Top Hit—and if this switch is on, Safari secretly downloads that page while you're still finishing your search. That way, if the Top Hit *is* the page you wanted, it appears almost instantly when you tap. But here's the thing: Safari downloads the Top Hit with *every* search—which uses up data. Which could cost you money.

General

- **AutoFill.** Safari's AutoFill feature saves you typing by filling in passwords, name, address, and phone numbers on web forms automatically (just for the sites you want). It can even store your credit card information, which makes buying things online *much* easier.

  The AutoFill screen lists on/off switches for the different kinds of data that Safari can autofill for you: your contact info, website account names, and passwords. (If you actually want to *see and edit* the memorized passwords, then open Settings→Passwords & Accounts.) You can also see your credit cards. Tap Saved Credit Cards to see or delete the memorized cards.

- **Frequently Visited Sites.** When you have nothing open in Safari, it likes to offer a page full of icons representing sites you visit often. Turn off this switch if your privacy concerns outweigh the convenience of this feature.

- **Favorites.** Your favorites in Safari are just ordinary bookmarks in an extraordinary folder. Here you can choose a *different* folder as the home of your favorites.

- **Block Pop-ups.** In general, you want this turned on. You really don't want pop-up ad windows ruining your surfing session. Now and again, though, pop-up windows are actually useful. When you're buying concert tickets, for example, a pop-up window might show the location of the seats. In that situation, you can turn this option off.

- **Content blockers.** This item appears only if you've installed any ad blockers. Here you can turn them off for all websites in one fell tap.

- **Downloads.** You know the new Downloads indicator in iOS 13 (page 501)? This screen lets you specify where you want your downloaded files to go (iCloud Drive, for example, or the phone itself), and how quickly you want the Downloads menu emptied out.

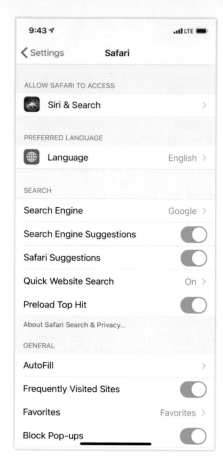

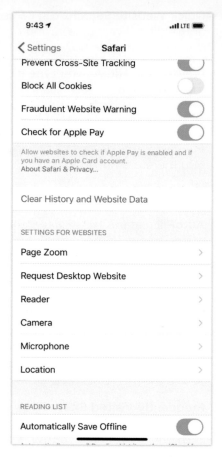

Tabs

- **Show Tab Bar.** In the larger phone models, this makes a row of tab buttons appear when the phone is in landscape orientation.

- **Show Icons in Tabs.** Do you want to see favicons—the little logos most websites design to help identify them visually?

- **Open Links.** When you tap a link with your finger, should the new page open in front of the current page—or behind it? Answer here.

- **Close Tabs.** People almost never manually close web pages after viewing them. Before iOS 13, therefore, they'd wind up with hundreds of open pages. No longer; see page 518.

Privacy & Security

- **Prevent Cross-Site Tracking.** This option prevents web operators from recording where you go after you leave their sites. As a result, advertisers have a harder time gathering data about you and what you like.

- **Block All Cookies.** You can learn all about cookies—and these options to tame them—on page 521.

- **Fraudulent Website Warning.** This option makes Safari warn you when you try to visit what it knows to be a *phishing* site. (Phishing is a common internet scam. The bad guy builds a fake version of Amazon, PayPal, or a bank's website—and tries to trick you into "logging in." You therefore unwittingly give up your name and password.)

- **Check for Apple Pay.** Some websites let you buy stuff with a quick touch of your fingerprint or quick peek at your face—but only if you let them offer you those controls by leaving this on.

- **Clear History and Website Data.** Like any web browser, Safari keeps a list of websites you've visited recently to make it easier for you to visit them again: the History list. And, like any browser, Safari therefore exposes your activities to any crackpot colleague who picks up your phone. If you're nervous about that prospect, then tap **Clear History and Website Data** to erase your tracks. This feature deletes all the cookies that websites have deposited on your "hard drive."

Settings for Websites

It's great that you can establish permanent settings for each website (text size, Reader mode, and so on), as described on page 500. But here you can set up the defaults for *all* websites. Including:

- **Page Zoom** is how magnified pages are when you first arrive. This screen also lists individual sites for which you've specified a zoom level.

- **Request Desktop Site.** See page 500.

- **Reader.** Do you want all sites to open up in the clutter-free, animation-free Reader View (page 520)?

- **Camera, Microphone, Location.** There aren't many websites that need access to these potentially spy-worthy components. But just in case evildoers try to access them, here's how you shut them down.

- **Automatically Save Offline.** The Reading List feature (page 512) is wonderful. But because it downloads entire web pages to your phone—and then syncs them to all your other Apple gadgets—it uses a lot of data. If you fear going over your cellphone plan's monthly data allotment, then turn this off. You'll be allowed to save sites to your Reading List only when you're online.

- **Advanced.** Safari recognizes HTML5, a technology that lets websites (like your Gmail) store data on your phone, for accessing even when you're not online. In Website Data, you can see which web apps have created these databases on your phone and delete them if necessary.

  JavaScript is a programming language whose bits of code frequently liven up web pages. If you suspect some bit of code is choking Safari, though, you can turn off its ability to decode JavaScript here.

  The Web Inspector is for website programmers. You connect your phone to a Mac with a USB cable; then, in Safari on the computer, you choose Debug→iPhone→[the name of the website currently on the iPhone's screen]. You'll be able to examine errors, warnings, tips, and logs for HTML, JavaScript, and CSS—great when you're designing and debugging web pages or web apps for the iPhone. (Experimental Features is also decidedly for programmers.)

News

Here you indicate whether the News app is allowed to Show Story Previews (where the first couple of lines of each news story appear right in the app). Restrict Stories in Today means you'll see only stories from news sources you've selected; you don't give News leeway to propose articles from other sources on topics you like.

Finally, there's a Privacy statement from Apple, and a way to Reset Identifier (the anonymous serial number Apple uses to remember your News interests—handy if you start getting stories on nutty subjects that don't interest you).

Stocks

The Privacy and Reset Identifier buttons are just like the ones in News.

Health

On your Health Profile screen, you can see which health and fitness apps are allowed to see your sex, date of birth, blood type, Fitzpatrick skin type, and Wheelchair status—and shut them down if necessary.

The Medical ID screen, meanwhile, holds the emergency medical and contact information described on page 81.

Tap **Data Access & Devices** to open the Sources screen, where you can see which apps and fitness devices you've permitted to store data in the Health app.

Finally, if you've given the Health app permission to access your online **Health Records**, you can see an overview of the data you've provided.

Shortcuts

By now, you know all about these automated software robots (page 182). What Settings wants to know here is:

- **Do you want** iCloud Sync to bring your shortcuts to your other iPhones and iPads?

- **Do you want them listed** on those other devices in the same order (**Sync Shortcut Order**)?

- **Are you willing** to accept shortcuts that *didn't* come from Apple's carefully curated, safety-checked Gallery (**Allow Untrusted Shortcuts**)?

Music

What you see here depends on whether you've subscribed to the $10-a-month Apple Music service (Chapter 8).

- **Show Apple Music.** When this is off, a couple of tabs (**For You** and **New**) disappear from the Music app. Which makes sense if you're not a subscriber, since they're doing you no good.

- **Add Playlist Songs.** Songs you add to a playlist get automatically added to your Apple Music library, too.

- **Sync Library,** formerly iCloud Music Library, is responsible for syncing your music collection across all your Apple machines.

- **Cellular Data.** Decide whether you're willing to use data for Music-related functions.

- **Downloaded Music** lets you see how much of your storage space is devoted to songs you've acquired.

- **Optimize Storage.** This option appears only if you use iCloud Music Library. It offers to auto-delete everything but 8, 16, 32, 64, or 128 gigs of songs. They're still yours—they're just online instead of on your phone.

- **Automatic Downloads** is another iCloud Music Library special. It means that any song you've added to your online song library also gets auto-copied to your phone for offline playback.

- **EQ, Volume Limit, Sound Check.** See page 277.

- **Use Listening History.** Each song you play on your phone helps to shape the Music app's "For You" recommendation. Also, people who follow you on Apple Music get to see what you've been playing.

- **Home Sharing.** Conveniently enough, you can access your iTunes music and movie collection on your computer upstairs, right from your iPhone, over your home Wi-Fi network. Here's where you enter the Apple ID that matches your iTunes setup. (In macOS Catalina, you set up Home Sharing in Settings→Sharing.)

TV

This is what you can adjust for the TV app:

- **iTunes Videos.** Use Cellular Data for Playback is a safeguard against eating up your cellular data with videos; leave it off to stream videos only over Wi-Fi. **Playback Quality** asks: When you're watching over **Wi-Fi**, do you want the best picture, even if that uses up more data? (Yes, some people have to worry about how much *Wi-Fi* data they use every month.) You get the same choices for **Cellular** data.

  Download HDR Videos is for iPhone Face ID owners, whose screen can show high dynamic range (HDR) video, with darker darks and brighter brights. **Purchases and Rentals**: When you buy or rent a video from Apple, do you want it in **High Definition** or **Standard**? (High Definition looks better but takes forever to download.)

- **Use Play History.** Do you want your viewing habits to affect the recommendations the app makes for what to watch next?

- **Show Sports Scores.** Ordinarily, the TV app shows the latest scores of many games on its Home screen. Turn this off if you intend to watch those games later and don't want to ruin the surprise.

Photos

You can read about most of this stuff in Chapter 9. Only a few items here are oddballs:

- **Upload Burst Photos.** Recent iPhones can snap 10 photos a second, as described on page 304. That's a lot of photos, which can fill up your iCloud storage fast. So Apple gives you the option to exclude them from the uploads.

- **Shared Albums** is one of the world's best features. But if you're a curmudgeon, you can turn it off here.

- **Auto-Play Videos and Live Photos.** In iOS 13, when you're scrolling through the Photos app, you'll see the thumbnails of videos and Live Photos playing, silently, automatically. If you find that behavior offensive, you can turn it off; now they just look like stills until you tap them.

- **View Full HDR** (iPhone X, XS, XR, XS Max, 11, 11 Pro, 11 Pro Max). You lucky dog—your screen can display the full range of colors and brights and darks in your photos. Don't turn this off.

- **Show Holiday Events.** You know the Memories feature (page 320)? It can create auto-slideshows based on the holidays in your country, if you want. If you'd just as soon not be reminded of these stressful times, then turn this off.

- **Transfer to Mac or PC.** iOS takes photos in a newish format called *HEIF* (high efficiency image file format). These photos take up half the space without losing any quality, which is awesome—but not all desktop photo programs can open HEIF files. MacOS versions since High Sierra can open them, but older ones can't; the current Photoshop version can, but older ones can't.

  If you're having trouble, turn on Automatic. That way, photos get sent as JPEGs, which every desktop program on earth can recognize.

Camera

Behold—the controls for the iPhone's amazing camera:

- **Preserve Settings.** The Camera app can remember the mode you had selected when you last used it—Video, Photo, Panorama, or whatever—instead of always starting with Photo.

  Depending on your phone model, it can also remember the last photo filter (page 302) or aspect ratio you used (page 336), what lighting effect (page 310), and whether or not you had Live Photo turned on (page 306).

- **Grid** turns the "Rule of Thirds" grid (the tic-tac-toe lines) on or off on the camera's viewfinder screen.

- **Scan QR Codes.** So cool! If you point the camera at a QR bar code (of the type you often see on movie posters and ads), the corresponding web link appears as a notification, ready to tap. You don't need a dedicated QR-reading app anymore.

- **Record Video.** This option controls the frame rate and quality of the video you shoot. The first number in each option (like **720p**, **1080p**, or **4K**) controls the *resolution* of the video (how many pixels make up each frame—and how correspondingly huge the video files are). The second, fps, controls the *frames per second*. Normal TV video is about 30 fps, so choosing 60 fps creates bigger files but smoother playback.

  On the Record Video screen, you may find an on-off switch for **Auto Low Light FPS**; in dim situations, you'll capture video at a slightly slower number of frames per second for a better image (at the expense of motion smoothness).

  A weird additional option appears here if you have a Plus, X, XS, XS Max, 11, or 11 Pro: **Lock Camera**. These phones, of course, have two or three lenses (page 4). Under certain lighting conditions, if you zoom while recording video, a little hiccup results as the phone switches from one lens to the other. But if you turn on this option you'll get no such glitch, because the phone will use only one lens the whole time. (You can still zoom—but it's a digital, fake zoom, and the image slightly degrades as you do so.)

- **Record Slo-mo.** Recent iPhone models give you a choice of slow-motion modes (and tell you how much space each takes up); 240 frames per second plays back at half the speed of 120.

- **Record Stereo Sound** (XS, XR, 11, 11 Pro models). For the first time, you can shoot videos with stereo sound! It makes a huge difference to the realism on playback. Why would you want to turn it off?

- **Formats** (iPhone 7 and later). Your photos and videos now occupy only half the space they used to—and look exactly the same. That's because Apple has adopted a format called *HEIF* (high efficiency image file format) for photos, and *HEVC* (high efficiency video coding) for video.

  Which is great—except what happens when you try to share one of your pictures or videos with someone whose phone or computer doesn't know that format? No sweat: iOS automatically checks before sending it to see if the receiving device can handle HEIF or HEVC. If not, it converts the outgoing photo to JPEG, or the outgoing video to H.264—the old standards.

  If you're having any trouble with this system, you can turn it all off here. If you choose **Most Compatible**, the iPhone captures photos and videos in the older formats (JPEG and H.264). As the note here points out, though, super-deluxe capture styles like 4K and 60 frames a second, and slow-mo at 240 frames a second, *must* use HEVC, no matter what your selection here.

- **Composition.** These options appear only on the iPhone 11 and 11 Pro models. Here's where you turn on or off Photos Capture Outside the Frame and Videos Capture Outside the Frame (page 299).

  Here, too, is Auto Apply Adjustments. When you've used Photos (Videos) Capture Outside the Frame and you begin to edit the photo or video, the app uses artificial intelligence to propose the *best* crop out of your broader photographic canvas. (A [⬚ AUTO] badge appears in the corner to let you know the app is making its suggestion.)

NOTE: For painfully technical reasons, the Deep Fusion feature described starting on page 301 doesn't work if you've turned on Photos Capture Outside the Frame. You can therefore think of Photos Capture Outside the Frame as the on/off switch for Deep Fusion, which doesn't otherwise have one.

- **Auto HDR** or **Smart HDR.** If this is on, Camera switches to HDR (page 300) whenever it thinks that lighting conditions merit it. If you turn this off, then the HDR button returns in the Camera app, so the choice is yours.

- **Keep Normal Photo.** When you take a photo in HDR mode, iOS saves *two* photos, one normal and one HDR. If you turn this off, you get only the HDR shot. This option doesn't appear on iPhone 11 or 11 Pro models, whose cameras are so proficient that they don't believe in the concept of a "normal" photo.

Books

These Books ebook settings are described starting on page 400.

Podcasts

These settings affect how often the Podcasts app auto-downloads new episodes, and how many; whether it can do so using cellular data (or only Wi-Fi); and whether you want the app to auto-delete podcasts you've already heard.

When you're wearing earbuds or using steering-wheel playback controls, the External Controls let you specify what the ◄◄ and ►► buttons do: Next/Previous track or Skip Forward/Back.

Best of all, you can adjust how many seconds those skip buttons skip.

iTunes U

Suppose you make notes while listening to these free college and museum courses. Do you want them synced to your other iOS devices?

Game Center

For millions of people, the iPhone is a mobile game console. Once you've turned on the Game Center switch and logged into Game Center with your Apple ID, you can allow Nearby Players to invite you to multiplayer games wirelessly, and you can create or edit your Game Center Profile (your player name).

TV Provider

As noted on page 281, the TV app is designed to let you watch all the shows you're paying your cable or satellite company for—on your phone. You can sign in here if you have an account from DirecTV, Dish, or some cable companies.

App Preferences

At the bottom of the Settings screen, you see a list of apps that have installed settings screens of their own. For example, here's where you can decide whether you want Feedly to use cellular data, change how many days' worth of news you want *The New York Times* app to display, and so on. Each one offers an assortment of preference options.

It can get to be a *very* long list.

PART FIVE

Appendixes

Appendix A
Signup & Setup

Appendix B
Troubleshooting & Maintenance

Signup & Setup

You gotta admit it: Opening up a new iPhone brings a certain excitement. There's a prospect of possibility, of new beginnings. There are those first few minutes—even before it's in a case—when it's shiny, spotless, free of fingerprints or nicks—a gorgeous thing.

This chapter is all about getting started, whether that means buying and setting up a new iPhone or upgrading an older model to the new iOS 13 software that's described in this book.

Buying a New iPhone

Each year's new iPhone model is faster, has a better camera and screen, and comes packed with more features than the previous one. Still, "new iPhone" doesn't have to mean the iPhone 11 Pro Max ($1,100 to $1,450). You can still get an iPhone 8 for $450, an iPhone XR for $600, and so on. (Thank heaven, the U.S. carriers no longer obscure the true price of the phone in two-year contracts.) And of course you can get even older models dirt cheap, used.

Once you've chosen the model you want, you also have to choose which cellphone company you want to provide its service: AT&T, Verizon, T-Mobile, or Sprint.

Research the coverage where you live and work. Each company's website shows a map of its coverage.

You can buy your iPhone from a phone store (Verizon, Sprint, T-Mobile, AT&T), from an Apple Store, from a retail store, from the Apple website, or even from the Apple Store *app*. You can buy the phone outright, or you can opt to have the price spread out in monthly payments. Or you can lease it.

All right then: You're in the store, or sitting down to do some ordering online. Here are the decisions you'll have to make:

- **Transferring your old number.** You can bring your old cellphone or home number to your new iPhone. Your friends can keep dialing your old number—but your iPhone will ring instead.

  It usually takes under an hour for a cellphone-number transfer to take place. During that time, you can make calls on the iPhone, but you can't receive them.

- **Select your monthly calling plans.** The carriers are all pushing unlimited-data plans these days, which come with a certain comfort.

  But the traditional "4 gigabytes per month" plans are still around, too. Of course, the problem with fixed data allotments is this: Who has any idea what 4 gigabytes of data means? How much of that do you eat up with email alone? How much is one YouTube video?

  As you approach your monthly limit, you'll get warnings by text message, but you can also see your data usage on your phone (page 605). Yes, it's a pain to have to worry about data limits, but at least monitoring them is fairly easy. If you use more than your allotted amount, some carriers automatically bill a surcharge—for example, $15 for each additional gigabyte.

  And all iPhone plans require an "activation fee" (ha!).

NOTE: The choice you make here isn't etched in stone. You can change your plan at any time on your carrier's website.

As you budget for your plan, keep in mind that, as with any cellphone, you'll also be paying taxes as high as 22 percent, depending on your state. Ouch.

Upgrading to iOS 13

If you've recently bought a new iPhone, great! iOS 13 (or one of its successors, like iOS 13.2) comes on it preinstalled.

But you can also upgrade an older or used iPhone to this new software in any of three ways:

- **Upgrade it wirelessly.** *Upgrading* means installing iOS 13 on top of whatever is already on your iPhone. You don't lose any data or settings.

This is the easiest way to upgrade. You've probably already seen the little red number on your Settings app icon (see page 69), and on the word "General" inside it; the phone is trying to tell you iOS 13 is ready to download. Tap Settings→General→Software Update to see the iOS 13 info; tap Download and Install. (You have to be on a Wi-Fi network, and it's wise to have your iPhone plugged into power.)

- **Upgrade it from iTunes.** If you wish, you can also perform the upgrade using the iTunes program on your computer (or a macOS Catalina Finder window). This method takes less time but, of course, requires being at your computer.

  To begin, connect your iPhone and click its icon (see page 555). On the Summary or General tab, click Check for Update, and then click Download and Update.

- **Restore it.** This is a more dramatic step, which you should choose only if you've been having problems with your phone or if, for some other reason, you'd like to start completely fresh. This step backs up the phone, erases it completely, installs iOS, and then copies your stuff back onto the phone.

  Connect the phone to your computer, open iTunes (or a Catalina Finder window), and then click Restore iPhone.

  After the Restore process, treat your phone as though it were a brand-new one as you read the following pages.

The Setup Assistant

Upgrading your iPhone to iOS 13 from an older version doesn't involve much more effort than sitting and waiting. When the upgrade is over, you get a Welcome screen, and boom: You're at your Home screen, ready to roll.

Things aren't so straightforward, though, if any of these situations apply:

- **You've bought a new iPhone** to replace an older model.

- **You've bought your first iPhone.**

- **You've upgraded your existing iPhone** to iOS 13 by *restoring* it (erasing it, starting from scratch).

All three of these situations subject you to the iOS 13 setup assistant—a series of screens that interview you to get all the settings right.

If you're upgrading from an older phone, you'd be very, very wise to take three preparatory steps. First, back up the old phone (see page 564). Second, transfer your old phone's SIM card to the new one (page 26).

Finally, iOS 13 can't open so-called *32-bit apps* (the ancient ones). You may own a few old favorites that you'll have to give up.

The screens you encounter, and their sequence, vary wildly depending on what phone model you have, whether you choose Quick Start and Express Settings, what backup you're restoring from, and other factors. But, in general, this is what you'll find when you turn on the phone for the first time after buying or upgrading it:

1. **Hello.** Your new phone's life begins with a screen that flashes "Hello" in various languages. (At this point, you can turn on VoiceOver [page 233] or Zoom [page 234] if you have trouble seeing it.) Tap Continue.

2. **[Choice of Language].** You won't get very far setting up your phone if you can't understand the instructions. So the goal here is to tell it what language you speak.

3. **Select Your Language and Country.** Now tell the phone where in the world you live. (It proposes the country where you bought the phone. Clever, eh?)

4. **Quick Start.** If you're upgrading from an older phone, you're in luck: The Quick Start feature is about to save you the tedium of entering passwords and setting up initial preferences. It works only, however, if your old phone is running iOS 11, 12, or 13.

    If you don't have another iOS 11, 12, or 13 device, tap Set Up Manually and skip to step 5.

    If you *do* have one, though, this is a blast. The Set Up Your iPhone screen (on the new phone) directs you to *bring the old phone close* to the new phone. The old one shows a Set Up New iPhone screen bearing your iCloud address; tap Continue.

    Suddenly, the new phone displays an animation that looks like a swirling cloud of glitter. Hold the old phone a few inches over the new phone's screen, so the animation fits in the brackets on the old one's screen. Boom! They're paired. The old phone begins to send encrypted data to the new one.

    You're now directed to enter the old phone's passcode on the new phone; it's going to become your new phone's passcode, too.

    The basic Quick Start process doesn't actually transfer much: only your Wi-Fi password, your iCloud password, a few settings, and of course your iPhone passcode.

    But when it's over, you're offered the chance to bring over everything else: all your apps, settings, and data from the older phone. You can tap Transfer from iPhone, which copies everything over Wi-Fi (or a Lightning cable and an Apple Lightning to USB camera adapter). That's slow but sure, and it doesn't require a computer or an iCloud backup.

    If you do have an iCloud backup, you can choose Download from iCloud instead.

    When it's all over, you get to skip most of the rest of these steps.

5. **Choose a Wi-Fi Network.** Tap the name of the Wi-Fi network you want, enter the password if required, and tap Join.

    Or, if there's no Wi-Fi you can (or want to) hop onto right now, tap Use Mobile Connection.

At this point, your phone becomes *activated*, which means it marries your cell carrier. If there's a SIM card from your carrier in your phone (page 26), this step takes only a second or two. If there *isn't* a SIM card in the phone, though, you can't activate it; you can't proceed to the Home screen. (The workarounds: Borrow a SIM card from your carrier, even from a deactivated account—or use Quick Start to inherit the settings from another iOS 11, 12, or 13 phone, as described in step 4.)

6. **Data & Privacy.** A little statement about Apple's philosophy: collecting as little data from you as possible.

7. **Touch ID or Face ID.** You're now invited to teach the phone your fingerprint or "face print" for the purposes of unlocking it without having to type a password. Start on page 54 for more on Touch ID and Face ID.

   You can also tap **Set Up Later**. When the time comes, you can revisit this process in **Settings→Touch ID & Passcode** (or **Face ID & Passcode**).

8. **Create a Passcode.** Whether you opted to store a fingerprint/face or not, you're now asked to make up a six-digit *passcode* for unlocking your phone. You'll need it whenever the phone won't accept Touch ID or Face ID—for example, after you've restarted.

You don't have to accept iOS's proposal of a six-digit passcode. Tap **Passcode Options** to reveal more choices, like **Custom Alphanumeric Code** (any password you like, any length, any characters), **Custom Numeric Code** (any number of digits), or **4-Digit Numeric Code** (like in the old days).

9. **Apps & Data.** This screen offers to reload all your stuff from your most recent backup. (See Chapter 15 and Chapter 16 for details on iPhone backups.)

   The new phone may guess about what recent backup you want to use. If it's correct, tap **Continue**.

   If not, tap **Choose Other Backup** or **Don't Restore**. Now you're offered a choice: **Restore from iCloud Backup** (if your backup was on iCloud), **Restore from Mac or PC** (if your backup was on your computer, like in iTunes or macOS Catalina), **Move Data from Android**, or **Don't Transfer Apps & Data** (if you've never owned an iPhone before or want to start fresh).

The **Move Data from Android** option prompts you to download a companion app on your old Android phone called Move to iOS. When you open it, the app (on Android) asks you to enter a number code that's offered by your iPhone at this stage. Then the Android phone asks what kinds of data you'd like copied to your iPhone: your Google account (email, calendar, and so on), web bookmarks, text messages, contacts, and photos. When you hit **Next**, the transfer begins, wirelessly and automatically.

10. **Apple ID.** A million features require an Apple ID—just about any transaction you make with Apple online, from buying a song to buying a laptop. Using iCloud (Chapter 16). Playing games against other people online. Making an appointment at an Apple Store.

If you already have an Apple ID, enter your email address and iCloud password here. If not, tap **Don't have an Apple ID or forgot it?** You'll be asked to provide your name, birthday, email address (or you can create a new iCloud email address), a password of your choice, and answers to a few security questions (you'll have to get them right if you ever forget your password). You also get to decide if you'd like the honor of receiving junk email from Apple.

You'll be sent, by the way, an Apple ID Verification Code—that is, a two-factor authentication code as described on page 662.

11. **Terms and Conditions.** Tap **Agree**.

You may encounter a step 11.5 here: Enter Old Passcode. If you've used this phone before (with a different passcode), you'll have to enter the old one to recover all your old passwords and the layout of your Home screens.

12. **Express Settings.** Do you want to set up Apple Pay (page 579)? How about Siri (Chapter 5)? Are navigation and other apps allowed to monitor your location using Location Services (page 623)? Will you agree to let Apple collect anonymous Analytics data about how you use the phone?

Here, Apple gives you the chance to say "Yeah, sure, fine" (tap **Continue**) for all these items at once, thereby skipping over a few steps in the setup assistant.

Otherwise, you can tap **Customize Settings** and walk through those screens individually before proceeding.

Some of these screens involve some setup. For example, Apple Pay requires registering your credit cards, and if you want to be able to use the "Hey Siri" hands-free mode (page 160), then you're supposed to speak a few sample sentences so Siri learns your voice.

NOTE: If your new phone is slurping up the backup from an older phone (if you used Quick Start, for example), you don't get Express Settings. Instead you get Settings from Your Backup. It serves much the same purpose—letting you skip the Siri, Location, and Analytics questions—except that it grabs the settings from your backup rather than using Apple's suggested defaults.

12. **Keep Your iPhone Up to Date.** Apple would really love it if you agreed to turn on Automatic Updates here. That way, every time it comes out with a new iOS version—which is usually more stable and richer in features—you'll get it automatically. (You'll still get a notification before it's installed.)

13. **Apple Pay.** You're now invited to store your credit cards, for the purpose of turning on Apple Pay. See page 579.

    If you don't want to use Apple Pay, or don't want to set it up now, hit Next anyway, and then hit Set Up Later in Wallet.

14. **iCloud Keychain.** Do you want your iPhone to memorize all your web passwords and sync them to your other Apple gear, so you don't have to? (Yes, you do.)

15. **Siri.** Want to set up "Hey Siri"? You can always do it later.

16. **Screen Time.** Apple invites you to set up Screen Time, to control your gadget addiction (page 383).

17. **App Analytics.** Behind the scenes, your iPhone sends records to Apple, including your location and what you're doing on your iPhone. By analyzing this data en masse, Apple can figure out where the dead spots in the cellular network are, how to fix bugs, and so on. The information is anonymous—it's not associated with you. But if the idea seems invasive, here's your chance to stop this data from being sent.

18. **True Tone Display.** This option appears only on the iPhone 8 and later models. It adjusts the screen colors in an attempt to keep them consistent under different lighting conditions (see page 615).

19. **Appearance.** And here it is, folks, the big deal in iOS 13: a choice between the traditional white-background look and the new Dark mode (page 5).

20. **Meet the New Home Button.** On the iPhone 7 and 8 models, this screen introduces you to the clickless home button—and invites you to choose how hard its click feels (page 609).

21. **Display Zoom.** At this point, bigger-screened phones (iPhone 6s, 7, 8, XR, and all Plus and Max models) ask how you want to exploit the larger screen. If you choose Standard, you'll see more stuff (icons, menus, lines of text) per screenful than on smaller iPhones. If you choose Zoomed, then you'll see the same amount of stuff, but *bigger*. You can always change your mind in Settings→Display & Brightness.

22. **Go Home, Switch Between Recent Apps, Quickly Access Controls.** These informational screens appear on Face ID iPhones. They're designed to teach you some of the gestures you'll need as you adapt to life without a home button.

23. **Welcome to iPhone.** Your phone is set up. Tap Get Started to jump to the Home screen.

If you've restored your phone from a backup, you're not quite finished, though; now your phone should sit in a Wi-Fi hotspot for 30 or 60 minutes as it downloads all your existing apps, music, photos, and videos from Apple's servers.

See, an iPhone backup doesn't include any of that stuff. Instead, iOS simply remembers *which* apps, songs, photos, and videos you had. After your backup is restored, your phone proceeds to re-download them from the internet; you'll see your dimmed app icons filling up as they arrive.

The benefit of this arrangement, of course, is that your backups don't take up much time or disk space. The downside: If you're trying to restore several phones from a single backup, you're going to eat up a *lot* of data and time.

In any case, this is an excellent argument for beginning the restore process when (a) you're in a Wi-Fi hotspot, and (b) you've got some time to kill.

Software Updates to Come

As you're probably aware, phone software like the iPhone's is a perpetual work in progress. Apple constantly fixes bugs, adds features, and makes tweaks to extend battery life and improve other services.

Updating Directly on the Phone

One day you'll be minding your own business, and you'll see a red number badge appear on the Settings app's icon. Open Settings→General→Software Update to read about the new update and install it. Note, though, that unless it's plugged into a power source, your phone won't install an iOS update unless its battery is at least half full.

Install Updates from Your Computer

Maybe you're not that adventurous and you'd prefer to install your software update the old-fashioned way. No problem: Connect the iPhone to iTunes, wirelessly or not (page 555). Then click the iPhone's icon in iTunes; on the **Summary** pane, tap **Check for Update**.

Two-Factor Authentication

By now, it's probably clear that *passwords* aren't enough to protect us from the bad guys. Even if your password is *é$*@çg45e+7r6ü*, someone can still steal it. There are all kinds of ways: An inside job. Poor security on a company's servers. Social engineering, where someone calls up pretending to be you and saying, "I forgot my password."

Fortunately, security experts have come up with a way to keep baddies out of your account *even if they've got your password*. It's a system called two-factor authentication—and it's no longer optional. (Let's call it 2FA to save paper.)

Here's how it works: Suppose you're setting up a new Apple device, or you're trying to log into *icloud.com* with a new web browser. You log in with your iCloud password.

Almost immediately, Apple sends a message to the screens of all your *other* Apple machines—devices it knows you own: "Your Apple ID is being used to sign in to an iPad [or whatever] in Hinsdale, IL" (and there's a little map).

And what if you don't *have* another Apple device? Then you can get the code via automated phone call or text; tap **Didn't get a verification code**.

And what if you're not online? No problem. You can make the older, trusted device cough up a code *on demand*, in **Settings**→**[your name]**→**Password & Security**→**Get Verification Code**.

If Hinsdale is not where you are right now, it means someone is pretending to be you! Tap **Don't Allow** and shut him down!

If it *is* you, though, hit **Allow**. Now your older device displays a six-digit code; on the new machine or browser, there's a box where you can enter it. You're in.

Sometimes the code and "enter code" box appear on the same device! What sense does that make?

Easy: You're using a new *browser* for the first time. The operating system treats that browser as a new "device," even though it's running on an already-accepted machine.

If some Russian hacker does get your password, he still can't get into your account, because he doesn't have the code. Sneaky, eh? And incredibly effective; 2FA almost completely eliminates the chance of someone else accessing your account. He'd have to have your iCloud password *and* your phone or laptop *and* your password for that device.

Each time, you're adding to your list of trusted devices. At any time, you can look over a list of them at *appleid.apple.com/account/manage*. (You'll get a 2FA code just to get into your account.)

This all works smoothly on Apple products. But what about programs (like calendar and email programs) that also need access to your iCloud account? They're locked out just as though they were hackers.

Fortunately, you can go to *appleid.apple.com/account/manage* to generate an *app-specific password*. If you enter this 16-character password as your iCloud password in your third-party calendar or email program, it will then be able to access your iCloud account as it did before.

Troubleshooting & Maintenance

The iPhone is a computer, and you know what that means: Things can go wrong. This particular computer, though, is not quite like a Mac or PC. It runs a spin-off of the macOS operating system, but that doesn't mean you can apply the same troubleshooting techniques.

Therefore, when things go wrong, let this appendix be your guide.

First Rule: Install the Updates

There's an old saying: "Never buy version 1.0 of anything." In the iPhone's case, the saying could be: "Never buy version 13.0 of anything."

The very first version (or major revision) always has bugs, glitches, and things the programmers didn't have time to finish the way they would have liked. The iPhone is no exception.

The beauty of this phone, though, is that Apple can send it fixes, patches, and even new features through software updates. One day you'll glance at your Home screen's Settings icon, and—bam!—there'll be a badge indicating that new iPhone software is available.

So the first rule of trouble-free iPhoning is to accept these updates when they're offered. With each new software blob, Apple removes another few dozen tiny glitches.

And sure enough: Within a few weeks of iOS 13's existence, software updates 13.1 and 13.2 came down the pike. And more will follow.

Six Ways to Reset the Phone

The iPhone runs actual programs, and as actual programs do, they actually crash. Sometimes, the program you're working in simply vanishes and you find yourself back at the Home screen. Just reopen the program and get on with your life.

If the program you're in just doesn't seem to be working right—it's frozen or acting weird, for example—then one of these resetting techniques usually clears things right up.

NOTE: Proceed down this list in order! Start with the easy ones.

- **Exit the app.** On an iPhone, you're never aware that you're launching and exiting programs. They're always just *there*, like TV channels, when you switch to them. There's no Quit command. But if a program starts acting glitchy, you can make it quit.

  To do that, bring up the app switcher. (If you have a home button, double-press it. If not, swipe up from the bottom of the screen and stop in the middle.)

  Find the "card" that represents your balky app, and then flick it upward to quit it. Then try reopening it to see if the problem has gone away.

- **Turn the phone off and on again.** If it seems that something more serious has gone wrong, restart the phone. If you have a home-button phone, hold in the side button for a few seconds. If not, hold the side button *and* either volume button simultaneously.

  When the screen says **slide to power off**, confirm by swiping. The iPhone shuts off completely.

  Turn it back on by pressing the side button for a second or two.

- **Force-restart the phone.** If you haven't been able to force-quit the program, and you can't shut the phone off either, you might have to force a restart. Thanks to Apple's fickle relationship with the home-button concept, the method varies by phone model.

  iPhone 8 later: Click the volume-up key, and then the volume-down key; now hold in the side button until the Apple logo appears.

  iPhone 7: Hold in the side button *and* the volume-down key simultaneously until the Apple logo appears.

  Earlier models: Hold down the home button and the side button until the Apple logo appears.

  In each case, keep holding, even if the screen goes black or you see the "power off" slider. Don't release until you see the Apple logo, which indicates that the phone is restarting.

- **Reset the settings.** This procedure doesn't erase any of your data—only the phone's settings. From the Home screen, tap Settings→General→Reset→Reset All Settings.

- **Erase the whole phone.** From the Home screen, tap Settings→General→Reset→Erase All Content and Settings. Now, *this* option zaps your stuff—*all* of it. Music, videos, email, settings, apps, all gone, and all overwritten with random 1's and 0's to make sure it's completely unrecoverable. Clearly, you're getting into last resorts here. Of course, you can then sync with your iTunes or iCloud backup to copy all that stuff back onto your phone.

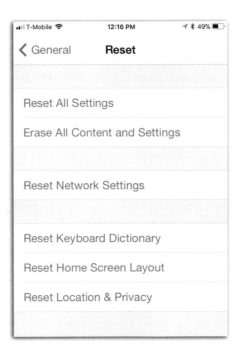

- **Restore the phone.** If none of these steps solve the phone's glitchiness, it might be time for the nuclear option: erasing it completely, resetting both hardware and software to a factory-fresh condition.

TIP: If you're able to sync the phone with iCloud or iTunes first, *do it!* That way, you'll have a backup of all those intangible iPhone data bits: text messages, call logs, Recents lists, and so on. It will all go back onto the phone the first time you sync after the restore.

If you backed up to your computer: Connect the phone to your computer, as described in Chapter 15. In iTunes (or macOS Catalina's Finder), click the iPhone icon and then, on the Summary or General tab, click **Restore**.

The first order of business: You're offered the chance to make a backup of your iPhone (all its phone settings, text messages, and so on) before proceeding. Accepting this invitation is an excellent idea. Click **Back Up**.

If you backed up to iCloud: You can restore your phone this way only if it's completely wiped empty. If it's not, then manually erase it using iTunes first.

During the setup screens described on page 655, tap **Restore from iCloud Backup**. You're shown the three most recent backups; tap the one you want. The phone goes right to work downloading your settings and account information. Then it restarts and begins to download your apps; if you're in a hurry for a particular one, tap its icon to make iCloud prioritize it.

When that's all over, you can get to work downloading your music (if you're an Apple Music subscriber).

iPhone Doesn't Turn On

Usually, the problem is that the battery is dead. Just plugging it into the USB charger or your computer doesn't bring it to life immediately; a completely dead iPhone doesn't wake up until it's been charging for a few minutes. It pops on automatically when it has enough juice to do so.

Recovery Mode

Phones, like the best of us, sometimes get confused. In a few weird situations, the iPhone gets so baffled that you can't even start it up. For example:

- **The startup process gets stuck** forever at the Apple logo.

- **The "Connect to iTunes" screen appears,** even when the phone *is* connected.

- **You've connected to your computer with a cable,** but the phone doesn't show up in iTunes or the Finder, or it says it's in "recovery mode."

The solution is the drastic, but effective, force-restore process (known to techies as the Device Firmware Update mode).

Open iTunes (or a macOS Catalina Finder window), on your computer. Connect the iPhone with its white USB cable. Now force-restart the phone as described on page 666. Keep the key(s) pressed until a message tells you that an iPhone in Recovery mode has been detected; click **OK**. (If you see anything but blackness on your iPhone's screen—an Apple logo, for example—the process didn't work. If the problem has not, in fact, gone away, you should start again.)

Now a message informs you, "There is a problem with the iPhone that requires it to be updated or restored."

By far your favorite choice should be **Update**, because that means you won't lose any of your data. iTunes will simply download and install a fresh copy of iOS 13. (If the download takes longer than 15 minutes, the iPhone exits recovery mode. Just wait until the download is finished, and then start this process again.)

If the Update process doesn't work, you have no choice but the bad one: **Restore**. That's where you wipe out the iPhone's contents and restore everything on it from a backup. (Of course you *have* a backup, right?)

Battery Life Is Terrible

If your battery seems to drain faster right after you've installed iOS 13, it might be because the Photos app is busy scanning and categorizing all your photos so it can use its object and facial recognition.

Or maybe it's just you *using* the phone more, checking out the cool new features.

If neither of those is the problem, then consult the battery-saving tips on page 37. And if the phone is more than a year old, it may be time for a battery swap (page 672).

Out of Space

It happens all the time. You couldn't imagine filling up 64, 128, 256, or 512 gigabytes of storage, so you saved some money by buying an iPhone with less. And now you can't even take a photo, because your phone is full. You're frozen out until you have the time and expertise to delete some less important stuff.

Fortunately, iOS 13 is teeming with features designed to ease up the storage crunches so many people face. Some are automatic: The recent HEIF and HEVC formats, for example, mean new photos and videos occupy only half as much space as the old ones (see page 648).

But when it's time to make some space, you have a few options.

The iPhone Storage Screen

The Grand Central of storage management is in **Settings→General→ iPhone Storage**.

Here's a master graph that clearly shows what's eating up your space. This screen also lists every kind of file by category (apps, photos, mail, and so on) and how much space it's using. That should make it easy to delete the fattest ones to make the most room with the least effort.

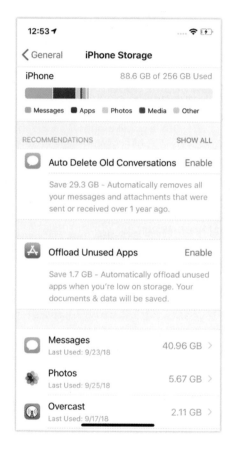
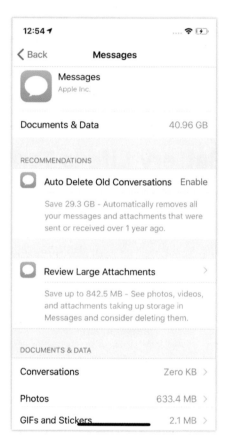

The biggest space hogs on your phone are video files, photo files, apps, and music files. Heck, deleting just one downloaded movie or TV show could solve your storage crunch instantly.

Better yet, this screen *suggests* ways to free up space, like deleting messages that are older than a year; looking over and maybe deleting big email attachments; or storing your messages on iCloud.

Offload Unused Apps

One of those suggestions is to **Offload Unused Apps**. It makes the iPhone delete the apps you haven't used in a while, but preserve their icons (dimmed) on your Home screens; just tap an app if you ever want to download it again.

This option has its own master switch in **Settings→iTunes and App Stores→Offload Unused Apps**. You can also hit the **Offload App** button for individual apps in the master list at **Settings→General→iPhone Storage**.

Offload Full-Resolution Photos

Also, for goodness' sake, don't miss **Optimize iPhone Storage** (page 355). It transfers your full-resolution original photos to iCloud—but leaves much smaller versions on your phone that are just right for viewing on its little screen.

Offload Music

Deep in **Settings→Music**, another Optimize Storage switch appears. Turn it on to automatically remove music from your iPhone that you haven't played in a while, freeing up precious gigabytes.

Warranty and Repair

The iPhone comes with a one-year warranty and 90 days of phone tech support. If you buy an AppleCare+ contract (from $130 to $200, depending on the model), then you're covered for a second year. Note that you have to add this coverage within 60 days of getting your new phone.

> **TIP:** AT&T, Sprint, T-Mobile, or Verizon tech support is free for both years of your contract. They handle questions about your iPhone's phone features.

If, during those two years, anything goes wrong that's not your fault, Apple will fix it for free. In fact, AppleCare+ covers damage even if it *is* your fault—if you drop the phone or something—at a rate of $30 for screen damage and $100 for other damage, plus tax. Maximum: twice.

There's a second tier of protection, too, called AppleCare+ with Theft and Loss (another $60 to $100 for two years). This one's for true klutzes: Apple will give you a brand-new phone if yours is destroyed or stolen—up to twice a year—for the low, low price of $200 to $270, depending on the model.

When something bad happens to your iPhone, you can either take the phone to an Apple Store, which is usually the fastest route, or call 800-APL-CARE (800-275-2273) to arrange shipping back to Apple. In general, you'll get the fixed phone back in three business days.

NOTE: *Back up the phone before it goes in for repair.* Apple often just hands you a new (or refurbished) iPhone instead of your original.

Also, remove your SIM card (page 26) before you send in your broken iPhone—and put it back in when you get the phone back. Don't leave it in the loaner phone. The carrier can get you a new card if you lose your original, but it's a hassle.

Out-of-Warranty Repairs

Once the year or two has gone by, or if you damage your iPhone in a way that's not covered by the warranty (backing your car over it comes to mind), Apple charges from $270 to $550 to repair an iPhone, depending on the model. (Apple usually just replaces it.)

Battery Replacement

Why did Apple seal the battery inside the iPhone, anyway? Everyone knows lithium-ion batteries don't last forever. After 300 or 400 charges, the iPhone's battery begins to hold less charge (perhaps 80 percent of the original). After a certain point, the phone will need a new battery. How come you can't change it yourself?

Apple's answer: A consumer-replaceable battery takes up a lot more space inside the phone. It requires a plastic compartment that shields the guts of the phone from you and your fingers; it requires a removable door; and it needs springs or clips to hold the battery in place.

In any case, you can't change the battery yourself. If you have AppleCare+, though, a battery replacement is free. If the phone is out of warranty, you must send it to Apple (or take it to an Apple Store) for a battery-replacement job. It costs $80. (As an eco-bonus, Apple properly disposes of the old batteries, which you might not do on your own.)

What to Do About a Cracked Screen

Keeping your iPhone in a case may lower the chances of your breaking it or scratching it—but it can't prevent bad luck. An incredible number of iPhone screens meet an untimely end, even with cases on.

Apple will happily replace your phone's screen for $280 to $330, depending on the model. It'll do it the same day if you take the phone into an Apple Store, or you can mail it in and get a replacement in three to five days. (As noted earlier, if you've bought AppleCare+, then a replacement screen is a flat $30.)

There are plenty of other companies that can repair a cracked screen, sometimes for less money—but you may not get an actual Apple screen.

And then there's the do-it-yourself technique. You can buy a screen-replacement kit for about $60 online, complete with the special tools you need to open the iPhone and do the job yourself. It requires care, patience, and some dexterity (Google can help you find the step-by-steps), but it's a good option if you're technically savvy.

Where to Go from Here

At this point, the iPhone is such a phenomenon that there's no short-age of resources for getting more help, news, and tips. Here are a few examples:

- **Apple's official iPhone User Guide.** Yes, there is an actual download-able PDF user's manual for iOS 13. *help.apple.com/iphone*

- **Apple's official iPhone help website.** Online tips, tricks, and tutorials; troubleshooting topics; downloadable PDF help documents; and, above all, an enormous, seething treasure trove of discussion boards. *apple.com/support/iphone*

- **Apple's service site.** All the dates, prices, and expectations for getting your iPhone repaired. Includes details on getting a temporary replace-ment unit. *apple.com/support/iphone/service/faq*

- **iMore blog.** News, tips, tricks, all in a blog format. *imore.com*

- **MacRumors/iPhone.** Blog-format news, accessory blurbs, and help discussions. *macrumors.com/iphone*

- **iLounge.** Another great blog-format site. Available in an iPhone format so you can read it right on the device. *iLounge.com*

Index

THE MISSING CD

There's no
CD with this book;
you just saved $5.

Instead, every single web address, practice file, and piece of downloadable software mentioned in this book is available at missingmanuals.com (click the Missing CD icon). There you'll find a tidy list of links, organized by chapter.